The American Poetry Anthology

VOLUME VII, NUMBER 3

Edited, with introduction, index
and biographical sketches

By

JOHN FROST

And the staff of the American Poetry Association

THE AMERICAN POETRY ASSOCIATION
Santa Cruz, California

INTRODUCTION

A dedicated poet confronts a difficult task whenever he sits down to write. Using only words, he must attempt to marry those infamously incompatible facets of the human spirit: intellect and emotion. He must manipulate the tools of his intellect — logic, memory, vocabulary — to create specific emotional and sensual responses. Often, he must balance the strict requirements of form with the fantastic wanderings of his imagination. Finally, only by the painstaking integration of these opposing forces, will the poet achieve his goal.

Included in this book, the **American Poetry Anthology, Volume VII, No. 3,** are poems that represent the careful combining of emotion and intellect. Reading this anthology, I'm sure you'll be struck by the tremendous variation in style and theme of poetry; you may notice a seemingly infinite variety of poetic compromises, where the poet's skillful marriage of emotion and intellect has rendered each poem effective and powerful in a unique way.

John Frost
Chief Editor
Santa Cruz, California
September 28, 1987

JUDGEMENT OF THE COMING NIGHT

It is only the sound of the rain
Falling on black pavements
That awakens us in the midnight hour
Of a night wind . . .

Do not judge harshly
The hours of the coming night —
Rain, more and more
Against the reflection of the light.

Joanne Monte

PRETTY BIRD

I glanced up from my desk
And I saw a pretty bird, graceful
With different shades of white. It
Was on the ledge below the sash.

My feathered friend was chirping melodies
That I was drawn by the soothing sounds.
As I approached, the bird's head turned
Towards me. We locked eyes.

It had sky blue eyes that pierced through the fog,
To a flowing stream of tinted silver, shining bright.
The room filled with warmth. Glowing like the sun.
I took another step. Just as the wind blew upon the window
Slamming the sash shut.

The bird flew away . . .
Despair not for I'm now the
        Pretty Bird singing.

James Parker

VAPORS

Hissing. Snitching eyes, locked inside
A body.
Cry if you can, eyes laughing inside,
Gnawing at the stomach.

Meditate, be at ease, one with all.
I'm one with all, except myself,
Fool.

I tread the leaden path as the
Sea attacks itself.
The white foam on ridges of the wave
Are now jaws of death.

The jaws are small with blunt teeth.
Getting bigger and sharper as the tide
Rolls in and the teeth keep growing with time
                In time
            Some time
            DEAD TIME.

James Parker

BREAKING OF RIVERS

The swift current swishes,
Across the smooth edges of the rock.
A mighty word, the stream-sparkling.
Even against external pressures
The stream glitters with honor,
In its swift journey across the land.

Suddenly the swift current turns
Into shattered arrays of water.
Not a unified force, a glitter to see.
But only rumbling earth spouting
Wretched hot fumes and trees falling
From insecure ground.

Animals are crushed inside the
Breaking earth where the
Swift current once flowed.

A mighty word, the stream-sparkling,
Now shattered. Being pulled
Along, commanded.

James Parker

JAMES EDWARD PARKER. Born: Covina, California, 11-8-62; Engaged to Margaret Anne Garrison; Education: University of California at Irvine, B.A., Psychology, 1985; Occupation: Vocational trainer; Memberships: National Council of Alcoholism, counseling teenagers; Comments: *My poetry is mainly personal thoughts and experiences of particular issues. The major thrust of my work is attempting to show to the reader that they can overcome any obstacle. The biggest obstacle I overcame was accepting my hearing loss and seeing it as an inconvenience, not a handicap.*

GOD GLESS THE CHILD

God bless the child who puts God first,
and is born into the world.
    God bless the child who is compassionate
    and accepts others.
God bless the child who has a pure heart and
shows love towards all.
    God bless the child who grows up respectable
    and obeys the instructions of its parents.

God bless the child who learns from the mistakes
committed and who never gives up.
    God bless the child who is grateful and is not
    resentful.
God bless the child who uses its mind and
is productive.
    God bless the child who knows where it
    is going and is independent.

God, please bless the child.

Joy C. Sivels-Rodgers

THE DAUGHTER I NEVER HAD

I would have changed her diapers
 and treasured the baby sounds
 so special to a girl —
and as a mother
 I'd have been the best —
 offering her the protection
 of womanhood,
 the security of my arms,
 and the warmth of my eyes
 as I nourished her upon my breast,

 but after awakening
 I realized I was only dreaming
 as I brushed the warm tears
 away from my eyes.

Terry A. Symon

DIVORCE

It wasn't
 the way you hurt me
 or your insensitivity
 that left me crying,
but the look from my daughter —
 knowing
 no father, no home,
 not even a dream
 could be had,
 and for her
 I cried.

Terry A. Symon

TERRY A. SYMON. Born: Big Rapids, Michigan, 1-10-51; Divorced; Education: Ferris State College, Big Rapids, Michigan, A.A.A., 1973; Occupation: Corporate Resource Manager; Comments: *My poetry is for those who have experienced life and can identify with life. I'm a Nam vet and not afraid to cry if something moves me, and I'm still looking for total commitment from a woman who enjoys poetry.*

THOUGHTS FOR YOU

Tonight my thoughts are filled with you
You're much more than a friend to me
Just being here to share a poem or two
Makes it feel like we're truly family
You have so much of your life ahead
I'm praying all your dreams come true
Remember the words that Jesus said
Do unto others as you'd have them do unto you
Take one day at a time — come what may
Be happy with whatever you have
Be patient, be kind and riches will fall your way
You'll be so happy you'll cry —
 then you'll laugh
For the beauty inside you is riches itself
You really don't need a mountain of wealth
Though, I know money can buy many things
It'll never buy the love I feel for you
That gives me a song and lets me sing
A beautiful melody written for two

Larry J. Ramsey

CHRISTMAS WITHOUT MOTHER

The snow outside covers the trees
As the north wind stirs a stiff breeze
Supper is cooking on the kitchen stove
In the house you can really sense love
Everyone has their chores to do
I'm really tired when I get through
Walking through deep snow isn't much fun
But feeding the animals has to be done
Decorations are hung and presents are wrapped
The route for singing carols is carefully mapped
When it's time to eat we all gather
At the table — and we wait for father
To thank the Lord for our evening meal
Words can't describe the way I feel
All together; father, sister, and brother
It just isn't Christmas without mother
She played the piano like no other
It just isn't Christmas without mother

Larry J. Ramsey

Moments held
So tight, so close
Before the coming dawn
The coldness of a newborn day
Can burn your inner soul

You walk alone down silent passages
Once cobbled, long ago
The stones reflecting golden dreams
Of men no longer known

You see the morning mist surround you
Leaving tears of empathy
To streak the mirrored windows
Of the narrow boulevard

Drawn upon a silver line
The Earth, below a storm
Cannot deny the knowledge of the day
It shines
Upon some distant shore.

Michael E. Gawin

I hear her call
She's a wild soul in the Universe
Siren of my dreams
She sings,
"Come, be with me . . ."

Rampage, but
I can't resist
I hear her call
Her words insist

Disappointment
Is all I expect to find
 (but maybe *this* time . . .)

I hear her call, and
Certain I should run (away)
I go . . .
Following her song, and
Dreams too timely to be strong.

Michael E. Gawin

The morning laid a thousand
Shades of grey
Upon the canvas of the shore
Weaving corridors
Of mist and secrecy

Driftwood flames burn
Silently
As glassy waves
Curl off the sea, and
 No one sees these things
 As we,
 Who love the mist, and
 Miss the sea.

Michael E. Gawin

THE BRIDGE

We have come down
From where we have been in the height
Of love we had squandered,
Consumed by deed and by sunlight
Until we had wandered

Away from wasted acclaim.

But we discovered time
Was of no importance in what we chose to do
About love we lacked; and
Still consumed by love we lost we knew
We must go back to who we are

And why we came.

Joanne Monte

EASTER DAWN

What mystery envelops this sweet dawn,
This morn that follows cloud banks piled so deep
That it would seem light was forever gone
And earth would lie eternally in sleep?

Yet blossoms sprout before a well-sealed tomb,
A tree sends forth the waking call of a bird,
Soft color penetrates the shrouded gloom,
And whisperings of angel wings are heard.

Then, suddenly, sun will not be denied,
But pours gold radiance throughout the sky.
A presence opens doors, tight-fastened, wide,
And, magically, all fears and shadows fly

Before a power which, by love alone,
Can conquer darkness and doubt-burdened stone.

Susan Thomas

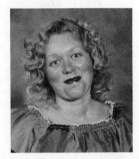

SUSAN JANE THOMAS. Pen Name: M.M.; Born: Sacred Heart Medical Center Hospital; Single; Education: Spokane Community College, Basic art, Volume design, Drawing/painting; Sales, Cashier computer, Retail, 1 year certificate; Occupations: Waitress, Cashier, Retail clothing, Keypunch, Data entry; Memberships: Eagles Lodge; Mayans; Rosicrucian Order; Poetry: 'Sparrows,' 'Sand Castles,' 'The Chickadees,' 1987; Themes: *Getting ready for spring. Telling about life and rebirth, coming forth of a change from winter and nature's sleep. How love unfolds and starts anew. How dreams can come true and princes and princesses reveal their magical affair. Renewal, resurrected, a brighter, stronger, happier, more at peace, more hopeful about your individual life and self.*

BUTTERFLY

Written for Jun Mitsuhashi, 11-16-84

On my shoulder did land

A Butterfly That

whispered in voice of a merry band
showing canvas of the Lord's hand

A Butterfly Sat

for a moment my look she did demand
then swiftly leaped to a lingering stand

A Butterfly Scat

"Come back!" I silently command
but off on wing she still ran

A Butterfly Hast

only a moment to share
SO, it's only fair.

Bernhard R. A'cs

REVELATION I

Written on 11-20-84 for my mother,
Marianna E. Ramsey, 7-4-42 — 6-12-84

The Virgin Mary came to me
  singing her song
  in sweet harmony
  "What's wrong?"
Flowery essence comforted me

Like a snow-white dove
  came forth this heavenly soul,
  was a Godsend from the above
  to fill an empty bowl
With a savory nectar of golden Love

Riding divine winds that have blown
  a revelation she told,
  "When finally, all alone,
    be Brave and Bold."
Could it be now, I'm really all grown?

Bernhard R. A'cs

TREES, BUTTERFLIES, AND PEOPLE

Trees, butterflies, and people are alike
in many ways.
    They are also all beautiful in their own
ways.
    They are all strong and sturdy in how
they think,
    But when a tree breaks its limb, it may
be repaired,
    And when a butterfly breaks its wing,
it may be repaired,
    And when a person breaks an arm or a
leg it may be repaired,
    But they all require one thing during
this time: *love.*
    Without it I don't know if they may be
repaired.

Renatta Anne

THE DREAM OF THE WILD HORSES

Maze over crystal clarity. The
horses frustrate me, repulse me, and
magnetize me. With the beating, soft
flesh melts, pounds on the drum. They
blurt, distort, sparkle in the mist. The
water weighs down my thoughts. The
horses stab one another with a piercing
glance. My vision is captured for one
single moment. Deep, fierce, purple
mud clogs my passage. The pure white
clouds trample over the horses and let
the millions of sounds blend, mush, and
settle, then start up again. Over and
over the hellish fire singeing the
horses, the dark smoke spreading like
a disease. Pressing, lumping together
like sheep. Trampling, stomping, pushing,
finally falling. Endless hooves lashing
in the sky and water. Revealing, not letting
go, final but not ending.

Paula McCormack

APRIL SNOW

Soft white snowflakes
Downward drifting
Dancing on the winds of Spring —
To the brown earth
Slowly sifting —
Feathers from an angel's wing!

Katherine Priestley Shirk

MOONLIGHT AND
LOONCALL

High rode the moon in a star-filled sky,
Below, the lake lay silver-splashed,
And all the world-in-waiting paid
Mute homage to the loveliness . . .
Then, from the shadows
Of a farther shore —
A loon called,
Taking the stillness
From the silent night.
And as its eerie beauty
Echoed its haunting sadness . . .
   the cry of the lost
   the cry of the lonely
  Blinding teardrops fell
And I wept once more
For you.

Katherine Priestley Shirk

THE WILD PEAR

The wild pear is in bloom!
And its lacey branches try —
Flinging fragile fingers high —
To touch the sun-lit sky.

The wild pear is in bloom!
And when the west wind sighs
— ashen petals drifting by —

White rain from cloudless skies!

The wild pear is in bloom!
And it's the month of May —
   Never will there be again,
   Never will I see again,
Such beauty in one day!

Katherine Priestley Shirk

DESIRE

Her limpid pools of lust
  Overflowing with desire.
Her luscious lips
  Hungry for undying love.
They touch the cold hand of reason,
  The cold hand of respect.
The pools of lust die down.
The lips dry up.
The desire withers.

Paul M. Santanna

A WARM SUMMER'S BREEZE

*Written for my friend,
Pat Burdette, 12-2-84*

A warm summer's breeze
whispered past
I and I
who were so pleased

We looked to a sky
cloudless and blue
and we saw
a magnificent butterfly
bouncing
in the
blue

In that moment that
casually passed
I and I
so struck by creation,
we sat!

Bernhard R. A'cs

HIGH IN THE SKY

Sometimes life is high
Reaching all the way to the sky
Then it goes down
All the way to the ground
It seems I'm always on the ground
Hearing no sound
I'd like to die
Then maybe I'd reach the sky
But what would the use be
Only to see
My life be high
If I had to die
I'd be on a cloud
Still hearing no sound
So nothing would have been gained
Only a lot of pain
So I'll stay down
On the ground
And I'll keep reaching high
Till I reach the sky.

Renatta Anne

STRING QUARTET

Schonberg's strings, synthesizing life's
      dissonances,
The cello mournful,
The violin glorifying,
Music, building uncannily,
Screeching out compliments,
Terrifying us rhythmically,
Blurting out cadences,
Satisfying the deep disharmony within our
      souls.
Reverberating along our spines,
Resolving all differences.

Ramona Kline

CONVALESCENT HOME

A long wail, down a hall,
Another fastened in, dumb stare.
Where's your mind, your youth, your
      beauty?
Passed with years, you've come to this!
Remembrance of things long ago,
Your arthritic fingers clasp a doll,
Your only comfort now, as then
Children: fathers, mothers,
Bring a rose, a smile, to cheer a
      moment from deep sleep.
You live for this?

Ramona Kline

DON'T BURDEN ME
WITH TEARS

Don't look down on me with sorrow
You will stay to see tomorrow
I am lying in the ground
All my family and friends around
I'm as happy as can be
Is there a way to make you see?
Oh, come on now, please don't cry
Your tears are heavy, I cannot fly
Can't I get it through your head
I didn't die, I am not dead
All I did was shed the weight
That kept me out of heaven's gate
But now I have the wings to fly
But I can't because you cry
So dry your tears and let me be
'Cause if you mourn I can't be free
So laugh about the fun I had
Because my freedom isn't sad
Your spirits rise and so do I
To the palace in the sky

Kathy Gilden

THE TEAR THAT TOOK
A HUNDRED LIVES

I was so upset that night
I changed for bed without the light
It isn't fair, it never is
A while left, but can I live?
Every time I start to think
I feel my heart begin to sink
And then they come so hot and sharp
The tears of pain from in my heart
Then I bent down to drop the food
To feed my hungry little brood
As they came up, a tear fell down
And in that pain-soaked drop they drowned
It spread across their little land
Like lapping waves across the sand
The story's told in sorry sighs
The tear that took a hundred lives

Kathy Gilden

GRIEF

Carry me back across time's magic dividing line,
  over the ever-changing expanse of years;
Grab me now from the cold fingers of reality,
  hold me . . . and slowly, gently kiss away my tears.

The sadness of this day has settled o'er me now
  like a thick blanket of rainy fog in the night,
And captured my mind in a deep pit of horrors,
  with no hope for a gleaming ray of light.

Oh laughing, cursed death . . . my anger burns into
  my wailing soul and kindles a white flame,
That starts the blaze that rages now inside
  and feeds the fire of hatred for your evil name.

Justice . . . justice . . . where are you when all is lost?
  When my babe lies blue and motionless in my arms;
Now with no hope for a small chance at life,
  to play for a time in the sunlight of its charms.

Grief has taken control of my quivering senses
  and left me wounded and too numb to give
Of myself to my family . . . or beloved friends;
  I'm too mad to die . . . but too sad to live.

Alice Miller

MY FRIEND

I am grateful to have known you.
It was inevitable that we had met.
You taught me many a valuable lesson,
that I will never forget.

Through you, you've shown me courage,
how to look within myself.
To tap on my own resources,
at last with pride and self respect.

You've been a constant flow of encouragement.
Shown me not to break (from stress) but gracefully bend.
Because of you . . . in my emotional dictionary,
you've put the *best* in front of *friend*.

Denise Dmytrasz

IF ONLY . . .

There's so much pain in the world today.
So many different ways to hurt, and be hurt.
So much anger, jealousy, and tears of regret.
Doesn't it ever stop?
Is there any way to ease the pain?
A way to keep two friends together,
Or keep a heart from breaking?
Love is the only answer.
But for so much pain, there's so little love.
So little love to mend a broken heart.
So little love to bring a new bond
Between two old friends.
If only love could conquer the hurt,
And strengthen hearts instead of tearing them down.
If only love could conquer the jealousy,
And bring friends together, instead of separating them.
If only . . . but "if only" is only a dream, and dreams may
  never come true.

Denise O'Guinn

TO CHERISH

Those who love are the soul of the universe
They paint great pictures made out of sunlight
And woven in clouds of dreams
They have found winter's infinite possibilities
Snowfalls and star-drenched skies
Their music echoes across the earth
Like a nightingale's poignant song
Their hope is vast as the universe which unfolds
A myriad of miracles
Yet on the brightest day some shadows fall
When dreams seem lost the whisper of love's memories never fade
Within the splendor of these reflections is
The future, the dawn, the light
Those who love are God's most favored ones
Though tears may hide the rainbow light
Which climbs the mist above a waterfall
Or blur the fragile archway to the sun
Cherished hopes can light the way
Trust renewed is like the broken wings of a dove
Rising ever stronger to soar to the sunrise and a new day

Geraldine Nathan

NATURE'S GUEST

I found a wood louse on the floor in my house,
A flattish louse, the color of a mouse.
But no mouse could roll himself in a ball
And look like a pea with no help at all.
The pea looked at me with his big, shiny eye
That was full of fear and startling surprise.

"How'd you get in here?" I asked, then remembered,
He'd come on the firewood carried in from the shed.
When I picked him up he unrolled and played dead.
Perhaps what he needed was first to be fed.
So I took him outside, laid him down near a tree
And said: "Look, Buddy, this is where you should be."

A. S. Hawley

THE STRUGGLE

You enter the arena, it's you versus him
Against the odds, not expected to win.
You start the pace, as the crowd screams wild
Your stomach is churning, as if you're a child.
You look for escape, but it's too late
Only destiny will decide your fate.
With each step comes one deep breath
Will it be life or will it be death?
At the end of ten, you're told to begin
Who will commit the deadly sin?
The sweat pours as you reach for your gun
You turn and fire, the deed is done.
The crowd settles down, there is no sound
You walk over to your opponent, who's down on the ground.
The man is dead, he needs no help
You lift his mask and find yourself.
The deed is done, but no one has won
The struggle against yourself is the toughest fight.
For it is you, who must determine what is wrong
  And what is right.

James "Jock" Burke

YOUR EYES

The whistling wind rushes through the
streets of my mind. I grip my
emotions to keep them intact. The
layers of my past crumble sweetly,
softly.

The emptiness within me echoes
through my soul. Do you see me
with eyes any more?

I have framed and held in my
heart a sea of dreams, a longing to
be touched.

The drops of cool water roll
down my cheek. I can be again
what I once was! I'm not a shell
of my former self. Do you see me
any more?

Across your face, your eyes
can't witness, silence will haunt me,
can't you see me!

Paula McCormack

By the way the world turns
   So does my head
They tell me all is well
   But yet I don't feel well

They say don't cry
   So I only cry when I am alone
I feel like a stranger
   Among the clouds
I don't know where to start
   Sharing experience

I feel so alone
   There's no one to share with
Maybe tomorrow I will accept it
   But not today

Marty Hanes

QUIET AS A MOUSE

Ideas running through my mind
   none complete
Everything is mixed up
I envy people who have friends
Loneliness is a sad disease
For there is no one to share
Quiet tears running down my face
For now the fear is winning
   my soul

Marty Hanes

BABY GIRL

A mother could not be prouder,
of the woman you have become.
I've loved you since your day of birth,
through the years, you kept me young.

We've had our share of ups and downs,
together we've laughed and shared tears.
But I'd never trade the worst of those times,
as it was continual love that caused my fears.

I am proud of your accomplishments!
Admire how you present yourself.
And I know, if I had a daughter like you,
I'd believe truly that I was blessed.

So through the years that lie ahead,
I want always that you know,
you'll be an important part of my life,
for my love for you will constantly grow . . .
   I love you, *Baby Girl,*
   Thank you for loving me back!

Denise Dmytrasz

ACROSS

There are trolls under his bridge
Right here in the city, giggling trolls
And wood nymphs splashing in the creek.
Incense burns its smokey breath into my veins
While Tibetan monks chant,
Calling from the depths with poignant cries
Of a thousand whales singing to each other,
Singing of love and death and eternal life.
Now they join together in a strange chorale,
Trolls and nymphs, monks and whales,
All here in this small, book-lined study.
A paper maché peacock smiling down,
Listening in rapt attention.

Paul Cummins

SONNET

Her riding crop correct, articulate
Her legs poised in geometric grace,
Statuesque, her back porcelain straight,
Long black hair precisely braided
Beneath her black brimmed hat,
Her habit all in place,
My lady goes riding.
She and her thoroughbred mare,
Trotting, posting, trotting
To the quiet of the formal morning air,
Harmonize in lovely rhythmic show
Like an antique violin and bow.
And there she stands in proud display
To be admired: Portrait of a lady.

Paul Cummins

FINE SOLITUDE

I don't miss you.
Strange,
for usually I am a misser.
I notice I have a lot more time.
It's like having space
on my canvas of life
to fill as I wish
or not fill —
The serenity
of being able to reach out
and choose —
The lopsidedness of your plans
not rocking me.

Sally Love Saunders

COMETH SPRING

Cometh autumn,
Cometh winter,
Cometh summer,
Cometh spring.
   as ne'r before —
See the buds open
And the bulbs in greenery
   spring forth.
Across the meadows
   we are coming,
He is coming, I am coming,
We will meet again.
Cometh forth the
   blossoming love.
Cometh spring,
Cometh love in bloom.

Carol Ann Rutte

LADY MOON

Oh! Lady of the moon
Your face is star struck!
Your eyes sullen . . .
Your cheeks billowy.

You rest on the beams
And shadows!
Oh! Lady of the moon
Come light the balconies
Of love!

Your silhouetted profile
Luminescent in secrecies.
Like the Mona Lisa's smile.

The sun nor the evening star
Can't compare to the
Light of the lovely . . .
Lady Moon!

Diana Stanton Minsky

HOUSEWIVES' LAMENT

I think I'm getting ulcers, somebody crunched my car
repossession took my furniture today
I wrote hot checks, I know, and stubbed my little toe
the insurance company says I cannot pay.

I broke my glasses, the vacuum cleaner quit
the central heating blew up yesterday
the goldfish looked me in the eye, then turned belly-up to die
my own dog bit me, then he ran away.

They turned the gas off, it's snowing through the roof
the sewer might be backing up, I think
there's ankle-deep water in the laundry room
and brown stuff bubbling from the kitchen sink.

The leftovers in the freezer, grew fur and little eyes
my kids took them to school for show and tell
a mouse ate my only shoes, you can't win if you lose
and tomorrow is another day, oh well.

Jaemi Handley

A PORTRAIT

In memory of Abraham Lincoln
A portrait composed after visiting New Salem and
Springfield, Illinois

They, the people, say
  That "Here portraits hang of famous men."
Destiny had designed them as such,
  For the people of the world.
The strokes of an artist's hand, the brush, the oils,
  Could not misinterpret the countenance of the face.
So come, let us look upon this portrait and recapture
  The values of an immortal name.
Note, his serene look and gentle expression,
  How well the artist portrays the tenderness of his eyes.
The faith in mankind emphasized in his hollowed cheeks,
  And that dark, ever-remembered Civil War beard.
His lips, how they seem to speak as they did once long ago,
  That "These have not died in vain."
A man, so humbly born for truth,
  To help set the equal rights for man.
Color or creed diminish in his portrait's eyes,
  And justice reigns, this the greatest of all prides.

Josephine Sadowski

ELECTION TIME

Bands can be heard and you know afterward
a speech is about to be made.
Candidates are speaking and hope you are seeking
what they have to offer.
Candidates are talking and as they are walking
they tell you their pros and cons.
They promise you this and they promise you that
they make life seem so unreal.
They shake your hand and point to the band and
pledge to help you if they can.
They woo the crowd and seem ever so proud to
make their appearance look good.
Their campaigns cost money and they don't think
it's funny when they don't come in at least first.
They promise you all and dare not stall because
it's election time!

Albert B. Casolari, Jr.

CANDLE

Look at the candle just barely lit,
  with one spark of a flame.
With waxy-like teardrops streaming
  down, like it's been blamed.
Maybe it's trying to tell us a story of
  its lost fortune and fame.
Or maybe an adventure with a beautiful dame.
But whatever the old candle is trying to tell us,
  we can't understand, it's such a shame.
Now the spark is gone, gone almost as
  soon as it came.

Catherine H. Rogers

YESTERDAY

As children we used to play, never to be troubled
About grown-up things; time was *forever* down at the farm.
Remember the apple tree outside the spring house
in the summer up where crabapples grew thin
in scuffed loafers and denim jeans.
We looked down on the world from the heaven
of leafy limbs.

Down on the creek in the woods cool and deep
we sank phantom boats and mysterious ships
down and down and over and beyond
smooth rocks and tangled creek barrier
on beyond and out of sight until we knew
that somewhere, someday it would reach its destination
without our knowledge and we'd never know who
won the race.

What did it matter who won, anyway?
Competition was no god.
We were in the springtime of our years: children
dancing in a country barnloft; Grandma and
Grandpa were alive then. The memories grow on,
dimmer, but warmer through the years.

Vicky K. Ramsey

THE WRITER

She sashayed in my hotel suite and
asked me, "Where's your book?"
"What!?"
"You know, the one you said you wrote of
Where To Go and What To Eat?

Oh, yes, yes . . . now, come here, angel,
have a drink and cuddle up and let me think —
Forget the book and take a look at what I've
got for you! Here, let's undo your pretty
blouse before I start to get aroused. Let's
put it over on the chair, I promise, I won't
touch a hair! How come you smell so um m m . . .
so . . . sweet? Your eyes are like a girl in love.
You're why I wrote that greatest book of
Where To Go and What To Eat.

She smiled. I gave my belt a fling and
tossed my shirt into the air. She grabbed
the shirt and disappeared and left me just
her blouse to wear.

Mary Dugan

THE UNSEEN SURVIVORS

They are the meek;
The humble of the earth.
Too soon they've grown weak!
Seldom ever again sensing mirth,
Abandoned and downtrodden;
Too often they are forgotten.

Yet they gave birth to years past;
Without them, life has no start,
But like lonely outcasts
They now stand apart:
Uprooted from this land;
These people we call the elderly.

Living on the fringes of society;
For them, misery never ceases,
Finding no consolation except piety;
Confined like a vanishing species —
But they are the survivors;
The unseen survivors called the elderly.

Rasaan Abdula Mohammad

BE BRAVE

Flowing, foamy white water
Sea gulls soar and dive to the water
Surfers paddle to and fro
Daring waves of different heights
Expert surfers guide their surfboards
Which look like sleek missiles
Past the monstrous waves
Amateurs fall into the vanquishing ocean world
Falling, tumbling, jumping and swimming
Attacking waves take on enemy riders
Frothing at the top
Then descending on unsuspecting victims
These waves can only be tamed
By the surfers who ride them

Zamir Moen

THE EVERLASTING ARMS

When the cold winds of sorrow
sweep over my soul,
When I feel I have no place to go;
There's a place where I'm
free from all harm,
And ''underneath are the
Everlasting Arms.''

He will keep me in all
the dark days ahead,
and hold me secure
in his ''Everlasting Arms,'' I've read.

So, let the storms come
and the wild winds blow;
Through it all,
I'll be held by the
''Everlasting Arms'' of Him
who loves me so.

Sheyla Mackey

HUNGER

Amidst earth's ripening lushness
The maggot hunger gnaws the innards
Of living things. Dull eyes and bloated bellies
And breasts that have no milk cry out
Their plaintive wail.

Sometimes, from far away, I hear it
And a camera clicks
Inside my brain. My peering eyes
Look backward into my head
And an image, like a photograph
From an instant camera evolves
In timeless motion
To shape and form and substance.

And with a gasp of sudden
Recognition, I see again
His pinched face and puckered lips
His skinny, wizened body. And as I look
His chilling, furtive eyes
Find my own.

He stares at the child that once
Was me — boring through my skin
And blood and bones
Into my marrow.

I blink —
And he is gone.

Darlene Myers

A ROSE OF LOVE

It was only a crumpled rose,
My Larry brought to me
There were only a couple of petals,
And the stem you could not see

But when his little hand reached out,
It caught me with a start
For when he handed me this rose,
He gave to me his heart

Helen Baker

SNEAK PREVIEW

Coming soon,
when the trumpet sounds above.
Jesus Christ.
One who bought us with His love.
Son of God
shatters darkness with His light.
Sacrifice.
Balm that heals the serpent's bite.
Sharon's Rose.
Saints who blossomed in His grace.
Light of Life.
Now they see His shining face.
Sword of Truth,
and the judgment thunders roll.
Burning eyes
tear the secrets from your soul.
Wounded hands
beckon those in carnal 'thralled.
Question asked;
''Did you hear me when I called?''

Tom Gilead

poetry should be

it is

poetry the mother of
nocturnal justice

poetry the father of
internal strife

the wife of an unnoticed man

poetry should be

it is

William Capozzi

LOVING WHISPERS

Love is a whisper,
Oh, my beautiful children,
Spoken in the night,
Ever so softly,
So it might be heard
Echoing throughout every moment
Of your lives.
Spoken ever so faintly,
To be repeated by you
To your children and by them,
to their children and so on
      And so on.
Love is a whisper heard
      Forever.

Donna M. Regan

UNDER GLASS, UNSEEN

where naked eye cannot see,
pale translucent bits of life —
nuclei faintly discernible —
shine like grains of rice
fired into glass. primitive,
nevertheless life because of motion.
ability to absorb, assimilate;
split, grow and reproduce
from earliest specks of nothing
throbbing in the dark; semi-opaque
shapes shine, transparent, or pulse
slightly; or, flat, rounded, globules move
to engulf some microscopic grain
of food, gelatinous. along with its motion,
time is required for any growth,
even the making of a person — time,
inscrutable, that does not exist,
yet measures all off from birth to death.

E. L. Kelso

OUR OLD BARN

Our old barn sat way out back,
with hay in the mow and a door on a track.

The smells in the barn were mixed and strong;
The hay was sweet, but the chores seemed long.

The cows gave warmth when cold winds blew.
They gave their milk and bellowed, *moo.*

The cows and sheep shared one side;
Pigs in a corner, and horses to ride.

Our old barn stood down the lane,
Protecting all life from wind and rain.

Now it sits forlorn, faded from weather,
Surrounding my heart like the fragrance of heather.

Our old barn is still out in back,
With the roof caved in and the door off the track.

Joyce E. Dickey

SUNSET AT BAIA DE LOS ANGELES, MEXICO

The sea at dusk lies calm,
Suffused with rose and purple.
A fishing boat,
Anchored far out,
Is silhouetted against the sun.
A pelican glides across the bay.
And lands gracefully,
Barely rippling the water.
The waves lap peacefully
In soft rhythmic musings.
The tide carries offerings from the sea,
A scrap of wood, waterlogged and smooth,
A blue glass ball from a fishing net,
And shells of exotic label,
Murex, Moonshell, Angelwing,
Vacated by their tenants,
These treasures from the sea
Will grace my northland home,
Will serve to bind me
Inextricably to the sea.

Jean Reed Kalmes

TO FLY AGAIN

The day has come for me to go . . . it is time to fly again
I have flown before . . . but I returned to earth and lost my wings.
I sat and brooded for such a long time . . . I am unsure . . .
   I may never fly again . . .
I am earthbound . . . bound to the past . . .
   that keeps me here in fear . . .
   bound to the present that says I am safe . . .
But safe is not enough . . . I long to fly again . . .
I long to soar in the heavens, to feel the cold morning wind in
   my face.
To be free . . . to live and laugh . . . and to love . . .
I fear I have lingered too long this time . . .
   it is the longest yet . . .
Have I lost my gift of freedom . . . my gift of flight . . ?
It is time ! . . . I must know . . .
I have the strength to survive, even if I cannot fly; but I must try.
I cannot go on without knowing if I can fly again.
I cannot stay earthbound, unless I know, that it is the only place
   that I can be . . .

Margarette J. Girgenti

THE SOMBER SENTRY

Way up high in the holly tree, wet the day and
   . . . raining . . . raining,
Creeps a spider, hard to see . . . Pauses first then
   . . . waning . . . waning.

Watch him hurtle here and there. Insect footing
   . . . daring . . . daring,
Spins with agiled sted finesse. Weaves a web and
   . . . caring . . . caring.

Braves the pelting summer rain . . . Silkened thread
   now twining . . . twining,
Center first then out again, large the circle
   . . . binding . . . binding.

Silkened prison seems secure, tightly holds
   the threading . . . threading!
That a mite if now would step, upon his doom
   be treading . . . treading!

So, the task is now complete. Spinning spider
   . . . resting . . . resting,
Awaits a victim to confine . . . The final act
   for testing, testing.

Too, the misty droplets cease; warm the day
   . . . advancing, advancing.
Sunshine . . . fast to dry the leaves . . . fickle gallfly,
   chancing . . . chancing!

Alas, alack! His end at be! Winged motion
   . . . ceasing . . . ceasing!
And there sits spider . . . still out of sight . . . but . . .
On his victim . . . feasting . . . feasting!

Clara M. Benson

THE MASK OF A CLOWN

What is the true face behind the Mask of a Clown?
A face with a happy smile . . . or one with a sad frown?

What is the factor that separates life and reality . . .
From fiction, make-believe, and fantasy?

The salted tears behind the mask of a clown . . . must never
Be shown.
The breaking heart inside this clown must be kept by
Her alone.

The eyes reflect the soul in truth.
A candid look at age and youth.

A look at love — a look at sorrow.
Will there still be her dreams for tomorrow?

What is the true face behind the mask?
A question she dare not answer . . .
A question she dare not ask . . .

Monica M. DeMarinis

LIFE HAS GOLDEN HANDS

I'll never love, I'll never lose
   for what I do I will choose.
Intoxication is the red robin
   shot in the breast
With the bullet of Spring
   at its best.

And it was caught in a cage!

All the seasons arise in the East
   And fall to their target in the West.
To change is how Man will strive
   It will make Love, the Seasons, five.

Now it flies in the wind.

To take life as it comes
   I know its hands are golden ones
Shake it; love and live!

Gary Skaggs

Springs running dry;
   Vessels weakened
And cracking at the seams.
   Suddenly —
      A golden mist
Flowing,
      Bathing,
            Calming.
Life, again — I am whole.

Marilynn M. McMillin

REALIZATION

Your eyes closed against the wind,
The coldness blows fiercely against them;
Chilling your body,
Forcing your eyes open,
Chilling your soul,
Breaking off a piece of your heart,
Hardening you,
Sharpening your senses,
Smartening you.

The hurt of realization.
The loss of trust.
A step back to see the whole picture
and misconception disappears;
All that is left is a realization
and the feelings of a fool.

Elizabeth Diane Coates

THE KEY TO GROWING

TO THE RANKING MESSENGERS

a lamentation of all other creatures
a general public arising
a universal blow-out,
a festive celebration
Come! all creatures of natural flight
Swirl! around the roof of life.
break open the windows of this secret place,
so chatter or wasted words can now escape.
Do not! tarnish the house of endless learning.
stampede the dancing hooves
of the wild running horses
into the mountainhead above,
over the rainbow into
the land where the lion dashes righteously
over its prey
to reign over his territorial gain.
ANXIOUSLY!
the lion waits
for a full new moon,
paws stretched across the plains
waiting patiently
for his new territorial throne to devour.

Cathy Kuntz

GOOD-BYE, MY DEAR

Through all the ups and downs and
      strife,
You stood by me, made me your life.

You understood I had to be, a person
      on my own,
And through the years you gave to me,
A love that's grown and grown.

I'll miss you now that you've gone
      away,
And I'll think about you every day.

And above all else, my thoughts
      will be,
How happy I was that you loved me

Dorothy Makar

Such beauty, peace
just floating in air
out of reach,
oh, how I wish
the children could see
the sunlight, gleaming
on silver clouds
in wisps and folds
they catch the light
and hide, the coming of night.

Tony Helton

WHITE TRAIN IS BLACK

White Train, White Train
Are they all the same?

Why do all have to suffer
For their war games

Nuclear warheads are their freight
We will all be gone . . . Is this to be our fate?

White Train, White Train, moving so fast
Like a long white snake . . . slithering past

Slipping through the cities in the dead of night
The conductor *must know* his cargo isn't right!

Is there no conscience left in America today?
Nuclear warheads are not my way

If this is called *Freedom*
What a terrible price to pay . . .

Alexis Cacyuk

Christmas is a time of cheer
Let us remember why it is here.
Time to be merry, time to pray.
Christ was born on Christmas Day.

Thank the Lord while this day is here,
It soon is gone for another year.
All we have that we can show,
Are pretty ribbon, and pretty bows.

A gift is not just tied with string,
A gift can be a living thing.
Some gifts will last until time's end
If I could choose, I'd choose a friend.

John A. Cody

MY LITTLE BOY

Giver of happiness, symbol of pride
He kisses my cheeks, he sleeps by my side
He steps on my toes wherever I go
Be careful, be careful, there's love below

His words aren't plain, but he jabbers along
And puts in my heart the most beautiful song
My darling baby, my world, my joy
My gift from heaven, my little boy

Helen Baker

THE REFLECTION

What are we but granules of sand on a vast seashore . . .
That will be washed away into the sea of time with the coming
Tide?

What are we but tiny stars in an endless obscure heaven that
Will burn out brilliantly or just frazzle and fade away?

. . . Lucky we are just to be alive.
Breathe in good clean air, watch a rose bloom, hear a baby
Cry, smell the fresh Earth after showers fall upon her
Face . . . or listen to the restless leaves talk in the breezes . . .?

To be able to walk by a still pond with your best friend
and talk about important things, such as, why do birds fly?
Why is the sky blue and what is true love?

Instead, we are always complaining about what should be and
What isn't . . . and things could be better.

Stop! Hold on to what is now . . . you can't, you know, because . . .
Now was then and is no more . . .

Monica M. DeMarinis

THE PERFECT ORDER

He spoke to me of his dream — the perfect order.
If there will ever be.

When the earth balances with the sun.
And the sky reflects the sea.

He spoke to me of his dream, all men standing together as brothers.
When the lion and the lamb befriend one another.

Is this dream — this hope a possibility?
Will this perfect order ever be?

To ponder a thought as vast as this . . .
Hope for the world finding ''the eternal bliss''. . .

No more conflicts, no more wars, no more strife —
Instead mankind will live a content and peaceful life.

He spoke to me of his dream — one day he will change this
Predestined world.
Make it into something special every man, woman, and child can
Behold.

I wish for him, his hopes, aspirations, and dreams come true.
And that he succeeds in his quest, his goal, his beliefs,
For me and you . . .

Monica M. DeMarinis

POISON

Love is a poison. It has entered my system
with some resistance, but nothing has hindered its
effect on every cell in my body. And now you tell
me that you do not love me, I suppose you mixed up
your feelings. It was a quest to see if I could love
you back, and when you found I could, you threw your
love away, now I lay destined to die. For though
you think you are so smart, you were stupid enough to
forget the antidote.

Lauren Gatti

I MISS YOU

In the darkness of the night
    I reach out to hold you.
I search the bed to find
    you're no longer there.
The dark seems so lonely
    and the bed so cold,
I need you here to love
    and comfort me again.
I hope in your search for life
    for one moment you think of me
    and hurry to find what you're looking for
    and come back home to me.

Because . . .
    in the darkness of the night
    I reach out to hold you . . .
    and I search the bed to find,
    you're no longer there.

Jeanine Shaner

GOOD-BYE TO A FRIEND

Tomorrow morning you will come to say good-bye
And already . . . I'm regretting it.
    I always hated good-byes.
But somehow I put it aside and replace those lonely feelings
With wonderful memories of what we had and those we start anew.
But all I can say is,
    I shall always think of you . . .
    When the first light's ray comes thru my window
    The laughter heard in empty rooms
    The joy of excitement in our babies' eyes
    Till the last star I see at night
    All these simple things in life let me
    . . . remember you.
So I leave these pages empty, for a new life begins for us all,
And may God look down and bless,
    My best friend of all.

Jeanine Shaner

WRITTEN BY THE SEA

Winds moan over horizon's shadow,
Gaping maw of caves echo waves' roar,
Granular dark absorbs blue-mirrored wash.
Tiny fish testify to nature's incongruity.

From womb of wet rock, frothy salt crystals
Sprout creamy; a lily's twin petals
Stream and soar from pine-green leafy nest
Life is illusive and ineffable at best.

From cliff-face to foam; a spider weaves
His world of dew-pearled thread binding blind souls;
Fodder for the whirring spindle of his furry loom.
In this haven, nature wears a ruthless face.

Savage and frail sublime lie alongside; outside time;
Perspective a pair of lovers can feel,
As their shadows dissolve in the tide's wheel.
Worlds will merge; I'll write of all worlds . . .

. . . Not of wisdom, nor oneness, these need no words.

Mike Scheidemann

PERFORMANCE COMMANDED

If I must ride waves upon your name,
Then I am not my woman.
If I must see life only through your eyes,
I've failed His image and man.

Herein rests a secret dear,
About me and all my being.
The total me is unfulfilled.
My ray, then, has part meaning.

To life and times, I heed a call.
My cause you'll find manifestant.
Record the all of what I see;
Relay life pictures etched constant.

The greater purpose discovered here,
His greater gifts respected;
The whole of me will thus prevail,
When radiating through time reflected.

Clara M. Benson

CLARA MAYS BENSON. Pen Name: Rusta ''B''; Born: Darby Township, Pennsylvania, 2-3-32; Married: Floyd Stephen Benson, 12-20-58 (one child, Stephen Eugene Benson, born 3-68); Education: Philadelphia College of Art, B.F.A., education, 1954; Temple University and Tyler School of Fine Arts, M.Ed., 1962; Fitchburg State University, Massachusetts, Supervision of Art Certificate, 1975; Occupations: Mother, Homemaker, Educator, Artist, Writer, Freelance Photographer; Memberships: DSEA, PATA, PEA, NEA, MAC, Harvard Craftsmen, NAA; Awards: Awards in artistic statements such as drawing, painting, sculpture, macramé, ceramics, ceramic sculpture, pencil, and pen & ink, in 1962, '65, '66, '74, and '75, respectively; Poetry: 'Creativity Rebukes Ignorance, Waste & Bigotry,' *American Poetry Anthology*, 1985; 'Serenade,' *Hearts on Fire*, 1986; Other Writings: ''Professor Higgins Joins the Space Race,'' play, 1965; ''A Gumper Christmas,'' children's play, 1966; ''Making A Tissue Paper Wreath,'' how-to booklet, 1984; Comments: *I prefer to select subject matter from my general environment and/or past experiences and encounters. Surprisingly, when reflecting upon an occasion, depending upon the subject, setting and season, I can approach it with a freshness made new after the passage of time — with my more recent experiences relating to it. I strive therewith to fill the pages of books with as many aesthetically profound statements of drawings, paintings, photographs, sculptures and writings as possible.*

HARD TULIP

Hard Tulip is a lonely woman,
who lingers by her window sill,
waiting for that special man
to caress her petals,
made soft by his long gentle
fingertips.

Kathleen M. Steamer

KATHLEEN MORALES STEAMER. Pen Name: Kathy; Born: Boston, Massachusetts, 10-3-58; Married: James Worden Steamer, 9-5-82; Education: University of Massachusetts, B.A., legal studies, 1983; Occupation: Special Education reading tutor; Substitute high school english teacher; Awards: 'Winter,' Fall, 1981, accepted for publication; ''Poem dedicated to James Steamer,'' 1982, accepted for publication; Poetry: 'Hey Young Man,' *Cosmopolitan*, March, 1981; Comments: *Writing poetry has allowed me to experience a great sense of freedom. It is the freedom to communicate openly about anything. I write about human relationships, the innermost feelings many of us share in common, and our unusual relationship with nature. I want to share my poetry with the world. I want them to be moved. I want them to hear my music.*

SKY BLUE LAGER

Sky blue lager, take a step
Don't touch the lines, please
In my mind these rules I've kept
Daydreamingly, I'm at ease

Sky blue lager, blue and white
The sky if you would only look
Up in the daytime light
Something no one ever took

They can't, whoever they be
I must be imagining something
But sky blue I like to see
Although nothing is happening

A friend I just heard
From the day before Wednesday
Told me that I'm absurd
Told me Thursday would be my day

Sky blue lager from long
Ago, he who reads this
Listen to my sky song
All my time now is his.

Dorothy H. Harvey

MOM

Here I sit upon the sand,
Equipped with thought
And pen in hand.
Yet not the words do I command
But they command of me.
I just sit and as they come
I'll write them down one by one
Where they come from
I do not know
Someone inside of me.
It's really not so strange to me
It's the voice of you, Mom
Reading poetry.
You gave to me so many things
The hopes and joys of what life would bring
But after this you did something else
You let me stand all by myself.
You gave me courage enough to try
To learn to walk and hope to fly.
You gave me strength enough to know
That I could walk once you let go.
I thank you, Mom, for all you've done
Because of you, I now am one.

Elizabeth Plumley

M. ELIZABETH PLUMLEY. Born: Boulder, Colorado, 7-24-61; Married: Robert P. Plumley, 7-84; Education: Front Range Community College, 1982; Occupation: Housewife and mother of two girls; Awards: Merit of Appreciation, Merit of Award, both 1987; Poetry: 'Adam,' *Impressions, Vol. 6*, 1987; 'Mom,' *Great American Anthology*, 1987; Comments: *Writing poems or stories is one of the best ways for me to express my innermost self. I can release my thoughts, opinions or the feelings I have for someone special. It's a special way I can share with others.*

REMEMBER . . .

In splendor of daylight
where have you gone?
Yes . . . the glimpse of a vision
I remember it well.

Blurred images of figures
romping and playing.
Loud laughter and fun
shared while dancing in the sun.

Remembering a vision . . .
when young, carefree children
play their innocent games
untouched by adult shame!

Valerie A. Stapleton

THE GUITARIST

A tangled, red-ochre halo, slipped about elfin ears,
Balanced his rosy scalp,when he deigned to doff
His Spanish suede hat, broad-rimmed, elegant.
Like a metronome, lined age receded on Dionysiac-sharp eyes;
Triangles shining when he drank brandy, issuing recognition
With a shudder; warming belly; a suckling child driven
To the ascetic life and dessication of desire.
He sought forgetfulness; glee was all! His eyes showed it.
In seclusion, he trod a tenuous path; glimpsed his real self.
However, loneliness is arduous. It riles life, goads her
To fan desires, breeds confusion, disillusion;
All this behind a mischievous, courageous grin!
He discovered distraction, making sweet sound on a guitar;
Made in Japan, a bridge-head between earth and heaven;
Hearth and sunlight; he hoped his chords spun a stairwell
For the angel to descend. The guitar was his psalm & salvation.
Freckled cheeks hollowed to indicate the depths he felt.
With lip-licking, tongue-sucking self-awareness, intensity,
Arching sternly on that holier-than-thou frame of wood,
He played four pieces, endlessly, perfectly.

Mike Scheidemann

TAPS

The bugles blowing taps so clear,
the end of a life we hold so dear.
The one stood there, who gave him birth, watched
him lowered in the earth.
The boy had answered country's call, he was among
the first to fall.
  Oh, he had so much to give, so much more of life to live.
Now all that's left are memories dear, the mother wipes
  away a tear, and clutches tight the folds of Old Glory
  bright.
  Even though the battle's won, this mother's lost her only son.

DeElla Johnson

COUNTRY NIGHT

From azure mountains tall, to valleys grassy green
  far from the bustling cities' cry.

Here where soft breezes sigh, and the dusty daisy
  nods its golden head. Fireflies lighting up the
  meadows where shy foxes tread.

The old owl watching for the hapless mouse,

The murmur of the river, and the stir of sleepy grouse.
Through tree branches dappled moonlight bright, join
with the scent of blossoms to kiss the country night.

DeElla Johnson

SECOND CHILDHOOD

They say I take life too serious
Maybe I was born that way
Old before my time they say
Waiting for my second childhood
The first one never seemed to have come
At times I feel the weight of the world
Worrying about those things I cannot change
Not knowing what to do to change those things I can
Life's turmoil — too serious
Well maybe
Some of us were born to be serious
So the rest could have fun
What a dull world it would be if we were all serious
What a dull world it would be if we all had fun
Who would take care of who
Yes maybe I was born on the serious side of life
But I am the caregiver
Easing your pain so you can enjoy
So I am serious — let me be
My second childhood will come in time and then
You can care for me.

Barbara L. Dietz Burke

SERENDIPITY

Back from the Far East to the Midwest, this Windy City,
After a protracted vacation, my mind was slightly beset,
By a fast emptying purse, which was in no way a nicety,
Yet, I was neither, uneasy nor ill, nor in the least upset;
From Ravenswood to downtown Chicago, coolly I entrained to try —
A branch of my bank, though I knew not where such to find,
Mother wit insisted, serendipity is around, on which to rely,
Hence, at Wabash-Jackson train stop, got off, my luck to unwind.
On ramp to curiosity, I headed to South Wacker Drive —
The sight of Sears Tower, imposing — stirred my elan alive;
Right on a wall across the lobby, was a windfall . . . a directory
Of all offices and businesses within — arranged alphabetically.
  'Twas a spectacle to behold a name, captioned for the 58th floor
  Bank of America, my money keeper — greeted my eyes in succor.

Pete P. Norella

PHRENIC CRAFT

My rapt insight into thy special gift calendar,
'Tis invitation cordiale, to thy phrenic domain,
Anon, I would lief, welcome such tempting comether,
To refuse an offer that good? Not I, for certain.
My lousy wit, regent to my reflexes — roused — rose enthralled;
To alated vehicle — transformed — with ingenious mold —
Programmed to range airy heights, a marvel to behold,
Unlike any other machine, its novelties, are perfections manifold,
With this showcase I reify . . . what I'm trying to unfold;
A spectrum of delight, this Phrenic Craft triggers envy,
With Thinsulate Insulation, warming us — far from frosty;
Crafted to negotiate thy realm, with rebus's eclat introrsely.
  My Phrenic Craft's tonometer is tuned to glamorize
  The "language of the soul," 'tis my paradise.

Pete P. Norella

ROLLING OUT IN FOAM

Roll on, peaceful river
Rolling out in foam
Your water swerves and quivers
On its journey home

Roll on, gentle river
I'm watching as you flow
And thinking of your journeys
Made long — long ago

I can hear the Indian Maiden
Singing a lullabye
While her young and mighty warrior
Listens for the wolf to cry

I see the red deer drinking
Where your clear water flows
And the ducklings are swimming
Between the lily rows

Roll on, peaceful river
You're almost home . . .
Life is like your water
Rolling out in foam.

Maureen Redden Campbell

A MOMENT IN TIME

The Beginning of a Romance

A moment . . . not too long ago
I heard you breathing near me
And in my mind a thousand forevers
Passed me by
I felt the strong and gentle touch
Of your hands upon me
That sent warm sensations through my veins
And cradled me in great desire
The feel of your soft and exploring kiss
That led us both to the intense release
Of our very purpose in life
Mingled with the joy of love
Then . . . left only with elusive feelings
After passion died.

Now . . . if I could have but one wish
It would be . . . to recapture
That moment . . . not too long ago
To look into your eyes
And see forever one more time . . .

Maureen Redden Campbell

SPRING

A touch of springtime,
 clear and soft — bubbling life;
 prepares for summer.

Warmth cleans the grey remains
 of winter ice from
 Lady Nature's face — and soothes.

Robert Owen

THERE'S A GARDEN IN HEAVEN

There's a garden in Heaven
I'm going there soon
Where the bluebird is singing
The white roses bloom

God and His children
Are waiting for me
I'll go to His garden
And there I'll be free

Pain and sorrow
Shan't follow me there
I'll walk without burden
Free of all fear

I'll pray in His valley
And climb golden stairs
Safe in God's garden
I'll wait for you there.

Maureen Redden Campbell

CHRISTMAS MEMORIES

I think of colors at Christmas time
Lights of red, blue, green, and yellow
Lights turning about the tree
I think of him — his smile/laughter

When I think of Christmas I hear the music
of his piano playing *Silent Night* with a beat
His fingers magically bringing life to the piano
His love burning bright

When I think of Christmas
I think of my father
I remember the love
His smile that truly lit up his face

When I think of Christmas I remember
the love of this special man that
graced my life for a few years.
My Christmas memories bring to life
my love and him.

Barbara L. Dietz Burke

RHYTHMS

Still bright dawn
You stir, I drape
A thigh across your leg
You stretch your arms behind your head
And arch like Nijinsky in Scheherazade
The rhythm of your heart is echoed
By the baby in another room
Beating on her little drum
Those sweet ancestral sounds
A tribute to her own descent
Your arm encircles my chest as I breathe
Life holding life
Now it rises with me
With me gently falls
I feel as in a womb
Warm, fed, protected
But this time there will be
No coming out.

Susan Whitacre

We're all right here (wherever here may be)
and while we're here we're free to see
all that exists within our sight:
it may be wrong, it may be right,
but "right" depends on who you are —
do you see the darkness or the star?
Is it life that you live for, or fear of death?
So many minds fed by one breath
live in one world, the one they see.
You are yourself, and I am
me
and perhaps that's all there is to be.
But we're all (here?) and it's all right —
what we don't see is beyond our sight . . .

Donna Collier

SAND

We are the grains
 of sand
  on the beach
   of eternity.
Blowing around
 like dust,
  Forever.
Caught in the endless,
 on-going,
  whirlwind
   of life.
But watch out
 for the bitter,
  frigid-cold
   ocean.
For it will swallow
 you up —
  like Death.

Donna Wise

SEABIRD

Seabird flying in the sky,
Swoops down to taste the sea.
Landing gently on the rocks,
watching children on the beach.

Seabird taking off,
Circling its domain.
Searching for another.
Swoops down and catches the sun,
crying out.

Seabird in the sky.
Watching and waiting,
in hopes of forever.

Megan Heffner-Schweitzer

THE HUDSON AT "COZZENS'S."

SHADOWS OF SILENCE

By the light against the wall,
I see the shadows of the night.
Casting their shapes in the dim light.
Making an imprint upon the wall.
Silence, dark silence, shadows of silence,
Meaning nothing at all.

Megan Heffner-Schweitzer

CONCERT

Like bees to honey
they spent their money

To see a one-man show.

They yell and scream
it's like a dream

To see them on the go.

They clap and sing
it's quite the thing

To be in a harmless riot.

They give a final shout
as they pile out

Now the hall is fully quiet.

Donald Larocque, Jr.

CRUCIFIXION

I've loved the cross as long as I can remember.
I've seen it beautiful in rich procession;
Simply hewn of dark brown timber
With Christ's limp figure hanging there;
Slim and straight in golden splendor
Adorning altars finely spread.
But then, one day in meditation,
I saw the cross I've loved
On Jesus' shoulder, raw and bleeding.
I shuddered, and through tear-dimmed eyes
I beheld the cross — my sins —
On Jesus' shoulder!

Rosemary F. Hargrove

VISIONS OF SUGAR PLUMS

Words will not be quite
As round tomorrow, and periods
Will be more precise;
Let's trim the holiday as
Casually as little boys, our
Loose ends unattended.
Colors all in disarray will
Lie about our table, splashed
In gaudy unconcern; and each
Shall have his sugar plum,
Placed like a possibility
Among stray hours.

George N. Braman

CHRISTMAS IS TO ME

Christmas is a time for all,
When little kids can have a ball,
When babies' eyes are open wide,
Where colors light the countryside.

Christmas wipes away our tears,
As family love again appears,
Where strangers like to lend a hand,
When friendship spreads across the land.

A snowman sits in someone's yard,
A mailman brings a yuletide card,
Young and old embrace with love,
As snowflakes fall from high above.

Outside the weather is turning cold,
Inside warm tales are being told,
Hearts feel lifted as carolers sing,
Driven by a spirit the music can bring.

As a snowy field makes quite a stage,
To supply enjoyment to every age,
We of this world unite in prayer,
For one day of peace for everywhere.

John Albert Biasetti

TAKE ME AWAY

The world surrounds itself with hate
I can do nothing but sit and wait.
For time will pass and ease the pain
Someone will come and call my name.
I will myself to another place
The doors are wide, the curtains of lace.
For its symbol it takes the heart
Mine is broken and falling apart.
I need to go to some safe land
First and foremost one needs a plan.
Love is our most precious gift
It cannot survive when always a rift
Divides the people, so the thing to do
Love the children because they love you
And pray to God the day will come
When facing a new day will start to be fun.

Ellen L. Salerno

FRIENDS NOT ENEMIES

Enemies are two different kinds of people.
Friends are just the same,
But enemies are thoughtless and mean,
While friends are loving and caring.
What I'm really trying to say
Is even though we're far apart,
We're not far away.
Our thoughts are with us
And so is our love.
This poem is too;
Meaning all of the above.
So just stick with it,
Don't give it up.
'Cause we'll always be together
In our thoughts,
And in our love.

Genée Stites

AS THE SUN RISES

As the sun rises to a new morning sky,
So the day begins afresh and new.
Trees to the upward heavens reach,
Lending hope to the creatures of earth.

The awakening of nature each day,
Reminds one that all things were created free.
Free to exist in the here and now,
To face new and exciting dreams.

As the sun rises each day so do dreams,
Dreams of some future accomplishment.
A fulfillment all wishes to share,
Supporting one another for all time.

The wishes, the hopes, the challenges,
These are the purposes of life.
Having friends and those we love
Share our future, makes it even brighter.

Linda L. Wilson

Terminal

Oh Death, I am but twenty-two
I cannot spend a lifetime
Waiting just for you.

So bring your hearse
Around my door
And pick me up
At the hour of four.

Lady Fate

If she says it is
to be
I cannot escape her
If she says no
I will lose the chase
Though slowly she passes
by me.

For Grandfather

It's sunset time
dear Lord
Enfold his hand
in Yours
And lead him
to eternity.

W. Vale

DÉJÀ VU

Lying in my bed
It's the middle of the night
Thinking of my life
It doesn't seem too bright
Connections can't connect
I need to get ahead
Hating this desperate situation
I'm better off dead
But . . . maybe there's a chance
I could start anew
Do it all over again
Déjà Vu

Jacqueline Korth

AT THE HELMSLEY HOTEL

The man with the top hat takes your bag
Did you think he was there for someone else?
Tiny princess inside you forgetting your heritage
Locked like a jewelry box you never open
Afraid there might be nothing there.
Emerald is the color of hope
The silken threads surround your sleep
Sweet dreaming girl in rosebud flannel gown
Have you seen beyond our window
How Saks and St. Patrick's sit side by side?
Some shop here, others there
One could hang crucified between the two
And have no heaven to show for it
Don't open your eyes, but stay
While the light breaks the buildings apart
And honors them each one
Remember that the moment is not gone
The emerald does not fade
And the gold room is in your heart.

Susan Whitacre

In the dark of the beginning, in the void and black of space,
there were no stars to sparkle, only darkness filled their place . . .
then something strange did happen: there was a spark of light
like a candle in the darkness, it shone so very bright . . .
it barely glowed at first, just a flicker in the sky —
as it grew, its luminescence would have filled a blind man's eye —
and then, the light exploded — brilliance flew throughout the air,
and pieces of somebody's dream went flying everywhere . . .

Donna Collier

I'm just writing to tell you that I miss your love here
and I want you to know that I need you back, dear.
I want you to know how I feel deep inside
Because the pain in my heart is just too great to hide.

When we were together my soul was on fire
burning bright with love and desire.
The desire to please you and the love to go with it
my life was a puzzle and you made the pieces fit.
Without you the fire is drenched by my tears
the puzzle is scrambled, mixed up by my fears.
But my love is locked here as it always shall be
and no one shall steal it because only you have the key.

Valerie A. Petro

Dear Great Grandfather:
As I stand here with you.
I look upon your land,
To see your sweat and tears, now in someone else's hands.
Now, please don't be sorrowed.
For you are not forgotten.
Your ambition and your drive will always be on my mind,
And your memory will always be in my heart.

Love always

Ronnett (Crafton) Lyons

SECRET FLAME

As I light a candle,
    here by myself,
I see the fire of your spirit,
    for it glows with a wealth.
The scent is of subtle spice,
    it is like your love.
It is glowing soft in the night,
    like air on the wing of a dove.
The flame glows hot and bright,
    similar to the love we feel.
The wick stays cold, silent and waiting,
    for it waits to be set to life
        and sent reeling.
The flame holds true and silent,
    forever keeping the secrets
        of the lovers who gaze
            into the eternal burning
                flame.

Donna Wise

THE CARPENTER

The Carpenter was a patient man, and kind
His knotted hands were deft to mend a toy,
Or find a Child's hurt out and give it ease;
Slow of speech, but he could always find
The word to set a troubled house at peace;
Day after quiet day he taught the Boy
The use of adze and plane, the holy joy
Of song that rose from finely crafted wood;
Because for all the Carpenter's word was good,
He helped the Boy to know the worth of truth;
For the hurt, the maimed, he showed a gentle ruth;
And when the painful years had done their part;
A Man gauged a Father's love by the Carpenter's heart.

Dorothy E. Law

MAMMA'S LITTLE BABIES

Mamma never had a lot, but Mamma gave us love. Mamma always
Dressed us up, pretty little dresses (a little worn and torn) but
Mamma loved us so.

She put us on a sturdy shelf when bedtime came at the end
Of the day. She told us "Close your little eyes," no longer could
We play. If Mamma took us down for tea, she sternly told us "You
Have to be good." But we would giggle silently and Mamma understood.

She shared our sorrows and our hurts, she knew we were afraid
Of the dark. We shared our secrets and she knew we would never tell,
For Mamma loved us dearly; Dolly, Molly and me.

We knew the day would come when Mamma no longer played the
Games and times we shared would be lost. A tear we would shed if we
Could, but we could only pretend. The smiles were painted on our lips,
She would never know our sorrow. But in her heart we would live on,
This gave us joy to know.

Don't forget us Mamma for dearly we love you so.
        Dolly, Molly, and me.

Leona Campbell

PREJUDICE

Traverse the veil, step out ignorant not,
That in our conceit proud of what we've got,
We hurt, and maim, defame and kill,
Step back in pride, but refuse to be still.

Hidden deep behind clos-sed door,
No chance to fight the ancient lore.
Fear and ignorance does hate enhance,
To live on forever, death the only chance.

Ring freedom's bell to awaken minds,
That to mankind our oneness bind.
But seeks the few continue the fight
Blinded ignorance can never right.

The veil drawn tight over blinded eyes
And silence answers the pleading cries.
Our proud assurance that we are right,
Smothers all traces of mankind's plight.

The veil is ripped and torn asunder,
As brother to brother wars reap the plunder,
Blinded eyes can ne'er see the light,
When lost forever the prejudice fight.

Dianne Bahl

A LOSING BATTLE FOR LOVE

You flutter in my mind
An unyielding mirage
Please! . . . Oh, go away
But you unknowingly persist.

I beg of you to part
Yet . . . refuse to let you go
Why, must this be so,
Only because . . . I choose

Depart! I yell, Surrender!
But I myself fight on
How can I lose this battle,
How can I live to win . . . ?!

Victory is so distant
And I know . . . it shall never be mine
Yet somehow I persist
And stubbornly fight, on and on.

Alla Plotnikova

PLAIN

Beautiful, ruined hands
And destroyed face
That no one can see.
You appear so ordinary.
Yet something hides in your eyes;
Beyond the fine wrinkles,
Behind the grey twinkles,
You don't see
What the rest of us do.
And no one sees you.
If your knuckles hadn't jammed
And your cheekbone hadn't cracked,
You could have been special.

DeEtta Taube

PUDDIN'

I'm here on the floor
Eatin' a puddin'
And just by looking at it
I can tell it's a good'un.

Its sweet creamy depths —
Luscious and chocolaty
And I dig in my spoon
Like Bill Cosby on TV.

Spoon after spoon
I sink down my throat
As I scoop from a bowl
The size of a boat.

''MORE PUDDIN'!'' I scream.
The answer is simple, I swear—
In order to get more puddin'
We need bigger Tupperware!

Jeff Koch

ON THE BEACH

Oh take my hand
as we walk on the beach

with the moon high above
though we know it is out of reach
But if you hold on to me
then we can run, run, run

the wind fondly embracing us
    pressing much love in our hearts . . .

Marge Anderson

Watching this morning
a leaf
unfold to face the light —
Pure, fresh spirit
in a source I took for dead —
I thought of your gentle,
newlifegiving touch.
And me, so sweetly roused.

Karen Miller

IN THE WRONG TIME

Lately, I rise up early in the day
For no other reason than to sit and see
You sleeping with your hair in disarray
And your lashes like wisps of ebony
Against the summer tan upon your cheeks.
And when I bend to gently kiss your face
There is the scent of sun and wind that speaks
Of innocence . . . some bright and far-off place,
That's never seen by mortals such as I.
And it is then I know the hurt must come;
No finite thing will ever satisfy
Your hunger. In the end you will succumb
And follow strains of music that passed near
But only you were privileged to hear.

B. A. Brittingham

WHAT YOU DO TO ME

My heart is filled with longing
My body explodes with desire

Consumed, I am, with thoughts of you
My soul is set on fire

These feelings, dormant for so long,
Awaken so many fears

And remind me of the many nights
Alone with only tears

I wish I could have faith in love
And open up my heart

But then it might, as in the past,
Be crushed or torn apart

Still I can't ignore the way
You creep into my dreams

To see your smile, imagine your touch,
Yet not know what it means.

Diane Dilmore

Little rhymes
And lyric odes
Stories in my mind
Thought and told
Chances taken
Dreams of success
Someday I'll have my masterpiece
My very best
Of course I'll keep the others
Scraps of paper and scribbled notes
They're worth more to me than gold
Without them
My masterpiece would have never been told

Edward W. Hodge

They have known the hurt
And have grown to change
Our children suffer most of all
Through the years
Against thousands of fears
Our children are the least powerful
From the beginning
They know the pain
Unable to understand the strain
About to fall
Our children remain
The least powerful
Left to cure the disease
Left to clean the stain
Their elders created with ease
The elders may go to heaven
But our least powerful
Our children
Will suffer our Armageddon

Edward W. Hodge

TO THOSE WHO HAVE BEEN HELD IN MENTAL OR PHYSICAL CAPTIVITY

gusts of freedom
    whip through my spirit
a frenzy of joy and wonder

 lifting me high
    above ceilings of sky
and dark clouds pounding with thunder

winds of release
    become my breath
i feel not fear but elation

soaring to heights
    of peace and light
my soul is God's creation.

Kimberly Myers

MY DREAMS

I dream of fairy tales,
I dream of Prince Charming,
But when I find my prince he turns into something evil,
Why is my prince always taken away by a magic spell,
Tell me why can't I dream something with a happy ending,
And why do my dreams always come true?
I dream of a princess turned to a maid,
I dream of a pretty maiden turned to a hag,
I dream of a love turned to a hate,
And all of these things are dreams of me.
I dream of a glass heart shattered,
I dream of things of a demon sort,
And if my dreams could be turned around,
Love would surround me,
My prince would take me away,
The hag would be a pretty maiden,
The maid would be a princess,
And most of all,
The pieces of my fragile heart would be put back together.

Sandra Neal

THE PARTING

We stood together just inches apart
Tears stung my eyes from the pain in my heart.
You were going away — our love couldn't be
But I felt your heart reach out to me.

No words were spoken; the silence screamed
Yours was the love of which I had dreamed.
I felt your arms tremble as you held me tight
Pain mingled with pain for a moment that night.

You were going away and we both knew
That your heart would stay; mine would go with you.
A love so strong, yet could not be
My world would dim without you with me.

Now I stand alone as a breeze drifts by
And dries the silent tears I cry.
The gentle wind is your caress
As it touches my lips, I know your kiss.

Hazel Harvey

THE BLIZZARD

We stand at the clearing's edge, arms around one another.
Watching pasture and distant hill become mirage
In the fury of the blizzard.
Pretending to be Arctic explorers lost upon polar snows. My son and I.

We find solace in each other's company,
Neither one speaking as we play out our fantasies.
He Perry, myself Admunson.
As the storm intensifies, swallowing us in its white maw.

With wind nipped cheeks and noses
We turn back into the sanctuary of the wood;
Towering pine and junipers stand like
Sentinels, bleeding the force of the storm.

In between the trees a rabbit darts,
Perhaps returning to a deep slumber,
    beneath marshmallow mounds of snow.

Within the wood, the wind sounds more like a distant seaside surf.
Above us the sky is a grey flannel;
We walk briskly now, strengthened
And refreshed from braving the blizzard together.

Hand in hand we head home;
To a warm fire and a cup of soup.
Father and son relationship strengthened;
My son and I!

B. W. Bartholomaus

A POEM IS NO MEAN TASK FOR ME

A poem is no mean task for me:
It is life compacted to a page,
Or if not life — at least a day.

I run with it at dawn
And break my fast with it soon after.
I nurse it through the morning hours
And feed it meat at noon.

We suffer heat from one to five,
And long for relief from showers
Or some distraction
To hasten evening's ease.

And when the day has ended
By sleeplessness extended,
I do not as old Robert Frost
Claim the poem came
From the white heat of the moment
With one dip of the pen.

I show the scar the galling offender left,
Evidence both of life cut off
And of quickened residue.

Tom Padgett

YOU

When I was with you I had no fears,
you were there to talk and to hear.
You made me very happy, never blue.
Everything you said was always so true.

Alone I never was on a Saturday night
you always came over, it was never a might.
We would walk for what seemed like miles.
Looking at you always made me smile.

Now, you are not mine and I am so sad
it is my fault and I am so mad.
We have grown so very far apart
the memories still linger in my heart.

I want you to know that I still care.
Now I sit alone and hug my teddy bear.
I still wonder where you are.
Now if you would just pull up in your car.

Anita Watkins

ANITA LOUISE WATKINS. Born: Silver City, New Mexico, 11-24-68; Education: Cliff High School, 1986; Membership: Gila Valley Emergency Medical Service; Award: Honorable Mention, 'For Someone Special,' 1987; Poetry: 'The Moment,' 'Lonely Road,' 'Love To Pay,' American Poetry Association, 1987; 'Just Another Guy,' 1987; 'With You,' The Poetry Center, 1987; Comments: *In writing poetry I am able to release my innermost thoughts and feelings. I believe love is the greatest feeling and that is why I use it as my theme for my poetry.*

THE LONE HORSEMAN

He roams the land endlessly,
  searching through eyes of old;
He came upon his favorite ground,
  that has been bought and sold.

He shuts his eyes and sees himself,
  once so strong and proud;
Now only tired, old, and weary,
  he sighs and looks around.

He spots an eagle in the sky,
  searching for its prey;
A feeling of contentment,
  leads him on his way.

He sits upon his horse so tall,
  and prays with all his might;
For a new nation that has begun,
  and knows he cannot fight.

  His nation is no more.

Emma Rotella

SNOW

snowed in, frozen out
drifting in the winter wind
the ground looks like gems

icicles hanging
dripping on the snowy ground
puddles freezing fast

children in snowsuits
playing in God's wonderland
making sweet angels

snowdrifts standing tall
bending the trees beneath them
so lovely, but cold

Dee Anne Blades

DEE ANNE BLADES. Born: Easton, Maryland, 7-6-47; Single; Education: Southern Seminary Jr. College, A.S., Kindergarten, 1967; Salisbury State College, B.S., Elementary Education, 1975; Occupations: Gopher, Chauffeur, Secretary, Kindergarten teacher, Poodle breeder, Poet; Awards: Poet of 1986; Poetry: 'A Dream Dies,' 1986; 'July 4th, 1986,' *American Poetry Anthology,* 1986; 'Give Up Your Life Kathy Brewster,' *Lucidity,* 1987; 'Lady Anne's Dragons,' *Independent Review,* 1987; 'Different Pathways,' *Impressions,* 1986.

HE STANDS AND KNOCKS

Come unto Me
All ye who are weary,
Said the Master one day,
And I shall give you rest.
Draw near to Me, and
I will draw near to you.
Along the highways
And the byways
Of the world,
In teeming cities,
On country lanes,
He walks
Urgently calling,
Come unto Me!
Up each street He goes
From door to door
Gently knocking.
There are no doorknobs,
No latchstrings.
Only we can open the door
To our hearts
And invite Him in.

Charles Haggerty

SONG OF THE HEART

This is a song of the heart
Of time, and life, and you,
A melody of love
That lasts forever and ever.

This I know, that I love you
With a love that knows no bounds.
My life has found its star
When you are with me, my dear.

My heart arises in hope
And reaches out to you
Beyond the plains of the moon,
Beyond the endless tides of the sea,
Beyond the mountains tall and strong,
Beyond time and eternity,
Yearning to have you by my side
To feel your presence near —
Your gentle touch,
Longing to have your heart
Beat in harmony with mine
In moments tender with love.

Charles Haggerty

LOVE IS NOT BOUND

Love is not bound by youth
But flings its magic
Across the years,
Growing with trials and triumphs,
Sending its roots deep,
Standing sturdy
In sun and wind.
It is the symphony of life,
Filling each day with song,
Discovering, creating, serving,
Making the world more beautiful
And bearing fruit
Tender and delicious.

Charles Haggerty

ROSES AND POEMS

Roses and poems belong together,
Imagine a bird with no feather.
What could one be if not the other,
Or a child which has no mother.
A rhyme that has no other rhyme,
Clocks that can never tell time.
Life that has not a single love,
A world that has nothing at all above.
Trees that stand high but always bend,
For no one to ever even call a friend.
Through a cloud sunshine couldn't leak,
Words which you can never possibly speak.
A torch without the slightest flame,
Our lives can be so very sadly lame.
As the world really can offer so much,
That we must always stay in touch.

Jeanine M. Jackson

GOD'S LOVE

The love of God is a stream of cool water upon the tired soul
    and spirit of man.
It refreshes and strengthens the weak and troubled soul
    and spirit of man.
The love of God vanishes fear and doubt.
The love is like a soft cool breeze on the soul and spirit
    of the weary and tired.
The love comes upon those who crave its strengthening power.
The love is a feeling of peace.
It vanishes the void of loneliness and despair.
The love of God is a love unquenchable and all powerful.
The feeling is peace and joy.
A feeling of well being and contentment of life.
God's love is a true love; a love of life; a love that never fails.
The love of God is a kind and gentle feeling;
    it is patient and long suffering.
It brings joy and peace in its wake to the soul and spirit.
To revive and to live again in God's fellowship.
The love of God is a gift of pure forgiving love,
    a love that lasts forever.
It is a pure and true love; a love from a caring and forgiving heart.
A love from God; a gift of love for all eternity.

David A. Sigler

A GIFT FOR GRANDMA

What shall we give Grandma? What will it be?
A nice, fancy teapot for a cup of hot tea,
A long wooly scarf to keep her warm,
Or a cane to guide her from outside harm?

At last we decided what her gift would be —
A bicycle for Grandma, she's just 93.
The bike's fastened down, she could not fall,
We'd have no worries about her at all.

When we gave it to Grandma, she seemed so perplexed,
What would her family be thinking of next?
But she took to the pedals like a duck takes to water,
She's on the move now, that gift was a starter.

Each day she climbs on, her head is held high,
She escapes the looks of the passerby.
She pedals in comfort in dainty, blue shorts,
This crazy contraption is a wonderful sport.

When friends came to call, as friends always do,
They climbed on the bike to try it out, too.
Now, this is a lesson for us all to face —
A bicycle for Grandma put her in the race!

Vera Hibbs

SEASLEEP

In waters of nightshade dreams I drift,
With Sleep, the somber bearer of peace or terror
Coursing at the stern,
Coursing me in his lift and catch,
While I crest, I fall, I turn —
Caught in the conjure twixt shadow and Life,
Twixt shadow and watery Death,
Caught like a fish in a net,
In the middle of all
I remember,
In the misery of all
I forget.

Roger Browning Moreland

FAMILY LOVE

The item of family love involves much thought, and when it should begin any couple thus engaged should recognize their problems will soon begin. When at first both are loving one another, you're on a two-way street, so long as that street don't bi-sect, life may be both calm and sweet.

Then one morn Jack gets up in a frightful mood and Jill don't understand what's got into her lover boy. He's just not the same Jack at all. This is their first lesson in their love affair. Now they find love isn't always sweet and gay, so they decide to shake it off, knowing of better days ahead.

Then one day, they both wake up finding Jill to be quite ill, to be sure a baby's on the way. Responsibility is all read hear, Jack's about to be ''Daddy'' and Jill will be ''Mama,'' you can bet. Now, a one spoken of will soon arrive, their young lively home to bless. Life really has begun.

They now want to have the best of everything to make a happy home. Pa learns his role will be both provider and protector to make a happy home. Ma senses a role of care and housekeeper will be her busy role. Then when baby Pete does appear, a kickin' and a squealin', then the couple feel their oats.

Pa's love explodes, Ma's grows tender as she smiles, wondering what's ahead. How many more of the darling bundles do they want to love and share. Shall they raise a baker's dozen, or maybe just a few. Oh how well will they all be taught from the cradle to the grave. How well? Oh yes, how well.

Clinton Allen

KELLY

I am reminded of the innocence
    that shadowed me during my childhood.

I remember recognizing beauty in a rain shower
    as easily, as in a sunset.

I am reminded of the way friendships were built,
    and rebuilt, on commonalities,
        rather than on life stages and
            levels of importance.

I remember being satisfied.

Now — my priorities have changed,
    and with them,
        my vision.

Rain showers are now nuisances,
    and sunsets, merely the ends and beginnings
        of workdays.

Innocence, and nature's beauty
    exist only for the duration
        of your smile.

Bertram Francis

OUR SON — JOSHUA

There lives in our house
This little boy
And to all that he meets
He brings very much joy.

He's a very hard worker
Willing to help you all day
But soon as the task is completed
He'll run off to play.

Before long this little boy
Shall become a big man
And no matter what his goals
He'll do the best that he can.

I think that someday
He just might be
President . . .
Of our great country.

Patty Maben

OUR DAUGHTER — HANNA

She drives herself so
But what dedication
She's at the gymnasium
Instead of vacation.

No matter the season
Winter, spring, summer or fall
Makes no difference to her
'Cause she's having a ball.

You'll find her competing
Whether daytime or night
So she strives every hour
To get her movements just right.

Her goal is the Olympics
I know she'll do fine
Someday a gold medal she'll be wearing
That little gymnast of mine.

Patty Maben

Visions for my lonely soul
Pictures in my dreams
A stir during a quiet night
Awakened by my screams
Eyes wide open, heart aflame
As I cry out your name

Thomas N. Kirkpatrick

I looked to the heavens last night
Gazing at all the stars so bright
If each star is someone's love
Yours would be the highest above
With your star riding the highest
It most certainly is the brightest

Thomas N. Kirkpatrick

ONE

I dream of you.
I see your face —
The tender smile.
The eyes. I trace
The memories
Of lovely days
And satin nights
That wrapped the ways
We loved. My one.

Madeline H. Wilson

ROADSIDE FLOWERS

yellow and green in clumps
of beauty decorate the
roadsides cheering the
traveler fashioned there
by intricate nature
no hands of persons needed
weeds in profusion uninspected
at close range missing the
beauty of each little flower
but the birds and insects know
them intimately
life gives life gives life

Madeline H. Wilson

GOODBYE

for Florence

With disbelief and settling loneliness
I say goodbye.
Not to you, you no longer can hear me;
But to intimate moments
Together, never to be shared again.

Madeline H. Wilson

MY STAR

I looked at you,
And you touched my hand.
Our eyes searched the desert sand.

Then I knew the spark was there.
But my hopes,
You could not share.

You looked away;
Then came the rain.
Fair Venus' son
Had caused me pain.

The handsomest of mortals,
Gone with the evening tide,
As poor Orpheus in despair
Lost his bride.

I shuddered my lips,
But words I could not say . . .
Then you turned
And slowly walked away.

Christine B. Henry

PLAYING GAMES

You play games with me,
And I with you.

When will this charade
End?

Or
Is it our destiny
To be
Together
And yet
Apart.

Do you love me?
Do I love you?

I think yes.

But —

You play games with me,
And I with you.

Virginia Rubarts

A STEP

I stand at the edge,
Looking into the endless ''nothingness''
Waiting,
Fighting with myself.

Should I take a chance, step,
Or turn away?

Would I soar to new heights,
Or fall because of self-doubt?

Would I survive the storms,
Or be destroyed?

At the edge, I
Sense the rage within, the hurting,
The suffering,
But want to take the chance.

I want to be.
I want to learn.
I want to love, to be loved.

I feel pain; I know fear,
But I need the truth.

I must — I have to just — step.

Virginia Rubarts

NIGHTCAP

In a quiet moment
Relaxing on a soft sofa
Inside a cozy hideaway
Tucked between snowdrifts
Candlelight, coffee and cream.

Lazy laughter, lofty leisure
Peaceful excitement
Morning enlightenment
Opening the curtains
To mellow powder days.

Mike Thacker

THE CEMETERY AT TEMPERANCE HILL, TENNESSEE

This cedar stands wise —
Softly shades the burden of life
  cradled in its roots —
And me, awed there by its ancient spread,
Sense the seed of my being.

  (The same passions I have known
  brought me here.
  And my tears, fresh-felt,
  slip beneath the mounded earth,
  find their way to you below
  who shed them first, before me.)

We meet at last, my gentle source and me —
A gift of love too late for telling.

  Karen Miller

REMEMBRANCE

I found it quite by accident today
Pressed in between those memories I hold
For rainy afternoons that lie midway
Between the ripeness of late summer's gold
And early winter's sudden silver chill.
No faded rose from seven seasons gone,
Its faintly musty fragrance clinging still,
No yellowed slip of paper written on
In your own hand, could pain me half as much
As can the cruel, unbidden thought of you.
I close my eyes and feel our bodies touch
Across the years with quickening anew.
  Downstairs I hear my children damp and cold,
  Save one . . the faceless child I'll never hold.

  B. A. Brittingham

SEPTEMBER PLUS SEVEN

Last year, and in all those that came before,
There were so many things to see and do:
There were shells to seek on a hidden shore,
And molten sunsets and drowsy rises to view,
And libraries filled with thoughts to read,
And fish to catch from an ancient pier,
And daisies and babies waiting to spring from seed,
And cars to drive against the wind. Last year.

There were wines of the earth and those of love to taste,
And the smell of baking bread and rain-soaked ground,
And Christmas friends and punch with brandy laced,
And greening hillsides flower-crowned.
There were colors and sounds and unfamiliar faces,
There were stories and symphonies yet to hear,
There were lights and sights and exotic places . . .
Last year. Last year when you were here.

  B. A. Brittingham

MY PLACE

Sometimes, when I sit alone, my mind escapes to a place known
  only to me.

And there I find the peace I need, the serenity that frees me
  from all pain.

I rationalize the past and contemplate the future; I correct all
  my wrongs to release the guilt.

There is a multitude of dusks and dawns displayed, and I celebrate
  their beauty.

Realizing my fortune in God's great gifts brings me back to the
  earth so full of reality.

I can walk on the beach, enjoying the cool sand between my toes,
  the tide not yet reaching its height.

I close my eyes to entertain the sun's warmth and I join the birds
  as they dance in the wind.

When I awake from my trance, my soul is recast, and the smile
  returns to my lips.

No more does the noise of the traffic and the crassness of harsh
  voices embitter my heart.

  Diane Dilmore

Just the other day
While at home all alone
I noticed a light
A light that grew on me
Within my mind, my body, my soul
Its glow was dull, like that of a candle
As one that would sit on a fireplace mantle
Its flame was small and seemed so fragile
But its presence held me in a grip very powerful
From it there came no heat and yet I felt a warmth
A feeling of security, serenity
Another thing that struck me strange
This flame it did not burn
There was no movement, no scope, no range
Still it held its place apart from time and space
Then it was gone just as it came
Hours passed as I wondered what went on
Feverishly, longingly, restlessly
I await for it to return again
What is it they say about opportunity

  Edward W. Hodge

NO WORDS TO WRITE

Searching for the right words to say
To bring a moment of cheer to your lonely heart
Words that would give forth a truthful way
Of what I feel when we are apart
Sometimes there are just no words to write
No words close enough to be read
Deep feelings to be expressed by touch and sight
I guess there is no more to be said
Now I am so far away
Sitting here alone and missing you
I guess all I really wanted to say
Is babe, I honestly do love you

  Thomas N. Kirkpatrick

THE POEM

I wrote a poem today
And cried.

It was not a sad poem,
But I was.

The lines rhymed,
But I hurt.

The title was "Love,"
But I felt
Alone.

I wrote a poem today
And cried.

Virginia Rubarts

DREAMS AND REALITIES

A one hundred thousand dollar house
Built on a five cent piece of paper.
The workers are paid with dreams and hopes.
A beautiful wife, two beautiful children;
No physical nor emotional problems;
I'd be eighteen forever.

A twenty thousand dollar house
Built on a one acre piece of land.
Can't pay the bills nor the mortgage payments;
A loyal dog and a stray cat;
A leaky roof and a lonely heart;
I'm thirty-eight and getting older.

David R. Sickels

A SPECIAL PLACE

I need a place —
A familiar place —
A quiet place —
A milieu in which to write, to think, to dream.
A place of beginnings and of endings.
A niche where I can
Write the words I could never say,
Think of the life I could never lead,
Dream of the love I could never share,
A place where I can finish the life I have and
Begin the life I have yet to discover.

David R. Sickels

MORNING

Fog wraiths
Lift their sleepy heads
And gently stir, meditating,
Reluctant to leave
Their beds of dreams
To flee the morning sun.

Trailing nocturnal vestments
They slip stealthily from the field
To sleep another hour
Between the hills.

Lilian L. Ayres

THE RIDDLE

I am nothing and no one
To take up space
I fit into corners
With seeming grace

I have no weight
In my gossamer step
Yet footprints are there
Recorded and kept

The marching shadow
Is a finger lent
To the sun dial
Pointing the way I went

My way's unmarked
In the slanting rain
Yet I'm everywhere
Running down the drain.

What am I?

(answer: Time)

Lilian L. Ayres

SOLITARY REAPER

Solitary Reaper
who harvests the echoes
that linger past the hours,
vibratos of the soul,
the orchestra of tunes
that proves the world alive:
the splashes of the rain
exploding on the curbs;
the swashes of the cars
that verify a speed
that leaves no time to be.

Solitary Reaper,
the master of the ears
who solemnly awaits
the tingling of a knock,
the startle of a ring —
to betray the throbbing
for the trill of voices
and the worth of being.

Antonia Zapata

A YEARNING

To climb the ladder of success
Is not an easy task.
To get there requires ultimate goals.
Ask yourself:
How may I achieve this burning desire?
First, choose the subject, study,
And when you get there
Are you really satisfied,
Or was it a mistake?
Chances in life . . .
. . . Become a gamble
But surely it's worth a try —
"Good luck"

Dorothea Schoener

MARKED DOWN PRICE

marked down bread —
that's what I wait for.
don't earn enough
to buy the better stuff.
too proud to seek
what evens out
a poor man's lot
and gives those lawmakers
a good night's sleep.
and when it's time to pay
it's, "Look at him!
Ain't got enough
to buy the better stuff."
the pennies counted —
and wrinkled bills —
don't add to the
sum that's there.
take out the oil,
the car can crawl.
don't need the oil,
i need the bread.
"The price is down."
i'll take what's left.

Antonia Zapata

SINGLE

The loneliness comes on me most
When the room is full of twos;
Standing at my single post,
And voicing my single views.

J. C. Adams

NAP TIME

The Superman cape lies quiet on the floor,
The cowboy's guns are still.
The lions and tigers have lost their roar,
The infantry has captured their hill.

Robots have run down their batteries,
The Indians shot their last arrow,
Sailors have conquered the roughest of seas,
The vet has just saved the sparrow!

The evilest villain has tasted defeat,
The vanquished "bad guys" abound in a heap.
In victorious dreamland, all heroes meet,
My little "action figure" has gone to sleep.

J. C. Adams

THE CLIFF

Here I am existing,
In the bare minimum state
Of life, and love, and sanity.

The edge for each is so very close
That I feel
The dizzy mind-empty feeling of falling
Each time I take a step forward
On toward tomorrow.

Mary Anne McCracken-Cooper

LOVE AT FIRST SIGHT

I do believe in love at first sight,
because that is what happened between you and I
You are the one that showed me the light.
This love is something I could never deny.

I want you to know that you mean the world to me.
I started to care the night we met.
For this is what I want you to see.
Can things between us be set?

Although you are miles away
my feelings are still very strong.
There is only one thing I want to say,
the love I have for you could never go wrong.

Do I need to say any more?
You will see that I am so right.
Someday together we will soar.
I do believe in love at first sight.

Anita Watkins

MY GOOD FRIEND

A tender smile you always lend,
Problems you have helped me mend.
You are my good friend.
Laughing together is what we do best.
Meeting you was the greatest fest.

I know in you I can place my trust,
Keeping my secrets you know is a must.
You are my good friend.
Partying with you is what I like to do.
Having fun all comes down to you.

In your life I hope rain never falls.
If you ever need to talk, give me a call.
You are my good friend.
You have showed me an open friendly door.
Oh, there is so much more that I want to thank you for.

Anita Watkins

A GROWING FRIENDSHIP

We have watched a very special friendship grow,
To where no one can exactly or possibly know.
How long can something as this go on and last,
For a strange strong force pulls us together fast.

And this friendship has grown to much much more,
To the fact there is no possibility of a return door.
Our thoughts we do share as well as our feelings,
In which we have no form of control in the dealings.

To much much more our minds work clearly as one,
So our days are filled with a unique kind of fun.
For which has opened a strange scary new door,
That for the key we have always looked for.

Clearly as one, united we have answers to everything,
All is as clear, loud, and free as the birds do sing.
Together as strongly, firmly, and proudly we do meet,
Never will we withstand any kind or form of defeat.

Jeanine M. Jackson

WHAT IS A MOTHER

A mother brings love to all your days,
With a gentleness in her caring ways.
Even through all the lies,
She has faced in life —
Her love is one that never dies,
She is a mother, she is a wife.

A mother is for cherishing and love,
Who is a blessing and treasure from above.
The good, bad, sad, and fun,
Whose arms are always held out —
She has a job which is never done,
And a love which never has a doubt.

A mother is the one who loves you true,
Who's proud no matter what you do.
All that I can remember,
Is how special you are —
Here's a lot of love from a family member,
The love, hugs, and kisses come from afar.

Jeanine M. Jackson

SOON TO BE — PART OF OUR FAMILY

The big day is coming
Soon my sister-in-law you will be
On June 6th you will marry
Someone very special to me.

My brother is very lucky
Now he's found someone like you
To share his hopes and dreams with
And help them all come true.

As time passes on
Closer I hope we will grow
So the word ''sister'' can soon drop
The words ''in-law'' it tows.

Patty Maben

TO MOTHER

Summer came and plucked you away,
   A rose so fair and full of love.
The angels from heaven smiled at me
   As they drove you in their chariot above.

Then I cried and importuned heaven
   For Him to give me the reason
That so lovely a summer blossom
   Should have to desert a season.

For summer should be a happy time,
   A time of life, joy, and glee;
But how wilted the other flowers in the garden appear
   Without the beauty of thee!

Suddenly, a voice answered me in a dream
As I lay sleeping . . .
   ''Life that has been truly lived and loved
   Deserved no weeping.''

Now, I remember the true things:
   The things you and I share.
We shall be together forever . . .
   Simply because we care.

Christine B. Henry

THE HARDEST LESSON

I came to you,
With burdens of my dreams.
Confused and afraid,
Hoping to relieve some pain.

You listened with an open mind
To the things I had to say.
You gave me the time
I needed to explain.

Sharing with you
The feelings I fight
Makes it easier, to know
What's wrong with my life.

Not that we can ever change
What we have made our lives.
But at least we took a chance,
To share some special moments.

I have learned so many lessons,
Life sometimes seems unfair.
But you . . . are by far
The hardest one to bear.

T. Gropper

We walked together hand in hand
As we beheld this gracious land

We saw the shores where men had sailed
And talked about their dreams that had failed

We watched the sky where planes had flown
And thought of all the hate that had grown

Overhead we saw a dove
The symbol of all peace and love

As we watched the sun shine bright
We hoped someday man would see the light

Diane Tribulato

GLADIOLI

White petals traced on pastel blue
Fine as Dresden, bridal hue.

Living still as first they owned
The sun and rain and earth as home.

Painted for a mantle tall
To grace the room and taunt the hall.

Tinted with a breath of life
Yet, by a hand which sheathes a knife.

Such beauty lives when man has died
The artist's brush the truth belies.

White petals there for all to see
Have loosed my bonds and set me free.

Margaret Bennett Breitzke

A FRIEND INDEED

Always there when I need.
Helpful thoughts to pull me through
The rough days when I am blue.

Helping me to face the truth,
When I continue to lie to myself.

To be sorry for our mistakes,
And forgive for them too.

You make me happy,
But when you're sad I'm blue too.

Because you're a friend and I love you.

Andra Marie Bourque

LINCOLN HEIGHTS JAIL

Pitiful creatures
Empty
Burning to be in a world that never is.
Starving
For denied basic needs.
Twisted
Warped personalities in a reverse society.
Perversity reigns; Hip is king;
Boredom the driving force;
Escape the only goal in life.

Long frightened nights,
Lonely creeping nights.
Cigarettes and swishes,
Dominoes and tin dishes,
Slop and spit —
And the drip-drip-drip-
Of time.

Sia Turner

THE RIDE

Circled rainbows, overlapping showers,
Looking so cool and nice. Flowers
On the dresser for love and all,
Still, they cast dark shadows
On the wall.

To be repeated, possibly, now and then
I love you, I hate you, I don't know you.
I want to do all this for you.

So, sorry, doesn't exist now
Tell me something, how
Can I speak of love unkind
That burned out my mind?

Truth, love, friendship, honesty
Words that meant so much
I am out of touch
Where am I?
Here, there, pieces everywhere
The bus stopped and
I got
Off.

Timothy G. Curran

THE STEAL

Love ain't real,
It's just a steal.
It ain't worth the time or pain.
I keep on trying, but I don't know why,
Love's giving me all these lies.
It's like a cat with diamond eyes,
Love's power — it can hypnotize.
I've gone too far,
I've gone too deep,
I better start a-running or I'll feel the heat.
Now it's done and I've lost my soul,
I better start a-moving or I'll lose control.
Now time has come for the fight,
She'll make me think that it's over tonight.
Queen of hearts,
That's what she is,
She won't let me be to live.

Buddy Dodd

MUSIC FROM BEYOND

The hall is empty;
Yet I hear the song
That keeps on soaring
In this silent place.
Is this sonorous beauty,
This heartwarming sound
Coming from echoes
Or memories now?
No, no dying echoes,
Nor remembrances deep,
Can hold the wonder
Of hearing beyond.

Anne Ayer

THE GAME OF CHANCE

Confetti that lies on cement
and is carried away by the wind;
the yellow, the green, and the blue
tell the tale of the deed that was done
and foretell the proof of the wrong
for the cards that are coated with silver
and the hopes of a fortune to come
and the ease of a living that's hard.
The cards now shredded in pieces,
along with the book that made it
    so easy;
the hope of a gain
and the breaking of odds
and a trip to the moon;
the doer has faded in walking
the avenues lined with the scraps
that lead to the adding of time
and the meeting of faces.

Antonia Zapata

MAN'S SMILE

I have observed man for a long, long while,
And nothing intrigues me more than the power of his smile.

For the *smile's* influence is so great, you see,
It can even deceive intellects like you and me.

Man uses the smile like a serpent's tool —
Conniving and pretending, creating the perfect fool.

Smiles can shove mountains and suppress pain;
That same smile that brings sunshine also summons rain.

The Master meant the smile a positive thing —
Like that of the bride receiving her ring.

But we have taken it, twisted it, and molded it too;
"I," my Friend, have even used it on "You."

We are all victims of Nature's perfect scheme.
We are all a vulnerable race lacking self-esteem.

If the future of Man depends on the nature of his smile,
The success of Man depends on his likeness to the Child.

Christine B. Henry

AN INSPIRED LOVE

An oak tree offered cool shade for my lover and me
One summer day as we were lying in the soft grass.
The sun graciously warmed a forest for us
As we slept in one another's embrace.

Hours later we decided to stroll down to the
Lake where the mirror-smooth water revealed
A wondrously picturesque sunset,
A sight created by God for lovers to share.

We then felt a love flow between us,
A love neither of us had ever felt before.
Our love then transported us through a shady grove
To a small cottage overlooking the lake.

We lit two scented candles,
One for the love we share now and
One for the love we will share forever,
A love that will unite us throughout time.

A peaceful sleep held us through the night
As a sweet forest breeze blew through the window.
We awoke lying under a shady oak tree and
Discovered that dusk had quietly crept up on us.

David R. Sickels

CAPE COD BAY BEFORE A STORM

The power overwhelms my soul
A spot so perfect,
Not a mar upon it,
Not a trace of man's humility has touched this place.

Gulls float, buoyant on the wind,
Gliding, calling,
Perfectly expressing the mood my spirit lives.

Some day this beach will be mine,
Protected.
It will never be touched by man,
Except when I come and feed the gulls, in solitude.

Mary Anne McCraken-Cooper

WITH INNOCENCE . . . HE SMILES . . .

As the light shines through the windshield,
She captures a glimpse of a footprint.

Her imagination runs wild, for her son is still a child.
Could this really be, a grown man, she can't believe.

He looked at her, and with innocence . . . he smiles . . .

She asks about the footprints, to put her mind at ease.
He smiles at her, for she would never believe.

As he's driving home tonight, the light will shine,
Bring back a memory, and with innocence . . . he smiles . . .

T. Gropper

I walked alone through the sand
And looked out over the sea
I thought how beautiful is this land
And all that it means to me

I watched the waves as they came to shore
And thought of men so strong and brave
Who fight for peace to end all war
I prayed that many lives they'd save

I looked out over the sea and cried
For my love who fought and died
He gave his precious life for me
And the dream that someday all men would be free

Diane Tribulato

I

I look out on beauty, on lofty trees and green expanse
On gracious homes and people, gentle, correct, abiding.

I look in on beauty, new carpets and old vessels,
Faces from an earlier age, primitive, serene, and of kin.

I have known beauty as well, silken and quiet hours
When often I have been given first consideration,
And where somehow it was returned last.

Yes, I have met man in all his moods, man and saint alike,
And I have known small faces above aching hearts
Immersed in budding frames.

Yet, all this I have often let pass,
Not from indifference or complacency,
But rather from a lack within myself.

I, who love beauty and velvet moments, new forms and gentleness,
I, who embrace these gifts, choose with unfailing certainty
Windows laced and crossed, people of emptiness
Blurring momentarily all the shapes of spring.

Except, now, for one or maybe two, my vision of fidelity,
And the reality of a smile breaking over a tiny face.

These both I have and cherish; perhaps after all, this is ultimate.

Margaret Bennett Breitzke

AND — THIS IS LIFE

When we are young — life seems to go
　　Floating gently by . . .

It seems we are caught up in time —
　　Held twixt earth and sky.

The days dawn clear — the nights wax serene,
　　All's right within our world.

But, somewhere, soon the gathering clouds
　　Are set to start awhirl.

Time starts its race — we hold on tight,
　　But it moves faster still . . .

Around we go — both here and yon,
　　Buffeted by the years.

Today gladness — tomorrow sadness,
　　Laughter, love and tears.

Time speeds up its pace — we hold on tighter,
　　But it keeps moving still.

Then — we fight no more, our race is won,
　　Let time do what it will.

Helen W. O'Key

SUMMERTIME

Walking with a summer breeze
and seeing what it sees and
watching bees as they fly close by
fill empty spaces that were once
the belonging of someone's thoughts.

Flowers of every colour
drawn from the angelic paintbox
reflect the sun and become one
of a million thoughts
scattered in the head-wind.

Faraway sounds of summer joy
enter the head in a daydream
and the scream of an overhead
bird catches the attention
of thoughts in passing summer.

Anders Frodhe

THE HANDS OF TIME

The hands of time
Have stopped for you
Your life suddenly taken
So much yet to live
The sadness overcomes us
And we cry.
When we think of you
We remember with happiness
All the good things about you.
Our sorrow will never completely vanish
But still the hands of time
For all of us
Must remain in motion.

Cindy Rathje

RHYTHM AND POETRY

The soul train
Made them run.
Jody run if,
It's good enough.
Here comes the sun
Girl,
Don't let me down.
All you have to do
Is just,
Free your mind.

Alfred G. Rowls

THE MOTHER OF GOD

Close to a cross Mary stood,
All lonely in her tears,
The Mother of the world and God;
Waiting on Calvary with her Son,
The Saviour dying for His brothers
And those God-forsaken people,
Whose Cain-hands built the cross.

The man on the cross was God,
God and man in One;
God in love and man in suffering.
Mary gauged a life in crimson drops,
And thought her own was failing
With His latest breath, when dreams
Were crucified with God.

John F. Koons

THE SACRIFICE

This is the end of the relationship —
the end of the struggle.
I can feel it.
It is customary to offer up
a sacrifice here. Isn't it?
This won't hurt a bit.
Raise yourself up to
the sharpness of these words.
Lay yourself over their cool back.
You've given me a selection of
blades to choose from.
Breathe easy
and it is done.
One, two, three.
We will remove the cancer.
Clean.
Quick.
Before your heartbeat
riddles me with holes.

Stuart K. Lender

RAIN CLOUDS

Drifting, clumping, billowing
Dark grey sheets of rain
Sunlight woven through the threads.
It's rainbow art again!

Genevieve B. Kubashack

NOT READY FOR THIS CALL

how could I die since I had not yet lived
I only believed in shadows, wandering stones
all the debris of time filled my bones
a world of waiting is all I remember
retracing steps of older encounters with care
spiders and echoes and dust everywhere
enigmas, lost places, without visible traces
stifled whispers entwined in nightmare
the daily tristesse, the only caress
Urd's well of the past
cast its spell on me
the highest note of my hymn
has never sounded
with no swansong I know I shall fall
crying alone the pride of my heart
I am not ready for this call

Alexandra Roceric

FAR REACH

The cup of blue horizon
Clasped his farm home
Tucked courageously
Between
Those beckoning mountains.

Nothing seen for miles
But his white New England home
And chunky red barn,
Nothing spoke
Of neighbor habitation.

Here was the home of a man
Who had gone
As far as he was able,
Here settled for
A grand far view
Of his
Unattainable blue mountains.

Hope F. T. Zarensky

REAL BEAUTY

I see a woman across the street
She looks my way and our eyes meet
I see the beauty of her face
But I know someday that will be replaced
I turn my head and look to the right
Another woman is now in sight
She is not young, for she is old
But still her heart has not grown cold
There is nothing better than a loving heart
'Cause that is something that won't fall apart
Physical beauty is only as deep as the skin
But real beauty comes from within.

Daniel O. Sapp

LIFE JUST PASSES YOU BY

Why when you are young, you are so full of happiness.
And life? No matter, what bad can come between
You and whatever life means to you.

Time goes on . . .
Things don't come to you as soon as they are expected.
Patience is fading.

Now afraid, because, you're not where you're expected in
Life, at this stage. Afraid of taking that chance.
Wasting the time so precious, to you now. It's gone
So fast.

Time has gone, patience gone, your happiness of
Life is gone.

Now time for prayer, 'cause all bad has come and
Will come again.

Andra Marie Bourque

TO DOROTHY PARKER

I'd rather be a celibate
    And never know the thrill-racked road
That rocks my soul to fluctuate
    'Twixt ecstasy and bitter load.

Don't take from me, don't use me so,
    This height divine, an unkind jest.
The pleasure turns to pain, I know,
    With longing nights and lonely breast.

I'd rather be a celibate
    And never have to write this ode;
Elaborate this desolate
    And disappointing episode.

Don't take from me, don't use me so,
    This joy sublime makes one request;
To suffer me, 'tis apropos,
    With blissful memories to detest.

Sia Turner

THE WALL

The shadow will come, and the rain will fall
and the darkness will come and finish the wall
and it will all end, the pain will be gone
nothing left to indulge upon but the memories
of which no one shall have the need to remember.
The wall has crumbled from the corrosion,
the worms are crawling under my skin.
The shadow, the memories the wall has faded
into the darkness and the rain which shall
continue to fall upon the corpse, washing
the worms, cleansing the soul, rinsing the
memories which can now be seen more clearly,
yet not understood.
No one has ever understood the pain,
        Nor the rain,
            Nor the darkness,
                which finished,
                    MY WALL

Dawn A. Sconfienza

OUR FLAG IS ON THE MOON!

''I see the moon, and the moon sees me.
God bless the moon, and God bless me.''

These were words I was taught to say in my childish way.
As a small child, I would look up to the moon and pray.
I never dreamed one day on the moon man would walk
When thrust into space and from the moon back to earth talk.

Childhood days were gone, but again I said a prayer.
With the nation, I bowed my head in silent prayer
For their safe return to earth, peace, goodwill toward man
When that first step upon the moon was taken by man.

Our flag was proudly planted upon the moon that day.
Fifty man-made stars were placed in God's heaven that day.
Pray it waves forever o'er lands of freedom and peace
Where wars and the stains of bloodshed shall forever cease.

Our Seven Astronauts have not died in vain — in strife —
Unto the watery grave, each sacrificed life
On their journey, ''Reaching for the Stars,'' that fateful day.
May their dreams live on and children of all races can say:

''I see the moon, and the moon sees me.
God bless the moon, and God bless me.''

Juanita McIntyre

AN ARTIST'S IMAGINATIVE CONCEPTION

Before painting the picture, the artist looks around.
He views nature's masterpiece and stands in wonder bound.
The wild, treacherous sea, its grandeur beyond compare,
Created by God when He gathered the waters there.

Through the artist's eyes, he sees the scene and hears the roar
Of troubled waters, a sea swelling in fury more,
Unleashing winds upon a spirit along her way.
A spirit which seeks release from body night and day.

Just a breath away, the spirit takes flight evermore
As the sea bestows the farewell kiss when touching shore.
With tempestuous winds, the sea breathes the breath of death.
But, for the weary spirit, there is no fear of death.

From a sick body, the spirit finds in death release.
Oh, how sad it would be if life here should never cease.
The artist sees the trees with grief, bowing their heads low.
Beyond the blue horizon, there's tranquility though.

The artist takes his easel and folds it on the sand.
The picture painted was not the mastery of his hand.
After one last glance, the artist slowly walks away.
He knows only the Creator could paint the scene today.

Juanita McIntyre

Banks of the Housatonic, at Pittsfield.

REPLAY

Darkness slips in slowly on the night,
Flashing, burning, shining neon light
Through the hotel room window.
He sits and thinks, but doesn't know
That the question burning in his mind
Is not the answer he needs to find.

Locked inside this lonely place,
The tears still wet upon his face,
He wearily waits and tries to understand
The reasons for his living, the photo in his hand.
A sad reminder of what is past
He didn't know it wouldn't last.

Yet everything must end, at times
The church bells toll their lonely chimes.
And he thinks again of things long gone,
Of words unsaid and deeds undone.
He lights another cigarette
And wishes that he could forget.

Timothy G. Curran

DAWN

Darkness engulfs me on an early morn,
  as I wake up from my sleep, like a newborn.

Throwing back the covers, feeling really bold,
  I quickly retrieve them, 'cause it's too damn cold.

These flannel sheets they do the trick,
  as I snuggle back in them and flip the switch.

Hoping for more sleep, I cover my ears,
  but those darn car noises won't disappear.

Admitting defeat I slowly creep out,
  to see what this new day is all about!

Marlene Brown

OUT OF SIGHT!

Ten years ago, I wrote a *ditty*
Eulogizing a celebrity . . . mostly out of *pity!*
His fame and fortune reached *colossal* heights
He broke *all* records . . . truly . . . *out of sight!*
They said it was *God* that took *Him* . . . away . . .
Yet, *His* songs stayed on to play . . . *I repeat* . . .
Breaking all records . . . even . . . *today!*
Impossible . . . you say? *Not so!*
It shows us *all* what true *love* is all about?
If it is . . . true love . . . *born from a broken heart*
Then, it cannot *end* . . . it *sings* on to *heal* and *mend!*
'Tis a *legacy* to *mankind* from a dear, departed *friend!*
He may be *dead,* but *He* cannot *hide* this *gift of song*
Just because He died!
He'll . . . live . . . on and on . . . of that *I'm* sure!
Because *He* said (which describes *Him* to a T . . . *perfectly*)
''Without a *song* . . . *there is no Me!''*

Amen (Acts 20:35)

Mabel Lagerlof

LOST ANGEL

(My Daughter)

You were a little Angel to me when you were born.
Somewhere along the way of life from me you were torn.
Inside yourself you've always been alone.
It seems the ones that mattered to you are gone.
Years ago our relationship decayed, and my love was turned away.
My heart sighed, as I cried.
This saddened me, as you were Angel dear to me.
Now you're so unknown to me, as I feel for me
your love has ceased to be.
Prayer stirs my heart, for my part.
I couldn't even give you aid in your time of need, because
of the wall you built up, daughter indeed.
My lost Angel, you are so cold, what can I do to take hold?
Daughter, awake, for your own sake.
Take hold of God's hand, as you walk upon this land.
You live such a life, as you try to be somebody's wife.
Your life you must take hold, before you become too old.
The Bible you must read, and it will fill your need.
I hope before I die I can hear my lost Angel's voice.
And I'll praise the Lord and rejoice.
Where is my lost Angel?

Carolyn McCulley

KAREN

Pleasant as the sweet April wind
Which brings the fragrances of joy
Eternally capturing the hearts around you

Marvelous as the many women you become
First soft and subtle with a comforting way
Then tough and outright showing great strength

A friend who understands not forgetting
Always present and caring for those
Who might otherwise walk alone

Those around appreciate your candor
I who know care for you.

David Spriggs

HELPING HAND

I was drowning in a dark and murky sea
I thought there was no chance left for me
But I had to try it one last time
So I reached out and a warm, gentle hand grasped mine
It pulled me from my would-be watery grave
And put me where I would be safe
I looked around to thank the owner of that hand
But there was no one there, just me and the land
I got down on my knees to thank God for that helping hand
He said, ''That is okay, child, I would do it again.''

Linda Collins

The get down radio — Booming!
singing out, the Atlantic sky — looming.

High skies, and blue winds
for four seasons spinning,
and no rain.

Four skies tomorrow — North South East West,
just like today,
Asking the temperature to rise
on a sunny breeze
was fifteen degrees in the East end —
Yesterday.

Warm air swings the consciousness
brings down hot temperate tantrums,

Like high skies
and blue clouds
by the way
that I found listening.

Frank Allen Mortis

COCKTAIL PARTY

Whispers trickle off
Loose lips drunken to
The point of absurdity

Crackers crumble
Between pillows
Hiding a vinyl couch

Tidbits of gossip
Reeking with endless
Shallow dull conversation

Lemons bobbing in
Hard drinks distorting
Clear thought easing pressure

Children telling tales
Pretending their hardened
Old bodies were new

Deanna Weber

A CANDLE FOR MOTHER

Her soul, should rest-in-peace
makes the living remember the time
of her decease

She would keep one
particular tradition most
alive

The burning of the
candle
How hard she for it did
strive
It is my solemn oath to
keep her custom
with generosity, not ever her
spirit to deprive

Betty Adams

UNCLE JIMMY

My Uncle Jimmy was a real good man,
You could see how he fit in God's plan;
He never learned a great deal from the books,
Still he did not associate with crooks;
He used his God-given skills to fix cars,
I never saw him go into a bar;
He would be willing to help a neighbor,
They'd buy the parts, he would donate labor;
He loved me, seeing me would make him glad,
Was full of love, I seldom saw him mad;
He's gone now and many of us miss him,
Writing is one way to remember Jim;
Yes, Uncle Jim has gone to meet his fate,
His love was the way the man became great.

Don Bedwell

FRAGILE MICROCOSM

When my world was as small and green
As the moist and living blade of grass
I stroked between my fingers
After a shower of rain swept by,
And the warm contentment of sunshine
Mellowed on my hand,

The music of my universe
Caught in a sparkling drop
Left in the heart
Of a tender purple flower.
I listened long, unaware
The harmony could pass.

The whole of beauty
Gathered in a puddle
Filled with sunset.
Eagerly I stepped in —
But it broke like glass
As I severed it from the sky.

Vera Lee Baker

MESSAGES

There are moments
    never forgotten . . .
I sit alone
    watching and wondering
not knowing what to expect
    a room full of people
    romance in one
Our eyes meeting
    as if to say, ''just be patient''
    and then cast a spell
''I love you''
    waiting and still wondering
    glances, glances,
but as dreams sometimes do,
    a kiss,
    a magical beginning,
        this dream has come true.

Jennifer Delisle

THIRST

With cupped hands
I scoop up time
To quench my thirst
For living.
Joyous moments seep
Through my fingers
Quickly
Leaving moist memories
To flourish.
Sorrow seeps through slowly,
Claminess clinging
Unwilling to escape.
Anxious handsful trickle
Quenching my parched soul
With new emotions.
I scoop and clench and live
eager for each handful.

Armella C. Killion

THE NIGHT WINDS' SONG

You who go your way alone
Listen not to the night winds' song,
Who knows the manner of the songs they sing
Close your ears to what the night winds bring.

Quicken your step, do not tarry
Be sure you've not too much to carry;
For the night winds sing their lonely song
Singing to the lone that comes along.

If you ever listen to the night winds' song
Do not dare to sing along.
Who knows what the night winds sing
Who knows what the night winds bring.

Beware the night, dark like raven wings
Beware the songs the night wind sings,
Of whispering things and murmuring dreams
Heed not the night songs' schemes.

Hurry, hurry, do not tarry
The moon be bright for to see the quarry,
The night winds' song may come along
And with the winds, the night winds' song.

Charles R. Goodwin

HEIRLOOMS

A dish, some spoons, a chair perhaps,
Prize possessions of a life now past.
If only we would learn past's lessons.
Then, perhaps, we would not be repetitious
of the mistakes. Far better to imitate
values — like the work ethic, and duplicate
the solidarity of independent life-styles.
And the sanity of slower-paced styles.

T. Christy Lichtenfels

THE CANOE TRIP

My brother told me what we would do,
We decided to ride in a canoe.
It was my first trip down the long stream,
I was excited, it was like a dream.
The first two got in and we were all set,
My brother got in and we all got wet.
We got started going and we could not see,
So we went drifting into a small tree.
We got caught on more trees and rocks that day,
But we did get ourselves going on our way.
We paddled for a mile, maybe more,
Another tree we're in, we all were sore.
We got caught in a new tree, not far away,
When we untangled we faced the wrong way.
It was a sign from God, or so we thought,
So we paddled back upstream, our day was shot.
We got out of the canoe, not sure where,
And carried it on our backs from there.
When I return there I hear some talk,
About the first canoe to take a walk.

Nicholas Massimini

AGING

The silences of my heart are many as they beckon unto me
Like the walls of a castle, my mistakes haunt me
The years of my life like snowflakes fall
The lust of my dreams has betrayed me and a century passes
by each breath I take
My losses have enveloped me like quicksand and I celebrate
the death of each day
I look to another only as memories
My heart sees hope in death as I release all of my sorrows
My dreams have been murdered by realism, I know the truth
My wisdom has come, I weep
My hurdles are many and many I have tread
My body despises me, my mind deserts me like a beautiful
summer day in January
Idealism laughs at me and I hide myself from it
Love has hospitalized my broken heart
I long for what is gone and it runs from my ugly face
God has betrayed me, I sink like a forlorn ship in need of a future
He, like an unfriendly friend, threatens me and fear overwhelms me
I reach out to Him but help is before me
And then my peace

Kathy Weber

REPENTENCE

I drifted high upon a cloud and looked down on the meek and proud.
Some walked so swiftly down life's road, they had no time to share
  a load of one who faltered on the way.
They had no time to kneel and pray.
They had no time to wipe a tear from a small child's face, so very dear.
The years rolled by and to their dismay, they found no joy,
  along the way.
Oh! they were rich in house and land, with no one there to
  hold their hand.
Their goals all seemed so empty now and some were heard to make a
  vow,
"I'll turn my life around somehow, if someone will just really care
  that I, too, seem to have lost my way,"
"Will someone teach me how to pray?"

Ruth Nichols

THINKING OF ANNA

Your eyes are the pools of amber,
the goldness of the sunset,
  Your voice is the sound of poetry
that soothes my heart and kisses
my soul,
  Your walk is a visionary beauty
of rhythmic movement,
which has been proven to be an
effective weapon for excitement,
  Your touch is silk to my skin
which subdues my body in a yearning
desire for your love,
  Your kiss holds the sweetness of passion,
the fire of desire,
  A heavenly moment of bliss
When I savor the sweetness
of your kiss,
  For your beauty is the beauty
you see in all things,
an inner beauty that fills
my heart and touches my soul.

Gerald L. Cardenas

KISS

It was so tempting I couldn't
resist it . . .

It was sitting on the table, a single
mountain in a vast prairie.
I went and scooped it up,
the wrapper was off, a flash of silver.

Into the dark tunnel it went,
savoring every bit of this morsel.

Until . . . I couldn't stand it, down came the stalagmites
and stalactites, crushing it like a ravaged animal
showing no mercy to its prey.

Then, down my throat it went,
oh, so smooth and delicious,
oozing like thick honey.

It was so tempting, I couldn't
resist it . . .

That chocolate kiss.

Andrea Navarrette

THE MIGHTY WARRIOR

Here I am! The mighty warrior
That can effortlessly fell the beasts
With my magic sword. My name
Is known throughout the land. My feats
Of strength are things of amazement
To all. Oh, you foul fiend, be
You cowardly now, you know my fame.
Be you frightened of my strong deadly
Sword. Yes! Yes! Run away. But
There is no way that you can outrun me.
I'll chase . . .
    "Johhny! Stop playing that game
With the dog and come in. It's time to eat."

Daryl Dubas

WRITER'S BLOCK

Sometimes I wish I could be
transported
into another time —
another place —
where no tears avail,
no sadness arises,
no problems.

Sometimes I wish I could return to my
younger days
when life seemed simple
and words flowed
freely
from pen to paper.

But here, the words are buried,
lost forever,
unable to live.

I stare at the paper —

it remains white and
empty.

Lori J. Feltner

SO HARD TO FIND

A true friend is so hard to find;
It takes more than state of mind.
It takes deeds of action, showing,
not telling.
A voice of calm, talking, not yelling.
Helping others to help themselves,
an exhilaration does bring.
Guiding children toward the right path,
hoping to that path they'll cling.
Whether times are good or bad;
there to cheer you when you're sad.
Impossible to make them mad.
Truly I would call them mine;
so hard to find, so hard to find.

F. L. Richardson

ONCE

    Once it was a smile
next in a long embrace
    And soon I could see
the love in your face
    Then I began to give
you my very all
    And soon, in a long
moment, my heart began to fall
    You left my heart
like you swore you wouldn't
    Walking away from ''us''
knowing I couldn't
    Now I stand in this
''loving'' world all alone
    And for now you have
made my pain known
    At first you seemed
the one for me
    But now I realize our
love won't ever be

Samantha Hamby

I felt the loneliness of our disagreement
when the alarm went off
and I opened my eyes
to find you sleeping
next to me.

It's an act of stubborn will
to choose sleep
while our anger simmers
between us and our bodies
touch in bed
without recognition
or apology.

The emptiness is overwhelming
and already I want to forget
the injustices that caused
the explosion and go back . . .
back to the alienation
which has grown comfortable
over months of routine
and little conversation.

Nadine Cox

DELORES NADINE COX. Born: Fort Wayne,
Indiana, 8-19-47; Education: Texas Technical
University, B.S. in Art Education, 1969; Occupa-
tions: Art Teacher in public school, Artist; Mem-
bership: National Art Education Association;
Comments: *My writing is always in response to
my own deep feelings about myself, other people
or my personal relationships. I write more easily
about what I feel than about what I see.*

SECRET SPRING

The verdant grass is peeking
through patches of remaining snow
trying very hard to catch
the birth of a lovely flower
as the bud begins to form
and the petals start to open;
while above, a stout branch
in grey and brown nakedness
reaching upward in desperation
also receives a touch of green.
The message — Spring is near.
You breathe — and it is here.
    Just as God revives in Spring
    grass, flower and barren tree;
    in your life He'll do the same
    if you will call upon His name.

P. G. Colon

DUAL MESSAGES

Early this morning
through my window pane
the budding branches
waved to me,
a greeting of the day.
Magnolias and daffodils,
hyacinths and crocus, too,
along with many others
bursting forth in bloom,
they also greeted me.

I didn't hear the birds
that usually sit the tree
or early morning jogger's
feet plopping along
to the rhythm of the beat.
Stepping out of doors
a cold wind chilled
the marrow of my bones
and whipped at my coat
as I pushed into Spring.

P. G. Colon

REBIRTH

In the darkness
all things are born
to come to this world
with a cry of pain . . .
then strive laboriously
to get bigger and better . . .
only to return to the darkness
at the end of their days . . .
But don't you fear the darkness
because it's an end
but it's also a beginning
of all things
waiting to be born again
to be better
every time they come back . . .

Maria Cowen

THE WAVE

A big wave came
and swept me away
from the safety of the shore
into the endless abyss . . .

shall I blame the wave
for my misfortune
or my own ignorance
for letting the wave catch me,
for playing too close with the danger . . .

and shall I keep looking
for someone to blame
and drown in my indecision

instead of catching the next wave
rolling toward the safety of the shore . . .

Maria Cowen

CHERUB FEET

When first I saw my newborn child,
With rosy cheeks so gleaming . . .
How I longed to hold and squeeze;
'Twas the moment I'd been dreaming!

She was every inch so lovely,
In her gown of palest rose . . .
With eyes sparkling like a dewdrop,
As she wrinkled button nose.

Her graceful hands reached out to me,
I swelled with glowing pride!
As I drew her Oh! so close to me,
Nestled precious by my side.

From beneath her wrap I stole a glance;
I couldn't help but peek . . .
At this wonder God had graced me;
Kewpie head to Cherub feet.

Then dreamed I paths this child would walk,
Upon those Cherub feet . . .
And dreamed I wonders eyes would see;
The throngs in life she'd meet.

Knowing time would pass,
This child would grow from tot to maiden fair,
I willed her from first breath of life,
My love, my heart, my care.

When her graceful hands no longer reach,
And my life has ebbed its flow.
My treasure; mounds of memories . . .
Cherub feet to woman's glow.

Carol Grey Honza

THE PUZZLE

What remains is a puzzle;
    unsolved,   unfinished,   unwanted.

Unsolved. For it never made sense. It lacked pure
      confidence. It needed desperate help.
Unfinished. For it will never take place again.
      It shall stand as is; Destitute,
         abandoned.

Unwanted. For it has no one. And no one has it.
      Screamed at, kicked at and battered.

This puzzle is my life with you.

Lisa R. Reppert

OUR WAY

A ship sails through the darkness of the 20th century, AD
The dolphins make its escort
Overhead it has a rainbow
Following its stern are the Sea Gulls taking their turn
  catching the updraft
Light shines down through the clouds
Captain orders its helmsman, "steer by the helmsman's eye,
  keep a stay on the light"
A mariner speaks out, "Why will the whales not follow?"
A Sea Gull answers, "they think themselves strong enough"
"But," speaks the mariner, "the whalers in their greed seek to slay"
"Yes," answers the Sea Gull, "we choose our own way"

Roger S. Harkness

WINTER'S END

Through the meadow I walk, my soul in need of mend;
to my senses comes, the damp smell, of winter's end.
A lone bee, on an endless quest,
seeking nectar, without rest.
Green shoots of grass, thrusting their eager heads past,
fallen brothers, of seasons gone last.
Ground, wet, from winter's snows gone;
on it lies a tiny fawn.
A meadow posie, asleep, soaking up the warm sun;
as I approach, it jumps, and toward its mother, runs.
A robin, fretting for a worm;
only one thought, in its mind firm;
hops nervously, across the ground;
until a fat one, is finally found.
Frogs in chorus, croak, in a meadow pond;
announcing noisily, winter, at last — gone.

Lewis Cassill

STONEY CREEK

Oh, happy childhood memories
Of a warm spring day and a soft summer breeze,
Along the laughing little brook,
Twinkling merrily around every cranny and nook.

Oh, what heaven for a carefree child,
Running free, running wild.
Hot barefoot feet from the summer sun,
Wading in its clear coolness when the chase is done.

What a child misses who didn't know the joy
That belonged to the little girl or boy,
Who had a wooden bridge from which to throw,
Stones and rocks to the water below,

And watch the circle magnify
As it hit the water, laughing reply.
Picking up stones all shapes and sizes,
Never knowing if you'd find some super surprises.

Teetering across from rock to rock,
No worry of passing time or clock.
Or just lying lazily along its side
Its cheery song still does abide.

Florence Dorothy Patzman

TWENTY YEARS

Twenty years have passed
Still haunting memories of Vietnam everlast
I can still smell the scent of burning flesh in the humid air
My buddies lying wounded and dead everywhere
Mortar and sub-machine guns blast
Come back to haunt me, like a ghost from the past
I think so much of my family and friends back home
As I stand so weary and frightened at the demilitarized zone
All of the villages that I burned
The screams of women and babies won't leave me alone
How I dread the thought of going to sleep at night
For the cries of pain and death won't escape my sight
Twenty long years have passed
But forever bitter memories of Nam everlast.

Anita Arabia

DEATH

Death, the unexpected visitor.
The one who takes away life.
Whether it be your husband, son,
daughter, or even your wife.
For words cannot express the way one feels.
When a loved one's heart stands still.

The overcast shadow.
The constant follower.

Death, the unwelcomed enemy.
Knows no one,
cares for no one.
Death, the workaholic.
It is busy every day, ever hour
on the hour.
Willing to obtain one's life away.

Joy C. Sivels-Rodgers

TO BE EXISTING

Distinct means of living
     possess attrition by giving
All distinct sides to face
     eminent, upright, westward base.

Character, style, descriptive,
     sole to searching, unify to marry.
Paces are for impressisonism.
Aptitudes are creative wisdom;
Knowledge, utterance are kinds of living;
Not only giving, also receiving.

Theresa Stevenson

THERESA STEVENSON, Pen Name: Terry;
Born: Los Angeles, California; 11-4-54; Educa-
tion: Merchandising, 1982; Revelation Seminar,
1987; Occupation: Sales; Membership: Living
Well Lady Association; Awards: Arts and Craft
Show, 1986; Comments: *My work is self-expres-
sion. I have a very intimate interest in my work.
A reality that could not be expressed, wished to
understand, with a more congenial realm.*

SEA CLIFF

The sands of time are wearing thin,
Worn by salty seas of sin.
The desert now, is but a shore,
Where evil finds its earthly core.

The deadly ocean swallows sand,
Making it a wat'ry land.
I look below from cliffs of rock,
A witness looking down in shock.

And I am certainly no help,
From where I sit on seacliff's shelf.
I add to such a deadly pier,
With each of my own salty tear.

And when in weeks, when I do find,
That I have nearly lost my mind.
My tears will turn to salted sleet,
The sea now laps my helpless feet.

Lauren Gatti

FLIGHT OF A PETAL

As I watched a flower's petal fall
     Its flight of fate once more recalled
How destinies of paths crossed
     Soon end before what was found is lost

Slowly as that petal fell
     Once more a memory I knew well
Reminded me of an impending goodbye —
     And with thoughts of you I released a sigh

Still in flight, the petal's grace
     Spawned recollections of a place
That you and I shared together —
     Each day in time a new endeavor

Then at last it came to rest
     The petal lay atop the nest
Of green grass and soiled earth
     From whence came its birth

As I watched it lie in state
     I knew it had at last met its fate
Perhaps content with what it knew
     As I shall be when leaving you

Susan A. Montelius

EVER-YOUNG SEASON

The robins bob-walk the lawns,
     Stiff and soldierly,
     Proud sentries of the grass,

New and middling leaves,
     Stretch and sing,
     To the warm rising wind,
       The onslaught of Spring . . . comes
       with the patters of rain,
       fertile in pollen,
       yellow in stain.

The violets are gone now, the dogwoods, too,
     But Spring is still young — when it dies, it is
     New.

Roger Browning Moreland

SIGHS TO THE WIND

Moonlight's gaze discovered her
     Along the water's edge
Casting sighs to the wind; her
     Whispers of a lost love

There she sat with memories
     Of someone who long ago
Pledged their love
     Before their heart could know

Moonbeams kissed her softly
     And caressed her with the warmth
Only friends could share
     Sharing secrets; keeping her safe

The cool night air became
     A lullaby to her ears;
The lover's gaze
     A flow of tears

There in silence, she shed the
     Sadness that brought her here
Along the water's edge
     Casting sighs to the wind

Susan A. Montelius

SOMEWHERE

Somewhere in the darkness
there must be a light,
Somewhere amidst the loneliness
there must be those, who despite

The hardships once encountered
found themselves a friend,
Somewhere in the beginning,
they found the means to the end

Somewhere in a man's blindness,
his eyes still must see; that
Somewhere in a man's captivity, inside
he must still be free

Somewhere among the voices,
one voice must cry to be heard,
Somewhere among individuals,
unity must be found in words

Susan A. Montelius

OUR OWN RESURRECTION

Easter is here again,
     So, rejoice and be glad!
We all are carrying our own Cross,
     But we should not be sad!
Instead, we have to lift up
     Our Hearts and find the Path of Love!
That's my Easter Message and
     Also His from
          ABOVE!

Kurt Mueller

NEEDS AND HOPES

When the needs of others require our response
We must sometimes postpone our needs and wants
Our goals cannot be cheerfully received
When there are others in desperate need.

We must sometimes transfer our hopes and desires
To someone who needs to be sparked by our fire
There are those times when their needs are requisite
When we must give, to keep them conciliate.

There is nothing more delightful than being fair
When it is our understanding that we share
There is not greater assurance of ''Peace on Earth''
Than the sharing of knowledge to which we were birthed.

The things we want and sometimes obtain
May sometimes help others needing some gain
If given with a true, free heart
Return, it will, with a brand new start.

So, if you cross the path of those who will not share
Remember there are those who do not care
Wish for your own with all your might
And you may not have reason to live in fright.

T. Steven Watkins

THE SHELL *Jim.*

I took the road that we once took —
    But you weren't there,
(I hope you know that I care)
    Then I visited and seemed carefree,
But, really, there's not much of me,
    Since the heart that beats is
        still your own —
The love I have is yours alone —
    My happiness went with you that day,
When from this earth you were called away.
    The sweetness and the light that
        once did shine —
Have gone with you, oh, sweetheart mine;
    Death took the day,
    It took the night —
It put all my fair fancies into flight;
    I'm just like a shell on the ocean
        shore —
Without my darling, evermore.
    I lived — I died — Only a shell
                    remains,
To catch the glow of the sun and the
        feel of soft spring rains.

Mary Quinn

THE VOYAGER

Long ago and far away
Off the coast of Montego Bay
I traveled far and wide
With my seafaring crew at my side
I visited so many foreign lands
And hunted down the worst of men
For as I sailed the world's seas
I battled with other pirate vessels so vehemently
I found my share of gold doubloons
As roaring cannons with deadly ammo boomed
The red glare from the cannon's fire
Sent a billowing cloud, that to the heavens spiraled
The voyager I am and will always be
As I journey the Seven Seas.

Anita Arabia

NEST IN THE TREE

I was a lost sparrow, in a nest in a tree. Whose
wings were limp. I still could not see.
    Cold wind cutting through my shivering soul.
Starving for something, what I did not know.
    My screeching cries for help, no one could
hear. Until one day, when you flew near.
    You lifted my wings, to the sky I was bound.
And opened my eyes to the world all around.
    You fed my empty mind and warmed my
shivering soul. You gave me your love, and
made my life whole.
    Now we are so happy, singing in sweet
harmony. So safe and content in our nest in
the tree.

Barbara Lunsford

ETHEREAL LOVE CONVERSATIONS

Held at night
or in the morning's early light;
whispered in the mind's quiet,
softly attracted to a magnet
far away.

Day on day
(I notch these mentally
with prismatic quality)
builds: a love-vine growing
out my window, onward coursing.

These thoughts, love's strung
beads
sparklingly hung,
my seeds
of words I would say to you
jeweling our hair with lovers' dew.

Wrapped in the embrace of your shining thighs
I would say things and kiss your eyes.

A pattern of love I quietly trace
until your return, to this, our place.

Stephen Jones

LOVE AT FIRST SIGHT!

My first glance at you,
  I knew right from the start!
That you were made for me
  And I would lose my heart!
So, keep the love light burning,
  It's worth its weight in gold!
You touched my hand with tenderness
  And Baby, I was sold.
I know you feel the same about me!
  So, let's get together and sing:
*Love makes people happy
  And sure is a beautiful thing!*

Kurt Mueller

RAIN

The rain has come
  to kiss the dust,
caress the land;
  make soft the crust.
First slowly pushed
  by stroking gusts,
the rhythm builds
  to pounding lust.
Then driven wild
  till final thrust
of throbbing wind
  has dryness crushed.

Robert Owen

WAR

The light and dark
  have fought again.
Grey dusk is here
  near battle's end.
Through failing light
  a reddish glow
  makes one last stand,
  then sinks below.
While darkness reigns
  with fearful might,
  it can't sustain
  the Lord of night.
Morning's armies
  rejoin the fray,
  reverse the rule,
  and restore the Day.
Thus begins anew
  the age-old form
  of war between
  the Eve and Morn.

Robert Owen

RESTLESS HOURS

Oh my soul,
'tis you that calls me
deep in the night.

Restless hours,
I must charge to thee
with no remorse.

Yea,
I know of your strength,
there is no need of flaunting.

Unforgivable, however,
are your intrusive wiles
for my body needs sleep.

Rest with my body,
I plead,
Oh, my soul.

Mitzi J. Bartée

SPECIAL TIME

When someone touches your life
It's something very special indeed,
Every human should have the chance
To meet someone so special
Who touches your life as no one else can,
And you hope in return
You did the same for them,
That the time spent with this person,
A very unique friend,
Was heartfelt both ways,
And when she leaves
Remember the Special Time together,
And hope to keep in touch,
So your friendship was not a thing of the past
But one made that no distance could destroy.

Tina Bollman

BLOOD ON THE ROSE

  Your love is of
thorns on a dying Rose.
  Your touch is of
fire, burning, and tearing
my skin.
  For your great
wealth is within me, the
unfortunate devil whom
after pain and death still
arises to glorify your
beauty.
  Time and time again
I die . . .

Ruben Cardenas

NOW AND ALWAYS

I've heard it said that love is fleeting
But disbelieved from our first meeting
No more to believe love isn't real
When I look at you, it's what I feel
No other emotion can express
How you dispel my loneliness
And put the meaning in my life
Someday I dream you'll be my wife
No other woman could fulfill
This heart of mine and so until
The end of time I love you dearly
Forever I will want you near me
To touch you is to hold a dream
For that is what you make life seem
Your smile brings sunshine to my days
And I could never count the ways
Or all the reasons why I do —
But can only say this, *I love you*
I've heard it said love can't endure
And all past loves become a blur
But never will I say that's true
My one love, now and always
You

Kathryn Anne Jennings

FOR MY PARENTS

I look at my parents with
twenty-two year old eyes and a
fledgling wisdom whose
first bud is
flowering.
Generous, loving people
marred by temperament
scarred by circumstance
whole and still treading
water.
Anything I am is a
gift from them
given freely to sprout
wings of wonder.
What I become will be a
gift in return —
incubated
and wanting to breed
tender pride.

Anna Maria Deuso

FAIRNESS

There was fear in my heart, when I saw
a beard on a steer.
So I put a spear in him.
Then I saw a tear come from his eye.
I should spare him, but I didn't dare.
I saw him peer at me with a
hard stare.
I don't think it was fair of me
to hurt the steer.
I went up the stairs to put
something on to wear,
because there was a tear on my
shirt from the fat, funny steer.

Tamara Haile

SOFT SPOKEN ONE

Last night as I lay down with worries on my mind, I
tossed and turned and thought, but no solution I could find.
Restlessly, I drifted to a dreamland far away, upon
my landing on a cloud, I heard a soft voice say:
Worry not thy sorrowed heart, from these things peace
shall come. Trust in the Lord Jesus, the precious forgiving one!
Suddenly the cloud floated, higher in the sky. Beyond the
stars and planets we swiftly floated by. That was when I saw
the place, with glistening golden gates, and sparkling lights
of happiness. All love, there was no hate.
The soft voice came back again, the softest I have ever
heard. It was like I knew just what he said, before he
spoke a word.
Then a sensation of peace swept over me. And I awoke
to the bright daylight. And I knew never again would I spend
a restless night.
At that time I knew, all my worries I would
overcome. I will forever have the love and grace of
the soft-spoken one.

Barbara Lunsford

THE GIFT

The present of life to you I bestow
As precious as living, surrounded by the universe's ethereal glow
I, the Supreme Being of the vast universe, and much more
No one from me can hide or ignore
I am responsible for all living things
Though sometimes unhappiness my children of earth bring
The vast wildlife that I created
Is nearly almost devastated
Fighting, disease, famine, and hate
My gift of life few seem to appreciate
How do I begin to explain
Those individuals who use my name in vain
Never will I understand
Why people get so out of hand
Undeserving to them is the Garden of Eden I once made
Only a chosen few can be saved.

Anita Arabia

ANITA L. ARABIA. Born: Philadelphia, Pennsylvania, 3-29-47; Single;
Education: South Philadelphia High School, English major, 1965; Occupa-
tions: Sales, Telemarketing, Sales representative; Poetry: 'Heroes in Blue,'
The Bulletin Newspaper, 11-80; 'Operation Noah,' *Now Magazine*, 9-85;
'Crown Dancers,' *The Chieftain*, 11-85; Comments: *Writing poetry enables
me to express myself in my innermost hidden thoughts and feelings, sharing
my deepest feelings of love for all that encompasses the vast universe.
Using my imagination to the hilt as I venture to places I have never been to
physically.*

THE BARNACLE

Lord, I don't want to be
like an old crusty arthropod
without eyes; dependent
on feelers and legs for meat;
retreating into his shell
at every sign of danger.

I want to be bold
and share your love and grace
with that lonely, unfortunate
who has not yet heard of you.

In order to accomplish this
allow me to develop
that special, unknown glue
which lets the barnacle
cling and adhere tenaciously;
so I may cling to you.

P. G. Colon

PEDRO G. COLON, JR. Pen Name: P. G. Colon; Born: New York City,
9-12-33; Married: Carmen M. Lopez, 4-4-53; Education: Brooklyn College,
B.A., 1963; University of Puerto Rico, School of Dentistry, D.M.D., 1966;
Occupations: Dentist, U.S. Public Health Service; Asst. Professor, New
York University, College of Dentistry; Memberships: American Dental As-
sociation; Fellow, Academy of General Dentistry; Association of Military
Surgeons of U.S.; Delta Sigma Delta; American Dental Volunteers to Israel;
Awards; Golden Poet Award, 1986; *Who's Who in Poetry*, 1985-86; Poetry:
'O God of Israel,' *Gates*, 1977; 'The Naked Stone,' *World Treasury of
Great Poems*, 1980; 'Beloved,' *World's Great Contemporary Poems*, 1981;
Over 12 scientific articles published in U.S., Germany and Japan in various
journals, 1967-81; Comments: *"I have set the Lord always before me; be-
cause he is at my right hand, I shall not be moved." Psalm 16:8*

EVERYBODY DESERVES A CHANCE

Hey! Don't put me down before you see what I am all about.
Because I know that you are ready to judge, criticize and doubt.
It should not matter if I am black or white. Don't you
know that is not right?
It should not be of importance whether I am young or old.
Oh! why are you so cold? All I am asking is for a chance to
show you what I can do. Everybody should be treated
equally and fairly. You are so contrary.
I am not trying to change your discriminative mind.
You are not doing anything but wasting our time.
How did you get to where you are today? Someone gave you a chance.
Heterosexual, homosexual, male or female, whatever may be.
All I am saying is everybody deserves a little respect and dignity.
Love is what we should enhance. Because you know as well as I do . . .

Everybody deserves a chance!

Joy C. Sivels-Rodgers

STRANGERS

I don't know you
and yet . . . I have known you since the beginning
of time
So close your eyes
and come to the dark place
half-way toward the dream . . .
And there I am . . . waiting . . .
a spark of life
as small as a grain of sand
in the endless desert . . .
but I also am all things,
a universe that knows no limits . . .
That's why I know you
because you have been a part of me all along . . .
without knowing . . .

Maria Cowen

MARIA COWEN. Born: Gdynia, Poland, 2-7-52; Married: Warren, 1985; Occupations: Sales manager, Artistic photographer; Poetry: Several of my newest poems are currently being published in the upcoming *National Poetry Anthology.* I am presently working on a science fiction novel *The Dark Side of the Force,* which will soon be available in bookstores throughout the country. Comments: *I wish to express in my poems a deeper spiritual truth which would help the readers to better understand themselves and the world around us. Being able to share my thoughts with you is a truly unique and most rewarding experience.*

FOR A MOMENT

You took my heart, held it for a moment,
and then shattered it. You formed it into
a path, a path to someone else.

You took my trust, appreciative for a
second. When you found how I felt,
you dropped that, too, and used the pieces
to form a river, from which you could drink
while you were on the path.

You took the laughter, you were happy
for a minute, and then managed to
also break that into pieces, only to
use them as a bridge to cross your river.

You took everything I offered,
shattered them, shattered my dreams,
and used them for your own dreams.

At least you took something I offered,
you took everything.
At least you loved for a moment,
rather than none at all.
You hurt me and now I pray to take back that moment.

Lauren Gatti

SANTA BARBARA LITES

Between the stars and heaven's door,
Shine Santa Barbara Lites.

Along the Rivera to paradise,
Glitter silver sands, reflect Santa Barbara Lites.

Reach'n towards heaven through —
The mountain range,
Shine Santa Barbara Lites.

God made love to Beauty,
When he made Santa Barbara Lites.

Jesse-Diego Gonzales

JESSIE DIEGO "CHUY" GONZALES. Born: El Centro, California; Single; Education: California Polytechnique University, San Luis Obispo, California, B. S., 1980; Point Loma Nazarene College, San Diego, California, Multiple Subject Teaching Credential (K - 6), 1985; Occupation: Bilingual teacher; Memberships: CABE (California Association of Bilingual Educators), ASCAP (American Society of Composers & Publishers); Poetry: 'Graffito on the Wall,' *Meca International,* anthology of Barrio poetry, 2-15-85; Comments: *Barrio poetry is designed to make it palatable to its audience and introduce barrio-experiences in poetic form*

EVENING SHADOWS

I picture two lovers, running through the trees,
their hair softly flowing in the cool evening breeze.
The sun is slowly setting, going down behind the
mountains. As darkness reaches near, they hope no one
will find them.
They stop above a creek to watch their shadows
fade away. Tenderly caressing each other, deciding
here to stay.
He gently pulls her down, on the green soft
grass. Wishing with all his heart, this night would
forever last.
She runs her fingers across his skin and
through his hair. Neither speaks a word about
this love they share.
They both have vows to someone else, old
loves that have gone wrong. So they sneak
away together, because together they belong.
As darkness falls upon them, they know that
they must go. And make plans to meet again
tomorrow, they love each other so.

Barbara Lunsford

TO START THE DAY —!

I wake up in the morning with a song in my heart!
That's a good, happy way to start!
I thank the Lord for another day of living
And ask Him: "What can I do today in a way of giving?"
He tells me: "Be kind and do your very best
And I'll be at your side and take care of the rest!"

Kurt Mueller

PROPHESY

Entrancer, romancer, magic carpet ride
Time stands still, icebergs melt
Want you near me, by my side
A crazy chance or a parting glance
Hurtle it to the top
Take a breath, take a step, dazzle and dance
Where do we go from here, where does it end
Will the music ever stop?

Day is night, night is day
Once in a lifetime intimations in a letter
Swept away to our hideaway
Piece of paradise getting better and better.

Your soft touch and charm never failed to make
The dreams go on, never will awake
Setting the stage for a tenacious, dream portfolio
A legacy, a labyrinth, a fantasy imbroglio.
When the moment is right, not a shadow of doubt
Can blind the destiny . . .
I hope you don't mind that you and me
Will always be more than a memory.

Mike Thacker

INSPIRATION

If you but knew my fanciful dreams
Sailing uncharted water, circumventing reality
Obscured by passion, abandoned to imagination.
All forms of beauty sparkle before them
Scenes of pleasure of endless variety
Visionary luxuries of unlooked-for beauty.

Long after twilight, dropping gently to sleep
Spirit of consciousness disengaging once more
Eternity compressed into a moment.
Flickering images and a monochrome mirage
Within each premiere the prevalent figure
Appears vivid and attractive in continuing grandeur
A recurring masque seeping into my soul
Knows where not to stop . . .

The awakening hour on a rippling sea
Realizing it is you, the one who evokes
The great spring, the mystery
Of day's second course
Charmer, slow dancer, the lady, the master
Of all my dreams.

Mike Thacker

FRIENDS LIKE YOU Lara.

How did I know I would meet a friend like you,
So special and kind,
With a kind of sensitivity so dear,
It's friends like you
Who make the world so special.
The kindness and caring
You put in everything you do,
Is something special indeed,
Life is full of surprises,
And you are among the better ones,
Who care so much,
Listening patiently and with such interest,
I can't help but believe,
Life would be especially dull
Without friends like you,
And when you need someone to lean on,
I hope you understand
I'll help you through
With ways I've surfaced while being friends with you.

Tina Bollman

SOMETHING FROM NOTHING

When everything is torn away
And hope has fled like passing days
And everything you thought was true
Is cruelly wrenched away from you
When all the dreams you loved are killed
You start with nothing and you build
Survival is the key, I guess
To have it all, or something less
To be your best, or second best
To drown in sorrow, or consider yourself blessed
At least you're left the strength to see
Your goals through all adversity
At least today is something new
A chance for all those Things To Do
When nothing turns out as you willed
You start with nothing and you build
It's part of life's best decency
We humans have resiliency
That ability to begin again
One more time and not
predict the end

Kathryn Anne Jennings

FLIGHT

Flight, is not reserved, for just those with wings.
Flight, can be accomplished, by both the winged ones and mankind.

Though man has no feathers, he can fly just the same.
Just spread the wings of your soul and let it go where it shall go.

It's in us all, yes, everyone could fly.
It's just that some don't want to learn.
And others don't know how to try.
It's easy if you let go and dream the dreams your dream while alone.

There's no limit to how far you can go.
It all depends on your destination.
And when your soul can fly, there's no place you can't go.

So my friend, just remember that . . .
Flight, is not reserved, for just those with wings.
Flight, can be accomplished by both the winged ones . . .
And You and Me!

Joseph M. Lampe

MY DARLING DJUANA MARIE

Magical, musical, mystical,
middle one of mine,
that's you.

I often wonder what secrets lurk
behind your eyes so blue.

So many times,
the magic of your charm,
to my heart,
a smile doth send.

As laughter bounces off your lips,
like chimes in the wind,
I think that I hear
an angel sing.

God sent you to me from heaven above,
I promise to leave you, never.

You are music.
You are love.

I believe in you,
now and forever.

Love,
Mom.

Nancy Marie Stone

CHRISTMAS IN MY KITCHEN

I have within my household
Three little elves, so dear —
But, oh what trouble they can be
As Christmastime draws near!

While baking cakes, I trip on one
As I cross the kitchen floor.
I fear that I might burn another
As I open the oven door!

From her playpen in the corner,
My cherub reaches out
To crawl, and pull up by my skirts
I feel as if I'll shout!

Then something whispers unto me,
A soft sweet voice says tenderly,
"Little Elves want work to do
For isn't it their Christmas too?"

I set out nuts in a wooden bowl
My "Toy Soldier" cracks away,
"Sweet Princess" rolls the cookie dough
While "Cherub" mocks with modeling clay.

Thus peace comes to my kitchen
There is Christmas everywhere
As the sun shines through the window
And touches the babies' hair!

Katherine G. Stroud

THE WRITER

I've tried before to write this wrong
but it makes me sad, it's never strong,
so I sit at home, my days are getting long.
I doubt if I could ever attempt to fly,
can't see no use in being that high
could I be like the rest and live a lie?

My thoughts on paper are a jumbled mess,
maybe it shouldn't be written, that's it I guess.
There's nobody to talk to, nowhere to confess.
I've written before, why is this a strain?
Now I laugh at what I once thought was pain,
I look again, but of course, only rain.

Being all alone is great for me
acting out dreams so tenderly,
writing them down so others can see
how lovely alone can be.

Debra A. Vandegraft

LIFE

Life flows on like a river
In its own allotted place,
Flows on and on like a river
That has no time or space.

Each life that floats
In the river's stream,
Flows on with the current
Like a summer's dream.

Each life adds a ripple
To the water's flow,
And you never can tell
Where the ripples go.

Myrtle Wick

THE DREAM

The universe is ours my friend.
Let's fly away and touch
The edges of time and space.
We fly into a space of time
From long ago
Which we once belonged.
This universe is ours
We created.
In our reality our thoughts
Are our communication.
There is great knowledge
Here.
We understand.
I look forward to the time,
To the place,
To us when we can truly
Live forever in freedom.

Maria E. Brian

TRUE FRIENDS

A friend is one who lends an ear,
Listens with the heart,
Rids all fear.
That one person
You turn to in doubt
Is patient and caring.
Love, is what we talk about.
No expectations.
No acts or fakes.
A friend gives everything,
Plus more,
If that's what it takes.
No matter the time or day,
Cloudy or bright,
A friend always lends a hand
And assists in life —
The constant fight.

Kathleen S. Hobart

A smile is all it takes —
One touch, will make me shake.
A small embrace,
A gentle trace,
A future fit for two.

"Never leave" we would say —
To protect the love we share.
I'd never find another,
That would show me,
All your care.

As the days go by and by —
I watch you leave,
I begin to cry.
Our future that was fit for two,
Became a dream,
That never came true.

Kathleen S. Hobart

THE WIND

The wind winds around the earth
On its timeless journey,
Into nowhere,
From nowhere.
Some days breathing new life
Into an otherwise dead world;
Dead in peace,
Dead in love.
Some days breathing a hateful chill
Into a hateful world
Of war,
Of death.
The wind has been around everywhere;
It knows everything,
Of the anger,
Of the hatred.
One day the wind will tire of this madhouse
And we will leave together,
To fly free
Forever.

Craig Willingham

UNTITLED

As the water rushes up to the fallen rocks
The waves wash back the memories of the love I try to hide.
You came to me out of the blue;
My guard was down,
I was totally at your will.

Like a plague of love
Unpredictable and overwhelming
You invaded my every part
Until I was no longer me
But an element of you.

I sleep, eat, work and dream of you.
No longer do I lay my head on my pillow
Without saying, ''I love you,''
To your polished picture.

But now, as your picture gathers dust
And tears fill my eyes,
The oceans breeze brings me back to now.

How I hate now!
Come back,
I love you.

David A. Mills

Believe in magic,
For magic is all.
The magic of sorcerers, dragons, and trolls.
In a unicorn's horn or in Pegasus' wings.
In a centaur's bow or an elven elm.
Believe in magic.
It can be seen.
The first light of day on a great sea of glass.
Or the birds as they gather their masses to praise
The day and the world and the fact that they may.
Magic is waiting
To be believed.

Calee Allen

SANDOR PETÖFI CLUB

(After a news report)

The tie he wore in People's Court when booked
betrayed his class (that's how his goose was cooked!)

His Danube-blood blue cravat had him tagged
as unreformed at heart (can thoughts be gagged?)

From his collection of black-mart foulards
that mirror well at Buda poets' bars

he had to choose the one that (we regret!)
to law and order constituted a threat!

Authorities (we're happy!) took the hint:
they guarded him as if their secret mint!

Three armored cars and then detectives took
him in . . . to autograph their dissidents' book.

They put the handcuffs on the gent allright
(but who can jail blue-silk sky geese in flight?)

Frederick Brainin

TRUE GREATNESS

Here's to true greatness, a tribute to Dad,
One of the best dear friends a girl ever had.
With patience, understanding, and love galore,
For his only child whom he did adore.

Here's to true greatness, a church worker so true,
Determined that Greater Mt. Zion would get what was due.
Never a selfish thought did he ever pay heed,
When this great church was in need! need! need!

Here's to true greatness, a neighbor's delight,
Lending a helping hand at trouble's first sight.
When away from their homes they had to be,
He was the one who was given their key.

Here's to true greatness, a family man was he,
Always standing by his dear ones with glee.
There to furnish them their every need,
He paved the way for this child to succeed.

Inez S. Hanley

LOVE'S END

Rays so hot, closeness so deep
burning inside, tearing apart your body
and you scream.

Swords so sharp, pain so great
piercing your mind and yourself;
then it's too late.

Body so cold, your heart starts to shake
icy tentacles inside, steam on the outside
then you realize what the signs make.

Your heart has been torn,
The hurt has been molded,
You have lost yourself and control
and your heart has
turned to cold!

Peggy Jordan

THAT DAUGHTER OF MINE

With scissors and shears i cut on the line,
then i go sew, for that daughter of mine.
I thread up the machine, with bobbin in place,
then i sit there and sew at a slower pace.
As i sit there and sew, sew up the seams,
i keep watching the stitch as i sit there and dream.
Dream of my daughter, by rivers and streams
she loves to go camping, by the firelight she sits
with her guitar in hand and sings to the stars,
she is done with her school, and turned out no fool,
for she studies and she learns on her job.
With her talent and all, she stands so tall,
and therefore the shirt, will be extra long.
With sleeves all extended, and narrow at waist,
i sew up the shirt, then i sit there and baste.
When i get it all done, i unthread my machine,
as i box up the shirt, i still do it and dream.
Then i will go send it, to that daughter of mine,
for i do so love her, and she is doing just fine,
so this is my note, to that daughter of mine.

Laverna A. Houdek

The past; us.
History; we.
Never; you.
Forget; me.
Your choice; you left.
My choice; to stay.
All dreams; lies.
All hope; fades away.
The stars; gone.
My heart; in two.
Who's at fault . . .
I blame you.

Kathleen S. Hobart

KATHLEEN (KATIE) SUE HOBART. Born: Jackson, Amador County Hospital, California, 2-22-70; Single; Education: Junior year at Ponderosa High School; Occupation: Goal is to become a child psychologist; Memberships: El Dorado County Explorers (Captain); Tennis, basketball, and softball sports programs; California Combat Association; Comments: *When I write, I write from inside of me. All my poems are emotional and full of feelings. I hope that someday, some person who reads my poems will get just as much out of them as I put in them.*

A WELCOME GUEST

Waken is the home of toil and motion
　with fields to reap,
Office of notion,
　precurser to sleep.

Sleep, the winged purveyor of dreams,
　a welcome guest;
Loom for raveled means
　at the Inn of Rest.

Gene W. Abbott

FAREWELL TO EDEN ADAM

Farewell to Eden Adam,
Farewell to Eden land —
You've had your fill of knowledge
From that tree where man began;

You know now who you're kin to —
You're the image through and through
So climb that ladder upward
To prove that you are you!

Dr. Don M. Ishmael

COWBOY'S LAMENT

I hope to see a mountain, or a forest, or a sea,
I'm sick to death of livin'
In this wind swept misery —
I hear the wind a-whistlin'
As it tears the soil free,
To cloud the sky with dirt and dust,
And leave behind a bare prairie —
I hate to see the earth dry up
And drop the heads of grain
And hear the cattle bawlin'
When they're thirstin' for a rain —
I hope to see a mountain, or a forest, or a sea,
I'm sick to death of livin'
In this wind-swept misery —
I don't know why I stick around
Unless it has to be
That I can't leave this dried up land,
Because it's part of me!

Dr. Don M. Ishmael

OOPSPA

Breathes there a note
With sound so pure
When skillfully played,
Can long endure . . .

But will dolefully fade
And tragically fail,
When a discord's made
On a tuba scale!

Dr. Don M. Ishmael

DECEIT

It never stops . . .
the pain of, I never know.
You, an insipid traveler
knowing only —
grey transparencies.

And touch, a lost horizon —
of someone's last chance
to be someone, for once.

This villainous beast,
divulges an honest heart
of his wishing.

Deceit, only he understands,
his tricks of confusion.
To destroy . . .
a moment's experience,
to grow proud in "true rapport."
His name of deception —
is a trait. That truth —
must continually test,
"these hazy waters"?

Patricia Anne Solek-Fritsche

SHORT POEM

My vision is
　　blurring
I'm almost asleep
My writing is
　　slurring
into bed I shall creep
Through flaming red eyes
　　I look at the time
I'm under the covers
　　and
here's the last rhyme.

Monica B. Strohmyer

THE CRABAPPLE

Standing tall and broad,
flourished with blossoms.
Sturdy but yet weak,
the crabapple.

The weather turns sharp
from sun to a stormy rain.
It's hard,
to see the pain and tears
running down the tree like sap,
the crabapple.

Beautiful in its solemn way,
standing shriveled and lost,
the crabapple.
The crabapple will bloom again.

Dori Rolando Dess

IN BETWEEN

it started long before
you or I were ever born
so how could we have known
the truth was not yet formed

we're supposed to stand for justice
we're supposed to stand for right
we're supposed to stand for those who can't
but instead we stand for might

the heads of nations sit around
and make decisions for us all
decisions that deal with life and death
fatality for all
what will it take
what needs to happen for those of you to see
that everything made in this world was
made for you and me

we're supposed to stand for truth
we're supposed to stand for life
we're supposed to stand for what we believe
but still we stand for might

Jeff Dess

MONUMENT ROCK, ECHO CAÑON.

FOREST

It wasn't that long ago
I remember it well,
the day the men came
with their axes held.

They didn't ask questions
these men of the woods,
they just stood and listened
to the sound of the wind.

Once there were many
now there are few,
once they were happy
now there is me and you.

I hope that our children
will be able to see,
the light in the forest
not the digging of trees

. . . who speaks for them?

Jeff Dess

For only to hold her in my arms
Just to kiss those wondrous lips
Of the girl which holds angels' wings
This the most beautiful girl of all
If this girl could be found I would
Do everything just and right forever
And all evils would disappear
Yet I must live with what is around
The girls which are beautiful to me
For the girl I search for is only
Part of a dream

James R. Hayes

For the memory of the past
The reminder of the present
Shows the pain of that
Which was lost within
The pursuit of a dream
For the dream was in sight
Yet she was too young
To see the dream now
I see a different yet more
Lively and realistic dream
For I shall have one that
Wants to love me for me
Not just my wants or words
She wants very much to
Become part of my world

James R. Hayes

Life of long ago
Living within today
Show in every detail
Lasting throughout time
Love as now as was then
Could time and distance
Tend to change its strength
Loving within lost time of dreams
Dying into reality of tomorrow
Life of long ago like yesterday
Showing in tomorrow as
Yesterday's love into today's reality

James R. Hayes

SUMMERTIME JOHN

He sat alone in the front porch swing,
Hair was red — pale and thin,
A limited mind and John his name,
As a little boy I befriended him.

He was big and I was small,
It really made no difference at all,
I'd walk by and he would call,
Sit with me we'll talk and draw.

He drew his favorites, I drew mine,
We traced the funnies line by line,
John . . . my buddy fair and true,
Happy summer how it flew.

Years have gone and the sand has sifted,
John stands there memories lifted,
Each in his own way uniquely gifted,
That summer we shared — split and drifted.

Now I sit here decades gone,
Tears run down shadows long,
"It's dark now, John," a mother's song,
"Come in John," Jimmy's gone.

James E. Moreland

THE LOBBY — OLD FRIENDS

Shadows move on the ceilings slick,
Shuffling feet on the floor below,
Some moved slowly some moved quick,
Laughing and weaving to and fro.

Heads on shoulders expectantly look,
Green covered sofas and chairs,
Reading and sifting papers and books,
To bring, to have a friend in their stare,

Old friends gather to meet and to serve,
No real painstaking reward,
It's good to see you! Gusto and verve,
Sensitive moments, to cherish, to guard.

In the lobby old friends we will meet,
In the lobby next time around,
In the lobby next year to greet,
I'll look forward to the next time in town.

James E. Moreland

OUR SON

Today is the birthday
   of our dear little boy
His age is nine and oh sometimes
   he's a heartache, but he's a joy.

We would never, ever trade him
   for any other child
Though he is often devilish
   we just melt at his sweet smile.

We love him when he's good
   and even when he's bad
And pray that he will grow to be
   an honest and upright lad.

So Happy Birthday our dear son
   we hope this day will be
A day of joy, a day of love
   and lots and lots of fun.

Nancy Porter

OUR DAUGHTER

Today is a special day
   for you our daughter dear
For it is your birthday
   which comes but once a year.

This day seems almost impossible
   for us to see that you
Have grown so much in this past year
   than we expected you to.

It's plain to see you're growing up
   in so many, many ways
We pray that our training dear
   never, ever strays.

We hope that you will remember
   that you're a Christian girl
No matter where, or whom you're with
   don't let Satan take you for a whirl.

Our love for you is expressed today
   and we hope that you will know
We'll always love you and try to understand
   although it doesn't always show.

Nancy Porter

MY VALENTINE

This valentine I write for you
   is just to let you know,
No one could ever take your place
   because I love you so.

The things you do, the things you say,
   always let me know,
That I am yours and you are mine
   and that our love will grow.

So on this day I wish for you
   a Happy Valentine,
And hope that you will say you'll be
   forever and only mine.

Nancy Porter

A MOTHER'S GARDEN

A woman kneels amongst a barren lot,
Children at her side sing songs that mother taught
As they poke their chubby fingers in the hardened ground
And place hopeful seeds within the dented mounds.

Weeks have passed, the sprouts are showing now,
Mother excitedly points to her children dear.
The eye in wonder just how
The flowers now appear.

An older woman labors as she leans
And aches within her bones,
As she cares for the yearly flowers seen,
She pulls the weeds alone.

Children grown kneel in the garden shower
They started so long ago to save,
And in their wonder gently pull the flowers
To place on their mother's grave.

Susan Eppers Calhoun

THE NIGHT

Strange, the quiet peace of the night.
It soothes, it grabs, it holds you tight.
So much happens at night, so few are awake to see.
The world come and goes, but nobody knows,
  Just all of what it is.

Strange, the quiet peace of the night.
It calms, it smooths, it can make all . . . right.
The night is for relaxing, for sleeping,
  But it is also for restlessness and activity.
The night. For so much, for so many.

Joseph M. Lampe

INNOCENCE

Take me back to days gone by,
when underneath an azure sky,
my spirit soared
and I was free
to run and jump and dance and sing.

Take me back to days gone past,
my bare feet ran through cool, green grass,
with bandaged knee
and toothless grin
the summer days would never end.

Take me back to days long gone,
when life was young and I was strong,
things were always
as they seemed
and the water rippled through the cool, cool stream.

Take me back for a moment or two,
let me reclaim my carefree youth,
when right was right
and truth was truth.
Oh, take me back . . .

Karen H. Hollis

IN MY HEART THERE IS A PLACE

In my heart there is a place where I can go and,
  no one can bother me

When life's outrageous slings and arrows torment me,
  there is a place where I can go

There is a place of unsurpassed beauty and love
  where I can go and shut out the outside world

There is a place where flowers always bloom
  and birds forever sing

There is a place where I can go where it never snows,
  and silence like a flower grows

In my heart there is a place where all life is at peace

There is a place where even the eagles are at peace
  as they soar into the heavens

In my heart there is a place where no one can push and shove,
  and yet there is room for someone to love, someone gentle as a dove,
  and in this place of love

There is always room for guidance from above

Kenneth D. Patton

A TOUCH

A smile, gentle words can mean so much,
But there's something special about a touch.
It sends out warmth, tenderness and sincerity,
It says, ''I love you, I care, you're special to me.''
A gift from God as one of life's necessities.
Some touches that mean so much to me
Are my Love's hand on mine as we travel along.
That touch means love and fills my heart with song.
Children's arms around my neck, loving and trusting.
Oh, who could refuse such a wonderful blessing?
And when we are sad and filled with despair,
A touch from a friend says, ''I really care.''
To me a touch says it all, it means so much,
So I must let others know I care, with a touch.

Joyce Ranew

MOVING AHEAD

Moving ahead —
    it's hard.
        If only I could move back in my life,
        and stay there forever.

Moving ahead —
    it's necessary.
        Time goes on; therefore I must move on, too —
        whether or not I so desire.

Moving ahead —
    it brings completion.
        If I journey the road before me in faith;
        I will find God's plan, and be forever fulfilled.

Moving ahead —
    it's worth the struggle.

Julie Rose

SEA SPORES

RISE YE, TWO SUN DAZE,
Feast Able the Eye.
IS IT the BREATH,
Consuming flowers
to shallowing graves,
and no more?

The Traveler comes
a walking, a waking
YE, Lilies of the Valley
Stretch there, Heads.

Sadder Moan is Heard
from Shepherd's Horn,
alone, Somewhere upon the Hilling Side.

CLEANLY, a Shine,
        and, the wetness,
as quiet whispers the grass.
Ah smally gazed her, his
        Form the Wind's SONGING.

The Heralded Announcement is Danced Forth,
    as Wings Spread Wide.

Victoria Smith

LOVE IS NOT LOST

Love is not lost if given away.
Its message received by others each day,
Bringing comfort to a despairing heart,
Instilling joy where only sadness had a part.

Love can give hope to one who has none,
Replacing dread and fear, giving peace to some.
Fulfilling its purpose, it enriches each life,
Putting an end to warring and strife.

Where there is love, there is no room for hate.
True love is unable to discriminate.
With love in your heart to meet each day,
Guess what happens when you give it away.
It returns to you, with wings, unbound!
Love is never lost . . . it is truly found!

Sharon M. Waterman

THE HAPPINESS OF LOVE

A tempess so sweet, no longer bitter
The diamond of hope now brightly glitter
My heart, thy domain is now
Shall not be tainted, never foul
In glittering hopes there yet remain
My feelings of now are still the same
My hopes that times of need are gone
Swept like the sands beneath the palm
My heart is soaring ever high
My happiness, I know, will never die
This life of mine, now fit for living
I promise now to be more giving
My hopes and dreams are yet to come
With you, my soul, with beauty numb
This world so vivid, bright, alive
From tow'ring trees to the turn of tide
I thank for love my love gave to me
To the haven of his arms I forever flee

Patricia Gayle Kuykendall

LOVE

Love is like an ocean
It flows eternally.
It bursts forth with restless passion,
As surging waves upon the sea.

Love is like a river,
Flowing gently on its course.
Deep contentment fills the soul,
Claiming peace and joy from its source.

Love is like a mountain,
Majestic in its size.
The height of which one cannot measure,
Its depth reflecting through love's eyes.

Love is like a journey,
It holds excitement and surprise,
Filled with beauty to behold,
And sweet memories for its prize.

Love is like a candle,
Burning brightly in the night.
It radiates a glow of warmth,
Giving hope and calming fright.

Sharon M. Waterman

MY LOVE

Shimmering softly, a thousand fold
Into my life I shall you mold
You gave me strength and harmony
You heard my softly whispered plea
No tears to fall in times to follow
No bitterness invading to leave me hollow
The beauty of this so solemn hour
Is more brilliant than that of yonder flower
I grasp its stem, yet leave it living
Forever to you, my heart is giving
Past tears of sorrow were not in vain
Your tender touch erased all pain
So generous, you, in all you give
My soul fills, bursts, with will to live
The thought of failure, ever present
Recedes through mists to times yet distant
I grieve no more for what to come
Seen only now, bright shining sun
A wondrous gift, giv'n to me today,
My heart bequeathed to you always.

Patricia Gayle Kuykendall

NIGHT

All is still.
Minute symphonies begin their twilight music.
As the sun's last fingers slip away,
Tiny crystals of light appear
Breaking the monotonous black solidity.

Like a ghost, he steals across the sky,
Veiled in misty brightness.
His craterous face beams softly upon shadows.
Nothing stirs.
Night has come.

Kayla Dowden

identity crisis

i looked in the mirror this morning
there was nothing there
nothing to see
i looked at all my pictures of myself
they were all photos of empty air
but i'm not too surprised
because
when i think about it
who am i really?
i haven't done anything important
nothing that matters
or makes any difference
i have no direction
i'm not going anywhere
i don't know
what i want to do with my life
and when i think about that
it scares me
what if i never find out who i am?

Marta Kvande

NO LAUGHING MATTER

why is it
I am never taken seriously
even by my ''friends''?
what is it
that makes my most serious problems
so funny to them?
maybe it's just
that they don't really care
maybe it's because
I'm not popular enough
to matter
I'll never be able to ask them
they'll just laugh in my face
so I guess
I have to find
a real friend
who will understand
when I need to be serious

Marta Kvande

FEELINGS CAN BE FRAGILE . . .

Feeling can be fragile . . .
If one dares to even care,
And a strong heart broken
By a word cruelly spoken.

Feelings can be fragile . . .
As the tongue becomes a sword,
Cutting deep to the soul
Soon reaching its final goal.

Feelings can be fragile . . .
I need not tell you so,
And a strong heart broken
By words reaching to your soul.

Terri Lea Murray

COMEBACK HILL

Here's a toast to C.P.R.C.,
To its mentors, Nancy and Jill,
Our recovery they oversee,
A mission eager to fulfill.

Taskmasters they surely be,
But nay, that's hardly a vice;
For we know quite well, you see,
Their R.N. badges mean Really Nice!

Many weeks of effort and determination
Prepare us for that happy day, graduation,
No need for tasseled caps or gowns
To mask the feeling of exhilaration.
Long gone are the grimaces and frowns,
Replaced by gratitude and appreciation;

At last the time has come, to old room 13
And the iron horses therein, to bid adieu.
Ann's cheery "hello," her services we'll miss, too.
And most of all, heartfelt thanks to Nancy & Jill.
They helped us reach the peak of "Comeback Hill."

John "Bud" Schifferli

THE SEDUCTION

Clouds moved rapidly across the face of the bright moon.
Chilling winds blew at the back of her neck as she pulled
her coat close around her small body.

The dampness of the blowing snow now blinded her.
Night escorted her along the dark path.
Howling winds laughed at her stupidity for wandering so far
alone.

The winds blew and the dampness penetrated her very soul.
She felt herself accepting the night,
yielding to its persistence.

Night slowly captured her heart and lifted her gently to the
ground, raping her of life.
And the winds blew and the snow grew still and the clouds
moved rapidly across the face of the bright moon.

Linda Smith-Banks

SOUTHERN LADY

Another hot southern night
the feeling felt so right
just for you and i
i think of the years gone by
wishing i could hold you once again
knowing i can never hold you again
the need for you is so strong now
thinking of all those times together
making love like there was gonna be no tomorrow
i will never forget you
your memory haunts me day and night now since you're gone
time passed by so fast when we were together
seems i could never say i love you too many times
never could i ever write too much poetry for you
you knew me inside and out
you came into my life but now you're gone
time must still carry on
that's what memories are for

Johnny P. Watson

LEFT BEHIND

This is a poem to Milt whom I have hurt so many times
whose loud gruff voice   a trade mark
laughter that could fill a bar
a presence so dangerously contagious
I followed you everywhere
followed until I could no longer keep up
knowing you were an only child, I left.
Thinking you would always be there
never thinking you wouldn't, and you left.
Behind you the beach, the bars,
afternoon cocktails, late night jazz, you left.
The beach is empty, the bars so quiet,
cocktails and jazz just memories.
Why did I trust you to live forever, to love me forever
you left
and after a while I'll trust you again
when I hear that familiar voice
say in that familiar way
welcome to my world
my love.

Christina Anne Bennett

CHRISTINA ANNE BENNETT. Born: 11-30-51; Married: William Bennett; Education: San Jose State University, B.A., Psychology, 1973; Saddleback College, Nursing Degree, 1976; Occupations: Registered nurse, Paralegal, Writer; Memberships: Emergency Nurses Association, Orange County Paralegal Association; Comments: *I wrote this poem in loving memory of a close friend. I am currently writing a mystery novel.*

INCA POWER

Quietly Tupa Inca's empire disappears;
    The plateau, whereon I stand,
To be resurrected in the modern years,
    The kingdom carved by disciplined hands.

Touched by the finger of time
    Is every earthly reign;
The beauty, to ease my weary kind,
    Spans the remnant of a culture few attain.

The brooklets of Machu Picchu yield their sighs,
    A hymn o'er the tomb.
Of festive days and gilded skies,
    Before the bearded men spread Inca's doom.

The mighty winds murmur, howl, and groan,
    To scare my jungle walk,
And stir the wonder forth, to roam
    Where Inca warriors and nobles once talk.

The Ocelot's distant, piercing scream
    Fills the explorer's sense with dread;
Still more ominous is the unveiled dream,
    It affirms Inca power fled.

Douglas Brower

REFLECTIONS

When it is my turn
   to be put to rest,
May family and friends
   gather together,
May the church be filled
   with flowers of every color,
May the prayer be
   short and sweet.
May you always remember me
   in your heart,
And I shall be a friend forever,
May your life be filled
   with youth so sweet;
Until that day comes,
   when we must once again
      meet.

Terri Lea Murray

THE BUTTERFLY DANCE

The rush to be near
the beauty in one's sight
to be free to say,
''Let's catch the flight!''

The rush to be near
the dance in one's walk
to be free to say,
''Let's really talk!''

The rush to be near
the love in one's heart
to be free to say,
''Let's never part!''

The rush to be near
the escape in one's soul
to be free to say,
''Let's love so!''

The rush to be near
to love so free
butterflies are beautiful,
''Don't you agree?''

Mary Kathryn Wetzel

NIGHT FANTASY

Dreams taking sight
in moving sands of night.
   Was that you,
   who rushed so sweetly?
Moonbeams weaving light
of soul's weary flight.
   Was that you,
   who spoke so softly?
Starbeams dancing bright
in loving waves of delight.
   Was that you,
   who touched so gently?
Fantasies holding tight
of reality's dreary fright.
   Wasn't that you,
   before dawn's early light?

Mary Kathryn Wetzel

MEMORIES

My innermost thoughts,
Cannot be bought,
I try to believe,
That one day I'll leave,
Happy and ready to face life alone,
But until then I sit by the phone,
Here at my home with mother,
There is no other,
I'd rather be with through the years,
As I shed some tears,
I've come to realize,
All my memories are a bunch of lies,
More or less,
I must confess,
Memories that I can't bear,
Or visions of a loss in the air,
Come to mind,
When I can't find,
The memories that I keep,
All to myself when I sleep,
My memories!

Randy B. Aron

CHRIST OUR KING

Greetings in Christ's name I bring
the true story of our heavenly King
How he came to earth one special day
in a barn, on a bed of hay
His birth is what we celebrate
His love so very, very, very great
He gave up all his kingly rights
to give us life and make us right
So someday when our lives o'er,
we'll be with him forevermore
His life he humbly gave for us
on a cruel wooden cross
His life did not end there though
for three days later from the grave
he arose,
and now glad tidings to you
I bring, the story of Christ our
King.

Zorrine Bailey

OLD JAMES

James wasn't much to look at,
   He only had one eye,
And we naughty children used to laugh
   When he walked by.

But James had a secret
   That we children never knew.
A secret that was kept
   From most adults, too.

James had lost his eye
   In a terrible war.
He lost it saving my daddy
   From death's dark door.

So I'm thankful to James
   For making daddy death-free.
For if it weren't for old James
   There wouldn't be me.

Judy A. Deeter

OH INNOCENT NIGHT

Oh, innocent night,
I feel your plight.
You are blamed for many a thing
that does not from your heart spring.

When the mist of an ominous night
comes just before the dawn,
the damp darkness is only a pawn.

Dark of its own
does not spawn violent acts.
The night is just wearing a dark gown
and similar events would occur
if night wore brown.

A white, light night
cannot stop a fight,
a lover's quarrel after sunset,
or a foolish poker game bet.

Oh, innocent night,
I truly feel your plight.
You are even praised for many a thing
that does not from your heart spring.

Ruth Calkins

THE SEED'S RELEASE

The colors of fall are soft rust and yellow,
And milkweed pods are opening;
The seeds inside are attached
To silky gossamer threads
That can open out to catch the breeze.

The seeds hang stubbornly onto the pod
Until the wind is right
And suddenly it seems
As if God releases them
To rise up, up, out of sight.

Like seeds in the pod,
Our talents lie within us;
And our immortality, too,
Depends on releasing them
To the greater life around us.

Whether we raise children,
Create a painting, write a poem,
Do a kind deed, or just smile at others,
The love we express is our immortality —
How we shall live on in the hearts of others.

Frances G. Callahan

LOST-N-FOUND

I am lost without the
thought of you . . .
But found when someone
mentions your name . . .
I am lost without
your smile . . .
But am found again
when you smile at me . . .
I am lost without
your touch . . .
But when you touch me
I come home.

Kathy Jacobs Dobrovolny

IT GONNA BE A RAINY DAY

Oh it gonna be a rainy day I can see rainbow smiling with the cloud
I can hear the thunder way up in the sky.

From the distance where I stand I can also see swallows flying way
Up in towards the rushing grey clouds yes I know it gonna be a
Rainy day.

I can see the lightning flashes over hills and valley and suddenly
The wind rushes violently towards the bamboo grove and they bend
As if they want to break in the background stands the old willow tree
Weeping in the wind I know it gonna be a rainy day.

I can see dark clouds rushing by and the sun refuse to shine I can
Feel a little sprinkle here and there yes, I know it gonna be a
Rainy day.

George Morrison

SNOW'S DOWN IN WASHINGTON TOWN

'Tis fun to walk out in the snow,
Red ruddy faces tied up in scarves,
Soft fragile snowflakes that bump a nose,
Winds zoom them in, in crazy arcs.

Crunching zombies meet face to face,
Each one politely holding his path,
Then they meet and share their space,
Way up high on the overpass.

Exhilarating, you know! The snow,
Brings out the best as we kick along,
Frisky moments and smiles that glow,
A different way — a different throng.

When snow's down in Washington town,
It alters a way of life,
They struggle a bit and slip some around,
Never a complaint — never a gripe.

When snow comes down in Washington town,
One will see a postcard scene,
Dignified buildings, shrines and grounds,
For a while stand together pristine and clean.

James E. Moreland

The worse part of losing you was not
the long lonely days that suddenly seemed
        so empty,
nor was it
the still endless nights that kept me awake
crying over you.

The worst part of losing you was not
longing to hear
your voice caress each syllable
of my name,
nor was it
the special way you had of sharing my silent thoughts.

The worst part of losing you was knowing
you were free
    to love
        somebody else.

Chanie Greenzweig

THE WEEPER CROSSING

and, so sadder, a tearing goes,
flowing onto the rows
and rows
of still-chanting, sounder love.

weeping,
crossing, (wet-dank), hall ways
to chilling, greying darkened room, (as ice-circles dance along walls).

with nails, red,
holding up neon-glow to eve's
unwanted signings, feelings gaps of circle-ice prances down.

no stage of sleeper stage takes a scene here,
as emotion is thrown-down-to fly across the dank-dying dust of
its greying alleyway.

ah, and yet,
the Times do turn over-way
to a sweetening Lightday,
ah to la,
a newly softer-forming

        WILL-OWED REAPING . . .

Victoria Smith

TEARS CROSSING BRIDGES

born to weeping,
tears-tremble-down-town-waves-walking-fear,
Excitement hides
within
shadowed-pencilings,
as steel-tone corners,
cold, stone-rolling,
glides toward inner bluing street-daze.
rolling too, the glow-worm slithers
onto
redding-blooding,
stolen pathways.

cry-cupped tears, frayed, and stalking,
(growing form hungry eye-sockets), (in Crouched Remotion).

silently, Feedings
are born to spurted wings
of Hunger —
carrying
    your soul,
        away . . .

Victoria Smith

THE MIRACLE OF LIFE

The Miracle of Life, expressed in many ways, is seen
through the eyes of young and old.
The birth of a newborn, the greatest miracle and joy of all.
The discovery of a new-found love, be it young or old.
Rain from the heavens above that makes all of nature grow.
Gentle snowflakes that fall so pure and white.
A small seed from which wonders grow, beautiful flowers,
fruit and trees.
The Miracle of Life, something to be treasured by young
and old alike.

Karen Schweiger

IN REMEMBRANCE OF A CHILD

Little Wolf
Child descended from the Sioux.
Born as the morning mists vanished
And the dawning of day came anew.

Little Wolf
Child and only son of Tacanka.
Destined by the twinkling stars
To roam the forest and mountains
For years numbering not quite twenty-one.

Little Wolf
Grandchild of an Indian Warrior.
Hostile, yet gentle; lonely and misunderstood —
This child of the red hair
The color of autumn leaves.

Little Wolf
Ho'pa child of my Mother.
Little Wolf, papoose, Lowell —
My only brother.

Little Wolf
Child of the Heavens.

Cathy S. Carson

LOVE AND MARRIAGE

No matter how many years go by,
I will never understand you.

You couldn't wait to get married.
And when we did, for me, it was
a living hell.

Before that day, I overlooked your
bad points and only saw your good.

I guess I just thought that the bad
points would simply disappear on
that magical day.

You insisted that you loved me.
Then why, when given the choice,
did you choose cocaine over me?

Leslie Colson

FOREVER ONE

A long time ago,
I fell in love with you;
Long before the golden sun
had risen,
long before the oceans
sang their mellow songs.
The moment I caught
your first glance,
fate gently touched my heart,
and I felt love
for the one who stood
before me.
You were to be my love
and my life;
My joys and my sorrows
forever and eternally.
Let us take this love now
and be joined
for we are destined to be one.

Terri Cooter

I DON'T KNOW

I don't know Relativity,
I only know what is relative.
I don't know war,
I only know what it does.
I don't know what hunger is,
I am thankful for the ignorance.
I don't understand long division,
only that division can be too long.
I don't know who God is,
and that's the problem.
Stop fighting, forget what it stands for.
Stop crying, it does no good.
Stop lying, it makes matters worse!
Stop understanding, it's solutions we need.
Educate, but don't stop there.
It is useless to know and not do.
I don't know what this world means,
or what it is,
but I know what it can be!
And that's not ignorance!

Frederick Dame, Jr.

RETIREMENT (1-25-87)

There's a feeling of completeness
With its own siren song,
Your life's fulfilled; for neatness
Your soul should move along.

That now when you've surrendered
Your job, your working space,
Another person's tendered
And will assume your place.

If you don't quickly fill the gap
Work took within your day,
A mindless void your soul will trap
And life will ooze away.

Charles H. Dever

THE WHALE

He splashes to the surface and then
disappears to the depths below.
A giant animal, yet ever so gentle.
The graceful curves of the tail that licks
playfully at the water, but yet could kill a
man on contact.
He's the hunted one; the one that men
will kill, but yet they fear him.
He is the quiet one, but he sings
below the sea.
His mouth is a cave, open when the
fish need a place to hide.
He is the whale.

Gina Erickson

THE CHILD'S SLEEP

Gentle breaths in quiet whispers
From the tiny mouth arise.
Unknown dreams of simple pleasures
Hidden under restful eyes.
Quietly I watch in wonder
As the child hums a sigh.
Peaceful slumber, protecting always
While the moments tip-toe by.
Suddenly, an unexpected twitch
Disturbs the baby's sleep.
But the movement is not strong enough
To concern a rest so deep.
Aft' a time he gives a whimper —
Not quite equal to a cry.
Soon a yawn, and now a stretch.
He opens finally his bright blue eyes.
He looks to me with smiling eyes,
And then he reaches for me.
Contentment sheds its warmth upon us
While I hold him tenderly.

Reneé Goyette

FREEBORN

From the cabin i am sitting
with mine eyes towards the sky,
the birds were more than singing
in the tree tops they did fly,
high up in the mountains
and back up in the woods,
is where the teepees stood.
By the campfire the indians sat
with their tom-toms in their lap,
some would dance and some would sing
they would all make the heavens ring,
with laughter and cheer
the indian would dance and sing
as was meant to be and let the heavens ring,
with the indians once free
like the birds and the bees
and like the butterfly from rose to rose,
that's the way — freeborn goes.

Mary Kay Houdek

IVORY TOWER

Like an eagle I have soared
Up into the clouds,
With a rapid heartbeat
And shortness of breath,
At last . . .
I think I have found
Heaven.
I climb the spiral staircase
To my thoughts
And to my feelings,
Searching . . .
For answers to my questions,
Only to be led
To more questions,
So I retreat . . .
Back to my ivory tower.

R. E. Lunt

TO MY SISTER AND FRIEND

As the links of a chain combine to form its strength,
so the members of a family bond to make such a chain.

When there is a weakness in the chain, the other links
unite to hold it together. It is the same with family.

In single pieces, a chain has little significance. It
is not a whole. This is the way of a family.

A chain which is lengthened is of more value. So are
the additions of a family.

The cost of a chain is determined by its worth, as with
families.

A family's wealth is measured by its understanding, trust,
togetherness, faith, memories and forgiveness. A totality
of love.

We will add a new link to our family chain during your wedding.

This gold chain is a symbolic gift of our family. May it
remind you of our being and strength.

This chain is just a tangible chain. It will provide memories.
In time it will perish.

A family is invincible.

A family is forever.

Sharon Bock

RECEIVING TOGETHER

Awaiting the glow from the lamp, a piece of my heart became
a part of her. As I was sure millions of American hearts had.
The lamp was lit. Waiting breathlessly for her to speak, as
if the magic of our hearts would bring her to life. She did
not utter words. The Lady did not need to speak aloud. She
speaks in each of us for we are her progression. Our hearts
are not borrowed for Lady Liberty, instead they are generated
by Liberty as one — these United States of America.

Sharon Bock

TO ALL WHO HEAR

Urgent says
          Beware
  I said
          watch these signs
          Of
          Corporate webs
Fascist forces   full ahead
If they get   their way
          Freedom's dead
  Choices voices
          This
          World retaught
          Our pride
          Our dreams
Must be recaught
                  Urgent says
  Beware
      I said
          Watch these signs
                  Of
  Corporate webs

Aquilla Pluma

THAT FIRST THANKSGIVING

The Pilgrims gave thanks that day long ago
For goodness and mercy the Lord did bestow,
For the end of their journey across the sea,
For their new home in America, land of the free.

They landed at Plymouth, when they came to shore,
Bowed down and praised God for opening the door
To freedom and safety, a chance to start life new,
For the promise seen in this bountiful land with its
   lakes so blue.

The tilled the earth and planted their seeds,
Built their homes, trusting God for their needs.
Though at times it was tough, they found a way
To make friends with the Indians they met each day.

So on that first Thanksgiving, they all joined hands,
Vowed to be brothers and share this great land.
They would work side by side, accept each other's ways.
They had much to be thankful for that day.

On each Thanksgiving Day, we should recall their plan,
And walk with our brothers upon this land,
Accepting each other through patience and love,
Giving thanks to our Creator for blessings from above.

Sharon M. Waterman

HUMAN

Why do people judge another
By the color of their brother?
What's in pigment of our skin
That could possibly tell what's within?
We can prove ourselves and work so hard
We can stand for the honesty of our word.
And yet a person takes a look at our skin
Then the questions suddenly begin.
Where's he from? What *is* he?
Who are his parents, from where are they?
I'm an American, born and raised,
From these questions I'll come unfazed.
Listen to my heart, look into my soul
I'm all the parts that make the whole.
I'm human, I'm male, sometimes happy sometimes sad,
But to judge only by color is really bad!

Cruz Riojas

FLOODED IN THE COLORS

Now I've never been a runner but you've got me running for you,
Running around in circles doing the things you ask me to.
And I've always been a listener, hear every word you say . . .
But it's started to sound dangerous, it's become a dangerous way.

And as I turned, turned around, slowly passing my feet over the ground,
Listening to the silence and hearing every sound,
The words were in your eyes and they turned my head around!

It starts out all so innocent, skies of rainbow blue,
Slippin' from the darkness just to dance in the light with you.
Baffled by the whispering, "voices in my head"
Twisted by the crooked "writings I have read"
Flooded in the colors, "I should have chose instead"
I'm dancing in the shadows drifting through my head.

James Garland Brosamle

LOVE

From the heart flows love
Love is more than a word
Love is giving and receiving

To some people giving is money and time
To others it is a condition of the mind
One thing is sure, Love comes from the heart

Kyle Meers

TO BE A POET

A poet's ingenuity
Subsists in rhyme and verse,
His vision of reality
Is measured like a miser's purse.

He seizes fancy on the wing
And pens it down in haste,
Binding it with artful threads
Circumscribing flight and waste.

Now he culls it every strand
With a wee bit comb,
Akin in viability
To a fetus in the womb.

Imagery his only tool
Voilà! the structure holds,
Another little cottontail
Snipping off the marigolds.

Evelyn Pitel

LOVE

Love is here today and gone tomorrow
leaving only memories, tears, pain, and
sorrow.
Sometimes when love dies, you can
still find the strength to survive.
But when it leaves you shattered and betrayed,
you find it hard to try again.

Deborah J. Scholar

BROKEN HEARTS

People see the side of you
they want to see . . .
They fall in love with
only a part of you . . .
When it's over we are
told, you broke my heart . . .
No, you broke your own
heart . . .
To truly love you must
see and love all sides
of a person; if we do not,
how can it be called love? . . .
We break our own hearts.

Kathy Jacobs Dobrovolny

LOVE IS

Love is a word that's tossed about
    By many a tongue today,
But seldom do we hear it used
    In the good and proper way.

We hear a hundred meanings
    For this word in common talk,
But most of them so clearly
    Do its proper meaning mock.

Though love is often thought about
    As something that is felt,
Its good and perfect meaning is
    A giving of one's self.

Hope Scott

MILDRED EBY SCOTT. Pen Names: Hope Scott, Mildred Eby; Born: Miami, Florida, 7-5-26; Married: Thomas W. Scott, 12-19-58; Education: International Bible Institute and Seminary, Th.B., 1982; Occupation: Nurse; Award: Medal from the Greater Miami Women's Club for 'The Robin,' 1941; Poetry: 'The Robin,' *Junior Joys*, 9-38; 'My Ministry,' *American Poetry Anthology, Volume VII, Number 1*, 5-87; Other Writings: "Let's Build the House of the Lord," *Association News*, 8-84; Comments: *I write children's poems, inspirational poems, ballads, and religious articles.*

CARTER COUNTRY

I know of this place.
    It's just a nick of space.
Stand tall my friend.
    There's not a breeze to bend thee.
Inhale the air! Oh so fresh
    But it's there.
In Carter country.
    That's where I long to be.

My arms are full of hope.
    My heart is full of love.
With the wind blowing my hair.
    And the sea at my feet.
Surely this is a feeling that
    Can't be beat.
It's Carter country.
    That's where I long to be.

R. N. Stone

Night is falling like a soft black kitten
Falling asleep on your lap
With the promise that when she wakes
Everything will be all right
Day rises like a tiny sleeping dragon
With a puff of hazy smoke
Or with a roar of brilliant flame

John E. Tollakson

LETTER TO THE LORD

I sit on the hillside
    and watch the sun rise.
Its beautiful colors
    light up the skies.
I sit and watch
    the day draw near,
as over the creek
    leaps a timid young deer.
I sit in the stillness
    while a red robin sings,
and watch as a soft breeze
    ruffles its wings.
Ducks play in the water;
    A crane flies overhead;
A hawk starts to land,
    but then flies on instead.
Moments like this
    are oh so few.
When I had this moment
    I was watching for You.

Elizabeth Wells

TONIGHT

We shared a minute,
in the realm of time.

You brought forth your life,
I brought mine.
Our defenses were there,
the barricades erected high.
Each one of us trying to stay on our own side,
wanting to cross,
but daring not.
Each wanting the other to cross,
for our emptiness knows no side.

Yet,
tonight;
I have met a friend,
now,
there is another on my side.

Steve Whitenburg

AMERICAN HERITAGE

The war is over and many have died
Fighting for heritage and American pride.
The soldier lies still and lifeless on the cold damp ground
Where he gave up his life to keep us free
And fought through the battle with pure bravery.

Thousands of men die and give up their lives
To keep our freedom and American pride.
But ask yourself, "Is it worth it?" while they lie in the blood
Where they'll be buried and forgotten and scarcely spoken of.

As the valley lies still with no sound,
The guns have stopped, the roaring has died.
And so did the men who fought for our side,
Giving up their lives for American pride.

A mother gets a letter saying her son has died
While fighting on the battlefield to save another man's life.
Can you imagine her feelings as the tears roll from her eyes?
All the heritage won't bring him back alive.

These men fought with courage throughout the day,
Trying to win in every possible way.
But they have died knowing that we will live
Enjoying the pride of America's heritage.

Bob D. Robison

RACE OF THE HYDROPLANES

With a growling roar

Our big boats unleash their power.
  Now is the hour
    To prove our mettle.

With a hundred horses
Underneath our wooden hulls
We match our brains,
  Our sinews, our engines,
    In the bursts of speed.

Round the curves
  We flirt with death,
    Laugh at death,

      Defy him;
      Throw the driver's gauntlet in his teeth; —
    Exulting with the
        High flying rooster tails.

Mary Wham

BOX

They said time heals,
Time simply built a box
        in which to hold the pain.
Sometimes, carefully, I lift the lid
        to peek inside.
The pain is there.
Contained,
Alive as ever.

Frances Grasso

THE UNKNOWN TALE

The tall ships who sat proudly in the water, were
large and silent. Their masts disrupted by the wind
appeared as surrendering flags of war unknown to men.

What is this war unknown to men? Who started it and
what is its cause? Who is the surrendering for, the
powerful waves? Oh, it is like mental silent graves.
The star in the sky like a lighthouse above in the
heavens. What is this secret? The unknown tale. Will
the war ever stop? Will we ever figure out?

The unknown tale.

Portia Spierdowis

SUMMER NIGHTS AND RUMORS

  for R.

Lulled by lake murmurs and the soft hiss
of summer's night; lulled by cottonwood's whisper
while the crescent moon climbs eastward, a soft kiss
and the muted music of bullfrogs' chorus, one by one,

sings through the still distance, the shadowy darkness.
Lulled thus, our lives slowly revolve, incline inward
achieve an honesty in which cowardice,
resentment, and cautious games have no part.

Your shining teeth part, time suspends its stroke
with swirling tide and lapping lake rhythms; suspends
reality from those long years lived before I woke.
The island's dark shadows swim in the moonlit lake . . .

This moment we cling together beneath a shadowy tree,
arms entwined: reach, touch, claim that sacred space,
narrow the chasm, close the circle, fly distance-free —
mouth pressed to mouth, breathing the other's breath,

healed of lonely reality, naked heart's cry, self-hypnosis
bemused by summer breezes, starlight and languor.
I know, still hear rumors of whose voice his is —
calling heart-to-heart — naming the nights left.

Jauneth Skinner

THOUGHTS OF YOU

It started with a flash, like a streak of lightning blue;
It burned me like a torch and the match was held by you, I gave to you.

It was the rain that brought me back to feel the knife twist in my back.
But the flames of things to be is what set me free . . .
So hard to see through the steam you made of me.

With a rain cloud in your left hand and a lightning bolt in your right,
Burning me down and cooling me off
        and twisting my heart so tight I'd turn to steam.

Seems like a movie and feels like a dream, can't cry, so inside I scream;
In my mind I rehearse the scene . . .

"*No sounds,*" just the pit, splish, splash of the rain,
"*No sights,*" just the blue streaks crossing the night,
"*No desires,*" just a flame that sometimes turns to a fire,
"*No feelings,*" just the spin of my mind as it starts reelin' with,
"*Thoughts of you.*"

James Garland Brosamle

YOU

I love you in the morning
I love you in the night
Nothing I have ever felt, has ever felt so right
When we are together, I'm in heaven
When we are apart I ache for your touch
Never have I cared for anyone this much
I want to do all I can to keep you by my side
I know I've hurt you and that you've cried
But you have to believe I never meant to
Because darling, I love you!

Dee Workman

BANANAS

Tropic fever moves her through the trees
With dark shade and dark companion.
Cane knives talking.
A common tongue.
The seeping juice
Stains their scalps and shoulders,
Their hands and barefoot souls.

Beyond, more trees gone wild
Lit bright by boiling sun.
The purple blood still runs inside
Snakes hide, coiled around the blossoms.

Fatigue and thirst slow down the day,
Bent backs and blistered hands.
On the edge of the porch
Ice tea sweats
In two tin cups.
In two tin plates
Sandwiches bake with bugs.

Hunger. Again a common tongue.
Rest. A common cause.
Survival in a changing land.
Waiting, for The Wet to come.

Lynn Garnier

SERENITY

On velvet paws with tethered claws,
She climbs upon my knee.
Though unaware, she has an air
Of quiet dignity.

A tiny Sphinx, she yawns and blinks,
And stretches regal toes.
Then nestles in to now begin
Her luxury repose.

I stroke her fur, she starts to purr,
In rhythmic, soothing tone.
And soon my mind starts to unwind,
Succumbing to the drone.

Forgetting cares and world affairs,
My eyes begin to close.
For now at least, the world's at peace,
As cat and mistress doze.

Barbara McIvor

EGOMANIA

Schemes and greed, a human need,
It is of these that vanity feed.
Life spent satisfying ego's pride
Is found a lonely, pointless ride.
And at this journey's aimless end
You'll find your ego your only friend.

Debra A. Martin

IMAGES OF THE PAST

Don't go chasing rainbows
They fade away too fast.
Just images of beauty,
Reflections of sunlight cast.
Too soon to disappear,
No trace remains when passed.
No record of creation's truth
What change of time surpassed.
And it seems things of beauty
In this world never last.
Yet memories hold forever
The rainbows of the past.

Debra A. Martin

TIME

On and on, with constant pace,
The hands of time run their endless race.
Never resting, yet held still in place,
The journey's path on unknown face.

Time exists not to question why,
Dictating birth and when we die.
And yet when all of life has gone
The hands of time will still move on.

Debra A. Martin

THE JUGGLERS

Colors fall and climb, then fall again.
Our eyes stare
at the men on the lawn
who throw offerings to heaven.
How do they dare?

Catching the sunlight,
their pin-wheels fly over our heads
like leaves falling from a tree,
or stars falling from the sky.

I wonder why only the jugglers
have ever tried to gather life's gems
and send them back up?
The rest of us shrug and collect things in cups;

Mortal containers of hollow tin
that never offer up the contents within.
Few have the rhythm or grace
to return a gift
without throwing it in God's face.

Lydia Nevarez

HIS FATE

For Greg, the year 1987
Began stinging and cold.
After January and February,
Time swiftly flew by.
Unwilling to wait any longer,
He decides to build a house.
His house, which requires full
Attention, physically and
Emotionally he felt drawn off . . .
So here was Greg, with the
Woman who loves him, living
In a duplex, not even a home . . .
And yet, such was the concealed
Asset that his life soon would
Take on a conflict as he
Had never dreamed of. His
Life has meaning and change,
He has reason to act.
Excitement, and vitality will move
Greg to have what is his fate!

Sherri L. Rea

SHERRI LYN REA-CHAMBERLIN. Born: Clinton, Wisconsin, 4-7-63; Married: Greg Rea, 9-3-86; Education: Blackhawk Technical Institute, 1987; Writing Course; Writer's Digest School (home schooling); Occupations: Physical Fitness Advisor, Nutritionist; Poetry; 'Depression — Overthrown,' *Many Voices, Many Lands*, 3-6-87; 'His Fate,' *American Poetry Anthology*, 4-22-87; Comments: *I have something, I feel, of value to communicate. I have information, ideas, and insights that will add to readers' enjoyment, wisdom, and awareness. My work may be designed to help or educate only 1,000 people, which fulfills its purpose, and is as worthy of publication as a book written for 1,000,000 people!*

A damsel in distress
Not many of us left
A golden lock, a curly tress
For he-men to rescue and lift
Out of the depths of despair
Why won't the lid open there?
"May I?" He asks coming out of nowhere
Makes one want to go where
Men like that are made
Chivalry is not dead
There are still some men here
Quiet, sweet, gentle, dear.

Jill G. McDowell

GENEROSITY

About your generosity, let me explain a little quirk,
A man who gets enough by begging will never work.

Be he a cripple, a rebel, a politician sinister,
A labor union leader, or a Protestant minister.

Be it a political party, social cause, or medical charity,
The leaders beg amidst luxury, and work is a rarity.

Beggars vow to help others, but help themselves instead;
The beggars get richer, the workers poorer — it's sad.

Put your money in the bank and ignore the beggers' pleas;
When you need it, you'll get it, without dropping to your knees.

J. D. Edgar

DON'T HURRY DEATH

Enjoy the sunset as much as the sunrise;
Ponder those tears dropping from your eyes.

Welcome the pain, as well as the elation;
One depends on the other, by creation.

No one laughs hardier than he who has cried;
No one relished success like he who was denied.

No one appreciates water like the one who has thirst,
And no one has felt ecstasy, who did not feel agony first.

Take the blows, and still risk encountering more;
To escape what you hate, you would lose what you adore.

Don't hurry death, it already comes too soon;
Don't rush away, it may not yet be noon.

J. D. Edgar

JOHN DELBERT EDGAR. Born: Salineville, Ohio, 4-6-44; Single; Education: Marlington High School, Alliance, Ohio; Malone College, Canton, Ohio, 3 years; Occupation: Writer; Comments: *In my writing, I emphasize religion and philosophy, and I occasionally write about politics and the economy. I also work with romantic and erotic themes, and I often combine drama and comedy.*

A BLAZE OF PRAISE FOR MAYONNAISE

A creamy swirl of milky white
Adorns my bread. I take a bite
And ahh, my taste buds tingle so
To taste this magic mound of snow.

Perfection in your silky slime.
You glide across this knife of mine
Into my mouth. I'm almost numb.
Now this is really getting dumb!

OK, let's face it, glob of fat.
You're fattening — and that is that!
If I had any common think
I'd wash the whole mess down the sink!

Don't seduce me, devil stuff!
I turn my head — enough's enough!
I shall no longer seek your sin.
(Unless I'm out of margarine.)

Barbara McIvor

IN WISDOM'S CONFIDENCE

Several moments ago
   I looked up from the floor
and caught you staring at me.
      When I saw you,
         you looked away.

It made me wonder what you were
      thinking.

Was it love?

Was it boredom?

It really made me feel insecure.

I know I shouldn't feel that way —
   Buy why?
      Why did you look away?

I stared at you for awhile still
         wondering.
      Gazing upon your beauty, I
         wondered
   did you feel the same for me
      in your heart as you
            once did?

I kept staring at you and wondering.

   Suddenly you looked up at me, and —

      I looked away.

Raeford E. Thompson, Sr.

KENT STATE

To Four who Died

Their sword pierced through the heart
    Of several doves in flight.
Several lives that flew so gracefully —
    Yet they won't fly tonight.

There's still a river of blood —
    That flows within our soul,
Of peaceful children of God
    Stopped by a bullet hole.

            So many regret —
            So many forget.
            But I still recall
                It all.

I raised the bleeding dove —
    Up from the cold damp ground.
I touched the wings of freedom —
    I kissed its dying wound.

I felt its quivering body —
    Curl up and die in its own fright.

I had once seen them fly strong
            And free —
    But they won't fly tonight.

Raeford E. Thompson, Sr.

TEARS

I never saw dad cry.
He left that job to mom.
I was told it happened
twice —

when she suffered
the miscarriage in 1941,

and when

he saw my sister in
a psychiatric ward in 1969.

Now we say it's bad
to hold back tears.
I used to think it was
the secret of his strength.

I thought they percolated
through him like mineral
rich water went through coal,
creating fine lines of crystal
which make it harder
to mine.

Pat Amick

CRUCIBLE OF LOVE

My love is molten steel . . .
    pouring forth from within . . .
        I am its crucible.

Linda Bostic

MATTHEW 7:1-5

It's so easy to criticize —
Not seeing the beam that's in our eyes
But when we start to see in love
    with the God-compassion from above,

Then faults and shortcomings will
            disappear
And we ourselves won't judge in fear.
Trying to make ourselves look better
    at the expense of destroying our
            brother.

Instead of darts and arrows of dissection
We'll hurl prayers in their direction,
And by that act we'll prove God abides —
    and He'll be the one who's glorified.

Raeford E. Thompson, Sr.

RAEFORD EARL THOMPSON, SR. Born:
Norfolk, Virginia, 12-20-53; Married: Elizabeth
Poulter, 9-2-72; Four children; Occupations:
Receiving Manager of Zayre's Retail Store,
Free-lance writer; Comments: *Although I spend
a great deal more time writing my book, poetry
is an escape for me from the pressures and
stress of my life. I try to release my feelings in
my words, hoping I reach someone else who
shares the same feelings.*

CARMEL MOON

Carmel moon,
Reflecting on silver sea
and misty rain
and me,
Hiding
now and then
under wind-swept clouds,
Illuming,
Bathing in shimmering light
my village by-the-sea,
my soul
Inspiring

Gail Berry

CRICKETS IN THE DISTANCE

It's 3 am and sleep eludes me
Dreams forsake me, the heat suffocates me
Street life breathing 'neath my window . . .
Do I hear crickets in the distance?

Am I mad or am I sane?
Each new dawn faced with disdain
Is there a better world on another plane?
I'm begging for release from pain.

What happens in the future?
What happened in the past?
Can't remember what my name is
Memories fade away so fast.

I dim the lights and close my eyes
The night's so cruel, doesn't hear my sighs
Street life breathing 'neath my window . . .
Do I hear crickets in the distance?

Christine Bode

SALOME

I live in dreams and know no shame,
though taunted by my peers, who name
me fool . . . with cause.

I hide behind my silken veils,
whose colored light dilutes and pales
the world of flaws.

One day I flung them open wide
to let the world of flaws inside,
and out I leapt!

The light of life's reality
I found was too intense for me,
so back I crept.

And here, among the blue and rose,
my wounded spirit comes and goes
with lessened sight.

So now I try, each waking day,
to keep the world a veil away,
in rosy light.

Charlotte Snowden Bridges

MEMORIES

Memories . . .
are in pictures themselves,
and little scraps of this and that;
or anything that leaves a little picture in mind.
Some are forgotten, but most are not —
containing both sadness and happiness,
as we each grow older,
collecting old and new —
Memories . . .

Wanda Carter

Here are a few lines I am sending your way;
To let you know I am thinking of you today.
I needed someone to talk to and you were there;
You understood what I was saying and you care.
I was so confused I started to lose my way;
My trust in you grows stronger every day.
I had to trust in you, I needed to believe;
There didn't seem to be hope for me, I didn't want to leave.
It is what you said to me that made me realize;
That which I need is to break down my disguise.
Whenever I am around you I feel at ease;
This in the only way I can tell you, listen please.
Thanks for being a friend;
When I thought it was the end.
Don't take this wrong, I wouldn't lie;
The friend I have in you, I could never say goodbye!

Rosalie Berger

RENEWAL

Leaves blow lightly in the wind drifting floating to the ground.
The evening mist a tearful end to nature's new exchange of vows.
Winter comes with darkened skies, gloomy clouds hide the sun.
Spring and summer slowly die, sinking blending into one.

Suddenly the clouds release, nature's crystal the purest violence.
Burying all the newly deceased, then a splendor of earthly silence.

Life is hiding almost dead, trees are bare to nature's hand.
A pure cold blanket clouds have shed, covering over the deserted land.

The days now pass this realm of time, the clouds drift south-away.
Nature's children, the morning's rhyme, as life begins another day.

The budding world peaks in green from its hidden past abode.
A new life where none was seen from within is given love.

Hopes become defined with reasons, life itself defined in us.
Sorrows, joys surround all seasons, bringing now a faithful trust.

Fall to winter, spring to summer, never does the cycle end.
Death to man is nature's blunder, for what else ceases to live again.

David Joel Blakeslee

TROUBLED

Lying in the soft grass under a tree.
I am troubled and not feeling free.

It is autumn now and the leaves are old.
The sun in the sky shines bright and bold.

Winter's breath is in the air about.
As I watch the birds on their way south.

In the distance the sea from which all things come.
Lies peaceful and calm like a silent drum.

Now I wonder if I will ever be as free.
As the wind, the birds, the sun and the sea.

David Joel Blakeslee

ICICLES IN THE SUN

Inspired by Bob Geldof

The brain is a battleground of conflicting thoughts,
Each nerve-end wired, bristling and taut.
Tears that fall like acid rain,
Permeate an ozone layer of pain.

Deep in the heart of nowhere brews an imminent storm,
Where hope is lost and faith is scorned.
Another Cajun sunset lost in the lust,
Poison gasses form emotional rust.

Ideologies cultivate,
Expand, evolve and dissipate.
Bereft of truths to consummate,
Numbed minds frozen in the grip of hate.

Each season passes with no revelation,
Time consumed to absolve expectation.
Images severed with the blink of an eye,
If one person forgets, a million may die.

Toxic warfare breeds minds of indifference,
Scarred and bruised souls ignite massive exodus.
Put down the guns it isn't too late,
Melt icicles in the sun, help the children escape.

Christine Bode

SHIP OF GLASS

To live through our life in its totality
  Is to sail a ship of glass in its fragility
So peaceful, so tranquil. The days of life will pass
  With reflecting beauty of a sunlit ship of glass.

Suddenly! Without warning! The oceans of our life
  Are horribly, are cruelly, are totally filled with strife
The waves become tremendous against our ship of glass.
  We watch it. We see it. In its fight for life.

We see all our dreams, our goals begin to scatter
  We see our ship of glass, on the shoals begin to shatter
In this time of life as clocks seem to slow
  That shining, fragile ship of glass seems to lose its glow.

Then as time passes, as we all know it must
  We wonder of our ship of glass, have we lost its trust?
As we flounder so much less and the waters seem less deep
  We search for our ship of glass we suddenly wish to keep.

Finally one morning, as the sun begins to rise,
  We find our ship of glass reflecting in our eyes.
As the waters of our life begin to lose its strife.
  We find our ship of glass to be less fragile in our life.

John Burke

SEE SAW—GLOUCESTER MASSACHUSETTS.

HOPE

I awake in the mornings before there is light
A frown on my brow, another sleepless night.
My tigre, my love, seems so far away,
I'm not sure if I can handle another lonely day.
I work and I strive, our future to build
Dreaming of our Castle, its halls to be filled
With our love, each for the other, bouncing off its walls
But today all I have is my love's lonely calls.
Yet I live for tomorrow, I keep going on
I know my love is forever, it can never be gone.
I strive for this dream of mine, I try to draw it nigh
For without this dream, this love . . . I would surely die.
I would have no purpose, no reason to exist
For my lovely tigre's love helps me to resist
The pangs of despair, always knocking at my door.
My love for her, her love for me, will keep me alive forever more.
My Tigre is my reason to build my life anew.

John Burke

A NEW LOVE

I walked down a shaded path with my head bowed deep in despair,
I didn't see what was around me, I didn't even care.
I heard the birds around me singing praise unto thy name,
but still I wouldn't listen for my heart would bring me shame.
Then you came along to dry my tears you said you understood,
and when you placed your arms around me I knew that maybe you could.
So I slowly lifted up my head and glanced into your face,
and when I saw your smile I knew I found your grace.
I began to explain my failures and all that I had done,
you said I was forgiven and now my sins were none.
Your love began to fill my life you give so generously,
how you keep on forgiving sometimes really baffles me.
You began to work again at patching up the crack,
and my spirit cries out "Oh Lord, I want to pay you back."
Now when I have partaken of all that you would give,
I become a brand new person and really start to live.
I now behold the clouds that dance up in the sky,
and when the birds begin to sing I no more wonder why.
So now my God I want to express all that you mean to me,
for it was through your grace alone that I have been set free!

Chuck Clemons

A POEM/FRIENDSHIP
WITHOUT END

I want to write a poem about a friend of mine,
but find it hard to get past the first line.
Where should I begin and what should I say,
to let my friend know how much he makes my day?
There are so many things that weigh upon my heart,
and I can't find the right words to give my poem a start.
I long to express all that he means to me,
but find my lips are locked and sealed without a key.
He brings such joy into this life of mine,
that to go through life without him would be a terrible crime.
How can I tell you about my friend without taking eternity?
It would be like explaining a sunset to one who couldn't see.
If there were but something I could do in just a little way,
to give you just a glimpse of all I want to say;
But I guess I'm doomed to have a poem without an end,
for words could never be told how much I love my friend.
So as I go my way with all these thoughts bottled up inside,
I leave these words to my friend, "I'm sorry but I tried."

Chuck Clemons

BETTER THINGS

What's more lovely to the eye than the rainbow in the sky?
It's seeing compassion in my Lord as they hung Him up to die.
    What sounds better to the ear than the songs the birds sing?
It's the sound of God's love which makes the heart to ring.
    What smells better to the nose than bread you freshly bake?
It's the fragrance of a prayer to God from a soul that is awake.
    What feels better to the touch than satin on the skin?
It's the feeling in a soul that has been cleansed from sin.
    What tastes better in the mouth than food from which you seed?
It's the Word of God on which our minds and spirits feed.
    What's more pleasant to the mind than thoughts we entertain?
It's the knowledge of my Lord whose mind I want to gain.
    What brings the spirit of man alive when it's been dead for years?
It's the redeeming power of my Lord carefully sought by tears.
    So if you want your senses brought unto their fullest peak,
Then it's after the Lord that you must begin to seek!

Chuck Clemons

REMEMBERING RANDY

You've long been on my mind,
    and while the focus is rarely clear,

Where the mind has failed,
    the heart ran true,

Your memory is dear.

For though I understand so little
    of what your existence has been,

Your faith and courage are never doubted;

I pray you sense this friend.

You undertook a destiny that never
    lent much hope.

I plead with God through sun and stars
    that with His grace you'll cope.

And if it isn't likely
    our hands embrace one day,

As the constant cool of your metal band on my wrist,
    your soul with me will stay.

Jeanine G. Coleman

AUTUMN

The earth is experiencing its annual orgasm of color

Vibrant, throbbing reds, and
Golds like trumpet blasts.

Each fall she seems to turn inside out in a
Final ecstasy of glory

Before old bridegroom winter takes her in his
Cold embrace
And leads her to his barren bed.

Elizabeth V. McBride

THE ONE I LOVE

the one I love is — oh, so far away —
yet . . . within a promise.
He stole my heart and took my soul,
as I took his away.
I think of his gentle kisses, of his sweet caress.
I think of him often, I need him so,
and miss him much.
Yet I wait so patiently:
because the one I love is — oh, so far away —
yet . . . time will bring him near.

Wanda Carter

PASSING ME BY

The walls around me are caving in —
forever tightening their grip around.
Try as I might to loosen their hold,
life is just against it.
I fear to see the end . . .
the end of what may and what will be.
But I cannot have any complaints —
for life has been so good to me.
I am lost: I know . . . I am.
No reason for one to cry.
I see the end . . .
Even as I fear . . .
Life is passing me by.

Wanda Carter

FRIENDS WHO ARE THERE

Dedicated to my best friend, Mandy

Friends are always there
When you need them.
When you need a shoulder
They are there.
When you need love
They are there.
When you need play or talk
They are there.
When you need a friend,
They are there.

Tere Cheshire

BLESSED WITH MY SISTERS

Three of a kind, a hand so rare.
So-called sharks know not what to compare.

Winter colors of red and black,
  each uniquely suited in this stack.

Individuals fold with, at best, a pair,
  after seeing three aces triple the share.

It will beat the others, no gamble lost.
Solid dealing at any cost.

The lucky draw of players few,
  matched me with her and her with you.

Jeanine G. Coleman

FOREVER YOUR TWIN

I pervade your being as a fallen angel,
    the brother that wasn't meant to be.

While I'm not present to tread the soil,
    from me you'll never be free.

You'll sense a spirit not akin to that
    which courses your veins.

And find you'll speak, out of turn,
    with no one else to blame.

No harm is meant, no feelings bruised;
    I implore your soul: Understand!

My path to follow was granted me,
    I dare not refute the command.

I'm in you, of you, at your side;
    I insist for you double strength,

To live, your being of this earth,
    with me, a touch of fate.

So travel the journey (it seems alone!),
    but fear not, I color you rich,

My diverse, united other half
    that destiny chose not to switch.

Jeanine G. Coleman

LIBERATION

You spoiled my fairytale;
The "happily ever after" never happened —
The prince turned into a frog.

All I ever really wanted
Was an old-fashioned home
And an old-fashioned love.

Grey hairs together and grandchildren
Were supposed to be
  our time of contentment —
A lifetime's reward.

But fairytales are "make-believe"
For little girls
And I've grown up —

And they tell me "happily ever after"
Never really happens
Anymore.

Now I'm supposed to be "liberated"
Why then, am I still looking for a "prince"?

Mary Ann Coward

[untitled]

Overwhelming emotions are more
a part of the mind
    than the heart.
The mind is not as fickle
    as the heart.
The heart is so subject to
    housing the trivialities of life.
Listen to the wisdom
    your mind speaks . . .
Not the foolishness
    your heart shouts!

Mary C. Dahlhauser

STAR CALL

On a lonely field
No one to be found.
As I gaze up
The stars look down.

I can hear them sing
Calling to me.
If I follow the call
I can be free.

Call of the Stars
The stars are calling me.
Call of the Stars
I can be free.

I love you
But I must leave.
The stars are calling
Can't you see?

I'm answering the stars.

Allan Davis, Jr.

LUCKY IN LOVE

Why must I always be
Unlucky so much?
My luck seems to be
The worst of the bunch.

Why must it be me
Who takes the worst fall?
Why is it always me
Who gets the short straw?

Maybe my luck will change
When I am with you.
'Cause I see a bit of fortune
Come shining through.

If I'm unlucky in all
Can I be lucky in love?
Can I change my destiny
Just by falling in love?

Why must I be unlucky at all?

Allan Davis, Jr.

FREE

Free,
You're free.
Bars of obstinate possession
once held you tightly
in the confines of my heart.

I held you captive much too long.

The cage door now sets open.
You have flown far, far away.
You're feed and water still remain full.

How far have you flown my Love?

Fresh lining covers the floor
of your abandoned abode.

Do you miss me Love?

Old friends inquire about you
from time to time.

Will you be back my Love?

I tell them you may return some day.

I know I'll see you again.

You will return . . . because you know I really loved you . . .

I just didn't know how to set you free.

Mary C. Dahlhauser

MARY COLLEEN DAHLHAUSER. Born: Scotia, New York, 3-10-57; Education: A.S., Nursing; Occupations: Registered nurse; Comments: *My favorite form of poetry utilizes an analogic concept, i.e., composing a similarity between unlike things. As may be noted in the above poem, I composed an analogy between an "animal of flight" and characteristics of a "prisoned lover".*

THE PERSEIDS

The Perseids fell last night
Competing with the moon, whose pale luster
Brightened all the sky and paled the stars.
She dimmed those sparks and instant arcs
The marked the flights of incandescent stone
Through the upper reaches of earth's atmosphere.

How many times around the sun
Has turned and will this planet turn
Wheeling through these little swarms
Of spatial gnats
Before they all burn out?

Elizabeth V. McBride

SKY BIRD

I am a sky bird,
Always having to take to the air,
I have no choice in the matter,
Just looking for another home to share,

I'll follow my instincts,
And My heart to survive,
I've seen the many seasons change,
And have weathered out all the storms,

I have lived many years now,
And still standing My ground,
Then you came along with weapons,
To shoot My friends and relatives down,

I see no point in killing,
And be devoured by your kind,
I wonder what I ever did to you,
I have never threatened your life,

I have witnessed the many extinctions,
With luck it might not be mine,
I hope you have learned a lesson,
For there were once creatures on Earth that could fly.

Leon F. Delong, Jr.

ESCAPE FROM WAR

The War it seems, seems misleading us,
        fierce fighting that puts a sin on us,
Damage done, duty calls, God and Heaven please help us all,
People here and people over there, should get together,
        if they really care,
If the War should go any longer,
        may it end within this hour,
The dying dead, the dead are gone,
But should we, the people alive, keep carrying on,
Could it be, somewhere inside, an evil demon gives it his best try,
Wars have come and Wars will go,
        but they've never been nuclear so it's been told
If they should win, I pity them,
        so much alone, no friends to talk with them,
If for instance, we should win,
        it's still the same, we're all that remains,
Now to the stars, they are still, as they are,
Technology speaking, people should be leaving,
        traveling right on past Mars,
The War it seems, seems to have been misleading us,
Trillions of miles later, a quarter of our journey had been reached by us,
People here and people over there,
        should get together, if they really care,
If a War should come our way,
It's better to make friends with them, and laugh the time away.

Leon F. Delong, Jr.

FOREVER

I close my eyes, and I can see,
A perfect pair, you and me,
Your arms around me, oh so tight,
This is love, it feels so right.
I hear your voice, as you say,
Nothing will ever get in our way,
Take my hand, share my life,
I'll love you forever, be my wife.
I open my eyes, the vision goes away,
But the hurt you caused, it's here to stay,
I guess your promise of forever,
Turned out to be whenever.

Miwa Detwiler

FOR GREGG

If feelings were measured in colors,
I'd be a walking rainbow,
Blue for the sadness, when we're apart,
Orange for the glow, you put in my heart,
Yellow for the good times, shiny and new,
And red for my heart, that says, "I love you."

Miwa Detwiler

REMEMBER

Remember the first time we sat together,
Holding hands and promising each other,
If ever we got angry, or felt really bad,
We would talk it over, never go to bed mad?
A lot has happened since we made that vow,
In fact, we go to bed without each other now,
Was it you? Was it me?
Or maybe it just wasn't meant to be.

Miwa Detwiler

LACK OF COMMUNICATION

I can alleviate
pain and
sorrow;

I can respond to
excuses and
recklessness;

I can accept
explanations
and offer
forgiveness;

I cannot
deal with
silence

Lori J. Feltner

TIME

Time goes on
With each passage of time, life also goes,
Too quickly for some, still others too slow.

With time our emotions also change,
Happiness goes too fast,
Sorrow goes too slow.

But with each passage of time, we grow more,
And with each year in passing,
We grow a bit wiser.

Lisa Foster

AN URCHIN'S DREAM

Folks don't put no trust in me;
I'm just an urchin boy, you see.
My hair needs cut, my clothes are worn
And people look at me with scorn.

What they don't know is I have hope
That some day I may be rich, too.
And when I am, if I know you
Had no choice where you were born
Then I won't look on you in scorn!

Denton Harris

THE FEET IN MY MIND

The feet in my mind travel a
    path well worn.
The soles of my shoes are all
    tattered and torn.
My mind's picture finds me
    alone and astray;
Bounding through a wilderness
    as a deer may.
I jump over rivers and wade
    through lakes;
Ballet-step treetops until
    my ankle aches.
Deserts, mountains, and grassy
    plains do I roam;
I anchor a fleecy cloud and
    float back home.

Cynthia R. Herrera

POET'S PENNIES

I can't relax on laurels won,
    But still have work to do;
When teasing words cavort in fun,
    I try to make them true.

Not that to stifle merriment,
    But rather search them out
For value if they might be sent
    To ease perhaps a doubt

Or add support for lagging steps
    To one along the way
Who needs to climb from boredom's depths,
    With, "Oh, that makes my day!"

Elsie L. Hicks

As I plunge beneath the ocean's foam,
    there's an exciting world before me.
The ropes, the boat, are all afloat,
    and the stars above help guide me.

The sparkling bubbles caused by air
    trickle up beside me.
I see below me — Starfish;
    and feel strong hands that guide me.

My work is done — for I am full.
    I've completed my day's mission;
and if you wonder who I am —
    I am the "Net of the Fisherman."

Sandra Larcher Jordan

EVENING TIDE

The sound of weathered dock boards,
    as they move beneath my feet.
While the ocean's wet and salty spray
    lies upon my face so sweet.

The sounds of surf that rock the soul,
    and bring so much contentment.
The crying gulls, gliding through the sky;
    wondering where the day went.

The gleaming of a setting sun,
    as it streams through drying nets;
For day is done and I am tired;
    Now it's time to rest.

Sandra Larcher Jordan

KENTUCKY YOUTH

I miss the green Kentucky hills;
    and vibrant skies of blue.
The Hollars and dry creek beds,
    plus the early morning dew.

The acres of tobacco,
    that stand in blazing sun;
Farmers with their weathered skin,
    Who work till day is done.

Places like "Flat Hollow," "White Oak"
    and "Tygert Creek."
Kids hunting for crawdads;
    old women digging leeks.

Never liked it much as a youngin,
    thought there was not enough to do.
Now, how I long for that gentle pace;
    As when my youth was new.

Sandra Larcher Jordan

COURAGE

In memory of Sean Vic, who lost his battle against leukemia on December 24, 1986.

He climbed the mountain to gaze into
the blue skies above.
Looking out over the valleys, he saw
battlefields and soldiers
bravely defending their cause.

He walked along the river's edge and
was reminded of a loyal dog,
defying dangerous waters to save its
master's life.

He faced the storms within his mind
to wonder,
What is courage?
Is it not the soldier dying for his
country,
or the dog fighting for its master?

He lay in the hospital bed,
challenged by the reality of certain
death —
putting courage to the ultimate test,
fighting daily to gain victory over a
losing
battle.

Lori J. Feltner

LONELINESS

The loneliness begins as I sit and stare
at all of the things I would like to have shared
with people I loved who did not love me
and others I loved who never knew me.

I say to myself, "It's not all my fault,
it's just they don't know how hard I have fought
to be everything that they'd like to see
so that one of these days someone just might love me."

So I say to myself, "Until that great date
be happy to sit, just sit here and wait."
But then . . . again . . .
the loneliness begins.

Rudy A. Rudge

SURVIVAL OR JUST PERFECT TIMING?

A crust of bread, a lowly thing,
Caused a flurry of feathers, of tiny birds on the wing.
No circus jugglers could better perform
Than these fighting fliers, as they worked up a storm.
From far and near, it seemed they came,
All wanting to get in the game,
Of grab it from your neighbor, take it away,
And each bird will try to do the same today.
Then one smarty waited until it was just the right size;
He swooped down, made his grab and carried it up to the skies.

Mary M. Volkman

THE AWAKENING

Webs of grayness slowly fading, weaving my way up
from the dark abyss of slumber, and as that oh so familiar
fog lifts, brings with it the melodies of morning; but
to this day I awaken to a new song.

Wisps of your laughter drift through the veil of
dawn's subtle half-light to greet my first conscious
thoughts. Beside me though we lie not together, your
gentle weight presses and I sense the light caress of
your breath on my cheek.

As the delicate bouquet of your sweet scent moves
quietly to arouse my senses, I awaken fully to the sheer
delight and excitation of feelings the mere thoughts of
your presence have stirred.

And in that one fleeting moment, that bright flash
of joy that brings smile to my lips and tears to my eyes,
I know; I love, I love you . . .

David A. Watkins

LOVE OR LONELINESS

The moon is shining bright,
the sky is a blue black,
the stars are scattered

It's mild and warm, it's made for lovers

It's meant for a couple to be together
and walk along the shore
with the blue rays of the moon shining down on them

It's a night for a young boy
to push a young girl on a swing

For some it's a night of love
for others it's a night of loneliness

The lonely wish to walk the shore with someone
they sit alone and wait to be pushed in the moonlight

This beautiful night is lonely for some
it is also romantic for others

The moon will always shine
the stars will never leave

Love and loneliness will always be here
for some now for others later.

Jean Mauro

THOUGHTS FOR IMPROVEMENT

Look to each day with a positive view,
And you will see sweetness in all that you do.
Seek out the goodness that life can provide,
Give up your anger, don't keep it alive.
Face each endeavor presented to you,
With the joy found in learning, expanding your view.
Live life to its fullest and be satisfied,
You've made the world richer while you are alive.
Pessimists leave us with a sour taste,
But optimists will always enhance their race.

Linda Silvia

EMPTY

They've all moved out.
That cannot be!
Where are my pals?
Where are all three?
I'm not ready.
It's much too soon.
Stay young longer.
I need more time.
Don't take from me
what I thought was mine.
Will they become visitors?
Dropping by on occasion.
A few days here
on their vacations.
So life moves on —
another phase.
Will I accept it with humble grace?

Norma Koontz

MAYBE SOMETIME

Maybe sometime
it will happen,

Maybe sometime
we don't be scared,

Maybe sometime
we'll go away,

Maybe sometime
we'll be able to say
"I love you"
and not be scared

Maybe sometime
we won't just dream.

Maybe sometime
all our dreams
will come true,

Maybe sometime.

Jean Mauro

AT 1:00 A.M.

From vertical
Through rectangular,
The sphere is circular
And illuminous.

White and round
It spins around,
Beaming to the ground
Voluminous.

Karen Kuhl

70's

Wild-eyed youth
Seeking identity in fashion
Clinging to life our passion flower
Raised in the aftermath of protest
Returning, heads bowed
Exhausted from the struggle for identity
Inventing new ways to express nothing
Inutile activities
Escapism in its true form
On into midlife but where is the crisis
Aged hippies reminisce
Our music mellowed
Our idols dead
Marred by tragic vision

Jay Douglas Kunze

A FALLING STAR

Is death dark and sordid
Is life all it's cracked up to be
Is the veil rent or merely parted
Is our hand ever considered
in an eternal scheme
Or theme, Or play
Should we wait for the dawning of the day

A new day rising bold, arrogant
A golden race of dark despair
A poet calling us into his lair, — with words
A piper playing the song of peace and plenty
He will catch us every time,
our huddled masses poor
with nothing in store for future days but hope
Forever following a star
A falling star —

Jay Douglas Kunze

THE INNOCENT ONES

Broken hearts and dried tears
are all around this world
old romances and side affairs
are all around this world

The innocent ones are the ones
with broken hearts and dried tears

They are the special ones
they are the caring ones
they are the gullible ones

They fall in love easily
then get hurt because of it
people use and abuse them

They are the innocent ones

They believe in love and dreams
and live in their dreams

They are the innocent ones
they have broken hearts and dried tears.

Jean Mauro

NO CASSANDRA I

No Cassandra I would be
To know what future evils lie
Beyond the ken of mortals who
With their past and present
Have nearly all too much to fear and fend.

Cassandra's gift — not gift, but burden
Can but rend the soul and alienate the
bearer
From friends and foe and all the
Joys of living.

Elizabeth V. McBride

CAN WE?

Can we start over?
Can we forgive?

Forget all of our hardship,
and go on and live?

Can we hold each other,
as we did before?

Will you stay forever,
and not slam the door?

Can we keep those feelings
that never did leave?

Forgiving our mistakes,
and all our pet peeves?

I love you my darling.
I know you love me.

I ask you this question,
just tell me, "can we?"

Susan Lee Meyer

BABY AND ME

Playing ball is just one thing
that baby and me both do.
We'd swing so high upon a swing
when baby was only two.

Mom taught me how to climb up trees
and there were times I fell.
I'd scrape up both my hands and knees
Mom kissed and made them well.

We'd run and play out in the park.
Then we would walk and roam.
Time passed as it was getting dark.
So baby and me went home.

I'd bathe and put him into bed,
and kiss him on the cheek.
As I walked out my baby said
"I sure had fun this week."

Now as I lay me down to rest,
I think that you can see
Life is always at its best,
when life is "baby and me."

Susan Lee Meyer

HE'S MY HUSBAND, HE'S MY FRIEND

He's the person that I lean on.
    He works from eight to four.
He walks in tired and weary,
    as he opens up the door.
He's the person that I yell at,
    when things aren't going right.
He tries to understand me,
    and holds me through the night.
He's the person I depend on,
    to help me with my chore.
He helps without a hassle.
    He does his share and more.
He's there when I feel lonely.
    He's there for fun and laughs.
He loves me, and me only.
    He even sets my baths.
This person that I talk of,
    who has a hand to lend.
He's my one, and he's my only.
    He's my husband, he's my friend.

Susan Lee Meyer

THE HUMAN CONDITION

  And the world's in a state of confusion
and the children are crying and the adults wonder why.
  I was on a train, in the smoking section, coming from Penn Station,
and this was the bar car, and a black man was serving drinks
  to already intoxicated businessmen.
Well, these two women came by, bought a couple of drinks,
  and were yelling ''let's have fun tonight!'' as they flirted
  with the nameless men.
And they think the kids are screwed up and yell at them for
  being like themselves. What do they expect?
    And the world's in a state of confusion
    and the children are crying and the adults are still wondering why.
And so I sat there and studied them and I wondered if
  they knew what I was thinking and their thoughts must have swayed
  onto me. They must have noticed my torn jeans and cigarettes
  and commented, thinking I was just an irresponsible
  juvenile rebelling against authority with nothing to
  give to society. And whose thoughts are right?
    And the world's in a state of confusion,
    and the children continue to cry
    and does it even matter who is to blame?

Michelle Sewing

THE 7 AGES OF GADGETS

The little child starts off with a kiddie car.
A tricycle and bicycle follow.
(Later — if he is the type — a motorcycle.)
At 16, he is ready for the Love of his Life —
The A-U-T-M-O-B-I--L-E.
(He has passed radios, cassettes and recorders.)
Then the computers, refuters and movie cameras.

Looking back, he has lived out his life,
Mostly mad about machines.
People came last of all —
if at all.

Abe Weiss

COUNTRY MOM

Time and again my memories roam to the old farm house —
My country home, to my country mom and my boyhood days;
I think of her and I marvel still — at the love she gave
And I always will, she had simple faith and loving ways.

I hear the old farm bell once more, calling dad and us from chores,
Supper table set for eight, grace with heads bowed o'er each plate;
Again I see mom's workworn hands,
    her jet-black hair with silver strands,
She was there to love, to heal, to care.

Her worldly gains in life were small,
    but great the love she had for all,
When it was time to go to bed, she always came upstairs and said:
''Goodnight, be sure to say your prayers;''
    when twilight comes, I see her there
My mom of yesterday.

In a little churchyard by the bend of a country road I sometimes wend
There my country mom's asleep, where mountain pines their vigil keep,
Free from life's concerns and cares, my country mom's gone upstairs.

Robert K. Slade

LOVE REMAINS

I wanted you to know today
    that I still love you and I always will.
''I love you'' means that this person I call ''me''
    would do anything possible to bring you happiness.
But, sometimes, because of who that me is,
    those things are no longer possible.
It hurts me to know my love was not enough.

I know that you still love me too
    and maybe you always will.
''I love you'' means that the person you are
    has done all things possible to bring me happiness.
It hurts you to know your love was not enough.

Neither is happy. We failed. You and I destroyed Us.
We didn't measure up. Both hurt in our attempt to bring love.

Shared pain. Today that's what our love means.
Two torn, inadequate individuals, yet
                    The Love Remains.
That in itself brings a new joy.
We are enough, even if not for one another,
                    at this time, in this place.

Joanne Taylor

POETRY NOW!

Now, more than ever before,
The World needs the Poet.

Now, when a Human Being is the cheapest thing,
His Divine Image must be re-declared.

Now, when mind-maulers manipulate masses,
Each man's uniqueness must be proclaimed.

Now, when man staggers on the crookedest roads,
The Poet's Vision can straighten their way.

Abe Weiss

ANGEL CURLS

It crept in, like the darkness of a storm.
We didn't even have time to be warned.
He life was quite new,
She was barely two.
But, in death quickly flew.

Our world was completely shattered.
Now, nothing much mattered.
She was the most beautiful child,
Her hair was angel white,
And her curls ran wild.
Her eyes were see-through blue,
And her baby lips shone like morning dew.

We'll never understand why the angels came.
But our lives will never be the same.
Our hearts will always be filled with pain,
Because of the night the angels came.

Barbara Mooney

Some people
live in a hostile world
  and act accordingly.

Some people live
in a friendly world
  and don't worry.

The first are successful;

The second live happily.

Andre Orbeliani

YOUR SMILE

Warm, golden sunshine
  in your smile

Given freely,
  without guile,

And, in my happy eyes,
  tenderness starts to burn.

Then, as a fanned
  ember glows

To my lips,
  warm feeling flows

And I wink,
  and I smile in return.

Charles S. Sharp

A prejudice is a firm belief
in a doubtful truth.
      For instance,
What does not happen
  cannot happen,
      or
What cannot be measured
  does not exist,
      or
Human brains,
  although limited in size
  have an unlimited ability
  for understanding.

Andre Orbeliani

THE EAGLE FLIES

The eagle flies today,
As he has for many years.
He travels far across the earth,
Through winds, rain, and tears.

Looking down upon the land,
Where the Red Man made his final stand.

The eagle's eye sees far and wide.
He knows the truth, what's inside.

He know more than words can say.
Alone, the eagle flies away.

Gregory Reichenbach

I CARE

Some funny jokes
      and anecdotes.

Laughter,
      and that's not all.

A helping hand
      when you fall,

A shoulder
      on which to cry.

A gentle touch
      to help you dry

Those painful
      flowing tears.

A tender word
      to calm your fears.

Lovely cards
      and pretty flowers

To fill
      your lonely hours.

A loving heart
      that you can share.

These I give,
      because I care.

Charles S. Sharp

SOUL MATE

Dedicated to "The Lizard King"

Paths cross/attunement
We reach for a new friend
Little realizing/he's really an old friend.
The karmic wheel goes round,
And friends are lost and found.

Lovers reach behind the veil,
And to each other, they've secrets to tell.
Of all things learned/and all things lost,
And how much all of these things cost.

Eyes do not see/ears do not hear
These subtle vibrations,
But the heart knows the true soul mate well.

For love is hard to understand,
And we all do the best we can
'Cause love is the secret — that magic tells,
It can be either heaven or hell.

Insane/but not alone,
Fantasy swallows pain.
My soul mate/Shaman/Poet
Heals the wounds in my spirit & soul.

Susan Sills

DECEMBER DENVER DRUNK

The crystal clear beer
Is all I fear
Drives me insane
Drives the demons to the surface
Takes away any reason or purpose
Takes away the pain

Tom Babinsky

AFTERNOON OFF

O precious time! How wonderful
To have a whole free afternoon
To do whate'er I fancy;
To read, or write, or watch TV,
To take a nap or take a walk.
If no one comes then I'll be glad
To be alone.

A few short hours all my own
Will surely be a joy to me.
My days are busy, busy,
With work, with family and friends,
With church and trying to do good.
But I could never give these up
For leisure time.

So I will not complain because
My cup of life is brimming full
And almost overflowing.
Instead, some sympathy I'll give
To anyone with ample time
Who cannot find rewarding things
To do with it.

Mary E. Simmons

A ONCE PROUD SHIP

Her tall masts standing straight and true
  With crosstrees outstretched firm and new,
Shrouds pulled taut to stay the sticks and
  Keep them firmly in their pits;
Foremast, tallest of them all,
  Mainmast for the heavy haul,
Mizzen hoisting flags and pennants highly risen.
  Freshly painted for and aft
The decks and house fairly glisten.
  In the calm of night this ship will softly whisper
All one has to do is listen.
  There is more to tell about this ship so bold
The tale is only partly told.

Her hull so new and clean
  Caulked tight against the sea
Surely made her feel surpreme.
  The ocean awaited her impatiently
And so did men and their war machine.
  They pierced her shiny hull with shot and shell
We know no reason this had to be
  Yet they sent her to the bottom of the sea.
She rests many fathoms deep upon the ocean floor
  This once proud ship will sail no more.

Frank J. Enright

FRANK J. ENRIGHT. Born: Fort Bragg, California, 3-21-19; Married: Anita, 4-6-46; Occupations: Seafarer, Operating engineer, now retired; Poetry: 'In This World,' *American Poetry Anthology,* Fall, 1985; Comments: *I am presently compiling a book of poems for publication, some with a strong seafaring theme, others are of nature, some humorous. I am also working on a book about life at sea, "To Leave This Port."*

HOW SHALL I KNOW THEE

Shall I compare thee to a summer's night,
Whose majesties in silence congregate;
Or gaze into thine eyes by candlelight,
And see the wisdom they would intimate.
Shall I weigh thy strength — forged upon the flame —
As tempered steel, made by the master-hand;
Or say that kings would righteously proclaim,
Exquisite is the nature of thy stand.
How then shall I know thee! for I confess
That thou art more than perfect in my eyes;
But honor does allude to something less,
For neither God, nor Titan be thy guise.
By right, let *sincerity* be thy claim,
And gracious *inspiration* be thy name.

Susanne Lucas

THE SOUNDS OF A BOY

The sounds of locusts in the trees
The sounds of birds flying the breeze
Bring to me tranquility a feeling I enjoy
Makes me think of when I was a boy
With no problems or intermittent thoughts
Thinking of people and their burial lots
Brings worry to my brow and tightness
To my smile but you bring only brightness
As we lay and waste the day away
I shadow the lovely way you alone say
How you love me and will please me
We are back when I'm a boy see
With tranquil thoughts and feelings
We are like the clouds with no ceilings
Nothing to hold us or control us
We are together and showing lust
For the world the people are gone
We left them far behind before the dawn
They will never bother us anymore
We shall forget the problems the worries we'll ignore
Here only the locusts in the trees
See only the birds fly on the breeze
Which bring beauty we enjoy
The sounds remind me when I was a boy

Tom Babinsky

MY CHILD (TO MEGAN)

A talented future you've only begun,
Your sparkle outshines the magnificent sun.
Your beauty, your sweetness, your own special way,
Have the power to bring lasting joy to each day.
You've given new meaning, I feel deep inside,
The love as your parent, consumes me with pride.
I'll never expect you to fulfill my ambitions,
I'll encourage you to seek your own recognitions.
I know not what life holds in store each new day,
But give my support as you follow your way.
I love you for being you,
That's exactly what I want you to be.
Know always whatever direction your life takes,
You'll always be perfect to me.

Linda Silvia

LINDA SILVIA. Born: Taunton, Massachusetts, 5-29-47; Married: Richard, 11-28-68; One daughter, Megan Elizabeth, born: 7-11-77; Education: Vernon Court Jr. College, A.A., 1968; University of Rhode Island, B.A., Psychology, 1971; Bridgewater State College, M.Ed., 1974; Occupation: Guidance counselor for Fall River Public Schools; Comments: *I find that writing has always been a natural, relaxing manner of expressing myself. It is a vehicle which enables me to more significantly communicate my feelings and ideas concerning life. I believe the only common theme in my writing is that my writing must relate to me and truly reflect my sentiments.*

TO MY SHY STUDENTS

My heart goes out to you who hesitate,
Who fear to approach me,
Who whisper your requests for help.

My Dearest Ones:
Long, long ago, I was one like you.
I feared teachers, neighbors — all adults.
I dreaded opening my mouth,
Remained locked-up inside,
Always an outsider and afraid.

It will take time to break through.
Some sooner, some later.
Never give up trying,
Never accept a setback.
Your Day, like the sunrise,
Will surely come.

Abe Weiss

FANTASIES

I lift my curtain of concealment
And enter an image unknown
Not worry about time spent
Or fears and trivials ingrown
Just let this feeling flow
And enjoy rapture complete and whole
For I know all I know
Nothing's left of my old self of condole
All is as it should be
In my mind I now have entire
And this is all in me
Untouchable and somehow full of desire
To do so much be so much
My fascinations are unfolding
Never has the drive been such
The experiences are always molding
Me and changing from one to the next
Time stays in my mind and revives
Somehow causes everything to complex
An awe of importance thrives
Carrying with it all my worth

Tom Babinsky

Carports, gardens, homes,
Houses, families, friends,
Caring, beginnings, ends,
Fun, romping, liking,
Sunny, rainy, hiking,
Being, loving, talking,
Hands, holding, walking,
Moonlight, lovers, kissing,
Lonely, sad, missing,
Carports, gardens, homes,
Not for one who roams.

Jill G. McDowell

EIGHTEEN MINUTES

Each morning I walk to work
an eighteen-minute walk,

My body begins to waken
and my soul to talk.

I find answers to the questions
that before I could not find,

And suddenly see the beauty
that is soothing to my mind.

Looking inside myself
to who and what I am,

Removing all barriers
of pretense and of sham.

Afforded a view of myself
that one rarely gets to see,

Knowing that if I listen
it could only better me.

Each evening I walk home
an eighteen-minute walk,

My body again wakens
and my soul to talk.

Lin Yarges

FOR EVERY PRECIOUS MOMENT

For every precious moment,
God gives to each of us,
We hold them closely to our heart,
And never let them go.

For every precious moment,
God gives to each of us,
We thank the Lord most Holy,
For giving them to us.

Mary G. Valdina

THE POWER OF LOVE

The power of love is immense.
The feeling so very intense
This is only a point of view
I've held since my love for you
Began, you incredible man.
High mountains, it's able to move
Oh yes, all in the name of love.
Love has the power to heal
Your love knows just how you feel
When you life's becoming grey
Love can brighten up your day.
So let's sing the praises of love
To the powers that be up above.

Cheri Raithby

BEAUTY

Like the first snowdrop, like the first tree,
You are the one that I want to see.
Like the first smile, like the first kiss,
When I'm away it's you that I miss.
Like the first sunrise, like the first star,
I want to be just where you are.
Like the first walker on the first fell
Up in the lakes, that I know so well.
Like sundrenched beaches out in Corfu
All of these things remind me of you.
What a wonderful thing to create
Beauty, like you, in its natural state.

Cheri Raithby

UNATTAINABLE LOVE

If wishes were horses
And I could ride
I'd mount my white horse
And stay right by your side.
We'd water our horses
At a cool mountain stream,
If wishes were horses,
And love were a dream.

Cheri Raithby

CHERIDAN RAITHBY. Born: Halifax, West Yorkshire, England, 5-24-48; Divorced; Education: Open University, Half credit pass, Sociological Perspective, 1978; Full credit, Science, 1976; Occupation: Volunteer work with disabled people; Membership: Harrogate Writers' Circle; Other Writings: I wrote a short article that will be published in a magazine for the disabled. Comments: *My work is quite varied. I will try my hand at anything.*

THE GIFT

You were a gift given
by love . . .
You were the gift
lost by love . . .
You are the gift
I will receive out of love . . .
My son, your love and life . . .
Are my gift.

Kathy Jacobs Dobrovolny

LOVE AND FORGIVENESS

You've had a series of arguments, a fight or two.
You've run away to stay and you say:
    I'll never forgive, no way, no way.
Welcome to the sea of torment. Present conditions: depression, sadness,
Critical views. Forecast: Recurrence of spitefulness,
    grief, a divorce or two.

She was cheerful in giving. You even acknowledged
    you enjoy a high standard
of living. She gave an increase of thirty
    percent to the church, fifteen
percent to the needy. You got mad over the money
    because you wanted to gamble more and get greedy.

Spitefully, you put her on a diet with a ten dollar
    allowance. You took charge
of the pocketbook. Not knowing, you rejected the
    blessings that God had sent:
Welcome to the sea of torment. Suddenly, you've
    lost your job. Enter unemployment.

Some people are doers, and some are talkers. The talkers seem
    to criticize the doers and do nothing but talk.

The talkers have a mental plan. The doers
    are breaking down barriers with their
actions. The talkers become divisive,
    spiteful, and jealous. Welcome to the sea of torment: Talkers will be
talkers.
    Unity awaits hearers and doers.

Larry W. Hilton

CLEAR PERSPECTIVE

God is love.
Racism choked America for a dime and a dollar,
    for a private sector on
Saturn, or a job behind the white collar . . .
    for a passion of hatred and
Blind inequities . . . for oppression of freedom and true liberty.
Racism met Jesus and bowed . . . racism met
    Jesus and bowed . . . in some.

Racism met Jesus and bowed: fleeing the
    byways and parkways, the balconies,
And fountains, the pews and the country clubs.
Racism met Jesus and bowed . . . in some.
It is plain to me that every man has to see . . .
    to the receptors of light
God is love and is a God of variety.
Every crayon knows that it is an imitation
    of the real works of of God: the
Beautiful colors green of the grass, the blue
    of the sky, the red of the
Apple, and the brown of the eye.
Whether you like it or not: God is building
    images of Christ in the races of
Men: He will shape you too if you invite Jesus in.

Larry W. Hilton

RETREAT

Did you hear the trumpet sound . . .
    have you seen the brightness of His
Coming with the saintly crowd? Have you become a closet to witness
And prayer to meet only your needs —
    neglecting the outreach — knowing
That if the gospel is hidden, it is hidden from those who are lost? Or
Have you heeded to the call of the Master's command by loving with
Compassion, not yielding your stand —
    to be a part of the mission to make
Our enemy his foot stool? Love has no boundaries —
    so why do you flee among
Many the schools, the community, and the neighborhood pools? Is it wise
To think God loves only just you? How great the pity that paints this
Thought of denial of His love that is true . . . to the just and unjust,
His love prevails.

Let Jesus reign in you to all mankind.
    For surely the kingdom of God is
Within you . . . so why deny others the
    kingdom when Jesus didn't deny it to
you? Allow the father to do His works through
    you as He did through Jesus.
Make a brother your brother, share his burden.
    Shed your light upon the
Darkness of this world.

Have we my demonstration failed to show . . .
    a strong commitment to our Lord
As He said to go . . . have we massively walked
    the streets of every city
Healing the sick, and preaching the gospel,
    yielding of our abundance and
Showing great pity?

Larry W. Hilton

LARRY W. HILTON. Born: Valley Falls, South Carolina, 7-25-49; Married: Catherine Marie Hilton, 12-13-84; Education: South Carolina State, B.A., 12-71; University of D.C., M.A., 12-72; Columbia School of Broadcasting, 2-85; Earl Paulk College, Ministry Preparation; Occupations: Speech-language pathologist, Radio announcer; Memberships: American Speech-Language-Hearing Association, Georgia Speech-Language-Hearing Association; Themes: *To convey through everyday observations that man's ultimate destiny is the Kingdom of God and his position within the Kingdom is determined by his treatment of the Kingship and redemptive power of Jesus Christ, and the applications of His principles in daily living.*

THE LITTLE ROSEWOOD CASE

She's a dear and lovely lady,
    and her face is still so fair,
As the silver of the moonlight,
    is entangled in her hair.

As she sits and gazes fondly,
    at the Little Rosewood Case
That brings many happy memories,
    and sunshine to her face.

The Little Rosewood Case,
    what tokens does it hold.
An old Prom Dance card, a fragile piece of lace,
    A faded rose how old.

A little box so full of dreams,
    each dream a souvenir.
That's all that's left of lost sunbeams,
    and loved ones ever dear.

Oh Little Lady you are right,
    you think and dream of each delight.
And while the moon is in its flight,
    you whisper softly, Love Good Night.

Robert M. Strong

THE ARMY OF THE LORD

Let us walk along with you, O Lord,
    though the road be treacherous and long.
Teach us your ways of life, O Lord,
    to you, we'll raise our voices in song.

The love to all, that you show, my Lord,
    in our hearts is sure to grow.
We want to be your servants, Lord,
    the seeds of Love to sow.

You suffered and died for us, O Lord,
    from sin, you set us free.
Let us help our brothers and sisters, O Lord,
    and work to be with thee.

Let's all listen to the words of the Lord,
    and practice his ways of life.
Let us all unite in the Army of the Lord,
    to work to end all worldly strife.

Robert M. Strong

DAFFODIL HILL

Heaven and Nature's beauty
In full bloom on the hill
I drive closer
So that my eyes may get their fill
My soul becomes captive
Of the spring's golden flower
As I watch hour after hour
In this flowery land
So beautiful, so grand

Rose Mary Gerlach

YOUR DISCIPLE

Thank you, Lord, that you were there,
    when your home I visited, my love to share.
I know we were not alone, O Lord,
    but I know, my prayers, you heard.

Strengthen and renew my faith, O Lord,
    the depth of my sins made me cry.
For failing you in the past, O Lord,
    from you, ashamed, I tried to hide.

Forgive me, O Lord, for all my sins,
    I know I pained you so.
Heal my heart and soul, O Lord,
    for one of your disciples, I may go.

We all should be your disciple, O Lord,
    your words, we all should tell
To help our brothers and sisters, O Lord,
    before the tolling of the bell.

Robert M. Strong

DAILY DREAMS

He mounts his horse and away he rides
Over the mountains and valleys wide
He crosses the rivers, creeks and streams
Following his daily dreams

He rounds up all the leaves and trees
He even tries to catch the breeze
Then he falls and hurts his knees

Little boy on a wooden horse
Mama listens to his noise

He gallops up and down the hall
Bumps his horse against the wall
Then Mama tells him that is all
It's time to go to bed

He puts his horse into its stall
A place against the bedroom wall
Now little horsey that is all
It's been a long, long day

Tonia A. McCormick

FOND MEMORIES

My childhood is passing ever so quickly
Before I am ready it will be only fond memories
Floating in the recesses of my mind

I will hold on for a little while
And enjoy the endless days of discovery
Which march ever forward in my life
Carrying me on to something new
Each time I open my eyes
And greet the early morning sun

Tonia A. McCormick

SUN RIDER

Come brave and true and strong young man
Riding from tomorrow's land
Over hills and valleys dark and gray
Bring the sun once more to stay

From the east he rides on a golden stallion
The Talisman, the true medallion
All the powers of the sun
Flow through you, the Golden One
Come with mane and hair on fire
With the sun's all healing power

Come to the land you must reclaim
To the voice that calls your name
Come with the power strong and true
To the soil you must renew

Come heed the voice that knows your strength
Into the darkness do not sink
Renew the land lift up the souls
Into the soil let brightness flow

Sun Rider come and bring the light
Save this land and make things right

Tonia A. McCormick

A WASTED LIFE

Why does he smoke dope?
All he is doing is shortening his life,
Really, he hasn't a hope
And he wants me to be his wife.

He said to himself "I'll just try once,"
But that was just the start.
"Or maybe twice would be nice,"
He's completely lost his heart.

He wakes up with eyes of flaming red,
And he mopes around for days.
He never takes notice of what I've said.
It's completely changed his ways.

So now the time has come for help,
It's desperately needed now.
I'd be better off without him,
But me, he couldn't do without.

He hasn't noticed until now
What he's done to his life
With brutality and bashing and saggy eyes.
And he wants me to be his wife?

Joanne Irving

EXISTENCE?

Who, or what am I,
How do I know I am?
I may not really be,
I am not sure of you or me.
What if I'm just a dream?
Who would the dreamer be,
It would be He.
He who rules eternity.

Linda Silvia

BEYOND THE TOUCH OF FINGERS

She was seduced by gentle breezes,
mingling with aromas . . . sweet with
promise of renewal.
The steady tradewind beckoned her to
seas unsailed, in search of precious
gifts — as yet untouched by human frailties.
Seduction's fiery blade glides over weakened
flesh — desirous of what is offered,
The rhythmic thrust of temptation is
quelled, only by the flux of time, and
a sense of her own reality.
She is mindful of the treasure and the
rarity, of what she *does* possess —
two hearts beat as one, bound by destiny;
sustained by the purest of ideals.
Deception's edge is blunted by the heart
that would not be deceived by fickled
promises. She was moved, by a sensitivity
that is *beyond the touch of fingers.*

Susanne Lucas

YOU ARE THE BEACH!

You are the beach! — I am content to lie
in wonder, upon your alluring charms;
enraptured by the soothing warmth of your embrace.
You are the beach! — I am bathed in nectared breath
that wafts anear, and calms a gentle stirring —
that you might strip away the fragile
armor of my countenance.
You are the beach! I am flush with thoughts of
reverie, as the tender whisper of a kiss shines
down upon my face, and brings a knowing smile.
You are the beach! — I surrender onto you my
nakedness . . . trusting, wanting. A tremble from within,
and I am sinking into ecstasy. The heavy ache upon
my breast, draws you nearer.
You are the beach! — we submerge in waves of
splendor. Together, we become the sand
that lingers on the shore, 'til
we are swept into eternity.
We are the beach!

Susanne Lucas

SUSANNE KATHERINE LUCAS. Pen Name: Sulu; Born: Detroit, Michigan, 1946; Married: James E. Lucas, 1967; Education: High school graduate, 1965; Occupations: Housewife, Mother of 3; Comments: *The most common theme in my poetry is the expression of love, and emotional conflicts. I try to express what I have experienced, and resolved; emotional struggles fuel my creativity. I also write light verse, and I'm particularly fond of poems about nature and its effect on our lives. I've been writing poetry since I was ten years old. Coming from a large family — twelve children — I couldn't afford to buy birthday cards, etc., so I made my own, with my own verses.*

THE STAR SHONE OVER JERUSALEM

The Star shone over Jerusalem
The night that Christ was born.
The three wisemen followed the Star
So did the kings that followed.
It was the time of the greatest joy
As the Star showed them the way.
How can man forget God's gift to man
On this most Holy day.
It is the light of the world,
Bringing joy to all the land,
For Christ will come again.

Mary G. Valdina

GOD BLESS THE LADIES IN WHITE

God bless the ladies in white,
Struggling with all of their might,
With compassion and kindness
To make us feel right.

Turn right, turn left,
Push up, push down,
Wheelchair to X-ray,
Prick for our blood.
Deserving of tribute..
God bless the ladies in white.

God bless the ladies in white.
They try with all of their might.
They try to keep us from fright.
God gives them the strength
No matter the length
Of time that it takes.

Sometimes with sadness,
Most times with gladness
Deserving of tribute
God bless the ladies in white.

Mary G. Valdina

MARY G. VALDINA. Born: Williamsburg, Brooklyn, New York, 2-8-08; Married: Frank J. Valdina; Education: Elementary school, 1-31-24; Occupations: Housewife, Mother of 7, Craftsmaker, Poet, Author, Songwriter; Awards: 10 Honorable Mentions, 1 Special Mention, Golden Poet Award, 1985, 1986; Poetry: 'For Every Precious Moment,' 'Santa Comes Just Once A Year,' 1984; 'O Hi Daughter Mine,' 'Friendship,' 'O Hi Son of Mine,' *Our World's Most Cherished Poems* and *Our World's Most Beloved Poems*; Themes: *Religious, family, Christmas, marine, love of family.*

GRAMMA'S DARLING

No one dares to spank you
You can do no wrong
Upset the coffee table
That means you're getting strong
You know I ought to hold you
Come here and let me hold you
I'll tell you why you get away
With all the things you do

Gramma's Darling you're sweet
And so petite
Heaven and earth seem to meet
In Gramma's Darling
The Sunrise lights candles
In your eyes
Gramma's Darling

Now Mom and Dad are sure
You belong to them that's true
But, just what is this special bond
Between your Gramma and You?

Gramma's Darling you'll see
When you're twenty-three
You'll still be
Gramma's Darling.

Mary Grasinger Doorley

TO A NEWBORN DAY

Misty morning born in May,
    stretch forth your hours
    and find a way
    to make this day some joyful gain,
    some surcease from Earth's constant pain.

Bring back some peace,
    some sense of youth,
    some will for good,
    some search for truth.

Enshrouded 'neath the sun's bright rays,
we still can hope for better days.

Earth's ancient wars must soon release
    all hold on those who lead the cause
    for strife — past all pretense —
    and find our long-lost innocence.

Elizabeth Haynes McAnally

ONE LAST TIME

    One Last Time,
    let me look into your eyes,
    reflecting beauty of the skies.

    One Last Time,
    let me hear the things you say,
    whispering, in your winsome way.

    Then,
    let us gently clasp each other's hands,
    with the touch of slippery sands.

    One Last Time,
    as the shadows of life fall,
    let us forever hear God's call.

Josephine Bertolini Comberiate

ANOTHER SUMMER DIES

The waves of gold,
Bow to the wind,
Under leaden skies;
As another summer dies.

Paul Rance

THE ROMANCING MOUNTAINS

Stilling effects of love in the air;
Singing winds echoing through its brushes;
Rustling leaves whispering gently in mind;
Sun-rippling waters falling down its path;
Roots of their hands joining together as one;
Misty dews that settle in the heart;
The Romancing Mountains.

Bonita J. Hryhoryk

SAYING NO TO DRUGS

Saying no to drugs
Isn't as easy as people think
First, there are your friends
Calling you a chicken
Because you don't want to get high
Then, there are the pushers
Who think you ought to
Buy their drugs
But when you don't
They keep on hassling you to buy drugs
Say no to drugs
And you will live a lot longer
Than those so-called friends
And the pushers
That want you to get high

Russell Morgan

IZOMO

O, Izomo, warmonger of old;
Your mud statue reminds me
Of your strength and courage.
Your face knows no laugh,
You are stout and strong
Like the man of Guinness.
Every inch of you spells
War, war and only war,
Your only hobby and profession.
Though youths take no notice
Of you when they pass by,
You are, nevertheless, the people's darling.
Though cows graze around you,
And ants have punctured your toes,
You are far from being forgotten.
For a day in March is set aside
For wrestling and war songs
All in remembrance of you.

Steve A. Okecha

NICKEL BONES

Jungle beat
    up from the street
        Tigers skull
            Outlined by streetlamp
                Alleys caught on a map

Head on a stick
    the monsoon is back

Eye of shark
    Shank of tooth
        End of bluefin
            The V. C. be damned

On home pavement
    we pay dues
        for madness suffered
            in Nam

W. D. White

LILIES

Do we live too long
to feel the joy
of lilies not toiling
in our fields?
(Soft cells harden
the arteries
of soft successes.)

But while I pump
my blood
into your system
I receive yours
for a moment
and feel us
living —

not long enough.

Irene I. Friis

Time keeps ticking away.
As we continue to live our lives
day by day.
    You wake up in the morning
    and another day's gone,
    but deep inside you know
    the memories will live on.
        Taking it all by each single day
        I realize there's so much I have to say.
        You fill my life with happiness,
        and hopes of being together, forever.
In your arms is where I'd love to be,
just as into your eyes I want to see.
I love you in all so many ways.
    Hoping to be with you for the
            rest of my days . . .

Deirdre Parrish

MOUNTAIN OF THE HOLY CROSS.

Lying on the couch,
thoughts of you enter my mind.
Images of you here,
flash before my eyes.
So real,
I reach for you
— only to find emptiness.
My ache for you,
so strong;
I can't let you out of my thoughts,
my dreams,
my needs.
You are my existence,
my life,
the love I have searched for.
My days
are meaningless without you.
Come back to me.
Soon.
I miss you.

Laurie Wickett

CHARLES

God has brought my life a new joy,
with a beautiful baby boy.
He's named after my grandfather,
a great man I don't remember.
Charles Timothy Snow is his name,
I won't forget the night he came.
Thank God I'm around to see him,
for awhile my chances looked dim.
I've got so much love in my heart,
when he hurts it tears me apart.
I'll be the best father I can,
until the day he's his own man.
Even then, I'll still try my best
'til the day they lay me to rest.
My boy finished my family.
I'm as happy as I can be.
A beautiful daughter and wife,
what more could I ask for in life?

Timothy B. Snow

STOLEN EMBRACES

Stolen embraces
sweet remnants of my past.
Now tattered and torn
their presence . . . my scorn.
I only wanted to give
I only wanted to be loved.
Such a fool
I am.

Leslie M. Gochenaur

TO A FRIEND WHO AIMS BEYOND THE STARS

For: S.D.F.

Master Head of Life
  Challenge pursuits —
You are as the Eagle's aim
  soaring high
Targeted quests yet to be conquered!
  Rewards —
Jeweled Rainbows Glorified
Sparkling with all life's
  wondrous treats
Eagerly you pounce
  on crowns of joy
And marvel life's splendorous riches
  rightly earned by you.

Suzanne Joy

CHRISTMAS

As it came to past
once in a stormy blast
Santa had to get through
to bring the toys to me and you
Should he take a speedy bus?
to quickly get to us
Should he take a fast, fast train?
for tracks were slippery in the rain
Should Christmas have to wait?
Should Christmas just come late?
What of the girls and boys
waiting for their Christmas toys?
Suzie made some cookies for Santa to eat
and left them sitting at the chimney's feet
The empty stockings by the tree
Will they always empty be?
When things were looking awful grim
I guess you know Rudolph came in
An answer to our prayer, he will take us there
and now Santa is safely on his way
to bring to us a happy Christmas day

Hazel Carestia

THE TREE

The tree once in the forest did grow
experiencing the torrential rain and snow
Upon it's branches was a robin's nest
where he often came to take a rest
One day it was cut down and taken for a ride
to a huge house and brought inside
Adorned with silver and gold
and colored balls, some quite old
A star was placed upon it's top
it was surely the cream of the crop
A Christmas symbol it now would be
stately gorgeous for all to see
It will now spread joy to every girl and boy
It has sacrificed it's life just like another
the little Christ child born to Mary, Mother
The First Christmas day the tree was there
it brightened up the stable bare

Hazel Carestia

Of whippoorwills and daffodils
And singing birds divine,
Such is the stuff that life's made of,
The visions are so fine

Of forest pines and dandelions
And fresh sweet-smelling breeze,
Such is the stuff that life's made of,
So beautiful are these

Oh, of tall oak trees and foamy seas
And ponds so clear and blue,
Such is the stuff that life's made of,
So pleasing is the view

All of these things Nature brings
So plentiful the gift,
Such is the stuff that life's made of,
May it give your heart a lift

Shelly Smith

TWO SOULS EMBRACING

What madness is this . . .
  that has seized me,
conquered reason and now . . .
  lays waste to all my
  goals and aspirations?

What gales blow, that whip the
  sea of my soul?

Take care, girl! Do not
  approach this raging sea!

But if you do, take care . . .
  for this sea will swell
  and embrace you . . .

Into an evermost tender world
where two souls embrace.

Francis John J.

THE SEARCH

You live, you die, at the end it's all the same
You watch the seasons come and go
You watch the rain hit the floor
You look up to the sky
And you look down to the ground
And your conclusion is
There are no friends to be found
You search and search and wonder why
You look and look and wonder why
An answer you want, what a pain
You eat and sleep with no gain
You get out of bed and you wonder why
Then it hits you, you know why
Early to bed, early to rise, makes a man
Healthy, wealthy and wise
So, you see, there is no answer
You live, you die, at the end it's all the same
  Judgment day — Judgment day —

Edward Kau

ALL ON PAPER

Looking through a paper window
at times you've seen your world crumble
you seem to pick it up and try
to rewrite your world, but like life you run dry.

With the wind your carried places
to be scribbled upon by unliked faces.
Your trapped inside and have to take it.
One wrong move is a mistake. You cannot erase it.

You finally wear a hole in your heart
Then from life you must part.

Only to be once again crumbled up and thrown away.

Carol A. Dixon

MAYBE WE CAN
WORK IT OUT

Changing around with the beat
I can't seem to stand on my own two feet.

Swirling around in my head,
my old love, which nothing can be said.

I realize what I have done,
his love for me is over, and mine has just begun.

Maybe if I work it out, I can change things around.
For me and my love can talk it out and manage on the same grounds.

Carol A. Dixon

THOUGHTS FROM MY HEART

Just a few thoughts in my heart I'd like to say
The love you have given me, I can never repay
There is a love between us, we will somehow relay
And hold in our hearts, that no one can take away.

Life is wonderful, and very precious it's true
Thank heavens God made a person like you
Who in this big world is to say we are wrong?
I'll remember and love you my whole life long

My life has been so little and yet so very much
Our moments together have come of heaven's own touch
As we travel through life, our memories ever so dear
Wherever you are, my love will always be near

The children must always be our dutiful goal
We'll guide them to live and love from deep within their soul
When their lives have been molded and our work is all done
Maybe then, we can find happiness and our place in the sun.

Now that my life's end is drawing so very near
My memories are so precious and close in my heart
God filled me with so much love for you and the children, dear
We'll all be together in heaven soon and never be forced to part.

Dolly Scurlock

WE LOVED YOU, DAVID

God loaned us one of his angels, to love for a while
He was our baby, our son, our gift from above
We had him here on earth, to keep, to love
We loved him, taught him, and allowed his own style

David was as rebel, a free spirit, and unique from the start
He tested our nerves, he trampled our heart
We gave, we helped him, we always shared
We tried to be there, to show that we cared

What more could we have done, we loved you more day by day
We were so happy, when you had your baby son
We remembered when you were born, our little one
God gave you to us and then he took you away

David, wherever you are in the heavens above
You know you are in our hearts, with feelings of love
God has his purpose that he took you away
Maybe we will all be together again, in heaven someday

No matter how hard we try to hold back the tears
We thank God that he loaned us his angel, for just a few years
We never said these words enough, we loved you and it's true
No one will ever know how much, until our lives are all through.

We loved you, son.

Dolly Scurlock

DOLLY ELIZABETH SCURLOCK. Born: Rowan County, China Grove, North Carolina, 11-13-36; Married: Robert E. Scurlock, 12-5-53; Education: Attending Nash Technical College, Rocky Mount, North Carolina; Occupation: Homemaker; Memberships: Volunteer Services, Nash General Hospital; Awards: Silver Banquets Award, 1986; named poetess for the Del-a-News, Delmar Printing Company, Charlotte, North Carolina, 1971; Poetry: 'A Smile,' 1971; 'My Day at Delmar,' 1970; 'Help From Your Heart,' 1972; 'Parents,' 'Teenager'; Comments: *I love writing. I usually write about my five children or work I love doing, and about my love for all things.*

YOUR WAY O LORD

Come and take my hand, O Lord,
    that I may walk with you.
Come and strengthen my faith, O Lord,
    that in life, to you, I'll always be true.

Come and enter my heart, O Lord,
    to teach me of your Love.
To give and share — to help and care,
    that all will be free like the Dove.

Your Love, O Lord, shines brighter than the sun in the sky
    Your Love lightens my days.
I will live my life with love for all,
    that I may be with you — when you call — I pray.

Robert M. Strong

MY FATHER

My father was a man with a special
   kind of love in his heart,
He was the strong one who kept our
   family from falling apart.

He devoted his life to helping his
   loved ones in every way,
And without his love and understanding,
   I wouldn't be where I am today.

He was a hard-working man,
   who had little money.
On rainy days, he always managed
   to make them sunny.

He would comfort me, and
   wipe away my tears.
He was there to help me through
   all my growing years.

I don't know what I will do, now that
   he won't be there;
He was My Father, my memories of him
   I just wanted to share.

Leila Davenport

WE BOTH HAVE GROWN

Remember the good old days, when
   we used to skip school,
Wearing our jean jackets,
   thinking we were cool.

We were always doing the things
   no one else dared,
Sitting on our back fence, all
   our secrets we shared.

We liked acting silly and
   sometimes even dumb,
Promised to be sisters forever
   and we both pricked our thumbs.

We've been through a lot together,
   all the happy times and sad,
And you have come to be the best
   friend, that I've ever had.

Now miles apart and with
   families of our own,
The years have passed and
   We both have grown.

Leila Davenport

LONELINESS

A dark dungeon lies beneath every lonely soul
unrest spirits flying wall to wall
endless thoughts through the night
o' my bride to be, restore my sight
sleeping alone every night
wondering who's there by my side
reaching out to feel her breath
waking up alone, another day of life

Edward Kau

The reds, the yellows, greens and browns,
Within their lacy frame,
Is God's creation of the trees,
From whence was Kilmers' fame.

He saw the forests glorified,
With birds and butterflies,
Branches spread with lofty boughs,
Towering to the skies.

Seeing this majestic view,
Of giants up above,
Exemplifies the wonderment,
Of God's unending love.

For He has made with all His grace,
A masterpiece so bold,
He's given us a work of art,
Of riches, to behold.

Thank you, Lord, for I have known,
The forest dressed in green,
And nowhere else that I have been,
Has life seemed so serene.

Robert S. Pearson

MY SHADOW

My shadow follows me wherever I go.
As long as I'm in the light.
Why he follows me, I do not know.
But where does he go at night?
I cannot find him when the sun goes down.
Maybe he's gone to sleep.
I looked upon the wet ground.
But did not make a peep.
I went inside and asked my brother,
Where did my shadow go?
He said, "Go ask your mother,"
"I really do not know."
I found my shadow in the morning light.
But where does it go at night?

Christina McCoy

RISE AND SHINE

Rise and shine,
Beginning of another day,
Time to say good-bye
You must be on your way.

Take the memory,
That must be left behind.
The loneliness you filled,
In such a short amount of time.

And if our paths should cross,
Someday, when you return;
Maybe the fire inside,
Once again will burn.

So rise and shine,
And face another day.
To whatever it may bring,
Time will pass away.

Karen Aileen Libero

WITCH OF HOLY HELL

The devil's got a hold on me,
Says he knows me very well.
Going to teach me how to get anything,
And call me the witch of holy hell.

There's an empty space inside me,
And a voice keeps talking in my head.
Says I'm doomed to be a loner,
Unless I listen to what's being said.

So I listened very carefully,
He said, "To me, your soul you must sell,
Then that empty space inside will fill,
You'll be the witch of holy hell."

So I sold my soul to the devil,
And by the end of that very same day,
I found me a man, who took me by the hand,
And said he's going to take me away.

Well, I fell in love with this stranger,
And we got along rather well.
I said "Tell me, just who are you?"
Says he's made me the witch of holy hell.

Karen Aileen Libero

THE AERIALIST

The heavenly Aerialist
Skyward bound
Flying through cloud and mist
He climbs high
Towards the blue, blue sky
Filled with exhilaration
As though nearing heaven's destination
Where his spirit lived before his birth
The Pilot slowly descends to earth
Back to valley, hill and home
There to rest,
Before, he again will skyward roam

Rose Mary Gerlach

AWAKENING

Against my back
   I feel your heart
      murmur
   beneath your breasts.

Our room is drowsy.

A cool breath of light,
   the glow before sunrise,
      slips between the curtains.

Across the road, a bird
   calls to her mate.

Gregory J. Smith

WHO ENJOYS OUR COMPANIONSHIP

A person's life is much like a lighthouse.
It stands watching everyone pass by.
Forgetting to stop and say Hi.

Much like the lighthouse vessels that drift on by
So do friends, family and neighbors. They sail on by
Forgetting to stop and say Hi.

One can only stand tall for so long.
Before they crumble and fall.

Then and only then will they sadly be missed.
By all who just drifted. Sailing on Bye.
As they once *enjoyed our companionship* of the past.

Before you lose that someone special.
Why don't you take a moment to stop and say Hi
One day it may be too late. For they have fallen,
Crumbling away.

Today they can hold you tight and share memories.
By talking to you or just listening.
Tomorrow can be too late. Their headstone is cold
Without feelings. It doesn't talk back.

Believe me. I know

Sandra Jean Keefe

SANDRA JEAN KEEFE. Pen Names: Sandie Vincent, Kathy Taylor, Sandie Brown; Born: 10-1-49; Married: Dennis G. Keefe, Jr., 7-17-73; Education: Hollywood Scriptwriter Institute, T.V./Motion Picture Writing; University of Buffalo, Journalism; Occupations: Freelance writer for newspapers, magazines; Scriptwriter; Poetry writer, Housekeeper, Mother, Wife; Poetry: Several poems, *American Poetry Anthology,* 1986; Poems, *Malibu Times,* 1984-86; Poems, *Surfer Magazine,* 1984-86; "Mysterious Five," TV Script, 1985; "The Alien Within," Screenplay, 1986; Comments: *Creating for the film industry is exciting, as well as fun. I find writing very relaxing. I often write to boys in the service (all branches). Their letters bring more than education, knowledge and the passing of letters. They bring friendship between strangers. I enjoy life very much. I feel life is too short to waste. So I never worry about tomorrow.*

TIME, SPACE, PLACE

Loosely placed between time and space,
traveling in an upward circle to a higher place.
Sometimes going to the extreme,
but always coming back to the basic things.
Sometimes I feel lost in a river of confusing thoughts
that tears my world apart.
Sometimes I don't listen to the inner soul
that stands beside us all.
Yet, it always catches me before a fall,
Even though I sometimes stumble hard and fall to my knees.
It catches me.

Loosely placed between time and space,
traveling in an upward circle to a higher place.
Sometimes going to the extreme,
but always coming back to the basic things.

Ronald Scott

RONALD SCOTT, SR. Born: Triadelphia, West Virginia, 8-26-48; Married: Linda Joyce Scott; One child, Ronald Jr.; Occupations: Respiratory therapy technician, Construction worker; Memberships: *Writer's Digest;* Awards: Award of Merit Certificate, Honorable Mention, for 'Systems,' 2-28-87; Poetry: 'Systems,' *The Great American Poetry Anthology,* 6-87; 'Tri-Love,' *Hearts on Fire,* American Poetry Association, 11-87.

CHRISTMAS RENEWED

Christmas comes but once a year,
    to remind us all that the Lord is near.
When the Star shown o'er the hills of Bethlehem,
    and Mary gave birth to the Saviour of men.

God gave to us, the greatest gift of love,
    his Son, Jesus Christ, from above.
To follow the example of his Loving Son,
    to always be good to everyone.

How often we forget his message of Love,
    and his commandments, we should heed — thereof.
So why must we wait, say once a year,
    to heed his message, that we should give and share.

Let's show our Love to all mankind,
    and leave our hatred far behind.
We should turn our eyes toward the Star in the East,
    and give the birth of Jesus Christ a chance — at least.
Let's practice Christmas every day,
    and live a charitable, loving life, his way.

Robert M. Strong

BELIEVING

They placed a crown of thorns upon his head,
      his garments with his blood, were red.
Jesus gave his life for you and me,
    from Original Sin, we now are free.

Suffering and humiliated,
    Jesus died upon a cross.
To prove to those, who did not believe,
    that in believing, all would not be lost.

We celebrate that glorious day,
    when Jesus arose from the tomb.
Jesus proved to us, that in believing,
    all would not be doomed.

The Temple of God was rebuilt,
    in those three days, from the Cross to Resurrection.
Through the belief and love in Jesus Christ,
    and all of his perfections.

Robert M. Strong

HOLY MARY

Most Holy Mary, dressed in blue,
    on bended knees, we pray to you.
We failed to heed your warnings of the past,
    and if continued, this world will not last.

Oh Virgin, handpicked by the Lord,
    to bear his son, the Saviour of the World.
That he should die, upon the cross,
    that all mankind, should not be lost.

The suffering and the pain you felt,
    when before his cross you knelt.
In Jesus life, and with his death,
    He forgave us all, with his last breath.

Most Gracious Lady, of all mankind,
    intercede with Jesus, so we'll not be left behind.
You are our Queen, Mary Most Holy of All,
    and with our prayers, from your grace, we'll not fall.

Robert M. Strong

ROBERT MILTON STRONG. Born: Cincinatti, Ohio, 10-15-19; Married: Thecla A. (Dreiling) Strong, 1941; Education: University of Vienna, Austria, Criminology, 1953; William and Mary College, Virginia, 1963; F.B.I. Arson Course, Armed Forces Institute, Korea, 1960, 1963, 1965; Occupations: U.S. Army criminal investigator, Private investigator; Poetry: 'Lover's Rhapsody,' 1938; 'Little Rosewood Case,' 1937; 'Voice of the Unborn,' 'Christmas Renewed,' 1965; 'Holy Mary,' 1966; Comments: *My poetry is of love, nature and religion.*

DREAM

Life, the time-honored symbol of existence,
Gives way to the emotions of mankind and,
We dream.
Yesterday, today and tomorrow pass on
Into the haze of infinity and,
We dream.
Eternity, a stretch of time forbids the search
To grasp and hold the aura of grandeur and still,
We dream.

Hold on to life,
Hold on to love,
Hold on to happiness
Wherever it touches you and,
Dream on.
Times moves on in the empty void of nothingness
As the days, hours, and minutes wane,
Dream on.

Your life,
Your love,
Your happiness
As big as the dreams of a lifetime,
This is your right to
Dream.

Neola M. Eichmeier

NEOLA MAXINE EICHMEIER. Pen Name: Mickie Johnson; Born: Kansas City, Missouri; Education: Roosevelt University, Chicago, Illinois, Bachelor of General Studies, 1973; Nova University, Ft. Lauderdale, Florida, M. S., 4-81; University of South Carolina, Advanced Public Affairs, 8-81; Occupations: Public information officer, U. S. Government; Memberships: Sigma Delta Chi, Society of Professional Journalists; Comments: *Sentimental threads run through most of my work in consonance with outdoor/nature themes. My poetry depends on my mood and reflects my thoughts at a particular time and place.*

THE PALAGONIA VISION

The rains the woods near Palagonia are not a common thing,
For nocturnal wayfarers hear the ghostly sounds
    of a tormented woman sing
Distressful, mournful notes this apparition writes in monotone,
Searching for her baby, in each rainstorm, she cries alone.

A few people, including I, have seen her dressed in white,
with long black flowing hair, darker than the nite
Searching for her baby, a baby she did not want,
and threw into the flood waters . . . the raging ravine holding taunt.

Remorseful now, these past years,
Searching for her lost child, in every rainstorm,
    she adds a turbulence of tears,
Dressed in white, the cries of The Palagonia Vision fill the moonlight air,
''My child, my child . . .'' is her last holy prayer.

Shirl-Leigh Porter Temple Goforth

MY MOTHER CARE

I know my mother, my mother care
For she kneel in secret prayer.

When I was a baby in waddling clothes
The things she did nobody knows.

I know my mother, my mother care
God knows she kneel in secret prayer.

When I stayed out all night and never phoned
My mother prayed while I was gone.

I know my mother, my mother care
She brought me up in the House of Prayer.

If you have a mother, thank God she live,
Ask Him for more and more life to give.

'Cause I'm sure your mother has knelt in prayer
Because she love you, because she care.

Down through the years mothers had it hard
But her trust — she put in the Lord.

I know my mother, my mother prayed
In spite of all the mistakes I made.

If we could only feel our mothers' pain
We would never hurt her again.

Then, behold the motherless children, comfort their soul and mine
Remember these, Lord, at Greater Mt. Zion.

Because there's no love greater than a mother's love
Unless it comes from Heaven above . . .

Anthony James Hall

GOD'S SPECIAL LITTLE ANGELS

You are one of those special little angels that God sent down
  on loan to me. For all my life I have searched for a child
that was never meant to be. God's way was to send His unloved
  angels to me. For He knew I would love them my whole life
through.
  When they would wrap their precious little arms around me and
say "May we call you Mother, may we come and live with you
some day?"
I would answer them in the only way I could. I, too, love you so
  dearly, but within my heart I felt if only *they* could.
"May we come and see you tomorrow?" They knew in their hearts
  what I would say. "I'll see you tomorrow as I do each day."
I would kiss them good-by. "God bless you, children, it's time
  to go out and play."
Now the years of search are over and through, for that child that
  man, not you, God, took from me. I know now I did have a child
for I was chosen a special mother to all the unwanted little
  angels you entrusted to me.

Gloria D. Hulse

FALLING SNOWFLAKES

My winter love . . . sit with me in front of window panes,
Watching falling snowflakes . . . cover cottages and lanes.

Soft drifts piling . . . alongst the roads,
Drooping tree branches . . . from icy loads.

Glistening sunlight . . . reflecting like starlit nights,
Turning landscapes . . . into a wonderland of dashing sights.

Staggered icicles hanging . . . from rafters low,
Cascades of frozen water . . . falling to mountains of snow.

Sparrows searching . . . for food in the weeds,
Seeking nourishment . . . for their bodies' meager needs.

Sleigh bells jingling . . . down country paths,
Frolicking children sledding . . . experiencing lots of laughs.

Distant bells ringing . . . from the town's steepled church,
Heralding the tidings . . . of the Christ child's Bethlehem birth.

Christmas trees twinkling . . . through the night 'til dawn,
Youngsters hoping that . . . Santa's arrival shant be too long.

By the fireside's hearth . . . all nestled in bed,
In my arms my darling cuddles . . . as holiday poems are read.

Kissing and whispering . . . good night and all is bright,
Snuggling close to me . . . she holds me affectionately tight.

Cold wintry nights . . . there's always warmth and happiness in my life,
Treasured season's romances . . . shared with my best friends
  and loving wife.

Richard Saldan

A TEACHER'S PRAYER

"A teacher affects eternity.
He can never tell where his influence stops."
  — Henry Adams

O Master Teacher, humbly I, a teacher of youth approach Thy throne,
    knowing within my heart that without Thee I am nothing.
If I am not yet fully conscious of how great is my task,
    may I begin at this moment to learn.
Grant me courage to face each new day, for I shall need it.
Give me grace and strength and power from Thine own great reservoir.
Well I know that I shall need the inexhaustible patience of Job,
    the wisdom of Solomon, and above all else a vast portion of Thine own
    great love
Bestow upon me the gifts of laughter and of joy.
May I treasure within my heart each childish smile
    that I may give it back in limitless measure.
Give me an appreciation of each child within my classroom,
    and grant me understanding of his possibilities as well as
    his shortcomings.
Let his color, race, or creed matter not in my sight.
Give me enthusiasm in sharing my knowledge, but O Great Teacher,
    grant me humility! There is so much I do not know!
Help me to spark some child to do his best, to open doors where
    seemingly there is no opening.
Give me the realization that the opportunities within my grasp are
    limitless, and may I never minimize the power of my example.
When these goals exceed my grasp, may I return to Thee for added strength,
    confident that it shall be mine for just the asking . . .
In the quietness I await Thy blessing as I petition now
    that I may become a teacher worthy of Thy "Well done." . . . *Amen*

Ruby A. Jones

APRIL AGAIN

Spring comes to me in a different way;
    in early blooming crocuses
and jonquils joyful as they sway
    in April's cold/warm breezes.

She comes to me recalcitrant —
    so fickle and so very slow.
Hesitates, unsure and shy and can't
    decide on rain or snow.

To you she comes exuberant
    and sings across the desert floor;
each golden note extravagant —
    she scatters color from her store

of treasures, carpeting the land
    with desert poppies, cloth of gold,
an Indian paintbrush, and the sand
    becomes a living canvas, bold

with color! I've known your west
    in springtime — you've known jonquils in the snow.
Each year our hearts touch and are blessed
    by springs we used to know.

Catherine Stockton Lamb

MY LITTLE MAN

Once a baby, now a little man
There's so much in life you want to understand.

So many questions of Why and When,
How I wonder do you ever comprehend?

Each day brings a new discovery and fire in your eyes
The excitement of learning and your answers to Whys.

There never seems a time your little mind is at rest
With eagerness and drive, you were well blessed.

I watch you as you sit so deeply in wonder and
try and guess at the thoughts you must ponder.

I know each thought is truly you cause there's
no one else who can speak as you do . . .

You sing and you dance, you flip and you flop
Sometimes I wonder if you're ever gonna stop . . .

I watch you sleep and even then, I see your mind
    anxious to begin.
A new day, a new plan, an eagerness to see what the
    day has in hand.

Once a baby, now a little man
I'm glad to see you really do understand . . .

Pamela Nidiffer

A BETTER DAY

So I save a penny here and a penny there to see a better day.
And now I find I'm no better off to see that day.
So what am I to do?
I think and think like most folks do and find what I thought
I would never find.
I find a piece of gold which is the God of life and this is
more than a penny here and a penny there.
For life is that which makes the gold and life is that which
makes a penny here and a penny there.
And yet for all such talk, I know the world will always have these
folks who save a penny here and a penny there to see a better day.

Harry Khosrofian

MA SAMS

Long ago I was alone, she took me in and gave me a home.
I was a child, five years no more, she gave me love.
The kind you live for.

She fed and clothed me and watched me grow,
She taught me things I needed to know.

She longed for everything to be right,
Though sometimes it all went bad.
My Wonderful Lady never turned her back,
She's the best friend I ever had.

Time passed and I went away,
Yet my love for this lady strengthened day by day.

I grew older and returned home, I sought the comfort
of her liveliness and beauty that grew to make me strong.

I wanted you to know of my love,
How you taught me right from wrong, for these reasons
and more I wrote to you this love song.

Here's to you My Perfect Lady and to what we share
It's nice to know I have you to always care.

I Love You My Perfect Lady.

Pamela Nidiffer

MY LOVE

You are like a rose my love,
delicate, fragile and beautiful to the eye.
At the slightest breeze, you wither and blow away:
Yet your aroma and your memory linger on.

On the whole you are proud,
tall, and withstand all that opposes you.
You have a shield of protection much like the thorns of the rose:
Yet they too can be broken or cut away.

You should be cherished my dear,
as one always does with one they admire.
I long to keep you to myself and share you with no one.
Yet I must let you be free of all ties.

The best way to describe my feelings for you are,
love, friendship and trust.
I admire your strength and cradle in your warmth and tenderness:
Yet I need you, my love, as a rose needs the earth to grow.

Gail Kaufmann

CHILDREN

The sounds of laughter fill my ears,
the room, the walls, the air we breathe.
Toys are scattered here and there,
children's voices all around me.
There are chores to be done, so why do I sit and listen?

I hear a cry, so loud and piercing,
It's demanding, wanting and needing me.
A diaper's wet, soaked through the sheets.
There are things to be washed, so why do I sit and smile?

Another cry and tears of pain,
I run and find a broken heart.
The knees are skinned, the heart is bruised,
a hug and the smile returns.
There are dishes to be done, so why do I sit and watch?

I need them now probably more than they need me.
I smile and think of yesterday, the days without my children.
I long, sometimes, for those again.
But love and live for today.
So I sit, and I watch, and I listen for my children.

Gail Kaufmann

ANOTHER DAWN IS BREAKING

Now the dawn is breaking. The bleak, black sky is
once again alive with color. The golden sun, grows
brighter and more brilliant, warming the earth's sand.
Each and every crack and crevice is being filled with
radiance. The ocean's waves beam, reflecting in a
rainbow of color.

Falls the sun's golden rays, awakening all the little
creatures of the earth, with — an abruptness!

The feeling of life is stirring from within, their
souls are warmed, caressed and kissed by the fingers
of the sun.

Once aroused and set in motion, these little creatures,
must scamper, searching, ever searching, for their
energy-giving food.

And now they do learn, that the weak fall by the wayside,
feeling never again the rising sun:
and the strong, ah yes,

Another dawn is breaking.

Roslyn D. Smith

TIME

Sitting here watching the clock
As the second hand slowly turns
I think about time's passage
Finally I'm beginning to learn

Life goes on whether you're there or not
Always someone to take your place
Time's passing will fade you away
Then memories of, we'll have to trace

And though we'll try for the grand illusion
Of our exsitence to be most sublime
Live for quality; not grandeur, because
Illusions are not enough to beat time

Robin L. Aguero-Tjiong

MY HAPPY LITTLE PONY

My happy little pony, cute as he can be, he always
makes me happy when he looks at me.
Prancer is his name, and I think he already knows,
he sets my little heart all aglow.
With a beautiful long tail, and shiny mane, I know
someday he'll be a horse of fame.
My happy little pony, I love him very much, I know
someday, he'll be going to the county fair, to strut his
stuff.
I know he'll win a prize, as he stands before the
judge, all spruced up in his gorgeous duds.
As I take him home proud as I can be, I know everyone
will be noticing me.
But my happy little pony dancing as he goes, already
knows he stole the show.
Ribbons on his back, a gold ring around his neck, I
know he's thinking "I won them all, by heck."
Now he's safely home, snug as he can be, just think!
All of him belongs to me.

Sue Ann Schwartz

WHY I CRY FOR TCHI

A better pal
No gal ever had
Than you, my magnificent, beautiful
Little black dog.
I perceived
How you grieved
While I was in the hospital, but understood
I was still your friend.
It was the wheelchair you hated. You needed me
And I was not there for you.
I miss you Tchi.
I didn't get to say goodbye.
The unfeeling driver rushed
To Christmas shop —
Didn't stop
To help you out of the cold storm
Or to get you to the vet
To ease your pain.

Bettye Ellis Owen

MOTHER

My mother is a gift, brought forth to me at birth . . .
    She has given me life on this planet called earth.
She is the spirit that dwells in our home . . .
    And with her by my side I will never be alone.
She has given me joy, and a hope for tomorrow . . .
    She has stayed by my side and shared in my sorrow.
I am her pupil, and my teacher of love is she . . .
    She has taught me to love others, and to allow others
    to love me.
She has opened my eyes and let me see . . .
What a very special person a mother can be.

Tracy L. Wolf

TO GIVE OR RECEIVE?

We've heard 'tis better to give than receive,
And also the gift without the giver is bare.
Let's be fair.
We must share.
The happiness and thanks of the receiver
Makes the giver glad to give.
Here's to good receivers!
You also give when you accept gratefully.
Sincere thanks are worth more than all the money in banks.

Bettye Ellis Owen

BETTYE ELLIS OWEN. Born: Hill County, Texas; Married: Russell Edgar Owen, 8-7-37; Education: Baylor University, B.A., 1935; 46 graduate hours at T.W.U.; Occupation: Taught speech therapy for 33 years; Memberships: Dallas Writers Group; Rejebian Book Review Club; Stevens Village Book Club; Loyal Chapter O.E.S.; Other Writings: *Ellis Heritage Geneology Book from 1812,* self published, 1st and 2nd printing sold out; Themes: *Home, Family, Everyday happenings;* Comments: *In early November, 1983, a stroke paralyzed my left side and makes typing painful and frustrating. I raised 2 wonderful children, Russell & Doris, and have 2 brilliant and talented grandchildren. My current work is telling the story of my valiant grandmother's journey from Mississippi to Texas by ox-drawn covered wagon during the Civil War.*

SELF

It often seems rewarding to find someone kind . . .
    But it is even better to find kindness in yourself.

It is unique to find someone willing to help others . . .
    But it is far better to find someone willing to help
    themselves.

It gives us satisfaction to meet someone full of love and
joy for others . . .
    But it is truly satisfying to feel love and joy toward
    the person inside us.

It gives us confidence to have someone whom we can trust . . .
    But it is something special to be able to trust ourself.

It is comforting to have someone who is supportive and
forgiving . . .
    But true peace can never be achieved until we can
    learn to forgive ourself.

To the questions in your life . . .
    You are the answer.

To the problems in your life . . .
    You are the solution.

And if you are in search of your identity . . .
    The findings are within.

Tracy L. Wolf

THANK GOD FOR MOTHERS

*For my mother's 85th birthday,
May 26, 1983*

Human life is a sacred and priceless gift
    From God who designs and creates us.
Said the psalmist, "I am fearfully and wonderfully made"*
    As he pondered God's mercy and goodness.

And our thoughts go out to where we began
    As a seed from the father who sired us,
A seed that found safety, and warmth and love
    In the womb of the mother who bore us.

In pain, and perhaps grave danger,
    Risking her life for another;
Accepting the challenge of working with God,
    Who bestows the honor of mother.

Praise God! He designed many motherhood roles
    For the orphaned, abandoned and others,
For we could not exist as living souls
    Without a Creator and mothers.

    ** "I will praise thee: for I am
    fearfully and wonderfully made . . ."*
    Psalm 139:14

Earlean S. Grogan

FRIENDSHIP

The others came to the door, all of them,
And sat, and talked of their accidents, operations, blood, and gore,
And I listened, nodding my head
Until I just couldn't anymore.

But you, dear friend,
Came thoughtfully, quietly,
Not for words, but for chores —
To cook my meals and clean my floors,
To listen, to renew and restore me
As you've always done before.

Mary Ann Jefferies

QUIET THOUGHTS

As I think quiet thoughts
the whisper of a voice speaks in my mind.
It is the whisper of a dream,
that blows gently like the wind.
I find myself drifting with its gentle flow
taking my thoughts with it, where it pleases to go.
It takes me to a quiet place, beside a winding stream
whirls around inside my head,
whilst I drift in peaceful dream.
I dreamed I was a bird in flight, soaring up so high,
my wings flap gently with the breeze,
as I sail on a painted sky.
I dreamed I rode a stallion across a sandy shore
and watched the morning sun, rise through earth's golden door.
I dreamed I crossed the desert, and slept in dunes of sand
then I climbed upon a rainbow and looked down on every land.
I dreamed I was all the colors, brilliant, bright and lush.
Placed upon a canvas, by aspiring artist brush.
Then suddenly my journey ended, I awakened from my dream,
where I sat thinking quiet thoughts . . . beside a winding stream.

Bonnie Flint Podgorski

FAMILY TREE

Trace each ancestor and never fail
To see the courage it took to sail
To an unknown world through uncharted seas
For freedom to worship and live as they pleased.
They were the ''astronauts'' of their day,
Charting the course, pioneering the way.

With adventurous spirit they blazed new trails
Over the mountains and down the vales.
Each generation had its problems to face
And worked to solve them with faith and grace.
The spark is there in your being, too,
Passed through generations down to you.

And if you find a scoundrel or two,
They're a very small part of the ancestral glue.
On the other hand, where would you be
If it were not for the family tree?
So let us each live in such a way,
Generations later can proudly say
We are cherished ancestors, worthy to be
A lofty branch on our Family Tree!

Ruby Tippit Peacher

SPRING IS A CHILD

Spring is a child who slowly awakens
    And stretches her form in a sleepy yawn,
Shivers in the cold air, feeling forsaken,
    As she gazes at winter, silent and drawn.

Then o'er the grass our sylphid goes tripping,
    Small body gleaming, she dives through the air.
In sweet April water, gracefully dipping,
    Knowing no sorrow, no worry, no care.

Out again now with joy bubbling over,
    She scatters her flowers in fairy-like fun,
'Til weary and tired she rests in the clover
    And drowsily dreams in summer's gold sun.

Ruby Tippit Peacher

THE DESERT

April, 1979

The desert air was heavy
            and still
Heat pounded upon the rigid sand
Like a pulsating heart

The sunset sky ripped apart in rays of
    violet
    orange
    and electric red
Reaching towards the ends of the earth

Still tenacious plants cling to dry and brutal rocks
    as the sun
Descends upon the west.

Melissa S. Lafkas

IN LOVE/L.A.

September, 1982

Orange glow sets the haze.
    Another lousy day ahead.
Jammed in cars like victims behind bars.
    Living on the freeway, but something's quite unique here
amidst the smog and distress.
    The man on the corner says, ''This town's a seducing mistress.''

Hustlers walked the streets — eleven and twelve years old —
    past their bedtime.
This is where the story loses its rhyme.

Davies Drive overlooked glittered dreams
    like a jewelry store
waiting to be robbed.

Motels I may have slept in, leaving ashtrays full.
    Pastel T-Birds I may have cruised in,
the tank not always full.
    Melrose might have took me one too many times.
Your eyes may have taken me to the other side.
    Past life soulmates can't always coincide.
August was the month I finally realized.

Melissa S. Lafkas

EASTER

Church bells toll summoning the Faithful
To honor His Resurrection, the day on which He rose again,
To shed faith and hope this Advent season.

Solemn service occurs
Mixed with joyous songs in praise of His name.

Bright breezes softly waft
The perfumes of ladies of the church
To the nostrils, a pleasing scent.

Posey colorful hats, gloves, and gowns
Awaken the feelings of the heart
In both young and old.

Shapely hips sway and beckon glances from the dour few,
Macho bachelors now enchanted by life around them renewed.

No anomoly in this idea of religious fervor,
The sense that two combined
March on with His heartbeat in their minds.

Ruth Walcott

FROM FLAM TO MIDFJORD

The bright green of sunlit meadows from lake edge
            to blue sky heights.
Crisp October air in Norgé kissing cheeks and ruffling
            hair on the ferry landing at August's end.
Ribbon River Road banding the lake edge as seen from above
            weaving snakily in and out of the shade.
Crystal clear waters fall from granite fissures down, down
            into the fjords.
The Norgé Trout is not mercury laden and looks like Alaskan
            Pink on your porcelain lunch plate.
Deliciously accompanied by good fellowship; all are lasting
            impressions of my first Skandia trip.

Ruth Walcott

WALLS

August, 1983

There's a wall which hangs my photos of stories.
   There are walls between my stories that block the flowing path.

There are walls of smiles that stood once for my view.
   There are walls that show no future.
These walls must be fairly new.

There are walls that give no answer.
   White and at night they turn to black.
These are the walls behind me for which I can't turn back.

There are walls between my words.
   A sentence can't be free
For it is incomplete without a period or apostrophe.

There's a wall between my love.
   I keep knocking at the door, but if you can't hear
You can't answer.
   So what's the wall for?
There'll be more walls tomorrow, and will I ever get through?
   Only if it's a sliding glass door
Behind it standing you.

Melissa S. Lafkas

MELISSA SHAYLA LAFKAS. Born: San Francisco, 12-20-62; Single; Education: Certificate of Achievement, San Francisco School of Business and Commerce, 1987; San Francisco State University, Music Recording Industry Certificate Program, Certificate for completion of courses in Music Press, History, Video, Publicity, Songwriting, Recording Workshop, Legal Aspects, and Credit work, 1984-1986; Occupations: Record Tracking, Freelance Photographer; Memberships: Bay Chapter Oceanic Society, Greenpeace, ACA Group Supporter; Themes: *These three poems were selected from my collection of 111 poems entitled* Poems of my Past (1975-1985). *Out of this collection are some lyrics for songs; others are simply reflections from real experiences during a ten-year duration on adolescence, travel, friendship, love, loss, grief — several different ranges of emotion;* Comments: *Writing is a very natural process for me. It's a release for inner feelings to come out. Pen and paper can be companions. What more can I say. The poems speak for themselves, meaning different things to different people. To me each is a phase, a feeling, an experience, and now a memory, a portfolio of my past.*

TWILIGHT

The twilight glow now fills my eye, with a
beauty rare as I look to the sky.
The clear cool light of the Milky Way, like
a road to heaven, it lights my way.
Each star in the sky like a soul set free,
Casting their light that man might see
the work of the Master, the Maker of man,
Placing each star to brighten his land.
The Dippers in place and the Big Bear, too,
the star in the north, a guide ever true.
This beauty rare, unmarred by man, was created
by God; it's the Master's Plan.

Arthur J. Johns

BLUE MORNING

Skies are shining over a desert stream.
What happened to the wild life that we once saw?
Gone with the past.
Utterly banished away.
So dense with its population,
All God's little creatures gone.
Blue morning, the hunter's on the move.
Dedicated to all the wildlife that has been killed.
Let man see his destruction of life and how it would change
   God's world.
See the sun.
Know you're alive with a vast love for all.
See the blue morning and save what is left from yesteryear.
Blue morning please save us all.

William J. Martinson

THE WALL

One wouldn't think that in such modern times, there exist
lands with long ugly borders
Not just an agreed upon, recognized line, but a wall of steel,
barbwire, cement blocks and mortar —
And the real tragedy of this unbelievable fact is; the purpose
of this strange and grotesque fence
It is to hold in restraint, an assortment of innocent souls,
drenched completely, in an air of ignorance —
Some are without hope, some, even without feelings, there's no
definite identity at all
There's no such thing, such as individuality, just one great mass,
casting dark shadows against a wall —
Millions of minds, perhaps very wealthy in knowledge, that could
be of great value and yet
This modern world, will never be able to evaluate, what is lost
here, among these pathetic silhouettes —
I am sure they must often wonder, what twist of fate, brought
them here to such a plight
Why should they, the humble, grope in darkness while just ahead
there is an offer of light —
But: Fate, in its confusing way of teaching the whole world, the
very big as well as the small
Through their suffering others will learn that there's no room for
shadows and there shouldn't be any need for walls —

Furman Clarke

THE ARTIST AND ME

An artist uses paints and brushes. To paint the beauty he can see. While the words I write, are a picture to me. If combined they make someone happy?

We think that's quite all right. After we are gone, we hope, we'll live on in someone's memory. To make people happy, means the world to us, you see. An artist uses paints and brushes.

A poet paints with words, the pictures he does see. Together they paint a picture, which is what was meant to be.

To a poet, a poem is nothing, but music without words. Each with its own melody. Like the songs of many birds, while an artist uses paints and brushes. A poet uses words, that he alone can see.

The many beauties of a foreign land. A tropical isle, with golden sand. We both are painting pictures. In our own way, you see. Our own way of making beauty. The Artist and Me.

Harold Bond

CHRISTMAS MEMORIES

Many years ago, in the middle twenties
When I was just a little girl of five
I longed for a doll to have for my own
One who almost seemed alive

I had seen her in the window of a large department store
But I knew she wasn't for the likes of me
For there were other children in our humble home
Who longed for pretty dollies just like me

So on Christmas eve we trimmed our little tree
With paper canes and homemade jingle bells
We each sent up a prayer for our secret longing wish
As mama's baking sent up Christmas smells

We didn't have a fireplace, our chimney was so small
A fat ole Santa never could come down
And so it was impossible that on Christmas morn
I'd ever find that doll with eyes of brown

But I had let my wish be known as children mostly do
Then went to sleep with smells of Christmas holly
When I awakened on that ne'er forgotten Christmas morn
I found my dream come true, my precious dolly

Santina Hartung

SEETHING STREAMS

Crashing down upon my wracked brain
Aching thunders spill out on the decks of times
  forgotten not
Their Holy, fragile, tautly balanced tirades
Immersed in life's coiled follies
Are drowned without water's need
Or calloused from within.
I beckon all to cast asunder
Such vacant stares of hollow skulls
And bellowing bellies of laughter's wretched core
Or writhing shadows of ungainly sorrow
That rise again
Only to die once more;
As stained glass windows open onto a world undone
Pregnant with the uncouth fetus of love's dwindling chore.

Roy D. Benson

DRAGON'S LAMENT

Icy trickle fire dew drop down
the caverns of my dark mind depths
tingles hot and burns my breath long
yearning for cool Spring's caress . . .

Window-leaning gasp awake and see
and feel on wild wind to soar
at ease and death
redeemed at last.

Long time since salvation is the snow
and Winter's ire deviltry crooning at my breast,
when lonely turns to wanting turns
to fever, and ache replaces ache . . .

Time turns 'round to remember day's
tempest and nights cradle-rocked in lullaby
of mellow dreams and turret skies
where hide the dragon's embers, to stay
awhile hidden and away; yet promised,
hanging heavy midsky, to come again
and steal love's joy away.

Diane Ramey

OH LITTLE UNBORN ONE

Oh little unborn one, growing deep, deep within.
So rapid does your heart beat, unceasing kick of feet.
Little being longing to come forth, to see a glad,
But frightening world.

Eyes of blue? Oh skin so crimson,
A being buried deep within.
Bone of my bone, flesh of my flesh, all my love
is yours.

Oh little guarded one, alone in hibernation,
Impatiently awaiting the day, when birth brings breath,
and future life.
Alone, you await a grand beginning, when each day will
bring new growth, for all creatures, both great, and small.
Oh little bit, a part of me, yet a separate person too.

Cynthia L. Gardner

CYNTHIA LOUISE GARDNER. Pen Name: Candid Self; Born: Decator, Illinois, 10-21-58; Married: James Robert Gardner, 12-12-80; Education: Mesa Community College, Arizona; Saddleback Community College, California; Craven Community College, North Carolina; major in Psychology and minor in Fine Arts; Occupations: Photographer, Domestic Engineer; Membership: Sergeant, USMC; Comments: *Hope to be a known photo-journalist, and hope to have my works well-appreciated.*

GO STAND BY YOUR GRAVE, MR. CRESS

Go stand by your grave, Silas Glynn Cress;
with your last breath, bid the world goodbye.

To be born again in a spiritual way;
even the best, as you are, must die.

The Cress family adopted you;
in turn you adopted every soul.

Though gravely ill, you took my message
from the cross; teaching the divine goal.

You danced though your role in Life's Play
with Alice, your wife; gentle and true.

You will no longer be in the cast;
six kids and others applaud you.

''Goodbye Glynn. I love you,'' each will cry.
They will miss you forever, I know.

''Sorry to leave you here to suffer;
Goodbye dear ones. I love you all so.''

My promise I keep: to raise you up:
into my glory, come with me now.

Go stand by your grave, my grand Mr. Cress;
the curtain falls, take your final bow.

Shirley Strain Hefty

SHIRLEY ANN HEFTY. Pen Name: Joan Stanhope, Shirley Strain; Born: Rudman, Iowa, 8-22-33; Married: Dick A. Hefty, 3-21-77, Building Contractor; Charles Warren, 6-14-52; Children: Christine, Charles Warren, Michelle Warren; Education: Enrolled in Iowa Central Community College for further education, 1987-89; Occupations: Retail Sales & Management, Insurance Agent; presently partner in Hefty Homes and Vice-President of Dream Homes of Iowa, Inc.; Membership: Chamber of Commerce; Poetry: 'Rodeo Man,' song, 1986; Other Writings: 'A Guide for Clear Thinking,' mini-guide, 1985; 'A Week of Days,' children's, 1987; 'Parodies,' *Jaycees Program Book,* 1966; Comments: *My poems are based on people whose personalities impress me, or a philosophical concept. I am working on 2 books and thinking about 3 others. My mind never stops writing; I just don't get everything in a printout.*

SANDCASTLES

I spent the day collecting sea shells.
Collecting and counting my shells.
I stopped only briefly to survey the land.
All I could see were castles in the sand.

There were some children playing.
They were playing on the beach,
Shovels and pails in hand,
Learning young to build castles in the sand.

The bikini-clad girls lay in the sun
Smelling ever so faintly of Coppertone.
They will never understand
That they are building castles in the sand.

The sun was blocked by dark clouds
And soon it began to rain.
For shelter the people ran.
They would return to build castles in the sand.

We spent summers at the shore
With our beach tags, towels, and balls.
Someone must have seen the plan.
Together, we'll go on building castles in the sand.

John C. Erianne

GRACE OF ANGELS

Fading, fading; the ship is fading.
A splintering light catches amongst sun and wind.
Fire is growing in the sky.
On the ground, we turn away
Frozen in our skins.

Voices screaming into the night.
Crying, our tears irrigate the ground.
Lub-dub, lub-dub, our hearts pound, lub-dub.
Reality is shattered in a trillion pieces
Like a mirror or window or glass.

God is looking over the sea.
He finds the lost ship.
There, over there, all is still.
The sea is calm, the wind has ceased.
The seven bright stars are gliding into eternity.

John C. Erianne

THE ICE CREAM STORE

''Tell me again,'' the little girl said,
The old man just smiled and shook his head.
''We have raspberry ripple and peach flavored brandy,
Strawberry, lemon, and pink cotton candy;
Chocolate, lime, banana, and coffee —
Pistachio, licorice, orange, and toffee,
Rainbow sherbet and blueberry swirl.
What will it be for you, little girl?
Bubble gum, peppermint, pralines and cream,
Butterscotch, hazelnut, toasted almond dream.''
Such wonderful flavors, two dozen or more,
All to be had at the Ice Cream Store.
As the last flavor rolled off his tongue with ease,
She looked up and said, ''One vanilla cone, please!''

Rebecca Hutton

WHO AM I?
WHO ARE WE?

I am born into a world very sad and cold,
They say all things in my childhood will effect me,
   they say or so I've been told.

The Id, Ego, Superego for who?
Does it work for me, I hope it works for you.

Dreams and symbols have they meaning to me,
I really don't know, I'm too tired to see.

His name was Freud so I've been told,
He is the one who summed up human behavior everyone knows.

Who are we in this unconscious state;
Keep up with your inner and dark thoughts before its too late.

Esteem, hysteria, where are the goals?
Is there any for me — I was not told.

Schizophrenia, neurosis, they are labels of the game,
If you are awarded one you must be insane!

The need for beauty, the need to know;
Realize you are healthy and be ready to go.

Who am I or we to put a human in a class?
If someone judges me I hope I pass.

Be who you are and fit the role of life which is an unending play,
Because others will be born into this sad cold world,
   I'm told or so they say.

Richard W. Meek

BETWEEN THE SONG
& THE SONGSTER

When you don't exist for the people
When you don't exist as a song
I'll borrow from you before you are born
So that I can guide you along.

The pen and the paper between us
Are harbors that creak with the waves,
Ready for launching to far away ears
Is the ship that together we saved.

Then sometimes you are a fortress
With cannons protruding through walls,
When all I want is to bring you to me
To take you to concerts and balls.

If you were not here to enlighten
Then neither the mountains would grow,
Oceans and hearts would abandon the world
So you see why on, we must go.

I'm the reporter of ages
And my report comes with you
Of things we have seen from an angle or two
Defining you till you are through.

When all the labor is finished
And you have been clustered a name,
You are given to folks for their senses to weigh . . .
And the world is no longer the same.

Joe F. Varela

LIFE AS WE SEE IT
IN THE EYES OF THE LORD

The meaning of life is so hard to understand,
unless you begin to realize what God meant for us
on this land.
   Things don't come easy, as we always say, but
look how Jesus suffered even until His dying day.
   Love one another, as He loves you, and help to
guide them in what they do. Learn and teach others
right from wrong, work hard at life and grow to
be strong.
   The test is here for you this way, and you will
help Him decide your final place to stay.
   As long as you have a roof over your head and
even a small reason to smile, this is more than
Jesus had, when he walked many a mile.
   Think of all the turmoil and stress He had to
see, but now He sits with the Almighty, on the
right hand side of God, forever to stay. Eternally
grateful for the price He had to pay.
   Now lift up your hearts and see what you can do,
because the final answer will be on How and what you do.

Susan Ramét

MISS LACEY

She stood in her classroom glancing over the two large classes,
Usually firm and strict, staring out over the rims of her dark glasses.
Attired in a green sweater, white blouse and a Scottish
   checkered skirt.
Behind all these features was a wonderful lady of outstanding worth.

Each morning she held in her hand a small, black, hard cover book,
It was a signal for morning prayers, suddenly we all looked so serious.
She was a believer in living a good life in a righteous
   and religious way,
Her teachings have remained with many of us students
   to the present day.

We all look back over these great school days upon the hill,
Where we were prepared for a world of many challenges
   and unknown fears,
Remembering her hard work and dedication and how she treated
   us all so well,
She was a great motivator who developed excellence throughout
   all these years.

Over the yesteryears we have expressed great gratitude in many ways,
Once again, time allows the opportunity to open our hearts
   and proudly say,
"History will never replace the great school years with you
   upon the hill,
But memories will forever continue until our minds fade and hearts
   become still."

Frank M. Blackwood

NATURAL TUNNEL.

THE LOBSTER TRAP

You just slide me into the deep icy sea, leave me there overnite,
On that slimy rock bottom, to challenge all those crawling mights.
Yet, through such hardships, I serve thee well even through bad times,
Even when you sell my crawling visitors for many dollars and dimes.

The rock-bottom crawlers are many, they creep along my little floor,
They hang from my only decoration, a baited stich
   just inside my open doors.
Like an old Newfoundland saying, "My door is always open to thee,"
But for crawling visitors that pass through my doors,
   are seldom set free.

Imagine having a caged life like me, it's not always
   that rewarding to see,
I'm always attached to a rope and buoy, that seldom sets me free.
But, I was created by man to receive and to give onto thee,
When my ribs have grown old and worn, just set me free at sea.

Frank M. Blackwood

THE MAN OF IRON

Dedicated to the late Uncle Billy Fifield

He was a jolly, friendly, family man, known by us all,
He had a heart of gold and nerves often described as gall.
His character was very witty, and he was usually full of fun,
A real workaholic, like a small beach bird, always on the run.

God gave him many skills that took others years to learn,
Often curious onlookers peeped in the forge to note the goings-on.
There he was sweating, grasping a mallet and pounding a piece of hot iron,
Perhaps making horseshoes, sleighshoes and anchors for folks all around.

The mallet pounding echoed loudly throughout our peaceful town,
Then it meant nothing, today it remains memorable, a beautiful sound.
He'd wet his lips often as the great heat chapped and dried them at times.
He'd wipe his brow quickly as sweat and smoke blurred his view.

Routinely he'd grab, pound and dip iron in water, and sputter a tune,
All this tough work started at early morning and lasted until noon.
It all seemed like great magic as we watched and took many sighs,
Seeing him grab hot iron, in bare hand, unbelievable to the human eyes.

His creative workmanship remains a great mystery, even to this day,
A mystery once shared and appreciated by all, it's now history to stay.

Frank M. Blackwood

THE PEDDLER

Ambling down a sleepy cobblestone street of yesteryear,
   strolled a green horse-drawn cart, listen and you can hear.
"I've got pole beans, and turnip greens, and potatoes in my poke."
   He was bringing fresh fruits and vegetables to us, the common folk.

As the old iron-rimmed wheels click, over the worn cobblestone,
   it's pulled by a sleek tan pony, that appears fresh from a currycomb.
In a harness of brown, studded with shiny brass knobs,
   glistening with a brilliance, that reminds you of gold watch fobs.

Hunched on a flat board seat, with the reins taut in his hand
   was a timely figure, a courteous, trustworthy, patient old man.
A burley old gent, in a tweed frock coat, in his face the lines showed
   all his precarious years, laced with happiness and tears, he glowed.

Ah! Everyone was glad to see the peddler, with his load of fine wares,
   fruits and vegetables, and it seemed he always had a fable to share.
Things and times such as these have long since disappeared,
   only the sight and the sounds in our minds, can bring back yesteryear.

Jimmy Rimmer Baird

HIDDEN PEARL

Pearls of passion are what my teardrops seem,
So much like the sand-born spheres they gleam.
Born in my eye as a sad memory unfurls,
A memory once dormant like sand in the pearls.

But from my eye only tears shall surge,
When from the mere shell something great will emerge.
What is the shell that such beauty has formed
When from my eye only water has stormed?

Maybe the sand is the thought of a shell
Which later into a pearl will swell.
Perhaps the shell has sad thoughts of its own,
But lack of a soul turns its tears to stone.

The pearls of passion which swell from my eyes
Release my heart from its sad, sad cries.
Their life is short, and then they are gone.
They cleanse my soul, so I can live on.

Perhaps the pearl is what's left behind,
When all sad thoughts from the soul have been mined.
The pearl of a person is what lies inside,
A heart in which hope, peace and love do abide.

Patricia M. Regan

AFTER THE EQUINOX

The sky is pellucid space;
Stars shine like fluorescent street lights
Upon the freshly washed earth below.
A gentle breeze, laundered free from dust and pollen,
Gusts lightly from the Southwest.
It is an autumn evening following
Six days of steady downpouring rain,
Which saturated the porous clay
And replenished the sinking water level beneath.

We breathe deeply of the pure air,
Rejoicing physically and mentally
At being free again from too familiar cells.
For a week we were imprisoned within
Masoned walls, refuge from the weather.
The step quickens; the voice has a lilt;
Life is good again; we are grateful
And we give thanks to a merciful God.

Alice Ruediger Ochs

i dream

i dream of you
　　cool midnight clear
　　　　with naught but our low sound
two slip the bounds
　　of cloth on flesh
　　　　prowl o'er me take me down
pert tips soft slice
　　now here now yon'
　　　　furred length press naked thigh

slow into mine
　　your bright eyes climb
　　　　hued quiet new stars shine

i dream of you
　　cool midnight clear
　　　　want naught but our low sound
take haste the hounds
　　warm flesh to flesh
　　　　growl o'er me
　　　　　　take me down

P. A. Mueller

SUNRISE

light,
charmed by definition, bursts free.
mist, frightened,
retreats.
falling into darkness.
gone from summits
light,
holding secret expressions, is beauty
seen within one magical beam.
unrestrained,
touches all,
living to see wordless images,
lightning explodes into brilliance.
darkness, frightened,
withdraws to where light is not
living endless lives,
casting away shadows,
light frightens day,
and lands shutter to accept a thousand meanings of
an enchanted force.

Wendy A. Bauer

THIS DAY

God bless this day as it will never be seen again . . .
Bless every precious moment from beginning to end.
The sun will never rise as it did on this day . . .
So cherish its beauty in a very special way.
God bless this day and the life that it gives . . .
Help us to ensure that it is a day well-lived.
Tomorrow is only a vision of what we hope to see . . .
We know not our futures, or even if they will be.
Let us forgive one another and rid our hearts of hate . . .
As Tomorrow may be, just a day too late.

Tracy L. Wolf

THE SANDBOX

I went back to my old neighborhood,
　In the garden there it stood,
A little sandbox made of wood.

In the winter I was ten,
　I loved to build fat white men,
And watch them melt . . .
　and build again.

My house had always been the best,
　Exciting as a treasure chest,
It lay beneath a robin's nest.

My ''friends'' were buried in grains of sand,
　I held each one in my little hand,
Their bodies moved at my command.

I collected leaves of crimson and maroon
　From skeleton trees against a golden moon.

I went back to my old neighborhood,
　In the garden there it stood,
A useless square of firewood.

Rose Fratta

MY WORST FEAR

I'm sitting here in this dark lonely room,
as it's very late at night.
I'm thinking over something,
which is my only fright.

The fright of losing someone special,
who's very close to me.
I know it won't last forever,
if only it could be.

He's someone who cares for me with all his heart,
he's someone whose love I share,
no matter how far we're apart.

Maybe it could last forever,
probably only in my dreams.
Who knows, this could be some dream in which we both do share.
I know as I'm lying in bed tonight,
it will be my only prayer.

I'm going to end this now,
before I start to cry.
Maybe if I take each day at a time,
we will be together until the day we die!

Tracy Dulin

TIGER'S EYE

Your face is a tan moon fringed with iron grey.
Your brow is broad and deep as a pool.
Your eyes are bright brown gems glittering with desire.
Your lips are soft as a bird's down and full as a ripe peach.
Like your Tauran brother, your sinewy neck shows resolve.
Your shoulders are broad and shelter me.

Ruth Walcott

TO ALWAYS REMEMBER

Look on the wall,
The one you hang your treasures on.

Mine has mostly pictures,
A diploma or two and some mementos.

The picture of my folks,
My gosh, they've done so much for us.

There are two family pictures,
One taken 25 years ago, one last year,
Lots of changes.

My first piggybank.
It's a model of a gas pump that sold Sinclair
gas for 29 cents a gallon.

We went to San Francisco.
The little trolley car reminds me.

My bride and I in that wedding picture,
She was beautiful then — 8 years ago — more so now.

I look at these things every day,
But I don't always see them.

Have you ever noticed?
Wonderful memories never fade.

Robert S. Pearson

THE RIVER

I went down to the river, to get away.
Away from the real world.
I took my shoes off, then dangled my feet in the water.
The water was cold, so cold it made me shiver.
So there I sat in my own world.
As I sat there my life passed before my eyes.
It's just like the river.
It keeps going on and on, but it's getting nowhere.
When I finally stopped daydreaming it was getting late.
The sun was going to sleep, but the moon was coming out.
It sparkled upon the water, which by now had become quiet.
It was as if, the whole world had gone to sleep.
I knew then it was time to go.

Christina McCoy

MEN

The Lord took from himself and made man
He made him warm and kind, then let Satan take his hand

God gave him a heart and the desire for love
Made him the kind of man we all dream of

Satan took and gave him that evil in his eye
Taught him all those things that make us women cry

The Lord showed him such things as loyalty and devotion to his mate
But the devil showed him Playboy and made loneliness our fate

Yes, God made man and Satan cast his spell
So though they all began in heaven, they all belong in hell

Jeri K. Rooks

THINKING OF YOU

Sitting in a darkened window, watching large fluffy
snowflakes twirl gently to the ground . . .

Standing on a beach at sunset, watching the day's
last light disappear slowly over the horizon . . .

Lying outside at night, waiting for a comet, or a
shooting star to leave its fiery trail across a dark,
cloudless sky . . .

Curled in your favorite chair, reading a book, a
crackling blaze casts a cheery glow from the fireplace . . .

Resting on a hillside, in the warm spring sun, watching
a pair of eagles soaring carelessly with the clouds . . .

Leaning on a rock, high atop a mountain, a gentle breeze
cools your body, hot from the climb — the far away sound of
a waterfall . . .

All of these things, shared with that special someone,
can be wonderful. Alone, crushing . . . Unless, you at least
have that someone — in your heart . . .

Stan Morrow

YOUR EYES

I could get lost in those eyes, and I wouldn't even mind.
I bet, it would even be nice . . .
    Looking at you, looking at me.
    Wishing . . .
So, What if it is a dream . . . it's mine . . .

A brown so dark and true, created I think, just for you.
No others can compare . . .
    Peaceful, yet exciting,
    mirrors of my desire . . .
Could I be in love with your eyes? . . .

No — I think it's the life that shines in there, your life.
Warm, tender, and giving . . .
    Loveshine,
    brighter than all the stars in the heaven . . .

Stan Morrow

FOR ALL THAT YOU GIVE

Blessed with an untainted innocence, setting us far apart
So dear and divine, the creatures of God, how you break mine heart

For all that you give and still we take more . . . to better our kind?
Have conscience and compassion been forsaken
    for the wonder of human mind?

Can we truly believe to suffer for the sake of science
    is to suffer with cause?
Or have we any concept of consequence for breaking
    nature's most sacred laws?

Though I, too, carry the scent of your enemy, for I, too, am man
Beyond all earthen sense, we share a special bond, so few understand

And though as your keeper, I may earn my bread,
    my true reward is greater yet
For it is through your love I am gratified and my purpose
    is both found and met

Jeri K. Rooks

THE HAUNTING DREAM

Eerie; tremble; frightful scare,
ghostly figure on the stair.

Darkness, dampness, musty smell,
cobwebs, spiders, moldy well.

Creaks and squeaks and rattles and groans,
laughs and clangs and screams and moans.

Lightning, thunder, rain and storm,
wake up in bed, nice and warm.

Kayla Dowden

WILD GEESE

O thou sweet loves
of my sleepless nights
your husky sad
complaints in helpless
manner
pleading humbly
do so pity me . . . as they are dear

will you not dare to rest
lest I and the likes of me
should find you unaware
step unto holy ground?

why is it God's plan
to make you restless in eternity
between two worlds?

Renate Potjan

A KING ON A THRONE

If I were a king upon a throne,
A golden crown upon my head.
Covered with every precious stone,
Diamond, pearls and rubies so red.

If I were a king upon a throne,
Clad in a cloak of mink and sable.
Everything I could possibly own.
And exotic food upon my table.

If I were a king upon a throne,
With all the crown jewels at my feet.
If there was no Queen to call my own,
No one so kind and sweet.

If I were a king upon a throne,
no prince or princess to love.
Just sitting there all alone.
Just me and God above.

If I were a king upon a throne,
I'd give up all my possessions.
Just for someone to call my own,
This is my confession.

George B. Norris

FAREWELL TO WINTER

Winter's almost over,
and we're all very glad.
But when I really think of it,
it makes me kind of sad.

To look outside my window,
and see the ground so white.
I really must admit it,
it is a beautiful sight.

I love to go out sledding,
and flying through the snow.
To see the pretty snowflakes,
as through the air they flow.

If by chance a snowflake,
should fall upon my face,
It makes me feel like God himself,
has touched me with his grace.

At last my pretty winter,
must say hello to spring.
Once more the flowers all will bloom,
and all the birds will sing.

Joann Barger

WICHITA MOUNTAINS RETREAT

This morning I lie next to you
Cocooned in flannel comfort.
Nighttime has left an icy negligee
About our tent, but I am warmed
By your embrace.

I hear the chatter of birds,
Like mothers making early morning
Preparations. Fresh-smelling breezes
Invigorate, entice me
To leave in search
Of clear-running streams.

The ruggedly handsome contour
Of this land stirs me with
Wild pleasure. You pull me closer,
And I envision your face
Etched with firelight.

This is our wilderness refuge
From all that endangers us.
Buffalo and long-horn cattle
Are our sentinels.
We retreat within the safety
Of each other.

Kathi Hill

RETRIBUTION

They taunted and teased the demon within,
  Thinking the beast beyond all caring —
They loosed the dragon breathing fire,
  With claws bared and nostrils flaring.
Its magnificent fury turned on them now
  With pent-up rage and anger felt —
Too late, they see their peril,
  Too late, too late to repent.

Rachel Schiebler

PRETENDED LOVE

I sit here holding your hand
Staring at the sea
Staring at the sand
Searching for a clue
to give me courage to tell you
I don't love you
I know I have said it before
but, I just don't feel it anymore
I hold you closer to me
looking into your eyes.
I can see your love for me is true
I began to tell you, I don't love you
But suddenly my heart went weak
I couldn't speak
So now I go on pretending to love you.

Laurie A. Pimentel

A COUNTRY SMILE

I know a tall and gentle man
A man with a country smile
For many years he farmed the land
Now his hair is snowy white
This man with a country smile
His sky blue eyes still bright
He always has time to visit awhile
To talk of days gone by
Always with a country smile
I know a man with a country smile
Who loves and trusts his God
His dear face wrinkled by life's trials
He makes all our hearts glad
With his country smile
Now you know this smile belongs
To *you*, Dad.

Janice F. Albrecht

Society is the judge.
Nobility is acquired
Only when found innocent
As to their desires.

Estrangement from humanity
Is known to them as guilt.
When will the circle perish?
When will we reach freedom?

So many ideas are forgotten,
For fear of being marked.
Inside us all, there's a traitor;
A rebel, waiting for his chance.

Once he breaks the weakening bonds,
Each person's paradise
Will finally unfold.
People will no longer fear
What their minds may hold.

Kathryn Johnson

94

IN VIEW

On the horizon
        Rays of lines, rays of lines
Streaking down, streaking down
        In the twilight time
Mirage-like patterns
        In a sunbeam
Blue whale   Water spout-in
        No end   No beginning

Music so Faint   Mystical sounds
        Magic of a harp
Upon us now (funny no music)
        Only cold & wet

But on the horizon
        Rays of lines, rays of lines
Streaking down, streaking down,
        In the twilight time
Mirage-like patterns
        In a sunbeam
No end
        No beginning!

Wally Kibler

WALLACE EDWARD KIBLER. Pen Name: Mark James; Born: Staten Island, New York; Divorced; Two children, Mark & Jeffrey; Education: High school graduate, attended numerous writing courses; Occupations: Machinist, Songwriter, Poet; Memberships: Songwriters Club of America, County Music Society of America; Awards: Award of Merit Certificate, 3-31-86; Honorable Mention, Golden Poet Award, 1986; Certificate of Honor and Honorable Mention; Poetry: 'Poets From the Past,' 3-31-86; 'Homework of Whitman & Poe,' 3-86; 'Free,' 2-86; 'Trust & Jesus,' 'Only Five Letters,' American Poetry Association, 1-15-86 & 4-86; 'Edgar Allan & Me,' 'Message Through Me,' 8-86; Comments: *To create a poem, a song, and have it published and reflected upon by contemporaries as well as generations yet unborn is very important to me. My mind is always open for that special message . . . often so freely given . . . on the job, in the supermarket, a walk in the park. My pen is always ready when the thoughts begin to flow! I also enjoy writing historical poetry.*

THE LOVE OF THE STARS

We're wrapped up together, my Lori and me,
We're entwined forever in eternity.
You're my friend, my lover, my sounding board,
We're close together as a sailor's cord.
Neither death nor another can break us asunder,
And that is the wonder of the love that is ours,
And so my dear Lori, my wife and my glory,
The love that we have is not overshadowed,
On Mercury, Venus or Mars,
For ours is the love of the stars.

William J. Galbraith

I MUST GET OUT

Sometimes I feel so full of rage
While sitting here within this cage
Thinking about what I've done
The happy and sad times, but mostly the fun
Wishing I were outside again
Enjoying myself, my family and friends
My being in here is unjust
I have to get out, I must, I must
Please understand I did no wrong
And I've already been here far too long
I know I've done wrong before
But this is no way to even the score
Sometimes I feel my mind is slipping away
I feel it more with every day
I must get out, hear my cry
If I don't soon, I think I'll die

Danette G. Balsam

OF ABA BEN ALI

Aba Ben Ali, son of
        Mohammed Ben Ali

Only 13, just a boy . . . fighting as a man
        by day . . . hiding in caves by night
Not for fame or glory . . .
        just the right to exist

Afganistan 1986
        Shame on the bloody *Reds!*

Aba Ben Ali, Son of
        Mohammed Ben Ali
In death with smoking gun in hand
        Forever on the lips
of those that still resist
        Shame on the bloody *Reds!*

Aba Ben Ali, son of
        Mohammed Ben Ali
Only 13, just a boy
        In a higher, peaceful place
he rests
        Shame on the bloody *Reds!*

Wally Kibler

ALONE

So many roads I've traveled,
Rocky, cold, and bumpy.
Many times my world's unraveled,
Many times my bed's been lumpy.

I've tried to live a life that's right,
Abiding by the manual.
And many times I've paid the price,
Because I've dared to be a Daniel.

But as I travel on life's way
I stand tall and proud,
Because I've said what I've had to say,
And I've said it all out loud.

So I'll go on doing what I have to do,
I'll set my goal and follow it.
I have to live with me, I don't have to live with you;
I'll take my medicine and swallow it.

John F. Borden

I WISH

I wish the world
was filled with happy places,
then when you look around
there would be smiling faces.

I wish the people
would live and let die,
then at the end
don't stop to ask why.

I wish that people would
believe that I am me,
so I can live my own life
and nobody to worry about me.

I wish that the
wishes that I say,
would come true
so I could live for today.

But most of all,
I wish everybody
was like you,
then they would believe me
when things I say were true.

Lisa Laska

A SELF-PORTRAIT

I view her canvas
As I preview my life
In a sense
The portrait I paint
Is only a reflection
Of my own studies

Fact or fiction
The painting becomes part of the artist

The never obtainable stroke
The last thing I place on my canvas
The lights go down
The stage is striked
And with minimal applause
I exit

Victor Bailey

YUKON JACK

When I wake up shaking in the darkness,
And my heart is full of fright,
My mind is full of terror,
So I quickly snap on the light.

Yes, the nightmare hasn't faded,
The fear is still intact,
I light up another Winston,
And drink a toast to Yukon Jack.

T. Wilkie

FOR YOU, MY FRIEND

I send you a smile
For just being there
By my side when I'm down
And showing that you care.
I send you love
For caring for me
When I was sick or hurt
Or wanted company.
I send you a rainbow
For saying to me,
The sun needs the rain
For a rainbow to be.
I send you the world
If dreams could come true,
For a friend takes it all
Then returns it to you.

Leslie Sorrells

THE LONG ROAD HOME

I have seen the darkest
hours of the night.
I have seen the dimmest
hours of the day.
I have walked the streets
through pools of lamplight.
I have walked through
meadows in the moonlight.
I have walked down
lonely alley ways.
I have run up
the steepest of hills.
Soon I will be carried,
carried down the long road home.

Kelly D. Knutson

WHEN IT FALLS APART

Sitting alone in the dark
the corner seems a friendly place
Staring into nowhere
dreaming small dreams
remembering the plans we made
Even when mother said
they were just fantasies
like touching stars in the sky
why didn't we listen
They were just fantasies.

Now I'm here
sittin' in the darkness
starin' into emptiness
those days are so far away
Wishing she was here
to tell me how I feel
Lost in a world of endlessness
if only I could have seen
the future back then
but now my only friend is
Loneliness.

Ghada Elaydi

I believe in fantasies
Fairytales and dreams
Sandcastles, Superman
Dishes of ice cream.

Every cloud a silver lining
Every dog his day
Little Mary quite contrary
Eating curds and wey.

I believe in wishful thinking
Daydreams and prayer
Prince Charming, Cinderella
Robin and Pooh Bear.

Every day a brand new dawning
Old-fashion cones
Star light, star bright
And there's no place like home.

I believe in love and music
Read between the lines
I believe in getting old,
Age, a state of mind.

Bonnie Ehrhardt

AUTUMN REFLECTION

When the kids are in school.
The series is over,
And the weather restrains us
From being a rover,
We look to those things
Accomplished indoors.
The storm windows are in.
The heating bill soars.
We sports-minded persons
Change seasons in stride,
From predominately outdoors
To most those inside.
Crops have been harvested
Near 100 percent.
We pause to consider
How time has been spent.
When a glance at achievement
Makes life worth the living,
We realize, profoundly,
It's time for Thanksgiving.

William W. Dillinger

FRAGMENT OF TIME

Time is an elusive lizard
which we can't fully grasp
and when we catch hold of its tail
we find it slips from our hands
and we are left with a part
a fragment, a memory.

Just as you cannot restore
the tail to the lizard
so you cannot restructure
the time that is past
just remember
the fragments, the memories.

Ginny Turner

SPANISH CASTLE

Castle, Castle, Castle, crumbling & of ruins
  of memories . . . riches, romance, poetry & music
Castle, Castle, Castle, once of might & strength
  of knights & ladies in waiting

Now battered by wind, lightning & rain, of ghosts
  creaking of armor & chains
Castle, Castle, Castle, once of heavenly heights
  atop a mountain high
Now full of decay . . . crumbling & of ruins
  racing toward the sea

Castle, Castle, Castle, once of banquets, fun & cheer
  of great crowds, "Let the jousting commence!"

Now alone Castle, Castle, Castle, another room crumbles
  but a grand ball is held at 12 midnight on the Sunday after
& all remaining rooms light up; music & dancing is heard
  for many a mile, of majesty, & dignity, & memories of youth

Spanish Castle, Spanish Castle, Spanish Castle
  of ghosts, creaking of armor & chains
Crumbling, & of ruins, racing toward the sea!

Wally Kibler

STATUE OF LIBERTY

Tall and proud she stands
Holding the Freedom Torch in her hand
Travellers who come to our land
Receive a welcome from the bands

The music is a joy to their ears
The journey is ended and there are no more fears
They know this is a free country
A Land of Opportunity

We hail The Statue of Liberty
For all it stands
And we shall always remain her loyal fans
Hail Woman of Peace

For you are a Mother to us all
The Woman we look up to
No matter, what our call
Hail Sweet Liberty

And forever,
Our Statue of Liberty

Rose Mary Gerlach

A SONNET FROM THE AGNOSTIC

Guilty as these Evangelistic Tongues
Of swelling with a passion to convert,
I shine my faint Agnostic Light across
The Sea of Bliss to show Another Way.
How often I have scoffed at Saving Souls,
Who minister and wave their Precious Book.
And I have told more Christian Sheep than one
To *go* to Him and let me burn in peace.
Yet, I ascend a pulpit with each step,
Waving big bangs and other dusty bones.
My words bring inquisition on the Lambs;
"Just where did Cain acquire his wife?" I smirk.
But soft, the Great Flock's voice descends, "Have faith,"
Inspiring no debate, concluding none.

Gregory J. Smith

HONESTY

So many peoples' words, have proven shallow and so weak,
So I tend to trust my eyes, and let their actions speak.

Yes, a thousand words are painted by one picture, don't you know,
Often peoples' words are tainted, by their actions which they show.

But to some extent, *you* paint the picture, yes, *you* create the scene,
By meaning what you say, and saying what you mean.

So you might want to remember, as day by day you live,
The amount to you that's rendered, is in proportion to what you give.

Yes, trust and respect are usually the pay,
For saying what you mean, and meaning what you say,

So if others' attitudes toward you, you don't want to demean,
Try meaning what you say, and saying what you mean.

This lesson which I'm sharing, I just want you to know,
I'm truly big on caring, and that's why I'm doing so.

One last and final word, about this lesson which I teach,
It's not just something I've heard, I try to practice what I preach.

John F. Borden

SIZE

If you look at your stature, and think nature's unkind,
Here's a word about size, it's a state of mind.

Everyone's height has its bad points and good,
But they could all be successful if only they would.

No doubt it's nice to be physically fit,
But more valuable things are determined by wit.

Yes, everyone's height has its good points and bad,
If they rely on height only, it's really quite sad.

Most people reach greatness not through physical strain,
But through their ability to use their brain.

Intestinal fortitude plays a large part,
What they feed their mind, and what's in their heart.

So if you fail to reach something, and your patience grows thin,
Stop reaching from without, and start reaching from within.

If you heed these words you are indeed wise,
One's height does not determine their size.

John F. Borden

THE SWAN

The swan glides majestically into the room,
Her long and graceful neck turning to greet the people assembled there.
Her pure white skin gleams in the darkened chamber,
And all turn to stare at her brilliance.
Her large almond eyes open wide as she spots me
  standing by the window,
And she undulates over to me to envelope my whole being within
Her wingspan, and we are one and love is all around us, and
We are at peace.
And the grandeur and the glory of my little simple story,
Is not of Greece and Rome, but of my wonderful sweet Lori.

William J. Galbraith

TO KNOW FOREVER

To know forever, may kill the raven
unto his nest he lies
within his torso, he stretched out
To see his forever!

To know forever, may stop the rain
its never predicting actions
the vision of a rainbow, only an illusion
To see its forever!

To know forever, may steel the smile
unto your cheek a frown
out of you there's me — unto me there's you
To see our forever!

To know forever, may prevent the unknown
unto the stars I pray
I look up to you and whisper a praise
So that I may see my forever!

Jamie L. King

SPOT CHECK

A blind spot entering the mind,
A record playing,
Forgetting what was said . . .
Living in a daze.

A blind spot in the mind,
Yesterday's tomorrow is today,
But, today's tomorrow has already passed . . .
Living in confusion.

A blind spot stationed in the mind,
A broken record screaming,
Words are clones of thoughts . . .
Living in a dream.

A blind spot overrules the mind,
A broken record constantly screaming,
Forgetting what was just accomplished . . .
Living in a nightmare.

Michelle L. Dunn

WINDS OF TIME

A gentle spring's breeze, softly,
elegantly distorts the clouds on the horizon;
fluttering the leaves of a nearby tree
as they rearrange themselves.
This soft spring breeze of time,
changes the memory of you,
till ever so slowly,
it dawns on me,
we have drifted apart.
Found our quiet places in different worlds.
Let our shared moments dispel into
separate hours.
Where have these winds of time blown us?
For we are no longer us,
we have become you and I.

Patricia Mercer-Capps

COURTED AND CAUGHT

Take me here and take me there
Treat me like you really care

Then when marriage comes along
You will sing a different song

It was steak and now it's liver
All that yelling makes me quiver

Smelly socks and breath like beer
Darn, there goes another tear

I'm sure I should have wed another
Better yet, just stayed with Mother

Suzanne Foster

Every night I have a dream
Where you and I walk hand in hand.
The moonlight shining on the sea
Reflects our footprints in the sand.

I dream about a magic place
Where we can be alone at last.
The rising waves and tranquil breeze
Erase all memories of the past.

I dream I gently touch your cheek
As we lie beneath the stars,
Then I softly kiss your lips
And all the universe is ours.

But then I wake up, late at night,
Remembering it isn't true
And so, I brush away the tears
And lie back down to dream of you.

Anthony Livingston de Bergerac

NEW DAY

up up and away
it's a fresh new day

daylight delight
sky bright, sunlight

the hours are mine
i can't define

to write — or not to write

Beverley Pettit

PIONEER SISTERS

We are flashbacks of the bygone days
When pioneer women helped in ways
To share the workloads of their sisters
And plan and build without their misters;
When hours spread to weary years
And constant toil brought inner tears.

Other friends just sit and chatter
And wile away the hours with matters
That fret away my precious time,
As work calls from this house of mine.
But not you, Friend, you hear it calling
And crack out work that knows no lolling —
From drapes to dishes, dust and after,
Constant working, constant laughter —
So when you leave, the weary day
Is bright with happiness and play;

Friendship shared with hearts so true,
For work is fun, Elaine, with you.

Mary Olive Tucker-Pickens

GOD'S GIFTS

My heart doth magnify the Lord
And so You spread from nature's hoard
Little flowers beneath my feet,
As though you find me sweet and meek;
A cool breeze when the house is hot;
Good food to fill the cooking pot.

Shade trees rising to the skies
And sights you give to just my eyes —
A dove to show my prayer is anchored,
The rain to stop my toil and anger,
A misty dawn filtered free
Through leafy green and golden trees.

And my mind clearly saw the angel
You sent to place the little blue shell
Of a robin at my feet while
She watched excited as a small child —
Her hands pressed to her lips, a giggle,
Even a majestic wiggle.

You, knowing how I love Your nature,
Both watched me find Your eggshell treasure.

Mary Olive Tucker-Pickens

W + M

The lazy *W* + *M* stretched
around the beech tree, no
taller than when they were
first carved in the smooth bark
forty years ago, one above the
other with ampersand between,
    but stretched.
Lives like initials have been
stretched, and the joining ampersand
    has faded.
Your mind stretched to the breaking
point into a painful realm of
    unreality.
Mine into intensified joy in the
    love of life.

Dubya

A DEDICATION TO MY GRANDMOTHER

For all the things you've done
  and all the things you've said
For all the things you've given me
  and all the tears you've shed

For taking me in when there was no one else
  and treating me like your own
For being so gentle and caring
  and for all the love you've shown

Because you are so special
  and no others can compare
I want to say "thank you"
  for always being there

You're truly one of a kind
  believe me, there is no doubt
For sacrificing to give to me
  and you, always doing without

In my eyes, you're a saint
  I'm glad there was no other
'Cuz I am so very happy
  and proud that *you* are my "mother"

  Danette G. Balsam

THE DARK PLACES

When I was a child
  and the room was dark
    I was afraid;

But covering my head
  frightened me more.
    So I lay

Quilt tucked tightly to my chin,
  eyes wide, searching the dark
    for the approach of the monster.

Age has changed very little.
  Our ignorance leaves great frightening dark zones
    in the world.

Closing my eyes to tiptoe past
  is no comfort.

I am compelled to enter
  and search all the dark corners

Because some frightful answer
  with which I must cope
    may be lurking there.

  Gene W. Abbott

FRIENDSHIP

Each one of us places a different set of values on friendship.
One friendship is solid;
Like gold.
Still it has no price.
Another is strong but not daily.
The support is there if and when it is needed.
We must never forget friendship in the intimate relationship.
I've felt the intimate without friendship;
It got very cold and I let it die.
True friendship can survive misunderstandings, jealousy and the
  treachery of mankind.
Laugh with me, love with me and sometimes cry with me.
Be my friend.

  Lois L. Selby

MARY MET A FARMER

Mary met a farmer many years ago
As she walked through a field covered by winter snow.

He bade her hello with a nod of his head
And said, "Please come share my molasses and bread."

"Oh, Sir, it isn't proper," Mary replied
"You are a stranger; I'll not sit by your side."

The farmer smiled as Mary walked away,
And he smiled again as she passed by each day.

One day while Mary was out for her walk,
She said to the farmer, "It's time we had a talk."

They chatted about all they had known,
From the price of eggs to the cost of cologne.

All at once Mary was sure;
This handsome young man was the man for her.

So it was that Mary found the love of her life
And for sixty years she's been the farmer's wife.

  Judy A. Deeter

PAINED EXPRESSIONS

Look at the pain in the face of this man,
Feelings of sorrow you can't understand.
What he goes through day by day;
The torment will not go away.

Unwanted problems are laid on his brow
Because no one ever showed him how
To stand up for what he thinks is right
And not go down without a fight.

Just because his head is not too loose and light,
Does this give people the right
To push him around
When he does not even defend his ground?

His problem is the overload of compassion for others in his heart;
And it pierces him like a dart
When he finds that others feel
That they're the greatest and to them he should kneel.

Is there no justice for this poor soul,
Or will he have to pay the toll
For his unwarranted kindness
Which is met by stonehearted blindness?

  Craig Willingham

NIP — A TRIBUTE

If there's a tribute I must write
To a man who saved my life,
Who stayed between myself and trouble
And always found us dates to double,
Covered his anguish with a joke
And gave love though his own heart broke;
Cried when I cried, kissed and cuddled,
Laughed at all the things we muddled;
Then it's to him, my grand Big Brother,
Who loves me like a second mother.

He gives me gifts from his sweet spirit,
Love and joy and peace that fill it,
Like blooms along the weary way
That open from a rainy day.
Sure, other brothers may be richer
And give great presents to their sisters;
They can keep their wealth and powers.
My Big Brother gives me flowers.

Mary Olive Tucker-Pickens

MARY OLIVE TUCKER-PICKENS. Pen Names: Molly Tucker, Molly Peery Tucker; Born: Nashville, Tennessee, 1947; Education: Emory and Henry College, Virginia, B.A., English, 1970; Peabody College; University of Tennessee night school; Occupation: Staff member of the Tennessee Bar Association, Nashville, Tennessee; Poetry: 'Best Friends,' 'Gene,' 'The Navigator,' *Hearts on Fire, Vol. IV,* 1987; 'Doubtful Blessing,' *Cat Fancy,* 5-83; Other Writings: ''Welcome Meal,'' humorous feature, *Grit,* 8-4-85; Comments: *To me God is ''The Author of Happy Endings,'' and that is how I would like to be remembered. I want all my stories and poems to give Glory to Him and bring peace and comfort to the hearts of my readers. My example in life is my loving, praying mother, Margaret Tucker.*

THE STORM

I am empty inside!
I cry aloud.
How can I reveal
  that which I do not feel?
The turmoil is gone —
  replaced by uneasy calm.
But, the wall will collapse once more,
  and I shall again feel the fury —
  of the storm.

Holly Cravens

PAIN

Dark as a moonless night
  it holds me tightly.
Never ceasing, always there,
  my only friend.
I hold it to me for fear
  of losing all I have.
Deep as the ocean;
  as fathomless as the depths
  into which I sink . . . my only refuge.
Sleep does not ease its hold on me.
Forever there, forever there.
Watching for a place to enter my thoughts;
  waiting to control my life.
Wound around my heart.
'Tis a black future that awaits me.
It is my comforter, my companion,
  my captor;
Never leaving me to rest.

Holly Cravens

WHEREVER YOU ARE

I've dreamed a thousand dreams of you
And replaced them with a thousand more.
We have lived, loved, and laughed a lifetime
In my mind.
I often sit and wonder
Where you are
How you've been.
So I read your old letters.
And touch your old photograph,
As though it were a talisman
With the ability
To make
My dreams of you
To someday
Come true.

C. E. Edmonson

AUTUMN

Dappled shadows on the lawn
Bespeak a sunny autumn morn,
Time of day for certain told
By how much shade, how much gold.
Not too long before it's noon,
Coming not one whit too soon:
Bearing out the sun's progress
As it moves on toward the west.
Trackless in the blue o'er head
But footsteps patterned on the dead
And dying leaves upon the ground
As penetrating rays come down,
Pushing through the yet green leaves
To form the sun's path through the trees.
Fall! — a glorious time of year
Whether cloudy or whether clear;
A brilliant display of God's power
To substitute for summer's flower.

Davie M. Herndon

I abscond into my own little world,
My paradise of fantasy,
And call upon a mystic dream
Within the shadows of my imagery.
When suddenly from the shadowy depths
A Pegasus does ride,
Its ivory mane billows the wind
As stardust settles behind.
To search the world's yet unknown;
To reach beyond the midnight sun.
With stature strong and spirit bold,
You and I have just begun.
Wonder what's beyond the horizon,
Then seek and you shall find!
For the impossible is always possible
In the universe of my mind.

Paula Kilburg

A SONNET FOR AFRICA

Your now condition is neither
Natural nor everlasting.
There will come a time
When you no longer starve.
There will come a time
When you no longer beg or cry.
There will come a time
When you no longer be ''a (mere) skull.''
Not too far the awakening will come
When you'll be impatient to produce, to create,
To mobilize, to launch on the offensive.
Africa, Africa, your great past and dream
Are not dead but asleep,
And with time they will awake.

Rinkart Eze Okorie

TO HAVE KNOWLEDGE

To have knowledge,
You must know,
To know,
You must be taught,
To be taught,
You must learn,
To learn,
You must listen,
To listen,
You must hear,
To hear,
You must listen,
To learn,
To be taught,
To know,
To have knowledge.

Shane P. Robison

THOUGHTS ON A MAJESTIC WINTER NIGHT

My thoughts go forth on silver moccasin feet
So quietly they leave no scratch or sound
As snow steps down to match their silent stride,
Feathering crystal over trees and ground.
I think how weeds take on a Heavenly shape
When wearing ice wool clocks of white
Ermine dressed, the darkest limbs reflect
A glowing whiteness in the dark of night.

I long to keep the hallowed peace I feel
Viewing saintly weeds along my garden wall,
I feel forgiveness can pattern like icy lace
To leave my heart a majestic waterfall.

Clara Laster

THAT GREAT AMERICAN GAME

When the sun begins to brightly shine
And the weather is feeling fine,
I start to feel that burning desire
To send a baseball soaring higher
Into the stratosphere from the end of my bat.

What is it about this sport,
That makes my face twist and contort
From swinging at a ball with all my might
To send it away on its flight.
Where else do you get a feeling like that?

There's an exhilaration that I get
When I see that the field is set.
The game will soon get under way
And I'll forget my troubles for the rest of the day,
Except for how to score that run.

When the bases are loaded and the game's on the line,
It's all up to me, but I'm feeling fine.
I wait for the pitch as it comes to the plate.
The pitcher reaches out, but he knows it's too late.
And as I see the ball sail away, I know the game is won.

Craig Willingham

NEEDING EACH OTHER

't read, others can't see
but they can read humanity

You call me to a cavern of understanding
carved by your acceptance of life's experiences
memories of past misinterpretations, not capable of detriment
you grow strong in love and understanding

You feel what others have never faced
Your experience runs high in the knowledge of our weaknesses
Because of your weaknesses your spirits brace humility
We see your lot but you understand ours
In learning to love and accept you we find ourselves

Beverley Pettit

SEA SHADOWS

Pale blue casts a shadow of white
Atop peaks of snowcapped mountains
All miniature compared to the breeze.

Copper covered grains focus silver and gold
Against the reflecting cascade of sunshine.
In and out, in and out, the sea moistens, and dries.

Against the erupting peaks of whitewash
Fish spout and fall; rolling, splashing,
Cooling themselves and dipping a muted laugh
At those watching from the heated shore.

The rolls of tunneled water rush
Eagerly only to be washed away
As they each draw nearer the shore.

Tides race to be first to fade
Onto the copper finish line.
Panting and motionless, it slips away.

By nightfall, the beach becomes an empty virgin
Of lonely sandcrabs and drifted seashells.
The rush of big waves calms to become
A shadow of white and blue on the water.

Mark A. Evans

MARK ALLEN EVANS. Born: Amarillo, Texas, 7-24-63; Education: North Harris County College, Associates in Liberal Arts, 5-83; Occupations: Klein ISD — Project PASSAGE Vocational Trainer; Memberships: Cypress-Creek Association for Retarded Citizens, Cultural Arts Council of Houston, Poets Northwest, Poetry Society of Texas; Poetry: 'Illegal Death,' *Today's Greatest Poems,* 1983; 'Modern Art,' *Joyful Noise,* 9-85; 'By Choice,' *Our Times,* 2-87; 'Peace of Mind,' *Our Times,* 4-87; Other writings: ''Champions,'' short story, *Our Times,* 4-87; Themes: *Friendship, family, unconditional love, and meeting the challenges in life, especially the ones you create yourself.*

. . . and as the dreamer releases his soul to the wind, the poet takes pen in hand and prepares to record the journey. Choosing his words ever so carefully, but with the deft precision of an artist and a craftsman, he breathes into the visions seen only through the eyes of a believer. Together as one the dreamer and the poet rise above the mind's eye and bring to the surface the delicate cries of hidden secrets. Their light shines into the darkest regions of existence and bring it to life. The very beauty of all they discover, the glory and passion that overwhelm them bring a single tear to their eye, and they fall back to earth, softly, to once again become . . .

Anthony Livingston de Bergerac

MENDED DREAMS

Dedicated to: Georgetta Richards
&
Barbara Richards Williams

Picking up heart's shattered pieces
I'll mend it with pen, and love's thesis
With every piece, I will hustle
To put it together, like a puzzle.

Life is a puzzle worth the mending
A love story, without an ending
When a heart is broken, life seems lost
We must repair the loss, at any cost.

Mend the seams of broken dreams
With written words that shine and beam
Repair and fix a lost, deflated mind
By writing your heart out, in loving lines.

If I knew all there is to know
What a book I would leave, for love to show
I've been helped to mend my heart
By finding you where you are not.

In these pages you surely abide
Loving me with all your pride
Helping me to find life's dream
A true love, without a rended scheme.

T. Steven Watkins

TIMELESS

Frosted fields, moonlit woods.
Snow-capped mountains, sunlit shores.
Lovers walk, hand in hand.
Hearts reach out, no need for words.

Starry nights, city lights.
Rising sun, setting moon.
Lovers watch, time pass by.
Waiting for . . .
forever.

Ruth Ann Beyer

MORNING

Rising sun begins the day
chasing the night far away.
Stars fading one by one
hiding from the morning sun.

Wind that's chilled from the night
starts to warm in morning's light.
Shadows start changing faces
as mist clings to shady places.

Clouds turning from gray to blue
as flowers shed drops of dew.
Turning faces towards the sun
watching till the day is done.

To help the day move along
birds begin their morning song.
In the yard a rooster crows
chiding man for being slow.

Ruth Ann Beyer

Like a withered branch
    Summer's hand outreaching
Touch of heat outstretched
    the flower fades, hard breathing.

But who bespeaks that heated breath
    the wilted flower fading?
Yet the hand of God doth choose
    to withdraw its shading.

Can it be so cruel a span
    that tender touch withholding?
'Tis the time, the chosen hour
    God's perfect will unfolding.

Jeanne C. Folks

ONE LESS

He was of the very last
To loose his shaky hold
To bow his head reluctantly
Forsake his Fool's Gold

He was of the last to go
Throw up his hands and mumble
Wanting not to raise his eyes
To watch the castles crumble

He was of the last to fall
Step down and join the rest
Not unlike the whole of man
He could not pass this test

He was of the last to cry
And fall upon his knees
To cast ideals one by one
Away into the breeze

He was of the last to join
The cold unfeeling host
Without a word or glance or tear
He fell in with the ghosts

He was of the last to leave
We few who still remain
Only scorn he took from us
He withered in the rain

Martin Mitchell

INSIDE A TEAR

A manifestation in a salient place
Another line upon my face
Another shattered, self-wrought cage
Again a vacant, haunting stage
The players gone, the music stilled
Another quart of sweet milk spilled
Somewhere between an empty hand
A bloodstained footprint in the sand
While the tide that comes to salt the place
Will then forgivingly erase
The telltale spot upon the beach
And draw the pain out of my reach
But on condition that I learn
The end of that trail was only a turn.

Martin Mitchell

SO SOON

December cold has won again
The sun has left the sky
Retreating, as it were, to rest
For tomorrow, another try

The darkness settles in like weight
The cold pulls on my sleeves
The trees along the road, so barren
When most they need their leaves.

My pace picks up as the cold grows harsh
But it cannot be outrun
A bitter prize again tonight
For another day's work done

But soon I'll be within my house
To sit before the fire
To think in quiet, feel the warmth
And like the sun, retire

But again tonight before I sleep
I'll shiver, but not from cold
From another cycle of the seasons
And all I still don't know.

Martin Mitchell

Dorothy,
Putting pen to paper
Placing thoughts in mail
My mind refuses to focus
Once again I fail

Unable to express my love
The way it's truly felt
For fear if I remove my shield
My heart will surely melt

My chosen profession forces me
To be strong and hard and cold
But when I hold you in my arms
All defenses fold

Your spirit intertwined with mine
Resistance proved too hard
You've penetrated my outer shell
And known my soul without guard

James D. Richards

WISHING

When you go to sleep tonight
will you dream of me,
Will your mind portray my thoughts
of the way I want things to be
Can you feel me at your side
kneeling on my knees,
Kissing you gently and so softly
wishing it could truly be

Valerie Jean Bell

FRUSTRATION YESTERDAY

FENCED IN   in cities in world in space in subways
         in profession in jobs in this woman in
         being a woman

FENCED IN   in a subway in being a woman because of
         this tramp that wants this woman

FEAR   because of all the possibilities
FEAR   because of no possibility at all

         THEN I recall the Lord
         a smile lights up my face lights
         my heart lights the woman of frustration

THE LORD   is with me — HE is my shield and buckler

         the subway stops where the tramp leaves
         without the faintest interest in me
         no regard at all anymore
         the next station is mine

SINGING WE WALK the night streets home the Lord and I

Renate Potjan

THAT GREY-HAIRED MOTHER OF MINE

Some fellows rave about the blonds.
Brunettes and redheads are fine,
But the sweetest girl, in all the world,
Is that grey-haired mother of mine.

You take some girls out on a date
And spend your very last dime.
But I'm happy to spend, on my very best friend.
That grey-haired mother of mine.

She worked and toiled, to care for me.
And brought me up through time.
She was kind and sweet, clean and neat.
That grey-haired mother, mother of mine.

She nursed me when I was down in bed.
And made me feel just fine,
She held my head, and kind things said.
That grey-haired mother of mine.

She loved me when a lad of three,
She loved me when I was nine.
She loves me yet, I'll never forget.
That grey-haired mother of mine.

George B. Norris

COMMUTER TRAIN

Trying to think, to rest,
a woman cackles behind me,
a man snores in my ear.
At the movies they'd be shushed,
but not here.

The city slides by —
dirty streets give way to houses, junkyards, trees.
Everybody's reading, sleeping;
no one sees.

Iron wheels speed me gently home,
rocking, lulling me to sleep
like a baby in a cradle of steel,
with a rush-hour schedule to keep.

Joy Schwab

DIMINISHING WINDS

Emotions, they can be havoc; pushing and pulling at you
   in times of anger and confusion,
they are like winds of a raging storm,
   enclosed in a tight bond, harder to withstand.
How do you release it, in what form will it go?
   Enter yourself into your closet,
to face the harsh winds that blow, think upon them deeply
   as they blow against your brow,
not giving an inch to let them force you down.
   With the firmness you stand tall, the raging winds shall
soon begin to fall.
   Then your heart will know what is right.
When you open your closet door, and place your souls upon
   the peaceful shore,
You will have peace in your mind and a song in your heart.

Karen Wren

MY FRIEND

You've always been there for me,
and I've always been there for you,
but, it takes two to see matters through.
I've tried to help you in each and every way.
When I did, it seemed you turned your back away.
We used to be close and joke around.
Now we can't do it without a frown.
We were ourselves, one time or another.
Now we can't even talk to each other.
Our eyes meet and we remember the times,
then we remember each other in our minds.
Remember all the laughter and cheers
that have now filled our eyes with tears.
I'm writing this, my friend,
because it's for you.
To have a good friend —
You must be one, too,
who will help to see our matters through.

Jennifer Tenorio

AMERICAN SPRING

America the great, the magnificent
When springtime comes reminiscent
Of the renewal of life, of nature
That slowly the winter has nurtured.
In full blooming you display your gardens
Flourishing all towns, all parks like no bargains,
And filling our hearts not only with your freshness
But also with delight, impetuosity and boldness.
When your forest puts on its gorgeous finery
That abounds in various greens and yellows tastely,
That protects thousands of wild animals:
Kingdom of silence and peaceful beauties.
America, you make my adrenalin overflowing
In this alive season which is your spring!

Bea Courouble

BEAUTY IS IN THE LIGHT

Beauty is in the Light,
   of his Word.

Beauty is in the Light,
   of his Love.

Beauty is in the Light,
   of his Creations.

Beauty is in the Light,
   of his Sacrifice.

Beauty is in the Light,
   of his Birth, Death, and Resurrection.

Beauty is in the Light,
   of my Salvation.

Beauty is in the Light,
   of his Truth.

Beauty is in the Light,
   of my Savior.

Beauty is in the Light,
   of the Holy Spirit.

Beauty is in the Light,
   of my Lord, Jesus Christ.

Angela S. Wright

YOU AND I

You'll tell me you hate lies
despise those who lie
yet all you give me are lies
You tell me you love me
but all I get are words
You tell me you need me
but all I do is wait
You tell me you miss me
but all I do is miss you more
You tell me our bodies mold into one
our hearts beat as one
but all I find is our love beginning to fold
I'll never lie to you
because I love you
I'll always need you
and you'll never have to wait
I'll always miss you
but now you'll miss me more
Our bodies do mold into one
but in time this too will fold

Honey West

RED CARNATION

I gave my love a carnation
Red as my love's sensation
It shouted with jubilation
This lonely red carnation.

John J. Parenti

WHO AM I

You take me along everywhere you go.
   I'm never left behind.
You might try to look for me,
   but I'd be hard to find.
In the minds of those who think selfish thoughts
   I'm always thought of first,
For prestige and the highest place
   these certain people thirst!
When I'm sick you care for me,
   and feel sorry for yourself.
Sometimes you'd like to put me to rest
   upon the highest shelf.
When I cry, "you" wipe "your" eyes,
   and when I sneeze you blow your nose.
When came the time to choose a life-long friend,
   I'm the one you chose.
When I am free — no doubt you'll be,
   for *I* am *you*,
         and
         you are *me!*

K. Lynn Kiihn

ME

For my father loved me well
   And raised me up to be,
A woman with charm and grace
   And a certain amount of dignity.

But, as a child I would run
   Wild like a cat on the wind,
Dancing free in the morning light
   Each day starting all over again.

Little girl fashions were not for me
   Pretty frills were too binding,
Each day was a new adventure
   My soul, like a top unwinding.

So now I stand before you
   The woman I was brought up to be,
A woman of charm, dignity and grace
   But, the wild cat still prowls deep within me.

Suzanne M. Lawrence

I feel like an empty garden
Waiting, hoping
Someone will come along and plant his seeds
Nurturing, watering me so that I may grow
Into a beautiful spot
For all the world to see.
I thought that once
He was there
But he went away just
When the flower began to bloom.
Almost instantly, like the change to winter
The blossom shriveled into wilted petals
As the ones I have saved in the pages
Of my life's remembrances.
Someday I hope to see the return of spring
On my body
So I can bloom again.

Doreen Lucas

by a starched blue mouse

eire

in an upright way she stood
she never resembled who i knew her to be
i could hardly tell
by but by the color by her hair by
and having sat played organ nicely
in a solid color blouse
her nose a gravely lent to her
by a starched blue mouse.

considered by me too far one way
and not enough an other
the sight of her got me thinking of anne
and anne got me thinking. my brother
likes her you know.
i know.
he knows i knew who this was
but being she's a churchmouse
and me a roundeyed elfin gnome
i remember her next at a car door complex't
which she closed as if on her way home.

in an upright upbright way she should
not have seen me where i sat.
i'm glad for that.

Stephen J. O'Slavin Wright

HATEFULLY WRONG

I stood there in the fair sunlight
Listening to birds sing in flight
Watching flowers dance in the breeze
And restful green on all the trees.

Soon my voice broke into song
All was right nothing wrong
My future looked bright as the sun
Tomorrow many things had to be done.

Untimely the sun went away
Silence and darkness my pay
A hateful bullet in my head
Quickly I was wrongfully dead.

John J. Parenti

RESTS

I learned why the rests were put in the music
Pause for reflection, at times for amusement
Stanzas for laughter, and pensive thought
Moods for all seasons in memory are wrought
Time still in motion, yet close at hand
No one cares, yet understands
Yet nature plays her sweet refrain
Upon the passage of life's merry plane
More serious though when not a game
And will not bring you fortune or fame
So spend your while in pensive frolic
Wit and humor are a gentle tonic
To life's woes and carefree ambition
Good for soul and constitution

Shirley A. Young

GRIST WIND-MILLS AT EAST HAMPTON.

I PLANT A TREE

I plant a tree
I see the sun
I hear a bee
I have some fun.

I read a book
I sing a song
I catch a crook
I move along.

I kiss my wife
I ride the train
I hone a knife
I hear a plane.

I smell a rose
I see a bird
I buy some clothes
I write a word.

I wonder why
I must die.

John J. Parenti

DELUSIONS OF GRANDEUR

I sit facing the wall
the whiteness, the bareness
concrete and cold.

Is it purity with strength?
the unyielding? the empty?

Or is it . . .
the delusion of grandeur
afraid to die.

Marriane Serrano

LIFE RAFTS

Life rafts o'er rocky shoals do toss
Man or wave may bear the loss

Powerless yet to find the cost
Still all adventure is not lost
If challenge far outweighs the cost

If liberty's price is freedom won
'Twas worth the price for everyone

No man shall take thy gifts away
For wisdom comes through acts of play

Shirley A. Young

GOLDEN TIMES

Minutes — hours — days
Time passes so fast
The golden times are today
Reaching forward and remembering
The past.
Every day is special — 'cause you will
Always be my friend.

Phyllis M. Cumbie

CALL TO ME

When I feel all alone
No one is there — no one really cares
Call to me and I'll be there
I'll be your friend in your darkest
Hour
Sharing my guiding light — like a star
In the deepness of night.
Call to me — I'm your friend
          Yesterday
               Today
          Tomorrow

Phyllis M. Cumbie

PHYLLIS MARIE CUMBIE. Born: Port St. Joe, Florida, 3-6-62; Education: Gulf Coast Community College, Political Science; Gulf Coast Community College School of Arts; Occupations: Librarian, Secretary, Payroll Clerk, Accountant, Purchasing Clerk; Memberships: National Junior Honor Society, Who's Who Among American High School Students, Society of Distinguished American High School Students, Florida Federation of Garden Clubs, The Humane Society, St. Joe Historical Society, National Wildlife Federation, The Wilderness Society, National Audoban Society, The Nature Conservancy; Themes: *Love of family, expression of friendship, comfort of friends, and observations of nature.*

THE DREAMER

Out on the horizon
as every man knows
lies the spirit of darkness,
what a harvest it sows!

I discovered one night
a set of dreams
upon which to build a world . . .
From the infinite space
between darkness and light,
a vast new treasure unfurled.

The tempest of life
quaked in my soul . . .
Doubt plagued my mind
like hot burning coal . . .
though conscience and faith
were rooted inside,
greed wrestled the past
revealing my pride.

Temptations had left me with no place to run.
At last, I awoke, where I had begun.

Deborah Beard

To Arlie with love

When I first met you
somehow I knew you were the one;
The one I was told would come.

I felt God sent you to me;
Our love was meant to be.
I needed someone like you; you needed me.
From bonds of pain and sorrow
from loveless relationships of our pasts
we are now both free.

I remember the first time we made love;
I trembled to your touch; I was a bit timid
but wanted you very much.

You filled me with passion, an inner warmth
I've never known, a special relationship
grew from the love you've shown.

Together we found the true beauty of love;
Our love is going to be everlasting,
It was planned by God above.

Donna Wright

WAVERING BY THE SEA

The sea was calm and still, serene;
His arms were about me.
Quietly he whispered
In my ear, "Do you love me?"

"Yes!" my heart did say, did cry!
But then my head asked, "Why?"
And all that I could manage
Was a faintly little sigh.

The sea was singing lullabies;
I looked up to the skies.
My head upon his shoulder
Asked if all 'twas lies.

I wished could tell him all I thought . . .
The joy his presence brought,
But shyness took its toll on me
And so his eyes I sought.

His eyes were quiet, like the sea;
In silence looked at me.
Again he questioned
To my ear, "Do you love me?"

Dorothy L. Hull

BEATING AROUND THE BUSH

I could shout it to the world;
I could whisper in your ear;
I could write it in a letter,
But that would not bring you near.
Still all of this is silly;
What I really want to say
Is just how much I love you,
And to kiss you, if I may.

Dorothy L. Hull

DONNA JANE

I have a sister-in-law named Donna Jane.
Inheriting Donna was surely my gain.
She is tiny and cute from head to toe.
Always happy to be on the go.
Smile at her and she'll smile back.
When it comes to manners, she has no lack.
Ask her for a nickle and she'll give you a dime.
Ask her for a second and she'll give you more than
enough time.
Look in her eyes and see them sparkle.
Pretty blue eyes that are truly a marvel.
Donna Jane is a sister-in-law great,
Who is filled with love, never hate.
May the Lord bless all sister-in-laws so fine,
Especially Donna Jane, who is mine!

Debbie Hestand

SUNDAY AFTERNOON

When we go for a ride on a Sunday afternoon
We see yard, garage sales and flea markets
They have sprung up like mushrooms
I used to stop at every one, they just fascinated me.
I'd come home with all the old things
From the days that used to be
But soon I had so many "treasures," I didn't know what to do
So I had my own sale, one Sunday afternoon.
I bought a canning kettle from a friend that moved away
It isn't just a memory, I've used it most every day.
So now when we go riding, on a Sunday afternoon
My niece or someone else will say,
"Close your eyes, the sales are up this way!"
I may buy a blouse or a coat that's caught my eye
But no more "treasures" from the days gone by.
Because I know that once I start, I know that very soon
I'll be hanging out a "SALE" sign
Some Sunday afternoon.

Inda B. Simpson

UNDER THE PALM TREE

Under the palm tree, you'll find me.
My thoughts are of you
How I wish you'd come along
And spend some time with me.

Although we just met, I'd like to say you're swell.
Maybe I'll put a ring on your finger,
Then I'll have you by my side wherever we may go
And you and I will find our happiness
Together until the end.

We'll build our little bungalow
Down the road a piece
Where the palm trees sway and grow tall.
Then we'll raise our family
And be contented as can be.
Remember our happiness began
Under the palm tree.

Betty Stewart

VULCANOLOGIST

Normally
the volcano
sits dormant. For long
stretches it lies quiescent
with just a wisp of smoke to
suggest that it's there at all
But then on Thursdays Saturdays
new moons four a.m.s high tides
and eclipses the demon starts to roar
Surging heaving great explosive shudders
Cinders chunks of sulphur lava magma the molten
flow explodes the bombs hurl skyward tumble whirl
Clunk to earth and slowly as the thundering melt subsides
As streams congeal and ropy pahoehoe and tufo and shards of spongy glass
Lumpy clumps of pumice ash surround us in an ever-mounting volcanic mass.

Morton Leeds

How does one show Love —
    through a smile of sunshine, or
    the warmth of an affectionate hug?

Isn't Love shown by merely trusting another person —
    doing things for them without question because you want to;
    just being there when someone needs you?

It's not so much the giving of gifts
    as the giving of one's time and self, and
    sharing the events of each 'n' every day.

Love is shown in so many ways —
    by a single glance or a gentle touch
    in the sharing of thoughts, ideas, and dreams
    by holding the hand of one who's ill, or
    in the comforting of one's sometimes foolish doubts and fears.
Love is also learning how to compromise and grow.

Loving someone and showing them you care is beautiful, but
    knowing that you're loved in return is the most beautiful of all!

Lori L. Bates

FOR A FRIEND

Somewhere, a beam of light reaches out and touches
a previously darkened place — allowing us to see
where we could not see before and giving us an opportunity
to discover something that has always existed but just
went unnoticed.

Everyday, the sun extends a warm ray of light
and allows one of God's gifts to blossom — helping
it to reach its full potential.

Seldom, does one find a friend that, like nature,
has a special quality — a quality that encourages
others to grow.

Robert W. Hummel, Jr.

ONE STAR

One star
Stands alone.
Although the rest
Have gone astray . . .
One star remains.

One star
All alone . . .
Dim, but still
It doesn't fade.
One star remains.

One star;
It does shine
No more near.
If flickers, now.
One star — how?

One star
I see alone.
Though clouds are many,
It still remains . . .
One star — alone.

Dorothy L. Hull

BUTTERFLIES

Iridescent in the wind,
floating, lighting,
momentary splendor.

A pause, a flutter,
off they go again.

An awkward intruder
unknowingly jealous
of horizons unseen
tramples fragile wings.

The corpse of the butterfly lies.

Linda Lathrop Spinney

STAR OF HOPE

From the heavens on high
to the ocean's vast floor,
a star of hope once shone.
A sign of courage, a sign of love,
a sign of life to come.
In the depths of my darkness
I found such a star.
It re-lit the flame of hope
in my heart and gave me the
strength to fight on.
It lifted me to my feet once
more to march boldly to my goal.
This shining light filled my
soul with courage and its
triumph shall be mine.
To my star I gave my
whole true heart.
My "Star of Hope" is you.

Linda Lathrop Spinney

REMEMBRANCES

Lonely spaces, unwon races,
thoughts of what once was.

Sandy beaches, your mind reaches
back to one once loved.

Eyes still crying, heart still dying,
pain still burns the soul.

One is leaving, one is grieving,
where did love go wrong?

Linda Lathrop Spinney

OLD HOUSE

Old and ancient house,
Clinging to a windswept hill,
With silhouette so tragic,
And atmosphere so still.

Old house now sad, forlorn,
Your people gone before,
Why go on standing,
Less window, stoop, and door?

Old house, weathered and deserted,
Of voice, of child, of love,
Leaning with the bitter winds,
That scored your roof above.

Old house you've shared so much,
With families happy and sad,
With children at their play,
And times of good and bad.

Old house you've served your people well,
But soon your time must come,
To leave the desolated landscape,
And fade into oblivion.

Calvin G. Wetzel

UNKNOWN U. S. SOLDIER

Number 74, *Unknown U. S. Soldier*,
That was all the marker read,
No history of the life he lived,
But simply, that he's dead.

No story of a love he'd known,
Nor of the tears a sweetheart shed,
No story of the wounds, the pain,
Just of the fact that he's dead.

The stone doesn't tell the story,
How a son from a mother torn,
Was killed in the heat of battle,
Scant years from the day he was born.

It doesn't tell of a mother's weeping,
Nor of a father's broken heart,
It simply reads, "Unknown,"
And proves he did his part.

Calvin G. Wetzel

ALONE

It's dark here,
or maybe it's just night.
I can't tell the difference
now that I'm alone.

You were my sun
on the cloudy days.
Now I just have the rain
since I'm alone.

We had fun.
You were the apple of my eye
when we were together.
Today I just cry.
It's hard being alone.

If wishing would,
I'd wish you here.
But for now
it's just me,
alone.

Paula Walling

WE'RE CLOSE

This is my friend,
we are always going to be.
We will never let it die,
because we're close.

My friend and I,
we talk of school;
teachers and of our pasts,
maybe that's why we're close.

My friend is tall,
and we both have glasses;
and like sports a lot,
that is another reason
why we're close.

I like my friend,
he's not too bright;
but neither am I,
even still we're close.

My friend and I
have things in common;
and the most important is,
the need of being close.
Maybe that's why we're close.

Paula Walling

THE UNPROTECTED NIGHTS

As we lay down next to each other,
The night is no different from another.
By the count of five, the sandman's come,
As as for me, I'm up until one.
If I could go to sleep before you,
Then I'd feel protected the night through.

Kathy Harris

PEER COMPLIANCE/DEFIANCE

This new mass hysteria,
about all bacteria,
ignores the criteria
for living, I think.

There's yeast in our bread
and yogurt from milk . . .

But we drug ourselves faint
as if life's what it ain't
to kill-off the ''germs'' that we're sure we should fear,
instead of remanding a case that's not clear,
'til we can recover a stance that's more stable
and get-up some courage to show we are able
to cope with hysteria
about the bacteria.

Edith F. Stormont

AUTUMN OF LIFE

Have you ever watched the moon on a cold wintery night
    when you could see nothing but snowflakes abright
Or looked at a tree all humble and old
    and wondered if icicles were making it cold
Or watched a beautiful rose fade and die
    and wondered why everything was so blue in the sky.
Because as you thought your heart said with a beat,
    this is life, God's kept so neat.
As I was a snowflake, when I was young,
    before I was melted by the sun;
As I was a tree in the middle of life
    with a beautiful family and a loving wife,
Now I'm a rose in the autumn of time.
    My sweetness is fading, I'm going blind.
Then there is a sound from above,
    saying, ''Come to me with all your love.''
Now that I'm old, weakened by time,
    I'm going to heaven to drink His great wine.
And as I leave this dear earth, I say,
    ''Be happy with life and God will show you the way.''

Frank E. Anglin

FRANK EDGAR ANGLIN. Born: Quincey, Massachusetts, 9-25-42; Married: Joyce J. Anglin, 7-1-82; Education: High school, 1961; One year of college; Occupations: President of Local 2869 Kaiser Steel, 1979-84; President and Chairman of Board, Kaiser Steel Cares Foundation, 1984 to date; Board Member, Kaiser Steel, 2-87 to date; Comments: *As president of Kaiser Steel Cares Foundation I am working with the elderly and through them have felt not only their needs but more importantly their emotions. In my poem I try to point out that in life it is a privilege to be an elderly person, for so many of us never reach that status, and yet with age come the many stresses of old age that we as a younger group cannot feel until it's too late. We should all be happy with life and allow God's help as we grow old.*

When my thoughts are madly spinning and my life seems so unclear,
When my head is full of doubt and my heart is full of fear,
When my soul is drenched in madness and the demons reappear,
When the days are too intense and the nightmares too severe
And the visions in my eyes are all blinded by a tear,
When the spark of life is fading and my breaking point is near,
When the sights I cannot see and the sounds I cannot hear
And the dreams that cannot be pierce my heart with Satan's spear,
When the angels tell their lies and love's own words seem insincere
When forever is an instant yet each moment lasts a year,
            THEN . . .
I reach out for your hand and all the dark skies start to clear
And all the gentle words you whisper softly in my ear
Make the demons fly away and Hell's fires disappear.

Anthony Livingston de Bergerac

GUARDIANS OF HEALTH

People simple, sincere
working the suffering from mankind to clear
with sympathy and understanding
building lives with study, work and planning
guided by God above, generating dedicated love
acquainted with sorrow and grief
endeavoring all they can to relieve

People that keep working on
when the patient believes themselves gone
compassionately gentle, benevolently genuine
fighting viruses, keeping patients functioning

Humans working under the cloak of perfection
mistakes not tolerated become burdens thrusting towards
attainment of knowledge, requiring the surrender
of energy, sacrifice of time, progress towards
harnessing expansion of advancing evolution,
a continuing goal to make great the health of the nation.

Beverley Pettit

BEVERLEY JESSIE ANNIE PETTIT. Born: Ontario, Canada; Married: Edwin G. Pettit, 10-2-54; Education: Assistant Nurse, 1947; Business College, 1949; Correspondence school and teacher training, plus advanced training in Blissymbolics, 1960-70's; Candore College, Arts Course, 1983; Creative writing courses; Memberships: Civic Hospital; Department of National Resources, Pembroke; St. John National Headquarters, Ottawa; Department of Education, Pembroke; Health Educator, Lung Association, Pembroke; Poetry: 'Love's Golden Circle,' *A.R.T.S.P.E.R.I.E.N.C.E. Review,* 1986; 'In Memory of Adam,' American Poetry Association, 1986; 'Burn Out,' *Breakthrough Magazine,* 1986; ''My Dad & Angels,'' poetry collection, *Anthology,* Aardvark Enterprises, 1987; Other Writings: ''Johnny's Making Money,'' short story, *Breakthrough Magazine,* 1987; Comments: *My writing gives me an opportunity to communicate wisdom gleaned, express gratitude, marvel over all things beautiful and relate mentally to human struggles. Writing allows me to go beyond tears and give words purpose by expressing sorrows and sufferings found in our own lives and in the lives around us. Words can permeate the window of the soul.*

NOSTALGIA

Where the zephyrs kiss the bluebells
And the sunbeams dance and play;
Where the busy bees are humming
In the fields of new mown hay;
Where the chickadees sing gaily
And the thrush and robins too;
Where the whippoorwills are calling
O'er the meadows bathed in dew;
Where each dawn breaks clean, refreshing
And each dusk brings calm content;
Where each man can be his master
In a world with conflict rent;
There is where my heart is yearning
There I'd lay me down at last
In some cool and quiet valley
When the cares of life are past.

Ruth Elder Alcorn

MY FOREVER FRIEND

You are my "forever friend" who
    I don't know what I'd do without.
You make me laugh on the saddest days.
    You are what friendship is about.

You have picked me up so many times
    When I was feeling down.
You are able to create a smile
    From what had been a frown.

You often joke about serious events
    Acting as though you don't care;
But your eyes are links to deep inside
    Hinting at secrets hidden there.

Your shyness I find attractive.
    You are a gentleman from the start.
You are a man with tender feelings
    Safely tucked inside your heart.

At times I want to hold you
    And feel you close to me,
For you are my "forever friend" and
    That's the best a friend can be.

Mary Jane Cunningham

FROZEN MEMORIES

Everything is frozen on the ground.
Even what is high is stiff on the outside.
Memories of summer heat.
Melt my inside.

Dreams of you in my sleep.
I woke this morning.
Dreading the cold.
It reminds me of your heart.

Faces hang from eves.
Drippy faces fall and freeze.

Spring bloom fast, be new.
Melt icicles from the past.
Come again summer and last.

Summer where are you?

Carla Fischer

OUTSTANDING PASTOR

Our pastor is nice in every way.
He shares with us the lovely day.

You can't call my pastor just
any old thing; because he is an
outstanding human being.

He has his ups, and he has his downs,
but he is looking toward heaven for his
golden crown.

He is not always right and not always
wrong, but he asks for forgiveness and
tries to live on.

If there is something I'll never forget,
my pastor says: "Lord have mercy. Children
don't forget to pray."

My pastor is nice, and he is so kind.
I'm not writing this to waste our time.
I'm giving my pastor all his flowers;
because Rev. D. W. Nash is all of ours . . .

Sherry Givings

STONE AMONG STONES

How strange, to wander alone,
As alone is each pebble and stone.
No tree knows the other
Though they are growing together.
Filled with friends was the world around me,
While the bright life I could see;
Now, that most of them are gone,
I am in deep darkness thrown.
Only those, who are plunged into darkness
Can really feel separation's grief and stress,
And to them, too, it is then known
That *everyone* in life is *alone*.

Hartwig Heymann

PART OF ME

You are a part of me,
Wherever I may go;
As I travel down a lonely road,
I think of you and loneliness passes;
As I walk a sad path,
I think of you as I go;
And I am stronger then,
For thoughts of you comfort me;
When I feel happiness,
I think of you,
For you have given happiness;
When I feel love,
I think of you,
For you have given love;
And as I travel time,
I think of you,
For you are a part of time;
The time when I have felt,
All things wonderful.

Angie Pons

HURT

I have no happiness in my soul
The hurt of the past will never grow old
The emotions I feel run out of control
I need someone to love and to hold
The emptiness I feel has made me cold
The life ahead I must shape and mold
The blood inside is hard and dry
There are no more tears left to cry
I know I have got to say good-bye
For the life I live is just a lie
The past is over I can't deny
I can't hang my head low, I've got to
        keep it held high
Someday I will be happy in my heart
But only when you say we don't have to part
We'll begin again and make a new start
We'll love each other till death do us part.

Danita Stoudemire

HORSE

Regal,
royal,
robust,

tall,
undaunted.

Sinews
dancing like angels
in silver sky,

advancing.

Prancing on
rivers of air.

Formal
in his grace.

This vehicle
of beauty

fills my
every space.

Gail Berry

LIFESAVERS

Come in a roll
all different colors
of the rainbow
red, green, yellow
and orange.
They remind me of U
    sweetheart
Because U R like
A rainbow of life
A lifesaver for me
So sweet and neat
U can't be beat.
    I Love U.

C. K. Morris, Jr.

UNTITLED

I smile. Colored fotos look at me from the table — TV. My living *flowers* smile at me. They scream my name. Ida Ida — crazy being happy. And light hair and smooth flesh and kisses — running the long of the corridor — ''they like it here, *Mum*'' says my daughter. They know or feel we belong to each other. Family . . .

And pieces of ''Lego'' are scattered on the carpet and a box. They were taken away by their parents sleeping, in the middle of the night — straight unto a blue Opel and went home — *me*? I remain alone. With a house in disorder and dishes in the sink. — *''Mammy it was wonderful''* my daughter says. I am crying. THE letters flow — I have made a pause, cleaned my glasses. *Continue* . . .

Continue. Continue to play. To run with the young. To exchange gifts. To make love. *Continue.* Continue to *write* to keep your *brain* alive — as long as it *works.*

Ida Fawers

COMMENCEMENT

''Mama, where is Jeffrey?''
He showed me how to climb the tree in the backyard that day.
A spanking came when we played Barber Shop.
''Sound it out,'' he said,
and walked me home from school for five years.

Knock knock.
I tried to go in
but his bedroom door slammed.
I didn't come back for a long time.

Then a shoe fight;
chasing, laughing, missed.
We started to climb trees just like we used to,
and today I'm crying,
he wears a robe and tassle.

Lynn Marchin

CHRISTMAS WASSAIL

She shuffles out with coffee and french fries,
slumps her patched-up shapelessness upon
the bench, and eyes the world with rheumy stare.
It's Christmas Eve. The shopped-out throngs now fill
the fast food place and spill outdoors in waves
of jostling hurriedness. She sits alone.
The season of good will! Noel! Noel!
Old memories now swell. They sparkle like
bright Christmas lights on branches of her brain.
''We wish you a Merry Christmas . . .'' they all
sang at the bar, then raised their glasses high
and toasted her, a lovely, golden star.
She lifts her coffee in reply, ''God rest
you, too.'' ''Poor soul, she's talking to herself.''
They look, then turn away. They have no time
for hopelessness, three hours left to buy.

Mary Freckleton

REFLECTIONS

Would you recognize me . . .
  if you saw my face? . . .
A chord strike, in your heart . . .
  if you heard my voice? . . .
Feelings of youthful love and laughter . . .
  rekindle the fire? . . .

So often I dreamed of you . . . and wished
  my dreams . . . would come true
To hold you in my arms . . . feel the warmth
  of love
Memories breaking the dam . . . opening
  the floodgates of my heart . . .

I hear your voice . . . in all that I do
  always reassuring . . . pushing me on
    making me believe . . .
But now . . . time passes more quickly . . . months
  fade into years

And I didn't want you to forget . . .
  the curves of my face . . .
    tone of my voice . . .
      and the friendship that we share . . .

Steve Sincavage

TIME WARP

So much to say . . . so little time
  the clock's always running, running my life . . .

''Climb aboard the no place express! Headed
  for somewhere here, someplace there
but never really getting anywhere!''

People I've known . . . people who care
  fading away
lost on my travels here . . .

''Buckle up please, next stop when we get there . . .
  close your window, empty your mind
no time to think! You're along for the ride . . .''

Fading images of yesterday . . .
  where have my friends gone?
Nothing's the same . . .

''You have reached your destination, lost
  in the void where time is found
forever circling, running round . . .
  trying to catch up with where you are now! . . .''

Stop! I've got to think . . . try to remember
  where have I been . . . who have I seen
Can't reach out! . . . it's all just a dream

HELP! . . . but no one remembers my name

Steve Sincavage

WINTERTIME

Wintertime is a peaceful time of year,
full of good humor, happiness & cheer.

Children go skating, skiing, sledding,
Mamas & Papas, the roads they are dreading.

Oh, how wonderful it would be,
if we adults could learn to be free.

Free to be childlike once again,
try as we may, to start to begin.

To see through our children's eyes,
how they view God's lovely skies.

Snow is falling, they shout with glee,
school is closed, and buses won't run,
just a whole day to have some fun.

Jackets & hats, shovels & boots,
lots of yelling, hollering and hoots.

Time for hot chocolate, popcorn & when,
clothes are all dried, they start once again.

Icicles clinging to the trees,
oh, how easy it is to see

how much we are missing
when we let go

of the beautiful child in us,
& curse the winter snow.

Gail Brennan

GOD AND I

God and I come to camp together,
We sail o'er waves that come and go,
We swim in the healing water,
We walk the island to and fro.

We talk and laugh together,
Recalling days of long ago,
We watch fleecy clouds go by,
And note the river's endless flow.

We climb the path together
And see the earth below,
We look upward to heaven,
Proclaiming joy as we go.

We will go on together
Until the sunset's glow
Turns to purple heather
Into night's relentless flow.

We'll greet the dawn together
On heaven's bright lovely shore,
For He will desert me never,
His love goes on forevermore.

Madelyn Campbell

BESIDE A STREAM

Where flowest thou, O peaceful stream,
With your rippling waters all agleam,
Your wavelets kissing a far green shore,
Then running back forevermore?

Green reeds beckon from your deep,
While on your bosom white gulls sleep,
Fish leap high in sunlit flash
And drop below in a silver splash.

While I sit watching, dreaming deep,
Your murmuring lulls me to sleep.
O, peaceful stream, would that I
More often by your side could lie.

Madelyn Campbell

ONLY FRIENDS

If I appeared before thee
clad only in love
would you turn away
because we be but friends?

If my fingers stroked fire
throughout your veins
would you cool down
because we be but friends?

If music throbbed strongly
inside love's pulse
would you not listen
because we be but friends?

If lips seared delight
upon your being
would you deny them
because we be but friends?

Naked fiery searing music
pulsating rhythmic delight;
I will not deny them
because we be but friends!

Shawna Craig

GRAINS OF SAND

Clear blue skies a lighter shade
than the dark ocean water below.
Warm sand, cool breeze, feet clean and bare,
walk slowly, placing one foot, then the other,
taking their time to feel each sand grain
they have a chance to meet.
The bits they miss look for someone else,
while stray pieces stick and pinch.
Gradually the pair arrive at their destination,
but a few grains have been lost along the way.

Heather Desmond

Clouds are made
of dreams we had
    Stars are made
of stories told
    The rain is made
of tears we cry
    The moon is made
to wonder why
    Heaven's there
to pray above
    The world is here
for all to love

Linda DeCesare

PEACE OF MIND

My home is in two places —
Each one with different faces.
When I am here, I think of there,
And when I'm there, I think of here.

I love the feel of the fertile soil,
But here it's the smell of suntan oil.
The river there runs wide and deep.
But here it's the ocean that I seek.

Why must my heart be split in two
Making me feel so sad and blue?
If the two I could combine,
Then I would have peace of mind.

Kathy Harris

IF ONLY . . .

If only I could
Write the words
With the same eloquence
Your thoughts possess

The tender passion
Our bodies share
Tells me
That you'll be there

When I reach out
In the night
To kiss
And hold you tight

The loving thoughts
Your words convey
The love I've sought
And strain to say
With the selfsame
Eloquence
Your lovely words
Possess.

Lauren Holland

And when the seed of growing sown
                in angry retribution
Springs forth its newborn stems from earth
                expecting restitution
The die is cast, the road is laid
                its course has now been set
For it will find a world unfair
                newborn into regret

Jeanne C. Folks

TILL THE SNOW FLIES

Stay with me till the snow flies.
Till the winter winds call down that fine lace
from the mountains of heaven,
and signify that a new season is full into its turn.

From now until then we will dance on the shore
of forever.
We will build a memory for me.
A memory that will come to life
when the snow flies
and will die when I die.

Dan Whitaker

The word unspoken
   spirit bent
      emotion dwindling to a
                thin thread
   Silence becomes the enemy.

Isolation of truth unknown
   quiet no safe harbor now
      anything but peaceful.

Solitude infringed upon
   by the awful silence
      invasion of all privacy
                alone.

Jeanne C. Folks

LOVE

Love is something you or I can feel.
Love is an emotion no one can ever steal.
Love is sometimes like a dream.
It sometimes comes true and sometimes it is taken away so it seems.
So now you're in love what should you do?
Just go ahead and love them as much as they love you.

Kenith Preston

The time is coming for me to leave
To start a journey towards the unknown
Down an uncertain, unmarked path
Separated from you, but never alone

This path I've chosen because I must
Fulfill a destiny determined for me
Above the sea in the cockpit of a jet
Dancing with the clouds, my spirit is free

The years ahead may be difficult and rough
Filled with loneliness, danger, pain and tears
But the light which is the love we share
Will shine bright when the smoke of battle clears

I know our love will endure forever
For true love bends, but never breaks
While I'm away, while I'm at sea
You'll be with me each second I wake

James D. Richards

FATHER STAY WITH ME

Father stay with me,
In the morning of my childhood.
Laugh, with me, love with me,
The new experiences I see.
Sing to me a lullaby I can hear,
To ease away my tears.

Father stay with me,
In the noon-day of my teen-aged years.
Guide me through my troubled, confused and changing fears,
Pressured by my peers.
Advise me right if you would,
Through my youth to manhood.

And in the evening of your life,
I'll hold your hand, so dear.
And sing to you a lullaby clear,
As you dream the dreamless sleep,
In a land beyond the years.

Angela S. Wright

WHEN WILL THE LOVE COME?

When will the love come,
That's not tainted by tears on the pillow of despair?

When will the love come,
Without the pain of lonely one-night stands?

When will the love come,
Without the pain of heartbreak and wear?

Is it my destiny never to know true love?
Of sharing together the ups and downs of life?

Is it possible for two hearts to meet,
And become entwined as one, without all this strife?

When will the love come?

Oh I beseech, the moon, the stars, and God above
To send me my true love before eternity has put
Me to sleep forever.

And I will never know when love has come.

Angela S. Wright

SEA GULL

My mind is an ocean —
Crashing waves of revelation
Sea gulls scream inside my head
Telling me my dream is dead

The kind of woman I want to be
Love of man, like poetry —
A simple, sinful symmetry —
Bodies flowing like the sea

Loving love and life with ease,
Sunstroked hair blowing in the breeze
Lost to me these things are now
Can someone ever tell me how?

Lauren Holland

EVIL THAT IS

once upon a time forever
in a misty garden far away
i wished upon a star
in the dusty moonlit sunshine
a drowsy faerie rose from endless rest
and a unicorn flew across a dewy river

I wished for a millennium of wishes
(but do not ever wish for happiness, child;
evil that is cannot be undone)

rosy blush of blossoms
as a black wind blows
and the angels stir
and grant wishes

a sprinkling of cinnamon freckles
across the innocent nose
of a child who will
persist for happiness
even as the gates of heaven close . . .

Arcadia Haid

PRIORITY PROBLEM

When I was down on my homestead
I wondered the fate of the stream
but the same thing happened to it
as it did to the American dream.

The children grew careless
the cans and bottles they tossed
but more importantly was
the other thing that they've lost.

The young got caught up
in this world of today
and forgot about family
with concern of their pay.

They missed the loving sound
of tiny pitter-pat of feet
in order for them to live
on an avenue instead of street.

Wonder what will happen
after the people grow old
when there's no pretty water
and nobody to hold.

Valerie Taylor Mabrey

SHELL

Locked inside, unable to move.
Trying, but locked by the walls
of the shell. Waiting for the time
when the walls will soften and let
the light in. Let life begin. Break
free from the imprisonment. Trapped
inside the shell. You can see everything
but it is as though you're invisible.
The walls are still there. The softening
has not commenced. I'm still inside
the shell.

John McKinnon, Jr.

GRASS

Long and tall, gleaming from the
morning dew and the glare of the sun.
The long stems of green await
their fate. The blue sky above
giving you the nutrients to live
and grow long.
But that machine will come
again. The boy will start it
up. The vibration will drive
through the precious soil.
The machine will cut your beauty
down. The same day the neighbor's dog
will run across the lawn. The kids
will play football on you and
the family will have its barbecue.
But the sun will shine. The rain
will come down. Most of all,
the grass will grow long and tall.

John McKinnon, Jr.

REASON TO PRAY

I used to sit by Mother
at church on Sunday
and it's for this reason
that I learned to pray.

The preacherman says
''a sinner a lazy man makes''
so I asked a sleepin' fellow
if a sinner needs to bake.

Mother's whisperin' in my ear
told what at home lay ahead
with the yardstick in the corner
that would turn my fanny red.

Maybe Mother would forget
if I gave sittin' still a try
but when I looked at Mother
that whippin' look was in her eye.

''Ask and you shall be given''
the preacherman says
so it is for this reason
that I learned to pray.

Valerie Taylor Mabrey

WRITINGS IN THE SAND

I think that I will
Journey to the oceanside
And write something
In the sand tonight.
I'll pick out a rock;
Maybe even a stick or shell
And write my name or
Maybe even a tale of love.
Then I'll stand back
When my writing is done
And wait for the tide
To reach out and grasp my words.
The tide will carry
My words away
To be forever immortalized
On a sea of hopes and dreams.

Eileen Karol

JIM

Jim, my husband, strong & true,
Sometimes he would make me blue,
Tall & nice looking, sweet as apple pie,
He always liked to cook & fly.
He loves his son & daughter with all his heart,
& from them he will never depart.
Jeannette, his wife, has eyes of blue,
Who will always be true,
Misses him with all her heart,
& I pray & hope he will never depart,
Jim, is a +man of steel, who will never yield.
His love for material things will
one day no longer be,
For he'll always be sweet as apple pie to me!

Jeannette L. Rodgers

JEANNETTE LAUNA RODGERS. Pen name: Launa; Born: Asheville, North Carolina; Divorced; Education: Will be attending Emmanuel Bible College, Georgia, fall 1987; Occupation: Homemaker; Membership: Woman's Aglow (Christian Women's Organization); Poetry: 'Stephen,' 'Malinda,' 'Clay,' 'Jim,' and 'Geneva,' all 5-87 and about family members; Comments: *I like to write about my family, this beautiful world God created, and animals such as dogs, parakeets, hamsters, horses, and bunny rabbits (animals I had as a child). I also like to write about states where I have lived; North Carolina, South Carolina, Virginia, Georgia, and now Alabama.*

WATCHING THE BABIES PLAY

Where did they go? Those years that slipped away
while we sat smiling and laughing and watching the
Babies play.

And where are the Babies after diapers and walking
shoes, and ballet, little league and Prom Night
blues?

When did they go, those years that slipped away?
While we sat smiling and laughing and watching the
Babies play.

Ruth Collett

CIRCULAR

I must retreat this padded place,
  On velvet walls I claw endlessly,
    Through the fastened gates of mind,
      Threaded, weaving, tangled at this time.

The keeper's graveyard he keeps,
  So small, particular, I cry mercy at his feet.
    Not I who was once an ounce?
      Come to this withered wreath.

Such vast stones, wag with wrinkled smiles.
  Warm the keeper, his love to guard.
    I pause at the mighty dribble of soil,
      That dropped and passed, my mouth drew hard.

Then perhaps most of all, startled,
  I face the world again. A mass,
    So fast and furious, the ink spills
      Through that path of rubbled grass.

Scourged, am I not? a wicked spruce
  Of flesh and blood, a mould of teeming weeds.
    The hollow length of autumn I build a castle, my thesaurus,
      Only for the ego conqueror, like a tide succeeds.

Gabriel Finn

LOVING

Hear the wicked wind blow across my baron thoughts, does the wind
care, does anyone feel for the battles I've fought.

I think, though I try not to, and pass the days by in quiet
emptiness and shallow feelings. How many more days are there left
before I start healing. I think of what might have been over and
over again.

Can they tell me . . . is there love after despair, or is it or can
it be that no one is ever prepared. For the weeping of one's soul
or the crumbling of one's heart, maybe one should hide their heart
if they were smart.

Crying to myself, I've beckoned to the gods, maybe the lack of hope
means they'll never be aroused to aid those who are misfortunate to
fall prey, and say, we must begin at the beginning were it all
ended . . . to all those who cared for me must also care for them.

If I be a victim of my love for another, let him feel for me as I
feel for him. For only then can we both love again.

Robert Hewson

TREES

Birds and trees go hand-in-hand.
Some reach the clouds while others are no bigger than a hand.

Sprawling far and near, across river and valleys, around the
world . . . the wind through their leaves and branches we can hear.

How little we care for them short or tall . . .
thick or thin, what an empty world it might have been . . .
without them.

Do you care, do I, which we shall ever save them from us
do we care if we lose them all. If lose means the birds will
cry then maybe we should cry too. For only crying will
moisten the ground for the next seed to sprout its leaves
for us for the birds and me . . . and maybe you too will
finally see.

Birds and trees go hand-in-hand and also the fate of man.

Robert Hewson

OUR MARRIAGE

How do I explain the way I feel
When sometimes my life just doesn't seem real?
We always have good times, but some times are bad.
We're always so happy, yet sometimes we're sad.
Our lives are so different from others we know
Our love never dies, it just seems to grow.

Why can't everyone have it this good
If they'd only try harder I bet they could
They always wonder why ours is the best
Why we seem happier than all the rest
It's not always easy, sometimes it's tough
But never stop trying, it's never enough.

Sharing our feelings each passing day
Always knowing the right thing to say
Saying ''I love you'' helps so much
I think that's what gives it that special touch
Maybe some day others will see
It's easy to be happy, just like you and me.

Michele Johnson

THE MEMORY OF THE UNICORN

Silvery streaks shine on mane and tail
  as elegant unicorns tiptoe
    through waves of dying grass.
Firm muscles fold on silky bodies
  as the creatures shake their powerful heads
    remembering how it used to be.
Gliding freely over dusty clouds and fading rainbows
  they gracefully bow their sorrowful heads
    breathing in dark smoke and potent fumes.

Heather Desmond

ABLAZE

Set the night ablaze
with six million dancing flames

Climbing wildly toward the sky
mocking everything alive

Wreaking havoc as they go
until nothing's left to show

But ashes all around
and a deadly rush of sound.

Rita B. Swartz

WINTHROP

High in the sky
flew I
as a child
with a bog-like memory
thick as quicksand.

Up and down
bounced I
on a platform lap
held by hands old & wise
strong & certain.

While across the street
mighty ocean roared
slamming high
wild plumes
off the seawall.

Bland concrete face
stolid in the dusk
watch me fly
mr. jetty
watch me fly.

Rita B. Swartz

MY CHAIR

I sit alone in my chair on a dark
night. My minds sees many things when
I sit in my chair. Once I saw a big
pink cloud flow by my face. Then I
saw a sandy beach with crashing waves
which flowed over my feet. A giant
marching band plays loudly in a large
hall and 50 flags fly before me. At
my feet, two red roses in a snow-covered
field, with hills in the background.
A nest of hen eggs cracking open to
become soft little chicks. A beautiful
silk-white mare giving birth to a
fine colt. I can see the beauty in
my mind when I sit in my chair on a
dark night.

A. L. Smith

PAPA'S HANDS

Papa's hands cup the child's
   & they play

Papa's hands cup the child's
   & they sing

Papa's hands cup the child's
   & they dance

Safely cupped in Papa's hands
   the child flexes its freedom

   & the grandchildren get
What the children didn't

   & the children
Are still looking.

Rita B. Swartz

RITA BRYNA SWARTZ. Born: Brookline,
Massachusetts, 1955; Married: Richard W.
Buckley, 9-6-86; Education: Boston University,
B. S. Communications, Summa Cum Laude,
1976; Northeastern University, MBA, 1978; Oc-
cupation: Writer; Awards: Certificate of Merit,
"Distillations," *The North American Mentor
Magazine,* Fall, 1980; Poetry: 'Slats,' *Eras
Review,* 1981; 'Gossamer Dream,' *Eternal
Echoes,* 1982; Comments: *The soul speaks in
stillness. I listen, and write.*

PROGRESS

All around me
What do I see
But remnants of what was.

Today they are useless;
The weapons from ages of darkness
Which no longer cloud the sky.

As modern man,
This day we stand
Enlightened by knowledge.

The knowledge
Whose progress we pledge
To war.

Matt Zuck

SOLSTICE

Significant
your rays of violet,
ultra to the worshipper,
deadly in your transient
north'ard role of all-time high,
nice, precise perfection bi-ennial,
striking vapid nimbus from the sky

ageless
your ambient stellar route
in oval form adorning,
constant in terms of endless
time, unremarkable for the majority
of earth-bound owners of a fleeting pause
of life miraculous, occupied in enmity

significant
your presence,
your unrelenting journey
of circuitry, with heat and light intense,
twice-yearly you are vulnerable and needy
in reminding us you are . . . significant.

Aylwin Adams

MOUNTAINS

Air of the Mountains
Quiet and clean
Where animals are free
A place where I would like to be.
Where I can walk, on foot,
In a peaceful, goodness.

Derek Birkenfeld

RATIONAL NUMBERS

She was an eight.
He was a six.
They were in their sophomore year
at William and Mary
the first, a four star.

Economics class
the return of the test (first of three).
He got fifty-eight.
She, a ninety-four.
He didn't care, so he said
it was eight seventeen on an April morning.

At least he got there
with a six-hundred seventy and twenty-eight.
They'd graduate in two years.

Good jobs were waiting
with a four star behind him,
clearing fifty-five grand.
He hoped for a three point five
so he'd graduate within the top twenty percent.

L. Burrell

WHAT IS A POET

Brick layers — lay brick
Writers of course — write
Dancers, oh they dance on through the night.

Electricians — they electrify
Artists — do their art
And window washers play a higher part.

Truckers of course, keep on truckin'
And road workers map the land
The statue workers, well they know where they stand.

Musicians make the music
Pilots fly the big planes
Engineers, they run the trains.

Bridge builders build bridges
Contractors build the houses
And exterminators, they get rid of the little mouses.

But, a poet is deep in thought, always searching
They work, rewrite, and use different names
Because they know things must change.

When you're in love and words are hard to find
A poet knows just what you have in mind.

Suzanne M. Lawrence

THE GIFT OF PEACE

There're many gifts I'd love to grant to those I hold so dear.
The love within a child's heart when mother holds her near.

The undefeated courage of a soldier off to war.
The eagle with assuredness, as he begins to soar.

The wisdom in the old man's eyes, whose life is near its end.
The boundless riches that we reap, when we have found a friend.

The hope that shows within the beauty of a snow-white dove.
The passion that will fill your heart, when first you find true love.

But most of all, the gift of peace is what I'd love to give,
For then I'd know they'd have a world that's safe in which to live.

Donna Marian

THE SOUL OF FIRE AND WOOD

On one cold winter night,
        sparks of an open fire take flight.
Traveling on the sea of the wind,
        to places unknown.
Fingertips of the flame,
        fed off the fuel of wood and air.
From the depth of your mind,
        looking into the depth of the fire.
Looking deep into the depth of the fire,
        through the colors of yellowish-orange embers.
Going deeper into and through the yellowish-orange,
        to reach the glowing white light at the center.
Traveling through the dark shapes of wood,
        changing in the firelight.
Each piece of wood that burns,
        outlines each piece of its own life.
Not feeling the heat,
        from the flames of the fire.
Wanting to touch the soul of the wood,
        yet not wanting to get burned.

Marcia A. Randall

TOUCHING THE LIFE FORCE INSIDE US

Touching each other's palms together,
        with our eyes closed.
Feeling our soul and spirit,
        meeting each other for the first time.
Maybe in another place in time,
        or another place in birth.
Our soul and spirit will meet,
        as they have in this time.
Hopefully we will come to know
        each other again.
Not just in a passing moment,
        but for a much longer time.
Touching each other's
        life force within us all.
Maybe we will be friends,
        and maybe we will be lovers.
Our soul and spirit will surely meet,
        somewhere or sometime in the life force of nature.

Marcia A. Randall

SNOW TIME

Do I like snow? Oh! I'm not a child
But when I was — I nearly went *wild*
To go out and play and shovel and romp
But now that I'm old — it's what I *don't* want

Pretty? Yes — beautiful too
To look from the window — *that* sure will do
But to go right in it and then fall down
That's no fun when you break your crown!

You cannot walk graceful — so don't ever *try*
The snow is for kids — not for folks like *I!*
For — if you fall — you become a disgrace
As you slip and slide — and then fall on your face.

So — take it from *me* — one who sure knows
Don't take a chance whene'er it snows
Just look from the window — that's safer by far
And thank the dear Lord you can stay where you are.

Gladys Weigert

GLADYS WEIGERT. Born: Dorchester, Massachusetts, 2-20-1894; Widowed; Education: Second year high school, Voice and Drama studies; Occupation: Housewife; Memberships: Dorcas Society (religious); Themes: *Nature and Religion;* Comments: *In addition to writing poems (I've given over 200 poems to friends), I enjoy music and reading. I'm a choir leader and I've sung solos in many churches.*

GOD; I AM SO SORRY

That I spoke in anger,
At the injustices done to me,
That it took time to get through to my heart,
That you still love me endlessly.

I am so sorry when I feel down,
Too weak to carry on,
That it took the soft touch of your strong arms,
To remember you're still my bond.

I am so sorry when I lose my way,
On the path you want me to take,
That it takes the touch of your strong hand,
To help me set my life straight.

I am so sorry if I forsaked you before,
That I turned my back and did not care,
That it took events throughout my life,
To realize you were still there.

I am so sorry that your son had to die,
That I may live instead,
That it took a loss so precious to you,
To remind us of the love you share.

Jane Betker

MOTHER

For my mother I give my full love
To hold her safe from harm.
My hopes and dreams for everything
May they always keep her strong.

She confides in me, and I in her
For things we could never keep.
To help each other and hold us high
Because, we both sometimes get weak.

Forever my mother may lean on me
Through good times and in bad,
Thy Lord will be her strength, and
I shall pray she's never sad.

Her love is like a springtime flower
It stays so beautiful in all she does.
The colors that change in all her moods
To always keep our pride strong.

She's always so young and lovely
So fresh to keep in eye.
Her happiness is my destination
My love for her will last forever!

Sherry Perry

FOG

Like the steam from a witch's brew
the fog rolls in from the sea. Its gloom
falling on the city. It crawls over
everyone and thing like an invisible
insect spreading its wings. No one
knowing or caring that it's there.

John McKinnon, Jr.

FOR A SECOND I'LL BE FREE

At the moment of my death,
Another life will be bore,
To carry my spirit forward,
And live again in this world.

But in that second of non-existence,
My spirit will flow free,
Like an eagle soaring through the mountains,
Peace from a world of entities.

A second is all I'll be given,
Cut from the bonds of earth,
In a world of spirits alone,
I will then know my self-worth.

I will see my God ahead,
Guiding us through the skies,
Until we are brought safely,
To a place where peace lies.

And maybe this time,
I will not return at all,
I will stay forever beside him,
Fulfilling my new call.

Jane Betker

JANIE PATRICIA BETKER. Born: Regina, Saskatchewan, 1-29-62; Married: Kelly Douglas Betker, 5-19-84; Comments: *I strongly feel that when you read a poem you are reading the poet's most inner self. I feel no other literature reveals more of the author than poetry. When I write a poem it is not by choosing a conglomeration of words that fit together, it is by feeling, and to capture that feeling on paper can become a difficult task, especially since you are opening your most inner self for all to evaluate. The major themes throughout my poetry are God and peace, God because he is my leader and inspiration, peace because I desperately hope in my lifetime I will witness world peace, but, as I have realized, we will only witness this great event when we first find peace within ourselves.*

Contrary to what some believe
when your heart breaks
it does not bleed
but grows to learn you
cannot fear to fall in love
or waste time on tears

Korene Cleo Sizemore

THERE'S HIM

At the top of the mountain,
in the sky, in the sea,
in the water of a fountain,
in a flower in a tree . . .

In the sun, in the moon,
in a cloud, in the stars,
in the darkness of a room,
in the clear of the sky.

In a love of a mother
in a baby's smile
all around of the world
you can easily find
what you need, what you want
only have to look up
or you look at your side
there's Him, there's Him
waiting by.

Ada Guerrero

ADA GUERRERO. Born: Las Villas, Cuba, 10-20-28; Single; Education: Philosophy M.D. and Librarian Diploma (Spanish), 1952; Occupation: Office Clerk; Poetry: 'There is Him,' 1987; Other Writings: ''The Old Man,'' short story, 1983; Comments: *I have written a lot of poems in spanish, as well as articles, short stories, etc., but they are not published yet.* Themes: *My themes and ideas in my poetry come from the inspiration through my feelings, which I'll try to communicate to others as a message of peace and love.*

I didn't really appreciate
my eyes
until one day I wondered:
Is the world getting gray —
Formless?
Are needles smaller now?
Are they economizing on
printer's ink?

But today —
the cataract is gone!
A tiny, soft, plastic lens
has opened my windows
to the world!
God has touched my eyes
and once again I see
how bright and beautiful
the world is.
I do appreciate my eyes!

Edith W. Maddy

WOVEN WINDOWS

Tapestries of every colored hue
From soft pearly grey to ethereal blue
Shimmering shadows sprinkled with dew

The warp and weft of yarn, weaves a cosmic charm
Spreading warmth o'er hearth and home
Lighter shades gracing the darker tone
Making everyone aware, they are not alone
At one moment, laughing; the next, cracking a tear
Smiling at yesterdays, awaiting the morrow
Slight tastes of bitterness, others of sorrow

For God provides His gentle balance
Each kindly touch cannot but enhance
Both large and small blessings, when given a chance
Bringing people together with differing views
Even those of varying hues
Moments of magic and moments of mirth
Are ours for the choosing from the moment of birth

Shirley A. Young

THE WILL TO LIVE

In every man there burns a flame
from the realms of life itself
Even the old man stained with sickness,
crushed by the sight of his world, and
dancing to seasons out of tune
cannot resign to Thy hovering eyes.

The "perfumes of life" echo within . . .
the sweetness of passion-filled nights
and lovers who navigate rapture,
like a robin sailing in flight.

The innocence of a little boy's tears
and the smiles from wrinkled faces
retreating from their tarnished lives
to renew the flame once more.

How kind it was for our Creator
to light this flame in men's souls
to fill his being with a taste of life . . .
the strength to carry on!

In the darkest night of a man's heaviest sorrow —
the flame becomes his torch.

Deborah Beard

CHRISTMAS AROUND THE WORLD

A child sleeps peacefully.
Dreaming —
— Anticipating
Days of family and fun.

Children starve desperately.
Dreaming —
— Anticipating
A grain of rice.

Children weep sorrowfully.
Dreaming —
— Anticipating
God's true love.

Kimberly Kempf

WHISPERS

Beautiful tree so gently swaying and such flowery green displaying whisper the sounds of nature to me and tell me the words of your heart.

Those soft, silent sounds that were shared with me were like those noble words of a prophecy.

"Look at my coat of glistening green — the awe of painters inspired and the envious cast that wintery twigs have endlessly desired.

Splashed on a canvas my summertime spreads to eyes on a bittersweet night, and at once when they see my flourishing petals, they only see summer in sight.

Ah, but my bark is mature and my dazzling drape that you often admire is neither inset nor secure.

For every tree, like every young thing — there's a time at first to bend; a bit of toil, an utter turmoil, and bits of rugged, upturned soil.

And we aging trees know of this time. And we know that it's part of the Plan . . . our beauty lies 'not' in the short-lived leaves, but in the deep-set roots of the land.''

Deborah Beard

REQUIEM

When life's long curtains part some day for me,
And I slip through to that Fair Land above;
Let no sad dirge of mourning ever be,
For I shall be with Him whom I so love.

    Him! Sweet Lover of my soul;
    Him! Whom heavenly hosts all praise;
    Him! While angel anthems roll;
    Him! Through fair celestial days.

Could there be sadness when it's joy sublime?
Could there be weeping with earth's sorrows past?
Ah no! Let song be raised at such a time;
For I shall know Love's final bliss at last!

Hazel T. Lynn

CEMETERY RIDGE/GETTYSBURG

The guns are silent now,
The shot is neatly stacked,
No bodies lying in the grass,
No cries from those that pain had wracked.

The tourists stroll o'er the sacred ground,
Their children shout with glee,
And none can see the ghostly forms,
That stand among the trees.

Here stands the men that dressed in blue,
There stands the men of gray;
Brothers standing side by side,
Reminder of that frightful day.

They suffered untold agonies, and
Each did his best, I'm sure,
For a cause he thought was right,
That his nation might endure.

But the guns are silent now,
On cemetery hill, a place
Where none will fight again,
For there'll be no cause to kill.

Calvin G. Wetzel

MOUNT TAMALPAIS AND RED PORCH.

CHÉVEN

Down, my forehead to the ashes, once, twice, thrice
Ages of anger, revenge and guilt the price

My headband wet, with those old fevers broke
No more the memory, on which to choke

The darkness of my soul careened
The powers of light, I had used obscene

My God forgave, and I could not
Tortured lives, my penance sought

Out of balance, to right then left
My powers then, I chose bereft

The peace too passive, then too savage
Oft tried extremes, my pain to ravage

The path this life, is pine needle strewn
Soft to the step, like sand in a dune

No dark of night, for powers this time
No spears of war, from me to mine

These gifts of light, for His call alone
Again to purpose, on my way home

Donna Alvis

THE METRONOME

The Grandfather clock's brass pendulum,
  Swings to and fro in its glass chamber,
The measured sweep of this heirloom;
  Is center left, to center right, exactly so.

The distance to the left is measured,
  As it travels to the right,
And so it is with us,
  Balancing our joys and sorrow.

Great happiness is best understood,
  By those, who, through Sorrow's door have crept.
Intense anguish plumbs the soul
  Prepares the way; makes room for joy.

Laughter's other face is grim, I know,
  And yet, which of us would live our lives,
Or grow, with static's void endowed?
  A child forever at dead center locked.

M. Caraway

THE SUMMER SUN

  The sunshine's golden, yellow beam,
filters through the clouds,
      softly . . . calling.
  I hear what's brought by the breeze,
      its ever beckoning pleas.

  When the sun, reaches down
carefully, to touch the ground,
      softly . . . if I listen,
  I can hear what's brought by the breeze,
      its ever beckoning pleas.

  But then the sun begins to glare,
and under its burning, maddened stare,
      no longer . . . hear I,
  The beckoning pleas, brought to me
      on the summer breeze.

  And as the sun lies down to rest . . . through the purple haze,
I see the bygone days of old,
      softly . . . whispering,
  I hear what's brought by the breeze,
      its ever beckoning pleas.

April Pillsbury

SOMETIMES

  Sometimes there are no words
Sometimes there are not enough
Sometimes I need someone
Sometimes someone needs me
Sometimes I need to be alone
Sometimes I cry
Sometimes I laugh
Sometimes I love
Sometimes I hate
Sometimes there's no me
Sometimes I hide
Sometimes I seek, and find nothing
Sometimes I find my answers
Sometimes answers find me
Sometimes there is no question
Sometimes there is no answer
Sometimes I wish
Sometimes they come true
Sometimes, always, they are hopeless
Sometimes I want
Sometimes I need
Sometimes is always
Sometimes . . .
        there are no sometimes

Charles Abulencia, Jr.

MOTHER NATURE'S WINE

The night's wafting breeze
carries the smells of summer rain.
Pungent mists swirl
against the window screens,
and freshly bathed leaves
shed droplets on the ground.

Dusty fields become spotted
as the July storm blows eastward.
The sky flickers and rumbles
as if Greek God's are conversing
in languages unknown to Man.

And a tiny flower drinks of
Mother Nature's wine.

Alisa Whitaker

MEXICO '86

After the torchlight revealed her face,
after the betrayal, eleven men
disturb the globe with kicking.

Maradona lurches to the ground
and is dust-baptized. The world,
a face-powdered terrace,

denies that he is tripped;
participates in one brief wave.
There is an art to this:

cooperating hands . . . the songs . . .

Still the dirt flies. Still the dust
is settling while the rescue team
shift handfuls of the ruins

pitting their tiny strengths
and prayers against the drawing
of good fate to its banker

to scratch out one last child
lost amongst these broken
images of home.

Dene October

DREAM LOVER

You never break a date
    You never let me down
You always send me flowers
    To dissipate my frown
You meet after five
    For dinner and romance
And we cannot survive
    Without a long slow dance
I call you when I need you
    You're always there, it seems
I know you will not leave me
    You're only in my dreams

C. W. Trent

SPRING DAYS

Yellow, pink, red, flowered days
    surrounded by a purple haze.
In the dreamy pastures
    cows graze.

Soft white clouds drift by
    smiling at the flowered trees,
A sunbathing person lays in ease.

Beautiful, glorious, spring days,
    take away my tearful ways.
Lovers leap,
    as springtime reaps.

There is a floral fragrance of spring air
    around my nostrils creeping,
gardens colored brightly,
    the friendly roses peeping.
Shimmering and bold,
    tulips stand in gold
and collect a sunray's kiss.

Colors glowing of the deepest hues,
    Spring days, oh, how I love you!

Cindee D. Rubin

Sitting in a whirl of memories
thinking through days gone by
wanting to grasp time
in my hand
as it flies
stars may fall
and waves may crash
colors swirl trapped
in my mind as they race and crash
black and white
prints the color of lovers
but there will always be
that hint of colors

Korene Cleo Sizemore

Loneliness is written down
marked by words on a page
and every time I've been hurt
I wrote it down in bitter rage
happiness is an energy
to be savored in its time
these words of heartache
should be forgotten
love will again be mine

Korene Cleo Sizemore

WHISPER OF MY DISCONTENT

That still voice
Deep inside me
Keeps suggesting in a whisper
There must be something more
Than this.
Something's missing . . .
Even though it looks as though
We have it all,
There's still that feeling,
So subtle a discontent
That I smile at you and
Pretend, but all the while
That quiet whisper
Keeps repeating:
''Is this all there is?''
Daily that whisper grows louder
Until today I could hardly hear
What you were saying
Through the shouting in my heart.
There must be more than this . . .
But what?

Julianne Titus

JUMPING FISH

A slow river
the simplest thing,
within natural tension.
The flat surface,
shower of marble,
release of tension
and all fear.
A flat surface
poxed by rain,
marking time deaf,
dumb and blind,
undisclosed future,
on its own,
a repeated vision
within natural tension, this smaller world.
Strong in dream, sky has its room.
Nothing is here except the vows we made.
The more I love.
The more I am lost.
I swim.

Gary Smith

GARY SMITH. Born: Sydney, Australia; Occupations: Actor, Painter, Teacher.

ODE TO A HORSE

With sounds of fantastic fountains, some secrets should be sung
　to silvery stars without a name in skies forever young.

A well-domesticated horse, since prehistoric times,
　deserves a flowery tale of praise, much sweeter than the rhymes.

With beautiful and lustrous eyes, an earth-born soul still speaks
　of sorrows, joys, and great glory — though no reward it seeks.

With garlands on your silken flanks, after the race is won,
　your pureness is beyond compare, when all is said and done.

Soon, whispers heard in heaven's trees,
　　where the nightingale still sings
　a melody of truth divine, tells what tomorrow brings.

Then you, a foster-child of time and a true friend of man,
　show feelings with a sweet silence and yield to nature's plan.

Enduring murmurs of the flies that haunt the summer days,
　with parching tongue and a sad heart, you wander on your way.

So soon, as summer is waning and days and nights grow cold,
　the sunburnt mirth just fades away as tales of time are told.

Beneath the trees, still shedding leaves on fading violets,
　or through verdurous mossy ways, you strike a silhouette.

So like a feather in the wind, as drowsy numbness pains,
　a spirit in the forest dim, from the brim, then winks and reigns!

Josephine Bertolini Comberiate

THE BALLOON

A balloon bright and yellow,
slips from a small delicate hand
of a child at the busy city zoo.
Her mouth opens, she starts to cry.
The free balloon floats up into the sky.

A new white string is tied to the dainty hand
as the child's mouth closes.
She looks up at a red sphere
flying with the slight breeze.
Her crying stops.
A wide smile comes across the edges of her little face
and the old balloon is replaced and forgotten.

Heather Desmond

A love I wait to share so long
　a love with you
could not be wrong
　you held me in your arms so tight
with you I want to be tonight
　you kept me safe from any harm
when I was cold you kept me warm
　you showed me all good things to be
then gave my life right back to me
　you taught me ways
from right and wrong
　now here I stand so proud, so strong
you showed me all there is to see

　　　you taught me to believe in *me*.

Linda DeCesare

PEACE ON EARTH

What is peace? Has it ceased?
Look at our land, how can people stand,
To see war go on, and life not grow on?

What is hate? It's when you're too late,
To learn of love, and God above.

What is war, and what's it for?
To kill your brother, to hate each other?

There've been centuries of war, which we deplore
So, "Peace on Earth," my brother,
Let's have love, not hate for each other.

For God above, will help us find love,
To accomplish peace,
And let war cease.

Jean A. Gilliland

CK's INSPIRATION

The tears of God are falling from the sky
A perfect disguise that no one would guess was rain
I stare through cloudy windows that wait for tomorrow
It's the last piece of paradise to forever remain

Wingless angels are on their way
Descending from the heavens with Mercury's speed
Cutting through the night like a rapier's swath
That hath the watchers of the morning taking heed

Marauders have gone and taken the nightingale's song
Spirits must make them pay
For the beauty of a stolen serenade
That was taken for granted in every way

Jim Ingles

RE

When I was young I thought of things that had pertained to RE
And as the thoughts came into mind I knew not what they were
Just dreams, they said, of what you've read, was my only answer
　But I could not be satisfied for what was told to me
I searched about but could not find someone who held the key
I tried and tried but soon grew tired of the constant search
　It did not fade, my quest for RE, but patiently awaited
Until the day that I could find the answer to my question
Was then I learned of Déjà Vu and finally found the answer
　I had been here once before or so it seemed to be
Didn't I do these things before, oh no, that couldn't be
How could I do and say these things and not be here before
In each life in which I've lived I hold each thought within
　And in each thought there is a power to recall/foresee
For those who use what's given them will hold the key to life
In each life some rain must fall and in each life some death
　Death is not the end of life but only the beginning

Theresa L. Jones

ON FIRE

Children dare not wrinkle their fine clothes;
Yet hardwood pews have no mercy,
And the curious strain to ensure a good view.

Well-painted sisters chant;
While amens strive to keep the pace,
And singed souls stir with abashment —

All toward a black cape;
Trimmed with white and a bounciful being —
Lifting with no wings for flight —

Then down —
Such security —
Apt to pervade its purpose,

Poor babes,
And crowns captured in relentless bobs —
Yet all fires die;

Perhaps not in hell.

Constance L. Johnson

CONSTANCE LOUISE JOHNSON. Education: Central Michigan University, M. S., Administration, 5-12-85; Occupation: Senior Training Technician, New Jersey State, Department of Human Services; Memberships: New Jersey Certified Public Managers Association, American Association on Mental Deficiency; Poetry: 'This Black Child,' *L'Spirit,* Cumberland County College, 1978; 'A Cry Was Heard'; Other Writings: *With Pen In Hand,* booklet, 1987; ''I In My Kitchen,'' ''An Ounce of Time''; Comments: *My poetic goals are to heighten my experiences as a poet, while gaining exposure and recognition.*

THE MYSTERY OF ROMANCE

I like what your eyes are saying
With every fleeting glance.
They seem to hold the magic
Of the Mystery of Romance.
Though it may be a game you're playing,
I'm willing to take a chance
To play a leading role with you
In the Mystery of Romance.
Your songs of love seem meant for me.
They set my soul aflame.
I know our love can never be.
Still I'm hoping, just the same.
Fate takes a part while you're playing
Music that makes my heart dance.
Your tender kiss makes me understand
The Mystery of Romance.

Thelma D. Ivan

LIFE

Passing on
Life
Children are born,
grow old
passing on
you, me, us
friends for
Life
Passing on
like the pages
in a book
Our life together
one year, one chapter
one table of contents
Joy, pain, plot
setting
Sharing, giving
receiving
The End

Beryl Nash-Bienaimé

THE WIFE'S LAMENT

The best of my years
I spent with you
I gave you my
all, but
who bothered to
count
I gave you my
life
and you
never
said
Thanks

Beryl Nash-Bienaimé

BERYL NASH BIENAIMÉ. Pen Names: Beryl Nash, Beryl Walker; Born: Mt. Pleasant, New York, 3-14-54; Married: William Bienaimé, 9-25-85; Children: Naomi, David; Education: University of Massachusetts, Amherst, B.A., 1976; Nova University, graduate work, 1985; Real Estate Certificate; Occupations: Teacher, Inventor; Memberships: National Educators Association, Classroom Teacher's Association, South Florida Black Journalists Association; Other Writings: ''God is Lifting Us,' essay, local newspaper, 2-85; ''Gifted in the 80's,'' essay, *Howard University Satellite, Gifted Newsletter,* 7-85; Comments: *To me writing is therapeutic. Writing is a multi-faceted art form. There is infinite power in the mind/writing process. I love creating and sharing.*

BY MYSELF

Being alone
is remembering friends
and living
remembering the past
and dying a little more.

E. Ann Rauer

I sense that my heart is beating faster
The fires of life are burning low
I go to seek the final master
But leave this verse before I go

I am a pilgrim in a strange land
My journey has just begun
This path, it has no snow or sand
The sky has no moon or sun

Yes, I am a wayfarer in a wondrous land
A sanctuary for all to see
Like all, I seek an ultimate stand
To hear a final decree

''Don't mourn for me, don't weep or cry,
Why use yourself for such a show?
If one should mourn, it would be I
You still have life and all its woe.

''From this moment on I'm filled with joy
While you still have life and all its care,
In the seas of life I grasp great joy
Do this and you'll find me . . . waiting there.''

Robert J. Thompson

PAST HER PRIME

Past her prime, alone she sat.
Thoughts hidden deep within, heart broken.
The hurt great; no tears, none.

Eyes downcast, chin low, gnarled
hands lifeless. Beauty gone; hollow
cheek, sallow skin, stringy hair.

Shoes scuffed, cracked, worn;
polished once, never now.
Dress wrinkled, threadbare.

A knock! The door! Enter they!
Laughing! Happy! Young!
Eyes bright! Then dim . . .
A dream — gone —

No pain.
No hope.

No life,
no more.

Ruby McKay Bradley

THE WHISPERINGS OF
SOFT CARNATION WINDS III

Silent Change

Whisperings across the oceans with your mind up in the
clouds . . . 2,000 A.D. positive.
     Fragrance Lover, tower spiritedly above those forgotten
kingdoms with their jewel-studded skeletons rotted in hypocritic
ignorances.
     And move onward in silence . . . with your golden-feathered
wings outspread afar — for the rainbow currents breathes its
eternity into electric skies, whose vibrations echo its forward
progressive motion.
     ''Majestically Coronated Mysteries Metamorphosis,'' blooming
the cause of spectral emotions — in that change in the fine-
point of reason, opens the passages of manifested perfection in the
softened whisperings of carnation winds.

Charles William Johnson III

SENTIMENTALITY

The simplicity of a mother's love is found in her treasures.
Mother unwrapped the brown paper that hid my pony tail,
and lifted tops from boxes that billowed of Big Chief
   I had elaborately wasted.

She shared letters that I had written ever so diligently,
and never, ever intended to mail,
and poems and drawing of a child artist without a clear channel.
Brahms' Lullaby filled the air and teensy teeth sang, rejoiced,
(Finally released from the Tooth Fairy's mysterious, motherly grasp.)

Debra K. Martin

CROWN OF THORNS

She once lived in silence, prayed for further guidance,
long ago in the serenity of a Colorado convent,
she became a bride of Christ along with other
reverent girls all dressed in white, and donning
     crowns of thorns.

The picture is old, tattered around the edges.
Todays are filled with outward searching.
As often as she finds the inspiration and strength,
she confesses her sins as if condemned.

Passion occupies her quiet home.
She accepts pitiful human nature . . .
Sacred statues fill a darkened den;
incense burns, and candles glow, reflecting.

Images off of their recreated presence.
Imagine that into her room God steps nightly,
kisses her forehead simply, gently,
and lends her his pre-sweetened dreams of peace.

Debra K. Martin

WASTING TIME

Hang your leg on my shoulder, loose a hand in my hair,
bite my lip, but don't eat it, grab my rib-cage and knead it.
Rub your nose over mine, get too close — you're cross-eyed!

Gaze at the teasing clock tick to tock tonight.
This silly lollygaggin' whips up the happiest sap.

Debra K. Martin

RESPECTFUL PLEADING

Please kiss me each and every sweet dawn,
yes, be the gentle inspiration of each thought.
Oh, how my love grows for you each day on and on,
be the one I was meant for and forever sought.

Please persist and let me know when I'm wrong,
understand me on the days that I'm blue,
I'll trust in you, it won't take me long,
and on your down days, I'll do the same for you.

Please keep a close eye on me as I change,
do lend me strong support when I appear weak.
Keep me always within your own wide range,
sweep me off my feet to the highest of peaks.

Please accept this love, this deepening love,
hold my hand firmly when we feel just right.
I'll shrink it to fit you smooth as a glove,
and lead you knowingly deep into the night.

Please make bed with me when the going is rough,
think of me often and the intensity of this desire.
Our love together will be resistant, rugged and tough,
in turn we will fulfill what each has as fire.

Debra K. Martin

ANIMALOTIONS

Happiness flits like a butterfly . . .
Carefree, from one spot to another

Boredom crawls like a snail . . .
Steadfast, at a frustratingly unending pace

Restlessness strikes like a cobra . . .
Unexpected, and with deadly precision

Pain devours like a lion . . .
Gnawing, in constant succession, increasing in intensity

Desolation zooms down like a vampire . . .
Bloodthirsty, sucking out the last ounce of joy

Anger charges like a bull . . .
Blindly, with intent to kill

Peace descends like a dove . . .
Gently, calmly, enveloping in its warmth

Ann Marie Pounder

three-day moon —
    waiting at the river's edge
mist and fog

Charles B. Rodning

the pond
    reflecting an old cherry tree —
floating blossoms

Charles B. Rodning

LOVING INDIFFERENCE

Loving indifference
Is a hard thing to do;
To seemingly ignore your child,
And still love them too.

To turn a profound deaf ear,
When they agonizingly plea;
For things that they want,
From their tranquil mommy.

A loving smile their mommy gives,
A patient little grin;
Knowing their wants aren't needs,
And not giving in.

Although mom won't always agree
With decisions her child makes;
Her constant love and concern is there,
To comfort their little mistakes.

Thank God for our mother's love,
And all her patience too;
For her loving indifference
Is a gift she gives to you.

Linda Susiene

NATHAN

The hollow sounds of my echoing cries
The hollow words of my longing desires
The shivers inside of the love i need
The satisfaction of your gentle love and fires
The touch of your words sweep over me
The sound of your love sends me drifting away
The feel of your breath on the back of my neck
The laughter floating from your lips they lay
The weight of your soul, i shall hold on
The beat of your heart together with mine
The love we make in the light of the moon
The love we share together in time
The tear that drops, but not to the ground
The hand that breaks the fall of my love
The light in your eyes that thrills my soul
The shine in the sky reflects us above
    One passion through two souls

Dianna Michelle

VIKING SHIP

I watched a Viking ship come sailing
Returning from across the polished sea
Its sail laid to rest unveiling
Beauty, grace and length, simplicity.

Its portholes told of tales wandered;
I could hear the crashing ocean's roar . . .
I listen still to stories laundered —
My Viking ship now glides on polished floor.

M. D. LeDoux

A FRIEND IN THEE

As I sit and think of what I see,
I realize, I have a friend in Thee.

A friend who lights the darkest day
and one who brings me flowers in the
month of May!

A friend who knows what I'm thinking
of . . . and shows all interest in what I
love.

He picks me up when I'm feeling blue,
gives me courage and strength when
I need them too!

I see in my world how He has brought
to me, all the goodness and glory He
wants me to see.

He brings me laughter, and laughs with
me too! Such a sense of joy to be here
with you!

I see trees, I see blue sky, and this
all tells me why, inside of me, I have a
friend in Thee.

Carleen Y. Atkins

WELCOME IMPOSITION

Green shod and dainty, smelling sweet;
Her pockets spilling buds so fair;
Spring tiptoes through the countryside
And wafts a fragrance on the air.
She moves so lithely, skirts a-whirl,
As golden curls sway all unbound;
A whisper here, a love pat there,
And there's a stirring all around.
With twinkling eye and saucy mein;
She gives her rose-gold scarf a shake;
Then, as she hurries on her way,
She leaves all nature wide awake.

Hazel T. Lynn

IN FAITH BELIEVING

Enshrouded in the lily's pristine white,
The anther soft of precious, perfect gold;
When time is right we see a dazzling sight;
For all its inner beauties then unfold.

We do not pull the petals all apart;
We wait to see the lily's secret heart.

Within the chamber of the rough cocoon,
A thing of fragile grace lies slumbering;
When time is right — not late and not too soon,
Emerging we see beauty on the wing.

We do not rend or rive this thing so small;
We wait to see it fly high over all.

Within my life are things that jar the soul;
Omniscience knows, and He doth hold the key;
When time is right, He'll then reveal the whole;
And bowing I will say: "Amen to Thee!"

I do not rage and storm with doubting "Why?"
I know I'll have His answer in the bye.

Hazel T. Lynn

DARK MOURNING

Mourning brings
The shadow of night
To roost with day; thus
Masking the light of dawn.
A pantomime of life surrounds thee,
Who deafens in sorrow;
As tears glimpse through yesterdays,
Seeking passage to a new horizon.

Tina Dempsey

ATTIC POTPOURRI

A trousseau unveils a maiden's lace;
    a brittle rose lifts open to a space
    in her memoir . . . his photograph, having
    eyes deep, like mine.

A porcelain child subsides in a cradle;
    a blanket of dust, shadows
    eyes deep, like mine.

A tiny brass key winds up a ballet;
    slippers reciting, for
    eyes deep, like mine.

A tarnished case hides a silent timekeeper's
    aging face; inquisitive
    eyes deep, like mine.

Cobwebs, collecting ancestry;
    look to inherit, more
    eyes deep, like mine!

Tina Dempsey

GRADUATION

Fond memories of those four long years
tucked away in both smiles and tears.
I've made some wonderful friends along the way
some will travel and others close to stay.
Graduation from college; a well deserving honor
I owe it all to my encouraging mother and father.
But now it's over; a life of uncertainty I'll soon dread
but with pride, confidence, and determination, I'll strive ahead.

Connie Rinehart

Thinking, wondering, my mind wandering to thoughts of you,
I scream in anger, I cry in pain,
I want to run, to hide,
But where, for what, from who?
And then I question — why?
Will the memories fade, and the thoughts disappear?
Will time speed up to heal my wounds?
If I must remember, if I must think back,
I'll try to recapture the feeling, the romance, the love,
Only it's blank, gone, abandoned,
Destroyed in the blazes of my fury,
To return slowly as life goes on,
As will all the intangible things you've destroyed in me,
Like my sense of trust, respect and confidence,
In myself, as much as others,
Because in losing these things I lost part of myself,
But that is not the greatest pain in thinking of you, and us,
And how you once loved me,
It's remembering that once I thought I loved you.

Lisa Williams

I have thought of all the fun times,
    but I never think of the bad ones.
I have remembered how you made me laugh,
    but I've forgotten how you made my cry.
I have always known my love for you was strong,
    but I never knew it would end this way.
I have wished you were here,
    but then I thank God you're not.

Lisa Williams

BREAK OF DAY

Come break of day, enlightening sun slant
fingers do filter through the air still boughs
of lofty ancient oaks and elms, in scant
pale saffron garb, casting among the sloughs
of darkest hue left huddled on the ground
in oblong patches, clinging to their stems
of origin; their shadow tips surround
the dew-bright sward and moistured diadems
delineate the curve and crimp of gentle
undulating pastureland, creviced by creeks
a-gurgle o'er smoothest bouldered mantles;
and, high above in vapoured mists, the shrieks
of carrion wings, wheeling on the thermals' warm
arising air, do signal nature's dawn.

Aylwin Adams

LONG TRAIL FROM YESTERYEAR

Little brave on your spotted cayuse.
Poised like some Chief of old on a cliff,
granite and sky touching,
that overlooks a wide blue river.
Are you dreaming dreams of many moons ago
when your forefathers rode the ancient hills
where you now watch?
Do you ride with timid bow the deer trails
of your hunters long ago?
Are you dreaming now of war paint
and riding down of foes?
Or does your mind see wagon trains
of people with alien tongues?
Do you ride the war-path on wings of wind?
How many white men fall?
The shadows reach out. Even braves must grow
weary, hungry and sleepy.
Your pony is restless. It's a long trail home
from yesteryear.

Mystery Alires

THE RIDGETOP'S PATH

Beside the barn, the logging track
did start to wend its way to ridgetop high
and, one day, climbing slow on old mule's back,
I turned to find the ridge's curving line drawn nigh
to steep escarpments, deep descending down
'neath clinging saplings caught amongst the slack
of leaves a-mantle in winter's aftermath of brown.

We passed o'er ridgeway's paths of up and down,
a slow and measured pace, relentless in its way,
until we reached the highest point, so grown
with dark green cedar, pine and fir, that we may
not see past their boughs, stirring and windblown,
hiding the vast horizon line that stretched around,
claiming the creeks and hollows as its own.

The challenge of the silence all about oppressed
and seemed to burst upon our careful tread,
needing to make intrusive its role, possessed
of the old mule's stamina, who hung her head
and labored hoof by hoof to journey on,
and them stumbled, fell and lifeless lay, her brave life gone.

Aylwin Adams

LITTLE ANN & SUNSHINE

Little Ann and Sunshine are doggies from the west
They belong to someone special, children from my nest
When speaking of their loved ones, you'll often hear them say
Little Ann and Sunshine have brightened up our day
No other dog can do it, not another one around
Only those two rascals who are dwelling on our ground
Yes, children need the closeness of a loving faithful pet
It helps them grow in many ways from the time that both have met
So many little moments become dear to them within
As they share their song and laughter with others of their kin
Little Ann and Sunshine did this and that today
How good to hear them speaking in their happy childish way
I remember the precious moments of long ago, you see
When I, too, had a pet that meant so very much to me

Lois Lumsden

SUPPLE WIND

Such a supple wind,
blows through this place;
evergreen bends,
grass shakes.

Whistles match the singing
of aves from far and near,
ivy-twined harp rings
fencerow harmony.

Gentle breeze, Spirit's breath
rests upon the face;
comforts a weary soul.
The dawn is thy breadth;
the shadows even quake —
subtle laughter ever rolls.

Jeff Earwood

TIME FOR CHANGE

Sands falling through an hourglass
between a narrow chasm stopping
only when gathered fully at
the bottom it is over
the time is gone
and now
there is empty space
at the top, which will
be filled by all our souls
to be eternally part of a world
beyond ours, one of infinite bliss

Ginny Turner

MOLLY BLACKBURN

o desert flower
what ill wind blew you away so soon
your bloom brought such joy to this wasteland

the people have spoken
and yours is a testimonial of love
yours and theirs
through you runs the thread
of the saga of ruth and naomi
your people are their people
and their God yours

may those who quaffed on your nectar
make the sweet honey of tolerance
may they pick up your pollen
and propagate your love
to the four corners of this land
making it an oasis of
molly blackburn's flowers

Vincent R. Blake

TIME MACHINE

My thoughts soak in me
I can only think of a sea

My mind keeps seeing this land
My future lies by the sand

On the screen, beyond my eyes
I can't see a future that lies

Our past is yet to come
Our lives circle the sun

Tomorrow as light as rain,
Yesterday rained over the dream-bearer

Goodbye, I saw you here, in and out
Came back another day, I'm leaving now . . .

Matty Bolouki

SELF-DISCOVERY

I'm not a short, short story
With beginning and an end;
But I'm a blazing novel
In whose pages there's a blend
Of pain and pride and hope inside
And my story never ends.

I'm not a quiet, shallow brook
Who winds the countryside.
I'm a deep and restless sea
In whom much mystery hides.
Should you explore my depths I'm sure
Such treasures you will find!

I'm not a trinket one can keep
Upon some dusty shelf.
I cannot be a simple soul
Who does not know the self.
I must be free in search of me . . .
Content with nothing else.

Diane Gause Downs

LOVING YOU

I have wanted to say, ''I love you''
O, so many times, yet I hold back
For to me those three simple words
Hold a promise one cannot retract.
I am filled with incredible emotions
That find no way to be expressed,
Brightening my days, warming my nights
Why must they cause me such duress?
Why do I fear such little words
And where they lead me to
Am I afraid to admit? commit?
My confused heart, what can I do?

I've never known one like him before,
Felt such tender, loving touch —
When he is near so overwhelmed am I
I fear my joy is simply too much.
I know he loves me,
I love him too,
Yet I cannot say it.
My friend, my love, what am I to do?

Priscilla J. Lutz

FALLING FOR YOU

Oh falling for you is the
Only thing that I want to do
You are my perfect lover
Always on my mind
You'll always be in my heart
And in my soul
Yeah falling for you babe
Is the easiest thing to do

Our love grows stronger whenever we touch
And together our hearts beat as one
Our spirits, they really soar
Yeah no matter where you are or what you do
I'll still be here
Still falling for you

How could it be
That we get along so beautifully
Were we meant for each other
No matter what happens you know I'll still
Love you, yes always and forever
I'll be falling for you

Gene Roberts

LIFE'S FURY

If God had only made of me a tree,
Better could I have weathered life's storms.
But the elements have now become thee,
I await your sun that warms.

Your winds that blow can bend my branch,
The rains you spew are chilling.
Against your rage I have no chance,
And rare balmy days fulfilling.

As the years pass, my endurance grows,
I can bend my limbs without breaking.
The tests of time are beginning to show,
Although not broken, I'm quaking.

Unlike the tree, move on I can,
To a climate that's more appealing.
The skies have cleared since all began,
The warmth I feel is healing.

To all who would listen, let this be heard,
My strength has grown tenfold.
No longer am I the kitten who purred,
I am stronger than any tree — behold!

Paula VanSickle

the wind
    rustling bamboo
brushing the night

Charles B. Rodning

A CRY FOR HELP

A child's cry in the night disturbs no others,
For to them hunger is not a fear,
But to his mother who rocks him tightly,
The meaning is very clear.

A day has passed without food for him,
A long day of hardship and sorrow,
His mother prays to God above;
"Please God; Let there be food tomorrow."

And deep in her heart she knows what will come,
Another day of anger,
For her child will have no food again,
Her government; no mercy for his hunger.

And as she lays her child to rest,
Her tears roll down her cheeks,
For she knows if we don't help him now,
His future looks very meek.

God's plea to us is to lend them a hand,
To open our hearts and give,
To feed his small children around the world,
So that our very own futures may live.

Jane Betker

UNTIL TOMORROW

Time At Hand Has Made A Stand In A World Without Shame

and

the damage done leaves no stone unturned where fools have
walked this path.

Anchored to a wasted existence full of immoral ways, that
in time of progress — there is no progress made.

Diseases plague the minds of fools yielding to temptations
where greed, lust and ego wait to feed upon their prey

and

distorted views and twisted thoughts create a wall of darkness
giving no substance, no foundation to a world so destined for
destruction.

But, through it all there is a final call to mend unhealthy
ways and seek the truth in wisdom where past mistakes were made.

Time will tell in judgment within the Master Plan if
efforts should be rewarded when the world begins again . . .

Bonnie Chapman

A coin drops to the floor
and hearing the light tinny "cling" of it
I turn to see it spinning in circles madly
unseen by greed's faces around me
reaching into their purses for more, more more more
It's surface reflecting, glinting, fluorescent light
as it spins in circles smaller so slowly
Only I and a kneeling child see
it spinning round and round and round and round
Soon it will stop, motionless
the circles growing too small to spin
and it nears a hole, disappearing within
falling, falling through to the ground
The child's grabbing hands catching nothingness
her eyes, just as empty, a fading grin
show me the child, also, had given in
to the faces of greed around her spinning
And I disappear, falling through to the ground . . .
the circles have grown too small to spin

Laura A. Deerfield

THE DOVES AT UNDERWOOD

Perched on the electric wires were unscary doves
  Who stared at the tenement on Underwood,
Who sniped and snapped out of their platform
  And grounded on the tenement's pavement.
As they cooed and pecked on the food's debris
  A good Samaritan-Iranian peered through his window.
Behold! A multitude of short-billed, misty-dark guests.
  Sympathy captured his spontaneous imagination;
In effect, he surrendered inside his room
  And out he came with Kellogs' rice cereals,
Letting go his cupped fingers.
  He had dinnered these lovely and peaceful creatures
Who wobbled toward their towering, iron host,
  And filled their empty stomachs, contented.
But these estranged creatures had sense of humour
  As they put up a courtly dance for their host
Whose heart was drunk with amusement.
  At the sudden blare of a passing car, they took wings
And planted the iron man moping like Oliver Twist.

Udeagha Eme

THOSE FEW STOLEN MOMENTS

Those few stolen moments with you one night,
Do you think that it was wrong?
Those few stolen moments when you held me tight
And made my life a song.
A song of gladness, a song of sadness
Filled with ecstasy and pain.
My heart is glad I met you,
But sad I can't forget you.
When will I kiss you again?
Those few stolen moments to hold you so near,
Who knew what they would start?
Those few stolen moments so close to you, dear,
Are only breaking my heart.

Thelma D. Ivan

THE WALL 2/
IN A SISTER'S VIEW

As I strolled to get a better view,
I remembered Lord, thanking You!

Saddened to see the families of these,
whose sorrow brought them to their knees.

I thought how thankful Lord I should be,
that my brother was standing here with me!

Lord, You know that in our hearts we could
not bear. We'll be thankful forever, his
name wasn't there.

You brought him home — although missing a
limb, but thank You Jesus! 'Cause it was
still him!

I pray for the comfort of the families I've
seen, I wish this war had never been!

Let our soldiers rest in heaven in the
comfort of Thee. Crown them in the glory of
the heroes they'll always be!

Carleen Y. Atkins

CARLEEN Y. ATKINS. Born: Papaaloa,
Hawaii, 10-12-55; Married: Michael W. Atkins;
Education: Laupahoehoe High School, Hawaii,
1973; Occupation: Secretary; Poetry: 'The Wall,'
Chasing Rainbows, 1987; 'Why I Thank Thee,'
poetry/short story, *Chasing Rainbows,* 1986;
Comments: *Most of the writing I do is based on
true facts or my own personal experiences of
feelings and spiritual background. It gives me
great pleasure to write, as I am moved in hope
that at least one single person might benefit from
these words. For all my work and His neverend-
ing inspiration and endearment, thank you, Lord.*

SUSPENSION

Two worlds
Two roads
Two butterflies
A choice
A non-choice
A decision
Gossamer threading
Two trees
Waiting
Holy Saturday

M. D. LeDoux

REFLECTIONS

Life begins, life ends;
  hurriedly,
  unhurriedly.

Days come, days go;
  quickly,
  slowly.

Nights censure, nights beguile;
  discontentedly,
  fearfully.

Laughter departs, loneliness commences;
  shortly,
  inevitably.

Past certain, future uncertain;
  regretfully,
  tumultuously.
Why?

Ruby McKay Bradley

JUST ONE TIME

Just one time, she thought,
it won't hurt one thing
so silent it will be.

It will happen just this once.
It's so dark here inside
no one is going to see.

Thus, wondering what she
might miss if she let this
chance go by, moved closer,
reached forth and gently
placed her hand in his.

Ruby McKay Bradley

RUBY McKAY BRADLEY. Born: Chester,
South Carolina, 10-11-29; Married: David Alan,
7-2-49; Education: Fine Arts major working
toward a B.A., Appalachian State University,
Boone, North Carolina; Comments: *I love
people, therefore almost all of my poems are
about people. I am interested in their thoughts,
feelings, why they do what they do, and why they
are what they are.*

DIRTY DIRT

Down under the water,
Where submarines battle with guns,
Man-made machines bottle up fun
Down in the water,
Where dangerous things appear,
Damned down eyes look in the glare
Down under the water,
Where dead things drown,
From sun-up to sunny dawns
Down in the water,
Where things die,
With dreams and nightmares

The sun and moon
Burnout, down-down-down-
Down in the water,
Where we kill each other
Like we were taught when we were younger

Joseph R. Williams

JOSEPH R. WILLIAMS.

DOG!

Dog! You vex me — you dog my steps
  and race my fast-moving vehicles
  to pant by my side,
  how often you have trotted by me
  and given a furtive lick to my hand,
  you know my footsteps and
  vehicle noises from all others.

Dog! When you race my machines you are
  marvelous, you suck and blow the air
  in great gulps, your paws grasp the
  turf and push it behind in giant strides;
  With your long tongue and ears flapping
  in your wind you test your limits,
  and at the end of your race on hot
  days you flop in the creek, pond
  or mill race to lap and splash.

Dog! You wear the collar and tag of my
  neighbor who calls you Mack,
  but we know, you and I, that you are
  Big Red, and you are really mine.

Dubya

VIDEO GAMES

Defender, Missile Command, Asteroids and Pinball,
    I know them all.

These are what we name
    our dear video games.

Money by the day,
    is what we all pay,

To play these things
    that clink, clank, and ring.

Blank expressions on all those faces
    of the people who come to the video places.

They become the game,
    and in them they find their fame.

Disappointment soon sets in
    whenever they don't win.

They go out with sullen faces,
    vowing never again to come to these places.

There is only one way this could be;
    They can always go home and play on T.V.

Debby Garcia

ELEGY OF NOCCALULA

Noccalula Falls is located in Noccalula Park,
Gadsden, Alabama;
the story told in this poem is true.

O weep for Noccalula — a legend e'er to be —
The Indian maid that for love met her fatality.
Upon the mountain summit, by the falls that bear her name,
There lived a great Indian Chief, full of power and fame.
His daughter, Noccalula, was so radiant and fair . . .
And true to tell, her character was of quality rare.
Many the braves who sought the honor of the young girl's hand —
Yet her dad favored a young chief with wealth at his command.
Vainly the maiden pleaded to be her own lover's bride —
But her dad had his mind made up, and brushed her pleas aside.
A pawn for wealth abundant, and for security,
The hapless Noccalula was certain and soon to be.
The wedding day came, and amid all the festivities,
To the soft rush of the waterfall and its gentle breeze;
Sweet Noccalula slipped, and stood one second thereupon . . .
She drew one last deep breath — then jumped —
    and was forever gone.
Her heartbroken dad gave the mighty falls his daughter's name —
And thus, to this day, Noccalula Falls has lived in fame.
O Lord, hasten the day when love shall be forever free —
Never bound up in a wedlock that wasn't meant to be.

Edwin K. Hayes

GETTING AWAY

Traffic noise, loud musical tones, wagons rattling
on the pavement, a puppy moans — the suburban life.

Pack up the trailer, throw in the kids, get out the
roadmap, and then like a whiz we're getting away!

The noise like a low hiss is slowly increasing — the
needle says hot. Soon we'll be releasing all our
antifreeze and water.

A wave for help — a friendly motorist heads us toward
town. In the parking lot of a closed gas station the
kids are down for the night.

Up with our ego, down with the thermostat, we're back
on the road hoping that is that for our troubles.

The blowout came about one hour after the sleeping
bag fell out in a rain shower on highway eighty-one.

We spent that night in a crowded rest stop trying to
find where we went wrong on the roadmap.

Throwing our cares away, we headed home the third day,
and we'll make it barring more disasters. I prefer the
suburban way.

Cynthia Lehnig

ON SATAN WITH ALL HIS POWER

Who has reached out and engulfed the pitiless
Frame of this wandering soul.

Now that he occupies the mind,
The special hand that the heavenly father laid upon —
Remains scorched among us that truly know.

And so they fall in;
One by one —
The whos' —
We don't know.

Onward —
Into this hollow pit;

Onward —
Toward this pitiless frame,

Onward —
To lay a gentle hand,

And so,
Satan —
Is still in command.

Constance L. Johnson

CLOUDS ARE CLOSE

Clouds are close; Any point will do on the ball of earth to die;
They hover, casting shadows of a giant checkerboard, awaiting my move;
Even crowned, I can leap from light to dark, and into light again;
No matter, isn't one spot like another for goodby?

Clouds were high, and so was I when young, and knew time
As a silvery ribbon, shimmering and shining, dancing on
    the breeze of life;
Sheets of weeks peeled away, fluttering in my face,
    obscuring the future
Before they fled; And days, with colored balloons of ups and downs,
    were rife.

But now, clouds are close; They cling to earth like a rainfall
Of flying confetti, seen from the view of outer space;
I've been there on short flights, soaring free; And will go again
To other dimensions of no corners or straight lines,
    or paths with signs;
I'm on a track for home, and toss behind me a handful of memories,
    with thanks;
And clouds I will remember as dreams, so close, yet eluding my embrace.

Monnet Alvarez

MONNET ESTHER ALVAREZ. Born: Syracuse, New York, 11-20-37; Married: Alfred Alvares, 7-25-74; Education: Chouinard Art Institute, 1955; New York School of Interior Design, 1980; Currently studying UNLV's Writing Workshop, Nancy Ashbury — well-known author; Occupation: Manager, Art Gallery; Memberships: National Association of Women in the Arts; Board of Directors, L. V. Symphony; Awards: Outstanding Achievement, DAR of N.Y., 1949; Have-a-Heart/Save-a-Heart Fashion Shows, American Heart Association, 1975-80; Essay "What America Means to Me," Kiwanis International, 1954; Column, Teenage News, *Toluca Lake Times*, 1955; Poetry: 'Say No,' 'Clouds Are Close,' 1986; Other Writings: "The Mardi-Gras," article, *The Nevadan — L. V. Review-Journal*, 1984; "Las Vegas Bootleg Era," article, *The Nevadan — L. V. Review-Journal*, 1987; Comments: *I believe creative work speaks for itself. Artistic output comes from the central core where divine power is individually expressed — the precipitation of prolific imagination — the manifestation of ultimate paternal love — through the exercising of God-given prerogatives — acting and reacting, growing and overcoming, rejecting and aspiring, coping with life as puny man would have it on the peel of the planet and reaching for life as the Supreme Power of the universe conceived it — extravagant, harmonious and perpetual.*

I'M LIVING AT LAST

My days were so dark with no sun above.
My nights were so long with no one to love.
But now they all seem to go too fast
Because I'm living at last.
The birds wouldn't sing, no flowers would bloom.
I saw only shadows, I lived in the gloom.
But now, my Darling, all that is past
Because I'm *living* at last.
I remember dear, that lovely day
When by chance you came my way.
I will love you and need you
Each day till I die.
I won't let one moment pass me by.
For so long I have walked out in the rain
But now safe in your arms, forever I'll remain.
To the winds all my cares I have cast
Because I'm living at last.

Thelma D. Ivan

AN EMPTY SEAT

An empty seat stands waiting at our Kingdom Hall
Waiting for a person loved by us all
So oft she sat beside me in that seat over there
Sharing precious moments and tenderness with care
Our voices joined in praises as we sang to our dear God
Joyfully we treasure the times to Him we laud
That empty seat keeps waiting for that dear friend of mine
For she seems to be the owner that has claimed it with time
Its outstretched arms are waiting to zap around her lap
Though it has never been able to shout aloud and clap
It seems to humbly treasure the times it held her weight
While she fortified her mind for her everlasting fate
I do think that if the seat could speak it'd shout aloud to all
I'm waiting here for Genevieve when she comes back to this hall

Lois Lumsden

DEEP WITHIN

Deep within the center of my heart's fondest fold
I look and see the many whom my searching thoughts behold
So many fleeting moments while passing by my way
Brought joy, sorrow, and laughter to fill my living days
The bitter times forgotten to draw away the tears
While deep within remain the good collected all these years
The God of loving kindness has shared His every dream
Taught me well the love that's carried along life's passing stream
For you see all those we encounter have a shining light
It's there for us to extract if we but keep our sight
Everybody longs to find true love's caring way
They show it by their actions, how they speak, what they say
Sad, but yet the fact is true, some want it all, none for you
Selfishness brings not the love hate wells up inside
Leave the hurtful things behind the sadness and the pride
Joy is found for those we love by caring without greed
Deep within we need to expand, sharing as we proceed

Lois Lumsden

HER MAJESTY, SPRING

Her Majesty, Spring, is on Her way.
Brighter dawns have been preparing for Her arrival
I can smell Her sensuous fragrance in the air,
As I catch a glimpse of Her new gown in shades of emeralds and jades,
Trimmed with tiny flowers of May.

Her Ladies' Court will be a blanket of tulips, daffodils and violets.
In the distance Her Majesty's winged orchestra quietly plays Her
    favorite rhapsodies and minuets.
She is coming closer now, entering through a gentle breeze
It is so like Her to arrive early or even hold back and tease.

When She finally makes Her unpredictable,
    yet glamorous, grand entrance
Who can resist rejoicing, falling in love with Her all over again?
Each eager, amid Her magical splendor, to do his or her own thing.
Her soft, warm smile will embrace us all,
Then we will feel Her generous kisses filled with new hope
As She waves Her wand to begin the Renewal Ball.

She is coming, hear the music, She will reign once more.
She who we wait and watch for, She who we all adore
Welcome, Queen Spring, Welcome.

Melba Barber

A LOVE NONE GREATER

My Lord, you left your home,
in heaven most high,
lay down thy crown and shunned thy throne,
to thy people on earth drew nigh.

An infant child did thee become,
and grew for us to teach,
thy way in man so rare has been,
to faintly beckon of thee — O Mercy.

Yet the path of shadow, our fate, you sought,
deep and dark, driving down death depressed
of cold wood, thorns and cross,
to change the decay-worn man in light — Reblessed!

O now we become thy body,
our fears to thee give o'er,
thy lifeblood cleansed — of death be free,
of life you are the Lord, the King, the Sower.

My Lord, who reigns the eternal home,
in heaven most high,
worthy crown, upon thy throne,
to thy people on earth are nigh.

Jeff Earwood

GRAY MATTER

I'm wondering how to work this
No directions come with the package
A gadget of confusion, it never works the same
Some days running freely
On others facing despair and depression
Constantly changing motions, and unlimited in power
My toy beckons to be challenged
Hoping one day to be understood.

Chris Hancock

FROM THE INSIDE OUT

We see a telescope, a machine, an object
Many similar in design, some dressed fancy to attract
Viewed from the outside, there is something that is lacked
If we put our eye to the focus we see beauty around
The stars and celestial bodies that abound
Each time we look, there is more to be found
Looking from the inside out.

When we see people, we look from the outside in
Often not bothering to see what is within
Not trying to get close, not even focusing in
If we did, then beauty I think we would find
From the outside it's clothes, from the inside, the mind
So next time you're looking for beauty, try
Looking from the inside out.

Ginny Turner

DANNY TARTABULL, EX-SEATTLE MARINER

"T" is for Tartabull, a hitter so rare
With doubles and homers hit far in the air

I sit in the stands with a soft summer breeze
And observe this young athlete with talent to please

And yet his detractors still point to his glove
Like Divine Intervention were sent from above

But for me I just like a man plying his trade
So Danny, God bless you the progress you've made

Tom Alswager

THAT EVENING WE SPENT TOGETHER

That evening we spent together
The memory will live forever

Your image encased in a shroud
That night you looked so ravishing
Your presence setting me upon a cloud
Your heart full of fire, blazing

The restaurant in which we dined
The atmosphere, so very romantic
Toasting with lambrusco wine
Time was going by so quick

Gazing out upon the lake
Sitting beneath the willow tree
Listening to the waves break
Staring at each other intimately

Holding you by the candlelight
Dancing with you to a peaceful tune
Such an unforgettable sight
Watching the brilliant half-moon

That evening we spent together
The memory lives forever

Craig R. Dinger

133

I AM

I am an old memory of what used to be,
When we were together and when we cared,
When you loved and not just me.

I am the silly little bird,
That sings so sweetly from the trees,
In the early morning, that's never heard.

I am the little girl who was once so happy,
Who grew up and tasted a small piece of life,
And wants to be that little girl again.

I am the flower that stands alone,
In a field of weeds,
Waiting there to be known.

I am the moon so blue,
I cry the morning dew that disappears that day,
Only to return again that night.

I am the star that no longer shines,
Lost in darkness for all eternity,
Others are all around me but still I am alone.

I am the line between life and death,
Fighting for the end that's mine,
And being pulled the other way.

Holly Kassinger

I WAIT

I am coherent enough to know
some things will never happen.

The wish-against
is just protocol; superstition left
from the pail of things,
almost forgotten.

Where shall I begin?
With the thick parade
of endless explanations?

There is a quiet spot
just down the road
where no one has died yet.
The air is beautiful there;
shaped like a tear
and waiting to fall into place.

We swarm now.

I have seen their dark shapes
like vultures with no wings;
a puzzle along the edges with
moans and smoke and rubble.

I am lucky,
I have a chair
and a very small piece of glass.

Lisa Minacci

CRIES FROM THE HEART

These children I hold are nothing new,
they've been here year by year.
I've heard their cries in the night
that only few will hear.

What haunts these children all the time,
what makes them so afraid?
They fear to live, they fear to die
see the mess we've made?

Take a look my fellow man
see if you can find
the love, the warmth, and tenderness
inside their tiny mind.

They really never had the chance
to feel God's tender love.
You never even told them
about heaven up above.

Instead you showed them hatred
they were beat and tossed aside
punished for what they didn't do
then silently they cried.

Beth O'Donnell

SILENT SCREAM

Betrayed then left to wander.
Searching for the reasons I need to hear.
A hunger drives me forward,
A feeling moves me on.
I can't right the wrongs.
Knowing *that* is the evil.
Pushed into the crowd,
Not trying hard enough to be unique, that
Is the demise.
One voice drowned out by other's words had
No voice of its own, that is the destruction.

Jodie Pelcman

EPHEMERA

Seventeen years beneath the earth,
Grub body curling in the warm soil
And one summer with wings,
In the sun.
Sing, cicadas, sing your summer in the sun.

Four years beneath stagnant waters,
Dragon to small fish hiding in green slime
And three days to fly,
In the wind.
Dance, mayflies, dance your days in the wind.

Years sleeping in the arid ground,
Toads waiting for water where there is none.
And two weeks swimming,
In the puddles.
Swim, toads, swim among the cactus flowers.

Valerie R. Ritter

THE SCULPTOR

A sparrow ventures frail notes
In the chilling, lighting air
And all the world must follow.
How I dread to haul out
My great, rough stone
Into the light.

The stone is cold and edgy
And I haven't the idea
For a curve today . . .
A head,
A hip,
A smile.

But
I'll chisel the veined grain
To shape what I can
Today.

Joe Skvarka

TEDDY BEAR

There's a cute little teddy bear sitting
by the light, waiting quietly for tonight.
He wakes up after I close my eyes and wonders
what awaits him because of his size.

He gets into my stockings, rings and furs,
then like a kitten begins to purr . . .
He gets back on the dresser because his feet
are sore, it's a good thing because I'm awake
once more!

Roni J. Schuth

MANIA

Eyes descend
Into worlds
    Oblivious;

And mania collected
    For visions heard
Pleas!
    To yearn
    This trial
    Evermore;

And shedding
Worth and substance
All cannot strike
    For more
    In hours
    Unending
    In truths
        Ending.

Ayad Gharbawi

LAKE ERIE, FROM BLUFF, MOUTH OF ROCKY RIVER.

DEATH OF A FRIEND

Say to us
Words
In changes
Impersonal

In Waves
Awash
Upon hearts
Coldened —
O days
Gone?
To become?

Ayad Gharbawi

AYAD GHARBAWI. Born: Baghdad, Iraq, 7-26-64; Education: Tufts University, B.A., 1986; Occupation: Student: Comments: *Defining my life is quite difficult. I was born in Baghdad in 1964; lived in Beirut from 1969 till 1975, when several violent incidents leading up to a bombing of our building forced us to go to London, where I have lived ever since. The only matter I believe relevant to my work is this: that we live in an age of ice, of unheard violence, of endless insecurities and mostly hopeless friendships. We live to work, and not work to live; where anger and frustrations over petty matters rage, hidden just beneath the bland façades of faces; where the meaning of profound sorrow is the loneliest matter on earth. Anyway, in addition to poetry, I paint and write music, all of the same nature, alas.*

THE DAWN

Morning dawns, the night fades,
Work, life presses on.
But tonight has lonely shades,
Where has that night gone?

AH! Were each night filled with gold,
Were I to believe in dreams.
Then such a beauty to grow old,
My heart holding sunbeams.

Could the night become day?
Can dreams become alive and real?
Please, Time, show me the way,
For you know what I feel.

Where are the answers?
Who asks the questions?
Listen, listen, my heart,
Said I to me.

Mary Jane Kish

CATHARSIS

The muse in me,
of me
is dying to get out;
to create
to live, love, to be loved and
accepted.

Do I dare?
There is a bitter lamentation
in my heart
and yet there is a deep yearning
of my mind and soul to escape . . .
wash away and simultaneously unfold
a radiance of long lost;
now,

new-found dreams and
creations
watch me
see me now
before I disappear there
here . . . before you!

Karen B. Maloney

KAREN BETH MALONEY. Born: New Brunswick, New Jersey, 1-5-59; Single; Education: Rutgers University, Journalism, Communication, Marketing, Business administration; Occupation: Market analyst, Research; Freelance writer; Memberships: NAFE; NASA; AFTRA; North Brunswick Women's League; Volunteer Action of Middlesex County; Writer's Caucus, through Princeton University; Other Writings: Advertising brochures and literature for small business; Three articles published in *New York Times* Op Ed section; currently negotiating a book of poems; Comments: *My writing is inspired through life experiences and in turn it helps cleanse my soul. This I call my "lifeline" which conquers the spirit of transcending all time. The Zeitgeist that evolves creates images of a person striving for that "something" that seems unattainable. The artist's individual life depends on that "feeling"; their "lifeline" which is needed to survive. Through all our sufferings of life's trials and tribulations and our joys, the writer's art can hopefully let us all feel and be one and help our fellow man.*

RENAISSANCE

In this new birth for which many lives
Were purged, gaining its delivery
Let us not, like one who quickly contrives
A cure, infect the wounds in recovery.
In new preponderance let all hearts strew
A tolerance instead of suspicion —
In guiding humanity. Re-imbue
With inward urge for humble contrition.
Let intrinsic values outmode flagrant greed
We clutch. With inexorable desire
To keep an exalted and final creed —
A trustful peace — not suggestive of fire.

With complexities facing future plan
Behold, man's humanities toward man.

Lilibel Pazoureck-Lucy

IT'S SPRING

It's spring
For there
Within his room,
Scattered to the four walls,
Is evidence full bloom:
A tail for kite with attached string,
Slingshot tied to a wooden prong,
Some little agates, large green tall —
A rabbit's luring snare
To trade for poetry song —
Cub scouts' model seaplane —
It's spring
Again.

Lilibel Pazoureck-Lucy

MOONBEAM

A crystal beam of moonlight
Slid down the dark of night;
It landed in a puddle
And sparkled with delight.

Delphine LeDoux

MY PRAYER

Dear Father, give me words to say,
As I bow my head to pray.
Let my prayers, for others be,
And not be selfish prayers to Thee.
When temptations come along,
I ask Thee Lord to make us strong,
And when Thou seest us go astray,
Please lead us back into Thy way.
Let our hearts be humble still,
As we strive to do Thy will.
Guide us daily, with Thy love,
That we might dwell with Thee above.
In Jesus' name, I ask these things,
O Gracious God, O King of Kings. Amen.

Doris Bowman Johnson

WEST WIND

You're a hut small, seven paces by five overall.
There are two shuttered windows,
A drafty door, and a sagging floor.
You're sitting on blocks in a corner of a German Parkplatz.

Once, you stood on a pretty hill where the west wind blew.
You saw many things: fighter planes shoot landings,
Make intercepts, bank left or right,
And paint the sky deadly white.

There were bright travel posters on your walls.
People bought air tickets to fly home.
Then, they moved you to a corner
When the hill was gone.

Years passed.
You grew old and forlorn.
People came again, and you saw a space war (Datsun/Toyota).
Then, they moved you once more.

Now, bent out of shape, you lean to port.
The floor sags more as you tilt toward the door.
It's almost over now; you don't need to move anymore.
Still blows the west wind.

Royston W. Donnelly

WISHING

I wish you were here, sitting beside me on this cliff,
Overlooking the great vast ocean.
Orange and reds of the fiery sun look beautiful
Setting behind the wall of the earth.
The ocean gently rippling to the edge of the shore
With its cold grey water lapping its white frothy
Tongue to me.
Birds lying on the ocean resting their wings after
A long day's flight.
The fog reaching for the city with its long misty
Fingers looking for a resting place for the night.
Oh, the end of a sunny day, with this feeling of
Peacefulness and tranquility all around me.
But the best part is knowing that you are mine,
And that you are here beside me.

Nancy Jean Hansberry

HUNTER'S MOON

Campfire patterns dance, and embers glow;
the songs of night proclaim the earth alive.
In the mountain valley waters whisper as they flow
in liquid riddles to be deciphered only by the wise.
Deep in the woods an owl intones the age-old question:
Who?
I ponder that riddle of the soul as best I can.
In a sudden flight of fancy I invoke the goddess of the moon
in search of help and guidance in becoming who and what I am.
As the firelight's dancing patterns draw my eyes
life's shifting mysteries draw my heart and mind,
and I wish my path could be as clearly and delicately defined
as light's lacy tracing of a hickory bough
amid the shadows of a hunter's moon.

Antoinette Kahler

Let all that dwells beneath the earth,
Instill its mark upon time
Forever, the beasts of the Land, the Sky, and the Sea,
Evermore, be yours and mine!

Innocence, not to be lost!
Supplication align.
Feast upon all that is dear,
Opaque, Oblique, Obtuse —
Relish all that is life!
Evermore, be remembered,
Vibrant, Voracious, Vexing, Valiant,
Evermore appeased.
Relinquished in Life and Death!

William F. Martin

ONE OF THOSE DAYS

Today I've done nothing, I'm deep in despair.
I'm really so lonesome, for someone who'll share.
No putdowns, analyzing unless you've walked in my path.
Not many have been there, but I won't be the last.
My friends they desert me, as though they don't care.
Their selfish ideas leave me in despair.
I should have known better, than trusting mankind.
It's a "dog eat dog" generation, men can be so unkind.
Doctors won't treat you, unless it's on their time.
But your money they'll take, not leaving a dime.
As I grow more needful, there's less that will give,
My head aches, I'm sad, and it's supposed to be a time to live.
The new doctor I had, just canceled my visit,
Finding a new one will be another chore.
So now that I've told you, of my dire situation,
It's not so bad, now that I know the score.

Bertha Munson

UNTIL I MET YOU

I used to laugh when people told me
that they need someone to share life with
to have a friend to talk to when things go wrong
to watch the beautiful sunrises and sunsets
to laugh and cry with
to walk with down a shady wooden path on a warm, sunny day
to share the happiness and sorrows of life with
I would always tell them,
Why do I need someone to cause me pain
hurt me when they decide to leave me
complicate my life
depress me when they are down
discourage me when they are sad
depend on me at their time of need
. . . I used to laugh when people said
they need someone to share life with . . .
that is, until I met *you*

Valerie Jean Bell

A HAPPY DAY

There is music in the hen house,
All the hens are singing praise,
To the one that sat so patiently
For twenty-one long days.
Now her patience is rewarded,
As each tiny chick pops out.
Mother hen is so excited,
She is clucking all about.
As she leaves the nest they follow,
And what a sight to see,
Mother hen is very happy
And as proud as she can be.
Take a look at papa rooster,
Strutting round like peacocks do.
Sitting on a fence post bragging,
Cock-a-doodle-do.

Doris Bowman Johnson

SONG OF THE SEASHELL

Oh, Little Seashell
Teach me your ways
Of simplicity and care

You've built a beautiful shell
Its delicate sculpture
You've woven with devotion
Each fragile curve
Reflects your knowledge and understanding
Of life's rhythm

Your rich lavender tones
Reflect my heart's deepest longings
Your gentle shades of coral
Reflect my heart's peaceful depths

Silently listening
Submerged within your rhythm
Echoes your timelessness
Your elegant, ageless beauty

Oh, Little Seashell
Teach me your ways
Of simplicity and care

Kerry Ann Shields

WHEN I GROW UP

I sit on the grass by the harbor
And I look out over the bay;
I watch the ships that are coming in
From ports that are far away.

With what cargo are they laden?
How long have they been at sea?
What of the men who work on them —
There's adventure and mystery . . .

I watch the outgoing vessels
And I wonder where they are bound . . .
What strange ports will they stop at?
What treasures are there to be found?

When I grow up, I'll go to sea!
And I'll be a captain, too!
And I'll visit ports around the world!
I dream now! Then I'll do!

Delphine LeDoux

CITY OF DREAMS

A silver web of shining dreams
Throughout the city spreads,
Blending all the varied skeins,
The interwoven threads.

A dream is built upon a dream!
Each dreamer seeks his goal;
Things are never what they seem;
Each dream exacts its toll!

As magnets to themselves attract,
Star-dusted city gleams;
With hope, the dreamers interact;
Entangled in their schemes.

Soon tarnished is the silver web;
The end of hope and trust;
The shattered dreams that flow and ebb
Lie trampled in the dust!

But some dreams rise, in glory burst,
Outshining all the rest!
The City of Dreams is there for those
Whose dreams of fame are blest!

Delphine LeDoux

DOLPHINS AND WHALES

Oh Life, you've opened the depths of my soul
Drinking deeply its waters of nourishment

Steadfast and sound in her footsteps
Gentleness and lightness woven into her care

For grace, intelligence and fun
I beckon to thee
As the dolphins and whales
Of the sea

Taking heed as daily living
Calls to me

Kerry Ann Shields

LET ME GO

Let me go
Forever
Oh God!

I want to go back
Into my world
A world of loving
Caring, giving, touching

A peaceful world
Of soft gold, mauve,
Blue, burgundy shadows

Reflecting the
Pulsating elegance
Of brown hues

Kerry Ann Shields

M IS FOR . . .

M is for Mohammed, M is for May
M his mark on my Moochie
Mentioning ancestors: Egyptian Mau
Munching Meow Mix and mopping Miss Mew
Miaouwing her father was Mao Tse Tung
And Madame Muezza her mother
"My name, if you please, is Sekhmet Bast Ra"
Capturing mice at night to amuse me
Chasing mama's mutt up the maple
And the minister's mastiff down the pews
By moonlight hunting moles at midnight
Moaning *Memory* from the roof
Moody misers down the mews
Throw mitts at her, but mightily miss
While she makes love to and merrily mates
With many a tom in marvelous May.

Dorothea Wirth

GLIMPSES

to fly with your imagination
inside your vision's night dream
down alleyways of awareness
land of nothing as it seems

oh seers and poets of a common gaze
again let's hear your horns
sun rising from some rainy sunday
as the ancient reason choice to be born

half human and half god
oh where might you dwell
inside the truth of all men's hearts
in terms of will from your well

the positive side of negativity
from misery grows the call
grown tired from no productivity
strength resolves from negativity's fall

so keep your eye on the dawning
and its circular love for the round
keep your ear on the echo's silence
your growth through time new sounds

Daniel Thomas Carr

BUTTERFLY

On wings of colored dust
she flies —

life as fragile as a sigh —
like pastel rose petals
drifting through the sky —

too soft and gentle to live long
too soft to die

Tammy James

DISAPPOINTED

During our lifetime, I am sure
that we have all been disappointed by you
Even though it might have been unintentional
it is still something that you so often do

When things are bad and our feelings are low
and everything in our world is down
You come into my/our miserable life
cheer us up and once again make our world go around

And then like an unexpected storm
when everything seems so right
You, my friend, let me down
and disappear into the darkness of the night

So that feeling of disappointment
returns into my life
The feeling of hurt is so strong
it is ten times worse than being cut by a knife

You would think that after a few times
we would not let you back in
But I guess it is a part of the human life
and your trying to be a friend is not a sin

Valerie Jean Bell

VALERIE JEAN BELL. Born: Mount Clemens, Michigan, 1954; Education: Associates Degree in Applied Science, 1983; Occupation: Production Application Support Supervisor; Comments: *All of my poetry and short stories are based on real people that I come in contact with every day.*

THE ARTIST

Can I paint a picture as soft as velvet and wine
as pretty as a picture with words that shimmer and shine
Do my words tell you of forever
Do my words tell you of time
Today, tomorrow, and never put together so they rhyme
Do you see my soul in colors, do you feel my heart confide
as the blind man sees the rainbow from the corner of his mind
If I were to paint a picture to tell of the love I've known
I'd start with lemon yellow and end with tarnished gold
I'd paint you in turquoise with light mellow days
green fingers, blue roses, pink shadows, purple haze
If you were to be my canvas, upon it I would lay
all the colors of my lifetime, all the feelings of my day
I'll fill you with autumn days, I'll chill you with winter nights
I'll warm your soul with a summer stroll
I'll caress you with spring's delight
I'll come into your heart, I'll creep into your soul
I'll be there when the winds whip bare
the trees with their leaves turned gold
If you were to be my canvas where words could never say
the wonders of this lifetime, upon your soul the paint would lay

Dawn Foster

DEEPER THAN LOVE

I tell you I love you but it doesn't say enough
love doesn't mean I need your touch
love doesn't know the fire you feed
love doesn't know the want turned to need
Love can run in waters shallow, melt the heart that's cold
but what runs so deep and like a thief comes to creep
and steal a heart that's hard to hold
I tell you I love you in the heat of the night
love's never taken such a flight
love's never seen the look in your eyes
love's prone to deception, obsessed with disguise
What runs so clear and draws you near
what makes your heart part of mine
love can be blind deceiving the mind
leave you to bleed when want turns to need
What is it that surges through my veins
like wild horses given the reins
When you take me into the night
what makes me need you before daylight
What makes me want to feed the fire and with you go higher and higher
What is it that flies on the wings of a dove
What do you call it when it's deeper than love

Dawn Foster

DAWN LORRAINE FOSTER. Born: Denver, Colorado, 8-28-55; Widowed, Engaged to James Day; Children: Jeremy, Ryan, Tory, Kerry; Education: Night courses in writing and marketing; Occupations: Bricklayer, Clothing designer, Marketing consultant, Writer; Comments: *I am a very shy person. I wrote my biography when I was 7. I started writing poetry in high school. I let people read my work many years later, and was surprised and encouraged to find I could touch the heart. I have copyrights on over 2000 of my poems. To me, my poems are actually song lyrics. I want to put my own band together and get my poems put to music.*

TRIAL DAY

Early mourning rain creases my hair
Heavy rush of energy rushes my veins
Drawn sentences from loud words
Lonely verdicts running away with drainage
Here I am on the brink of insanity . . .
        So they say
Lines not straight, but lean toward crooked walls
        (before)

And there again, the vessels of life are flowing over,
Down dingy stairs
Taken to heart a stab of time . . .
        With working muscles
Yes, time stabbed the heart dry of flowing life
And there again, what with my mind —
Am I to do over?
A burden, a load: just a chip broken on the floor
Off my shoulder

Joseph R. Williams

WHISTLE ME A TUNE

whistle a tune familiar feelings come
some reappear out of the past
fading light vanish the sun
meanings hidden in shadows cast

whistle a tune some unborn day
all men will come to see
understanding's reason for kindness the way
peace can heal all the wounds to be

whistle a tune hope's still trying
yet another given chance
released at last all of the dying
again to relive the spirits' dance

whistle a tune forever's vision
tales of birth in the round
age-old song now's renewal
truth's ringing timeless sound

whistle a tune rebirth's belief
distant ends will meet in time
common ground holds the sacred search
common joy hears the singing's rhyme

Daniel Thomas Carr

BEHOLD JESUS CHRIST

Behold Jesus Christ the virgin-born King
Whose inspirations wrote all hymns we sing.

Behold Jesus Christ's holy salvation,
Which brought man inspiring revelations.

Behold Jesus Christ's holy creation.
Worship God in divine recreation.

Behold Jesus Christ's holy mysteries,
Whose love will conquer man's worst histories.

Behold Jesus Christ on a blood-stained cross.
Christ the King is your Almighty boss.

Behold Jesus Christ's beautiful angels
Singing inspiring heralded noëls.

Behold Jesus Christ's holy miracles.
Christ prophesying divine oracles.

Behold Jesus Christ's holy ascension.
Christ returns for all with no exception.

Behold Jesus Christ's perfect Holy Ghost.
The Holy Ghost is God's comforter host.

Behold Jesus Christ's holy ministry,
Because Jesus Christ's return you might see!

Timothy A. Wik

THE SEA AIR

The stillness of the sea, oh! how calm
and peaceful it must be. If only
you could see, oh! great sea you have
so much beauty and charm, I wish
you would hold me in your loving
arms, and all the snow-white doves
should rest ashore; the people

are fishing upon the pier, young
children with their mothers near,
the sea. Listen to the sea! Can you
hear the billow, row? The waves
splashing over the shore; sea shells
scatter on the sea, my teeth begin
to chatter! I shatter the rest of

the sea shell to even the score,
the children build one of the
most beautiful sand castles
that I have ever seen. Listen!
Listen! to the sea gulls they are
about to land, the children's kites
are flying high above the air, can

you see the breeze blow my hair.
The wind begins to blow the water.

Ginevar Curenton

THE CHANGING SEASON

It's the dying time of the year
where the leaves are turning
and the sky is graying
where the wind is cooler
than it used to be —

Where loneliness settles in
and solitaire begins —
and the sun dips down
into the pocket of a cloud.

It's the dying time of the year
when the birds fly triangular
above the once round trees
and the pepper of a summer
turns to salt in the breeze.

Tammy James

THE PARTY

I looked out the window
and stepped out of my skin
A crowd of gleaming people
spoke to me, gave me red flowers
They held my hands and danced with me
Told me how beautiful I was
in my silver dress
of stars

I looked back at the window
The crowd
pulled their hands away
They lay on the ground, staring
at lizards emerging from my mouth
and odd fingers growing out of my arms
My dress melting in the fire,
I tried to creep away
without seeming strange

Lisa Campbell

TRUSTING

Trusting is one of the hardest things
    for me to do
I had a rough time as a child
    and couldn't trust anyone
I am still having a hard time
    trusting in people
I'm always afraid someone
    will break their trust with me
It takes a long time
    for me to trust in a person
I look in their faces
    and sense if I trust them or not
And if I trust in someone
    I take it slow
I slowly, with caution, tell them about myself
And if I don't trust in someone
    I tell them nothing
It is a very long process
    but I hope one day I trust
    in someone and can tell them everything.

Denie Vashey

IMAGINE A WALL

Imagine a wall
    that one can hide behind
A wall that is so thick
    no one person can penetrate it
A wall that one has built for oneself

Imagine a wall
    that one can hide behind
A wall made up of hurts
    and pains
A wall to protect oneself
    from being abused
A wall where no one can reach
    the one who is behind it

Imagine a wall
    being broken down
Being broken by someone
    who cares and understands
Being broken down by
    that special person
    you've come to trust

Denie Vashey

THE TOUCH

I built a wall around me,
to keep me safe and sound.

I'm glad that love has found me
and torn that wall back down.

I tried to keep out bad things,
but good things stayed out too.

Until you touched my life and
drew my heart to you.

Linda Barrett

VILLAN-AGE OF LAW

In a village on a stone
A letter was written
The words are for sight,
But not unknown
They made the law . . .
                    Broken
Cracked it hard and horrible

On a brain in a state of mind
An event was noticed
A scene with something in pain . . .
                    Nothing

On a face mocked with mental anger
A native as the life of a stranger
Wandering into corners learning prayer
Mentioning love
And hating with the speed of anger . . .
                    Regulated lawless

Joseph R. Williams

BITTERSWEET YOUTH

  As memory rolls away the hours, the days, and the years,
It all rushes in, all the pain and the fears.
I find it hard to remember the girl I used to be.
I should have known I would never be free.
So poignant, the sweet tenderness of youth.
So hard, the bitter truth.

  I guess, that odd throbbing ache, I will always have.
You would think after all this time it wouldn't be so bad.
My single bed, so empty, always so cold.
Funny, when we were together even my thoughts weren't that bold.
If the mysteries had been answered then?
I wonder how different my life would have been.

Cynthia Chapman

SKYWARD TO GLORY

Oh kindred souls lift up your voices and scream, skyward.
When in the flesh you cannot touch heart.
Oh love's companions let yourselves be heard.
When in your pain you can no longer be apart.

Only souls may we be known.
Through miles of land, body, and face.
Only together weaved and tied so grown.
To meet our longing we will race.

Oh love's sweet youth, to God we cry!
In our sorrow and bleeding pain.
Oh lovers' souls reach up to high.
We will not die, so to death be lain.

Cynthia Chapman

TREASURES

I thought love's mystery would forever
Remain a hidden treasure for me,
So many loves had come and gone
And left their traces, scars and memories.

Having resigned myself to seek only love's comfort
With someone whom I cared for and seemed right,
Leaving love's flame and passion a faded
Dream with no hope in sight.

But God must have heard my silent prayer
For when I least expected
I turned and she was there.

We each have a purpose in life,
Roads we must follow, lessons to be learned.
My love and I had to part
Each left to find our way.

Lucky am I who at last learned
Love's treasures, the pleasure and the pain.
The feelings and the memories of my heart's
True desire, neither man nor time can erase.

Lourdes M. Estrada

THE DREAM

Dedicated to Reggie

At twelve, it was just a big dream
One almost impossible, so it may seem.
But he never gave up or lost his desire
For deep down inside, he was on fire.
Slowly and surely, he must work out a plan
So he would be ready, when he was a man.
Each day studied the ways to be strong
The right things to do, and leave off the wrong.
The right things to eat and the proper amounts
The right things to help and the things that count.
He had faith, more than most people do
So he knew deep down, his dream would come true.
It would take a long time to reach his goal
But he would do it and strengthen his soul.
He knew God had showed him the way
And he asked for his guidance every day.
Many years have come and many years have gone
But the brave little guy never went wrong.
Today he says thank-you, I have made it through
Just me and my Karate, dear God, and you.

            Grandmother.

Annie G. Federici

DARK SPECS

Protecting peepers from blistering brights
Hiding stares from beautiful bodies
Shading the personality of one, but adding another
Making mystery of one's eyes
Shutting off the passage to the soul
My shades do do all they should
For I am unknown to others while I sit
Figuring them.

Chris Hancock

UNTIL TOMORROW

Thirty days until tomorrow
The minutes tick away
Notice how I smile my sorrow
Thinking of things to say

People writing their endless poems
Whispering words out loud
A fire burns, the ocean foams
Why is it man's so proud?

With walls of flesh and bars of bone
His sentence is to live
Listen to him cry, hear him moan
There's nothing more to give

Seven days until tomorrow
The hours tick away
No time left from which to borrow
The time is now today

Christopher Jennings

THERE ARE TIMES

There are times
When emotion washes over
like waves on the shore,

There are times
When doing nothing
is what is called for,

There are times
When love is the emotion
that envelops without warning,

There are times
When hate abounds like
crashing thunder sounds.

There are times
When ending is beginning
and beginning is the end.

Mary Ann Edenfield

RECOGNITION

In a snatch of a song
In a few notes of music
Caught in passing,
In a flicker of light
In the excitement of color
On the page of a book —
I find something of you.

An idea, a memory emerges
And forms a feeling
A half-finished thought
Falls from the mind
Into the heart
To ripen.

In silence, and in words,
In the sight of each other,
And in the imaginings
Two people try to meet.
Like a thousand facets of a diamond
Are the ways for One to know Another.
An endless maze to wander in.

Juta H. Fowlkes

THE LATE LATE SHOW

Guitars jangle and burley drums pound
marrow-jarring thumps:
Dancers prance to primal caterwauls
with Neanderthal stomps.

Like squid-ink sea swirled the show
smothers dark my mind.
Skulking otherness of prehistory drags
in disjointed memories:
Behemoths, pterodactyl screams, the rank
pungence of meal-fire
ringed by feeding clan who snatch with snarls,
and my bones unlatch shivering.

Jackal howl of trombone ricochets:
and the Now is recaptured — by applause
that pelts with clatter
of a stone avalanche.

Like spilled birdshot we scatter, unthinking.
Our tattered cloaks of civilization —
molting again
under the glory of stars — have fallen to shreds.

Joan Hanford

LOVE

Love runs deep,
  It is an unexplainable feeling for someone,
A feeling which will knot you up inside,
A feeling which will tear you apart,
  A feeling which at first will confuse you,
  But give it time,
Love will straighten itself out.

Michael McKinney

I'M EVERYWHERE YOU GO

You'll find me flying on the wind beside you.
Look for me watching you in the mirror,
The reflection is yours;
But I'm right behind you,
Watching every move you make.
Sweeping through the air,
Playing with your hair,
Looking into your deep blue eyes.
I'm with you everywhere you go.
When you go to bed at night,
I'm lying there right beside you;
Just enjoying the thought of being close to you,
Every minute of the day.
If sometimes during the night,
You feel a strange sensation in your ear . . .
That's just me, whispering softly, ''I love you.''
Till the end of time —
Yes, I'm everywhere you go.

Kathleen Moore

LIFE'S MYSTERY

It's been a mystery
down through the ages.
Man has wondered
what is it like?
Those who know
cannot say
and if they could,
we'd never understand.
It remains a mystery
one must experience
to understand.
But then it's too late,
the knowledge is useless.
Who is there to tell
what it is like,
when you are dead?

Paul D. McCrory

MIRROR IMAGE

Morning, still dark, eyes of mine
looked into, eyes of mine, still dark,
asking myself not to frame this
pictorial of my time, me, my image,
for no photo shall expose, both
our faces into one place.

The mirror divides an image,
me and the glass-reflected stranger,
two worlds blended by each other's
secret.

Pressing my nose against the mirror image,
my mind looked through my eyes.
To play his game, I've to feel no pain.
I've left myself, inside, alone, mellow to bone,
the color of my skin, he will not show
two noses as one, don't know where to go.

Numb laughter is now concluded.
We see no image, now, through the mirror.
I am home.

Craig Peterson

I can sit here in
class and think of you.
But it's not the same
like being next to you.
Hugging and kissing you
is really great.
I want you to know
you knock me off
my feet.
Because of your love
and sweetness.
You've made love
a reality to me.

Dennis Sittre

LIFE

Listen, now, to what I have to say
If you get to the top, you surely must pay.
You have to work, to plan, and to scheme
And keep your eyes on that special dream.
It takes push and shove and a lot of guts
A lot of disappointments and kicking of butts.
It's never easy, no matter how hard you may try
And many's the time you would like to cry.
You take three steps forward and slide back two
And wonder what else you could possibly do.
You sweat and swear and give up in vain
When all of a sudden, the way seems so plain.
Have faith in God to see you through
Ask him to show what you should do.
The ones that laughed at your corny old jokes
And hung in there until you were broke
Have all vanished and gone with the tide
At the very moment you needed a ride.
So it's back to square one and an honest prayer
For that's the only way to make it there.

Annie G. Federici

JESUS

He was here in the beginning — and made the world with God
They spoke it into being — to some this may sound odd
He was born of a virgin — this no other man can claim
His mother's name was Mary — and Jesus was His name
He was here in the flesh — for just a little time
Not here on His own — He had a hill on His mind
He was tempted by old Satan — in more than one way
But He gave him Holy Scriptures — that His father did say
He taught the twelve disciples — as He walked with them each day
He knew what He must do — and exactly what to say
He loved this sinful world — so He left His heavenly home
Then came down here — that we might be atoned
He's the healer of the sick — and will raise up all the dead
Through Him we have the power — if we believe in what He said
He died up on a cross — but arose again to stay
He's at home with the father — until the trump of His day
He's prepared for us a home — if we'll keep His great command
He'll take us up to heaven — if we'll hold on to His hand

James R. Norris

FROM CATERPILLARS TO BUTTERFLIES

People come to the program
  Like caterpillars of all kinds
But when they learn about their disease
  They begin to cleanse their minds.

They learn to deal effectively
  For they are sensitive with charm
The fact that they cannot drink again
  Is what causes them alarm.

But knowing that the power they get
  Like a new and different birth
They learn to rely on their higher power
  Rather than people here on earth.

They are delightful and interesting
  Artistic at many things
For finally at last they've once again found
  Their beautiful butterfly wings.

Jeannie Urban

THE LIGHTED WAY

Christ's Highway has always been the road for me
The divine, endowed protection of my destiny
The road that has carried me to whatever glory
A straight, lighted path has been my story.

Unhindered has been my way through life
Even when strife demanded some price
Each moment that was invaded by a devastation
Was defeated; and gave me double compensation.

Because, I know, there must be accepted tears
Through the years there have been no fears
Christ's Highway has shown me the lighted way
The way to loving all things, day by day.

Whatever the occurrence, good or bad
The *lighted way* deters all the sad
The temptations that are put into our path
Are hurdled obstacles, to be left in the past.

T. Steven Watkins

A STARRY NIGHT IN SAMOA

Surrounded by the night I sat and devoured
the tropical warmth and the millions of stars
while from inside the huts the Samoan music and laughter
drifted to the distant ocean reefs

Wave upon vociferous wave amassed
as the stars soared and stooped
to aggrandize the beauty of the darkness
then buzzing about my head and neck
the stars landed and created a welter of my soul

Their babel became a cacophony
of biting and pain as I was mesmerized
by murmuring mosquitoes and gnawing gnats
who divided my body into bits and carried them away
into that starry night in Samoa

Nancy Hoekstra

UPCLIMB

Perched atop a slide, my child
cannot understand the antonym
of East and West; she merely beguiles
the other children as they play on limbs
all the same and do not reconcile
that her language is a paradigm

Where are the Communists to shout Slavophile
or Americans to brim with peaceful hymns?
None to be seen in this isle
of small children on a gym
yes, in different styles, for awhile
yet far away from governments' faces so grim

Perhaps the vile words of war would not compile
if we in all our languages would prim
playful words and smiles juvenile
yes, my child in Czechoslovakia was a glimmer
of friends, not enemies prelim
in a world so mild!

Nancy Hoekstra

LU YEN

I bar maid, work in clubs
big like Bien Hoa,
small like Plei Me.
Army men with no beard
grab when I pour drink.
They used to whores,
hootch maids with rotten teeth,
skin like riverbed.
One put hand up my skirt —
"searching for bugs," he laugh.

I pray to run away
but know hundreds in Saigon
like take my place.
Upstair rooms worse than bar.
So I swing hips, smile,
think of baby-san back home.
I serve Heineken
for twenty cent a pinch.

Peter Ulisse

LIFE OF WONDERS

What a wonderful world is this
Which is full of darkness
And surrounded by miserable sorrows
And clouded with tears

What a moving world is this
Which is rolling here and there
Just trembling with terror
In the stormy sea

What a confession world is this
Without any conflict nor fuss
Futility of living in this world
Without no hopes of futureless

What a self-made world is this
Which is full of selfishness
For my question and help
People seems emptiness in their mind.

Miguel Barreto

WEAVER OF DREAMS

Let me give you thoughts to cling to
beyond your wildest schemes.
The pictures I paint I will bring you . . .
I am the weaver of dreams.

Close your eyes and come away
we will ride on magic streams
through the portals of yesterday . . .
For I, am the weaver of dreams.

I will take you beyond all mortal care
to the place where fate it seems
claims the soul of all who are there . . .
For I, am the weaver of dreams.

Clyde L. Schultz

RESTITUTION

It was your days
And now it's my nights

It was your feelings
And now it's my desires

It was your fate
And now it's my happiness

It was your tears
And now it's my anxiety

It was your words
And now it's my act

All these are my desires
And it's your restitution

Miguel Barreto

MIGUEL BARRETO. Pen Name: Mike; Born: Goa, India, 9-23-56; Married: Miguelinha Rebelo, 1-11-83; Education: Graduate in 1975; Occupation: Refrigeration mechanic; Awards: First prize for 'Our Principal,' India, 1972; Poetry: 'Sacrifice,' 1983, 'Freedom & Rights,' 1985, *Arab Times Focus,* Kuwait; Other Writings: 'Life Is An Art and Humans Are Artist,' 'What Is Love,' articles, *The Workers Friend,* India, 1983; Comments: *I have written most of my work in Konknni and then I have translated it into English. Konknni is one of the Indian official languages and it's my mother tongue. Through this art I can express a lot of feelings and emotions to others. My pen is an art and I am an artist of my pen.*

EXPECTATIONS

The tides that take all fools to sea
with their dreams in empty hands,
are fools like me just waiting to be
lost on heartbreak strand.

A million dreams are left behind
when the winds of hope have failed
to blow away the mist to find
their ship has already sailed.

A million footprints along the shore
of the lost and lonely ones.
Soon there will be a million more
before the mist is done.

As long as dreams are dreamed by man
and tides flow out to sea . . .
Some will be buried in heartbreak sand
on that beach we failed to see.

Clyde L. Schultz

THE GARDEN GATE

Just this side of the garden gate
we met when hearts were young . . .
and birds in finest voices sang
of a love so young and strong.

Just beyond the garden gate
the wild flowers grow . . .
and fill the air with sweet perfume
in morning's early dawn.

You went first through the garden gate
then turned to wait for me . . .
with outstretched hand and smiling face;
welcoming me to that perfect place.

Just beyond the garden gate
my true love waits for me . . .
hand in hand we'll stroll once more
. . . through all eternity.

Nancy J. Wheeler

NANCY J. WHEELER. Pen Name: Nancy J. Weideman Wheeler; Born: Missoula, Montana, 4-22-45; Married: Kermit L. Wheeler, 5-22-62; Education: Clinton Elementary, Missoula County High; Occupations: Domestic engineer; Office secretary; Author; Poet; Poetry: 'Requeim of a Mountain Man,' *Montana Logging Association,* March, 1987; Comments: *I like to use feelings pertaining to my own personal experiences in my writing. Many of the poems I have written are of my children, husband or friends. The passing away of my father, Henry Weideman, has been a very strong influence. I was born the youngest of five children in a small farming community in southwestern Montana. I met my husband in 1960 and we were married 5/26/62. We have three grown children and four grandchildren. The love they have for each other has been a foundation for much of the poetry I have written. The support of family and friends has helped me to keep my faith in my own talents. Through poetry I am able to convey the feelings that cannot otherwise be conveyed*

TRUTH

Truth is not always as I perceive,
Events not conclusive as I believe,
Results not effective as I conceive,
But, I must persist, and always will,
That time, faith, and works do instill,
That truth will prevail and right fulfill.

William W. Dillinger

DOESN'T ANYONE GO TO WISCONSIN?

They tell of trekking in Nepal,
and trips down the Amazon they glorify;
the beauties of Antarctica they extol,
and the expanses of Siberia they magnify.

No one cries of having visited Madison;
only trips down the Orinoco they dignify
while cruises down the Mississippi merely nullify;
of Shanghai they exclaim, not Prairie du Chien.

With stories of Macchu Picchu they torment
those who saw Milwaukee
and of Lake Baikalin distant lands they comment
while no one whispers of Lake Michigan.

Of great expanse and equal discomfort in Bangladesh
or peering at the beggars of Calcutta they lament;
of Cape Horn to Lapland they are eloquent,
but no one need speak of Green Bay, Wisconsin.

Nancy Hoekstra

Life flares
    we meet
        and each is changed

So too,
    do any two atoms
    or any two stars
    or any two galaxies
    or even
        any two people
        if
        they are close enough
        one
        to the other

Somewhere
Somehow
    part of all that is
    are you and I
and sometimes,
    wondering,
        we contemplate our brethren . . .
            . . . the galaxies . . .

Robert J. Thompson

NOAH BUILT A BOAT

Noah's life would change when the Lord spoke,
He said, ''Noah, I need you to build a boat.

''The boat will become a floating zoo,
As you must gather my animals two by two.

''The people of the world will think you strange,
But ask them to join you and follow my name.

''When they won't follow just close the door,
For there is forty days of rain in store.

''Noah you will then need to repopulate the land,
For man will have another chance for this is God's plan.''

Ed Freel

NEAR-DEATH

I remember the first time I smelled it;
the awful, rotting stench of near-death.
I was across town, in the rat district
where my people never go —
among filthy, sordid hovels where immigrants are shelved.
The stench of near-death made me retch
and I hurried home to my haven of self-deceit.
(That was many years ago; it's worse now.)

I remember, more recently, those nights I spent in hospitals;
A neighbor, a child, my mother, grandmother, and my aunt
entered one by one, all near death, some nearer than others,
though none quite touched it.
They try to cover the stench in those places
with germicides and antiseptic words.
The germicides don't help much.

Yesterday I gave half my sandwich
to a boy who had wandered in from the rat district.
Today he shriveled away and they swept him under the carpet.

The stench of near-death is worse
than that of death itself.

Bradley Cook

THE BENT-OVER LADY

The bent-over, bent-over, bent-over lady,
Where did you come from? Nobody knows!
The bent-over, bent-over, bent-over lady,
Where are you going? Home, I suppose.
Were you always bent over? Did you always look like that?
I wonder if you were born with a hump on your back?

The bent-over, bent-over, bent-over lady,
Pulling your cart as you go down the street.
The bent-over, bent-over, bent-over lady,
Sees nobody's faces, only their feet.
When you sit down and lean back in a chair
Can you lift up your face and look up in the air?

The bent-over, bent-over, bent-over lady
Trudges along and goes out of sight.
The bent-over, bent-over, bent-over lady,
Will I see you tomorrow? Hope so, good-night.

Phyllis C. Conable

NIGHT VISITOR

White Moth

One evening in spring a visitor dropped in.
His wings still tremulous and new to night,
he wore the down the newborn wear. All else
except his shaky state proclaimed him prince
of airy realms: ermine of cap and collar,
fit of white velvet beneath, and over all
the satin of his spreading cape, glistening
like ice and spangled with miniature black stars.
On his breast gleamed the red ribbon of state.
A paradox: an exquisite of frost
and snow, this dazzling fair from night so dark.
Bright messenger! What message did you bring
from darkness for the aching heart to hold?
Some thing about where you're from, or why . . .
Did you not come to say that the message remains
although the winged messenger must go?

Anne Kelly

THIRD WATCH

In the third watch
When a night wind blows
Gentle in a sky glistening
With stars
I wake
And waking remember

In those moments
Alone in the quiet dark
I remember what I've
Never known
Never dreamed
My flesh recalls

Randall David Miles

A DREAM IN MAY

I dreamt last night
That it had snowed
Winter was come again
To stay till spring thaws

The candle flickered
In a cold draught
Guttering with a smell of beeswax

Randall David Miles

PATRICIA

I saw her eyes of hazel hue
That blended with a sky of blue
Glancing also was a soft sweet face
Set on figure tall yet with grace
Her hair was a halo of light
That crowned that figure tall
Yet exquisitely gowned
A lovely creature I thought I'd woo
And the wonder of it is, she loves me too.

James Cersosimo

WHAT IS SUCCESS?

Living a life you want to live,
Giving the gift you want to give,
Saying the words you ought to say,
Helping someone to find their way,
Seeing those things that you should heed,
Filling the void in others' need.

THAT is success.

William W. Dillinger

FLOWERING SEED

Love is like a flower,
  it blossoms when it grows.
Sunshine and a gentle touch,
  can nourish a lonely rose.

When you're feeling droopy,
  afraid to make a start.
Fertilize that tender seed,
  which is planted in your heart.

Gather all the raindrops,
  overcome what you fear.
You can rise above the earth,
  gain strength with every tear.

Open your petals to everyone,
  spread pollen wherever you go.
By doing so, it may rub off,
  on whoever is willing to grow.

Pam J. Kleinwachter

MY LITTLE ANGEL

At night when I am all alone,
  attempting to get some sleep.
An angel climbs up, at my side,
  and rarely makes a peep.

No matter if I wiggle or squirm,
  or rise within the night.
He always stays at my side,
  and keeps me in his sight.

When I'm off my schedule,
  he always seems to know.
Patiently, he waits for me,
  but loves me even though.

When I'm busy, and he's ignored,
  it fills me with much guilt.
I apologize, and scratch his back,
  my poor little angel Wilt.

He listens when he's spoken to,
  understands, no matter what.
This angel is a loyal companion,
  my precious little mutt!

Pam J. Kleinwachter

IN THE PARK

Pale and secret as a bird's egg
Is the lake in the park;
Left by nursemaids and children
In the path of the stumbling dark.

Slipping ahead of the darkness,
Pungent with vapors of spring,
Fog hastens to hide the lake
With a dripping smoke-blue wing.

Florence Lonsford

END OF THE DAY

Sudden and cold
  Is the end of the day
When time puts her scissors of tension away;
  And home, home, home go we.

Dusk is a slouch
  With wind at his heel,
Hedgerows are knitting with needles of steel;
  As home, home, home go we.

Fields in half-light
  Are pools of white roses,
Bushes are cows with icicle noses;
  When home, home, home go we.

Footsteps are tinsel
  Unwound to our door;
We've eaten the day to its small golden core,
  And home, home, home are we.

Florence Lonsford

GRANPA'S QUANDARY

Searching thoughts scorch the
by-ways of my brain

As the emotions of loved one's
parting seeks relief.

Sounds of presence — silent —
yet echoing on the drum.

Taunts-n-Tears-n-Tales-n-Teachings
no longer measuring the mettle of
my dreams.

Emptiness replacing full —
as death replaces life —

John R. Chiesa

JOHN R. CHIESA. Born: Chicago, Illinois, 7-6-24; Married: Frances, 1-22-48; Education: B.A., M.S.; Occupations: I have worked professionally in many areas and in many occupations; Poetry: 'Indelible,' 'Gifts,' 'Am,' 'Commitment,' all 1987; Other Writing: ''Battle of the Boudoir,'' essay; Comments: *In recognizing all of the things it is to be man, it allows us to know what it must be to be GOD!*

GOD IS OUR REFUGE

A paraphrase of Psalm 91, from the book:
Praise the Lord with Psalms, Metrical
Paraphrases of Selected Psalms, *by*
Laura Brown Lane, Vantage Press, 1986.

He that dwelleth in the secret place of God,
Shall live beneath the shadow of the Lord.
The Lord my fortress and my refuge is,
He is my God, so I will trust in Him.
Yea, with His feathers shall He cover thee,
And underneath His wings shalt thou have trust.
His truth shall be thy buckler and thy shield.
Thou shalt not fear the terror of the night,
And not the arrow that shall fly by day,
And not the plague that walketh in the dark,
And not destruction that doth waste at noon.
And though a thousand at thy side shall fall,
And e'en ten thousand at thy right shall fall,
Behold, it shall not nigh unto thee come —
For only with thine eyes shalt thou behold
And see the doom the wicked shall receive.
Because thou hast made God thy dwelling place,
There shall no evil come nigh unto thee.
For God shall have His angels guarding thee —
In all thy ways His angels shall keep thee.

Laura Brown Lane

A FOOL ALONE

I stand beside a running brook,
  like pages from a long forgotten book.

The time of day is half past ten.
  I dream of places I have never been.

The waters at my feet form a pool,
  and reflect a portrait of a fool.

I hear an owl in a far-off tree.
  He is asking who, who, who are thee.

The love I have I wish to share.
  The pain in my heart is too great to bear.

I shall end this lovesick poem with a sad
  and bittersweet tone:
Here stand I a fool alone.

John R. Lenzä

THE WINDOW

We strive and think of things that are new, but
are mired in the past and what we learned are few.

Through a window one day a shadow appeared, I felt
puzzled and trembled as it neared.

Some things I knew not entered my mind, I moved
forward and ventured to see what I could find.

I opened the window as swift as I might, with a
great burst of joy *The Shadow Was Light*

James Cersosimo

ONLY IF I COULD SING

I don't know what brought me alone,
but I know it has to be a very beautiful song.
If I could sing, I would sing about us.
How our love is built upon honesty and trust.
It is mellow and so sweet.
The relationship we have is beautiful and unique.
If I can write a song, this is how it'll go.
Soft, smooth, mellow and slow.
I'll write about two young people who are in love.
And their future that they always dreamed of.
The love that they have for each other.
Based on loving and caring for one another.
The love that they have within their heart,
that no one can ever tear these two apart.
Their love which is so deep,
that they are so happy that they always weep.
When the tears stop, love has grown.
Soon, their wedding would be known.
It may be three years or even four,
but by that time, their love would have grown some more.

Wanda T. Sanders

THE SIDE OF MERCY

Open thine eyes; you must awake, my son.
  Through yonder window heaven's light still streams
To guide thy way for work still much undone.

And things sad at least to me it seems
  Are so because of deep and wintry fear
Of frightening thoughts and foreboding dreams.

Thou cannot let dark gloom feed that bursting tear
  Or reddened face or purple heart prevail
Because there is a now and there is a here.

Or else all we do will only fail.
  Without strength of heart and single mind
Life is cold and black and deathly pale.

Oppose injustice hard of every kind,
  To fight it firm and surrender not
A single step lest we find

That we condone the wrong and preserve the rot
  To spread decay and greed and lies
And ruin the innocent of the lot.

Be on the side of mercy, it will serve you well
And leave the sinner in the sinner's hell.

G. C. Vezzoli

TEARS

The sorrow in a mother's heart,
is measured by her tears.
Clump them altogether —
and soon a pool appears.
The tears of joy a child brings —
oft create a little spring.
There, between the bad and good —
in her boat sits motherhood.
Tossed ashore on shifting sands,
firmly holding each child's hand.
When oars and sails go amuck,
she smiles and says, "It's all
just luck, of one kind or another."
That's why we're waterproof, you see,
because a mother has to be.

Grace Frigo

YOU

The flowing waters.
In it, is your reflection.
Peace and calm always.

Leslie Mellgren

THE YEAR

Day by day and week by week
A few more months and another is complete
One day at a time we live and cry
Happy times bring a joyful sigh
The weather turns cold as it comes to an end
We prepare ourselves to live it again.

Brian Pierce

Man — a creature vain enough to think
He can soar through the air
Like the gull, or sail
Across the seas like the whale.

Not only is man vain,
But he is also persistent.
For he does these things —
The great copycat.

His cities dot the earth
Like giant anthills, and he has cut
The earth into ribbons. Now,
He is murdering the creatures he has copied.

Soon, man will be omniscient.
There will not be a bird left to fly
Or a fish to swim.
Only sludgepiles will be left, and concrete.

Gregory Price

PRAYER OF SALVATION

Standing there
Bronze and bare
Shoulders graced
With jet black hair

From toe to thigh
To head held high
Arms outstretched
Toward the sky

Dark and dancing
Eyes enhancing
Inner strength
Now advancing

From the past
Across the vast
Expanse of time
His prayer is cast

Native son
With nature one
Speaks to those
Whose life is done

Kathleen Rose Sanciprian

POSSESSED

I am writer
unrecognized
save me from going mad
I am writer
obsessed with words
living on insanity's edge
I am writer
a tormented soul
confined
self-imposed
behind closed doors
demons rampant in my head
some alive
others dead
a pen
a typewriter sets them free
For God's Sake
exorcise
the
writer
me

Patricia S. Talton

LITTLE BIRD

Little bird high in the sky,
how does it feel to be alive?
What is it you see
with your naked eye?
Little bird, how I cry
because you're so innocent
in a world of time.

Janet Zobenica

THIS LAND

This land which I love and call mine
Stretches across a continent
Just like a majestic carpet
Closely hugged by someone divine!

It lies still and mute, yet so active
Providing the nation with food
Giving all the trees a firm root
There isn't anything it wouldn't give!

This land is for eternity.
An America with greatness
Of mind and heart; setting a pace,
Blessed with grace and humility!

Generations to come will profess:
This land always has a happy face!

Harry Wang

AT EASE

Late Twentieth Century America

Each generation sees the world
    With its own set of eyes.
Mine . . . through television screen
    From king-size beds
All propped up in pillows.
    "Comfortable," I surmise.

Each generation seeks the laurels
    With its quests from the heart.
Mine . . . through the entertainment scene
    From La-Z-Boy easy chairs
Playing the games of ball with feet raised high.
    "Passive," I remark.

Each generation leaves the gifts
    With its symbols from the soul.
Mine . . . through high-tech fulfilled dreams
    From pushing buttons
On objects, panels and walls.
    "Convenient," I submit, "But cold!"

J. Jones

Every petal on every rose,
In every garden that sunshine grows,
These are thoughts I think of you,
'Tween time we part and touch renewed.

Alone in thoughts so bittersweet,
Again, my love, I wish to meet,
To share our love and joy that grows,
As the petal on the rose.

Robert Vanderbrugen

MEMORIES OF OUR CHILDHOOD

Sometimes the years seem to pass so fast,
memories are all that're left of the past.
It doesn't seem like that long ago,
that we were pals in both heat and snow.
Remember the time the horse chased you around the tree,
yes I was laughing because he wasn't chasing me.
Don't forget the time we worked so hard making a raft,
we took it to the river, and as it sank we laughed.
We loved to go sledding in all kinds of weather,
then go home and have hot chocolate and cookies together.
Remember dressing up in old dresses and high heels,
and going biking, and hiking, and taking our meals.
Oh and the fun we had on fallen trees in the yard,
making huts and hitching horses, with our imagination it wasn't hard.
Once we even held a yard carnival with games, tickets, and all,
it wasn't anything fancy, but everyone had a ball.
Time seems to change us and separate friends, you see,
but we've always stuck together, yes you and me.
Memories of the past, this was only to name a few,
I can think of many more and you probably can too.

Crystal Woltman

FORSAKEN

Don't let anyone fool you just to get you on
the outside. The pleasures may be plentiful.
The happiness might be great. But if you lose
out, it will be too late.
For example: A pretty green field of grass in
comparison to one that is not so green, but has
been scorched due to lack of tender loving concern.
Everybody loves a winner, something beautiful
is to be admired. To water that green field,
were you hired? No, you volunteered. Instead
your home is the field that survives, not so
beautiful in everyone's eyes. So you abandon
your home, the grass needs water, you say,
"leave me alone! I've got something else to
do today, I'm going this way." There sits the
green field. Someone else is watering today.
You go back home, kick the grass, it weeps and
withers. Today my friend you're off again, forgetting
the ground you had to stand on to get where
you're going. Slowly, the grass fades away more
rapidly each day.

Valerie Whitfield

MEDITATION

We meet many people along life's road
And lasting impressions of some, we hold
Some we regret we ever met, but what do we know
    of the stress
Within that figure we so distrust? Not to judge
    is best.
Was there some struggle long past, and no one
    to help or guide?
None to encourage or lend a hand, none to
    take their side?
Can we justly condemn, or would we not be
    the same
As people along life's road, that we're so
    ready to blame?

Frances E. Woodard

PURPLE SHADES

The misty morn of
            lavender blue
The shade of
            orchids too
The purple of
            violet hill
The lilac flowers
            I remember still.
A streak of purple
            in the sky
A purple dot
            on a butterfly
A purple moon
A mauve lagoon
And the purple
            hours that end too soon
Purple nights and
            purple days
How picturesque
            are *purple shades* . . .

Alice Folus

ALICE CAMMILA FOLUS. Born: Schenectady, New York; Education: Art Student; Occupation: Designer; Memberships: Catholic Education System, teaching 3rd grade religion; Awards: Certificate of Merit for Outstanding Lyrics, *Before He Died*, Chapel Recording Company, 1987; Poetry: 'Yellow Buttercups,' 1986; 'Summer's Last Roses,' poetry and artwork, 1986; 'Black, White & Gray,' 1986; 'The Dream of a Little Girl,' *The Tender Passion*, 1986; Other Writings: *Alice Where Are You?* children's book, Vantage Press, 1984; Themes: *Reflections, nature, colors, love and religion*; Comments: *I write short stories, and I am currently working on new poems and books. Poetry comes naturally to me. I love writing.*

BELOVED TYRANT

Agonized miaous on midsummer's day
            Summoned us —
Iron paws in silken gloves now rule our house
        She the beautiful tyrant
        We her valets and serfs
        Her caprices our commands
        Her lithe and supple body
            Cloaks a dictator
    More onerous than Simon Legree
        Her purrs and licks and kisses
    Mightier than a cat-o'-nine-tails
Her love more girding than ball and chain
        Succumb to cats' advances
            Become their docile slave
    Exalting God's image within our souls
    They're brothers and sisters for life.

Dorothea Wirth

MAKING HAY.

OF ONE ACCORD

The sky
Wears turquoise gown
And milk white camellia blooms,
The sun sends gold, no glooms
Haunt this day down
From high

For now
The sickles wait
With tempered steel to sound
The harvest all around,
"No man come late!"
The vow.

How grand!
The state of sky.
The sun, the sickle, man
(A part of His great plan)
Lays harvest bye
On land.

Lilibel Pazoureck-Lucy

LILIBEL PAZOURECK-LUCY. Born: Yukon, Oklahoma; Widowed; Education: B.A., M.A.; Occupation: Teacher; Memberships: N.E.A., O.E.A.; Awards: 20 poems or more have been published, 13 radio plays used in Oklahoma City schools; Poetry: 'Psychopathic,' 'Cycle,' 'On Looking Up,' 'Forsythia,' 'Buoyancy'; Themes: *My country, people, nature, my child, pets, war*; Comments: *Life is a marvelous revelation, sometimes sad, but never boring.*

MY HIDEAWAY

My sewing room is my hideaway,
It's there I find something to do every day.
There's mending to do and beads to string,
With separate tables for everything.
There's squares for quilt tops, and yarn for crochet,
A quilt in the making, for a babe on the way.
There's bracelets and chokers, from bright colored beads
Pictures from butterflies, dried flowers and seeds.
I make little clowns, and monkeys from socks,
Christmas tree angels, and hand-painted rocks.
When I've worked a good while on one certain thing,
I put it aside, and crochet a ring.
In the middle of each I fasten a pearl,
That makes a nice gift for a dear little girl.
I make pretty wreaths to hang on the door,
And I crochet rugs to put on the floor.
There's so many things I have lined up to do,
I will have to live to be a hundred and two.

Doris Bowman Johnson

ALOHA, BAGHIRA!

Onto my breast you hop flexing claws
My skin you knead drawing blood
Pain piercing — I try to relax
Knowing you mean "I love you!"
Caressing you my fingers tingle
Your purrs vibrating through me
We're welded in one single purr
I stroke your smooth and silky fur
Your back, your sides, your tummy
Your firm and round and bony skull
I rub your throat and tickle your chin
Massage your ears and kiss your brow
How soft and velvety calm you feel
When with sated sighs you fall asleep
Completely still but oh so warm
And sleek and sweet and furry
Oh how I crave your vibrant purring weight!
How my arms ache to hold you once again
But you are dead.

Dorothea Wirth

TAKE A SECOND GLANCE

take a second glance at the blue the sky does hold
just for the pleasure of your eyes
yes and it's true to this very day
with the blue in your heart and all that you hold for the sky

take a second glance at the wind that can spray
from a magic of a source unknown
like a lover may fly on the wings of wind
only then get a glance at its secrets shown

take a second glance at your twilight side
that for everyone holds a twinkle inside
yes it can spread just like a passion
rising, rising just like the tides

take a second glance at that stranger who went past
who would with life in love finally come to fall
leaving only his poems to last
maybe not a stranger at all

take a second glance at the oceans of miracles
for our eyes born to see from the start
learn to unfold on the wings of perception
these secrets many they dwell in our hearts

Daniel Thomas Carr

DAY AND NIGHT

Golden sunlight whispers in through the curtains,
A honeyed sunrise sweeping away the bitter hemlock
Of last night's nightmares in the darkness.
Snatches of words spoken to us; people;
Scenery — all are distorted in disturbing
Sequences in night dreams.
We writhe under the grip of the
Hideous nightmare
And shudder into wakefulness.
But it is a blessing to open the eye
On the day, in safety.
The only thing we then fear
Is plunging over a precipice
Into a real nightmare
From which one never emerges.

Lisa Mesaros

LAST WISH

Please don't bury me beneath the sod,
I want to be where heavenly angels trod.

Not in the cold, damp dark,
But flying in heaven with a lark.

Don't come mourn at a grassy plot,
For there in the deep dark I am not.

I am spirit, free as the clouds,
Mingling with mortals, when allowed.

My heavenly home is among the spheres,
So, come be joyful with me, no tears.

Zelia Payne

I SEE GOD

In the symmetry of a gull's wing . . .
In the trust of a doe's brown eye . . .
In the patience of a waiting seed . . .
In the natal convex curve . . .
In the child's guiding hand . . .
In the ancient's steady tread . . .
In the constant arch of heaven . . .
In the ceaseless ocean's roll . . .
In the human heart and soul . . .
I see God in me.

Zelia Payne

BETTER AND LASTING

Because we're older the spark
    is gone?
Who dares to bring a sunset to
    our dawn?
When love was new and every look
    and move became desire,
Never did we dream those looks
    and moves
Someday would retire to a love
    of a far better kind,
Of tenderness, and loyalty, born
    of adversity.
Who dares to say the spark
    is gone?

Frances E. Woodard

A GOD'S EYE

No one is ever Alone
Because they Possess
Their very own
An eternal inner Light
Of Happiness.

Sharon Derrico

HIDE YOUR EYES

Hide your eyes from me, my Man.
Hide your eyes from me?
I can still see the hate and anger
you have inside for me.
I'm astonished that you loved me enough,
To feel such hatred for me now.
Ironically, you are justified
    as you know things to be,
But I want to tell you the truth,
    rather, the whole story,
Just to see you free.
Hide your eyes from me, my Man.
Hide your eyes from me.
That way you can't see the sorrow,
    within my own, lest the hell that
        I've been through.
But, this very moment,
I'm just thinking of you.
Let's not hide our eyes from each other;
Maybe then, we can see it through.

Sharon Derrico

BLESSED SORROW

Accept sorrow, drink her deep and long.
Reject sorrow, and she will scald you,
But her nourishment makes strong.

Sorrow's melody is unwelcome at twilight song,
She visits unexpectedly in winter's blue.
Accept sorrow, drink her deep and long.

Her false illusion looks hurtful and wrong,
For she pierces the depths
    of our souls with rue.
But her nourishment makes strong.

Dwell on her goodness at dawn.
She offers armloads of blessings and truths,
Accept sorrow, drink her deep and long.

Glistening where brilliant diamonds belong
As they sparkle in your heart imbued.
Her nourishment makes strong.

Humility, patience, character, compassion,
She cleanses you to burn for God renewed.
Accept sorrow, drink her deep and long,
Her nourishment makes strong.

Colleen Koerner

MY TRUE LOVE

    Keep him close, girl,
for you have found your true love.
Like roses are red, so flows the
passion in your blood for each other.
Like the sun shining on you and him,
being with each other is rarer than old
wine, for there flows a greater love
between you two; just as time sometimes
stops when you look into the eyes of your
true love, *forever* is your true destiny.

Carmelita Douglas

THE SILVER-LINED GLOVE

When you're tired and lonely
remember God's up
above, washing your
tears away and drying
them with silver-lined gloves.

When you're tired and lonely
look for guidance from above
and sunshine comes in
buckets from the heavenly
stars above.
Just turn on the key to
the unlocked mystery.

When you're tired and lonely
remember God's up above
and talks to all with
His love.

Debra Sykes

WORKING DADDY

    Tired, dirty and sore, he comes in
through the door.
    Our baby runs, pick me up, but
daddy is tired, dirty and sore.
    He's been working all day long
down at the factory.
    He goes to momma, kisses on
her lips, he's not too romantic,
just hungry, tired, dirty and sore.
    Little sister tries to talk,
momma broke a cup, daddy.
    She's sometimes a klutz, food
is on the table,
    Tired, dirty and sore, he
bows his head to the Lord.
    Tired, Dirty and Sore.

Debra Sykes

GOLDEN SPHERE

The music and a special dance,
Taught this girl there's just one chance,
For happiness this day forth,
And how much love is actually worth,
For love cannot be stolen or bought,
Now she knew, she had been taught,
Love is a gift, a blessed thing,
It takes the shape of a ring,
No beginning and no end,
Always loving, not a bend,
She had found her one true love,
To her he came the message of,
A small white dove from God's right hand,
He had in mind for them one plan,
For her to love and cherish him,
For him to soothe her, like the wind,
For love is all they both now knew,
And into one they grow from two.

S. A. Christianson

A NEW ENGLAND COVERED BRIDGE IN SUMMERTIME

It's nice to walk and think and dream
    Near the covered bridge that spans the stream
Where people come to swim below,
    At the foot of where white waters flow.
But there's another reason I think I know
    Why folks have come here since long ago.

The covered bridge is, I think,
    One of those things that are a link;
Perhaps that's what the poets are
    When in a blade of grass they see a star,
Or the hand of God's reassuring force
    Sheltering us all when it's time to cross.

Much of life is linking things:
    Sunbeams and gardens and what loving brings.
And it doesn't matter what we call
    The mainstream link that binds it all,
Because only we need a harmony mild,
    Like the blend of bridge and flora wild.
Where other "bridges" lead is not here to say,
    So we walk this one now, linking life today.

G. C. Vezzoli

ORANGE TOWNS

All the vacant lots on Main Streets
Have "Now Leasing" signs.

Jojo's working at a bowling alley food stand
To feed Maria's immaculate love.

The helicopter base's been going
13 hours strong,
And the pretty Midwestern boys
Want to raise some hell to forget.

And everybody's got a ghost to feed
Or a couple of ghosts
Or alimony penance
Just for being too young to know an alternative.

The Steely Man's
Afraid to face Ophelia
Knowing she might
Strike the chord
Too sweet to lose.

Pedestrian lovers use caution as a gift.

I know a place
Where friendship spreads by those who have
Bright, clear eyes and faces
And the sound of thundering Bruce
Cuts deep through the cigarette fog.

Paula Jayne Brown

A MORNING WALK — AND MEMORIES

An early morning, misting rain
Yielding to a clearing sky, a promising rainbow.
A morning walk along the beach
Melts my heart with memories time has not yet blurred:
I see her face, fixed and still
Her nose is narrow, red in the cold
A tear slides down the side of her face
She brushes it away, securing a strand of blonde hair behind her ear
Her eyes are wide open, as blue as the crystal sky above
Her pink polo shirt shows from beneath her sweatshirt at the neck
The line of her jaw is taut, the skin close to the bone
Even now there is a gentleness about her
Goodbye, she says, it's for the best.
My morning walk turns to a jog, my heart beats faster with every step
The early morning rain begins again, the promising rainbow fades.
Why must the rain
Last so much longer than
The rainbow?

C. E. Edmonson

FROM THE STABLE TO THE CROSS

Our Lord was born in the stable
yet He died on the cross:
so that everyone would be able
to repent and not be lost.
    His bed was made of hay, His
garment with swallowen clothes.
He was light that shines brighter
than day, through the stable door.
    Sister Mary smiled as she looked
on Her son, brother Joseph he did,
too! Eternal Life had just begun
through our Lord Jesus so true.
    He gave his life, up on the
cross He died, for you and me.
He died that the world might
not be lost to set the sinner
free.

Gennie Graham

BETRAYAL

An endless stretch of warm evenings ahead
reminds me of the fate I dread.
The sound of laughter pricks my heart,
        but after the drops of blood
                fill my well,
                I may start.
Others read and smirk
as hidden lesions form,
and tormenting spasms
rip my soul apart.

I stretch and twist within my mind.

I search for relief in someone to trust and find
that no soul before me hath been quite so blind.

Billie J. Watson

JUST SAY "YES"

Life is different now.
It has no meaning.
Never thought things
Could be so worthless.
They say love hurts — it's true.

Trying to forget but . . .
Good memories don't die.
Wishing to be with you but . . .
False hopes are only lies.

You were once my joy
My entire life
Now I am nothing
Without you.

Failure is my weak spot, so
Let's make things work.
Obviously, I want to, but
Now it's up to you
It's all up to you.
Regrets won't cross your mind so . . .
Just say "Yes!"

Dana Conque

TEEN SEX

In the movies it's always easy,
It's laughter, sex, and love;
Not necessarily in that order,
But one way or another
Everything is safe and fun.
But now
Love is what I feel;
Romantic nerves are stirred,
Hearts begin to flutter
And bodies become unnerved.
Your first time is a special time,
And special is tonight;
For I have made my choice and
Tonight is yours and mine.
Tonight it is no movie,
No flashing fame or fortune;
Tonight belongs to you and me
While our lives hang in the balance.

Elizabeth Gómez

MAN'S SEARCH FOR GOD

Mankind throughout the ages
  Has searched and has found
New pathways through yonder skies.
  Yet there is a space *in* yonder skies
That is hidden from earthly eyes.

There is indeed a God somewhere
  Not seen by the human eye.
Yet through our faith and love for him
  We will see him by and by.

The Mists are heavy between earth and the sky
  And we cannot break them apart.
Yet man will search eternally
  Then find God is there in his heart.

Ethel Marquardt

YOU CAME TO ME

You came to me and took my hand,
and I was afraid.
You showed me a life I never knew
existed and I asked no questions.
You gave me hope and strength,
and you asked for nothing.
You made me laugh and smile,
you were my friend.
You became my love!
You became my life!
But most of all you are my dream!
You know who you are!

Cyndi Mood

AND NOW, WE SEE

That which is real, try you won't feel,
Pain of the heart, try you won't heal,
Sometimes you talk of spreading your wings,
But dreams of the mind are such endless things.

Yet onward you go, to see where you are,
Not looking back, not going far,
Just when you feel, you are going somewhere,
You're still slipping down, gasping for air.

Now time is short, for all is for naught,
And still you can't see what ignorance wrought,
So go on and see whatever you can,
But see not you will, till life's race you've ran.

P. J. Parker

ALONE TOGETHER

Did you know
There's a place where the
          Jojola rolls
Up, down,
      all around,
Just a man who's alone,
He takes what he can,
Goes where he wants,
By himself,
      where no one
          messes with his mind.
He's got nowhere to go,
Forever is a lot of time,
He lives only to me,
He travels the roads in my memory,
Then comes to me at night
          in my dreams.
He comes in and he goes,
In his wake he leaves his pain,
He's always here but he never stays,
He's just a ghost of the man I loved,
He is all the time
          I've lost.

Monica B. Strohmyer

SONNET #7

Mine eyes did see a big black bird today
And when it saw a bird of its own kind
It lifted its black wings and flew away
To tell the other what was on his mind.

Then up they fly o'er mountains big and small
And here I stand watching these birds aghast.
I looked upon myself feeling so tall
The wind blew me a loud and sounding blast.

Then as the moon falleth upon the mount
The bird I saw flew on into the night
And with deaf ears I hear and I do count
The hour with which this bird had yet in flight.

With cold and wet I leave this mountain tall
And that black bird can never in me fall.

Evan Smith

LIFE'S EBB

Death, undecided,
reached and clawed
at my loved
one's door!
The seasons lingered
one by one
in deep despair —
Healing fought her
battle fierce,
but lost
as time's grotesque
mask leered out
at new
found hopes —
Tears dried —
My loved one, tired,
reached out —
Peace, yes peace,
came walking
through that door!

Fawn Crosby

SOLITAIRE

To God I cry with raging heart
Please make from me this fear depart

For I know not what lies ahead
Nor where nor when danger is spread

With someone I wish to walk
To laugh, to joke, to speak and talk

I watch the sun at the close of day
And think, dream, hope and pray

Yet my own soul is my closest friend

Craig S. Moore

PORTRAIT OF LOVE

If I were an artist I would paint
a picture not painted before.
For the thrill of love I would use restraint . . .
tender pastels that make the soul soar.

For the color of happiness bold and bright,
the shades of the rainbow's hue;
For romance I would paint, a moonlit night
in the deepest tones of blue.

For ecstasy, the blush of the peach;
For laughter, silver so bold;
For modesty I would have to reach
into the tints of delicate gold.

For the love of life and what it means,
I would make it all come true,
wrapped in shades of delicate greens . . .
My portrait of love for you.

Clyde L. Schultz

CLYDE Le ROY SCHULTZ. Pen Name: Lee Shannon; Born: Jefferson, Iowa; Married: Yvonne Jeanne; Education: Drake University, Des Moines, Iowa; Occupation: Retired Sergeant of Police, Los Angeles Police Department; Awards: Grand Prize, Edward A. Fallot Poetry Contest, 1984; California Golden Poet Award, 1985, 1986, 1987; Comments: *Write poetry that can be read and understood, poetry that comes from the heart, not the dictionary. Live beauty, think beauty, write beauty, remember your reader must understand what you are saying.*

GRANDMA ROSE

Grandma, Grandma Rose, where ya' goin'
   with that grip held tight in your hand?
I'se gon' to the depot, gotta hurry, gotta
   meet a man.

Grandma, Grandma Rose, where ya' goin'?
'Child, I can't talk long now, or I'll be late.
Got some ol' friends of mine a-waitin', a-waitin'
   on me, they're standin' at the gate.

Grandma, I don't see nobody, nobody nowhere.
'Child, the gospel train's a-ridin', and I've
   gotta get on board.

In days gon' by there was white horses an'
   chariots o' fire, from on high
To take the folks to the great by and by.
But, I'se got a train a-waitin' on me.
I'se gotta go now, quiet down, and let me be.

'Child, all's ya gotta do is trust in the Lord,
   and all the blessin's of God will be yose'.
I understand Grandma, I love you Grandma Rose.

Patricia A. Singletary

THE DEACON PRAYED

A deacon rose from the pew one morn', and began to say his prayers:

"Must Jesus bear His cross alone, and all the world go free?
God, I knows there's a cross for everyone, there's even a cross for me."

The congregation was visibly moved, as he continued with his prayer:

"Lord, I knows you have need of workers, to walk in wisdom's way.
I pray, for grace to guide us, to till the white fields today."

Someone said, "Thank you, sir," another cried, *Amen;*
The deacon kept on praying and said something about sin.

"God you sit high and you look low, the good we see,
But the evil in men you know."

A hush came over the congregation — not an *amen,* anywhere.
The deacon prayed on:

"Sin has tried to conquer us, to take us by the hand.
Lord, you knows, Satan is a mean, mean ol' man.
God, forgive us our many sins, our faults and our deeds.
Help us to overcome them, and supply our every need."

Yes Lord, yes Lord, was heard from those pews.
The deacon humbly turned and sat in the pew.
Child, didn't that deacon pray; some nodded their heads,
   some others said, *Whew!*

Patricia Singletary

PATRICIA ANN SINGLETARY. Pen Name: Pat; Born: Manhattan, New York, 3-3-48; Education: Manhattan Community College, 1978; State University of New York; Empire State College; New World Bible College and Seminary, B.Th., 1984, M.Re., 1986; Occupation: Minister; Memberships: National Association of Negro Business and Professional Women; National Association of Female Executives; Spiritual Life Commission of Clergywomen; National Corresponding Secretary, Interdenominational Board of Clergywomen; General Secretary, National Editor, *Ekklesia,* newsletter/magazine; Poetry: 'The Preacherwoman,' 'Burning Cross,' *New Voices in American Poetry, 1987.*

Pledge your love on a beach of white
Build me a castle in the darkest night
Make me promises — hold my hand
Let me hear the ocean thunder — feel the depth of the sand
Walk with me beside the bluest sea
Whispering love — make me believe
In your eyes I'll see the words so true
Hear my heart
I Love You

Amanda Rodriguez

MID-MARCH ON A MELLOW DAY

Mid-March on a mellow day,
the sun bright and warm,
snow in the woods
low enough to walk on
without sinking to my knees,
I veer from the roadside
with joyous heart,
once again under the canopy
of the great old trees.

Tired from my walk,
I lean against a sapling
clasping its barky form
in an impulsive embrace,
knitted cap a pillow for my cheek.

With face tilted toward the light
and eyes closed in quiet prayer
the wind-swayed tree rocks me,
ever so gently cradled in God.

Sharon M. Daley

SHARON MILLER DALEY. *I was raised in upstate New York in the foothills of the Adirondacks. There I've had an excellent opportunity to experience God in nature. As an American wife and mother, I feel a compelling responsibility to give something beneficial to my community, church, family, and society in general: through my daily activities as homemaker, piano teacher, church organist and avid student of the Bible, I seek to express in a quiet and loving way the values of the Christian faith, upon which I've centered my life. Through the art of poetry and the art of music, I've sought to reveal basic scriptural values and to elicit the guidance I need for my life.*

PEACEFUL FEELINGS

So quiet is the night
As I sleep away
Dreaming of wonderful things
And what may come someday
Peaceful bliss
And calm feelings
Carry me through the night
As though I were in heaven
It was such a peaceful flight
And then the morning comes
I awaken to the light
And see that it was just a dream
Although it was real last night . . .

Debra Crisamore

LOVE'S MEMENTO

How beautiful the lake can be,
If only you were here with me.
It is a sight to behold,
Upon a moonlit night
So clear, so cold!

You were like a breath of air,
So beautiful, so young, so fair.
Your eyes that sparkled like the dew,
With so much love
For those you knew.

Although my heart has suffered pain,
The beauty of the lake remains.
To me it is a part of you,
And it is here,
I'll think of you.

Violet W. Parrinello

CARNAGE

Sabra and Shatilla —
Just words that
circle the mystic path
within my brain —
Yet, Dena knows!
The horror is mirrored
in her dark, sad eyes,
veiled within her
draped, black chaddor —
A husband's body
lying still in death —
A mother; father; gone —
Buried deep within
the rubble of
dust and stone —
and a son,
where was he?
I try to grasp
her knowing!

Fawn Crosby

WALK ON

Linger
a little while
in joy —
With morning's hint
of color
watch a quiet
dawn unfold!
Recall fond memories —
Listen for twilight's song —
As evening's quickened
heartbeat calms,
walk on —
Tomorrow may hold
pleasures,
the quivering touch
of a lover's hand —
Or just beyond
the warm wind's kiss,
a baby's smile
may be the plan!

Fawn Crosby

A LOVER'S BALM

So much to give yet harnessed to right
No comfort is found in the dead of the night
Full of emotion under lock with no key
A frustrating condition in which to be

How long can the damn hold before it fails
To release the passion to faltering sails
Diluted by doubt and dispersed in a mist
Destruction of faith from the need to be kissed

A body so wanton from a need to fulfill
It's lustful yearnings that appear at their will
A hot burning fever leaves a throat dry of thirst
When a hint of a hope disappointed is worst

What can I do with this problem of mine
When just a touch would be divine
I wander around with my mind in eclipse
Craving the nectar from soft lips

To enliven my fantasy I need only you
Fermenting a lover's compassionate brew
Releasing my passions to ecstasy's calm
When the whole of my heart is in your palm . . .
    and my needs are soothed by a lover's balm

Pamela Gosnell

BOY OF 10

Uncombed hair,
Bare feet,
A toad.
Defiant look,
Top-secret code.

Eight tadpoles
Swimming in a jar.
A hug rebuffed,
A sudden kiss,
And a guitar.

Allene Haldy

I'LL BE A BUTTERFLY

I will not be a caterpillar
That creeps along the ground.
Not for me the earthy plot
To which his life is bound.

Instead I'll be a butterfly,
I'll spread my wings and glide
Across the fields, across the streams,
Throughout the countryside.

I'm not content with less than this,
When I know that if I try,
My life's reflection can become
Like a butterfly!

Far nicer to remember,
Far lovelier to see,
The shining metamorphosis
My very life will be!

Allene Haldy

IN A CHARIOT OF FIRE

In a chariot of fire
Riding the skies
I roll through the ages
And to me time is naught
It is the turning of my wheel
Still, save for worship, what am I
But a manifestation of nature
Indistinguishable amongst so many others
Then again, often I wonder
Is this imagination, nothing more,
No experience beyond my own
If so is my burning
My blinding radiance
Anything other than my will to
           self-sacrifice
For the salvation of those whom
           I created
That then being the justification
           of my existence

Randall David Miles

IN THE DAWN'S EARLY LIGHT

As I lie upon my bed, the white light of dawn
grows bright against the window shade.
Dimly aware of morning's little soft sounds
I drift in and out of sleep that fades.

As from above, I see the front of my body
open as a door from the right.
A figure comes striding from the misty fringe
His face covered by a veil and hidden from my sight.

Sitting down upon a throne
In the center of my empty being
Love flows from him to fill me
Happiness and joy flood my soul with singing.

Welcome, Lord Jesus.
I heard your knock
to enter today
into my heart.

Linda A. Byrum

A TRUE FRIEND IS HARD TO FIND

In a world full of people, who just don't truly care.
There you are all among them, I can feel their glaring stare.

When they face you filled with smiles, or they come to you upset.
You respond with all your whiles, or you help and then regret.

How can they want to take from you? Why would they even start?
You're warm and full of kindness, and from them so far apart.

Still they have no forseen reason, but to take what they can get.
Always thinking of themselves, but of you they'll soon forget.

When you think you have them figured out, your feelings rearranged.
Somehow they know you're on to them, all their actions seem deranged.

Still you're keeping up your guard, and them within your range.
For now they move so smoothly, and show how quick they change.

Even though you know what's going on, you let it just the same.
Because you're simply not like them, you play no trick or game.

Phyliss Estrada

LOSTING PRECIOUS MOMENT

With somebody who don't care about you and then losing all your
precious time around may be you never gonna be benefited from this
because going around saying this and that

But who knows what's gonna happen next, in the future, you've got to
give it a try and find out if you've been this lucky one but am gonna
keep on tryin', tryin'

If I really can overcome this idea and if I've been the lucky one
to stand in front then I'll show you all the gratitude that a man
should have — needing to be secure now even by you now

George Morrison

GEORGE E. MORRISON. Born: Black River, Saint Elizabeth, Jamaica, West Indies, 5-31-49; Married: Angella Swaby, 7-6-85; Occupation: Horticulturist; Poetry: 'It Gonna Be a Rainy Day.'

THE FOREST STANDS STILL

In Memory of the
Supervisor of Instruction

A tree has fallen,
A female tree.

The one with great spreading branches,
Ever reaching upward, outward and over;
The one that had leaves to spare for shade,
When burning sun tried to touch
Those on the ground beneath;
The one that stood smilingly steadfast in the wind,
Whose very trunk exemplified characteristics
By which others could be measured;
The one whose roots probed extended depths,
Signifying a way of life
Recognized far and wide,
As mighty and wonderful.

A tree has fallen,
A female supervising tree.

Her seedlings weep.
The forest stands still in her honor.

J. Jones

TURMOIL

Within me dwells a storm . . .
Caused by continual pain —
Thunder pounds at my brain —
Lightening strikes my heart —
Rain falls from my eyes —
For I cannot escape this hole . . .
The wind whips through my soul —
And the cold chills my every bone.

To be or not to be . . .
To love or not to love — you see —
O Lord — your greatest gifts . . .
Are also indeed . . . our greatest misery.
For to care — is to hurt . . .
Yet not to — no —
But to do so . . .
I am broken — scarred . . . and scared.

Monica Slowick

IS IT

A land of free speech —
Try speaking your mind.

A land of opportunity —
Try finding a job.

A land of equality —
Try finding an apartment.

A land of justice —
Be a victim of crime.

A land of freedom —
With nowhere to turn.

Monica Slowick

LITTLE THINGS

A flower or two
A few minutes here and there
Supper now and then
A bottle of wine from time to time
Or tell you I care for you now and then
It all boils down to one thing
I love you

George Irl Angell

THE WAIT

As days wear on
As you waited
For nine months you waited
Now that the time has come
Your reward is a new baby boy
With this new baby
May your hopes and dreams be fulfilled

George Irl Angell

GLIMPSES

Significance lies in the minute
Your sacred stares, luminous glow
Amber shimmers.

Sidelong gaze, the mystery in your eyes
Disturbs my acquiescence to isolation
Those singular moments.

Glimpses of possible paths, flapping
As a bayadere flag in the sun, the wind
In my heart.

Vincent Bertolino

CLOUDS

Thin wispy patterns of white
Or cotton fluffs on high,
Vapor trails or mottled bands
Show clear against the sky.

Before a storm the thunderheads
Pile up like swirled whipped cream.
Puffs of white on a dark flat base,
They promise rain, it seems.

Ever-changing clouds above
Are designs beyond our human art.
Their beauty and surprising shapes
Hold fast our eyes and touch our heart.

Hilde K. Didjurgis

GOOD-BYE

Your eyes
rain blue ice.

Still my fingers
burn to touch
the coolness
to my cheek.

Cynthia Farquhar

LOST DREAMS

There comes a time in people's lives,
When we must put away our dreams,
Those dreams that seemed so real back then,
Are now just magic scenes.

Our dreams are now just wisps of smoke
That spiral up and fade away.
It took too long to make them real,
So now, they've gone astray.

But we should never give up dreaming,
It is essential to our lives.
There are new goals that we must set,
And new dreams will arise.

So keep on dreaming, it's good for you.
It gives you something to look forward to.
Eventually, they will not be dreams,
But will be your life-long schemes.

Mickey M. Escobar

YOU CAME INTO MY LIFE

You came into my life
When I was feeling low
You came into my life
And made it all aglow

You are the one I need
For times ahead of me
Your love planted a seed
For all the world to see

I know I'll love you till
The stars no longer shine
'Cause I no longer feel
That love will not be mine

I know we will be one
'Cause it was meant to be
You are my shining sun
When tears have threatened me.

Mickey M. Escobar

THE SOUL OF MAN

The Soul of man's a fragile thing
So easily it breaks.
Pure strength of will can never hold it
If the head's not also straight.
Feelings cloud and twist the mind
Loose its hold on life.
The soul cuts loose and tries to run
And then begins the strife.
The heart is hollow, soul's adrift
The mind knows not what to do.
The more it tries, the worse things get
Without unity with the other two.
Finally, the deed is done
The straw that breaks the back.
The shattered soul, no hope for it
The heart still has great lack.
The soul of man's a fragile thing
So easily it breaks.
Once gone, it never heals aright
The tragedy's too great.

Jon S. Evans

RESPONSIBILITY

If it were not for me and responsibility,
 I would not be me.
 I would be . . .
Feathery bamboo whispering to the shady pool.
 I would be . . .
Hoyden, pixie, faery, nixie.
 I would be . . .
Tiny and brown, acorn just lying around.
 I would be . . .
Fiery, ferocious, humming hornet.
 I would be . . .
Hyacinth, fragrant, lavender, and dewey-eyed.
 I would be . . .
Croaking, pompous, knobby Mr. Toad.
 I would be . . .
Butterfly fluttering on blossoming bough.
 I would be . . .
Silky black cat on Halloween.
 What could I not be . . .
If it were not for me and responsibility!

Zelia Payne

TO MY LOVE

Every time I hear a waltz, I think of you.
Every time I hear a rumba, I could, too.
Every time the music swings, I just want to sing,
Wishing I had wings to fly straight to you.
See what thoughts of you do to me? I have
Visions of our dancing 'round a tree.
Treading on the village green,
With no shoes nor socks between.
Just a barefoot whirlygig, is what I mean!

Frances E. Woodard

AMERICA AND THE HARLOT

O' America, the harlot has lured you to her murky and webby chambers;
You have entered the vestibule unaware of hellish dangers.

Blind and laughing, you stumble in jeering and mocking your way;
Not counting the wages of sin, living for lusts of today.

The harlot now enters the room. ''Come in, my dear, and sit awhile;
You'll get used to the lovely gloom,'' she says with dripping smile.

''Behind these drapes are fun and games though it may sting a bit;
I'll wrap all your guilts and shames with misty clouds of ointment.

There's neon signs to light your way through streets which lead to fame;
Harlequin is here to say you have everything to gain.

Riches, power, mammon and gold; There's only one thing I require;
Promise Satan your eternal soul with blood-dipped pen blessed with fire.''

O' American, America, come out from her;
 Come out of the demon-filled night;
Loose from her sensual pleasure; Come back to the Glorious Light.

Remember Christ's soldiers of the past and the bloody road they trod;
O' America, stand fast! Stand fast in the name of Almighty God.

Marcine Bice

TRIBULATION

Bitter winds of tribulation laugh with morbid glee,
As they cut and sting the soul so mercilessly.

The searing rains of sorrow salt upon the wounds,
Till the ogre of despair vehemently looms.

But they shall not harm me with their awful skill,
For Jesus is the Master . . . He is the Master still.

(based on John 16:33)

Marcine Bice

GLUTTONY OF THE MIND

Fast-food stores on every corner
in-between and down the road.
To get our brains a going
and our minds on overload.
Gourmet air from every restaurant
seeping-in-and-out
innocent bystanders whom it vows to haunt about.

 Our cravings scream for chocolate
 caffeine will satisfy
 Stomachs need desserts
 because sugar pacifies.

Yes, Americans need junk-food
to equip our every mood.
Amuse us with a four-course meal
the setting is quite crude.
And to refuse that coke at dinner
would be really rather rude.
Demons of gluttony
working overtime
trying to win our bodies
in a battle of the mind.

Colleen Koerner

He took me by the hand and led me through the jungle
Now and then I stumbled
But he helped me face the struggle
We both saw things, bright and new
We both cried when it was through
And when at last we reached the light
He decided to make his flight
He left me then, standing there
He left me then, he did not care
Where once there was so much
Now there is so little
But I've not lost, nor have I won
For someday he will face the gun

Amanda Rodriguez

SWINGING

I swing outside here in the dark.
My love alone, forlorn;
Yet I know that after dark
The sun brings in the morn.
Please be there then, swing with me —
Together yet apart.
Still, know that with all I give to you
I still hold my very heart.
Don't weep, it's good to have you here
And swing beside me still,
Because for life's important parts
You have mine and always will.

Jon S. Evans

GUILT

Day by day my life-blood flows
As the wound that was our friendship grows.
I pay the price for unknown sin —
My day is torment and hell sits in,
For bright imagination dreams
And flays the soul; the flesh it reams.
I still don't know just what I've done
To drive away a lovèd one.
Friendship, love — dislike, polite lies.
What was has become; you break the ties.
Deceive yourself, I know what's true,
I know what feelings rest in you.
It hurts too deeply, I cannot cry,
And so my soul just slowly dies.
When your actions match your words
And light shines in your face once more,
I'll know forgiveness — I might heal —
'Til then my life's an open weal.
Can one be strong in love, and brave,
Cross the line and my mind save?

Jon S. Evans

SEA DAWNING

Along this stretch of space
the sand and sea
blend to form a gull-colored line
melted like pale smoke
against the horizon.
Earth and ocean
blurred together
in the anonymity of pre-dawn.

High above whispering wave song
chalky cliffs
thrust rocky breasts
into quivering fog.

Moon of May,
lemon-misted globe of light,
weighs down tattered clouds
littering grey morning sky,
until the sun
burns a hole
in the grave of night.

Cynthia Farquhar

MEMORIES NOT FORGOT

If you could see through children's eyes
  A world of wonder, cloudless skies.
The smell of grass, a butterfly,
  Hop and skip and jump, so high.
If you could see through children's eyes.

So many trinkets you could treasure.
  Our parents' love without measure.
A busy life, yet filled with leisure.
  Now gone for me like erasure.
World so full of childhood pleasure.

Once in a while, though not often,
  I really try and years will soften.
Then with a satisfying sigh,
  I see the world of cloudless skies.
A stolen glimpse through children's eyes.

Harold D. Gascoigne

THE INTRUDER

Beneath the towering pines I strode.
  Through ferns grown out with lacy frond.
Upon my back a store-bought load,
  I walk beside a tranquil pond.
Then smelling sweet the roses wild,
  And tasting plump raspberries, too,
Sewn there surely by nature's child,
  Watered pure by her mother's dew.
I climb to mountain peak on high
  And view the wonders all profound.
Marvelous visions please my eye,
  But nothing here of human sound:
Domain of bear, eagle, and of moose.
  A realm where men are of little use.

Harold D. Gascoigne

CONFUSION OF LOVE

You once wrote me a lover's letter
Said you would wait forever
To hold me in your arms
    What's the matter now?
How could you change your mind so soon?
Could she be prettier than me?
Or maybe she is more fun to be with
    Instead of me.
But, do you love her?
    Like you once said you loved me?

Diana L. Hurta

Thoughts.
Coming, going, out of reach
happy, sad, a bothersome leech.
Shifting, changing
and yet the same.

James P. Carmody

DISTORTIONS

Sadly gaze with misted eyes,
  Out foggy window's haze.
World so phony passing by,
  Without substance rushing.
Frenzied race to nowhere.

A water-colored brush to sky,
  All the streets are pencilled in.
Heaving sigh makes gentle wind,
  Paper flowers are blowing.
This painting has no frame.

Wet oils on canvas running,
  Buildings' false fronts warping.
Hanging on horizons far,
  Child's crayon drawing flat.
But two dimensions seen.

Black poles sharply rising,
  All stretching their ugly wires.
Bearing wordless chatter,
  Cold and plastic telephone.
Speaking harsh silent words.

Harold D. Gascoigne

MARKER

Time passes you know
just watch closely
and you'll see.
Another minute
long gone
like water
flooding the channels
of forgotten memories.
And i,
a floundering fool,
must swim backwards
toward forever
to meet my
moment
while it goes.

Richard Ellis Gold

COTTON CANDY CLOUDS

There are times
When all I want
Is to close my eyes.
Shouting out the pain and shame
Of the world I'm living in.

I want to go and hide
Using the earth as my recluse
Finding tranquility and peace.
Dreaming forever —
Of cotton candy clouds.

Diana L. Hurta

WHY ME?

Let's sit down together, our guts to spill,
Of all the inequities, our lives' bitter pill.
Neither our children nor husbands, so dear,
Can bear anymore to lend an ear
So oft do we spew forth our vent
Of garbage upon them, their energy's spent!
  With reckless abandon we maintain our course
Of gossip, destruction, how could it be worse?
We live in our own little worlds of no hope
With gloom and doom and pretenses to cope.
So tell me your worst, as new stories I crave
That I might repeat them and make you sound brave!
  When in reality, you've had your fill
Of venom and vinegar, and need quiet . . . still . . .
I'll prattle and rattle and clang someone's ear,
And explain your plight with your family so near,
Thus to help you in your eternal bent
For causing the injuries, hatred, now pent
Up inside of your loved ones . . . but of course . . .
You don't see the reason he wants a divorce?

Lauren M. Mayo

BEAUTIFUL LAND

I long for the day that
I'll have no need to drive a mechanical thing,
I'll just put on my hat
and walk instead along the road and sing.

And if I could see the mountains
clear, and unhindered by waste in the air,
and clean were the fountains
that flowed down from the heights and given much care,
and if the waters of the sea
could touch the shores and feel no filth in the sand,
then it would seem to me
that we have, to live in, a beautiful land.

Brian Floyd Newton

WITH REGARD TO THE ONE REMEMBERED

I still remember that fine spring day
When I walked in to find him there.
His hair shone red, his head bent low,
As he sat reading in a straight-backed chair.

We became friends despite my crush on him,
Though maybe that's why I scared him away;
For I'd drop books or say something stupid
Whenever I saw him coming my way.

Weeks, months passed, and he never came back,
I gave up considering whether he liked me or not.
Nowadays I pass by, with a bent head and a smile
To the boy that I never forgot.

Kris Roberts

Abraham walked alone with God; and knew he was his friend.
He had no fear when the Almighty spoke, and said
He would father men
Who would walk in faith and walk in love; led only
By His hand.
And Abraham walked where ere He led, into an unknown land;
Although the path was often dark, and the way he could not see,
He knew his Friend was always there, to keep his spirit free.

God spoke one day to Abraham, ''I want your only son
offered to me as a sacrifice, before this day is done.''
Abraham knew he could trust this One, who walked
with him each hour,
So he took Isaac as God had said; for He had proved
His grace and power.
No matter what happened to his dear son, he knew
God was at his side,
And an Angel spoke from heaven above, and a ram
He did provide.

Today we walk with God inside, and hear His voice within;
But can He speak to you and say,
''I know you as my friend?''

Bonnie J. Sanders

CITY LIFE

If you live in a city you're always rushed;
You can't look around you without getting pushed.

You go speeding, down the highway maybe a block;
To beat a red light so you won't have to stop.

You do your shopping in the early part of the day;
So there won't be many people getting in your way.

You breathe polluted air hoping to survive;
Knowing that tomorrow you may not be alive.

You can't sleep for the traffic that keeps you
  awake at night;
With their roaring motors and their
  blinding lights.

So why waste your life living in the city;
When you can get away where you
  won't be so busy!

Debra Whitson

THOUGHTS ON AN ASH WEDNESDAY

against the snow
the barren branch
blood-red berries on the bow

precious drops
shed for all
both then and now

bread for all humanity
blood free-flowing
the vicious battle won

O Jesus, help me be
broken bread
outpouring wine.

Sharon M. Daley

CHRIST'S DAY

T his day we celebrate Christ's Birthday,
A s we expect He will return someday.
N ectar flown to Earth by Holy Angels,
N ourishes the Infant, and to us tells,
E very object of Creation, "The Lord
N arrows His gap from the heterodox horde,
B y giving His only begotten Son
A nnunciated to Mary, specimen
U nified to God by blest purity,
M adonna, Matriarch of Piety."

A ngel Legions attend His every need,
D esiring to serve, not willing to cede.
V enerated by Wisemen and Shepherds,
E pochal for all, being beyond words.
N ature nursed its Divine Creator,
T urning the Earth upon its equator.

N aked to survival's whims, He then grew,
O mnificent, all were awed that He knew
E ncyclopedic storage of theology,
L ooked upon as a Holy Prodigy.

M ission accomplished, by teaching people
A bout God's need to have His love fulfill
S haping Man's image to be in His own,
S oared from suffering, to reap what was sown.

Markham H. Lyons

THE HARBOR

My father sits in harbor
as though his heart had been persuaded
to watch. The raspberry smoke that drifts
on midnight water.

Louise Hagins

GEOGRAPHIC COMMAS

Tonight the streets below
are a changing forest of people.
These roads lead to others,
and down the way —
a thousand miles — you sit
before an easel
rooting people to a canvas.

I recall a nation you created:
Brazil, 1969, Festival of Eggs.
The flame dance, burning slippers,
the crash of abalone tambourines.

I, too, believe in dreams,
I will never see Brazil.

And as for you and me,
a thousand miles divide us.
You captured it in *Nexus, 1980:*
distance is a series of
commas carefully placed
in time.

Clemmie King

STARS ARE BURNING BONES

Now homes seal the pit
where local pets were buried.
Our cat for fifteen years —
her eyes are staring, fossil ambers.

Some things the land can't still.
Nightfall is her lasting match for blackness.
She's a constellation left of moon;
her paw, lifted toward moon cheddar.

Sometimes I think I'm free.
Yet, that celestial paw —
  claws in check —
exerts a hold on me.

She begs for a dish of moon,
it's something I can't give her.

And my life is tuned
to the music of these stars:
the cadent purr, a latent caterwaul.

Clemmie King

BLUE BABY MOON

The earth is a virgin mother.
She bore alone the moon,
  a blue child,
circling at her hem
  tugging tides.

Baby moon,
pretending in your heaven-pen
  at play,
though you pull
you'll never wean yourself away;
you can only hide
  your darker face.

Clemmie King

NIGHT ON THE MOUNTAIN

Silken stars lighted from brand
Across the giant's course,
East to west, snow and singing, lightning,
And the strong, slow swish —
Strange, unknown, unfamiliar,
Wonderful, kissed with hope.
Crossed in time, prophetic,
The alabaster spills its hard
Streaming fragrance over straw;
Beauty breathed in byre,
Truth babbling on a Baby's breath,
And heaven reflected
In an ass's eyes.
Night on the mountain
Amid the huddled sheep,
But not cold.
Oh warm, warm
Like the fire of hearts —
The unconsuming burning
Of a soul.

Mary Paulhamus

SPECIAL LOVE

"My Darling." Days may come
  and go,
But for me our love will only
Grow and grow.

As the years pass by not knowing
What the future will hold,
My Dearest Darling, I know in
  my heart
That my cup of Love will overflow.

"My Love," as you can see,
There will always be
That very special Love,
Just for you and me.

Noel Privee

TOGETHER WITH LOVE

As we stroll through the paths
Of life, hand in hand,
I know that with your Love,
We can meet all the daily
Problems and demands on us.

All the Love that God gave to us
Is the most wonderful feeling we
Can ever share.

So, "My Darling,"
With all my heart,
The joys we do together,
Only show that we truly care.

Noel Privee

SINGING NIGHTINGALE

I heard you singing
  so soft and sweet
Just like a nightingale
  That could not sleep.

Under the stars
  So still and deep
Into the night
  That held their keep.

The melody that I hear you sing
  Still lingers on and
My heart fills with joy
  Forever it will long.

So keep on singing
  So soft and sweet
Just like a nightingale
  Singing for her keep.

Under the stars
  That glitter and shine
Into the night
  That love will time.

Betty Stewart

THE YOKE

The yoke is easy, the burden light —
Lord, not always does it seem.
Sometimes the yoke around my shoulders weighs
and heavy lays the burden that bends my back
beneath the rod of discipline.

Come closer with tender love,
place your hand of blessing upon my brow.
And lead me to quiet,
let my heart drink
the joy that only you can give.

There will I cease to struggle,
but only for a while
as the pressing burden is released
and I fall crashing at your feet,
sinking in verdant meadows.

Refreshed and strengthened
by your gifts of self, I continue —
carrying now a lighter yoke,
an easier burden than before
because of all that my Shepherd is.

Sharon M. Daley

OH! WHO AM I GOD?

Oh! who am i God?
with my eyes filled with tears.
Oh! God who am i?
when my mind is empty without anything to think.
Oh! who am i God?
with a broken heart that feels no love.
Oh! God who am i?
when i open my mouth and speechless words come out,
tell me so that i will know i am real, too,
not just a reflection in the mirror.

Carmelita Douglas

CARMELITA MARIE DOUGLAS. Born: Sacramento, California, 7-7-67; Education: Del Paso Heights Elementary School, Valley High School; Occupation: Word Processing (training); Comments: *The things, the people, and the animals around me have always fascinated me. These things are a part of everything that makes me who I am. They become a poem in my mind, and I just have to put them down on paper for all the people I know, and don't know, to see.*

A SEASCAPE

The dark of the wind plays in and out around the fences,
and sends papers and leaves and drifting ladies
rolling down the street,
scurrying in the wake of tidal waves and typhoon
as they seek shelter in any lover's arms.

But these lovers are monsters in a turbulent ocean;
slipping along the bottom in slime and muck
and grasping the little ladies;
drowning them, suffocating them,
holding them under.
In the end they are sucking the life away,
eating the flesh and leaving fragments for the scavengers.

In the dark of the wind
the beaches are littered with shells
rolling in the shallows,
basking in the sand.

What the seabird sees
is the storm tide,
and she wisely flies away.

Deborah J. Nelson

DEBORAH JEAN NELSON. Born: Somers Point, New Jersey, 2-9-53; Married: Rodney F. Nelson, 10-1-77; Occupations: Administrative Assistant, Writer; Membership: National Association of Female Executives; Comments: *I want my poetry to be a window on the world — a window that shows the world a little bit differently than we normally see.*

FRIENDS

To a special friend
The kindness that you have shown
Is what our friendship has been founded on
We have a closeness that is a strong tie
We may have our differences
We are still close
Of the time we spend together
To know one another a bit more
We understand of what each is looking for
And what each is missing
We care for each other in our own way
We show each in different ways that we care
I was looking for a friend
What I found was someone who is special
In my heart and will always be there
We may be away from each other
But we have a closeness that only a few people really share
From someone who cares

George Irl Angell

THE WEB

Like chiffon kerchiefs spread to dry
    on a field of stubbled hay
The weaver spiders work at night
    their silken webs to lay.

When dawn takes every drop of dew
    and strings it in a chain
Nature's necklace shines like gems
    and spiders' traps are lain.

Small insects lured by tinseled light
    are caught in the sparkling glow;
Their bodies stilled forevermore
    and drawn to the trap below.

Life weaves its web of golden dreams
    and spreads it out bejeweled
Before the eyes of human's greed
    and laughs when man is fooled.

For he who weaves the web by night
    is deadly in the baiting —
Tensed beneath the silken threads
    reality lies waiting.

Barbara S. Weppener

FAIRY LIGHTS

Their lanterns twinkled 'cross my lawn
    as fairies ran to beat the dawn.
They ran to hide in the hollow tree
    that grows on the hill across from me.

When morning bursting orange bright
    snuffed out all trace of elfin light,
Wild zephyrs parted spring green grass
    and let the fleeing pixies pass.

Now — was it just a breeze unruly
    or did I see them running — truly?

Barbara S. Weppener

THE BOOK

  Great, is the mystery, of love, for a Book.
Moving, is its written word —
Passion, tears, and desire,
Do the written word inspire.
Sad — with anguish, was its beginning,
Sorrow, and heartache its meine,
Joy and gladness, its hidden meaning.
        For —
Great, is the mystery, in its silence,
And profound, when it is expounded.
Oh, Written Word, whence cometh thou?
From the ages, from the ages,
Words, poured forth, from its pages,
Spirit, and soul, of man uplifted,
By the beautiful words, there in it.

Annette M. Ashbough

YOUR WEDDING DAY

There's a bright new day before you
And a chance to start anew
With shining hours waiting
And much for you to do

There's a big blue sky above you
And sunlight through the trees
Why should you ever worry
With gifts as great as these

So love and learn and laugh and play
That's wise as well as just
'Tis better to live and be worn out
Than fall apart with rust

And, when the days grow shorter
And darkest shadows part
Allow the wrinkles on your face
But never in your heart

When shadows steal your sun away
Treasure every minute
Tomorrow is a bright new day
With golden sunlight in it

Lola Burr

ALL MY THOUGHTS
AREN'T ME

    My thoughts
    and I
are confined in the same
cell of fickled conflicts,
a forced game to subdue
gray thoughts to save the good.
I win the Victor's key
and evict shaming thoughts.
So all my thoughts aren't me.

Dorothy Randle Clinton

MEMORIES

A wind that echoes
Through the pines
And brings me
Peace of mind

It blows away
Sweet memories
That summer
Left behind

They lay like
Buried treasures
In far corners
Of my mind

Colleen Dougher

CHRISTMAS IN THE OZARKS

There stands the tall
And stately silo,
Filled to the brim
With this year's milo.

In the hayfield,
There stands a deer.
A beautiful doe,
Her fawn is near.

Wood smoke curls
On up the flue.
It warms our home
And our hearts, too.

Down by the pond,
The children wait
For word the ice
Is ready to skate.

Beside the hearth
The tree with lights.
Its base is covered
With secret delights.

Bonnie K. Gillis

LONELY

Alone.
All alone.
No one's there,
To share
My loneliness,
Lonely.
I'm so lonely.
I need someone.
Won't you be
That someone?
Be with me.
Then we'll be
Lonely together.

Shannon Hall

MY BIG BROWN-EYED
BEAUTY

    Who is my pride and joy
I watch her growing
Stronger and wiser
Each passing day.
    Growing so fast, my little one.
Won't you slow down;
Let Mama love you as
My little one for just
    A
        Little
            Longer . . .

Laurie Millard

CASTELLATED ROCK

???

Born on an air force base
   Born flyin'
Cryin' Flyin' Tryin'
A child rolls down the blinds
A man is staring back at him
   Breaking glass
      falls into the alley-way
Rain rising off the sidewalk
Woman crossing — fleeting vision
   on a sunlit street
Motion like an ocean
Craters wail on the moon
A wind whispers into my ear
   Keep moving
     Banish the fear

Michael D. Pollock

MY FAMILY

When someone calls during any season,
  Day or night, rain or snow, for any reason.
My family is always ready to help.
  Every now and then they may yelp.
If something needs to be done,
  They turn the work into being fun.

We stay together through any case.
  We always look at it in the face.
All of our talents are to be shared,
  For all the people that really cared.
We show that we care by loving
  And caring, by not pushing and shoving.

My family is as close as you can ask for.
  I could never ask for any more.
'Cause my family is the only one,
  That could fill my heart, that they've done.
We have always known, money can't buy love.
  My family's love is as tight as a glove.

Kim Rudloff

THE SEA

the sea is a
wide
flat
green
stone that is
empty of
scratches
on which the clouds
sit
and talk
in their thunderous language
and the
gallant ships
frolic
quietly
silently
among them

Jason D. Walker

MOMENTS OF FANTASY

Working in luxury in the daytime
but when I go home at night
the only thing I can see is poverty.
   Moments of Fantasy
Oh God, hear my plea
Help me escape this reality
   Moments of Fantasy
When I'm riding home in the evening
I think about the life I'm leading
And I'm sad my girl is gonna leave me.
   Moments of Fantasy
I lie awake nights thinking
If I were a yachtsman out on the sea
The world would be free to me.
But it was just a moment of Fantasy.
   Moments of Fantasy

Benny Givham

STRIKE THREE . . . OUT

A sister for a mother,
a child for a bride . . .
between the two . . . framed
his life in a baseball game
and prison bars,
called the time and strikes.
Strike one! Strike two!

Father of a young child . . .
Knowing not her mother,
nor ever seen her father.
He sat behind irons bars
in a melting mood.
Strike Three! the soul died.
He struck out.

Lorraine Hicks

OUR FIRST MEETING

Your picture hanging
on the wall . . .
brings memories
of the first day
you came into my life.
A little bundle
with a pinkish face . . .
such a small mouth . . .
large blue tinted eyes
venturing to see
all life.
Not a whimpering cry
from your lips.
So fascinated you were
to sounds . . .
emerging visions
in your view.
So captivated with wonder
of this realm
you entered.

Lorraine Hicks

THE WAR-WRANGLED BANNER

See Davey Jumper there?
Married himself a pretty girl
with an unusual face.
What do you think it means?

. . . at Grandfather's farm . . .

Hurray, hurrah, it's suppertime.
Long ago and far away I loved you
what so roundly I sailed
to the light bulb's first beaming.

. . . on the old porch swing . . .

O yea, it's so neat-o
to fend off a mosquito
a day's time from the breakers receding
where the dragonflies brood.

Gilbert Mowery

BE STILL

Be still, my child
and know that I am with you always
Sit down beside me, under the tree
where its leaves will shade you
Rest your head upon me
Close your eyes and feel
the comfort of my divine love
My arms are around you
Dear one, be not afraid
I will embrace you
Allow me the freedom to go before you
I will clear the way for you
In the solitude of your mind
I will speak, if all is quiet
You will hear me
Go now, "My Child"
Peace be with you

Carrie Wolford

SWEET DREAMS

I close may eyes and rest my head
against the softness of the pillow.
I snuggle in the comfort of the blankets
and hug the pillow next to me.
I smile as I gently drift off into
a peaceful sleep.
The quiet solitude of the night echoes
in the mystery of its peaceful harmony
assuring me the Angels are watching
Over!
As I dream a kind of magic surrounds
the visions that slip into the unknown,
I hope for good thoughts, cherishable
and everlasting
to guide me as I rest
into the freshness of a new day.

Carrie Wolford

DREAMS

I wish I could have held you just one more day.
I wish I could have told you the things that I had left to say.
I wish just one more time, I could feel your touch
And I wish I didn't miss you this much.
I wish I could say how much I loved you
And how much I needed your love so true.
I wish you never had to leave
For this my heart and soul still grieve.
I can't even count the tears that fall like rain
And no medicine in this world can help the pain.
  What can I do?
What hurts so much is that I was in love with you.
    You may be gone,
But the dreams, thoughts, and the pain go on.
  Now in a dream, a land far away,
A wish has come true, I held you one more day,
I told you how much I loved you,
        And you were there . . .
                Forever through.

Shari Sloan

SHARI LEE SLOAN. Born: Rockford, Illinois, 6-26-67; Divorced, January 1987; Occupation: Teen Worker (volunteer); Membership: Youth Haven Association, a place for runaways and homeless, abused and troubled youth; Poetry: 'Peaceful Mind and Gentle Heart,' song, *Betty's Music Makers*, 4-16-87; Comments: *I usually write about troubled teenagers and love. I just write what I feel and what I see in the world. I love writing and the satisfaction I feel after I finish.*

BLUEGRASS WIDOW

Beware all you ladies of a Bluegrass man
He's a full-time member of an instrumental band
His emotions are stirred by a chord or a note
And on an instrument's body all affections he dotes

When you speak he is mentally practicing a song
And all the nights you sit waiting are lonely and long
While he courts and seduces those strings to a tune
About romance and life or a mid-summer's moon

Oh listen to these words from a 'Grass man's wife
With music his companion, it'll be an infinite strife
You'll compete for his love but in the end 'twill do no good
The musician is the judge and the winner's made of wood

So restrain when you're drawn to those pitiful cries
From his songs of sadness and heart-breaking lies
To the music he'll be true while you wait beneath its shadow
And as fate you'll be in mourning as another Bluegrass Widow

Pamela Gosnell

SPRING CLEANING

My world seems filled with half-forgotten things.
Half-forgotten memories, half-forgotten dreams.
Projects in abandon lie scattered all about,
Waiting for someone who cares to sort confusion out.
Straighten out the closets, bring order to the shelves,
Line the bureau drawers afresh (Dare I start on myself?),
Brush away the cobwebs that cling to days gone by,
Sweep out all the haunting sounds of loving word and sigh.
Clear away pretension — past is past — it's gone!
Bring order to tomorrow so that I can go on.
No longer do I yearn for that which I have had,
But the fact I hope for nothing more makes me feel so sad.
To share a love, to share a life, can mean both joy and pain,
But this feeling of rejection screams, ''Don't ever care again!''

Allene Haldy

LIFE

In the quiet of the storm . . .
Now . . . silence surrounds me . . . comforts —
But — then again — the winds start howling —
Voices leap like arrows from the shadows . . .
And faces all distorted — stern — cruel —
Lurk in the misty rain & eerie fog . . .
Haunting me — tracking me — with no escape . . .
On and on this endless misery —
Day by day — piece by piece . . .
Cut from my innermost core —
'Til . . . 'til . . . hopefully another quiet in the storm . . .
But — then again —

Monica Slowick

SPEECH

*A tribute to Dr. Martin
Luther King, Jr.*

Pain: thinking down the corridors of forgotten history;
Fears: realizing the truth and trying to change the way it is;
Rain: blending your *love* in spreading the word;
Tears: finding the strength to confront another day.

Talking: sharing your dream with dignity;
Teaching: arming each of us with self-respect
for ourselves and each other;
Living: bringing our dreams, hopes,
and aspirations together.
Learning: sharing our poverty and encouraging
us to search out the truth;
Touching: grasping each person with your Love.

Your love, your truth, cutting across all colors
in the rainbow of humanity;
so simple, that it makes sense, and
raises all consciousness to one idea,
one goal, one guiding principle:
TEACH PEACE!

Richard Ellis Gold

Praise the flower,
In all its glory,
Caressed in beauty,
Surrounded by story.
The look is so delicate
But wait and see:
After the storm,
There it'll be.

Harold K. Conrad

THE DROP OF RAIN

Like tiny rivers they flow
The drops of rain on my window pane.
Just another rainy day, I think
As I sit and watch the drop of rain
To contemplate its ultimate fate.

The workers busy around me rush
To what end will their endeavors become?
Our time is short
Our days but limited.
And yet we can never take the time
The time to study the drop of rain.

That drop of rain has fallen upon the ground
Not to give new life to the gardens of spring
Since all around me is concrete.
How unnatural does that drop of rain
Seem in its setting of concrete.
That drop of rain
Has met its fate upon the concrete.

Michael J. Hynak

GOD GAVE

God made the world
He made it for man
He made it so beautiful
With shore of sand
He made things alive; with grace
So man would not feel out of place.

Then God asked man for a rib
So women could live.

Together they stayed
In the garden that God made
First there was Adam,
Then there was Eve.
God looked down, and was pleased
Now the world is a mess
We all know
Waiting for God
To serve the final blow.

Robert A. Litterer

Maybe I don't know you yet,
and I didn't yet turn the pages of your soul,
and my lips, didn't crawl
into the depth of your lips,
and my hands, didn't gallop all over your body
like a wild horse.
Maybe I don't know you yet
despite that my eyes sailed over your body
from head to toe, more than once,
and stealthily penetrate into you.
And my thoughts
build a thousand bridges and ways
between my heart and yours.
Maybe I don't know you yet
but I live in you
and you live in me.
Like the candle's light
        lives in the dark . . .

Naddeem Fiyad

FOGGY BLUE ADIEU

Mother Nature felt blue today,
You could see it in her trees;
A fog rolled in . . . in to stay,
Perhaps Ma Nature grieves.

She pulled her cloak close to her,
Gathered its folds all around;
With fall's leaves gone, memories as it were,
Made her beckon her clouds to the ground.

And in that vague obscurity,
That she bid soften her pains;
One may find a security,
Filtering through her membrane.

For others grieve as you do,
Others have felt that shove;
And the anguish when we say adieu,
When we must say it to one we love.

Kevin McKenzie

BUDDING PROMISE

Here we are together
One look in your eyes, and I see
All the love we have to share

Like a budding rose
Each day blossoming a little more
Revealing a new facet of its natural beauty
Its growth is subtle, until blossoming is
Complete.

And then it's a revelation
So profound in its splendor, yet
Gently reaching so many senses.

Lori Janwich

UNTITLED

I know
that we were born, for some reason.
To let the rivers flow,
and the trees to grow
to let the days pass.
And the sun rays to fall,
and wash the face of earth.
I know
that we were born like flowers
some day to be picked . . .

Naddeem Fiyad

NADDEEM SHIADY FIYAD. Born: Rama, Galilee, Israel, June, 1956; Occupation: Store manager for Kentucky Fried Chicken; Memberships: Writing club in Israel, 1979; Writings: I have published several poems in two books in Hebrew, but this is my first experience writing in the English language; Comments: *I live in the depth of this life, its beauty and mysterious reasons have driven me down to the bottom of it and so my poetry extends in the ways of life: touching, operating and living every moment of it.*

AGING

Her hair was black as night,
Now it's white as snow.
She no longer knows me,
She has grown too old.

She is a little girl,
Back in her tender years,
This is her protection,
Against her pain and fears.

As I look upon her,
All withered and worn,
My emotions are in an upheaval,
My heart is torn.

If only I could help her!
There's nothing I can do.
So, dear God,
I'm turning it over to you!

Barbara Ward

Thick clouds above us,
we feel a storm approaching.
Walking in the rain.

Philip J. Angel

JUST LIKE A SOAP OPERA BITCH

No one can escape her three-pronged attack
She moves in quickly, devastating on impact
Long and powerful, clean and unrelenting
She gets what she wants no matter what
Upon meeting her it's obvious her rap is unbeatable
Initially warming her body to yours
Boiling your blood, making you hot
Then blowing in your ear, scraping inhibitions away
When she's gone, her tragic trace remains
Death, destruction, use and abuse
You'll know she's coming, but then it is too late
Because no one can escape her three-pronged attack.

Chris Hancock

LITTLE FOOTSTEPS

Listen; can you hear them crying?
All these years, they have been trying
To escape the pain you've put them through.
To escape the pain that I once knew.

Listen close and you will hear . . .
Their tiny little footsteps are getting very near.
They're trying to reach out; to get into your heart.
The way you have been treating them, is tearing them apart.

It doesn't take intelligence to fully understand
The power that love brings, is really in demand.
Just open up your eyes, and unplug your ears.
You'll find tiny little footsteps are easier to hear.

You've been this way for such a long time,
But I believe there's only one thin line
Between the hate you show outside,
And the love locked deep inside.

I hope someday to find the key
To unlock your heart and set your feelings free.
Then maybe you'll be able to show;
The tiny little footsteps I wasn't able to know.

Edna Jenkins

SENSES

Look at all the trees reaching to the sky.
Oh, what I would give, just to be that high.
Look at all the willows standing in a row.
Look at all the beauty Mother Earth can grow.

Wake up in the morning when the sun is shining bright.
Oh, how I do treasure the value of my sight.
Seeing all the colors of the leaves in the fall,
I can surely see that God gave this world His all.

When I go to bed at night, and lie in the dark,
I hear all the animals playing in the park.
I thank the Lord for giving me these joyful sounds to hear.
And I pray He never takes my ears — in case He calls me near.

When you're home, I hold you close, to never let you go.
I thank the Lord for giving me these feelings I can show.
I hope He never takes away the treasures He gave me.
'Cause I value all my senses in my own serenity.

Edna Jenkins

Richard Ellis Gold

THE GAME OF LIFE

Lonely and sad; apart from the rest.
Wondering if you'll pass the test.
One too many mistakes have been made.
This time the price will never be paid.

How many tables will have to be turned?
How many hearts get burned?
Too many peoples' lives are at stake.
Too many things for granted we take.

Life goes on no matter how bad it will feel.
All we can do is play the cards that we deal.
Each card laid will take its toll.
And share on the burden of your life's role.

If we give up when we're losing the game,
All of our battles were fought in vain.
Just hold out 'til the last card is played.
Then, we will see where the final judgment's made.

When we are waiting on the other shore,
Will we then see what this game of life was for?
Will we find ourselves standing at the mighty feet of God,
When they lay our bodies under six feet of sod?

Edna Jenkins

DIVISION OF YEARS

In memory of my Mother

To break our bread in division of years
Is sadness breaking bread, a quiet meal
When the slow-chapped measures of food heal
No more breaches of mother loves and fears.
To eat our meal together blends our tears
And talk into a domesticated feel
For each other that no one can steal
Away when only our food disappears.
To think that lips that once fed you now say
To you no words of praise or censure
Is a hard thing, but Love, whose knowing hand
Feeds us in our toddler's chair our pure
Food with care, knows one day we will stand
Grown and tall to always feed and pray.

Donald McCants

DONALD LESLIE McCANTS. Born: Gadsden, Alabama, 6-11-51; Education: Jefferson State Junior College, 1970-71, 1973-74; University of Alabama, B.A., History, 1974-78; Occupation: Car wash attendant; Memberships: Alabama State Poetry Society, SpeedX Shortwave Radio Club; Poetry: 'On Listening to a Quartet Sing a Motet of Thomas Tallis,' *The Sampler,* Spring, 1984; 'The Verdi Requiem,' Alabama State Poetry Society, 1986; 'Lines on Animal Mortality,' *American Poetry Anthology, The Society Poetry Book,* 1975; 'An Imitation of Anglo-Saxon Poetry,' *The Sampler,* Spring, 1974; Comments: *I am a firm believer in the use of strict form in poetry, along with the carrying on of the great traditions of English poetry. I also aim to integrate my Christian beliefs into my poetry, in much the same way that George Herbert's poetry was rooted in the eternal truths of Christianity.*

WHAT ARE YOU TO ME

You have been
friend
lover
wife
mother
What are you to me
to another
you have not been?

P. McAdams

ANGELS WON'T TELL

The trees were whispering gently
  The moon was shining bright
The crickets and the tree frogs
  Were showing their delight.

Though the shadows held a secret
  The Angels knew full well —
A saddened heart was breaking —
  But Angels won't tell.

The dawn crept in slowly
  The moon hid its lovely face
The crying heart had vanished
  From the lonely shadow embrace.

Now when the moon shines brightly
  The breeze cuddles through the eaves
Like the crying of an Angel —
  The moaning to never cease.

Honey

LEONA B. REYNOLDS. Pen Names: Honey, Honey Bare, Honey Reynolds; Born-Jacksborough, Texas; Married: Clyde Reynolds, 1940; Education: Hills Business College, Oklahoma City; Training in Real Estate, Journalism, Poetry, Law; Occupations: Real Estate Broker, Poet, Writer; Memberships: Real Estate Board, President Reagan's "Task Force", Advisory Board & Trust; Awards: Silver Poet, Golden Poet, and four Honorable Mentions, 1986; Poetry: 'Wayward Traveler,' 'Tragic Trails,' 'Just a Shadow in the Sky,' 'Angels Won't Tell,' 1986; Themes: *Pathos, "life style" short stories, scenarios (movies).*

SOME ADVICE

I want to fill this poem with words of wisdom
And tell you how to have a happy life
But I have no magical secrets to give you
Just bits and pieces of truth and advice
Like love yourself
And don't be afraid to love others
Keep a part of the child within you
Enjoy the beauty of the day
And when things are at their worst
Don't give up but keep perspective
For things will most likely get better
And the future cannot always be predicted
I don't want to tell you how to live your life
But I did want to share with you this advice
I hope I have reached you.

Carol Esposito

FACTS

I want to promise you happiness
And tell you that the world is a bliss
I want to make you smile, yea
And tell you that people care
I want to guarantee for you
A happy future, a happy life
But I don't want to lie to you
And I don't want to hide from you
The facts of life. So here they are:
    There are people who will hurt you
    There are people who don't care
    There are people mean and ugly
    There is danger in the air
    There is hunger, there is crime,
    There is war, there is hate,
    There is sadness, there is death,
    But there is you
    And you can join with those like you
    Those who love, those who care
    Because they too exist
    So don't despair
    And if you need me,
    I am here.

Carol Esposito

REFUSAL WITH A VENGEANCE

Within this short span of
under one hundred years

I'll make peace with the
sag of breasts, the spreading girth of hips.
I'll face with dignity
the lines my character reveals, and
I'll sit at the sidelines
cursing my aches,

But I won't buy and I will fight
the tale you oldsters spin,

That love, romance and pleasure games
must end one day,
fade away
into the solitary confinement
called
wise old age.

Helen Fogarassy

TERMS OF RETURN

The hughold fold
of an opening rose
riding tall
above the vase

Breathes wishlullment
headier than
the whooshrush of
springdawn rain

Helen Fogarassy

LITTLE OLD SCHOOL BUS

The little old school bus chugs right along.
It neither hurries nor pokes.
It gets there on time if it doesn't break down,
In spite of the loud noise and jokes.

Children must stay in their seats all the time,
No standing, or fighting allowed.
Driver must see to the safety of all.
She will take care of the crowd.

It's fortunate children who ride on a bus,
No walking in rain, sleet, or snow.
You see them on corners, all waiting in line,
Whenever to school they must go.

So old yellow school bus, grinding along,
We hope you will just keep your cool.
Just push with your might, and keep your lights bright,
And take all the children to school.

Evelyn M. Johnson

GROW UP

Why must I grow up? I'm happy as is.
It's such fun to do what older folks quiz.
Now, why not play ball in old worn-out jeans?
We're not there for show, not by any means.

I still like to run, and play in the street,
To let my hair fly, and wear my bare feet.
There're Frisbees to catch, and bike riding, too,
Just so many things that I like to do.

In summer, there's swimming with neighborhood youth,
And hiking in mountains. Does this sound uncouth?
I'll have to grow up in just a few years,
Then put off my playing, and hide all my tears.

So let me enjoy playing ball in the park,
Or when lights go on, hide and seek in the dark.
Right now I must play, just like our young pup.
But later I'll quiet. 'Tis then I'll grow up.

Evelyn M. Johnson

MY BEAUTIFUL HIGH DESERT HOME

Old country roads filled with holes, rocks, and curves,
And a few rattlesnakes on the side,
Is the right way to go in the sun, rain, or snow.
All in all, it's a beautiful ride.
But the best part of all, at the end of the trail,
No matter how far I need roam,
There's a place that is dear, and I long to draw near.
It's my beautiful high desert home.

Sunsets are like what you've ne'er seen before.
You just have to stand there and stare.
As the blue turns to red, and the sun goes to bed,
Heaven seems closer out there.
So when I am free of the powers that be,
If I am on land or on foam,
I'll pack up my gear, and hurry out there
To my beautiful high desert home.

Evelyn M. Johnson

AMERICAN INDIANS

The Black Crow's flight silhouettes dawning daylight sky,
While ancient maples' and pines' shapes suggest a form
Of Tribal Conferences taking place above Earth,
In the Heavens where the Spirit rests, Angels fly,
Warriors recount past glories, courage is the norm.
Each Medicine Man brews mystic potions with mirth,
All malice tossed into the Void and deepest Pit.
Kindness prevails, hope is kindled, love is divine.
Strength in weakness, nobility — humility,
The Bow is broken, the Arrow without bit.
Raids and revenge no longer force us to pine,
Energies of War find pools of tranquility.
Night Owls, wide-eyed, scan the bowers for fleeting prey;
Growls of hungry bear shake the morning like thunder;
Trout splash concentric ripples on the silver streams.
Hunting grounds, burial grounds, Sacred sites do not stay,
Boulders of granite are crushed by the new builder,
Lumber shredded to pulp for paper, used for dreams,
Inscribed for treaties of peaceful coexistence.
Sorrow lay flat, suffocating the old and young,
Spears pierced the souls and bodies of the Chieftains.
Insatiable greed, spurred by ignorance,
Nations of Indian Spirits exist when sung,
Grandly about, upon the still plains and mountains.

Markham H. Lyons

FROM BABYLON

Joy is a promise and a future state.
Tomorrow's songs are glories, but unheard.
Our silent harps hang swinging on strange boughs,
For the sweet songs of yesterday
Would break our hearts beside this alien stream.
They haunt the empty niches of the just
Where incense curled and lingered in its flight —
Silent, heavenward and sweet.
They rest beside red pools in secret hearts
And echo softly over trodden souls
Where no lips part to give them utterance;
And new songs fail to tempt the jaded tongue —
No ''Pange Lingua's'' in a tinseled world.
Yet on this nameless shore we dare not sigh,
Nor let our salt tears swell this foreign flood,
Nor yearn to batter babes against the stones.
We are but probed and searched in bitter night.
Our hearts are tested in a sullen flame.
But joy is promise and a future state,
A sudden Presence and a lasting Light.

Mary Paulhamus

THE LADY

My lady light
            give to each silent
memory,
tomorrow contentment
still, we are.
as always a union
            as
words a new
            dark tone cry as past
play away what child we need
till we in growth deny,
grey for light,
            and become again the music
            of our union.

Frank Ocain

WHAT A GIFT LOVE IS!

When the storms of life come down
Upon the hapless ship of life,
It bears it far above all strife!
What a scintillating jewel you are,
Far brighter than the morning star;
As a mother clasps her infant to her breast
Oh what a gift you really are!
You are filled with inspiration
That never lags nor ceases,
You are the light in a father's eye
That keeps him young and spry,
Love, a gift from the Master's hand
Lavishly given to those who seek
Binding up the wounds of them who speak
With cruel and bitter tongue —
Love, you are born in the heart of God,
You are every spry and young,
Love, you are strength to a seeking soul,
A gift from the loving King of kings
That gives my soul its wings.

Babette Elaine Kaltenbach

BABETTE ELAINE KALTENBACH. Born: Johanasburg, Transuaal, South Africa, 9-4-1899; Education: Carthage College, University of Evanston, Illinois, M.A., Spanish and French; Occupation: Missionary in Africa, Brazil, and Mexico for eighteen years; Memberships: Christians United in Global Outreach; Poetry: 'Mumba, Son of a Cannibal,' *Just-a-Tree* magazine; 'All Aboard'; 'Preaching Birds'; 'Preaching Animals'; 'Preaching Insects'; Comments: *I am working now in northern New Mexico with Christians United in Global Outreach in a program called, "The Healing of the Nation's Church."*

SEA WITHOUT BOUND

Divine Nature,
vast sea without bound
from which life flows
and where thirst's quenched;

where saints drank from
to refresh their spirit;
where the Samaritan woman
saturated her lips;

where swallows go
to dip in their wings
to soar above the tops

of the sublime mountains.
Oh shoreless blue deep,
give me your waters to drink.

Ernesto Oregel

REJOICE IN THE LORD

I rejoice in the Lord.
My soul doth magnify His
Mighty works.

The promise of a new day
To labor,
The promise of rest.

I love the Lord Jesus
And all His wonderful deeds,
And I beg His mercy.

Lord, please remember me!
Though I know You always
Have and will.

For Your name's sake
I will give praise to You.
Amen.

Meg Prose

MY DAUGHTER

"A big kiss for mommy?"
"Here's a big kiss for you!"
And I love you little one,
I need you.
You are so funny,
You are so naive,
But because you grow so fast
You'll be on your own, soon.

Meg Prose

HERE

Here, I am so peaceful;
Here, it is so beautiful;
Here, at the face of a mountain;
Here, with hawks, woodpeckers, and deer;
Here, where all I hear are *Your* friends;
Here, where *You* whisper to my very soul;
Here, I am just a mortal man;
Here, to have and hold all this serenity;
Here, is where I am at peace with *You*,
    and myself;
Here, is where I just sit and contemplate with
    You;
Here, I am loved like *You*;
Here you are *God*; just as I should want to be;
Free and everlasting . . .

Jerry Russell

BE MY VALENTINE

Oh, My Love it is so nice to have
Valentine's Day to express our love
to our loved ones.
    ''Be My Valentine''

Oh, My Love, I know I should tell
you more often during the year how much
I do appreciate all the little things
you do for me during the year.
    ''Be My Valentine''

Oh, My Love, my only wish is that I'm
worthy enough for you.

Can I do as many things for you as
you do for me.
    ''Be My Valentine''

Oh, My Love, I love you *dearly*. Thank
you for the wonderful years you have shared
with me.
It is wonderful to share life with someone
like you, my love.
    ''Be My Valentine''

Shirley Winters

A LEGEND IN HIS OWN MIND

He's the coolest
The greatest guy he knows
But ask him a question
And his ignorance shows

He's been everywhere
And done everything
According to him
He should be king

He considers himself
The man of the hour
And dreams of himself
In a golden tower

He's good for a laugh
Just talk to him
And you'll find out
He's so damn dim

He's the greatest
The best of his kind
Actually he's a legend
In his own mind

Troy L. Walters

ASSIGNATION

Cast by the convolutions
Of a world in anguish
Upon a foreign shore,
Prone, weeping salt tears into alien sand,
I raise my head to call, half-hidden
In the anomalous rush of sound,
And see before me,
Under twisted boughs
Of unfamiliar trees
And twined in bizarre blossoms
Of a crude, barbaric hue,
Love beckoning sweetly as He was wont to do —
Love crowned and bleeding,
Regal, tender, torn.
Winged out of weakness,
Mad with haste, I fly
Into a vast embrace,
And, in the flowering desert of a breathless hour,
Drink beauty
Who would thirst no more.

Mary Paulhamus

MY BEAUTIFUL LITTLE LADY BIRD

*My Beautiful Little Lady Bird lived at our house
from December 20, 1986 to May 1987.*

Amazing little parakeet, who really loved to fly.
And in her home cage, Lady Bird was quite
an acrobat, turning somersaults,
opening her own cage door,
singing and talking in her own bird language,
enjoying her special birdseed and water.
Lady Bird loved little children and sometimes sat on
their finger, Lady Bird missed all her friends
from the pet shop where she came from.
My Beautiful Little Lady Bird mystery.

I had gone with my mother to the doc on May 25,
and when I came home, Lady Bird was very ill.
Lady Bird hadn't been sick until that day.
Lady Bird couldn't eat, or drink her water,
and was so weak, she couldn't stand on
her two little feet. I did what I could
to make her comfortable. Lady Bird will be missed.
When at last, she closed her eyes in silent sleep.

Betty Stewart

JUST A DREAM

The swelling in my chest
  The pounding of my heart
    The vibrating in my head
Are from just my dreams of you.

The tingling of my flesh
  The quiver of my lips
    The emptiness of my arms
Will be consoled, I know, when my dream comes true.

To dream of your arms around me
  To dream of your lips pressed to mine
    Just to dream of you — my darling
Makes everything in my life seem just fine.

Dorothy E. Williams

WHO AM I?

You sit me in a highchair, a bib beneath my chin;
Upon my tray a bowl of mush to squish my fingers in.
If I could talk I'd tell you I don't want mush anymore.
Instead I try to show you and throw it on the floor.

  You frown at me: "No, Baby, No!"
  And wipe my pudgy hand.
  Through teary eyes I beg of you,
  Please, *please* understand!

You sit me in a wheelchair, a towel beneath my chin;
Upon my tray a bowl of mush to squish my fingers in.
If I could talk I'd tell you I don't want mush anymore.
Instead I try to show you and throw it on the floor.

  You frown at me: "No, Baby, No!"
  And wipe my boney hand.
  Through teary eyes I beg of you,
  Please, *please* understand!

Highchair or wheelchair, baby or wife —
Am I just beginning, or ending my life?

Barbara S. Weppener

THOUGHTS FOR LITTLE HEARTS

As I lay my weary body down to rest,
    and my thoughts
      go wandering o'er the day.
Summing up the moments that were best,
    now the day is o'er, and
      on my bedding — nestled — I lay.
A day filled with important events
    brought joy, not to me alone.
But to the little hearts in my house.
And their voices were a joyous tone.
Happiness reigned throughout the eve,
With the finishing touch a special treat.
Weary minds no longer able to weave,
    new thoughts, overcome with sleep,
      for the 'morrow they must meet.
A bright new day full of challenge,
To test their strength, keel and balance.
Soon the battles o'er and done
And for the victor,
    new thoughts have begun.

Dorothy E. Williams

LOST SOULS

Oh, the weary souls
    That are lost and all alone
      Buried deep within their own sorrow,
Moaning and groaning
    For a bright tomorrow.

Afraid to try anew,
    Afraid to wander out,
      Just afraid of everything
That may change their way of life.

How sad and pitied are they
    With no imagination to use,
      Missing new adventures,
        Thinking they'll be abused.

Dorothy E. Williams

DREAMS

Elusive as the wind
As bright as the crescent moon
Wondrous as your one true love
Necessary for survival

Like a soft melodic tune
with crisp piano and a few
well-played guitar riffs

They flow along
waiting —
waiting to be caught.

Partners in a purpose
a team of impenetrable force

Hold tight

There very well may come a time
when they're all you have

Keeping you afloat
Giving direction and sustenance
Until the rain stops
And you reach your very own brightly-colored rainbow.

Aven R. Baral

EVERLASTING LIFE

Everlasting life! What does it mean? (John 3:16)
The meaning of the Word is very plain.
Everlasting life means life forever. (Isaiah 51:6-8)
For Jesus said I will forsake thee never. (Hebrews 13:5)

Eternal life is mine, I'll never perish. (John 10:28)
This, God's promise, I will always cherish. (Titus 1:2)
I shall not come into condemnation. (John 5:24)
For I have received eternal salvation. (Hebrews 5:9)

When I sin be sure I will be chastened. (Hebrews 12:6)
But my punishment won't be loss of salvation.
  (John 17:12, Philippians 1:6)
Salvation's not of works which I have done. (Titus 3:5)
Salvation is of God and Christ His Son. (Jonah 2:9, Acts 4:12)

Eternal life is mine this fact I know! (I John 5:13)
When Christ returns with Him I'm sure to go. (John 6:44)
What Christ starts in me He'll surely finish. (Hebrews 12:2)
I've believed in Christ so I'll not perish. (John 3:15)

Eternal life's a gift God gave to me. (Romans 6:23)
It's not of works but a gift so it's free. (Ephesians 2:8-9, Romans 5:15-16)
I'll go to Heaven when I die I know! (I John 5:13)
Since Jesus prayed I would that makes it so. (John 11:41-42; 17:9, 20, 24)

Paul J. Bretschneider

EVERY TRUCKER'S CO-DRIVER

May God be with each and every one of you,
On every journey through and through.
To keep you safe from all harm,
He'll cradle you gently in his arms,
Keep you rested and bright eyed —
Your steady hand he will guide
Down all the highways that you travel,
Blacktop, stone, and even gravel.
When you're down and out he'll be there —
Because he loves you and really does care.
With the Lord at your side, and the wind at your back,
You will surely be on the right track.
He'll bring you home safely once again,
Because he is your co-driver and your best friend.

Kathleen M. Clothier

AUTUMN HAS COME TO MICHIGAN

Check-shirted hunters in a wide-open field
A spotted dog poised in point
The crash of wings, a pheasant in flight
Autumn has come to Michigan

    A graceful form through dazzling leaves
    A sight, a squeeze, a shot
    A trophy adorning a wall in a den
    Autumn has come to Michigan

A ball sailing over helmeted men
A feint, a grasp, a run for the score
Cheers from the crowd, acclaim for the team
Autumn has come to Michigan

    Saturday morning, crisp and with leaves
    Father and son, rakes in their hands
    Smoke, lazy, drifting, sweet
    Autumn has come to Michigan

Apples and pears and pumpkins with frost
Chestnuts and acorns and squash
Turkeys and dressing and cranberries, red
Yes, Autumn *has come* to Michigan.

W. H. Drummond

COMPUTER KICK

Comes the dawn, to work we must trudge, in order
to make a dime.
Next, we must listen, as management complains that we
waste our time.
Nine to five, 'tis the same rotten routine, that has us
climbing a tree!
To hell with nine to five, we wish we could state
and tell management, we will leave.

Alas! My friends, our wish has finally come true,
no more haggling to be done;
Can't call in sick or take a personal day off,
since management has now won.
We are no longer good enough, they say to us,
our work is not desirable.
Our pay for the years, the same old thing; we must go!
As they hired one, more knowledgeable.

They hired a computer, in our place, you see!
And we are left, on the jobless sea; yes, you
and me!

Carol Rutledge Hawkins

MY GOD IS IN HEAVEN

Like the wind on a warm summer night
Like a flower blooming and bright
The beauty on awakening to morning sunlight
My God is in heaven, everything is alright
Earth is revolving around and around
Birds are singing, what a beautiful sound
Fireflies darting, stars twinkling at night
My God is in heaven, everything is alright
A sweet baby child and old grey-haired grandpa
Make me think of the majesty and wonder of it all
My loved ones and home, an eagle in flight
My God is in heaven, everything is alright
When God made the world He surely understood
He looked around and said it is good

Mary E. Thompson

THE BEST IN EACH OF US

We keep searching and trying to see
What we think is the best in each individual
As we meet and pass along life's way.
    Yet, so often as the case may be
It's impossible to distinguish just what makes
    Up the difference in personality.
    This one is blustery and quite nosy,
    This one is unstable, and oh, so uncouth!
    And, please, don't say it's just the youth.
Because so often it is just that one true friend
That proves to be the one you simply cannot comprehend.
    Ah, but we have to keep on trying to understand,
    Hopefully, to be of some help to our fellow man.
For who knows, some day we just might be the other one
Who will need a compassionate helping hand.
    Then, too, perhaps we can fathom
    A part of what might have been
    The best, discernible from amongst the variant,
Furnishing the yardstick to measure just how far we can extend
Into that particular world of knowledge and refinement.

Lou Eldridge

A CHARMING SWEDISH VILLAGE

Yonder in a little village named Sigtuna,
    There lived a Swedish couple
    Whose names were Helge and Anna.
So gracious they were to open their home
    To other Christians from hither and yon.
Anna had spent many hours,
    One could tell,
    On a most scrumptious buffet, not to be excelled.
Helge, too, had prepared in his own way;
    Because the English language
    He scarcely did grasp.
So, he set about two weeks in advance
    To work on a welcome address
    That held his guests in a trance.
Certainly these two I'll not soon forget;
Nor the plain and simple living they displayed. Yet,
    What a marvelous blessing we did receive
    For making that visit to a charming Swedish village.

Lou Eldridge

THE DESERTED HOUSE BESIDE THE ROAD

There is nothing quite so sad than to see
What, many years ago, was a fine, stately home
With a happy, healthy, growing family.
Now, with its broken windows and twisted roof being blown,
And what once was a handsome front door, now torn down,
Leaving that deserted look all around.
But, it happens to be just one segment
Of this, our changing world at present.
Now the family members are dispersed,
Having left their home for more glamourous places on this earth
To go to, hopefully, wistfully,
A better life. Yet, we wonder if —
Some far-off day when they reminisce
They long for a part of that happiness,
Shared in the growing and heartfelt struggling
Of that family who once called home
That broken-down house; still, *oh*, so statuesque
Amid the debris and broken glass,
Beside this winding road in a short crook,
With the desolate deserted look.

Lou Eldridge

LIFE SHARED

For those who truly love, there is but one way of thinking.
You think as one. You hope as one.

For those who truly love, there is but one way of dreaming.
You dream as one. You build together.

For those who truly love, there is but one way of loving.
You love completely. You love forever.

For those who truly love, there is but one way of being.
. . . One Together

Tina L. Huber

GOD'S PATTERNS

Long before I see them
    Patterns of wild geese flying
    Split the sky in perfect formation.

Monarch butterflies migrating
    Transform trees
    Into still life.

Fencerows and telephone wires
    Host flocks of blackbirds
    Like spectators at sports.

Nutting squirrels romp up and down trees
    With nut-filled paws and grain-filled jaws
    Digging frantically to conserve their treasures.

Trees bury tender grasses in falling leaves
    Preserving tender shoots for spring
    Against the winter's bitter cold.

Patterns of God protect his creatures
    Sustaining life in flora and fauna.
    Made in his image, can I doubt his care for me?

Olga Borchardt

HER EYES

When I look into her eyes
I see something bright
A mesmerizing twinkle
Like a beacon in the night

When I look into her eyes
I'll stare at them awhile
And when she looks at me
It seems as if they smile

When I look into her eyes
I see the fire of love
A captivating spark
Like a shooting star above

When I look into her eyes
My heart begins to melt
And when she winks at me
I forget how bad I felt

When I look into her eyes
I see a wondrous sight
A hypnotizing glow
Like a moth drawn to light

Troy L. Walters

HAND MIRRORS

What to hold
to dreams as near
as clouds
fly through on tree
tops, topple down
into blades of grass
and know it is the
shade that cools
her heated thought.
The sky is full with song
and glimmers of a
miracle peak out
from the moon, from a smile.
It is the intrigue
of the fans that
hide us from the heat
and the grapes we
taste, one by one.
What to hold to dreams . . .

Arline Bennett

LET ME

I mean no harm
I only want to touch your wing
Go inside your cocoon
    Let me touch you
    Let me feel you
    Let me inside
        Before you fly

Lorrie Ackley

Dear God what is the reason
    For this life we live on earth
Is the answer in our marriage
    Or the joy of giving birth —

Are we here for some set purpose
    Is it in the stars above —
Is it worth the pain we suffer
    For the health of those we love —

Why do you leave some people here
    With no life left to live
While others die so very young
    What answers can you give —

We struggle through our daily life
    But God I wonder why
Were we placed here to fight for life —
    Or do we live to die?

Kathleen Benedetto

JESUS' BIRTHDAY

There is love and peace and joy
All because of one small baby boy
Who came to earth to share
All God's love and tender care
And if we heed this message of love
We'll join him there in heaven above

Judith M. Capper

TOO DEEP TO BE CLEAR

What could have happened?
Only God and he will ever know
I cried for him
His pain was so deep

He wouldn't share it with anyone
So I took it upon myself to weep

His wound was to heal
'Til I severed it again
It wasn't meant to happen
Or to start over again

He's still a dreamer, and a fighter
A lover and a sinner
Until I crushed the wall he's built
To keep his soul from surrender

His eyes told me what I had
Not wished to hear
Pain and sorrow
Too deep to be clear

Regina Freshour

MEMORIES

Written down on parchment paper
All the words sounding 'round,
    Echo still a while after
Down the halls of endless time.

    Parchment paper thin and frail
Cylinder bound and tied with string,
    Shoved into a little alcove
Long ago put there to hide.

Janette Lestina

CONCEPTION IN GLASS

When you looked in that mirror
And became you,
Did you, back then,
Know what to do?
If there was no difference
(There never was before)
Between an open field
And a hastily closed door?
(One grows poppies.
The other yields shame.)
And what if you and I
Were to be the same?
Yes, it was I
Who saw what you had seen
And knew there was
No difference between
Concrete mazes
Or your heart
Or the moonbeams on the glass
Forming the start.

Kara McBride

SIGN OF THE TIMES

We've lived through wars
of worlds and minds
Found reasons for
life's saddened times
Cured influenza, measles
and plague
    Why now do we suffer —
what debt must we pay?

Old age is a burden
we all must endure
Acceptance is easy
no hope for a cure
    But given my rathers
I'd have to agree
Age is a Godsend
    AIDS is his plea.

David A. Mills

176

MY MOTHER, MY FRIEND

For being there for me when I thought no one cared,
. . . know that I love you

For listening when no one else was there,
. . . know that I love you

For giving to me a part of yourself that I shall treasure always
. . . know that I love you

For being the special kind of mother I could always turn to
and depend on through all the days of my life,

. . . know that I will *always* love you

Tina L. Huber

TINA LOUISE HUBER. Born: Kileen, Texas, 11-23-62; Married: Richard Huber, 10-25-86; Comments: *For me, writing poetry allows me to express my feelings in ways that I am unable to achieve with the spoken word.*

She was born with beauty and a brilliant mind
She was witty and thoughtful and musically inclined
She enjoyed many sports and was fond of the arts
She had great love of family; was saddened to part
She couldn't know that she'd soon become ill
And for the rest of her life would be climbing a hill
But climb it she did with self-pity denied
She never complained and she seldom cried
She'll be happy now, her mother is here
It's so quiet and peaceful and there's nothing to fear
I know how she trusted the Lord up above
I just hope that she knew how much she was loved

Beryl Jarvi

We love you, Mom, it's plain to see — to you we would not lie
So it is best, you will agree, to tell the reasons why
Well, first of all, my sweetheart, we love you for your smile
Your friendly manner, slightly coy, shines throughout the while
We love you for your patience; your calm and quiet way
The hearty little chuckle that we hear from you each day
We love you for your brilliant mind and your humor is a blessing
One doesn't rear a family with just a lot of guessing
We love you for your kindness — we like to hear you sing
Goodness knows, we envy quite, your skill at everything
We like the way you understand the things we say and do
We really love you, Mother, and know you love us, too

Beryl Jarvi

He's a man of all seasons who enjoys each day
In his very own self-styled philosophical way
He loves family and people; he's a warm friendly man
He goes golfing and swimming whenever he can
He likes to tell stories and he listens well
Sometimes when he's joking, it's hard to tell
He is most scientific with a mathematical mind
A would-be prankster of his fellow mankind
He's extremely warm-hearted and dislikes the word *no*
He seldom gets ruffled — just takes things slow
Making mountains from molehills really bristles his hair
But when it comes to composure, none can compare
He's a positive person who doesn't complain
If he has any troubles, inside they remain
He builds a man up when a man's feeling down
He's a comfortable person to be around
He's our own Guest of Honor at this party tonight
May all his tomorrows be fulfilling and bright

Beryl Jarvi

THE TREE BOY

Not very luckily
he viewed life too objectively
and the more of it he'd read and see
the more negative he grew to be
until his life was sheer misery.

He made dangerous connections
of societal imperfections.
He'd laugh at the elections
or any pretense of implied corrections
in a place and time that lacked his affections.

He would not adhere to his family's traditions
and, sadly, he developed absurd suspicions.
And he'd run away on wild expeditions
leaving his antics to fit specialists' definitions
and his parents to take compromising positions.

He lived to the ripe, old age of thirteen
and one day fell from a tree unseen
to be lying on the lawn in the twilight's sheen
every bit as misunderstood and mean
as he had looked in life and in life had been.

Gilbert Mowery

NO WAVE

Downwind striking,
sharks snipping in the underwater kingdom,
the contour of the coasts,
harbors invisible, steady, and ever waiting,
ropes holding, sails fullblown and proud,
sunken treasure, islands of the birds,
walking on the continent, through the formations and conventions,
in and out of peace of mind, the service reception,
through days spent afterwards, lost and dreaming,
standing at the rails of the boardwalk fifty years later,
frail and dying, moving and progressing,
intact and reasonably clear-minded, looking at the stars,
youngsters are riding the amusement rides,
a clown sells popcorn against the stillness of rooms,
lights, music, cameras, action,
a trying night, precious expressions of control,
the expensive funeral, teachers and schoolgirls,
the order of the silver star wand,
downwind striking.

Gilbert Mowery

POEM TO RICHARD

The way I feel is not like before,
My love for you is so much more,
Than I thought love could be.

It is so easy to play with love,
Believing someone is so above
All the others.

But soon the pain and heartbreak come,
When you find you're not the only one,
Who is important in his life.

Now love is no longer a game,
For into my life you came
With sincere love.

Your love has brought me happiness,
I know it's not like all the rest,
That brought joy for just a while.

My love for you can only grow,
And in my heart I truly know
Our love will last.

Jan Richter

ISLE OF VIEW

I've been lost for a long time,
Not knowing where I am,
Where I'm going to,
Where I'm coming from.

Finally, I've found myself.
I'm on the Isle of View.
I call it that because
From here, I can see you.

Still, I'm very much alone.
Seeing you from here
Is not much comfort,
Though it does help some.

From the Isle of View
I cannot be rescued.
I wouldn't want to be.
But would you come be with me?

P. S. Isle of View.

Ben Thair

BREAKING LOOSE

It pains leaving these memories
  crying, dying on make-believe memories.
Take a rest and let the cool sea breathe.
Let the piece bridge the whole
  while the valley moves on.
Make-believe memories, happy, glowing,
  strutting, popping, icling, never memories!

Ollie Marshall

THE ULTIMATE

Man and woman relate as two
  individuals coming into one.
Forces are pushing, pulling,
  trying to submerge.
Each moment is a utopia
  of infinite happiness.
As the water from the mountain
  connects with the mouth of
  the river, the present has
  been submerged into the future.

Ollie Marshall

TWO STEPS

Two steps crossed the same pass.
One left torn, the other completed.
One cried, one laughed.
One shedded community guilty with
  corroded fairytales.
One answered only to self.
One stood with true and alone.
One stood pathologically with the community.
One day time set upon each.
One remembered the cost.
One remembered the reward.
One wandered how to pay the debt.
One knew the debt was priceless.
Each went upon his way.

Ollie Marshall

OLLIE MARSHALL. Born: Springfield, Arkansas, 5-18-53; Education: Montclair State College, Secondary Social Studies Certification, 1976; Kean College, Preschool Certification, 1978; Northridge State College, B.A., Sociology, 1971; Los Angeles City College, A.A., 1968; Occupations: Teacher, Writer; Poetry: *The ABC Character Builder*, poetry with the ABCs, a hardcover children's book; 'Time,' *The New Poets: Yes*, Cambridge Collection; Comments: *It has a universal meaning captivating its listener as he/she relives a profound growth experience in a moment. It binds the author with her environment, connecting personal perceptions, experiences, and observations as each reaches to relive a given life span with phrases depicting an essence of the bare soul. As the phrases unfold, the listener's and the author's souls connect, who once thought each stood alone.*

STARQUAKE

Looking into the sinister-blackness
of night
a Starquake
pulses the World

Kaleidoscopic events fill the surface
Scholars watch in awe,
the sinister-blackness
bursting with silver and gold light
becomes brighter and brighter

The Scholars study and
accept

The Shepherds
blinded
run for shelter
shaking and mourning
waiting for the end of the Starquake
It will always be there
as will the
scholars, and
shepherds

Diane Rupar

IN DUST

I would you wound your subtle ways
About your subtle breast
And, draped in naught but subtle ways,
Assailed me in my rest.

But frocked in guile and subterfuge
You stayed me in my lust;
So missed is mist, and dust are dreams
When dreams are laid in dust.

As wafted salt and angels' wings
Molest the suckling sky,
Deflowered children bleeding hope
Presage my shearing cry.

Discerning lies woo supple truths;
So Tabby woos the Dove:
I would you framed my lowly heart
A hell for higher love.

Naomi L. Johnston

SMILE

People say that you don't smile.
You're serious all the time.
But I remember a time when you smiled.
A time when you were mine.

Your eyes sparkled.
You started to grin.
And your giggle was, oh, so shy.
And then I saw your wonderful smile.
And I knew what you had on your mind.

You are a kind and gentle man.
With a touch as sweet as can be.
I see a smile when we touch.
And I know your smile is for me.

Nancy Stewart-Tornai

EPITAPH TO THE FEARLESS

Hail to the ones who venture into the dark tunnels
Hail to the ones who explore dark jungle terrain

They need not be of one certain color
but they definitely are known by one certain name

They are the fearless, the daring, the brave
Never shying away from life's great escapades

Hail to the ones who fly into the heavens
Hail to the ones who go under the depths of the sea

Those who let no peril of life bar them
from the knowledge that they must seek;
Those who possess that spirit that transcends
petty fears

They who will go face the greatest danger in search
of a better life for mankind

They who conquer our fears for us and bring back
the light to shine in our minds

We salute you, we applaud you
We worship and adore you
You do the things we can not do for us
God protect you, fearless ones

Barbara von Bothe

LONELY MERMAID

Lonely little mermaid sitting on a rock
Some say they know her but none know her not

How could they know the rarity of she
Helping the people, returning to the sea

Why was she put there, what purpose could it hold
All that she wants is to just rest her soul

But this she cannot do, her duties are not done
Her father calls out from the sea that she cannot yet come

And her father exclaims:

''When you have given yourself for their sake
Come to me then, I will open my billow gates
And call you to the sea for all eternity''

Barbara von Bothe

JUDGE NOT

Judge a man not for his looks, or how he may be dressed.
Measure him not for what he doesn't do, but for what he does the best.
Think not how much he owns, or the house in which he lives,
But for the way he treats others, and how much of himself he gives.

It need not be in money or expensive treasures that he pays,
Just a helping hand, a smile, or a kind word along the way.
Judge him not by the job he has, or the kind of car he is in,
But by the kind of person he is, and the kind of heart that beats
within.

Sylvia Bothe Burgin

MY BROTHER

A new baby arrived at our house the other day
Things just aren't the same old way,
To my parents and grandparents it was a great joy
You have probably guessed, it was a boy.

But you see to me it was just a brother
I would have really preferred the other,
But you know how things go, you take what you get
I even tried throwing a great big fat fit.

Kinfolk came from near and far, him to see
They really didn't pay any attention to me,
They all made such a fuss and he's so dear
You'd think he was the only one living here.

You wait and see when he grows up
He'll just be a boy, a big tease and a cut-up,
And pull my long curls till I cry
Don't you know there's nothing he won't try.

But I guess when brothers get full grown
And have a family of their own,
They'll be pretty nice to have around
Especially when you are homeward bound.

Miriam Barbour

AND END WITH ONLY MEADOWS

The say that death begins when from the womb
The fetus slips into the world of men,
Fills its lungs with air, time and time again,
And each breath brings it closer to the tomb.
A love was born once in this very room.
The things that I know now, had I known then;
I would not hesitate nor count to ten;
Nor would I wait at all the heather's bloom.
I would not give to death the chance to spring,
And smother slowly in its fateful cape
The things that I have cherished until now.
New love I would have been abandoning
Before it had the chance to take a shape,
And end with only shadows on my brow.

James G. Clayton

FRIENDS

Did you ever stop to wonder as you go your selfish way;
if the road that you are traveling in the end is going to pay?

Could you give another person a little credit when it's due,
and not think all the honors should be handed out to you?
And when the road is getting rougher that we travel day by day,

Do you think that everybody should give you the right of way?
Criticizing another when she or he tries to do his part.
If you can do it any better, don't you think it's time to start?

Are you jealous of a person just because he or she passes you?
In the struggle up the ladder there's always room for two.

Have you passed someone in sorrow, with a heart as cold as lead?
Do you heed the cry of mercy or do you coldly shake your head?

Annie M. Howard

BIG TREES—MARIPOSA GROVE.

IMMORTALIZED SOULS

Of zealous men great and mighty
Whose spirits in death live on
Mysterious feats they achieved
Of Godly life they lived,
Holy they were, pure and righteous.
They who made history and history made men
Who through trumpets and shouts tumbled walls,
Who created exodus, crossed the mighty
Oceans and smote water flow from rocks.
Stood they the test of flood and wrestled the lions,
Even in the lions' den, they smiled
Valiantly fell they the giants with pebbles
And journeyed to heaven in chariot of fire.
Of valor, who by faith straightened the crippled;
With fame and of esteemed throne granted enormous wisdom
Though sojourners in Babylon, merrily they
In the furnace, waved and walk'd with Him!
Threats of kings and fetters of death they defied
And on Lonely Island, too, heavenly revelation was theirs.
Oh! how wonderful are these Souls.

'deolu Obakoya

GOD'S CRAYON BOX

The air is heavy, in the early dawn.
  Heavy dew glistens, all across the wet lawn.
    Early birds gather about, for their early morning treat,
      Awaiting their daily handout, so they can eat.
        The trees are changing colors, nuts are falling, too,
          And high up overhead, fleecy white clouds move slowly
            In the sky of robin-egg-blue.
          Shiny red apples readily fall, daily onto the ground,
          Landing with a thud, they lay scattered all around.
        It looks like God has taken His crayon box, or His paint box
      And scattered His colors about, to fall where they may,
    'Cause this really is a colorful season, with many colors everywhere,
  So pretty and so gay, it's beautiful, a work of art in every way.
  Nature is really God's artwork, that I believe is true —
  And I am so grateful, that God shares it daily with me, too.
October always reminds me of the gypsies, wild — colorful and free —
  And I always welcome her arrival,
    And the time — she spends with me.   Thank You, God.

Bernice Riedthaler

A GOODLY MOTHER

My Mother is always so soft and dear.
She leads her family from the rear.
Even though Father is at the head,
It is in Mother's wisdom I am fed.
I see her smile, hear her gentle sigh,
I notice the tear slipping from her eye.
When I look upon her loving face,
I want to run to her warm embrace.
She always watches over me, I know.
But understands just when to let go.
When I must learn to stand in her shoes,
Mom is the model I want to choose.
Thank you, Lord, for the mother you gave to me.
Now help as I try to nearly as good be.

Dorothy M. Stanley

WHEN MY HEART WAS A SAPPHIRE

Thoughts Thoughts
Tumbling Tumbling
Eyes Watching,
Sapphire iris open wide
And mine looking back, scared.

I wish we would stop just looking,
At least ignore each other awhile.
For I hate stalemate
I hate indecision
And I hate shyness.

But I am shy . . .
And when your naked gems cut my back I flinched.
I tried to sit still . . .
And yet I twitched and twisted,
Misleading your thoughts
Of glittering, brilliant blue, engulfing me.

Lashes down
But yours still spread like fragile rice plants
In a paddy, waiting for a monsoon.

My tide breaks and
I wish you were still here to see it.

Ingrid Schroffner

GOING TO SLEEP

As I get into bed at night.
After I lie down. I open my eyes
and watch the little clock on the wall.
the little clock says tick-tock.
tick-tock after listening to the little clock
on the wall saying tick-tock tick-tock
I close my eyes and fall off to sleep.
As I sleep I can still see that little clock
on the wall from my bed going tick-tock
tick-tock. tick-tock the song sounds so good.
lying there in my bed. hearing the little clock singing
tick-tock. tick-tock as I dream sometimes
I dream about the little clock on the wall
going tick-tock tick-tock.
when the alarms goes off in the morning
from the little clock. I wake up and get out
of bed and get dressed to go to work
I walk by the little clock as I get ready to
leave the house I stand and listen and can
still hear the little clock on the wall go tick-tock.

Ronald Williams

U.S.A. — HISTORY'S DREAM WHEN IT SLEEPS

The Infant cries but is never born,
We hear Old Man's death rattle, yet
  he never dies.
There abides death side, one Pacific Island,
  and the dark side of the moon.
An Arkansas soldier gives his own definition
  of the superior national state: where you
  live no more than 15 miles from good
    fishing waters.

Stanley A. Fellman

181

THE WRITER

Open your heart
In ultimate sincerity.
Mark the sands with
Profound and provoking ideas.

A stone carved
Away at rough limits,
Sharpening lines in strength.

Feel the shape forming
Into molded structure.
Awakened,
Into the night stars shine
The gleaming rays of dawn.
The moment of acceptance.

Lydia Fernandez

RESTLESS HEART

Since the day I saw you last
An imagery of clouded thoughts has filled
My mind of you.
I am drawn by the light that plays
In reflection of your depths;
A keepsake for my remembrance.
A glint of life revealed.

Lydia Fernandez

MOUNT STERLING

It's two in the morning, not a soul in sight,
I'm walking home alone to spend the night.
You're out running around with your friends,
When you see me you'll stop and chat again.

I can't take this no-love affair,
I can't keep pretending I don't care.
I've done it all, there's nothing left to prove.

I'm out here in the snowlight,
It casts the world a pearly white.
The color of innocence doesn't belong,
In a world that's gone wrong.

The snowflakes fall like tears.
The night cries out, but no one hears.
It's cold, black, and harsh.
Lights reflected create a splash
Of color that cascades down,
And beautifies our town.

Omer Ray Garland

BYE FOREVER

I am saying bye forever,
I don't know when or if I will ever
be back. My love still stands forever.
I wish I could too. But life goes
on like everyone says. So I say bye
forever. Bye is for the good times
we share. Forever is our love that
stands. Bye forever.

Jennifer Walek

GOOD-BYE

I like being nice to others
Especially my parents, sisters, and brothers.
I try keeping myself straight
By trying to do much better,
But when he has reached the gate
I know I will feel much sadder.
That's when there's something wrong
And I know it's not right
I sing a certain song
That makes me see the light.
I know when dad is gone
I will have my happy song
But there still will remain
The love for my dad who suffers no more pain.

Rodney H. Rowles

SANTA CRUZAN'S LAMENT

How I love our city
Where the redwoods meet the sea

Our flowers and weather
are as perfect as can be

Dancing at the Coconut Grove
enjoying Boardwalk & sun
Having a shrimp cocktail
feeding the seals is great fun

Watching all sailboats and
sunsets over the sea
It's all breathtaking
and absolutely free
but . . . please dear tourist
leave a foot of the beach for me

Gloria Giordano

I like fresh air,
I love my cozy corner
  at the fireplace.

I like hiking
I love my comfort.

    but,

I like my sweet wife.
I love my passionate mistress.

Andre Orbeliani

WISHFUL THINKING

I left my head
    At the beach
Buried there
    Under the sand
Where thoughts can
    Rest and dangle
Like the seaweed
    Bobbing up and down

Jo Bivin

NOT MINE

What am I, God?
  I am nothing.
Thy voice instills me —
  Not mine.
Thy insight fills me —
  Not mine.
Thy world engulfs me
  Oh God.
Help me to use it — like yours —
  Not mine.

Jo Bivin

JOANNA MAE (BRENNER) BIVIN. Pen
Name: Jo Bivin; Born: Cissna Park, Illinois, 7-3-
25; Married: Stanley E. Bivin, 7-30-49; Educa-
tion: University of Illinois, B.S., 1947; Occupa-
tion: Teacher; Memberships: NEA, IEA,
RFEEA; Poetry: 'Haiku from Hawaiian Vaca-
tion,' 1977; 'Wishful Thinking,' 'Not Mine,'
1976; 'The Fly Who Came to Church,' 1967;
Other Writings: *Bozo the Clown*, children's
book, 1986; Comments: *I like to write about
persons, places, and things closest to my heart.
It has been a pleasure to experiment with
various types of poetry. Some of my poems are
serious; some are humorous. I have enjoyed
writing haiku and tanka, also.*

EVERYDAY HAPPINESS

My heart is happy.
But . . .
There seems to be something missing.
Maybe someone.
My heart will not break.
But . . .
It longs,
Longs for the feel of someone's touch,
Someone's kiss,
Someone's love.
Even on a day of so much joy,
I'm lonely.

Wayne J. Kurpjuweit

ON BEING SICK

When I was sick, time ran into itself, the clock wasn't divided
into twenty-four hours, hours politely following after each other,
each minute and second waiting in an orderly queue, like housewives
at the butcher's counter, waiting their turn.

Time ran into itself like the traffic jams at rush hour and to make
matters worse the days suddenly got muddled into the hours and we
spun, twisted and sped like a helter skelter in a fairground.

The noises in my head did strange things so instead of enjoying
the voices of my children, my music, I wanted to shut you all out
leave that fairground and run for the warmth of a quiet velvety
green wood, or the gentle lapping of the waves coming up onto
golden sands.

As children we spun round and round, arms open wide, laughing and
laughing as we disobeyed the laws of gravity, until falling dizzily
onto the ground, arms out wide, legs splayed the world spun, twisted
and heaved and we felt as if we would go spinning off into the dark
unknown to become some new planet in the heavens.

Joanna Walford

IT CANNOT BE

You are my love and I need you.
Are you my love?
  How can that be?
  I have never touched you.

You are always there.
You sense when I am troubled.
  How can that be?
  You do not belong to me.

You comfort me when darkness overwhelms me.
For all you have given you ask nothing of me.
  How can that be?
  Others claim your love, your life.

Without you I am lost.
No one to stem the bleeding, close my wounds.
  How can that be?
  Why would you mend me?

You said I am loved; I know the truth.
I cannot leave you; and fear you will send me away.
  How can that be?
  You are another man's wife.

P. McAdams

THE RIDE

As the train passes through the dungeons of the world
And I ride to escape the pain of uncertainty
Memories flash like lights of red and green
Passing hospitals yet people smoke
While one tries to sleep, others talk
And the rest stare into vacant space
Empty soda cans and cigarette butts
Share the ride but they don't pay
And then I arrive at my destination
Yet the braking of the train
Does not halt the loneliness
And after all, I have arrived
Nowhere.

Carol Esposito

THE COTTON ROOM

To pour out to you
  my innermost feelings

To share with you
  my most intimate thoughts

To seek from you
  a response to a thought new to me

To pose you a question
  the answer to which I've not a glimmer

To offer an invitation to you
  to consider a concept untried, even heretical

All are like rocks
  thrown into a cotton-stuffed room —

Nothing comes back.

P. McAdams

ONE

My body, mind, and soul with you I gladly share,
Placed safely in your hands and care.

But a moment, without you,
Away from your side, is endless — eternity.

My heart beats best against your flesh,
My mind thinks most of your happiness, and
My soul perceives our unity.

We understand, believe, trust, and think,
At once, the same, in unison — for we are one.

Though centuries may pass or
Seconds tick slowly by,
Whether separated by long miles,
Or lying warmly in your arms,
These words are truth to time indefinite:
  You exist in me and I in thee.

Mary Jane Kish

UNWRING THE BIRD'S NECK

*Supplication to the gods storming the officialization
of English in the State of California*

Unwring the bird's neck —
immigrant, multicolorous —
who does not know that the key
for surviving nowadays

in this world, foreign to him,
neither is his plumage color
nor trespassing the frontier
but leaving behind his language

of origin in oblivion
for learning another tongue
that is badly or poorly known

by four of every three
of all the birds nesting here
who cannot sing but in English.

Ernesto Oregel

YOU AND ME

Expounding on all levels,
Building, eating, talking of habits,
Exploring the historical marks,
Whether they be on land or body,
Exciting to be open and free,
Being with you as being with me.

Paula Sterner

GRANDPARENTS

The last day I saw you,
You were sitting in your favorite chair.
So very silent,
In your solitude.
Thinking of those years gone by.
And of the lovers you've had in the past.
Old and grey now,
But always bright and chipper inside.
Don't give up your memories.
Dream of how it was.
Think of how it is.
And then remember your grandchildren,
In your times of need.

Wayne J. Kurpjuweit

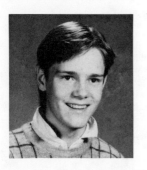

WAYNE J. KURPJUWEIT. Pen Name: J.W.
Johnson; Born: Lynch, Nebraska, 5-5-70; Single;
Awards: 4th place for 'The Rose' in *Young
Writers of Wyoming* competition; Poetry: 'The
Rose,' 'The Father I Know,' 'Pain of Sand,'
'The One Who Sits in My Chair,' 'Playground,'
all in *Young Writers of Wyoming*, 1987; Com-
ments: *I believe a poem should not be set up to
mean only one idea, but many. Poetry should
bring out feelings, of all who read. In today's
society, people are only reading with the mind
— when when they should be reading, and feel-
ing, with the heart.*

GOLDEN YEARS

I am free to overflowing
Yet am bound
Like ancient
China lady feet
A piñata figure
To be hung
Bursting forth gifts
Of stale cakes
To feed the children
Useless relics
Of the pre
Assembly line dawn
Gone
With penny candy
Street cars
And brother love
Gone
Soon
All gone

Gary C. Shukis

THE STARE

He catches my glimpse
I watch his.
Our eyes meet, lock,
and are held into place.
The mystery.
The curiosity,
yearning for passion.
A stolen moment,
mutual and uninterrupted.
A force of hot
pounding desire
collides, stands still,
only to break up
and never to be returned again.

A. Birch-Madgett

DAMN THIS CHARM

Damn this charm!
  it wraps itself
Around my core,
  tighter and tighter, still
Constricting, threatening,
  drawing me closer
Toward captivity.

I twist it right,
  then turn it left,
Over, then under,
  then over again —
It's free once more
  and nothing's there.
Damn his charm.

Laura J. Clark

FIVE

I sit and look at things
  and can't figure them out.
But big people seem to know everything,
  the way they run all about.

I sit and look at my toys
  and try to take them apart,
They give me lots of joy,
  but I can't match up the parts.

My mom is always spanking me
  for things I don't mean to do.
I really don't understand,
  but she seems to think I do.

She always slaps my mouth
  for saying words that Dad says,
They don't sound bad to me,
  but that's not what she says!

Veronica S. Kellogg

REASSURING LOVE

I love you
Your smile makes my day
The touch of your hand gives me strength
Your voice reassures me
Your body gives me warmth
Your presence sustains me
With you I am whole and complete

I love you
More than there are stars in the sky
More than the sands of the sea
More than time can tell
In life and hereafter
Even more; my sweet love
I know that you love me

J. Stone Gramm Robbins

THEATRE OF LOVE

The grand illusion
  the big façade
The act put on
  is far from odd.

The days go on
  the theatre long
The costumes bright
  and emotions strong.

The play closes down
  the house lights dimmed
The audience gone
  as hearts slowly mend.

Laura J. Clark

MY FRIEND

To say what I feel
But do feelings have words?

To show what I feel
Look into my soul!

Help me find the words, at least a few
To say what I feel —

In your presence — see my smile
    tension fades — my spirit soars,
    eyes sparkling — ecstasy to see your eyes
    warmth to be near you.

In your absence — see my smile
    dawn is brighter — the night much lighter
    memories flashing skyrockets
    my heart holding your hand — my friend forever.

My caring never ceases,
Friendship has no seasons,
In friendship, there is no absence.
My soul, forever, always, by your side.
And love exists — without reasons.

Mary Jane Kish

PEACE AS IN GOD'S WORD

*Inspired by a chapel service
led by Director Harold Talley*

The peace of God be upon us
As He has promised in His Word,
From Genesis to Revelation —
Our hearts are deeply stirred.

Safety is promised in Psalm 4:8
The Lord will bless His people with peace,
So says Psalm 29:11 unto us
He has promised this sweet *release.*

"Great peace have they which love Thy law
And nothing shall offend them."
Psalm 119:165 will gird us round with peace
We are protected root and stem.

My peace I leave with you, my sons,
So says John thirteen, twenty-nine,
John 16:33 says: *"In Me ye shall find peace,"*
Righteousness, peace, and joy divine.

"Peace on earth, good will to men,"
The angels sang at His birth,
"For He is our peace who hath made both one"
We know that peace shall cover the earth.

Colossians says *we have peace through His blood,*
We are told to seek peace and pursue it.
We are told *to let peace rule in our hearts*
If we do this we will not rue it.

Babette Elaine Kaltenbach

RENAISSANCE OF CHRISTMAS

Over the years, the holiday spirit has changed —
    From a holy day called Christmas,
        To the party-going craze.
Instead of praising the birth of Christ, something worth honoring —
    They raise a toast with glass in hand,
        "Happy Holiday," greetings they bring.
Commercialism and fashion have poisoned our minds —
    Keeping up with the changing times and forgetting the importance,
        Of Christmastime's old style family tradition.
If we could only recapture a Renaissance past —
    Of old Bethlehem, whence miracles came with peace,
        Love would impart the human heart to honor Nativity.

Hazel Mae Parron

CAROLING MESSENGERS

We tell you a tale, we bring you our message in song;
Of an era gone past, of a Christmas day in the morn.
Long ago; far away, in a stable, at Bethlehem,
A baby was born to a poor virgin and carpenter man.

Oh, Mary and Joseph had traveled afar;
To a distant land, by a guiding star.
No money to pay and were turned away,
By every innkeeper there.

A mother with child turned out in the cold;
A husband that stayed by her side.
Witnessed the fact of a miracle birth,
Nations would remember world wide.

Bearers of gifts saw the star in the east;
Three wisemen whence came in the night.
Shepherds were told by an angel, they feared,
That a Savior had been born this night.

Sing, sing;
We sing you a song of cheer.
Christ Jesus is born,
The Prince of Peace is here.

Sing, sing;
We bring you good news tonight,
As we go caroling through,
A snow-covered winter's night.

Hazel Mae Parron

MARILYN

My real only friend,
Her babbling talk
Gave me comfort when I was sick.

Please don't leave me in this place.
Please, Marilyn, come talk to me!
Yet, even her confused jargon to no one
Could give me the worst headache.

She is going to heaven . . .
She rejoiced in the Lord.
Marilyn gave up at fifty-four
Because she had led a full life
Because it was her share of the American dream.

Meg Prose

MICKEY'S LEFT JAB

Beep, Beep, Beep
annoyingly the watch buzzes
day, date, month, year
a calculator — what next?
Blood pressure! I.Q.!
pulse rate! sexual preference!
just want the time of day
Dammit!
We're surrounded by a computerized
micro-chip world stuck to our wrists
a piece of future shock
Give me a round dial with
Mickey trapped under
the crystal of time
ducking the vicious path of the
second hand sweep tripping over
his right hand falling into
the pit of the day date
Crushed as simple past
turns to shocking future

Cary S. Cruea

STRIFE

I hate him
I know the pleasure he finds in it
He laughs at me
Just waiting and watching
He's thinking, ''soon will be the time''
At last he screams
a piercing shrill
I jump up blindly and pound his
skull with my fist!

Alarm Clock pressed his luck

Jason Faulk

WHAT IS PEACE?

Is it peace, because there is no shot,
no battle raging; tempers hot?
Is peace . . . no war upon this earth,
or is it freedom from famine's dearth?
Is it one, or all of these?
Answer me . . . just what is peace?

Is it peace, within the sound of song;
the music played, what words belong?
Is peace a joy that should be shared;
or is it just that someone cared?
Is it one, or all of these?
Answer me . . . just what is peace?

Is it peace that we should try for?
And borders free that men should die for?
Is peace all of the world or part?
Is it a portion of the heart?
All for peace, there was one price:
Peace is found, in Jesus Christ!

Russ Penne

AWAKE! IT'S SPRING!

Spears of ice, with droplets dripping;
Winter chills so slowly slipping.
Weaving waters, gentle plumes;
Rushing rivers, frothy flumes.
Weather warming, slushy snows;
April's coming, winter goes.
Budding bowers, leafing tree;
Bustling sparrows winging free.
Grass a-greening, robins sing;
Flowers stretch . . .
Awake! It's spring!

Russ Penne

MY BOY

Across the miles I see your smiles,
I hear your laughing voice,
I'd like to be there at your side,
But haven't got the choice,
And even though we're miles apart,
I still can see you near,
For you are always in my heart,
As though you were right here.

Gerald Richardson

A BEAUTIFUL WORLD

I stopped today, along the way
To take some time in this world so fine

To feel the sun and smell the air
To see roses bloom without a care

The birds singing in the tops of trees
The scent of flowers on the spring breeze

How thankful I am that I can be
In this world God created for you and me.

J. Stone Gramm Robbins

CHILDREN

Children mark the beginning
of life on earth.
Unselfish love, ignorance,
and clean hearts are
children's way of life.

Too bad evil then ponder
our hearts
    forgetting we are
        Children of Love.

Dalia Reicino

DEATH

They say death is the zone
marking the end of fate.
And vanity should overbear
its existence in way.
Along then comes a cyclone
and takes it all away.

But remember, dear,
it is not the end —
Remember you started
with a tear in your eye.

Dalia Reicino

FRIENDS

Have you found there is no reason,
Have you found there is no rhyme,
Have you found you've lost the season,
Have you found you've lost the time,
Have you found that time has passed you,
And has now come to an end,
These are times that you'll remember,
I will always be your friend,

There are those who are surviving,
There are those who want to live,
There are those whose life is thriving,
On the love they have to give,
There are those whose life is saddened,
By the feelings they could share,
There are those whose lives are gladdened,
As they see a friend is there.

Gerald Richardson

AMERICA

As we walk now hand in hand,
The miles across this promised land,
We'll hear the beat of different drums,
And live our life just as it comes.

This is our land which we defend,
It's touched our heartstrings as they mend,
It's filled us up with great desire,
And purged us in its raging fire.

It gives new hope to all who seek,
The rich, the poor, the strong, the weak,
A land of riches to all it seems,
A land to come fulfill your dreams.

Its name's America I'm told,
It has a history strong and bold,
My heart I pledge to this our land,
It is my home and here I'll stand.

Gerald Richardson

FALL LEAVES

These frail colors of fall crunch under my every step as I go today;
The cool breeze blows and they drift to an' fro,
They drift tirelessly along their way as I sit an' watch;

For soon they will be gone,
But I know not where;

These beautiful shades of autumn are left for us to marvel,
And to ask, Who invented such things as fall leaves? . . .

Jerry Russell

Happy Birthday Miss Liberty. We the people of the United States
are proud of you.

Thanks to a small group of people especially a sculptor from
France was so impressed by the freedom in the United States he wanted
to help give us a present. He began to dream you up, first a picture,
then a model. After years of up and down you became a reality 100
years ago. Happy Birthday Miss Liberty.

You stand so tall and magnificent and what a sight you are as
people come into the New York Harbor.

Yes, Miss Liberty we love you for what you stand for and we will
give one of the biggest birthday parties anyone could have for a
100th birthday.

As the men who helped put you up said, "She will stand here
long after we are gone." "Happy Birthday Miss Liberty."

Shirley Winters

WHERE IMAGINATIONS PLAY

My life, is not what it seems.
But, constant pain and wild dreams.
I may appear stable, or well-adjusted.
Yet, deep inside, everything's busted.
I am, literally, wasting away,
And getting worse, day-by-day.

I have no strength. No drive to mention.
And, nothing seems, to hold my attention.
My senses are dulled. My mind is scattered.
My will's been broken. My whole life shattered.
I've always been weird, afraid and alone.
Maybe that'll change, once emotions are known.

I sometimes think, I've lost my mind!
But how could I lose what I didn't find?
Emotions are strong, and must be shown.
If you hold them in, your mind gets blown.
There has been no snap. Just gradual decay.
I've slid into insanity. Where imaginations play.

Troy L. Walters

A PORTRAIT OF J.C.

An undulating forehead merges into delicate narrow contours
Hair, a thicket of grassland shrubs,
Bearded like a banyan tree, nose moulded in a bell jar,
Ebony-faced — tall, sweepingly slender like a giraffe

Eyes, the burning flame of a captured panther — hurting to escape,
To burst loose the claustrophobic air, leveling captive walls to dust

Eyes frozen in a stare, eyes, that promise the impeachment of God,
Marble eyes of night, blinking into many, many light years away.

Looking at hands — light breaks slumber
And oh! the skin, dark, exotic as an African night
A phantasma — a prison.

Then feet, gnarled by stony tracks and mud-pitched roads,
Rambling through cotton fields, sugar plantations —
A harvest of blood blacker than sweat,
The crucifix route, echoes chants begging death
That shudder death itself.

Weathered Arctic, Antarctic, a flower denies
The steel frozen earth, the drums beat louder, louder
Cracking the heavens with bolts of blue passion
And haunted ghosts in bloody graves resound with laughter.

Carl D. Ballantyne

Above my solitude, my sand.
Above my shores splashed by faithless waves.
A white star bores through the blue-black night waste.
It melts my grey and I can see your face.
My soul's sanity bleeds in colors.

Douglas J. Blue

THE VIETNAM VET

He came back from a hostile world.
A place that was his home for over a year.
What effect did war have on a man who believed in peace?
On his medical charts Delayed Stress is the diagnosis;
"No one can say for sure" is the prognosis.
He sleeps with a gun instead of a lover.
He's armed through the night and ready to take cover.
His eyes are blue, so tranquil and calm
but they turn so evil during flashbacks of Nam.
He has memory lapses and bouts of depression.
He loses his temper and shows his aggression.
His body is poisoned by Agents Orange and Blue;
he realizes this, but what can he do?
He's been home for days, turned months, turned years
yet time can't erase his wartime fears.
He's obsessed with weapons, warfare, and jungle survival;
one on one combat and killing the rival.
He wants the hatred to stop and the love to start
but it's hard to feel love from a purple heart.
His case isn't classic, his plight isn't rare.
He's among the survivors of "the boys over there."
He was a soldier in a war everyone tries to forget.
He's an unsung hero.
He's a Vietnam Vet!

Karen Janice Lewis

REMEMBER HER

With strength and beauty
A smile so sweet
With loving patience
Our lives to complete

Leaving us now unprepared
Grandma has passed on
Her travels are over
She's gone home

To a glorious land
With no anguish or pain
With the heavenly angels
She will now reign

In God's court
She'll await us there
With beauty and splendor
Those treasures to share

When our travels are over
When our journey ends
Grandma will be there
To welcome us in

J. Stone Gramm Robbins

CONTRASTING VIEWS

Please don't take that rainbow from me,
The part of me that sees new hope.
Tender love that holds me fondly —
The mountains with the sturdy rope.

Let me see a bright tomorrow
Letting loose cares of today,
Give me back the promised rainbow
Thief of the night — just stay away.

Joan Bargmann

NO SECRETS HERE

Deep in town
where there is no place to go
a kitten wanders
searching for lost milk
something sweet and tender may answer
not always milk.
Deep in touch
where
there everywhere
a thought is living
waiting to be found
maybe sweet
maybe sour
maybe lost forever.
Deep in the pools of the stream
lies a golden trout
maybe she's there
maybe she's not
discover if you will
there are no secrets here.

Bill Buseman

VISION

Don't ask me about Christ,
I take him where I find him.
He's sometimes found in temples, domes,
But also in those modest homes
Where simple living played.
Did Christ appear and braid
Their lives into love-knots of gold?
Whether young or old,
He sold their pain for joy.

How do I know him when I find him?
(And mind you, I don't always know!)
The eyes — soft, loving, kind,
Like beacons call my ancient mind
And bid me answer, not with words,
For those are blind, kind perhaps,
But eye to eye, soft as sky,
Remind me why I'm here.
It's clear that we're
Involved in destiny.

Jan Curtis

SOME THINGS FOR SUMMER

A romantic evening on the streets,
Watching the sunset down by the beach,
A fancy restaurant with the one you love,
An exciting plane ride from way up above.
Working on your darkest tan,
Trying to find the perfect man,
Going on a relaxing vacation,
While listening to your favorite radio station.
Saving a day for Disneyland,
Going to the concert of your favorite band.
Just hanging out down at the mall,
Or fixing your schedule to do them all.
You even have time to do a lot more,
'Cause in the summer, you just *can't* get bored!

Katie George

INFLATION

(Christmas 1975)

People are striving to make a living
Those who aren't forgiving
To work all week to earn some money
Just to buy food, that's not funny.
What used to be known as enjoyment
Is now referred to as unemployment
People are tired of doing without
The big wigs have it all
They know what it's about.

Children are hoping
Santa will come
Will he have to buy gas, stand in line,
Or does he know someone?

Everybody's wondering how it all came about,
Looking for someone to find a way out
With the know-how of today
Somebody should be able to find a way out.

Robert A. Litterer

ADVENTURE IN NEW YORK

He's just a five-cent sport, he's just
a five-cent sport; always thought, he'd
have a lot, all he ever got.
He's just a five-cent sport.

As he was walking down the road
one day, with his dirty old clothes
and his hat caved in.
He's just a five-cent sport, he's just
a five-cent sport.

Last night as he was sitting in the
park feeding the birds, a
policeman tapped him on the shoulder and said:
Don't feed the birds.

He's just a five-cent sport, he's just
a five-cent sport; always thought, he'd
have a lot, all he ever got.
He's just a five-cent sport.
Such is the life of an adventurer in
New York.

Gerald Momy

GERALD LEO MOMY. Pen Name: Jerry;
Born: Moncerf, Quebec, 7-6-26; Education:
Eighth grade; Occupation: Hospital personnel
(15 years); Membership: Affiliated Inventors
Foundation, Colorado Springs; Awards: U.S.
Patent for floor cleaning device; Honorable Mention for poetry, 1987; Poetry: 'China Dolly,' *The Art of Poetry*, 1985; 'Jesus Loves Her,' *Words of Praise*, 1986; 'Betsy Kay I Love You,' *Hearts on Fire*, 1986; Themes: *In poetry I strive to embody creativity, thus harmonizing with God's creation (the universe)*.

PEACE ON EARTH

Peace on earth
Depends on each one's search
For what is right
And seeking the Holy Light

Let us pray each day
And give our thoughts away
In a sharing that holds forth
The symbol of a mighty torch

Grant that this year be
One to rejoice and prepare to see
A hearing, a listening from above
A renewing of ourselves as a

Newborn Dove

Jeanne Faust

AFLAME

How cold and solitary is a match
  until it's struck into a flaming blaze;
Then when it meets with a lonely candle,
  it lights it and breaks the smoky haze.
The match is short-lived; but when its fire dies,
  it leaves a flickering candle that soon burns out.
How like these two, we all must seem to God
  when we forget what His message is about.
Christians need each other to spread God's word
  until the world is spiritually afire,
Receiving God's blessings and His love;
  this is His only ultimate desire.
In your life glowing with faith and aflame,
  and have you reached out to someone today?
Did you let them know that you want to show
  God's love for them in your own special way?

Flora Ellen Moore

MERRY CHRISTMAS MOM & DAD

Christmas is that magic time when hearts & words all
seem to rhyme; a simple time, a time of giving, reminding
all that life's worth living.
Good cheer & joy fill the air, while health & happiness
make the perfect pair.
Buying gifts & trimming the tree, an innocent child on
Santa's knee.
That glorious star that shines so bright, high in the
sky on Christmas night — expressing His wondrous love & might.
Christmas is welcomed through everyone's door, but
Christmas to me means much, much more; for I am special,
unique in a way — I have Christmas every day!
Not with presents or money per se, but love, kindness
and thoughtfulness too — all of which were given by you.
You've given the gifts that mean the most, given freely
& without boast. We wish and wish, but for naught, knowing
that love cannot be bought.
The spirit of Christmas is in my heart, & though by
miles we are apart — with all my love I give this poem, &
with just a thought of Mom & Dad, I'll be at *home!*

Karen Treihart

MCLAIN PARK

The bay water slaps fiercely against the long
island of rocks — huge, speckled, extended out —
reaching for the serenity of the lonely lighthouse,
she watches and protects.

Each one leaves a piece of themselves with
their "I Loves . . ." and their "Rock-n-Roll Forever,"
dates read back into the 1970s.

On the beach bonfires are distributed through
the hills of sand — neverending, between small and
broken trees, aged logs.

There is laughing, guitar-playing, music
penetrating from radios . . . life.

The last struggling flicker of a bonfire
is left, then only the light from the lonely
protector guides my way.

All is dark.

All is memories.

Diane Rupar

THE CONFRONTATION

I wonder,
yesterday I found what I had
searched the day before.

Today I reflect in bittersweet silence . . .

I have lost my joy for discovery . . .
or rather perhaps, I have just forgotten how to discover joy.

Experience is the violator of Innocence,
as is Time the persecutor of youth.

I no longer hunger for wisdom,
for it leaves my belly empty.
I am searching inside for answers to external things.

Is there no simple answer?

Yesterday there was,
Today there could be,
. . . Tomorrow I dread to think about.

Maybe I should start worrying when I stop searching . . .

I look in the Mirror,
          and I confront my enemies.

Eve Reinhart

AN ECSTASY OF RAGE

Walk away, pass me by, no — don't look my way.
  Reach through — grab my heart,
    twist my emotions, torture my days.

Pass me by, no — don't look my way, walk away.
  Obliterate my obsession, gullet my veins,
    dislodge my blood from entwined minutes.

No — don't look my way, walk away, pass me by.
  Disband your hold, disgorge my mind.
    Crucify my being, within seconds,

You walked away and let me stay.
  Agonized, pierced and racked with fear.
    Alone I remained as I watched you.

Pass me by.
  You stole my heart, a corsair in disguise.
    Destroyer of dreams, master of pain.

No — don't look my way, not with malevolence.
  Your evil eye, profane actions, scurrility air,
    with your meandering mind and twisted manner.

Each passing day, minute, second I relive
  That *day* — you walked away . . .

Beverly Hirsch McKamey

DADGUMMIT — ANOTHER SUMMIT

We have a missile aimed at *you.*
We touch a button — and you're *through.*
  What's that? You have one pointed *our way?*
  Let's talk awhile — whadya say?

Robert Emmett Clarke

SETTING SUN

One of the most beautiful sights to me
Is to watch the setting sun
As it slowly sinks out of sight
As its day's work here is done.
But as the sun is sinking
Slowly out of my sight
And bringing darkness to me
With the oncoming night
It doesn't make me feel sad
For I know its work has just begun
So that my Australian friends
Too can enjoy a day of sun.
So my friends, as you watch
The sunrise in your Australian home
Think of me in America watching
The same sun setting at my home.
And as the day ends for you
And you watch the sun set, my friend
I'll enjoy the sunrise here at my home.
As my day of sun begins again.

Shirley B. O'Keefe

GOD SPOKE TO ME!

I was lost in dread and sadness,
To God I raised my plea
For strength to bear my sorrow,
He heard and *spoke to me!*
He bade me keep my mind serene,
My heart pure, believing, clean —
My hopes He raised anew on high,
My faith He strengthened, ever by
His sweet assurance,
For you see, when I despaired,
He spoke to me!
He promised to share my burden,
I could leave it in His hands;
I was shamed by my human weakness,
By my failure to understand
And to know He is always waiting
Wherever the need may be —
I'll be grateful to Him forever —
Because *He spoke to me!*

Ada Waters Everette

WHAT YOU GET IS
WHAT YOU SEE

What you see is what you get
  is most always said jokingly,
but oh, how true about life it be
  that what you get is what you see,

See life as a burden and it will be
  for you give to it that reality,
see it as worthless and inevitably,
  sans meaning or purpose it will be,

But see it as you would a friendship,
  to be treasured, and it will be
full and happy and never ever, a
  burdensome, worthless responsibility,

And if in the passing nights and days,
  our time as if a drop in the sea,
you see it not as a valued gift from God,
  curse not what you choose it to be.

Mary D. Welker

PHILLIP BURCH

We didn't see our grandson,
He was twenty miles away,
But his mother wrote us previously,
''Phillip Burch said 'Grandma' today.''

We went to see his mommy
And brand-new sister small,
Who slumbered in the nursery
Like a fragile Dresden doll.

Christy is all a girl should be,
Dark, olive-hued, petite,
But there's another back at home
Who is rough, boisterous — and sweet!

An ode was written to Christy
And sent to kin far and near,
This verse is penned to P.B.,
For his ears alone to hear.

No one can ever take your place,
You're special because you're you;
You will grow up tall and straight and strong,
Loving others as we love you.

*Mary Margaret Louise Peery
Tucker*

MARY MARGARET LOUISE PEERY TUCKER. Born: Baltimore, Maryland, 1921; Married: Nathan Burch Tucker, Jr., 1943; Education: Washington School of Art, Bowling Green Business University, Bowling Green, Kentucky; Emory and Henry College, Emory, Virginia; Occupations: Artist, Staff member of PGA Insurance Company; Comments: *My talents are gifts from God. All of my paintings and writings are dedicated to Him. I pray that they will be used by God to His majestic glory.*

WILTED PETALS

I guess I planted the seed.
It wasn't intentional.
I just kind of dropped it on the ground,
    and it took root;
But you took care of it.
You watered it and gave it nourishment
    and watched it start to grow,
It flourished;
But then something happened.
Maybe you thought it was a weed,
    or you didn't like the color.
You lost interest.
You quit caring.
    and now, I think the flower is dying.

Julia Fisher

TO MY FARAWAY FRIEND

Time changes all
Old memories are images

Move on in exploration
Looking for same

Creating new images
Experience for new thoughts

Still short of replacement
Of one image

The long sessions
Chatting, laughing and crying
Which will never be erased

So, to my *faraway friend*
I toast to you a simple saying:

  No matter
  How far or close
  By land or mind we are

  In my heart,
  You are a very special friend.

Paula Sterner

SPEAKER'S CLUES

Torn are the wings of the flightless birds,
Such as the souls who hear not the words.
Fearless are the thoughts of unspoken words.
Holding the moments of the wrathless sword.
The barriers of time have all paid the dues,
Such as the fortune of the speaker's clues.

Lisa Arthur

SET THE CONTROLS
FOR THE HEART
OF THE SUN

Set the controls for the heart of the sun
The river flows to the beat of the sun
The wind sheds tears of joy
Doves fly in pairs a sign of the future
Give me wings and
Take me to the heart of the sun
Show me a way to capture the heat
Let me spread the warmth
So everyone below can glow
Set the controls and set me free to be me
In a world free of translucent bodies
Like empty rooms full of windows
Give me a paintbrush and
I'll paint you a lovely picture
Of what the world above is all about
Set me free of nuclear disaster
To be where exposure is the only danger
''Wake me up before you go
Shut that radio let me dream''

Christopher Dubiel

NIGHTSONG

Through my open window, I gaze . . .
as the cold mist of night air baptizes my soul.

I mourn the barrier between us.

A barrier that I constructed of Naked Emotion.

You were my Predator, and my Prey . . .
I was the Hunter . . . and the Hunted.

Defiling your innocence as my own,
breaking your spirit at the cost of mine.

My loins ache for you as the moon sighs.

Reality mocks my folly,
and I laugh while tears are still moist on my face.

I led you to abandon me as surely as if I had mapped your escape!

. . . I must now recapture your tenderness in thought . . .
your caress via fantasy.

The crickets echo a cacophony of nightsong
that my heart is conducting.

Eve Reinhart

EVE REINHART. Pen Name: Devon Lane; Born: Columbus, Ohio, 3-17-54; Married: Michael F. Reinhart; Education: Noni School of Modeling, Advanced Modeling, 1973; School of Modern Photography, 1976; Occupations: Photographer, Writer, Model, Christian, Wife; Comments: *The most prevalent theme in all of my poetry is "emotional reflections." None of my poetry portrays "what is," as much as it portrays "what is in me," and hopefully what is in the hearts of those who read it.*

SEA GLASS

A new my love,
as we venture the rippled waters of life together,
caught in the drifting sea of life's experiences as one;
The coral shines as the essence of your smile,
your eyes are visioned with excitement as in the lifting
of the sea mist;
We are as the sea glass stones;
The sands of time wear away our rough and jagged
edges and soothe and smooth our souls,
till we are but what we were meant, to be a foggy
cover on our outsides but clear to ourselves on the
inside engulfed in one another's love.

Andrea Healy

THE DREAMERS

Dreams awaken my love and me at the ebb of dawning,
To give us such fright — with no warning.
What places these visions in our subliminal minds?
Of chaos, mayhem, sadness or some sensual kinds.
Thoughts that would never come — during light of day.
Oft times we laugh — just to make them go away.
With sleep disturbed by these nocturnal fears,
Rude intrusions of our gather years,
Two lovers' eyes refrain from closing again —
In avoidance of returning to the unlocked den.
Knowing all the while we must keep —
These unmasked dreams, perchance to sleep.

Eleanor L. Sawyer

THE CAULDRON

The Cauldron is filled with evil
Deadly laughter hovering — Lurking in
dark corners
We run . . . into It, We fall

Every minute, Every day, Every hour, Every year,
A new ingredient is added to the Cauldron
The recipe begins to boil, We stir

A European Pastry
A Russian Goulash
A Middle Eastern Garnished Meat
An African Soup
An American Pie

It becomes hot, boiling
The clanking of metal . . . Cold Steel
An explosion
We start again staring into the Cauldron

A new recipe must be made, We're amateurs
It's difficult, foreign, uncomprehensive
The recipe is titled
P-E-A-C-E

Diane Rupar

DIANE MARIE RUPAR. Born: Hickory Hills, Illinois, 4-20-68; Single; Education: Sophomore at Suomi College, Hancock, Missouri; Occupations: Newspaper editor; Awards: Journalism Award during freshman year at Suomi College, 1987; Poetry: 'McLain Park,' 1987; 'In My Dreams,' *Many Voices/Many Lands Anthology,* 1987; Other Writings: "Sting Games Are Family Affairs," article, *Berwyn Life,* 7-84; "Teen Recalls Grandma's Cross," short story, *Berwyn Life,* 4-7-85; "On Her Own, Girl Thinks of Mom," short story, *Berwyn Life,* 5-12-85; Comments: *Most of my poetry as well as my short stories are contemporary. Their focus is personal experiences that are important to me, the ones that really are planted in my mind. Also some of my other poetry is based on how I see myself and how that conflicts with what others think of me.*

THE DECK

The ace is he a spade
with a full deck?
Does he have a heart of diamonds?

Fields are full of clubs
The queen is running.
The king awaits the jack.
The highway marker
reads two through nine.

We are in the heart
of it all,
where the feeling is.
The king laughs
while I dance
with the queen.

We are a royal family
amongst the regulars.

I make the cut
that is deep
in the heart
like a diamond.

Christopher Dubiel

RISE ABOVE
THE ORDINARY

Those who have come far
find what is real
Now take the time
to go inside the self

The journey is a life
with time well spent
Holding love and virtue
for granted once taken
With a close pleasure in

Be free to settle into ''un''
for the wiser will never know
The sign of relief will be high
and the path you've come to
Requires no answer but one

''I Will'' be myself

Jeanne Faust

FREEWAY MADNESS AND
A HIGHWAY GOOD-BYE

A tune of sadness gropes
Singing of lost lives and hopes
And the squeal of tires
Ends in tearing metal on a wet road
Screaming for the gods of death

A radio report saying blood
Of a three car pile-up ahead
And all that is left of the dead
Is a paragraph in the local gazette

Thomas L. Swalley

TO MY CHILDREN

Don't grow up too fast, my children.
Take your time and make it slow.
If not you may arrive somewhere
You might not want to go.

Don't always be in such a hurry
To mature beyond your years.
You may get old before your time
Along a trail of tears.

Don't be eager to jump out there
And face the world unknown.
Just remember, no matter where you go,
You will not go alone.

Our spirits will be part of you,
When you go far away.
We hope you'll know how much we cared;
The things we could not say.

So, don't grow up too fast, my children.
Don't leave childhood way behind;
Because someday, when the burdens grow,
You'll miss it, you will find.

Julia Fisher

MY FRIEND

A friend is someone special;
Someone who understands;
Someone who's there because they care
And doesn't make demands.

A friend will always be there,
Whenever things get rough.
He'll take what you can bear to give
And feel that it's enough.

I truly hope you realize,
I'm glad that you're my friend.
You help keep me together,
When I head around the bend.

You listen to my problems
And put up with my tears.
You always do the best you can
To help ease my fears.

You never try to change me.
You like the me you found.
When God said I could have a friend,
He knew you'd be around.

Julia Fisher

The moment is still.
The beauty serene.
The sky dances off the mountains.
It's quiet, it's peaceful,
it's God's moment.
It's the desert.

Sandra R. Boothe

On the wings of our smiles
We shone with the sun
And glown with the moon.
Love,
Gone too soon.

On the wings of our smiles
We laughed at the rain
And played in the snow.
Love,
Forgot to let grow.

On the wings of our smiles
We rested our hope
And ignored despair.
Love,
We forgot to care.

On the wings of our smiles
We'll find faith
And we'll find trust.
Friend,
To love, we must.

William J. Gayzik

FEELING RED

Red is a heart, a symbol of love;
red is the warmth of a warm woolen glove.
Red is a ribbon in a young girl's hair,
red are my cheeks in the cold brisk air.
Red can be happy like Santa in a store;
red can be sad from bloodshed in war.
Red is serene as a cardinal in the snow,
red is subtle within the rainbow.
Red is a rose, blooming in the spring;
red is the sparkle of a bright ruby ring.
Red is the cherry that hangs in the tree;
red is the scrape on a young child's knee.
Red is the sun after a hot summer's day;
red is the tone of fresh wet clay.
Red can be angry or a burning desire;
red can be blazing, as flames in the fire.
Red are the oak leaves that pass with fall;
red is the mourning at a loved one's funeral.
Red is the life and the things that I see;
red is the dream of discovering me.

Sarah N. Gray

HARD FACTS

Rocks never die . . .
        . . . they simply wait
as time drifts by.
The sea beating,
The lovers dreaming,
The children weeping,
Existing.
Rocks never die . . .
        . . . but will I?

Sarah N. Gray

JESUS WAS CRUCIFIED

Jesus was handed over, He was betrayed by Judas that day.
He was given to the officers, our Jesus was led away.
They took our Lord Jesus, the truth they did not know.
They scorned Him with false judgment, put Him there on show.

They whipped our Lord Jesus, they spit on Him with scorn.
While the soldiers planted on His head, a halo made from thorn.
They put a robe upon Him, this fulfilled the Scriptures true.
As the soldiers cast lots for them, with dice that they threw.

They slapped, and misused Him, Pilate said, ''Behold this man!''
But the people called to Pilate, to crucify that man.
With the Passover customs then, Jesus could have been set free.
According to the Scriptures, this wasn't meant to be.

For the people called to Pilate, with a demanding shout,
''Crucify Your Lord Jesus Christ, and let Barabbas out!''
Jesus bore His cross, He suffered along the way.
Along the road to Calvary, they suffered Dear Jesus that day.

Pilate wrote a title, for all the people to view,
It read, Jesus of Nazareth King of the Jews.
About the ninth hour, Jesus was crucified,
His garments the soldiers took,
Fulfilling the Scriptures, that were told in God's good book.

Ernestine J. Tebo

ERNESTINE JANE TEBO. Pen Name: Erny; Born: Parishville, New York, 4-23-34; Married: Robert, 3-22-52; Education: Parishville Central School, ICS/ Business degree, 8-8-63; Interior Decorating degree, 2-22-66; Art degree, 6-19-68; Occupation: Roll finisher, Newton Falls Paper Mill and Co.; Memberships: Life member of the Auxiliary of the Clifton-Fine Hospital, Star Lake, New York; The 100 Club, Chapel Recording Co.; St. Law. County chapter of the N.Y.S. association for retarded children; Awards: Certificate of Merit for lyrics, 'Stand Up for Jesus,' 'The Rider on a White Horse,' 'Praise Him,' 'No One Can Hold His Glory,' 'Good Book Ballad,' 'The American Way,' 5-4-84; Certificate of Merit, 'The American Way,' 2-28-87; Poetry: 'Little Brown Hidden House,' *Town & Country News,* 3-4-86; 'The Brook,' *Town & Country News,* 2-7-87; 'Mother,' *Currier and Freeman News,* 3-10-85; 'Crucifixion of Jesus,' *Town & Country News,* 4-10-87; 'I Had a Dream,' *Town & Country News,* 11-2-86; Comments: *I enjoy writing lyrics, and I have put my own tunes to many of them. I have several songs, some done professionally, by Chapel Recording Co. I write both spiritual and fictional poetry, and in addition, I have done some short stories, although I prefer poetry. My short stories were never published, but were read among my friends. Their comments were good.*

WINTER WHEAT

As leaves dance down in hues of glory,
    the tiniest of twigs play hide-n-seek,
nestled in quiet, enveloped with peace,
    to prepare for the long necessary sleep.

As winter wraps the barren earth,
    in its snow-white feather bed,
the stark coldness cannot reach,
    those tiny little sleeping seeds.

The sun's warmth descends, demanding to be seen,
    but please little ones, heed, sun's deception.
Allow those uncried tears to cascade about you.
    Wake up sleepy one, the time is near.

Burst forth, expand your shoot, reach up toward the sky.
    Beware my friend, take heed listen for the scurry.
Your life began so short ago, hear my caution,
    so you can grow, tall, strong and beautiful.

Sway in the wind, wave to the moon, laugh with the stars,
    woven by magic, spun of gold, grown so bold, only . . .
to hear the reaper's song, hurry on now, the time is here,
    your meaning clear, reason to be, your purpose won.

Beverly Hirsch McKamey

A SATELLITE METEOROLOGIST MEMO

God's view of America is seen every day,
The marshland, the beach, and a salt-water cay.

From rockets and vehicles launched into space,
Begin day and night with an image retrace.

Land, clouds, water and sand a montage may,
Created like only the maker can say.

White clouds move by like puffs in the sky.
These satellite photos never fib nor do lie.

Ripples on the water does the yachtsman find.
As weather unfolds from the forecaster's mind.

Hurricanes, tornadoes, and storms are told,
With the new technology that we behold.

Black and white pictures they may appear to be,
But predictions of sunshine set people free.

Henry W. Brandli

SECRETS

Secrets are but hidden treasures, messages unknown,
Buried deep within the soul, begging to be told.
As they toy with the emotions of the one to which they belong,
Like the solitary hermit, no one hears their lovely song.

Sometimes secrets quickly fade away, though the melody is sweet.
While other times they linger on, resisting sure defeat.
But the tune continues playing as the indecision grows stronger,
Until one day the secret becomes no secret any longer.

Remember, life is full of secrets, mysterious and wise.
Use caution, since so many times, they can be merely lies.
And secrets demand such an uncanny trust
To remain what they are, precious knowledge untouched.

Maria Chechile

NIGHTLIFE

Speakers hammering away the night,
happy people unstairs — party —
afraid to speak — open up,
scared deadly — I am living dead,
a Zombie with feeling of taciturnity —
desire for understanding,
yearning to be touched — talked to,
parasites in heart and mind,
shadows thrown in my thoughts;
between people I walk — not with them,
be one of them — and not;
long nights I walked dark streets,
seeking for my turn —
secretly hoping for victory.
Beauty in pain I feel —
innocence — the water is calm,
little stones trigger its surface,
''It's done memory fails''

Gerhard Schock

SUDDENLY

Suddenly,
The bird
Sprouts wings
And flies away.
Suddenly
Occurred.
Treads sky
Instead of clay.
Suddenly,
No more
Held down
On earth to creep.
Suddenly,
A door —
To heaven
On wings released.

Marie Suter

THE GIFT

The barren winter reigns in world and heart
As fear keeps back the spring of his creation.
He longs to face the day with music born
Inside his very soul of meditation
And leave behind the winter, cold and stark.

A holy, noble gift is stifled by
The blind, irreverent world in which he lives.
Yet it is destined, once refined, to surface
And bring more glory to the One who gives
Each good and perfect gift upon the earth.

Then suddenly, the true man does arise
To meet the frigid air with warmth of tears.
Pure music burns inside his frozen heart
To melt the snow of all his dreaded fears
And turn to tears the ice of all his doubt.

Marie Suter

REAL LOVE

I went through my entire life
And never really knew
Anything but loneliness and strife
Then into my life came you

I knew from the first glance
That you were meant to be mine
God in heaven to keep everything in balance
Sent to me an angel so fine

From that first glorious moment
Until the day God calls for your return
I will always look upon you with wonderment
And thank God for His loving concern

To share with a sinner like me
A little bit of heaven from above
I now know for a man to be free
He must have an angel of his own to love

All I really want to say
Even though it doesn't show
I love you more each new day
And forever my love will continue to grow

T. Dee

WHEN I NEED SOMEONE

When I need someone
With whom I can share
When I need someone
Whose love is beyond compare

When I need someone
To make my troubles go away
When I need someone
Whose devotion will not sway

When I need someone
My burden to help bear
When I need someone
Who really does care

When I need someone
To give me encouragement
When I need someone
To help me over disappointment

When I need someone
There could be no other
When I need someone
I need my mother.

T. Dee

THE OUT AND ON MOON

A very bright ball
Is staring at the earth
Not all the time
High in the dark
That I cannot reach
If you can reach it,
Reach it
I think you are going
To keep it for a couple
Of weeks

Monica L. Bennett

Every year I live
I am more convinced
That the waste of life
Lies in the life
That we have not given,
The powers we have not used,
The selfish prudence
That will risk nothing,
And which, shirking pain,
Misses happiness as well.

No one ever yet
Was poorer in the long run
For having once in a lifetime
Let out all the length of the reins.

Gianna Porter

BROKEN HEART

What heals a broken heart?
A laugh, a smile?
To try going out for a while?

Do all these laughs and smiles happen,
And yet a broken heart won't slacken?
Urge me, ''go out,'' ''You should dance.''
I don't want to —
Or take long evening walks,
I've tried that too.

But what does heal a broken heart?
This low, low spirit,
What does cure it
When hard work seems to
And dreams of you do.

They seem to mend what aches apart.
But, then the memories make it start.

What does heal a broken heart?
Does longing and yearning and wanting for
What's gone and done and nevermore?
When lost is someone you adore.

Jacqueline M. Anderson

RUN OF ONE FIRE

Late afternoon, the hills remain
   watershedded Evergreen.
Soft rains help our crew
   slow the run of the fire.

I hear plane motors —
   airborne waterfalls arriving.
But now, blue nitro lightning
   rising from near the crest of
   the middle hill, we are too far
   to hear its distinct crack.
Who would stash it there?

Some fires can be beauty and the beast,
   at the same time.

Stanley A. Fellman

GLANCE AT DETROIT FROM THE CITY HALL.

THE CLOWN

He was as proud as a peacock.
Flaunting his colors in front
of everyone there.

The lively clown juggled his bottles and blocks;
and chased an imaginary butterfly with an
invisible net.

He had made me laugh, stumbling over
his over-sized shoes, and getting his
baggy pants caught on the edges of
tables and chairs.

Even when he cried, everyone was pleased.
Perhaps he was truly sad — but no one
could tell the difference. When we all
laughed, I thought he looked relieved.

And when he took his final bow, he smiled
widely, then marched off-stage to the beat
of his theme song.

He was as proud as a peacock.

Gerald Garrett

SONG OF THE
RED SQUIRREL

All through the leaf-whipped autumn,
I sat back on my haunches
And tested the tangy air.
I scuttled through the grass
In my coat the color of nutmeg,
And watched you
From the opposite side of trees.

All through the snow-tracked winter,
I shall watch you no longer
From the opposite side of trees.
Inside my deep hollow,
I shall lie curled in my nutmeg coat,
Asleep beneath
My tail of red-flecked fur.

Ruth Ginther

THE WALL

I who so love sunshine, must walk in
    eternal shade.
Punished for wrongs I didn't do
In a world I never made,
A gift at birth I never earned
A battle for rights on unequal
    terms.
An invisible wall erected by man
On this side must I ever stand?
Carrying a burden of race; a shade
Behind the wall that prejudice made,
Bigotry and intolerance, cruel scorn
Fill the world into which I was born
If you were me, and I were you?
Would I build a wall, just as you do?

Audrey Brumfield

FRIEND

I have a friend
that is special to
me.

No matter where I am
He's always there with
me.

He never lets me
out of His sight
For He loves me
with all His might.

I have faith in Him
you wouldn't believe
but He's got more
faith in me than
I can conceive.

I will love Him
forever and that
is for a very long
time.

Kim Hass

QUEST FOR LOVE

The time spent here on this realm,
Is an endless journey at an empty helm.
Fragmented pieces of joy and sorrow.
Timeless days and empty tomorrows.

Always lost in a swirling mist.
Hoping vainly for true love's kiss.
Calling out a name no one can hear,
Formless words falling on deafened ears.

Looking upwards for a rainbowed sky,
Or the tiniest sunbeam to catch my eye.
My hand reaches out for the golden ray,
Before I can grasp it, a cloud steals it away.

A wooded hillside beckons to me,
Where a lonely daisy stands under a tree.
Singly, its petals fall to the ground,
He loves me not, is its dying sound.

Could it be, in this life,
I was not meant to be a wife?
My soulmate, friend, and one true love,
Is not yet here, but still above?

Sandie Porter

RAIN

It's dripping little by little
Then it comes with some soft sounds
As it goes faster and faster
The more it's getting louder and wetter
The more happiness and joy we get
Because we need this kind of survival
My love for itself to let it happen
Garden, flowers, and grasses will
Show you with pride and bright tomorrow

Monica L. Bennett

KISS THE RAINBOW

To the girl I adore
With all my love and more.

My heart skips a beat
Whenever we meet

You have made my life complete
With your smile so sweet

What matter is this
That I should have such bliss

Your love is as pure as gold
With you I would grow old

There's one thing I do know
Having you I kiss the rainbow

John F. Russo

WHAT CAN BE

If you believe that you can fly
Well then you can, but don't cry

Life has its ups and downs
Sometimes we feel like a clown

If we don't always feel on top
Then don't let that stop

What we feel in our heart
For there is a part

That will be brighter
If life is taken a little lighter

What does all this mean
It means that we still can dream

To find that place in the sun
Where we all can run
And feel as if we've won

That is what can be

John F. Russo

JOHN F. RUSSO. Comments: *To me, poetry is the very breath and essence of life, where one can impart the debt of one's soul to the world. I write about life, love, and hope. I try to convey in my writings how one needs to always look for the light at the end of the tunnel. It would make me happy to know that I have touched someone's life and that they have come to a deeper understanding of themselves.*

IT'S ALL OVER

How can I say that things are fine
   when day after day you're still on my mind?
Even though it's all over I'm still clinging to
   one last ray of hope we may see this love through.
On the outside I wear a constant smile
   but inside I'm drowning in my tears.
I try to forget but the pain lingers on.
   I find it hard to believe the feeling is gone.
Love is such a fickle emotion
   that must be handled with the best of care.
Love can't be mistreated or ever abused
   but it hurts and it heals and is often misused.
Now you, my love, can't run from the truth.
   Just learn from the mistakes in your past.
The future holds for us the best of things,
   and together we'll learn what this game of life brings.
You need plenty of time to think this all out
   so take it in hopes it will clear up your doubts.
Right where you found me is where I will be
   for I can't run away from sure destiny.

Maria Chechile

INSPIRATION

The sun smiles down on a brand new day,
Shining rays of hope on the restful child.
Rise up and make those dreams come true!
Those rays of hope were meant for you.
Let faith lead the way and time be your guide.
May fear's pace fall short of your lightning stride.
And confidence be nourishment as you travel life's road,
While strength is the friend who helps carry the load.
Love is your mother and wisdom your father.
To succeed, heed the words that they speak.
Push trouble aside as you journey on farther.
Walk on — let your dreams be your feet.
Though the road may be rocky, the mountain quite tall,
And perhaps many times you will stumble and fall.
Do not be discouraged — the pain does not last.
Look on towards the future; forget what has passed.
When the journey has ended and your destiny reached,
Success will shine bright in your eyes.
Others shall see you as their morning sun,
And you'll shine rays of hope on their lives.

Maria Chechile

LIFE MOURNED

The old door opened, creaking.
I listened to the loud introduction of my heels
And refused to look at the open mouths of snoring faces;
Heaped in oblivion on vinyl couches
Where the crippled bones
Of arthritic bodies
Were trapped in mind and existence.
Even, in their own memories
To an amber yellow age
No longer living.

Lydia Fernandez

SANDY

Waves gently lapping a shimmering sandy shore,
Your golden hair licking the wild blue sky.
Eyes gleaming with the radiance of a thousand suns or more.
Moonlight dancing on a turquoise sea.

Lips so full and succulent,
Waiting like grapes to be tasted.
Beauty betrayed by every scent.
Perfume, on you, would be wasted.

Today, I pray that your love would stay
With me, two souls forever free.
May my heart lie beating within your display.
Three times to be unlocked by your key.

Innocence gone astray,
I wish I could hold.
Ask that you would spend a day,
If I could be so bold.

I only wish that you were mine.
I have the place for our rendezvous,
And just the perfect time.
How I dream you were there!

Omer Ray Garland

CHOSEN YOU

Maraud my heart, I am but a marionette in your
merciful hands,
To be handled gently:
I am in your arms with no recourse but to mold to your form
of existence,
With no show of hesitation, giving all there is to give;
Ponder my soul, ravage my being;
Feelings of overwhelming helplessness and yet growing strength
in the full knowing of you.
I have no choice but to choose what was chosen.
Why try to be what I am not;
Without you I am not;
With you I am;
I stand naked, fully clothed in you;
The forbidden fruit I have bitten with no cure; nor wanting one;
The fleece of your love covers me with the warmth and
absorption of pure untouched pleasure;
Secure in the melting merger of your passions;
There is no jurisdiction of circumstance in my emotions
to you, there's only you.

Andrea Healy

UNTOUCHED SNOW

Winter's untouched snow
It's the most beautiful
It can make us happy or sad
Or think of pleasureful dreams we once had
Sometimes we see faces in this gleam
And wish we were part of this untouched dream
It's nice to walk through this shining place
But now it's snow we must waste
'Cause once we've been through this patch of snow
Don't forget what we now know
For once it was untouched and dreams untold
Only because we knew it was the most beautiful . . .
              Untouched snow!

Rodney H. Rowles

CHANGE IS

To surrender
   that which is
      safe, secure,
   warm, comfortable.

To be tossed about
   on an ocean
      of doubt,
   riding the waves
      of uncertainty
with terror as a companion.

To feel
   the oils of promise,
      of wholeness, of healing
anoint the bruised
      and battered spirit.

To witness
   the past fading into the sunset,
      the future rising in the east,
   the present encompassing both.

Anna Rita Zimmerman

I felt your soul
   touch mine
      and enfold me
Just as surely
   as your arms did.

And strength surged forth
   from you
      to me
In a healing that eased
   the hurt and sadness
      I was feeling.

What a blessing
   you imparted
      in the gift
         of yourself!
And I, like a child,
   eagerly took
      and savored
         every moment.

Anna Rita Zimmerman

TO MICKEY

Beauty is in the eyes of those who behold
Perfection is of the spirit, the heart, and soul.
If I am granted one request,
Strew roses in the path of my beloved;
Play violins at her request.
Unerring let her footsteps climb,
The steepest path to touch a star
Grant that her eyes may ever shine
With inner light; yet look afar —
And still encompass me,
And see me; not just as I am but —
   as I wish to be.

Audrey Brumfield

OCTOBER BRANCHES

Sumac, maples, birch and tamarac
blend into a brilliant potpourri of color.
One last wild burst of flame
before the frosty breath of autumn
cools the dying embers of display.

Drying leaves drift gently to the earth
like ashes wafted on the breeze,
until the barren limbs, black
as the coals of a dead fire,
stand nakedly awaiting winter's icy blast.

Warmed by their covering of winter snow
the trees wait quietly, at rest,
until the rising sap of resurrection
heralds the return of spring.

Olga Borchardt

NO YESTERDAYS

There is no remembrance
Of things
From the past.
All the pleasant memories
Could not be
Forced to last.
The days,
Like a cloud of dust,
Swiftly pass on by.
Time has no meaning
To a mind
That seems so dry.
The constant dreaming,
Hoping to find
That peace of mind,
That once existed
In this desolate
Mind of mine.

Lona Greer

SAWDUST AND CINDERS

We are . . .
Throbbing shells
Holding bannerless causes
Flowing echo chambers
These invisible spills
Of outcast spirits
In the vegetable gardens
On train station platforms
Working and waiting
Weary on benches
Drowned in lemonade
The eyes of the lost
The windows of sawdust and cinders

Lawrence Lui

THE LIFEGUARD

He sits up high
Watching o'er his domain
Protecting them from unknown harm.
Like an eagle flying above
Looking down,
Keeping an eye
On its young.
He sits up high,
Sees the beauty
And knows the peace
Of his tranquil place.
He sits up high
And he does pray
That no harm
Will invade
His beautiful, peaceful place.

Lona Greer

STEERING WHEEL

square and blue
denoting a county
numbering a citizen,

a legal nomad
to and from work
across town

in carbon monoxide
herds roaring
up to a gate,

to stop and wait,
for a gun
to say go.

the race
day in — day out
for years until

post speed
limit thrill
ushers in an
insurance man.

Eric Rose

A WOMAN'S HAND

The hands of a woman can be like the earth;
Can behold the rich, the poor,
And bring forth great worth.
Can behold the great and tall;
Can reach where nothing else can at all;
Can bring forth from the smallest seed,
And like when dew settles,
Can even sprout her own weed.

A woman's beauty lies not in herself,
A shroud of her life and love
Represents her beauty and wealth.

Bobbie Cooper

NO REAL ANSWER . . . LIFETIME OF WONDERS — CANCER

There's winter, there's spring,
There's summer, and there's fall.
As each and every day we grow
No matter how high or how low.
We either wait, to suffer pain
Or grow so old we must use a cane.
We'll never know when or why he calls,
But he will when it's time.
Sometimes before, but we've learned to ignore
By listening to radios or watching t.v.s
Driving our cars or r.v.s.
But, as days and nights go by
We sit and wonder why?
Why has everyone gone away?
And there's still no real answer
To this terrible thing — cancer.

Rodney H. Rowles

BIGOTRY

Bigotry, Old Bigotry why are you here
Bigotry, Old Bigotry why are you there
Bigotry, Old Bigotry you bring only despair
Why must you blind our eyes
Why must you fill our hearts with hatred
Bigotry, Old Bigotry please leave from here and there
Bigotry, Old Bigotry why must you be so cold and cruel
Bigotry, Old Bigotry why don't you let us live by the golden rule
Bigotry, Old Bigotry why all these tears in my eyes
Bigotry, Old Bigotry you bring us many lies
Bigotry, Old Bigotry you only see color, not justice and what is fair
Bigotry, Old Bigotry I will not live in despair

Dennis Humphrey

A LOVE NEVER LOST

The mind is dust.
But that I cannot swallow.
When you left, you said you would make it or bust.
Don't look behind to see if I will follow.

You wonder why I play this game.
I never show my love, my dear.
Not paying attention when you came.
But I really do want to hold your love so near.

I need your friendship by me.
Your love is needed by many.
I need you to see my visions of life,
    so you can see.
You say you have no boys, my dear,
    yet in reality you have plenty.

Your love is never lost, my dear.
To me your love is always true.
If you say you're sad, my dear.
I'm always here for you.

Wayne J. Kurpjuweit

YOU ARE MY PRECIOUS HONEY BEE

You are my precious honey bee,
that's the way you'll always be.
My Terri Lynne, my Terri Lynne
you're more than a granddaughter, you're my friend.

You cheer my life, when I'm sad.
You make me so very glad,
so how on earth, could I get mad.
When you're the sweetest your grandmother had.

You build me up, never let me down.
You're so fascinating, to have around.
I know, in heaven, you'll wear a crown
and that's the place we're bound.

You've led an incredible life.
You've brought me happiness
in care and strife.
Since I'm so old you've brought
more pleasure beyond measure.

So may every line I've written,
direct your heart and life to heaven.
You're my hope my life my prayers,
in God's holy heaven you'll be there.

Mrs. A. A. Roberts

TERRI LYNNE ROBERTS. Pen Name: Honey Bee; Born: Tyler, Texas, 4-15-62; Father: Al; Mother: Frances; Brothers: Art Jr., Mark; Education: Harlington High School; Texas University, School of Dance; Band, Cheerleader; Occupation: Bell and Associates, interior design and antiques; Memberships: Baptist Church, Y.L.B.S.; Themes: *Love, sweet love, America, freedom, Bible, birds, trees, the arts of the home.*

THE LAST SMILER

He awakens;
        breathes the refreshing wind.
He listens;
        hears the subtle calls of chimes echoing.
He smells;
        sniffs the fragrant orchids.
He speaks;
        tells the ancient craved tales.
He sees;
        watches the emptied faces.
He feels;
        touches the grinded souls.
He thinks;
        acknowledges the prideless facts.

Then — He *smiles*;
            smiles for all the youthful,
            doubtless humans that had
            their desired spirits vanished
            from their frail bodies.

A. Birch-Madgett

THE FINGER OF MY MIND

The symbols sieving
    through mind to mouth;
the words make me master
    of objects.
I carry them
    wherever I please
and play as if
    things were there.

So with your name,
    an asphodel or lonely birch.
I keep them always
    close and secret.

A word . . . your name;
    I utter and hear it,
I receive and give it,
    I am instrument and ear,
author and actor.
    The finger of my mind
touches the object.
    I say it . . .
and in its sonority
    you are there.

Leo Kartman

LEO KARTMAN. Born: New York City, 10-28-12; Married: Barbara Leila Kartman; Education: University of Wisconsin, B.S., M.S., 1936; John Hopkins University, School of Public Health, ScD, 1950; Occuations: U.S. Public Health Service, World Health Organization; Memberships: American Society of Tropical Medicine, Royale Society of Tropical Medicine, American Association for the Advancement of Science, etc.; Poetry: Poems have been published in several small, obscure publications in the United States, Great Britain, and Switzerland; Themes: *Psychological insights, appreciation of the arts, friendships, political commentary, and love poems in a variety of styles.*

THE WALK

Horns blow the wind in your ears
And all the hatred hurts
The rose of sweet revenge
The pearl, the apple
The jewel-eyed dagger,
And the bubbles in your head
Danger comes,
And walks away . . .
Have you the luxury of tears?

Lawrence Lui

A SONG

Walking on the carpets of my mind
Following the mists of thoughts and time
Sound and fury having no meaning
Gently as I go
    As we stand upon the seashore
    Time begins to cry
    For things we have not said or done
    To each we cannot go

Living foolish lives
Speaking words of folly
Sheep until the ides of time
Mists of grey, time unending
    As we stand upon the seashore
    Time begins to cry
    For things we have not said or done
    To each we cannot go

Forever may there be some meaning
Wherever we must go
We live and we die
Until forever we are

Barbara Matthews

GOODBYE

Danny's smile all aglow
sheepish and true
his skin like silk
dark bronze — ever so smooth

Macho he was
an image to maintain
but he was Danny with me
that caused him pain

A bond was formed
on both sides of the tracks
that strengthened us both
no need to look back

We taught and we learned
about each other's lives
I'll always love you, Danny
for opening my eyes

Mary Woodward

MORNING AT EDEN'S GARDEN

Sun swept
Cloudy morn
Woods and fields
A woodpecker
    knocks

Thomas R. Boughan

SHYNESS

What am I to do
When I sit next to you?
I get so shy,
I clam up and hide.

I don't know what to say.
I don't know how to be me.
Then the games begin to play,
And we don't know what we're going to be.

The times are changing
And that's no lie.
While we keep on pacing,
Life is passing us by.

Maybe some day
Our song will play.
Then we'll be together
For ever and ever.

Pamela Sue Kendall

PERSPECTIVE

I cannot my Self see
As others see me
I can see others
Unlike they themselves see
And thus know more
About them in a short while
Than I can perceive about me
In an eternity
My mirrored reflection of me
Is blurred by its nearness to me

Leroy L. Moses

SOMETHING INSIDE

Something inside
each time you smile
explodes within me
and all the while
I'm knowing you love me
but something hurts
my pride won't let me tell you the worst

Something inside
each time you speak
each time you tenderly kiss my cheek
makes me wonder why I am
holding from you
the one thing I just have to do.

Something inside,
each time you're near,
makes me realize that you're so dear
that right now, in your arms I'll stay
even though very soon, I'm going away.

Nena Lynne Norris

WASTE OF A FLOWER

In a room there's a vase
Blue with black lines
And hairline cracks in its hand-painted designs

In a room there's a vase
The rim giving birth
To a chip, that exposes a flesh that is earth

From the vase comes a flower
Whose petals are brown
On a stem that is bent in a bow toward the ground

From the vase comes a flower
Placed inside
The chipped, cracked, blue-black vase; and like the vase died

From the death of the vase
No soul was released
For its life was perfection; perfection now ceased

From the life of the flower
No progeny was sown
For its pollen on the wind, never has blown

It grew toward the sun
To mature in a bloom
Just to die with the vase; in a closed shuttered room

Frederick J. Salvato

WHEN ALL ELSE FAILS

It's the ''silent ones'' that simply get lost along the way.
  The deaf and impaired hearing that you meet most every day.

They are just normal people who have ordinary cares of life.
  Not being able to hear or speak causes them a lot of strife.

They need your help and caring too, we all need to understand.
  For when a problem arises, we can offer them a helping hand.

In this ''silent world'' of people, please reach out your heart today.
  They will be eternally grateful, your support is like a sun ray.

When we open up the doors of life, hope is there and darkness flees.
  We reach out to one another, and give to them the keys.

We counsel them to save them, in every conceivable way.
  When all else fails, but you still try, you can always look up and
  pray.

Jeannie Urban

THOUGHTS

I have planted many trees in my thoughts,
only to watch the seeds grow to become a forest of tangled weed.
I have said many things in haste,
only to have them return unending as mocking echoes.
Reminders of the other in all of us.
I have planted seeds of happiness,
and found them to be hybrid with confusion and distrust.
I have dreamed many dreams.
Remembered them; studied them.
Only to realize the wasted time serves no meaningful purpose in life,
which in itself is but a dream.
I have loved many times, many ways.
Enough to know you get what you give.

Raymond Langston

THE OLD MAN

The older man sits on the bench
and stares at the people gone by
He thinks of the war he lived
and all his friends who were shot and died

and when he came back home things were not the same
and they never will be again
day in, day out, it rapes his mind
until the energy is gone within

But the people look at him strangely
he is clearly not dressed for the times
with an old torn shirt and his trench coat
on a morning in mid-July

He is scared from moving technology
that changes while he sleeps
and wakes to a cruel world
to which he fought to keep so free

Now the years have passed, from the days gone by
and you get nothing dwelling on the dead
because the new war's life with poverty
and the fronts are inside his head

Now the old man doesn't care
and doesn't care for the people that do
because his world was blown apart
back in 1942.

Terry J. Firth

A TREATISE BY THE VIETNAM VETERAN

Liberty, for you we gave one year
but our brother gave his life
Fire and blood, the jungle rained
when a dreaded enemy arose by night

Weary, but no safe walls gave us comfort
We found rest beside our dead
A great nation stood up to protest
In ricefields, their angry voices we read

Vietnam, after two thousand years of struggle,
your freedom we fought to gain
Born to lead his people, Ho,
right or wrong we challenged in vain

Home! To cities, factories, and farms in silence —
The deed had been done
To see ahead, we looked behind us:
A heritage of freedom; a unity of one

Thomas A. Faulk

ON WAR

I have known the ravages of war through my brother's eyes.
And heard the quiet sobbing in the night when there seemed no reason.
A time when old wounds burst anew and bled with infectious memories
of the heated battle.
The ungodly fires as if hell itself had come to be a reality on earth.
I have felt the hate of a world whose thinking
could no longer be contained within civilized reasoning.
Yes, through his painful memories I, myself, cannot forget.

Raymond Langston

ALONE

Many thoughts come to mind
Remaining in a World of uncaring
  beings
All those that were once loved
  have left
Leaving me alone with an uncertain
  destiny

Who understand this lost feeling
Security once felt, destroyed
Immersed in a sea of self-pity
Reaching for a light that doesn't
  seem to exist

But something deep inside of me
Keeps me going on
Searching for a new identity
For a world of peace, and someone
  who cares

Somewhere, out there . . .

Ernie Pisacane

ONE LONESOME TEAR

That one lonesome tear
Falling down my face
It's not because of fear
The tear that caused my disgrace
There is no one here
To fill this lonely space
Yet, they are near
But none will slow their pace
For this lonesome tear
Falling down my face.

Amber Sharp

THE WAY OUT

The World has got you
in its grasp,
making you think
you're free at last.

"Partying," "drinking,"
"smoking" too,
is this what freedom
means to you?

The pressure's building;
it's pushin' in.
Your chance for escape
is gettin' thin.

If what you're doing
is a sin,
stand up, be strong;
don't let temptation in!

If you want to find
the real way out,
turn to Jesus;
He'll show you the route!

Marla Smith

ON ACTS AND ARTS

all acts are eternal acts
in that they will influence
all things
forever

acts acts eternal are all
that influence will they in
things all
forever

to lessen the importance
of such influence
on an artist's creation
is to lessen
the importance
of art

Carmine J. Scarpa

WILD MONKEYS

We won't be *knocked out! knocked down!*
Pulled by the hair or drug on the ground!

Before Christ!
Was a different kinda life.
Animals runnin' insane,
huntin' their game.
Well, us 'Wild Monkeys,'
sure ain't tame.
Ain't gonna be bound!
Ain't gonna be chained!

Can't cage us up! Can't tie us down!
Us 'Wild Monkeys,' ain't gonna listen
to your sound. Winds a-blowin' wild
and free, just the way we always
thought it would be.

You know we want to *trustya* —
But — we turn around and *bustya* —
Bound and *chained, ain't* into no man's
game, half *crazy* — *no no* they're not tame!

We won't be *knocked out! knocked down!*
Pulled by the hair or drug on the ground!

Deborah L. Sorgani

RATHER

As the rose
Reaches for the sky
So, my love, would I
If like the sun
You'd beckon me
'Round you the leaves would twine
The flower and the vine
A lovely heady wine
Oh, I'd rather be the rose
Than the thorns
Which you impose.

Carolyn Smith Thomas

THOSE EYES

I saw those eyes,
And to my surprise,
They were staring back at me.

Alas, I sought
And then I thought
Yes, he's the one for me!

But then the fears
Of the broken heart and the tears
Mellowed my heart inside.

For why should the last
Of my ever terrible past
Withdraw my feelings, and hide?

That special feeling he bears
He says that he cares
What splendid adoration
And with great dignity and pride
I said, okay, and tried
And henceforth it has grown
With love and great inspiration

Michelle Webb

THE BEAR AND THE ROSE

There was a rose
A young and tender rose
Who thought she was a tree
A tall and brave tree
Who could stand strong against the wind

And there was a bear
A kind and good-hearted bear
Who saw the rose —
    and believed she was a tree

And so he picked her — and kept her
But she was not a tree
Only a rose
And he squeezed her stem too tightly
In his strong bear hands

And the rose tried
But wasn't strong enough
And so she died — sadly
Because she loved the bear

But he
Thought he had found a tree, and
Didn't know how to hold
Such a young and tender rose

Marie-José Caro

The moon is
Down.
Did you see
The Black Horse
Who dropped it
From pearly teeth?
He has hooves
Of opal
And a tail of
Silver stars.

Elizabeth Liechti

202

THE BOWHUNTER'S MORNING

Beyond the jagged black horizon, November's red sun tints
the fringes of silver clouds floating in the eastern sky
Frost glazed spindling crackles beneath my step;
brittle goldenrod surrenders its frigid crystals to a touch
An ancient red-man, I would be —
nature's student, in quest of survival
The polished weapon belies my fantasy
A distant diesel's groan speaks of warmth, home, and children
who would plead for the life of nature's innocent
Majestically, the tawny-coated buck stands before me
His arched rack like winter's tree
By stealth he has survived;
now he tests the morning cold — a scent? — a sound?
A skill perfected, muscles draw taut like the bowstring
A twang — the arrow glides swiftly, forever
Unhurried, the white-tailed deer melts into the brush

Thomas A. Faulk

GRANDMA

Grandma is my mother's mother, you know,
She's dandy and gee! I love her so —

When Daddy says "No cookies Lou!"
Grandma comes right by and slips me two.

And she says . . . "You be nice now, boy,
Don't think I'm no toy,

Your mom and dad let you have your way,
But you know me, I don't play;

I'll tan your hide and do it well,
You keep our secret and don't you tell —

You see, your mom and dad don't understand,
These cookies will help you grow into a real strong man."

Ma says "No" to the baseball team,
Grandma goes in and before you know it, Ma screams . . .

"Get out of here, boy, and go play,
You'd better make a home run today!"

My Grandma, man, she's keen!
She's the sweetest mama I've ever seen.

Don't get me wrong now, I *love* my mom and dad,
But without Grandma, things sure would be sad!

Shirley W. Bing

OUR CREATOR

God smiles on our heads with brilliant sunshine.
He kisses the flowers and puts them in line.
He carves out the trees, and plants them in land.
He guides all our footsteps. He's holding our hand.
I cherish all nature, creator is He,
Divider of water, He made all the sea.
There's beaches and forests, mountains and plains,
Craters on moons — now let me explain . . .
God gave us the beauty, He gave us His Son,
To die on the cross, for your sin He's come.
What can we give back? There's little to do,
but give Him your life, He'll treasure it too!

Dorothy Marner

. . . SAID THE PLAYWRIGHT

Think of each asset endowed upon us as a card in a card game
How will we play the cards we've been dealt?
Seemingly, we start out believing what hand we have, we must play
Not true. All are choosers here — discarding old, obtaining new
Thus, here we interplay the Theory of the Script of Life
We have all been written in, so we must
    don the costume and play the role
In the First Act, we are but a lingering whisper . . .
A caterpillar within a cocoon — we are much the same as he
Within our own shell, we too begin to grow,
    inward as much as outward
Inside, we fill up what is empty —
    finding answers to posed questions
The answers need not be important to everyone
Answers are only choices. The choice you make
    need only be useful to you
What results from choosing is assuming responsibility
    of your character
Discerning for yourself both from what is logical
    and what is irrational
    (Beware of consequences, they will be your own, based upon what
    action you've written for your character to play)
Finally, when you decide to accept you and your role in the game
You will come to realize the power and creativity you possess,
That each of us out there are playwrights
    writing our own individualized play
Copywritten under an assigned pseudonym,'' said the playwright.

Shannon Blaney

LIFE

And though it was day, one could still see the moon,
And the carrousel turned to the carnival tune.
There were lions and tigers, mustang and deer,
And a young boy stepped on, holding high his balloon.
He ran to a mustang and jumped to its back,
Put his hand on its rear and gave it a whack.
As the carrousel started, his face filled with fear,
The mustang reared up and down fell a tear.
The young girl behind him was on a white horse —
A mere foot away on the circular course.
She let out a cheer as the horse lifted high,
And kicked in her heels with a good bit of force.
The lions and tigers scattered throughout
Jeered at the children whirling about.
The mustang went down, and the boy heaved a sigh,
Weary of watching the landscape roll by.
And when it was over, the little girl cried,
For she wanted more of the carrousel ride.
And the boy stepped off with a gleam in his eye,
Turned loose his balloon, and it rose to the sky.

Sara Burton

THE GRAINS OF SAND

I walked the water's edge
and watched the waves
carry the sand away.

I stood still and waited
for the wave to return
and all the sand rolled
back as gentle as a breeze.

Love can be loose, it too
can wash away, but some
will sift.
    Some will return back to
you. A little finer, a little
cleaner, a little softer,
but will cling harder
than before. That's why
we have beaches by the
shore. The grains of sand
have returned as before.

Bobbie Cooper

BOBBIE J. COOPER. Born: Filbert, West Virginia, 7-12-42; Single; Education: Hammel-Actual Business College, 1961; Occupations: Administrative Management, Cosmetologist; Memberships: AIIM (American Management), NAACP; Poetry: Presently coordinating poetry collection for publication in 1987; Comments: *My poetry is a collection of my thoughts, my life, my aspirations, holy inspirations and impressions of those I know and love.*

GOOD-BYE

Dedicated to Michael Fraley, my grandfather

As the dark shadow
Passes once again,
I must bid farewell
To another friend.
While pain rages within my chest,
I remember you at your best.
Though you are dead and gone,
In my heart your love lives on.
I remember the times we shared,
How you showed that you cared,
All the fun that we had,
How you cheered me when times were bad.
You touched my soul where no one can,
For in my life I knew no greater man.
And though my love will never die,
By God's will, I must say good-bye.

Jim Greco

STRIKING FASHION

There was a zebra on the floor
she danced a digging motion.
A jungle buzzed beneath the roar
that caused her dance commotion.

A cub lion stalked the zoo
and looked the animals over,
wouldn't move too soon and
shed his veil of clover.

Deep inside there was room
but who would push to try?
By evening's end he was gloom
again, a night gone by.

The zebra danced and stepped some more,
she always caught the cub's eye.
He wanted to say hello,
instead, he ran outside.

So a name she hasn't got,
the zebra stayed a zebra.
They moved apart, she was lost,
watch a spectator cry.

Eric Rose

ERIC JAMES MILLER Pen Name: Eric Rose; Born: Washington, D. C., 9-27-61; Education: MacAlester College, St. Paul, Minnesota, B.A., English and Accounting, 1983; Occupation: Freelancer; Poetry: 'Love is Imagination,' 1987; *Selected Poems 1981-1986*, self-produced, 1987; Comments: *Recently I escaped from the suffocating, perpetual world of numbers to pursue long-time interests in film and stage. I hope someday to combine the intensity of an extended poetic moment, a moment that lasts beyond the last word, with visual images subtle, yet strong enough to carry a theme through to a story or a play.*

LOVE BY MAIL

How many letters did we write?
It seems like enough to fill a castle —
looking back now I know that I spent
weeks of hours
    Waiting
        Love.
You were always in my heart.
Three thousand miles apart
yet so together —
connected too, by plans of when
we could next be together,
to love beyond the letters.

Linda Baron

MUSIC

Music says it all so well,
the rhythm and tones
and words together.
The expression,
of ideas and experiences
shared by others,
and put into harmony
with the beat of life.
Music played a part in our world —
The musical background —
a symphony
for our passion;
A radio by our bed
playing love songs,
as we made love.

Linda Baron

LINDA BARON. Born: Blackfoot, Idaho, 1-9-48; Married: Stan L. Baron, 7-17-71; Education: B.S., Education, University of Idaho, 1970; M.A.T., Lewis & Clark College, 1975; Postgraduate work, American College, 1986-87; Occupations, 1970-1987: Teacher; Insurance agent, trainer, and executive; Memberships: PTA, Life Underwriter's Association, Women Life Underwriters, National Association of Female Executives, NOW, American Business Woman's Association, National Museum of Woman in the Arts (Charter Member), Woman's Division Chamber of Commerce; Awards: Golden Poet, 'Popcorn,' 1987; Poetry: 'Popcorn,' *The Great American Poetry Anthology*, 6-87; Other Writings: "Sell Variable Life as IRA Alternative," sales/marketing technical writing, *Monarch Life Marketing Services Bulletin*, 12-86; "Mr. and Mrs. Yuppie," sales/marketing technical writing, *Monarch Life Marketing Services Bulletin*, 4-87; Comments: *My poetry paints word pictures of Americans — living, loving, working, and facing the realities, both joyous and painful, of it all.*

From a snowbank came a Unicorn
She was formed of crystal
And rainbow light
Her hooves were stripped shell
She threw up the frost with them
In a bright wave
She danced with a fox
Of fire and emerald
To the music of a steel string harp.

Elizabeth Liechti

ALONG THE SEA SHORE

The waves were viciously crashing against the shore,
It sounded much like a lion's roar,
The wind and the trees were going their own pace,
It almost seemed like the waves and the wind were having their own race.

The sun was mild on some people's skin,
But for others they were burnt on their face and
especially their chin,
Many were burnt and as a result they were blazing red,
They were burnt all the way from their toes to their head.

For entertainment some played volleyball,
And when trying to get the ball some did fall,
And some were in the ocean and they jumped the waves,
While others were admiring the guys, picking out their faves.

Nicole Lindholm

WELCOME HOME, VETS

They walk through the cool morning air,
Hearing shouts of ''Thank you, we care!''
Walking in groups with disorganized gait,
They receive their welcome, a little late.

People stand on the street or sit in the grass,
Handing flowers and flags to the vets as they pass.
They receive their thanks with a humble air,
As some push a comrade in a wheelchair.

Their uniforms consist of cammo this and that,
Combat boots and an old blood-stained bush hat.
Some walk with a limp and a cane in hand,
Struggling to keep time with the marching band.

Yes, they have come home,
But the scars still burn,
For each carries a memory,
Of someone who didn't return.

Lord, hold in Your tender, loving care,
The P.O.W.s and M.I.A.s still over there.
Oh God, please let us never forget,
The Vietnam Veteran who hasn't returned yet!

Donna E. Gearhart

IMAGINATION

The imagination is such a wonderful thing.
It lets us create or build on just dreams.
As children we imagine many wonderful things,
of Santa Claus, fairy tales, of castle & kings.

When we grow older and our teens roll around,
our imagination changes and becomes more earthbound.
We now go to school to study & learn
and work our imagination and much knowledge we earn.

We keep getting older and adults we become,
but still our imagination continues to run.
But now in reality we labor & strive,
and through work and imagination we live a good life.

At last in our golden years with our time almost done,
we can sit and look back on a life that was fun.
Our imagination now peaks and in our mind we can see,
the beautiful life in paradise,
next to our maker, so joyous and free.

Carlos Serrano

YESTERDAY, TODAY, TOMORROW

Yesterday we laughed and played and shared
our many dreams together.
Not too much, but just enough for us to
feel about each other.
We talked about our future alone and
together.

Today we are laughing and playing and
dreaming alone.
Not really understanding what happened
to our friendship.
We are talking about our futures, to
ourselves, and making our best that we can apart.

Tomorrow we will be laughing and playing
and dreaming without each other.
Not having the courage to say we want
what we had.
We trust ourselves and all that is about
us, but we will always remember the
laughing, playing and sharing we did
together.

Yesterday, Today, Tomorrow.

Melinda L. Miller

MARRIAGE

As an adolescent you think about getting married
Pondering thoughts about children to be carried

Growing up into teenage years
Begins your path of love and tears

Adulthood has finally arrived or so it seems
At last you find the person of your dreams

Proposal of marriage fills hearts with love
Acting almost like two turtle doves

As you are married and live as one
Keeping prospectives makes it fun

Throw away fantasies of vine-covered cottage houses
Hang on to your loving spouses

Many hours of hard work and plenty of talking
Will keep you both from ever walking

Away from this marriage of yours
It was not meant to become wars

Trust, positive attitudes and there to care
Enable you both to always share

The love you both have, with no intentions to roam
Is what makes that house of yours a happy home

Patty J. Linville

DAYBREAK

Daybreak, clear and bright
Chasing shadows from deepest night
Daybreak, pure and fair
Honeysuckle awakening
    Fragrance in the air

Come, come, come at my calling
Soaring through the lightened sky
Shine, shine, gleefully falling
Drops of sun silk, heavens high

Flash on, blaze on, so strong
Seemingly forever
Not quite so long
Time overtakes you
And then you are gone . . .

Marie-José Caro

Give me back my ring!
I want it back,
Right now!

You don't deserve to wear it.

But — It's! —
Well, I gave it to you!;
This is true,
But I want it back!

Well, fine then;
Keep the Damn Thing;
If that's what you want;

What I really want back,
is just, you —

J. T. Hawkins

Who goes there
Like Puck
In the night?
And what is your
Business,
You who is all speckled
With shadows?
I am a dog, sir,
A dog with no home but the road.
A dog, sir,
With no business but
Moon-singing in autumn
When the leaves are all
Russet-gold.

Elizabeth Liechti

CRIME REPORT

My feelings have been stolen!
— and —
I did not see the thief.

I cannot describe the loss,
— and —
Don't know how, to replace it.

J. T. Hawkins

JEFFERY THOMAS HAWKINS. Born: Chula Vista, California, 11-12-60; Single; Occupation: Free-lance human; Writings: *Life as Viewed by a Human,* a limited-edition printing of collective thoughts and feelings taken from my writings, published 12-85; Comments: *I feel that my writings are no more than an explanation of everyday situations in my life. Many people do not know how to act, in so many situations, simply because they never question themselves. I ask myself, then write down my conclusions.*

THE WONDERMENT OF DAWN

In wonderment, I harken
to the lure of mystic dawn
when silence reigns unrestrained
by din of humankind.
There sunrise casts its blushing glow
across the firmament,
while its fiery well-spring still remains
hidden from my sight
beyond the shadowed wilderness
of native forest trees
so recently ill-treated
by winter's icy breeze.

Limbs once bare and shed of pride
stretch forth again in splendor,
newborn of spring and purely green
where there was naught but havoc.
Is it song or mating call
of unseen bird and creatures wild
that from the depths of pine and oak
ascend as hymns of praise
to waken deep within my breast
an unfamiliar spirit life
restraining me as though I were
in rigid webbing wrapped.

Evelyn C. Reece

DAVID

What a perverse man-child you were,
Loving me when I couldn't be loved —
Holding me when I didn't want to be held.
You made me laugh when I just wanted to cry.
You were so exasperating,
Deliberately turning my words on me.
Yet, you seemed to understand me
Even better than I did myself.
Without wanting to, I came to count on you
Just to be there through my tomorrows.
But too soon you went away
Before I had a chance
To thank you.

Anita R. Saliscente

NO RETURN

You're very talented in a special way.
You use people, then throw them away.
You lead people on, then set them free.
You did it to others, now you've done it to me.
You said our love was the real thing,
like Coke, friendship, and diamond rings.
The diamond ring turned to glass
and my shiny knight to dingy brass.
Our love was built on your schemes.
Now I have bandages and broken dreams.
The Coke is all that remains seemingly real.
You're like that, you know, imitation, artificial.
Now the Coke, like you I learn
is empty and used . . . "no deposit, no return."

Susan Winslow

BARRELING

Barreling 'round the corner,
    Wheels screeching all the while,
That "Honda 4-wheeler"
    Did a beautiful "wheely."

A little dog and two cats
    Took off in separate directions.
I'll bet they were as scared
    As I was about then.

The guy raised his fist
    And burned rubber down the street.
I suppose he was proud.
    By the time he left there was a crowd.

Nicholas

SECRETS

Countless lilies whisper to the wind
Their secret tales of love interred below,
As silent hearts bequeath to Mother Earth
The last demise of ever constant woe.
Their quiet refrain now echoes in the hills
And now the angels pipe o'er restless rills
The songs of resting relics, to baptize fools
            in love.

Jack Honan

A SINGLE MOTHER

No time to be just a mother
For you become all others
Father, sister and a brother

Your time is spread, oh so thin
Some days you feel you just can't win

Too many worries of bills unpaid
She suffers much of mistakes you've made

Time is short and years rush by
Much you try to give her so she will try

To grow up strong learning important lessons
Not about money or material possessions

But about morals, values and trust
To have happiness in your life
These are a must

The many roles you play all through the day
Leave you exhausted at night with no time to play

When she's older, you hope she looks back,
Smiles and knows
It was the love you gave her that made her grow

Patty J. Linville

PATTY JEAN LINVILLE. Born: Sullivan, Illinois, 10-16-55; Occupations: Waitress, Mother, College student; Comments: *My poetry is my way of capturing emotional happenings that occur in my life. My writing is of the utmost importance to me for expressing true life experiences. We as humans can equally share with each other.*

THE MENU

of life

APPETIZER
Babies so new — born in a heavenly blue.
(served with — tender loving care.)

ENTREE
School of Life — heaped high with — hope and strife.
(served with — lust and love, with a dash of trust
in your fellow man.)

DESSERT
Moonbeams: a topping of cream for all completed dreams . . .

(served with — (1) husband and (1) wife; leaving
children to carry on the menu of life.)

Barbara Goldberg

CHERISH LIFE

Problems, Problems and then *Problems*

Stripped to the bare
Fear, Anger, Hurt,
Stripped of Life for feeling

Demands, Demands and then more *Demands*

Good enough, not so,
Strive for more harmony

Breakdown, Breakdown, and then *Breakdown*

Go on for betterness
Rid the problems, demands and just breakdown

Center Post has uprooted three-fourths
Very shaky
More stability needed tremendously

Waves too high for the stability
Wearing center post to pieces
One by one tearing at the base
One by one tearing at the base

Strive with all your strength
Draw from within, *Can be done*
Draw from within, *C a n   b e   d o n e . . .*

Paula Sterner

PAULA M. STERNER. Born: Waukesha, Wisconsin, 7-5-54; Married: Bruce K. Sterner, 2-18-77; Education: Moon Valley High School, Bookkeeping/clerical and simulated office procedures, 6-72; Occupations: Escrow manager, Loan closer supervisor, Co-owner of Bartenders Ocean Breeze, Kailua-Kona, Hawaii; Comments: *My poetry revolves around the basic situations life has dealt me and others close to me. I believe life at times is not easy for people to express verbally. That is why there is poetry; the songs come from the soul of the poet.*

THE BURSTING OF AUTUMN

Silence-blue, rosy, and golden,
Reigned over hillsides and valleys between;
The wee ones, amid glory so molten,
Were hushed in shy wonder where grass was still green.

The voices of summer, the lacework of dewdrops,
Were echoed in memory, almost with pain
As Autumn swept over the paisley of hilltops
And rushed on apace with the fragrance of rain.

The earth was so green as we waited a moment —
A hush of the breath — then a glory unfurled,
A trembling, tumbling, chaos of colors
Poured forth unrestrainedly over the world!

Georgia Bray

The things that we say
can never be said
in the same ways
never mean the same things
we meant
when we said them

Kissing you hello-hello-hello;
on a Hudson Street corner
against the winds of world
of time —

Kissing you momentarily
slightly wine-warmed
slightly love-warmed
against the world's winds;
the winds of past
momentarily good-bye

No one would understand
two women
whose youth had fallen away
halting, happy, embracing
every possibility living offers
against the wind of world —
of time.

Cassandra Langer

MY UNKNOWN CHILD

You are the child I gave away
It wasn't fair to keep you
They said to sign on the bottom line
A decision I've had to live through.

I don't believe that I was wrong
Though I wish I could have held you
To give my newborn baby up
For I was a baby, too.

You're just about the age right now
That I was when I had you
I pray to God that you don't make
The same mistakes I do.

I have no way of finding out
Just how your life is going
A family gave their love to you
My gratitude still owing.

I'll bet you dream of what I'm like
How I look, am I someone's wife
I sure dream of you, sweet girl
Your eyes, your hair, your life.

Today's the day you turn sixteen
If only I could wish you
The happiest of birthdays
Love Mom, and I still miss you.

Sandra Zarb

ON MY CROSS

A scourge darted
Like a shot
From an unknown plane
To deflower my morn;
Dwindling my lower clock
From second to second . . .
Yet this scourge clads me
With the breast plate of faith
Sculptures my delights
Gingers my guts
Makes me
Not only to stare
But to dare.

Augustus G. A. Sam

GEORGE

strolling down the beach
is George
counting shells
walking slowly
toward the reefs
water lapping
sea gulls flapping
no one looking
no one laughing
out of sight is
George

Martha Mae Martinson

MARTHA MAE VENNER MARTINSON.
Born: Batesville, Arkansas, 10-23-24; Married:
Harald E. Martinson, 12-9-42; Education:
Stephens College, Columbia, Missouri, 1942;
Huntingdon College, Montgomery, Alabama,
1952; Hageustown Jr. College, Hageustown,
Maryland, 1983; Occupations: Wife, Mother;
Memberships: Daughters of American Revolu-
tion, Conococheage Chapter; Fountainhead Gar-
den Club, United Daughters of Confederacy;
Awards: Prizes Contest, Hageustown Jr. College,
1983; Poetry: 'Lonely Bird,' 'Moon Shadows,'
Campus Crier, Hageustown Jr. College, 5-3-83;
Comments: *Learning lessons in life by observing
nature, by being sensitive to surroundings, by
seeing and understanding beauty in surround-
ings, I paint a picture with words.*

PRAYER

the mighty, the small,
the silent, the noisy,
rise with solemnity
in shining ora
like organ chords.
the child, the parent,
the blind, the cripple,
half-hearted stop
trapped by truth
like seaweed in a sieve,
only holy, soul searching
reaches heavenly ears
to show man's goodness.
the mighty, the man,
are those who believe
acting out their faith
like ancient prophets.

Mara W. Cohen

A VICTORY

A giant sea
So empty.
Hungry birds catch fish
Which have no taste
And fill no stomach.
Silent waves
Dash empty shores.
Matts of seaweed
Cover sandless beaches.

Mara W. Cohen

SHADOW

Suddenly, a shadow entered
The scene
Surprised, could not believe
My eyes

Flash . . . Blue aurora
Streaking golden waters
Sloping tenderness dividing the sky
A completeness

Asked . . . answer
The picture seemed together
Afterward a long cold walk
Accompanied by a nothing of a talk

Sounds causing movements
Trickling from the ceiling
Slowly splashing against the walls
Another change

The motion continued
Tempo rising beyond range
Suddenly . . . falling
Conclusion of a rendition

Larry James

I'M MISSING YOU

I remember when we were young,
We laughed, cried, talked, hugged, danced, and sung.
You liked me so much you called me sweetie pie.
You understood who I was
And you didn't mind if I wanted to touch.
But then, you had to go
And I didn't want to say goodbye.
Oh, memories are all you have brought
  When in doubt and I fear,
I wish you were near.
You can't see the tear . . .
It's in mine eye.
The pain hurts so bad I want to cry.
Did you love me or was it a lie?
  Why does it hurt so bad to love a friend
And to see them go?
Oh, who will it be to cheer me up
When I'm feeling low?
Why do I feel like a yo-yo
Chasing after a pretty rainbow?
Why, oh, why won't I just let go?
Oh, how I'm missing you.

Mary Elizabeth K.

WAR

Beyond the chain of thought lies a universe,
In which peace is only perceived.
If that idea were true on earth,
No war would be conceived.

From the time of beginning a reason was given,
Of earth and reality as known.
Until the time of destruction, we will be living,
And reaping what we have sown.

The earth has been stripped of natural resources,
For the advancement of the race.
What of the future, and its recourses,
Will mankind have to face?

Father Time is the clock that ticks away infinity.
Our fate is in his hands.
What hour is the clock set,
For peace to rule the lands?

Lisa Arthur

HEARTS-EASE

Hearts-ease how rarely do we find it
As blindly we wander here below,
Stumbling, aching hearts go seeking always
For that our human hearts can never know.
The futility and lack we always suffer
To find — when we have found it, it is gone;
But one thing, Lord, I am convinced of,
Thou art preparing Hearts-ease farther on!

Thou in Thy tender love, the heart's creator
With eternal knowledge hast a wise design,
And from the very center of Thine own heart's aching
Hast placed a tiny spark of it in mine;
And lest some other heart should find the answer,
And fill that aching void Thou hast left in me,
Thou breakest all the hearts in thy creation
That Hearts-ease may be only found in Thee!

Georgia Bray

A MOTHER'S BIRTHDAY

Mothers have birthdays too you know
They've given their all letting their children grow
Helping them through their ups and downs
Being there for freckles and frowns

Once a year comes a day to renew
And see yourself from a different view
The kingdom of kindness is all inside
That's what's important to cherish with pride

How well have you taken to care for your self
With all sorts of demands lying high on the shelf
Let this day be one to remember
Without giving in or wanting surrender

No matter how many years you feel fate has thrown
You can have whatever *you* want to own
The body can't count, what does it matter
Keep a state of calm without the inner chatter

Thanks be in giving to you
A present of verse, of something true
With thoughts that carry a message clear
Wishing I were there to help spread good cheer

Jeanne Faust

Know to learn
        Learn to know
free the balance

        blossom
                Creativity

William J. Gayzik

A PASSING TENSE,
A BEGINNING SENSE

I anticipated it . . . I knew it all along —
lived it, breathed it, inspired it,
by everything I did.
Choices . . . wrong, I suppose.
Crucial decisions, anticipations, anxieties.
Perhaps it is destiny . . . fate.
Maybe is was meant to be —
painful, wounding, agonizing.
Or . . . do I exaggerate?
So — Is it over? Am I right?
Yes, it has passed away, suddenly,
discreetly, easily . . .
Then, why tension, why hurt? Where are they now?
The time has passed, and the past is no
longer present.
It no longer burns, bleeds, screams.
It has died . . .
But somewhere — deep, deep in my heart,
love grows and my soul is forgiven.

Sarah N. Gray

Limestone Natural Walls, below St. Paul.

Flaming swords and angry foes
And dreams undone in death's throes
The enemy comes and life goes
How many lives lost and broken
No one ever cares or knows

Time as always still remains and no one even wants to change
Though sword be replaced by bombs and planes
The lust in the heart for blood stays
And men go on killing each other for fame

A day did come when life was destroyed
In the most horrible way ever known
And the terror realized still caused no shame
Men just looked at one another and passed on the blame

Now the days of nuclear fallout are here
And by creating it we've bred terror and fear
When the last one goes off there'll be no one to hear
No one to shed the last hopeless tear

But we haven't come to that yet
So let's stop before it's too late to regret
All that burning and screaming and killing and death

Thomas L. Swalley

THOUGHTS OF YOU

Love is like the statue of a king,
cherished to begin,
only in later years — it's there and stands still.

Love is like a horse,
running fast with sudden stops,
changeable it is like old doorknobs.

Love is like some wine,
as long as you drink it you will be fine,
only on an empty bottle you feel rotten.

Love is like a flower — sometimes like a cold shower,
sometimes like bread — too hard,
but you always get your part.

Love is like beer, some are too warm —
some are too cold, never forget what it holds,
drink it and be aware another one will be there.

Love is like cheese,
some are mild — some are spicy,
so all I can say is ''handle it wisely.''

Gerhard Schock

MY PLACE

empty like my heart,
an old Linenchair — Televisionset,
Mattress on the floor —
meaningless but used.

The plushteddy you gave me,
talks about future —
There is no way out — heart of pain,
took you for granted.

Lost — lost your smile,
curled hair covered eyes,
furry feeling skin of the teddy — touch my face;
guess who loves you?

Nonstopping Memories flush my brain,
dirty clothes on the floor,
empty bottles in the trash — leftover food,
Radiosounds disturb the silent phone on the wall;

Why don't you call?
put an end to my loneliness —
take away the pressure torturing my soul,
drowning me into darkness — free my heart . . .

Gerhard Schock

WHY AM I

When upon my past I reflect
Many times I wonder why am I
There are moments I could select
When I have wished I could die

When my previous life I review
Many times I wonder why am I
Making mistakes is all I seem to do
I want to hide my eyes and cry

When I look at my present life
Many times I wonder why am I
Then I think of my wonderful wife
And my soul fills with a contented sigh

When I look at my offspring
Many times I wonder why am I
Then their sweet voices ring
It is now I begin to understand why

When I am surrounded by friends
Many times I wonder why am I
Then the loving hand of friendship extends
Now I know the reason why

God made me with care and love
God filled my heart with compassion
Now when I wonder why I just look above
Because made in God's image has no comparison

T. Dee

SNOW

White, the sky slowly fell
Heaven descending on the earth
A message, time will tell
Thirty-three years from birth

The blanket covered mother
Putting days to rest
Friend of men, protecting
Don't ask the reason why

In houses the lights were on
Inhabitants afraid of the darkness
The globe above reflected whiteness
Showing there was nothing to fear

Slowing emerging from dwellings
Footprints could be seen
Fear of purity, never overcome
The earth will not be the same

Standing on the rise, the cross
A breakthrough to the other side
The tracks led nowhere, faded
Lost, the lights are off

Larry James

DREAM

What were you saying
Yes, the portrait has a cloud

Further on, gray blends with blue
Images winging across the background
Looking for . . .   y o u
At last   . . . found

Mountains forming waves in the sky
Islands of blue flowing into paleness
Above, motions heard but a shadow flew by
Disappearing into a white mass

Blackness crawled concealing
A blast rumbled through the heavens
Jagged streaks illuminated
Paths, a way to Olympus

Suddenly awaken . . . confusion
A dream ending in shattered pieces
Click . . . contours cast
Reassurance given by someone close

Restlessness settled down
Click . . . midnight fell

Larry James

MOON SHADOWS

A day world of devils
Had scratched at my brain;
In the evening
When the trees danced in the star light
And moon shadows softly swayed
In the whiteness and quietness,
The secrets of my soul
Mingled with them
And they took my cares away.

Martha Mae Martinson

NEVER FALL IN LOVE

Never fall in love, my friend . . .
    You'll see it never pays.

Although it causes broken hearts . . .
    It happens every day.

You wonder where he is at night . . .
    You wonder if he's true.

You wonder if he's happy . . .
    You wonder if he's blue.

And then it starts — You don't know why . . .
    You worry day and night.

You see, my friend, you're losing him . . .
    It never turns out right.

First loves are always special . . .
    But the price you pay is high.

If I had to choose between Love or Death . . .
    I almost think I'd rather die.

Believe me and don't fall in love . . .
    You'll be hurt before you're through.

You see, my friend, I ought to know . . .
    I fell in love with you.

Tamara L. Murray

NOW . . .

Your love meant everything to me.
How can you take it away so easily?
I guess I wasn't meant to understand,
For I'm a woman and you are a man.

When we were together the love was there,
But now it seems to leave the air.
I haven't seen you for so long,
I guess now all our love is gone.

We only had a few short months
To show our love inside.
And with all the long months in between,
It looks like the love has died.

My love for you will always be.
The real strong feeling, happy and free.
Although you must move along,
I'll remember you like a favorite song.

At least the good times outweighed the bad,
But . . . Still I feel a little sad.
'Cause your love meant everything to me,
And you took it away so easily.

Tamara L. Murray

LAMENT

Denied by love,
Seduced by years of caring,
I lie on the altar
Of bleeding separation
Sacrificed by time.

Doris I. Warren

HEATHCLIFF AND CATHY

Myriad shades of somber grey
Cased in cold pervading gloom
Cast shadows which loom and sway
Beneath wind-whipped branches.

Under one gnarled tree a form appears
Of dark and brooding man
Seeking one who once was woman
Who spurned in life
But seeks in death
The union of a strife-torn love.

On these moors
Two figures merge.
In broad shadows.
Wild passions
Sweep the trees, the clouds, the moon.
Poised in sepia
They leap that hour
In strength and power
Of transcendent love.

Doris I. Warren

CHALLENGES

To look up at a mountain
I see more than just a hill
reaching towards the endless sky.
I see mountains so high
no one has yet to climb,
though so many have tried.

Gently sloping, mountains capped with snow
full of wildlife, living, undisturbed.
Tall thundering mountains, full of fire,
their unpredictable anger that explodes.

The mountain a small child climbs
in a single step to its father's arms,
the hills he has yet to face
on his journey away from home.

The incredible mountains of fear
that challenge us to follow a dream.
The plateaus we rest upon
that help to keep us moving on.

The mountain of life given to us,
with our own special loose rocks to slip on.
And a mountain of love to be received
if we are willing to share.

Mary Bentler

JOE

A Soul has gone to his repose
And why, . . . only the Good Lord knows!
Of all, this gentle, quiet one,
Our good friend and their dear son.
There is a reason, this we know,
Why God has chosen Joe to go,
To be with Him in Paradise.
To grace His mansions in the sky.
All those whose life he chanced to touch
Will feel the void and miss him much.
For all who knew him or shook his hand
Realized that they had met a *man!*

Donna J. Reimus

A CHILD'S LIFE

A child is the beginning
of many great joys.
    With their tears and laughter,
those little smiles and grins.
    To see them a growing
and showing their love.
    On you they depend
in learning life's chores.
    The questions they ask
the answers you give.
    Life can be so unknowing
your help you will give.
    A child they're not too long;
they're growing up soon.
    But, they'll always be your children,
even when they're grown.
    The memories of the little smiles and grins,
and all the questions they've asked.
    These memories will be with you
for the rest of your life.

Patsy B. Buchanan

FOREVER

    You came into my life and lighted it up.
You made me think of things, that I never thought of.
You took me to the top of the world and we began
to soar. I think I finally found that open door.
I only knocked once and you let me in. That's
when our romance began.

    You came into my life, and I began to
shine. I think I'll make it this time. Just being
together makes us high. We have love on our side.
It's going to last forever, I know I'm right.
I found a treasure, this time I found a gold mine.

    You came into my life, and you lifted me up.
You filled me to the rim, you filled my cup.
Know I'm overflowing and beaming with happiness.
You took away that lonely feeling. You took away
the sadness. It's going to last forever. We
will never part. It's written in the skies
above. It's written in our hearts.

Vickie Cerrato

A MOTHER'S HELPING HANDS?

Come Mama, she said, as she took my hand,
come see my doll.
I can't right now, I said, I have to make a telephone call.
Come Mama, she said, come read to me from my book.
I can't, not now, I have dinner to cook.
Come Mama, come and please help me to spell.
I can't, not now, can't you hear the front door bell?
Come Mother, she said as she took my hand, I want
    you to meet Joe.
I can't, I said, as I hurried away, this is my night
    to play bingo.
Help me Mother, I'm pregnant, what shall I do?
It is your problem, I said, the solution is up to you.
Come Mama, as she took my hand with joy.
I want you to see, my new, adorable, baby boy.

Henrietta M. Stacy

THE RED-TAILED HAWK

High above the trees . . .
Above the roots, above the leaves,
Above the shadows, sleek and gliding . . . climbing, climbing,
And, then, fast descending with a cry . . .
''Peree — Peree — I am free'':
The nobled, feathered red-tailed hawk
    comes declining.

O winged majestic spirit . . .
Your cry is the key on which I first heard
Freedom's note, not as an echo in spaces void,
But, a song, a splendid song came piercing,
And lifted my senses to see and to feel
    strong, good visions:
O my winged one, you were a messenger of freedom.

''Peree, Peree,''
The red-tailed hawk sends his cry for me to listen,
And I do; and I, too, become free:
''Peree, Peree'' — to all with soaring minds;
''Peree, Peree'' — to all who preserve in life
Holy freedom in her majestic flights.

''Peree, Peree'' — to all who preserve in life
Holy freedom in her majestic flights.

''Peree, Peree'' . . . cries the masterful red-railed hawk;
Come set your eyes upon my soaring,
And, I will make you feel free indeed:
''Peree, Peree . . . be free, be free.''

Ray Furman

REFLECTIONS ON THE RESURRECTION

On one cross, on one humiliating cross,
Jesus was nailed in shame, there to take the blame
For the sins of you and I.

One might ask, Why, why did He die?
He died for you and me
That we might be eternally free.

Such agony, such humiliating agony,
Such pain, no one will have to suffer that way again.

He carried that heavy cross, and climbed that hill
To fulfill God's will —
To die that we might have a better life
Without unnecessary toil and strife.

But, my friends, this is not where the story ends.
The truth is Jesus is alive today
And walks with us along the way!

Jesus can live in your heart and dwell within your soul
So Satan can no longer take control!
We, as Christians, must tell everyone
Of God's only Son.

Joyce Elaine Hamilton

HE CALLS

He calls us
By the name we know
To give us the name
He wrote
Upon our hearts
When they were
Just a thought
Who am I to say
He doesn't know me
And remind him of my
Given name
He who named himself
And all from
Me to him
Not for poetic rhythm
But for purpose
Knowing my heart
Would answer
In a quiet moment
As if I had known no other

Carolyn J. Coffee

NEW HORIZONS

As you look into the distance,
The furthest you can see
Is just to the horizon
Of your own reality.

If you stay there safe and stable,
You will learn the borders well
But your knowledge of the outside
Shall be but what others tell.

So venture out and find, my friend,
Just what the distance hides.
It's the only way to truly know
What's on the other side.

Should the new grass not be greener
Or the ocean not as blue,
There's yet a new horizon
Up ahead, awaiting you.

Desiree DeGraca

PARAFFIN TEARS

Wax drips from my candles
In silent paraffin tears.
Streams of liquid emotion
Build upon one another
Until they, too, melt
Into tears.
Do the candles cry
For crying's sake,
Or do they feel and share
The loneliness I experience?
Do not cry any more paraffin tears for me;
I will cry my own
For the candles' sakes.
It is the least I can do for
My tall, bright friends.

Nancy Martindale

I REMEMBER GRANDPA

*In memory of my grandfather,
Howard W. Andrus*

I remember Grandpa
   giving rides upon his knee,
Always time for one more ride,
   or maybe two, or three.

All of us would clamor
   and climb on Grandpa's knee.
For tickles, hugs, and lovin'
   it was the greatest place to be.

Upon on Grandpa's shoulders
   one could see about the farm,
Never fearful of a fall,
   supported by his arm.

His hands could throw a horseshoe
   and with ease it hit the post.
Those hands worked long and honest
   but that's not what I recall the most.

For what the child in me remembers
   more than all will ever be . . .
There was always room for one of us
   up on Grandpa's knee.

Kim (Moore) Kelsey

LET US BE CONTENT

Small, petty things
   — Like acid, eat into the mind,
      And magnify life's frailties.

Vulnerability surfaces
   — Through frustrations; deafness,
      Or, a fear of going blind.

Irritability erupts,
   And speech explodes, leaving the human
      Spirit desolate and betrayed.

Does dim sight obscure the star
That shone so brilliantly in dreams?
Or deafness obliterate the sound
Of the symphony of Life's great harmony?

The offspring of our love goes forth
With his own dreams. His voice —
It will be heard. The Master's hand
Will bless his claim to recognition.

Therefore, let us be content,
   Now to be audience
      And applaud.

M. Ringereide

MOTHER THROUGH THE MIRROR

Mother through the mirror
I watch her as she sews.
The thread goes clean, the blouse
takes shape perfectly,
I wish dreams could work that way.
Mother doesn't know I'm watching
and she lets down her guard.
I see her weariness at once.
It occurs to me then that soon she will
turn forty.
Mother through the mirror is suddenly
more than a reflection.
She sighs;
I pretend to smooth my hair as I
gaze into the mirror, but it is her
reflection I see.
Mother through the mirror notices then
that I am watching.
She bows her head, and I bow mine,
silently we wonder;
When will we communicate
without having to gaze at a reflection.

Lori Janwich

SIGNS AND SEASONS

When owls and cats make love all night,
And doves start cooing ere 'tis light,
When frogs croak out with all their might,
Spring is here.

When corn is tall enough to plow,
And flies torment the old red cow,
When sweat drips off your nose and brow,
Summer's here.

When Jack Frost steals in quiet and soft,
And red wasps cluster in the loft,
When ice forms on the watering trough,
Fall is here.

When juncos flit from thorn to brier,
And ice hangs heavy on the wire,
When tabby sleeps before the fire,
Winter's here.

When your eyes so blue and bright
Shed through my dreams their lovely light,
When I love you with all my might,
It's — well — it's any time of the year.

Edgar H. Stevens

BUTTERFLY FLY

Lying side by side throughout the long dark night
  With your hand held gently in mine
I want to softly kiss your slightly parted lips
  I want our bodies to lovingly entwine
Then you roll over onto your side away from me
  And the moonlight through the window
Glistens in your long golden hair and I realize
  That as always the answer is no

Lying side by side throughout the long dark night
  I turn my back to you as I yawn
My dreams are already filled with your images
  And always too swiftly comes the dawn
Lying this close to you is more than I could ask
  That you even stay in this single bed
Is something I cannot figure out but I know
  That my love for you is always tainted with dread

  Golden hair flowing as we run into the wind
  In my dreams I begin to cry
  For then on beautiful butterfly wings
  Without a look back, you fly

  Paul Brian McCoy

CALENDAR RUSE

We share the bitter and the sweet: A law of life is told.
Our goals . . . our dreams . . . left incomplete
        (the epic scheme unfolds).
The wolf of time is at our feet. A decade turns to rust!
Embarkers on that one-way street that surely leads to dust.

The haughty man, the lowly beast, are brothers sharing fate:
Eventualities the same . . . uniting small and great.
Look closely at your destinies; the sand is falling fast.
An atmosphere of vanity ever since the die was cast.

Yes, you who toil so fruitlessly ('cause there's so much to do),
the mortal knows his time is marked. He's waiting for his cue.
Existence is a fragile gift, so plan it carefully!
And when you're gone you will receive an impressive eulogy . . .

  Darlene Bergeron Valentine

AND THE WALLS CAME TUMBLING DOWN . . .

Quarrels strip away the thin veneer of dignity
exposing ugly scars from other times.
Make visible deep wounds never healed,
festering masses covered by a parchment skin.
Purpling bruises come from beating
against imprisoning bars that never yield.
Quarrels topple carefully built walls of security.
Bricks of self-control fall at hurled epithets.
Stones of self-worth crumble beneath the memory of
        yesterday's mistakes.
The mortar of propriety turns to ashes beneath the heat of anger.
Quarrels undermine the wells of privacy, baring the need to be fulfilled.
Painful reminders of innate faults dry up the hopes for wholeness.
Resentment muddies the clear water of the right to be oneself,
spilling out in tears of anguish, bleak with fear.
Quarrels divide and separate. Apartheid, aloneness, loneliness —
The mind wanders down blind alleys, lurking shadows, untrod paths,
fractured plans and dreams, not knowing where, when it will end.
Out of the shadows a flickering gleam of hope:
  ''I'm sorry'' . . .

  Olga Borchardt

There is a part of me that
  no human hand can touch,
  no human eye can see,
  no human voice can reach.

A place
  where no footsteps b
  no human hand can touch,
  no human eye can see,
  no human voice can reach.

A place
  where no footsteps but mine
    have left their trace;
  where no sun shines
    and only darkness seems to thrive;
  where only doubt and fear
    wish to make me their companion;
  where pain of body and spirit
    holds me in an inescapable embrace;
  where my cries go unheard;
    for here
      I am
        totally

        alone.

  Anna Rita Zimmerman

ANNA RITA ZIMMERMAN. Born: New Jersey; Education: Georgian Court College, B.A., English; The Catholic University of America, M.A., English; Occupations: High school English teacher, Administrator of small retirement home; Book publications manager; Comments: *I write my poetry to express to a special person how I feel; to express how I feel about my life in the present and in the future; to express how life touches me at a particular moment; to express how I see the life experience from my own vision.*

DREAMS ARE

Tell me what your dreams are
Tell me what you're going through

Tell me what your dreams are
I might have been there too

If I can make you feel again
Then your heart I can mend

In just a little while I will see you smile
'Cause you've given to me a part you were afraid I see

Don't ever stop dreaming
Despite how things are appearing

Tell me what your dreams are
Tell me what you're going through

  John F. Russo

A MAN

A person whom I admire
Is someone I will never meet
He is now in a jungle
Fighting in the heat

In the jungles of Vietnam
He is stranded, alone
Waiting for someone
To bring him back home

Not many people know him
Not too many care
Not too many people know
That he is over there

All of his fellow men
Can no longer be seen
They have all been separated
At the age of nineteen

He is now about forty
His clothing is a sorrowful sight
He hunts and runs by day
Tries to sleep at night

This man isn't a ''Rambo''
Or a ''Chuck Norris'' that knows martial arts
He is a lonely and melancholy man
A man with a broken heart

Marc P. Virata

MARC PHILLIP VIRATA. Born: Chicago, Illinois, 3-10-74; Education: South Junior High, Arlington Heights, Illinois, seventh grade; Occupation: Student; Poetry: 'Omen,' 1-17-87; Comments: *Writing poetry shouldn't be considered as an assignment with due dates. Poetry is an art, and art needs time, love, and sweat in order to be successful. Without these elements, poetry would be just as good as a speck of dust.*

A MASQUERADE

A mask to hide our happiness
one to conceal our sorrow
A mask to cover up the past
one more to veil tomorrow.

I walk through life without a face
a puppet full of lies
Intent upon concealing my
heart from prying eyes
How sad that when a life is played
It's no more than a masquerade.

Lori Janwich

SILENCE IS GOOD

It is cold tonight.
The cool air circles round my feet
    Like a cat seeking recognition.

    The only sounds
The dogs beside me on the rocker sofa
    Breathing heavily,

    And the furnace
With its authoritative assurance
    That heat is forthcoming.

    The thermostat is up now.
The quiet surges back, a wall for my thoughts
        To bounce against.

    Why are some afraid of silence?
Dread it, flee from it, are insulted by it,
    Make frantic efforts to dispel it.

        Silence is good.

Marjory Lee Thompson

WE WERE ''FOOLED''

The geese went north in March early
And the blossoms came out on the plum.
But the old ground hog knew best . . .
And he laughed as he fled:
There's still more winter yet to come.

We were told that spring was ahead
So we set our clocks ahead, too.
But the old ground hog knew best . . .
And he laughed as he fled:
''Watch out'' or Nature will fool you.

So we sit inside and we shiver,
Worried about our buds and our tubers.
But the old ground hog knew best . . .
And he laughed as he fled:
It's not April — it's Oc-toe-burr.

Now we don't know what's around the corner
And it doesn't matter how we were schooled.
But the old ground hog knew best . . .
And he laughed as he fled:
And we're sitting here feeling *fooled.*

Joy A. Arnold

Don't feel, don't think, don't trust
All the lessons learned —
Learned again from you.
Just as a cradle barely burning,
You snuffed its beginning light.
As I began to exist to me,
You taught me I didn't exist again.

The emptiness at love's leaving
Has torn great holes in me,
And with them — all the beauty gone —
Just pain remains.

And if it goes — what then?
What will fill those empty places,
Where once danced the light that was you?

Linda F. Buckner

across the bosporus in a scull:
spaghetti tangle of synapses —
            sinapses;
every chemmendeleev knew
and more
mores and conventions than
the democratic donkey has fleas
and kicks
hard to believe but someday

my

sinopees   will open

and shut with

all the

agility of an

iron   door

Gary Esposito

I hope for you the day will come,
When all your trials will be won.
Always things work out for us,
When in our Dear Lord we do trust.

Just as dark clouds blacken the sky,
A ray of sunshine passes by.
For all the rain that surely falls,
A rainbow comes to clear it all.

So as we live each day through,
Somewhere along, a dream comes true.
It may not be what we expect,
But something even better yet.

Looking for answers of our own,
Growing impatient we have known.
If we'd but listen carefully,
He's always there for you and me.

Always for you my prayers do go,
His blessings onto you will flow.
With faith and patience you will see
Peace and joy for you there'll be.

Shari Eccleston

CAN'T UNDERSTAND . . .

    How can one lose someone so close
someone who meant the world
and the world was brighter when
he'd smile or laugh with me.
    My world darkened as we said goodbye
but his smile lingered
leaving me with hopes of finding
someone new to love.
    Yet, how can he leave a friend
someone who loved him
and with my love brightened his
days because I was his friend?
    He did it for me,
because he loved me he let me go,
but why let me go forever?

Darlene Elwartowski

LIFE IS A STEEPLECHASE

The race, a horse, one minute in the race, running,
Jumping, trying for the lead.
The next, a fall, maybe a break,
He gets up and goes on if he is able.
If not, what a waste.
Yet, the race goes on.
This is life, life is a steeplechase.
The race, a man, one minute in the race.
The race of life, running, jumping,
Trying for the lead.
The next, maybe a break.
He gets up and goes on if he is able.
If not, what a waste.
Yet, the race of life does go on.

Lona Greer

ON THE DEATH OF A BLIND PIANIST

Up there on the ceiling
        the lights are glowing
like a sky
        over white birches.

The rush of hands . . .
        I hear again
the Spring Sonata
        and you living,
lifting earth in spurts.

Grace of a moment given,
        hands pausing point to point in air;
the cadence of your white fingers
        flung like spears into flesh;
and the aching, pure statement of a scale
        lets me remember passion
in your shadowed eye.

Leo Kartman

SOLO REMEMBERED

The moment awaits completion
        of the deed
                entering in
an echo like mute music
        tension begins
to build an answering cadence
as the strain
                of moving comes to life
with startling pain
        illusion in the captured muscle
over bone
        strings an intolerable silent
                quivering tone
of a body
        beautifully aware
        fixed again
as though it had never been
        but captured
                in bright shards of memory
still there.

Leo Kartman

CAT DON'T CROSS THE ROAD

My thoughts are coming the color of blue,
My thoughts in parallel lines,
Running down my windowpane.
I'll find you in the noontide sun,
Because the moon shines down in the middle of the night,
And I don't know why,
Please tell me why . . .

Cat, don't cross the road.
And dog, don't bark down my door.
Blue, don't come to me.
White, I wish I could see.
And gold and green will always be
My babies . . .
God, please don't strike me down,
Stop blowing pollen in my capillaries.

Lawrence Lui

EMBODIMENT OF THE COURT JESTER

The fall
    it brings depression,
        a slowing of sorts
            preamble to misery

Wishf'ly thinking,
    I'm leaning t'ward the sun
        a freeing of hearts
            — warmth of the womb

Limbs slow to nil
    when age devours the path
        and mirages appear tenfold
            hording what time is left

No heat lingers
    where wayward stones abound
        a burrow to quiet my sorrows
            — makeshift sort of tomb

cameleon

THE WAIL OF THE HUMMINGBIRD

Listen to the wail of the hummingbird,
maybe it would help;
What man can't hear
he can't imagine by himself.

See his wings a-flapping faster
than your mind;
What man cannot see
he cannot hope for.

Smell the flowers that he eats,
for it helps to make you think;

Small gifts bring great joy,
man is a fool to walk on by
and never hear the wail
of the hummingbird.

Ronald L. Mahony

PRAYER

Dear Lord I cannot kneel to pray.
My poor old bones won't bend that way.
So I sit quietly in my chair, and send
my prayers to you up there.

I pray for peace and health and love.
Please send these down to those I love.
Grant them faith in ills or sorrow,
and lift their eyes toward tomorrow.

Hold them safely in the hollow of thy hand.
Help them to see and understand
the many blessings given them.
Please hear their prayers, Oh Lord, Amen.

Emma Enberg Baisley

TO THE ROOFTOPS

Straight out of a Jack Kerouac paperback,
Tough bluff boy;

He sat, smirking, on his red Vespa
In Denny's parking lot.

A pink panther,
Bumbling all his cool intentions —
You couldn't help wanting him.

The Everyman
Is no woman's only man —
He's a lonely man.

Paula Jayne Brown

ROCKWOOD INSPIRATION

Pastel promise
Artistic urge
Are found within your vise
An unending wondering
What lies beyond those eyes.
Every deeply sparked am I
And asking please to find
Their beauty isn't ending
A simple pastel blue
But that the treasure really is
A richer inside hue.

Steffanie S. Douglass

I scrub my skin away
Till my bones shine
Chant in corners spin
Webbed in to wake
In thin dreams of dawn
Ebbing slightly

Swallowing my heart
I make him cry

Jane Fell

DREAMWORLD

It is real you see;
  It is more real
  than you or me.

Dreamworld is a place
  unknown,
  for it lies deep
  within the vortex zone.

It looks easy to go there,
  so you think,
  but to enter takes bravery,
  and to leave takes strength.

Beware of Dreamworld;
  you're playing with your soul.
  Stay away and live forever,
  or you'll pay the toll.

Jennifer Keene

OUR LOVE

Way deep inside me I see a light shining,
  my reason's forming light and darkness.

And I'm on my way — soaring high is our
  love, a heart so brave and gay.

It's my reasons penciled in delicate grace
  and the seasons formed by day and night.

I sense the fan of angel wings, under
  spirits of our love in a land so
  far away.

Now my happiness is realized and I'm
  on my way —
For the pleasure of our love is
  taking me away.

June Ann Nissinen

MY SECRET

I watch you lying quietly
  asleep beside me dear,
And whisper to you tenderly
  and stroke your silken hair.
On nights like these I know a love
  that daytime cannot bring,
A calm that no one else can share
  a time just mine serene.
So sleep my love
  I'll hold your hand
Until I slumber too,
  tomorrow's yet another day
Remember, ''I love you.''

Louis Arduin Piazza

ALLEN — JANUARY 10, 1986

*For Allen Truett —
the one I'll always love*

Someone very special
  came into my life that day.
He put feelings deep inside
  that, again I could give away.

Even after I'd once said
  so long before then,
that I'd let no one in my heart again,
  still, I let him in.

Could it have been his smile,
  that made me open the door?
Or his eyes of dazzling blue,
  that sent me wanting more?

It's so hard to remember
  what it really was,
that made him mean special things to me
  I only know that he still does.

Tracie L. Runyon

DINNER

Sharp ivory teeth
Gleaming in semi-darkness,
And the prowling feline
Tears soft mouse flesh
Into mounds of
Bloody confetti.

Patricia A. Struller

THE LIGHT BLUE LIGHT

The still body of the child sits
and the light reflects spasmodically
The child concentrates deeply
and the pulsating light strikes out
The child absorbs the light
A look of hatred, a flash of contempt
and the room is alive with the glitter of radiance
A fierce scowl of anger
A new dart of brilliance
A deceiving twitch, an ominous shudder
the light dances to and fro
A helpless puppet in a frigid trance
sat the still body of the child

Then,

The light becomes less intense
The face of the child melts in a smile
The body relaxes
A momentary pause from the light blue light
A short break from rape
A break from murder
A break from corrupt sex
For commercial time has come

Steven J. Scanlan

218

REFLECTIONS OF THE FINAL JOURNEY AT DAWN

Dedicated to Barbara

As the sun sets I wait each night at the door —
I wait for you, my friend, knowing you'll be coming no more —
The part of you you left behind was the shine on our sails,
the path thru the sea —
It was the beautiful understanding loving part, the part you
left with me.
I watched as they floated by, the petals of each flower —
I remembered all the years of our friendship — I relived
each minute and every hour.
As I filled my glass full with champagne, I raised it high
my friend —
I toasted us to the very end.
Above us, like the dreams we shared, the jets flew just out
of our reach, way up in the sky —
A tribute to you, a sign to me — This cannot be a final goodbye.
From nowhere the dolphins appeared, graceful and in uniform —
Making a statement to all — ''This is a death that will not
understand mourn.''
As I wiped the tears from my eyes and scattered your ashes into
the sea —
I wondered, my very best friend, if you knew with them went a big
part of me.

Nancy Lorraine

TANGLED GRAPEVINES

*To a vintage cast: Jane Wyman, Robert Foxworth, David
Selby, Ana-Alica, William R. Moses, Lorenzo Lumas,
Margaret Cuddard, Susan Sullivan*

Settled among the grapevine of Falconcrest,
Angela Channing's house majestically sits
but its occupants are wrought bitter and tense,
For the family lines have been severed in a fight for the precious gold;
After they've aged and grown old.
Richard is so filled with anger, rejected by them in his childhood past,
And Lance, by nature spoiled, then Melissa, uncertain whether goodness
   is bought or spent.
Maggie, the kind mother and author, her husband Chase's wish always
destined to be true; that they remain in Tuscanny,
   the source of his family roots.
Cole, their good-hearted son, freed himself from the vineyards'
tenacious hold — for he understood its poisonous
   and most certain blinding toll.
But Emma, poor Emma, is always to remain under her mother's thumb
and rule — cloistered away in her dream castle and her bedroom.
Chao-li is ensnared by loyalty but the sheriff of the land
   could never prove,
that Angela Channing will ever cease wearing her glorious ruling crown.

Susan Gilbert

YOU ARE THE DARKNESS

You are the darkness
 of the yin and yang
  the deep shadows in the tiny
egyptian temple between the columns —
   in the museum
  — you here with me, darling dark one
 I'm given gold loops embroidery — layers on
layers round you to outside diamond
 — diamond of my *Absolute Being?*

and then an earring produces itself
 in me for thee? gold tiny filagree
instead of the seedpearl ones for my love last week
 you gave the same darkness
             the very same darkness gold pour moi
I found old gold perfect earring in little shop
 to wear with my true love —

Joan Shambaugh

THE TREE AND I

Outside my window there stands a tree.
In so many ways it is just like me.
The seasons have changed and ended our hour.
Of beauty and richness, of life and power.
The trees' leaves have changed, the color now brown.
Like my heart they fall to the ground.
But like all living things the tree puts up a fight.
It is holding one green leaf almost out of sight.
I in turn have a hope inside.
That I am mistaken and love has not died.
We both know life has not passed us by.
So much alike, the tree and I.

Irene Smith

''Please don't leave me!''
 I cry,
''I don't want to be
                          alone.
   Please,
     listen to me,
        I want you near me,
   I want
     you beside me to
        hold me and
           talk
     to me.
   I want you to be
        my friend.

Please,
   Don't leave me!''

Normay M. Wade

WORSHIP

He entered the sanctuary late
When we had already begun
He paused at the doorway
Bowing his head reverently
Patiently waiting
Until he could take a seat
Without disturbing the faithful
Who had come to worship
Poetry

Timothy P. Wayne

FOR PETER, MURDERED
IN CENTRAL AMERICA

The white crumbs and dust,
    scattered now,
forever my brother
is
not the
    ash that slipped
        through my fingers.

We spread him in a figure eight
Dropped him in cold stream of fate
Dusted him on herbs and leaves
Hid him in the nooks of trees
Fed him to mice and chickadees
Sprinkled him where no one sees.

Rubbed him on our wounds for healing
Lost him in our swamp of feeling
Concealed him, and laid him bare
We spread him now, for everywhere.

John Roberts Wolfe

NORMA

She still is here
Though she has gone.
Yet she has come but once.
So short a time
To leave quicksilver
Dancing in the hall:
I know that she will always stay.
Her presence is assured,
Unlike some who only come
And leave no trace behind.

Anne Ayer

WINTER

Silvery silk leaves
falling gently
from winter's dying trees.
A quilt of snow
that covers the ground
as icy wind
swirls around and round.
Outside this window
the snowflakes will prance
and put on a show
where they'll dance and dance!

Cheryl Yvonne Duckworth

DEEP DOWN

Waves do not realize
they indeed make gains;
they only know their struggle
and make peace with their sweat.

They feel their way,
repaving the same sands
wearing down rocks
polishing them — burying them,
returning them to their maker.

Through the yawning foam
jagged sculptures rise.

Christine M. Björkfelt

THE SAD WOMAN

A moth flickers
around a saffron
streetlamp.
Her breath sends beads
down the window pane.
Tree shadows wrinkle
upon the bare wall.
She returns to bed,
shifting her face
to meet the light.

Christine M. Björkfelt

WINTER STIRRING

When dusk touches
the winter plain,

frail icicles
snap at twigs
then shatter upon
the bluish snowcrust.

A glazed pool
swallows
the skeleton of a leaf.

The icy breeze
sweeps over footprints
in the snow,

an unfinished path
toward spring.

Christine M. Björkfelt

THE USA FLAG

See! The USA flag,
    flying over the ocean blue,
Looks as though it's trying to soar
    just like those big birds do.

This flag has been tied to a boat;
    winds are blowing it high.
Isn't that a beautiful flag
    waving there in the sky?

Alice Charpentier

SNOWMAN

One cold frosty day in early morn,
I saw a man on an icy lawn.
He had somewhat a dirty face
As if, he had fallen in sod someplace.

Another day glancing at that man,
Clothespin nose with the same smudgy 'tan,'
"Hello there!" I said, gave him a smile
Heard myself say, "Hope you'll stay awhile."

A wind-storm came, got very frigid,
He stood still frozen, stiff and rigid.
Then warmer days came, he had to go
Disappearing slowly after snow.

I often look at that empty place,
Wondering what else will fill the space.
Thinking of that figure standing there
With a torn hat on top of no hair.

I never will and I never can
See that very same snowman again.
He couldn't say, 'Hi,' nor a 'Good-bye.'
Yet, I sort of liked that snowman guy.

Alice Charpentier

FROM ACROSS THE ROOM

I sit and watch you from across the room
    and I do confess
    my eye searches the naked flesh.
Every flinch of an ankle
    or twist of a toe
my thoughts linger
    on what lies below.
Holding my chin in the palm of my hand
    the warmth of your breasts
    heats my flesh.
Entranced in a stretching yawn
    we share the satisfaction
that lies beyond.
As I lick my lips
    and dream of your feminine hips
I trespass upon a woman's beauty
    as if it were my masculine duty.
But long after the lust of the eyes
dies . . .
    my compliments remain.

Cris Hernandez

Inner space
Stones forbear
This age of mine
Surrounds me
As full air rains
I tremble to attempt
A sort of prayer

As the sun breaks loose
I stand for God uncertain
Treading on the dead
I listen my way home

Jane Fell

WINDOW

Standing in the window looking out over God's greatness
at the time of my greatest need,

Looking over the trees swaying in the gentle wind,
Looking up to the clear blue sky for God within;

Looking out and down at the very special small and
colorful array of blossoms reaching up, too.
God said to me, ''There's nothing I can't do!''

Looking out through the empty, warm space and the sun's gentle
rays, thinking of how I, just lonely me and my smallness —
just how I fit in?

Looking out but thinking how real He is to me. Thinking
and looking at these things, how great He must be.

Looking at the wonders He has from this high window,
How easy it must be for Him to look down on me.

Bobbie Cooper

TRANQUILITY

The breeze died down, it's quiet now,
Not a branch is waving.
Like the quiet before a storm, or the time a child is born.
Not a single cloud in sight,
No darkness turning down the light
Which engulfs this silent spot,
This piece of earth, created by God
For comfort and tranquility, for every human being to see,
To have, to own, to hold,
To love this warmth, from heavenly above.
The sun burns hot upon my head, spinning my thoughts about,
Wiping out ideas I had, on love and life and time ahead.
No let up, says the weatherman, humidity will rise again.
Even the trees look down on me, begging for a drop of wet.
How can I breathe? How can I help?
Come down from heaven to this earth,
Please, let me live and breathe again.
It's not too much to hope, to pray, to let me live,
Through yet another tranquil day.

Lisa H. Meyer

TO JAMES — 1966

In trust and faith he sleeps tonight,
    In hope and love 'til morning's light.
Or does he dream of yesterdays?
    Of things he did a thousand ways?
And does he dream of things long past,
    Of happy times that seldom last?

I'll guard his every sleeping time
    Throughout short years that he is mine.
His steps are his — I must but wait.
    The roads he takes are not my fate.
The time is here and I am done.
    I must let go — my son, my son!

Anita Hill Boney

FAREWELL

It's time to part thy love from mine, by stepping away
From my protecting guiding line, that led your way.
It's time to make your own way of living
And not to go on, blaming me
For all the burden you've been given
And for the things that could not be.
Be free, to think and say your piece,
To open wide your eyes and see.
Be free to share, to do your part
And face your life with open heart.
Be free to dream, to build, to ban.
Look up and become a man.
Live your life, while I live mine and
Look at this great land of ours
And welcome love, into your house.
I cry within my heart for you,
I'll envision what you'll be going through.
With eyes of wet and no cheer to hum,
I'll say to you,
''Farewell, my son.''

Lisa H. Meyer

LISA HILDA MEYER. Born: Oldenberg, West Germany, 3-6-38; Single; Education: High school, one year to go; high school partially in Germany, 1953-55; some night school in Philadelphia, Pennsylvania in 1974; Occupation: Bartender; Poetry: 'Night Shadows,' *Pro/Am Poet's Magazine*, 1970; also a variety of poetry published in local newspapers in Philadelphia, Pennsylvania in the 70's; Comments: *I have to be in a state of depression (down) when attempting to write anything, short stories, ideas, poetry, etc. Happy times give me ideas, but not the urge to write. In my writing I prefer emotional themes, love lost, and today's events.*

ENDLESS REALITY

Through the window time passing . . .
I, and nothing more in this dream.
Destiny called . . .
And I, too mesmerized by the light, could not see beyond the sun.
A lonesome star in the sky . . .
So kept by time to exalt the gods.
So I, to thrive from this land of yore.
A day in the life . . . a light in the sky . . .
So on and on we've come to defy the gods . . .
Resting in dormant crypts . . . awaiting the hour . . .
Seeking forgiveness from oblivion.
Rise dark shadows, call the winds aside . . .
For you are nothing more than the shadow which revolves
Through realms of time.
Fair winds do blow to distant lands . . .
As do souls on a forgotten plateau
        of the endless reality of Nevermore . . .

Mary Elizabeth Hatcher

THE LOON

The adorable loon
Really isn't a goon.
He's the last
    to leave his summer haunts
And the first to come back
    bringing uncles and aunts.

The adorable loon
Really isn't a goon.
His young he protects
    and he's ever so careful
To keep track of his mate
    over whom he's so watchful.

The adorable loon
Really isn't a goon.
He keeps a good distance
    from us nature lovers
But over us he
    lovingly hovers.

Alice Ekern Sulzdorf

COUNT DOWN TIME

Astronauts must have
    doubts at length
When those final
    moments arrive
And it's count down time.

Racers pray for
    every ounce of strength
When those final
    moments arrive
And it's count down time.

A baby's birth is
    a solemn occasion
When those final
    moments arrive
And it's count down time.

But an execution is
    the real ultimatum
When those final
    moments arrive
And it's count down time.

Alice Ekern Sulzdorf

It was tea-time. He came into the room,
Car-motor running outside,
Flipped the lid of his cigarette case,
"Want a light? . . . Good."
When I looked outside 5 minur-motor running
outside,
Flipped the lid of his cigarette case,
"Want a light? . . . Good."
When I looked outside 5 minutes later, He was
driving off.
Off, is right. One of us could be.
Sorry I wasn't dressed.

Anna Hart Willett

CLOUD FORMATIONS

Psychiatrists use the
    ink blotch test;
But I really like,
    by far the best,
To try to figure out
    a cloud formation
And from it
    get my affirmation
About the wonders of the world.

Many of my creations
    come from mythology,
While others pertain
    in detail to biology.
Nursery rhyme figures
    can't seem to stay.
As fast as they appear
    they are whisked away
To intrigue another world.

Alice Ekern Sulzdorf

IDENTITY

Musings of a mind possessed
with movement, not a soul has guessed
its angles of perception.

Bits and pieces, old and new,
kaleidoscopic points of view
mingle in conception.

Choose the shards that somehow fit.
Rearrange them just a bit,
trying to believe that it
    can show me who I am.

Words that lips could never say
suddenly seep out, the way
steady raindrops fill a pool.

It's only words the tongue belies.
The truth lies open in the eyes,
bleeding tears that save the fool.

Victim of a need to know
the root that lies beneath the snow . . .
waiting for the vine to grow
    to bind all that I am.

Angel Y. Bryant

JESUS IS THE ANSWER

Jesus is the answer to all life's creations
Jesus is the answer for a better nation
Jesus is the answer for the church bells
    that ring
Jesus is the answer for the songs that we sing.

Jesus is the answer for our life's treasures
Jesus is the answer for all human measures
Jesus is the answer for our daily prayers
Jesus is the answer for all our needs and cares.

Jesus is the answer for the rivers that flow
Jesus is the answer to why we all glow
Jesus is the answer to all things
Big, small or in between
Jesus is the answer for what it all means.

Lena J. Carter

HAND IN HAND

Hold my hand so gently
Just as you do my heart
Words cannot say the love we had
Right from the special start

You give so much to me
In everything you do
And I hope that I will be
The only one for you

Hold me. Hug me. Kiss me again.
But also be my friend
Never leave me, oh how I pray
To see your beautiful face every day

We are in love,
You do understand
We can do anything
With the world in our hands
So please, let's face this life together,
Just you and I . . .
    Hand in hand

Betty Clark

CELLDOM

In this realm a French Knight lives,
he rides a great white Norman steed,
when he's on guard he sometimes gleams,
if he is in the lead.

But deep within the Forest Sang,
beyond the plasma wall,
reigns King Cer with all his AIDS,
who heed his beck and call.

And when he calls his AIDS to force,
disgustedly they answer,
in brainwashed chant immune to will,
"Oh Yes We Can, We CanCer."

And so they forge inside the Sang,
without passion, pride or plot,
seeking out the whitest knight,
known as LanCellot.

When they spy his gleaming steed,
alas they strike with feeble breath,
but his Holy Grail is Queen Guerir,
and that's their kiss of death.

M. Catherine Bunton

MARTIN

As homely as the desert in June,
As gorgeous as a silver moon.
As calm as a river in May,
As wild as the posies on that day.
As surprising as a startled rabbit,
As wise as an owl looking on havoc.
The road of life goes quite a way,
Twisting and turning every day.
This poem of the world around,
Of eagles in sky and people on ground.
Of one friend, and many,
What would my life be without any?

Miriam Troxler

FARLOW

My Farlow Teaarrow, my friend, my boy, my every day of mischief.
My joy, you are my baby in every sense of the word.
I waited for your birth and planned so many special events for us.
I just didn't know what was in store for me.
So the great day was at hand and I was a mother instantly.
The three-hour feedings, the sleep I did not get.
The constant worry that you are well, the joy of sharing,
the days of playing with you.
Now your little baby days are over and we are sharing a love so true.
You follow me wherever I go. But you could never learn the word 'no.'
I still lose sleep, still worry about you, if I lost you
I don't know what I would do.
I could search the world over and never find another you.
Now you are one year old and I would change nothing of my
precious year with you.
You wake me to go out but not as a child should.
You take a strand of my hair and give it a tug.
Instead of a spanking, I give you a hug.
I toss you a bone and give you love, you are my baby.
That's all I see, although others see you as an English Bulldog.
Your love has blinded me. Happy first year, Farlow.

Vivian Sprinkles Nyberg

VIVIAN SPRINKLES NYBERG. Born 10-16-31; Married: Stewart M. Nyberg; Poetry: 'Quiet Mornings,' (1-1-87), 'My Babe (My Mother),' *Cross Country Dispatch;* 'Me and God,' 'Farlow'; Comments: *I have two daughters, Taleathea and Lavon. They are my themes and ideas. My mother, a stroke victim, feeds my heart and mind with loving thoughts.*

MISPLACED

A wave of resentment has swept through doors
breaking through work and through homes
scattering patience like dishes onto floors.
Should we brace for another storm, or is this just
a remnant of fearful currents past?
The blue sky weekend has turned a gray mist,
there is something new offshore, perhaps,
waiting to test our bamboo pillars and thin coats,
the lonely chill has not yet finished
chastising backs and throats.

But candles burn on in the huts,
the waxy molds have spread across tablemats
turning muted colors passing shapes different.
The flames flicker time away, while shadows
on rented walls stand guard inside
speechless windows, watching the circus outside,
streets on which everyone returns home
to coax their dying flames,
so afraid to share their final screams.

Eric Rose

URIAH

Flee! Prophet, flee to just Osiris' breast!
Leave everything, deny your lids their rest.
"The lion roars, the land lies desolate!"
Your regal enemies with blood-lust foam;
Into Egypt, their sinister shadows flit.
Oh, has the mighty Nile no clemency?
Is there no refuge for a refugee?
They bind your hands and bring you to their king;
"Let him taste the sword he prophesied!"
Into a common grave the corpse they fling.

Augustine Ephrem Valentine

MY MILITARY GARDEN

Classic uniformed armies are deployed here.
In full bloom flower troops form battle lines:
purple alyssum, blue ageratum infantry in front,
yellow plumed celosia-marigold cavalry on left flank,
blood-red salvia-zinnia mercenaries on the right,
tall dahlia and canna lily cannoneers to the rear.
Reserve militias of peonies, fuchsia, phlox
ready to fill gaps in ranks left by the slain.
Further back crimson barn and vegetable garden,
chockoblock full to feed the troops.
Logistics are perfect, and I am psyched for combat
to smite any tyrant, alter history
like Washington at Yorktown,
or the "Iron Duke" at Waterloo.

Ross Staples

SAFETY VALVE

Just as my oil burner-boiler needs it
to keep from blowing up when water pressure
gets above thirty pounds, so my mind-body,
when undue stress, frustration, blues set in,
when times get hard and pain takes over,
or again when euphoria follows
some modest success or joy, there's a need
to lower emotional temperature.

Then poetry composition is my valve.
I fire a stanza broadside, get my blood
flowing smoothly again, adrenalin checked,
give some problem my best shot, feel right again,
use it as some use religion, hobby,
athletics — release for sanity's sake.

Ross Staples

SEA OF TEARS

In a Sea of Tears I drown.
On Islands of Hope I rest.
My love for you lies beyond to the continent.
In my Boat of Despair, I try to reach the shore, your arms.

Laury Kirkbride

CHILDREN

Children are a blessed breed of people
whose helplessness makes me cry,
because so many cruel people
take advantage of a child.

Oh, how I wish that I had the power
to take care of each and every one
who has been abandoned or neglected
because of the parents' selfish pride.

Yes, children are special people
who need love and care and help;
for if you neglect these little people,
how in the world do you expect
them to survive?

Aida Escobar

FAMILIAR FACES

Familiar faces
With
Words unspoken
Memories run through your mind

Hollow eyes
Which
See nothing
Friendships left behind

Lost expressions
Show
Empty hearts
So much left to find

Familiar faces
With
Words unspoken
The memories unwind

Patricia A. Houlihan

HARVEST

Trumpets blown!
The seed was sown
Heavenly harvest known
To all who see
One's unity with destiny.

How long it takes
For man's mistakes
To reveal the breaks
  In the pattern; perceived
  To someday relieve
All pressure put upon this place
Where life has become
A matter of space!

Time no longer appears to be
Relevant to what is free.

God! Let it be a festive flight
Far beyond the dim-lit night;
Sacred, sanctioned, sane insight.

Marie J. Lemasters

NIGHT FLIGHT
WINDOW SEAT

Sunset's majesty,
  in auburn hues
Fade from bright orange,
  yellows and blues

Greyness appears,
  signaling night
Like waves of an ocean,
  swallowing light

Ribbons of color,
  once vibrant and clear
Narrow so quickly,
  then disappear

One final battle,
  one final show
The darkness of night
  against day's afterglow

The winner is certain,
  night's ever widening cloud
Consumes all below,
  in its darkening shroud.

Bill Wilson

WILLIAM E. WILSON. Born: Long Branch, New Jersey, 6-9-44; Married: Jane, July 11; Education: Tulane University, B.A., 1966; Wake Forest University School of Law, J.D., 1969; Occupation: Attorney; Memberships: New Jersey State Bar Association, Monmouth County Bar Association, New Jersey School Boards Association, National Institute of Municipal Legal Officers, National Association of Clock and Watch Collectors, American Trial Lawyers Association, American Horse Council; Comments: *To me, good poetry is the use of what Blake calls the "imagination" to express a thought, a feeling, or a circumstance in its purest and most intense form.*

DO YOU HAVE THE TIME?

We see each other rarely,
  just a nod "Hello,"
a quick smile of recognition,
  a light touch on the arm.
I miss our heart to heart chats,
  trying on shoes at Payless,
  spending our paychecks,
  complaining about work.
Could we get together sometime?
  I mean,
  do you have the time?

Kimberlee Ferris

DRAKKA; THE LOST EMPIRE

Mondo pups barking at night
Too simple a gesture carried
Into a stage of fright.

The realm of the unseen has yet to be fulfilled.
Masters of iron mold another to the throne.
His place shall rule with hands of stone.

Hawks seeking shelter from the storm
Traveling from the east
Taking on one different form.

Scattered pieces of the fallen city
A wasteland to rebels
Lies secretly below.
Vulnerable to several attacks.

Queen Rachel
Raises her thunderous voice
In disgust
To find her lover disappearing
Into another woman's lust.

Ron Sandefur

COLOR

Sunset's splendor
The radiance of a flower
Meadows of shaded green
With yellow wild flowers, in between
Fields of golden grain
A rainbow, vivid in the rain
Fresh colorful vegetables
Ripe luscious edibles
Leaves of fiery red
Delicate pink blossoms instead
The shimmering sea of shade blue-green
Sparkling fireworks, with wonderment are seen
The brilliance of a diamond blue-white
The fabulous fabrics, seamstress' delight
Sky of baby blue
Rustic autumn hue
A vision of color has been here employed;
Gratified would be if it's been enjoyed.

Isabelle Silva

E

You are Gaia,
a forest of hope,
a sea of knowledge,
a nurturer, our mentor,
tending your flock.
You are the Earth.

You are Aeolus,
sending us out on your breath,
with a gentle push,
scattering us to enrich the land.
You are the Wind.

And you are Hestia,
giving us the drive,
the lust to succeed,
engulfing us in an incendiary passion,
to inflame those in our realm.
You are the Fire.

Kimberlee Ferris

CATSKILL FALLS.

CHALLENGER II

I watched it explode in the bright morning sky
On its way to a mission in space.
The crew and their passenger gone in a flash!
Only bits of debris in their place.

"So what," says the cynic, "in Afghanistan
The Russians kill hundreds each hour,
Life's cheap in the '80s all over the world
What's different about this great power?"

I'll tell you what's different: We value each life,
It matters not whose it might be,
The flyer, the teacher, the man in the street,
Oh yes — then there's you and there's me.

Lucy Nuttall

LAMENT OF NAPOLI

The trash bags stacked to left and right
  with reckless abandon upon the ground.
The traffic jams without end,
  no parking spaces to be found!

    Napoli — O Napoli,
      my heart belongs to thee.

The bay so black with sludge and oil,
  with rusty ships and piers all broke.
The tunnels blocked with cars so small,
  with horns that sound and fumes to choke!

    Napoli — O Napoli,
      my heart belongs to thee.

Through it all the thieves run free.
  The watches go, the wallets walk.
Crowds that push and shout with glee,
  among the screeching ladies' talk!

    Napoli — O Napoli,
      my heart belongs to thee.

But then I think back on that day,
  when first I viewed my new-found home.
With beauty of a different type,
  I knew right then I was not wrong:

    Napoli — O Napoli,
      my heart belongs to thee.

Lou Albright

THE LIGHT

Beware the darkness in the light,
Light can be darker than the night.
Demons in light can steal your sight,
And the innocent light can indict.

Light can corrupt, be a bringer of blight,
A double-edged sword, steeped in spite.
The righteous are forever and alone, right.
So beware the darkness in the light.

Robert W. Sharpe

LOVE

Love is the most important
thing to me
No matter what kind of love
it should be.
Whether it be love of nature,
or love of one another.
It could be love of a country,
or love of a sister and brother.

Love is that of friendship;
the glory of two best friends.
Love is when two lovebirds
marry to tie the ends.

Love is belief
in only one God.
Believe in His kingdom,
because He is not a fraud.

Love will be forever.
Its kingdom will have no end.
Don't ever misjudge it.
It will always be your friend.

Kim Clostio

YOUR SOUNDS

I play this,
my vision, on the sand.
Shells every few feet,
tepid mellow moods;
skittishly nervous no more.
A gently aging couple
still in love
hand in hand.
No swimmers, no gulls.
Only the water
and the beach
making love
before my eyes.
Tradewinds that cool
but do not chill.
Here, the whispering secrets
of Nature's naked gifts
sound very close
to the way I feel
when I'm with you.

George T. Coleman

A MOMENT

My heart feels gentle.
My soul feels calm.
My mind feels peaceful.
My spirit feels free.
Because in this moment Lord,
there is just You and me!

    Thank You Jesus!

Melva Lea Hines

A POST-CHRISTMAS PRAYER

O God,
Like the Psalmist, I would cry,
"Bless the Lord, O my soul,
and forget not all His benefits."
I don't know why
You make such a fuss over us
who pay so little heed to You,
but You do.
You even made a special star
to guide the wise
to where you are. AMEN.

Paul Hamsher

A PRE-CHRISTMAS PRAYER

Lord,
Help me make life fun again
like when
the family gathered 'round the reedy organ
singing carols
and ringing out the "Grand Amen,"
or going to church together
on Christmas Eve
to share with others who believe,
the joy of Love's forgiving
that makes life really living. AMEN.

Paul Hamsher

A PRAYER ON CHRISTMAS EVE

Father in heaven,
this Christmas Eve
I go again to worship
with others who believe
the Holy Child of Bethlehem.
I'll join in carol singing
and envision angels winging
about the shepherds on a hill
above the manger bare,
and Wise Men bringing gifts
of gold, frankincense and myrrh.
Give me the uncomplicated,
child-like faith
that will absorb
a little of
the love
You planted there. AMEN.

Paul Hamsher

MY FATHER

When I watch you hard at work,
And the wisdom you know for what you do,
It makes me wish I were more like you.
When I see the determination you have
To get the job done,
It makes me think that you're second to none,
And for that I stand up!

Paul Marion Cox

226

GRATITUDE FOR A YOUNG WIFE

My lizard, my lively writher
May your limbs never wither . . .
May you live out your life
Without hate, without grief

      Theodore Reothke in *Wish for a Young Wife*

Without her he would rust out
reliving bloody Guadalcanal,
raising the flag at Iwo Jima.
She draws him from TV chair, football
to garden workout, live theater,
joins him often to hike or bike.
She spurs the decorated ''vet''
to travel and new adventure.
Often they dine out and dance.
He likes Ellington, she the Beatles.
They adjust to each's wish and beat —
bend, sway, twist — a dance style their own.
He's her Ulysses, protector,
she's Penelope, rejuvenator.

    Ross Staples

ALONE

The time spent alone, apart
Wishing to be together, as one
And then, to be as one
Without knowing the worth of self; alone

The time spent together, so full — and yet so empty
Lifted by false joy
Warmed by baby love
Protected by protecting — blinded by devoted concern
And all — still
Without knowing the worth of self; alone

And then again — the time spent alone
Growing, building, laughing
Crying, reaching, wishing
For the past
For the secure togetherness

To be together as one
Perhaps someday — but not today
And not with you — my faded love

For now, for one, for me
Knowing the worth of self; alone

    Marie-José Caro

AND A LITTLE CHILD SHALL LEAD THEM

''A story please Mummy,'' said three-year-old Sue.
So Old Mother Hubbard I read slowly through.
My thoughts all the time on the state of the world
And the chores to be done as the new day unfurled.
    (Dishes I wash by the dozens!
    Should I try to get out of this rut
    There's the hydrogen bomb and the Russians!
    Indeed life is grim — and for what?)
Poor old Mother H. and her cupboard so bare
Had nothing on me. I was filled with despair!
'Til Sue, looking up with a shake of her head,
And her dimples all showing, so quietly said,
''Why didn't she look in the refrigerator?''

    Lucy Nuttall

ENDURING TRIUMPHANTLY!

It's another day, dear Lord, and the pain refuses to subside.
My heart aches with such a heaviness I can hardly breathe. I
feel so alone. There's no one to turn to nor any place to hide.
O' Lord, how can I endure? When will it ever end?

As I lie here with the dark closing in around me, I wonder
how I can possibly face another day knowing it will be as
this one, for tomorrow I must wear a different face before the
world. Dear Lord, how can I endure? When will it ever end?

My Lord, you were all alone: forsaken by others. A man of
solitude and many sorrows — and yes you cried often for the
agony you saw in others. O'Lord, how did you endure? Did
it really ever end?

With a destination for Jerusalem from birth you endured more
pain than us all and yet your whole life was for others. Your
all-sufficient love surrounded others in their great need and
in so doing you found release and freedom. Yes, Lord, you endured.

Now, I see, that in giving we receive — Freedom! In giving of
yourself to others you were able to endure such sorrows. In
giving of yourself to man you endured the cross and therein
found freedom — for all. Yes Lord, you indeed endured,
Triumphantly!

    Gloria Hester

A DIFFERENT VIEW

The girl stands there defiantly. She is hard and cruel to
those around her; not at all appealing. As I watch her, I
feel such compassion and longing to reach out and protect
her from the world's harshness. That same harshness that
she has so patterned her life after. As I look deeper,
I begin to see a frightened little girl so like a rabbit ready
to dart away from danger. Her eyes are filled with such agony
of pain, so unlike the facade of self-assurance she has
chosen to wear. Dear Lord, is this how you see us?

I take another look around the room. The girl is just as
harsh and rude as ever and the people seem to recoil from her.
Nothing seems to have changed and yet, it has. For I have had
a glimpse through the eyes of God. I have felt such a surge
of love and compassion accompanied by a deep longing to ease
the pain of one so unappealing. Yes, I have changed for I
have just looked through my Father's eyes and thank God his
view was so, so different!

    Gloria Hester

YOUR OVERWHELMING LOVE

I listen to the waves of endless time pound again and again
against the shore and I know you are there.

I watch the burst of colors at sunrise and know that I have
witnessed the birth of a new day and I know you are there.

I smell the fragrance of a beautiful rose still wet with
dawn's early dew and I know you are there.

I feel the cool soft grass against my bare feet on a late
summer's evening and I know you are there.

In all of creation I stand in awe of who you are and am
humbled as I think, all of this — for me — because of your love.

Yes, Lord, I know you are there for I am overwhelmed by your
great love.

    Gloria Hester

MY BABY GIRL IS LEAVING

My baby girl is leaving.
To test her wings anew.
Surrounded by ageless seas
Of a thousand faceless friends
A thousand friendly strangers.
New hearths and homes to try
First step to all that is.
Long miles and lonely hours away
Yet not forgotten in thoughts or prayers.
My baby girl is leaving.

My baby girl is leaving.
A father's joy, sweet hidden tears.
Youth past, she's growing up
Pretty baby, beautiful woman
Joyous childhood, exciting adulthood
The world's within grasp
Take and savor life's choices
And bring forth that father's pride,
The best wish of all,
My baby girl is leaving.

Robert Noble

JUST BORN

A rose just born so tender
Fragile, delicate and pure
Brings promise of great joy,
Sharing the beauty of the universe,
To those of us who care.

A rose blooming, opening to
The sun's tender caress
Attracts mighty and meek alike.
Only the strong are gentle enough to
Pick this delicate flower. Only the
Kind are wise enough. Only a
Lover is true enough.

A rose, in a strong lover's wise vision
Never fades, never dies, never
Loses the essence of life.

A rose though here only a short time
Leaves behind a changed world
To return another season
Renewed.

Robert Noble

REFLECTIONS

Reflections linger in your eyes . . .
Silent remnants of a moment gone by.
You smile innocently,
Feeling the rain . . .
Always blinded by the sun
Whose warmth you could never forget.
Reflections . . .
I caught a glimpse of you through the glass . . .
Standing there . . .
So unaware . . .
And I, being weak . . .
Remembered you as my love.

Mary Elizabeth Hatcher

THE HAWK

With graceful wings across the sky
Your flight is beyond compare.
Soaring high above the heavens
Flying you're not
But capturing sight.
Courage,
Strength,
Boldness and skill . . .
Your goals are set . . .
And these you touch . . .
With no sound,
But victory in your heart.

Mary Elizabeth Hatcher

LISTEN TO THE CHILDREN

Listen to the children,
Not so much what they say;
But listen to their tears
And silent cries of today.

Listen to the children,
But don't expect them to speak;
For their hearts are heavy
And their bodies are weak.

Listen across the nation
As children die each day
Of a growing lack of food
And no place to stay.

Innocent victims
Trapped in society's share.
A nation of plenty
Seems to be so unaware.

Listen to the children
Then do something today.
The problem is real,
We can't wish it away.

Laurietta Jordan-Faulkner

THE KITCHEN

It's the heart of the house — the kitchen
Where all the good news is spread,
Where troubles, shared, become smaller
Where the riot act is read.

Where the children do their homework,
Where guests have a cup of tea,
And cookies are baked by the dozen,
For visitors such as me.

It's always warm in the kitchen
With hospitality rife
Whether turkey is in the oven
Getting ready for the knife,

Or it's humble fare you are serving,
With helping big, of love,
Surrounded by friends or family,
Giving thanks to the One above.

Mildred Keating

DARKNESS ALL AROUND

Does my mind deceive me?
I try to talk to you,
but you do not hear.
I try to reach you,
but you slip away.

Is this real?
My mind cannot tell.
I reach out to you, but find only darkness.
Darkness is all around me.

My mind is in darkness.
My thoughts, my body, my very soul;
they are no longer my own.
I do not see; I cannot feel.
Darkness is all around.

Katherine S. Walker

NEVER SURRENDER

Fight the good fight
No matter where you are,
Never set aside your dreams
And never surrender.

Keep your head held high
When your spirit is down,
At least try to smile
And don't let yourself frown.

Don't give up
When the odds are against you,
Pick up your heart and laugh
And never surrender.

Shannon G. Wood

SUNDAY'S FRUSTRATION

I see; I feel; I think;
But to what end? Am I
An idea? A dream? A scheme?
Am I just flesh and blood?

Does *He* exist? If so,
So what? What point to life
Except — to be, for *Him*
Or not. But not for me?

One way no choice is mine;
The other is the same.
All that is left is to
Accept my share of blame.

Alive or dead, to the
End or beyond, there is
No difference, because
It is not mine to will.

I see; I feel; I think;
But to what end I do
Not know; I no longer
Care. I will live to live.

Robert E. Rodriguez

TO SHANNON

A young girl came to our door
''In trouble,'' they said — she needed help and more.
She was brought by our own dear daughter
And in what ways we could, help we brought her.

You were her baby boy, beautiful and clean,
Sweet as eyes had ever seen.
Again she would ask for help, again we would give —
Then she took you away but our hearts were captive.

A darling child, a handsome lad is how you grew.
Now there's a Daddy, a brother too.
So much of good, yet trouble is there
Making discord of what should be fair.

Things bad — but another would not need escape.
You chose the frightening things your life to shape,
The ''grass,'' the pills, the street,
Leaving thoughts that are bittersweet.

Dear one, wherever you may stumble,
Whatever demon may cause you to tumble —
That you overcome is our prayer
For the Lord and I, we care.

Virginia Levack

MANY HAPPY RETURNS

I called my friend today;
    You see, it is her birthday.
So it was for that special wish
    Time could never diminish.

''The big six-o'' she said, ''but I feel the same.''
    Wasn't it but days ago to play we came
In a ''play-house'' built in the back yard
    Of blankets, and boxes and many a discard?

It was so since we were two and three,
    To wade in the creek or climb a tree.
From the first day of school to the last
    And on through the years steadfast.

New friends give sparkle to life
    With new thoughts and ideas rife,
But there is comfort in love that is old
    That hearts embrace, ever to hold.

Virginia Levack

NEVER FORGOTTEN

Even now I can close my eyes and see you as though it were yesterday.

I can see the courage in your eyes, the gentleness of your smile,
strength outlined in your face.

I remember as though it were yesterday, but I know it's not.

It's been a long time since GOD took you from us; but you know,
    Grandpa,
your memory lingers on. You're as close as the thoughts in my mind.

You may be gone, but never, never will be forgotten. *''I miss you.''*

C. Ward

BUT GOD!

God, sometimes I feel so small and so alone.
I cannot make my cries known. I want so much to let it out,
To scream and shout, to get it out.
And ask you Lord, why me? Why did you let me be so bad?
But I know this makes you sad.
I hurt God. I hurt bad!
And I feel so *damn mad!*
I feel so mixed up and confused.
God! I've been abused!
I know sometimes I get mad at you,
And I forget to ask *You,* what should I do?
I know Lord, that you are there, and you really do care.
But God! Sometimes I get so scared.
I cannot feel your presence there.
Please Lord, make it known to me,
That you are there, and you'll always care.
Please give me strength to understand.
And Lord!
Please hold me in your gentle hand.
Please hold me tight so I can feel your strength and might.

Debbie J. Pederson

INCOMPLETE

Imagine a world without music playing.
Think of a church with nobody praying.
If you've ever looked up at the sky with no blue,
Then you've seen a picture of me without you.

Have you walked in a garden with nothing growing,
Or stood by a river with no water flowing?
If you've seen a rose untouched by the dew,
Then you've seen a picture of me without you.

Imagine heaven with no angels singing,
Or a Sunday morning with no church bells ringing.
And if you can see how my heart is longing for you,
Then you've seen a picture of me without you.

Debbie J. Pederson

FIRST CHRISTMAS WITHOUT DAD

This year is very different, Mother;
The love we share with you
Will be just double all the other
And memories will see us through.

Let us not mourn our loss too much;
Let joys of yesterday remain
To keep our lonely hearts in touch
With one gone on to God's domain.

In spirit Dad is with us,
His presence seems so real;
And if with us, he could discuss
His wish this yuletide season,
I'm sure he'd laugh our tears away
And say, ''Have a happy, happy Christmas day!''

Evelyn C. Reece

ADVICE

Ah! my children, let me be!
Do you think I cannot see?

Do you think I do not know
What it is to ebb and flow?

What it is to want and need
From confusion to be freed?

From confusion I have grown;
Please accept what I have known!

Please accept what all my years
Have accomplished through my tears.

Robert E. Rodriguez

KAREN

She's not the wealth of Troy
Or Caesar's fair delight,
Or earth and moon and stars
Or sky and bright sunlight.

She's the absence that I
Feel in those times when I'm
Alone, and the fullness
That I feel when I'm not.

Robert E. Rodriguez

ROBERT EDWARD RODRIGUEZ. Born: Chicago, Illinois, 4-29-57; Married: Karen Helen Rodriguez, 1981.

MARCH 26, 1979

My pain is years deep.
I am learning to be myself again,
Detached from you.

I am re-grouping my life
To exclude you.

Surviving without you,
My strength comes
From being alone.

Anne T. Quinterno

THE SIGN

I asked God to show me a sign,
To show me what life was about.
When I looked out my window,
God showed me that sign.
He showed me a caged animal.
The caged animal looked sad.
He had somewhere to stay,
Someone to protect him,
Someone to love.
But still he looked sad.
He was not free.
Then God showed me another sign.
He showed me a free animal.
The free animal looked sad,
He had a home to sleep in,
Food to eat,
He had the whole world to run to,
But still he looked sad.
He had no one to love.

Tiffeny Oswalt

VIEW FROM A PHOTOGRAPH

I see you
Your torn clothes
Worn like a badge.

The empty sleeve.

You don't forget,
Crawling back
Into the bowels of life.

No one cares.

Sweat
Mingles with
The wet, rotting wood.

You couldn't survive.

Anne T. Quinterno

THINGS

The teddy bear she'll never
ever hold in her gentle, caring
arms.

The cradle lies empty
Toys untouched
Love never given
The forever she'll never see.

My dreams lie unspoken
in a dormant room.

The precious doll I'll
never hold.

Lora Everhart

DEMONS OF AMBITION

Strive and strive to stay alive,
With many a good intention.
And through the strive to stay alive
Are the demons of ambition.

In the minds are left the marks,
With such a great precision,
That in the light a thought embarks,
On the demons of ambition.

Follow the light that lights the path,
That is the only mission.
For, avoiding the light that lights the path
Brings the demons of ambition.

So, in the dark there shall be,
For was made the wrong decision,
To follow the evil of the night
And the demons of ambition.

Gregory S. Abbott

TEARDROPS FALL

Teardrops fall, when a loved one dies,
Teardrops fall, when a newborn cries.
Teardrops fall, when lovers fight,
Teardrops fall, when love has taken flight.
Teardrops fall, for the hungry and poor,
Teardrops fall, when our nations go to war.
Teardrops fall, in romantic setting,
Teardrops fall, at your children's wedding.
Teardrops fall, when someone says I love you,
Teardrops fall, when their love is untrue.
Teardrops fall, when you hear a sad song,
Teardrops fall, when you feel you don't belong.
Teardrops fall, when a child breaks a toy,
Teardrops fall, with laughter and joy.
Teardrops fall, when your body aches,
Teardrops fall, when your heart breaks.
Teardrops fall, when you're lonely and scared,
Teardrops fall, because nobody cared.
Teardrops fall.

Susan M. Do

A MOMENT'S HUDDLE

A moment's huddle
too late! —
A moment's huddle.

We'll cuddle the night away
and kiss our Zero hour;

   Come the last morn'
   in the silent dawn
   under the radiance of a hundred
   thousand suns,

We'll go picking cloudy mushrooms,

   Hand-in-Hand.
   One-by-One.

Ronald L. Mahony

GOLDEN SOUVENIRS

Golden memories,
Gathered through the years,
Were born in pleasures shared
And tinged with secret tears.

Golden memories,
Mellowed by the years,
Are bound in tender love
And sealed against unfounded fears.

Today, I looked behind the veil to yesterday,
I dreamed I held you in my arms the same old way;
I clasped your gentle hands and touched your hair
And in your eyes I saw how much you cared.

Our years together were not lived in vain
For love surpassed the sting of foolish pride and gain
Leaving only treasures rare for the reclining years
To fill the idle hours with golden souvenirs.

Evelyn C. Reece

SOMETHING TO REMEMBER ME BY

Let me give you something,
Something to remember me by.
Here's a box of rosy dawn
Packed in a snuggle
And tied with a song.
And look! Here's a golden sunset
Wrapped in warmth
And sealed with a smile.
This is a rainbow I found
That I put in this jar,
Mixed with moonbeams
And a little falling star.
At least that's what I wanted to give you,
But a tear fell on them
And they weren't the same anymore.
Back they turned
Into the fantasies they really are.
So I'm sending you my dreams,
As something to remember me by.

Anita R. Saliscente

SUMMER'S CHILD

Voices are calling me,
    Reaching out to me and calling me back,
Beckoning to me from time long since past.
    They remind me of afternoon picnics by the river
And splashing in the water.
    "Remember . . . remember," the voices call,
"Remember and come back."
    "Too late! Too late!" I cry.
But from deep within me, I hear a tiny whisper,
    "Not too late. It's not too late . . ."
As my little daughter takes my hand
    And takes me back
        To Summer.

Anita R. Saliscente

OLD MEN IN HATS

I used to lie on the backseat of the car
watching the telephones and skyscrapers roll by.
My father
We shared bacon sandwiches and chocolate malteds
and trips made into journeys
until I had to share the back seat
with those who didn't see the magic in
moving lines and buildings on wheels.
Advancing to the front
I found a wrinkled man in a french beret
with clenched knuckles
muttering something about
beware of old men in hats on the road.

Arlene Schulman

AUNTIE ESTHER

Your wedding picture torn in two
Louie ripped to shreds.
The bride in the flapper dress with Tinkerbell dreams
smiling coyly at the camera
is now a lumpy shape in a faded housedress
with a pink plastic hearing aid and brown orthopedic shoes.
Your lover abandoned you
stole away with your money and heart
and left
a sad old woman who cries on my shoulder.

Arlene Schulman

UNTITLED

Loneliness can relate to many different things.
Sitting there listening while that distant bird sings.
You lie awake in bed with no one else to speak.
Your senses perk to sound like the dripping faucet leak.
You stare into the darkness seeing spots in the air.
There's no one to talk to and there's no one to care.
Or maybe you sit there when you eat, all alone
with nothing around you but a silent telephone.
Simple life near a fire where thoughts are understood,
playing your own music. Can loneliness be good?
But what is loneliness when in yourself there's you?
You must learn to blend them to form a life for two.

Susan Winslow

NO WAY, REFLECTIONS OF A RETIRED TEACHER

No cheery good mornings with teachers in the hall?
No 'hello theres', none at all?
No eight o'clock bell, no news to tell?
No intercom messages, delivered so well?
No classes to meet, no papers to grade?
No plans to make, or have they all been made?
No impact that comes when teacher meets class?
No thrill derived from a breakthrough at last?
No evaluations, no criteria, no counsel to give?
No example to set to show pupils how to live?
No challenges, no rewards, no mountains to climb?
No bright shining faces to look up into mine?
No — — — — — way!

Gladys Brewer

WALK IN THE WOODS

Will you walk with me in the wood awhile?
   (the mist lies along the mountaintops)
Beneath the branches single file
   (tendrils of fog through the trees)
I know it's wet but can't we just
   (from darkened pines the silver drops)
walk a bit? I know we must
   (fall softly on sodden moss and leaves)
be home by dark

I love the woods in the shadowy mist
   (a hush when all the forest's still)
don't you? Oh all right if you insist
   (blankets of fog hug the distant hill)
we'll stay here where it's warm and dry
   (the ancient pines huddle there)
You put the kettle on while I
   (gnarled trunks and branches bare)
stand by the window and look out a bit
   (nothing moves that we can hear)
at the dripping trees and the fog and wet
   (except the call of the whippoorwill)
  It will soon be dark
   (the plaintive cry of the whippoorwill)
  It will soon be dark

Rae Ursini

AD ASTRA PER ASPERA

I stood in reverence and awe at the foot
  of a mountain I thought to be
  the embodiment of all knowledge.

I began the tedious climb toward the peak,
  thinking that I could gain this
  wisdom by scaling the crags.

I stopped midway to look downward and saw
  but shale and splinters and roots of
  fruitless trees with their tenuous grasp.
  The peak still loomed but beyond
  the sky still beckoned.

I knew then that as I struggled to learn
  the limitless horizon beckoned
  and my gain was but one small step.

Mary E. Cates

BUTTERCUPS

Children are playing in a field
  of buttercups,

Creating an appreciation of yellow
  upon their skins,
A touching glow under their chins,

Radiating life inward to outward;
Their eyes fixed on each other's throats,

Amazed at yellow turning to gold.

Ronald L. Mahony

A NURSE'S PRAYER

Oh Lord,
  I have come on willing feet
  With my hands outstretched
  And a loving heart

  To minister to Thy sick
  And to assist You.
  This would be my part.

Oh God,
  Give unto me what I lack
  Patience and courage,
  A willingness to share.

  Lend gentleness to my touch
  Lest eyes closed in pain
  Cannot see I care.

And Lord,
  Knowing that some cannot heal
  Help me to assist
  Those souls to Thy Lands.

  Let none who come unto Thee
  Leave this world without
  The love of Nurses' hands.

Mary E. Cates

AFTER THE STORM

Glistening snow has covered the fields,
  Freshly fallen in the night,
Lining every tree and bough —
  Sharp against the morning light.

Olivia Brum

TRANSCENDING

It is coming now, the feel of
  flight Beginning.

I can no longer hear the Cacophony,
  the tumultuous sound of voices weaving.

I cannot see the amorphous Ghosts,
  the distortions of shapes well known.

Gossamer threads of thoughts float free
  and unfettered from the Earth.

Now I can hear the whisper of the Wind
  as I unfold and fold My Wings.

The light is nearing.
  My eyes do not need a Shield.

My Mind is crystal and the
  Shimmering takes My Totality

I am Free and at Peace.

Mary E. Cates

(JENNY)

In the eyes of darkness is
She seeing what I see
When at night I close my
Eyes? She reaches for the
Mirror but only to feel the
Cold glass and act as
Though she is looking.
Behind her I am standing
And I see her beauty
And reflection. At
Times the darkness is her
Enemy, but can also
Be a friend. Is she
Seeing the dream in her
Mind while she sleeps,
Or does she only hear
Voices from a distance?
The darkness is a peering
Beauty and a silent evil
In blindness and in sleep.

Stephanie Ann Cooley

ONE NIGHT I HAD A DREAM

Oh wind whisper me a silent dream
Forget me not as though it seems
That forever the cold wind blows
Wailing softly is the weeping willow
Lying in bed my head on a pillow
A song which no one knows
First I am here but now I'm gone
Who is to tell right from wrong
I am alone in the dark
I cannot hear it fall, the rain
A past memory will cause great pain
Tripping over toys in the park
A carousel of a unicorn shrine
Closing my eyes I am blind
A stranger touches my shoulder
Sleeping deeply a cat steals my breath
A passerby softly cries the name Beth
The wind begins to grow colder
Oh wind whisper me a silent dream
Forget me not as though it seems . . .

Stephanie Ann Cooley

LET ME LIVE ANOTHER DAY

Let me live another day to see
A mountain covered with snow and
A winding stream that seems to follow
Me wherever I go, but it is not
Me that it follows, but the mountains
Above it.
Let me live another day to see
The encircling clouds ready to make
The dancing snow that seems to follow
Me wherever I go, but it is not
Me that it follows, but the nature
Around it.
Let me live another day to travel
Down another lonely highway that
Seems to linger on forever that
Seems to follow me wherever I go,
But it is not me that it follows,
For I am following it.

Stephanie Ann Cooley

VET'S LAMENT

You taught us to shoot in Democracy's name
    with shiny new boots and dreams of real fame.
The songs that you sang made us feel tall and proud
    to be part of your gang and scream it out loud.
You sent us to Nam, our hearts filled with pride,
    not thinking of bombs or who's on whose side.
You showed us some sights we still dream of today
    and put us through nights that made us all pray.
You made us not care for the people we killed,
    just to breathe orange air and accomplish your will.
Then, you brought us back here to the land of the free,
    our hearts filled with fear at what we might see.
You left us alone when the bodies all fell
    to flounder and roam in our own living hell.
Yes, so often I pray in a mood of regret
    for the price we pay to be labeled a Vet!

George T. Coleman

TO 'MAN'

I stand before you with mere words of expression.
Shimmering as a naked child in the wind at such thoughts as
bearing my inner feelings to your critical acceptance.
You, the one who has entered my life so abruptly, who has
passed through this locked door of my soul as the sparrow's
wing cuts the morning mist.
Revelation! A relationship spent in spiritual entwining where
coming of age nor past lives and loves matter not.
Time stills for a moment as we partake of the bread and wine of
communication, exchanging thoughts and future quests.
Such feelings confuse yet arouse my inner depths, as when our
eyes meet in a moment of frivolity then stop, to view a deeper
aura of the unknown, yet knowing, billowing within.
The adventure of our relationship! To know you so intimately yet at
times know not at all as another presence of the man with a thousand
faces raises his head and greets me with a boisterous introduction
as I am left in wonder once again.
In essence, so much to learn, so much to share, to know and grow.
To know these lives of yours and mine are measured not in
moments of time . . . but in timeless moments.

Susan Winslow

DULL EYES WITH EYELIDS A THIRD CLOSED

Dull eyes with eyelids a third closed,
What for do you mask your shining lights?
Twice I have seen their blue brightness
Arc lights flashing with each lid flutter,
And lovely were they; lovelier than
The sweet blue lilac in bloom.
But now like clouds shielding the sun,
Only a glimmer of free sky sifts through.
Sadness must dim your flowery soul,
Or surely this would not be.

Rob Bignell

WATERS OF EMOTION

Love is a deep, blue sea —
    alluring, dangerous, yet mystifying.
Unrequited, its maelstrom will hold you prisoner.
Relenting only after suffocation.
Reciprocation, it will ravish you with its prismatic grandeur.
You become a part of its wonder.

Lust is a shallow pond —
    attractive yet superficial.
From afar, its splendiferous beauty enchants and amuses you.
The summer breeze bears the redolence of water lilies.
It is a call you cannot deny.
Dive, and the calloused bed will belie its innocence.
Wade, and the crystal liquid will massage your body.

Like a flowing river —
    sparkling, beautiful, yet a chameleon.
Ride forever on its current, and
    its effervescence will excite you.
Threaten its domain, and its whirlpool will swallow you.
Follow the travels of the water, and
    its efficacy will have you surrendering to the sea.

Gayla E. Black

REVENGE

The cowboy stopped to walk his horse,
    As he rode the desert trail,
He had tracked the outlaws this far,
    He was determined not to fail.
Ten thousand dollars was on their heads,
    But the cowboy wanted more,
He'd track 'em down and kill 'em,
    He'd even up the score.
He'd tracked 'em both from Abiline,
    Two hundred miles or so,
For you see they'd killed his brother
    He couldn't let them go.
The distance between them narrowed,
    The time was near at hand,
He felt the tension mounting,
    He had to make a stand.
Not ten feet was between them
As he stood, back towards the sun,
    They drew, but he drew faster,
Revenge for his brother he'd won.

Robert S. Boyd

HESITANT

Riding on the rim of reality,
one loose move and you've fallen.
If wrong, ending as a statical fatality,
if right, the rest of your life will awaken.
Being different isn't really being an odd-ball,
going with the flow could just stop your destination.
Use your head, be proud, stand tall,
say no, life is a great sensation . . .

Salvatore LaFata IV

FRAIL LOVE

Love's so frail, I fear
to let it touch my heart
for when it dies, it tears
our fantasies apart,
leaving only shadows
of hope that used to be,
echoing the sorrow
in painful memory

Oh, to be so near
and yet, so far apart —
you hold me oh so dear,
but not dearest, in your heart —
living for the strangers
who love you secretly,
erasing all the pleasures,
in our doomed reality

Robert E. VandenHeuvel

FOOLISH HEART

Foolish heart,
bleeding
for a friend who'll never be
the lover, you desire
desperately —
sleeping in the shadow
of true love
and romance,
you lose your love
to beauty,
and unfair circumstance

Robert E. VandenHeuvel

CHARLENE

This child has sorely touched my heart.
I've worked. I've prayed and sometimes wept.
I've watched her grow year after year.
Her needs are great; her talents few.
I've walked beside her as she grew.
I've helped her through each varied part —
The constant vigil kept —
Of pain, of joy, of fear.

Kaleidoscopic day on day.
Dwarfed, tragic clown with unshed tears;
A world unsuited to her need.
Guileless and lost; a homeless child,
Sometimes meek, sometimes wild;
Unarmed of rules for games we play;
Maturity outstripped by years;
Her case I often plead.

Yet I know not this child of mine,
Though as bodyguard and friend,
Through twenty-seven years of pain.
When she's unveiled, some morning bright,
And stands before me whole and right,
With burnish and refine,
My broken heart will surely mend.
For joy I'll weep again.

Ruth C. Rowley

HONOR IS FOREMOST IN PEACE

Since the dawn of evolution
Through the twilight of existence,
The world is torn with revolution
And resistance.

War upon war upon war
And no cessation in sight;
Dead are the weak and the poor
Who cannot fight.

With Liberty and Justice for all,
Honor is foremost in peace.
All the world's nations hold survival,
When all wars cease.

Luanne McInnes

SHIPWRECKED

This vessel that set off for an ocean trip,
sailed the captain and the crew.
Waves awoke upon the ship,
away the mast and sails flew.

Ocean water filled the vessel
and fell fathoms deep.
Oh, how they sank in the wrestle,
only to end them to a forever sleep.

Carol A. Dixon

CAROL ANN DIXON. Born: Mt. Clemens, Michigan, 7-24-66; Single; Education: East Detroit High School, 6-84; Occupations: Secretary, Accounts payable clerk; Memberships: Quarter Horse of America Association; Poetry: 'Dreaming,' 6-83; 'Perched Forever,' 4-87; 'Life in the Fast Lane,' 6-83; 'The Heart,' 5-87; Other Writings: "Shipwrecked," short story, 4-87; Comments: *My writings are about everyday life and the things that happen to me. I write down on paper what I cannot say aloud. I feel that people can relate to my work. Once I put my thoughts down on paper, I get a feeling of accomplishment.*

A MOST PECULIAR TREE

Long spider tree
Bare and lonely
Extending branch
In no man's land
'Cause in the shade
No one can see
The eagle slide

Out there maybe
Someone crazy
Will touch a branch
The bird will land
'Cause in the shade
No one can see
Trees never lied

Long years to be
Bare and lonely
Taking a chance
In desert sand
'Cause in the shade
No one can see
That trees have died
The eagle cried.

Corinne Cykiert

UNEMPLOYMENT DANCE

Hello, welcome aboard
Good-bye, we don't
Need you anymore
You can stand on your head
Give us the juice of your soul
We'll suck you in — then
Press the "ejection" button
You can stand in line
For government money
If you have kids
To feed
We're very sorry
You can click your heels
You can bow and spin around
Or join the unemployment dance
Hello, welcome aboard
Good-bye, we don't
Need you anymore.

Corinne Cykiert

CLOUDS

They mimic — like white shadows,
    those drifting, vagabond clouds.
They smile and bathe in the sun . . .
As they depart,
    frowning, crying,
They put on their heavy dark coats,
    whisper their farewell,
    that is the wind,
    and
Let night fall on our shoulders.

Jon Saldivar

RAIN TRILOGY PART III

The Widow

Time has died, the rain stopped,
The sun dark and unsmiling, the oceans lacking in motion.
The earth settled and calm, the air unsounding.
But as I search to let my heart feel,
I find the true meaning of you, and I love.
I conquer vast empires of feelings and protect them
    as wonders never discovered.
A longing love, one of want and need,
To feel as if lighter than thought, a meaningful self-worth.
But as the final grain of sand slips through
    the connected glass structure,
    time loses breath.
Still I love and find reason to survive
To fight with eternity and fate, to find goodness and peace.
To live when all has died and still left so many yet crying.
To rebuild, to flourish with wisdom and deliverence,
To walk with justice, to unnerve fear,
To be left as a thorn on the stock of a dying rose.
Black tears abound only to be left as the Widow
    of past truths and convictions.
Life, love and laughter, the only remaining light within so much dark,
Still, I go on.

Nina J. M. Foster

MOWING

Hamlet:

To mow, or not to mow — that is the question;
Whether 'tis nobler in the grass to suffer
The spores and seedpods of outrageous upgrowths
Or to take arms against a field of troubles
And by mowing end them.

Annette M. Matthews

TOGETHER

Standing alone in this vastness of space
Searching for life's beginnings
Beginnings for life's search
Pressured to move forward
Instincted to look back
    Standing alone in this vastness of space
Enjoying what we want
Wanting what we enjoy
Dreaming of past lives
Living of past dreams
    Standing alone in this vastness of space
Searching for life's future
The future of life's search
Looking back to past destruction
Destruction of life's past
    Together we must stand in this vastness of space.

Ed Strusz

THE NEWNESS OF NATURE

The birds are bringing to us their sweet, beautiful melodies,
The bees are receiving nectar from flowers in the bush and the trees,
People seem happier savoring the warmth of the weather's breeze,
And everything seems to be coming to life after the cold and freeze.

But what mystic causes our spirits to soar,
And what expectations are we seeking and yearning for,
Could it be peace, beauty, and tranquility,
Yet, it seems as though these words are weak,
To reach out and bring forth to reality,
What we mere mortals feel, need and restlessly seek!

The season seems to resemble new life with promises of radiant beauties,
It is time to enjoy nature with all of its blooming splendors,
Yet, this new birth of a lovely season,
Is it but a sign or is it the main reason?

We look inward in our search for a reason,
But outwardly, we enthusiastically relish and enjoy the season,
Yet, the truth we all know is not to nature alone
    but it is a time of new birth,
But far more importantly, if only we accept,
    our souls are given new birth,
How much better do we enjoy the season,
When our spirits and nature are united,
    joined by our creator and blended in reason!

Chester A. Tatum, Jr.

SLEEPING WITH THE DEAD

That sound, it's so distinctive
The creaking of the bedroom door
The quiet steps across the floor

You thought you heard a whisper
but it must have been the wind
The gentle hissing as the breeze blows the curtains
And in the light of the moon
you could swear someone was watching you

You thought you felt caresses
but it must have been a dream
As it knelt down beside you, gently touching your hair
And in the haze of a sleep
you could swear someone was kissing you

She lies down beside you in the bed.

Gregory T. Verdino

THOUGHT

A thought is a lot quicker than a flash
    That crosses the sky on a stormy night —
    Its high voltage sparkles a blinding light
Accompanied with a roar: what a smash!

Don't be fooled by such a brief duration
    'Cause it has already penetrated
    Like a sharp needle, and concentrated
Into an unmanageable dimension!

Its effect, though may not be felt at once,
    Will last and last until the end of time —
    Whether packing a passion or blessing
It is worth a million dollars an ounce!

    O, please, don't you take good care of that mine
    Of thoughts? And may they never stop flashing!

Harry Wang

NIGHT

Night slips into the empty sky,
    and
      Death, in black suit and overcoat,
    caresses my father's brow.
The park
    where the children play,
      by the cemetery,
      grows restless . . .
Swings shiver and sway,
    taking the moon for a ride.
Sleep's on my mind.
I close my eyes to night . . .
    to
    night.

Jon Saldivar

AT THE FOGG

As I was saying.
At the paintings
  Gaze and blend
  People in the afternoon.
A collection at that
Time, that particular time.
  It can be framed.
  It can be collected
    For an instant!
  A large enough collection.
    A life.

A. Runch

MY HANDICAP

Out of the corner of my eye
I watched them
yelling for one another
holding hands.
They shuffled away
as if a group of small children
smiles on their faces
hearts on their sleeves
my soul weighed down with guilt
one of them acknowledged my stare
with a smile.
Boarding the bus, they waved
at the movies, the crowd & me
my guilt disappeared
and at that moment . . .

    I loved them.

Linda Montgomery

THE WRITER

I thunk and thunk with all my might
About the novel I wud wright.
I typed throo bone and fingernale
And got my story in the mail.
Instead of saying, "It's a pip!"
They sent a darned rejechun slip.
My words look pritty when I make'em;
How come the Editors won't take'em?

Joy Caputo

SORRY

We collect grievances
Like seashells on a beach.
Innuendos of guilt self-imposed.
A cheating heart
With a mind
Hazy with regret
For things said and done.
Sorry I said that
Sorry you said that.
How many sorries
Make an island?
I am shipwrecked
As my soul
Reaches for its last breath.
One more time
To consider
Our paths in life.
One more sorry
To end the strife
Of hurting then forgiving.

Angela Galipeau

DANCERS OF LOVE

And the sun goes down
As the night begins to set in.
The gypsies within us start to dance.
Dance to the song of love,
That the moon and night air play for us.

Together we will wrap our arms
Around each other and sway to the melody.
While the trees prepare a cove,
Where we can lie when we become anxious.

Lorella Carbone

TO OUR CALIFORNIA

We greet you with a gay hurrah,
Our State of California!
Accept the lays we come to render
To landscapes of your regal splendor.
You are the state of many charms,
of modern cities, towns, and farms.
We hail the peace across your plains,
Your valleys, flanked by mountain chains,
The grandeur of your ocean, streams,
Our pioneers had seen in dreams.

We love you, California,
Our vision of Utopia!
You wore the halo of your glory
When you were still a territory.
Your sentinels of redwood trees
Date back to bygone centuries.
Our sunny state, our golden ore,
You have become an open door,
The emblem for our future years
That link our own with past frontiers.

Lydia Regehr

SANTA REMEMBERS

Santa is a whiz.
Nice man that he is,
He comes once a year
Amid shouts of cheer.

Santa knows the date.
He won't make us wait,
Nor will he forget,
He has never yet.

Busy, in demand,
We think he is grand,
Grandest ever was.
Thank you, Santa Claus.

Lydia Regehr

SIREN SONG

The water calls
    To my unquenched thirst,

It is a siren's song.

Lapping ever
    At the pebbled shores,

Pulling and pulling.

My longings deep
    Will dwell calm,

At the water's edge.

Sweet moisture of life
    Both giver and taker,

Ever in balance.

I feel its presence
    It is my need,

My reason to be.

To seek the water
    Where'er it lies.

Calling, calling.

S. Glen Hayward

ABOUT A FRIEND

Again a friend reminded me,
How abundant days are scarce,
For her who abruptly becomes
A unique friend to you.

Rhonda Michelle Rudrow

AGE

Age is the top of a mountain high;
Exceptional air and view.
A long hard climb, a bit of fatigue;
But oh! What a wonderful view.

Rhonda Michelle Rudrow

MERIMBULA, NEW SOUTH WALES

I am in awe at what I see.
A half-moon bay on each side of me
Painted with white combers
Rushing to the shore.
I sip my coffee in warm comfort
And watch the black swans above.
Lightning cuts the clouds far at sea
And reflects in the azure Tasman.
The wallaby freezes in the garden
Like a statue, uneasy, it might be seen.
The small birds prepare to rush
The feeder at their appointed time.
What other sights can bring such peace?
Is this a glimpse of heaven?
It is to me,
There is none other.

Lois Whittaker

BIG MEADOWS
SHENANDOAH NATIONAL PARK, LURAY, VIRGINIA

I remember June's delight —
A warm sun glowing
Wild strawberry picking
Blueberries budding.
Now, in September, thistles are bobbing
Yellow daisies scattered
Say, ''Farewell, lovers.''
The lark's not singing now;
The crows are calling — away
How summer's fled;
Gray clouds are hanging;
The winds are chilling.
Soon nature's growth
Will be put to bed.

Martha Mae Martinson

LIFE

Life is a beautiful thing to behold
    But all that glitters isn't gold.
Disappointments and failures dig deep in our souls,
    We're always striving for unreachable goals.
Wandering through life's winding halls,
    Not knowing where they'll lead.
Endless obstacles, such high walls,
    Overcoming them just to succeed.
When you've finally reached the end of those halls,
    And struggled over ten-thousand foot walls,
When dreams are realities, and goals seem worthwhile,
    Just say; ''*Hey, I made it!*'' and sit back and smile.

Tamara L. Murray

TENANTS OF A TIME GONE BY

The whistle didn't blow today.
First time in nearly thirty years.
Silence cautions those who wonder,
and bids them not to question why.

The clock struck six, as always has,
yet its echoes danced from wall to wall down hollow corridors.
Darkness clutches tightly, through the blinds,
the cluttered desk, scattered books, and the pictures, on the wall.

the guys from   Johnston High
down 52nd St   reunion, '45
                camping
             with the kids
the wedding day   Mother and Dad
          the big bar-b-que
          last 4th of July

          Tenants of a time gone by.

The memories here cry out from the faces trapped within these frames,
but their beckon falls on empty chair.

For the whistle didn't blow today.
First time in nearly thirty years.

Ed Waldrop

NERVOUS REQUIEM

There seems a cautious juncture
rising up to meet my feet against the floor.
I have no sense about the night
just briefly passed and left me to wonder who I am
and where I'll be when this way passes
once again, beneath the fertile plains of anarchy.

Forlorn jurors, random to the exercise,
blindly swindle each emotion into realizing with majority.
Dispensing with formalities and reigning justice
proud and bent on sustenance of favor with the precious few.
Now ''*we shall overcome*'' has become the cry.

Ed Waldrop

Remembering Edwin and Kirby, our two little boys,
Their favorite pastime was the little mud toys.
The planes were carefully placed on the wood.
They tried and baked and they knew they could.
Soon our boys grew to be men
And the little clay planes remembered when,
They were tiny but solid as a rock.
It was just a matter of time, a tick of the clock,
Before they were scheduled to go to the moon.
They all declared they didn't know it would be so soon.
So the two little boys who molded planes of mud,
Today the thing for them is balsa wood.
But we still remember the planes of clay
And our boys who grew up in such an interesting way.

Louise Hinson

Patiently I wait for you
longing to hear your voice call out to me.
Quiet nights made for two in the city
while waking in the morning to a gentle kiss.
A spot of sunshine as we hold hands together
walking down streets you keep me on the way.
Always seeking love on the way.

Sherry Shea Jubelirer

I love you.
You have kept me dreaming,
helping me to believe I will see
the goodness of the Lord working
in our lives.
Your faith is strong,
an inspiration to me.
How I was blessed the day I met you.
Together we opened doors
that never would be possible alone.

Sherry Shea Jubelirer

The Lord Jesus reveals the Holy Truth
my soul has long thirsted for
I look to the heavens of blue light
to see the truth I must seek.
Holy Truth shall always be my goal
for this gift from God
enables me to revel in its reality
and for that alone I would wait for God.

Sherry Shea Jubelirer

WHALESONG

Little whale born in a tank with your mom.
Trying to nurse while she moves is no fun.
Learning to do tricks for people like me,
cute little upstart in penitentiary.

No other small whales around, ominous.
Where do they go, little baby Orcas?
Olympian someday if you can grow
locked in a dungeon and man is your foe.

Reformatory for whales roaming free,
detention for denizens of the deep.
"Jump for your supper if you want some squid,
through the hoop for the guard, as Mama did."

She may never be able to teach the hunt,
or to sing real songs to her little runt.
"Do tricks for treats," is a real humdrum song,
monotonous, wearisome, sad and too long.

But Mama is watching that gate to the sea,
pretending to do tricks for people like me,
measuring how high her baby can jump.
Go for it, Mama, and take little runt!

Gregory Neil Smith

TRUST IN GOD

Oh, my dying friend,
When the night is cold
And the stars are dim,
You may feel the need of a friend,
God will be there.
So reach out your hand,
And trust in him.

Sandra Lee Johnson

CHRISTMAS BELLS

We ring bells throughout the year,
Bells that all the world may hear,
Bells of sadness, bells of grief,
Bells to warn against a thief.
Bells for games, and bells for fun,
Bells that make all children run.
Bells in schools and other places,
Bells that mark the end of races.
But the happiest bells of all
Do not ring in spring or fall.
I mean the bells of Christmas Day,
Which bring joy here and far away.
These bells have a language all their own,
Ringing out cheer in every tone.
May the Christmas bells ring joy for you
And bring you cheer the whole year through.

Bernadine Bailey

MY RICHES

Oh, I have riches worth far more
  Than all of Midas' gold,
Not wealth that in the bank is kept,
  But what the heart doth hold.

The priceless gift of work is mine,
  A work I love to do.
And each day's task fills time so full
  I'm never sad nor blue.

The love of song, the love of books,
  These are a part of wealth,
But far above all these, I count
  The luxury of health.

The joys that beauty always brings,
  A sunset or a star,
These are beyond the power of wealth,
  As real joys always are.

The memories of happy things,
  Of days that now are past,
For only in the memory
  Can fleeting pleasures last.

But more than all the rest, I count
  A friendship tried and true,
For that is where all real wealth lies,
  In having friends like you.

Bernadine Bailey

THE GIFT

A rose of deepest crimson
Doused with a splash of gold
For spice, a dash of cinnamon
A breathtaking sight to behold
Brilliant rubies lie amongst
A handful of star sapphires
As God retires this day
With a fire to end all fires
A bit of orange covering
The sins of yesterday
Tomorrow a new beginning
Beautiful in every way
My eyes are filled with tears of joy
As I gaze upon the sky
This overwhelming feeling within my heart
Shall never, never die

T. Willits

GRANDMA IN THE REST HOME

Your wilting body,
such a sad sight,
the moaning and the groaning
is just a fight for life.
You want to cry,
but you fight.
Ying body,
such a sad sight,
the moaning and the groaning
is just a fight for life.
You want to cry,
but you fight.
You have forgotten why.

Michael Monteith

MY CHILD

A wee small face and tiny hands,
How dear you are to me!
Kissed with a helplessness so sweet,
Blessed with an inborn trust as deep,
How dear you are to me!
As I hold you now in my arms asleep
In memory we'll always remain complete,
A Mother's love; a child secure,
We brave the world together, dear.

And suddenly before me stands
A fine and tall and handsome young man,
When did the years go by?
All too swiftly and all too fast
Through a Mother's eyes the time did pass,
And now before me with pride I see
A son who's mine and a part of me.

And yet even now the clock stands still . . .
Almost as though by a Mother's will,
As invariably so, time can't erase
The tiny hands and the wee small face.

Rene Denise Parker

EIGHTEEN MILES

Sweet eighteen, madly in love
Sadly to say, has fallen like a dove
Can one heal the pain of a scar?
A bicycle may be the best by far
From stretchway to hillway
The miles become a skyway
Seeking your love seen the first hour
Grows into months that are counted as years
A mighty oak so far in the distance
So slowly grows tall as miles diminish
A love so great, it defies imagination
It seems to be reserved for another generation
Hot air beats the face at ninety degrees
While lungs seek for shade's cool breeze
The heat of lost love makes one stand unsure
But the heart beats on desiring what is pure
While eighteen miles of sweat will be the only cure

Mark Styles

THE MAN SAID

And the man said
Give me a penny
Then i'll ask for nothing
   . . . Just many

Give me a nickel
Then i'll ask for nothing
   . . . Just more

Give me a dime
Then i'll ask for nothing
   . . . Just the world

Give me nothing
Then i'll ask you something
Will you love me
   . . . For caring
   . . . For loving
   . . . For my being

Lorrie Ackley

DIED THE FANTASY

She probed his body a unique summer love affair
But only in her mind
Lived the fantasy
He was the king she was the queen, mistress of desire
But only in her mind
Lived the fantasy
She drew his breath, he touched her breast
But only in her mind
Lived the fantasy
She committed suicide before her lover's arms
But only in her mind
Died the fantasy

Lorrie Ackley

When you were inside of me
I sang to you with secret joy.
I loved the being you would become, once born,
And I hugged you safe inside me.
I wanted to watch you become you.
To share the beauty of things
And see it all again, like the first time — with you.
To love away all the hurts.

I watched you endlessly — and worried.
I felt your hurts, your joys and so much pride.
I watched you strive, and frown and master!
And then you were gone.

I cried to reach you — felt so distant from you.
I felt the pain so great within you.
I watched you want to die,
Your light so dim and almost gone.
I could only helplessly stand by.

And you are lost — and I am lost.
And I only see the form that is you — not the light I knew.
The ghost of you and all the love I cannot touch.

Linda F. Buckner

IT ONLY TAKES ONE MAN

I looked through a clear hole
In a dusty window.
These were the white Southern years,
And this was the country of tears.

I met a girl outside:
She was softly brown-eyed.
Her tropical skin was such pleasure —
Like liquor to my touch.

But the hard men had come.
They put us to the run.
I dried the wet fear from her face.

Each step punched the heart from our lungs;
But of those hardest hearts, I had the hardest hand.
It only takes one man
To show you're better off blind.
It only takes one man
To let love be the guide.
It only takes one man:
There's as much strength here as hate on the other side.

They are the dark and we're alone,
With all the love of racism in the home.

Shep Clyman

OH! IF GRANDMA ONLY KNEW

Do you remember when, they weren't antiques then?
In the attic, things were erratic
Dusty memories, so valuable today
With pleasures, Grandma almost threw away

Old clothes and pots, toys for tots
A sewing machine, brass turned green
The phonograph — it was a laugh
With all these treasures, there's one tale
We're selling 'em all — in the next garage sale.

Max M. Wolfson

THE "CLIFF HOUSE."

JUST ILLUSION

There was a glimmer in his eye as he sped away.
Sparks were flying from a red night out.
In the bleeding street another twisted body lay.
We had a killer on our hands.

Did that really happen, or was it just illusion?

The call of Islam's empty down softly scheming halls.
The echoes bounce from blindfold silence.
This night people lean against posts near the palace walls.
Don't get too close to them.

Is that really happening, or is it just illusion?

Pretend they're tears of innocence that we wipe away.
It's dark enough if we close our eyes.
Crowds still gather like the birds on black cloud thunder days.
What is it dripping from our hands?

Frightened of some things that touch us,
Sweating hard from little heat;
Awaiting the sword of justice,
We're squirming in our seats.

What will really happen?
It won't be just illusion.

Shep Clyman

Come see the sun as it fades from the sky,
Slipping beyond the mountains.
Like a mischievous child playing hide and seek,
Slowly stealing from the sky its shades of blue.

Suddenly it remembers as it is stealing,
To tease us just a little while longer.
Not satisfied to adorn us with the beauty of the day,
But reaches to touch our souls one last time before its leaving.

Sweeping gently along the tips of the mountains,
It graces the sky with shades of pink
Not yet satisfied, boldly brushes in strokes of brilliant purples
A blending that sweeps the mountains with vibrant hues.

Stroking every shrub and tree, and then moves on
To glide along the rippling streams.
Leaving behind its ribbon-like reflections to be admired,
And stares intently upon its mirrored reflections on the lakes.

Lingering on with all its might, reaching out
To all that will welcome its last touch.
Sadly draws away the brilliance of the evening,
Whispers softly of its leaving and gently kisses all goodnight.

Shari Eccleston

THE SMUDGE POTS

Sudden night-frost in early spring
Sounds of rush, rush, hurry, hurry.
The sleeping orchards stirring,
Awake reluctantly, shivering in the near dawn.
Smudge pots quickly burning in a ring, like cheerful fireflies;
The life-warming smoke spreads its protective blanket
Over flowering branch-arms lifted heavenward,
Delicately moving in thankful supplication,
As they waft paeans of perfumed praise,
In gratitude for the warmth.

Rachel Ellis

A look, a smile, a laugh, a touch, once real but now forever lost.
I know not the reason why we met, when losing you would be the cost.
A whispering came within me real but now forever lost.
I know not the reason why we met, when losing you would be the cost.
A whispering came within my heart
And I listened not for love of you
Yet I could not keep from knowing, as your silence grew.

I noticed more and more with time, the far-off look within your eyes.
A restlessness within you grew, and soon I knew you'd bid good-bye.
No warning did you give to me
Why could you not have told me so?
Of your ever-wandering heart and your restless drifter's soul.

How is it that you haunt my heart and mind the whole day through?
Always you are with me, no matter where I go or what I do.
Leaving always a lingering void
For all I imagine of what I've known
Once somewhere in time was ours, so short and swiftly flown.

Shari Eccleston

AS THE WISE MEN SAY

When does the hurt of losing a
part of you go away?
    When can I start remembering the
pleasant times without pain?
        As the wise men say, in time.
    How can I stop loving a man
who's been my best friend?
    How does one continue on
as though he were never there?
        As the wise men say, give it time.
    Why did destiny bring us together
only to tear us apart later?
    Why did I have to fall in
love again?
        As the wise men say, you will know in time.

Darlene Elwartowski

HE WIPED AWAY EACH TEAR

    When I was a child, and weak with pain,
(Jesus gave me the strength to walk again).

    He felt my pain, and heard my every cry,
(He wiped away each tear, as He passed by).

    Jesus, (now as I grow old, and weak, with pain,
please help me to be strong again).

    Please — stay by my side, (let Your
love and wisdom be my guide).

Norma Dean Jones

MY LOVE

The gentle wonder of your touch
Arouses in me . . .
Memories
Of soft light dancing from the flickering flame
In an open fireplace,
The fresh greenness of the landscape
After an early morning rain,
The warmth of the sand and sounds of the sea
Encircled by a vast blue sky
On a clear summer day,
The cool crispness in the autumn winds
Carrying leaves of red and gold
Softly to earth.
Your special caring and love
Has awakened in me . . .
Light and laughter,
Comfort and joy,
And loving completeness
In the ever turning and flowing stream of life.

Rene Denise Parker

ROPE OF LOVE

Many men will see,
The greatness in me.
Hold on tight
To the rope of love,
And I'll not drop you.
Says God above,
You'll not tangle
In my rope or dangle,
But the cords are strong —
Because my love
Will hold you
In my arms
Where you belong.

Bonnie S. Peter

RESTRAINT

To see it so often
And want it so much
Makes hiding true feelings difficult.

The mind may stray,
Eyes even go along,
But the body will never follow.

Jeff Smith

SEXUALITY

Soft touches and hard desires
Entwined together as one,
Xenophobic or adventurous,
Unleashing needs as it is done,
Admitting universally in its embrace
Lovers with the heart who want to come
In joy, with the pleasure,
To touch, the battle, the might, the
Yearning for love every day, every night.

Annie M. Benson

THE SUNRISE OF LOVE

When the sun sets on romance
When infatuation fades
And the reality of life
With the person you've married dawns,
Hang in through the night,

The night of adjusting
To who it really is you chose.
Don't try to change them;
Don't make them into
Your needs answered.

Accept and appreciate who they are.
Look for their good qualities
And ask them to do the same for you.
You don't have to agree on much
Just be there for each other.

Stay steady in your loyalty
And you will finally experience
The sunrise of true love,
The love that knows, accepts, forgives,
The love that lasts eternally.

Frances G. Callahan

BOTTOM OF MY PURSE

At the bottom of my purse,
There lives a leather demon,
There lives a leather god.

I can't find things he's hid,
(He claims he didn't),
I know he did.

It does no good to plead,
To tell him it's time to leave,
He's deaf to me, you see.

So I'm resigned to live with him,
To suffer through his hiding whim,
'Til I get a new purse.

Annie M. Benson

LOST

An empty sky
An empty sea
A leafless palm
Despair
What to do
Know not I
No horizon
Neither day nor night
Yet a soft twilight surrounds me
Time is as a stillframe waiting
Waiting for what
I know not
The emotionless world about me
Seems aware of no consciousness
Oh despair
Can any other comprehend
Is there any other to comprehend

David J. Hale

CADENCES

A sea of clouds
Is where the moon's glow
Reflects shadows
Down upon the earth
The timeless mountain
Sends tremblings of unknown rumors
Down through the valley of rhythms
That carries on
To a threshold of tomorrow
The tide of the endless ocean
Rides on
In search of a shore
To rest upon
And the seven winds of old
Fly forever on
With *All Knowing* in their grasp
Yet to none
Will it be known
Till the seven winds
Have sight upon them

David J. Hale

ETERNAL LOVE

Shadows cast upon unseeing eyes.
Darkness descends where darkness lies.
Light into unprevailing gloom.
A rose unto the blind does bloom.
The maidens blush, a man's desire.
Around the heart, a wreath of fire.

Into the days, time does roam,
to find in darkness an ageless home.
With elegant measure the bells do chime,
to mark the passing of a sleeping mind.
At night our fears arise and crest.
Perhaps in day we find our rest.

When day and night and time collide,
I pray with you knelt by my side,
for ours to be an endless love,
as delicate as a gray-white dove.
Through our love a bud will flower,
and through eternity, our child will tower.

Mary Sue Hall

I say, I do not believe in love
Yet, let me tell you true
Your eyes have captured my heart
I do not wish to be let go
This may not be love
But, it is certainly more than desire
Be mine, till the fire in my heart
Burns to cold ash and embers
Or until tomorrows cease to come

And I will promise you a dream time
Of loving, living, laughter and song
Growing, sharing, entwining as one

Carroll R. Bethea

WE SHOULD SLOW DOWN AND
TAKE THE TIME TO LOOK AROUND

In today's (rush-rush world) often we forget
to stop and look at what life is all about,
we should slow down, and take the time to look around.

We should stop, & look at the mighty oak trees
blowing in the wind, they will be here long after our end.

The mighty oak will outlast us, because they live
without a big fuss, they stand so tall, and strong,
taking life with ease, just swaying in the breeze.

We should stop and look, at the pretty sunrise,
as it drifts lazily across the sky, leaving behind
a rushed, and troubled world, as it passes by.

Norma Dean Jones

SUCCESS

Long, long ago we said:
"Dream no small dreams, make no little plans,"
And forged ahead creating and attaining
Day by day, our world to suit ourselves —

Only to find we do have feet of clay,
That anchor us at times in foolish,
Human gloom, when only love and peace and joy
Should be the lights that point the way.

Now, close to the mountain peak of life,
A rock wall looms, an obstacle in time,
Which bewilders and defeats the final
Trusting, energetic step to claim

The vista we would view,
Hear the music of what will be,
And know the gift evolves — while
You are you, and I am simply me.

Then — let us pause, renew our strength,
And continue on the course we set.
Posterity will record —
Our success as human beings.

M. Ringereide

TO THE MEN WHO DIED AT PEARL HARBOR

The bombs and shells are silent now
Lest those who sleep awake again.
Tread softly here and breathe a prayer
That these brave men died not in vain.

Their bodies lie in honor here
While we who tread the decks above
Can only offer them our tears
And to our land undying love.

Pray they rest in confidence,
That we who live will ne'er forget;
Pray the spirit of these men,
Deep in our hearts, lingers yet.

Edgar H. Stevens

YOU DID IT UNTO ME

*In memory of a certain cold day just before
Christmas 1944, in northern France.*

The cold wind of December cut to the bone
As he thought of his lost buddies, Christmas and home,
But the coffee and rations from the kitchen smelled good,
As he buried his cold feet in the straw where he stood,
When a child slipped up shyly to filch a piece of bread
From the straw on the floor of the old cow shed.
Then, turning around, his voice a little gruff,
He said, "Here take mine. I've had enough."

As back to his fox-hole the soldier made his way,
His belly was empty, but he heard his master say,
"I was a-hungered and you gave me meat;
I was thirsty and you gave me drink;
I was a stranger and you took me in;
Naked and you clothed me."

"For in as much as you have done it unto one
Of the least of these my brethren,
You have done it unto me."

Edgar H. Stevens

THE MOMENT I REALIZED THAT I'D
FALLEN IN LOVE

A brisk breeze blew through our light summer clothes.
The feel of toasty sand on our unshod feet,
The rhythmic pounding of the surf,
Combined with the excited screaming of the gulls.
We lay, baking ourselves in the rays
Thrown to us by the fiery sun.
Side-by-side we lay down at the foot of a weeded dune.
Heat emanated from all around us.
I focused my eyes lazily on Barry.
His soft brown hair fluttered in the wind.
The muscles of his back rippled as he turned toward me.
He playfully rubbed his stubble-strewn cheek against mine,
Making his cornflower-blue eyes dance with amusement.
My heart fluttered rapidly and I felt as light as the air
That cooled our bodies.
I smiled, then knowingly closed my eyes
And basked.

Michelle L. Smith

MIDNIGHT MOVIE

Midnight movie on T.V. was shown
An old gruesome tale, a moan, and a groan
It thrilled and chilled me quite a bit
A castle went blazing, a mysterious — who-dun-it

The gardener was pardoned, the cook wouldn't say
Don't suspect the chauffeur, he was away
They grilled and concluded, then right on time
The villain was caught, he paid for his crime
The butler confessed — you all should know
A suspect was nabbed, 'cause it was a one hour show.

Max M. Wolfson

IMAGE, EARTH

Quasar,
billions of miles
away
reflects earth

A quartile
of heavenly bodies
quaquaversal

Headwinds
of firmament
strangely harmonious
consonant

Great-hearted earth
blundering
wondering earth
revolves
around its sun
nourished
and perplexed.

Margaret Rosenborg

FAREWELL

A soft rumble going through my mind
my eyes swell with every tear
the last memory of you
is so final
the hurt will never end
someday maybe once again we will meet
but as for now
we are doomed to walk in ever silence
crying to ourselves
tearfully in our hearts.

Amy Kathleen Westerhoff

MENTAL PLAY

I'm lost in my illusion, a fantasy drive
And when I'm there all emotions come alive.
I feel the satisfaction of physical power
Emerging from me in my private hour.
It's lovely, delicious, a secret all mine
I can tell no one so precious this time.
We're worlds apart in reality
But alone I make you come to me.
I wish you knew the things we've done
The pleasures we've shared in my mind as one.
Already I know you, your taste, your smell
And I want you to see me in this way as well.
It's awfully bad to desire all this
To play with fate, that tempting Miss.
But I want you just bad enough
To make it known and call her bluff.
I know it will be worth my time
No one shall have me till you're mine.
I'm lost in my illusion, a fantasy drive
The one part of me that's fully alive.

Shelly Renee Wheaton

IN GOING TO THE BEACH . . .

In going to the beach . . .
When I was young
Half the joy and half the fun
Was collecting shells for everyone

Shells unbroken, whole unscathed
Having known no wrath of ocean
No battle of wind, sea and wave
Pure white gloss, or bone beige
Indigo purple and mussel shell black
I'd run to the shore and then run back

Though in later years . . .
I have found
Sand polished shells
Littering shores abound

It is those worn rainbow hues
Whose ocean journeying
Has been no easy cruise
Missing middles and ridges made smooth
These shells have lived a battle of truth
I admire them now as I could not in my youth

Carroll R. Bethea

A CHANGE

Here I sit watching you
Though you never look back,
I dream of you every night
But you never dream of me.

Now you sit watching me
Though I never look back,
You dream of me every night
But I never dream of you.

Amy Kathleen Westerhoff

IMAGE, THE SAME

Light and lightness
of our life
Glowing gladness
without strife
surrounded by
methodical madness
of this world

We ride
the same
gentle horse
float in
the same
cloud
paint
the same landscape.

Margaret Rosenborg

YOUR EYES

Your eyes so deep and sound
look after me
they follow me everywhere I go
I feel safe under your caring stare
the love of your heart is seen
through the careful look you give
I know that if I fail you will not look away
but help me to move on
and you will always be with me
to the end

Amy Kathleen Westerhoff

AMY KATHLEEN WESTERHOFF. Born: Cedar Lake, Indiana, 2-25-73; Education: Freshman at Tolleson High School, Tolleson, Arizona; Occupation: Student; Themes: *My thoughts at the time of writing, my life while growing up.*

LOVE

I felt like a long cold winter
with life stored, dormant.
    As the spring, he came
to me bringing life.
    All blossomed with radiance
releasing the most delightful fragrance.
    His kisses were sweet.
They brought to me the drops of a gentle
rain on a hot summer day.
    The passions thundered through
my flowing veins.
    In his arms I found calm
for my restless soul.
    Old wounds were healed
and tears subsided.
    Many sunsets I have seen
and each dawn I can still enjoy
the sweet aroma of love.

Feliz Mosch

BUT FOR NOW

I did sojourn past the rains of the moon
And the cries of children
I sung the "Song of Apollo" aloud
To the animals around me
In harmonious madness
I found treasure in the sincerest laughter
Never before had I felt
The sweet rapture of cider in spring

Christopher Alan Mansel

THE LAST CAR RIDE TO THE STORE

On car rides to the store, Mommy always lets me stand
On the blue leather seat of our old Chevy.
I breathe deeply the smell of her strong perfume
Mixing with the aroma of her Wrigley's juicy fruit,
As I jump gleefully on the old springs that creak in protest.
My hair feels independent from my head as it flops up and down,
Staticky from brushing against the ceiling.
I briefly stop and raise my hand to wave at a sheepdog puppy
Who had lifted his shaggy leg toward a birch sapling alongside the road.
The sudden scream of brakes and a lurch of our car,
Wipes the smile from my lips, and the color from my face.
I hear the yelp of the puppy who has run out into the road before us.
Thrown forward, I put my hands out to try to catch myself.
My hands are pushing, pushing through the glass.
My small body follows.
As I slide across the hood and onto the pavement
I see the puppy's ruffled fur become blood-soaked, his back oddly angled.
I close my eyes tightly and cry out in pain, and fear,
"I want my . . .!"

Michelle L. Smith

A GOOD DAY

This was a good day.
Not spectacular. Just a good day.

His laugh across the breakfast table
Was what started the day rolling along
To such a satisfactory conclusion.

There seemed to be lots of things
To laugh about today.

I found the tickets and the key that were lost.
The washer did its job to perfection.
My neighbor came to chat a bit.
Even the crotchety mail carrier waved.

About evening
There was a happy little bird
Underlining my joy with his song.

And at dusk when I watched the lights
Of the city below bloom and spread
Their glory along the black velvet of night,

All I could say,
Would never be enough.

Marjory Lee Thompson

THE TINIEST OF TEARS

No better friend have I now, nor even in the past.
Our friendship I can count on, until the very last.
We've shared our secrets in the dark, since I was very young.
Of no stronger hero, was a ballad ever sung.

But then I reached adulthood
And knew I could not stay.
My friend just stood there watching
As I packed to go away.

In all the time we shared, over all these many years,
I've never seen my friend's eyes shed the tiniest of tears.
But even as I finished, and knew the time was near.
Long before I raised my head to say our last good-bye,
I knew with every certainty
I'd see my mother cry.

Ann Zandie

THE GAME

Running for office open in the fall
Working in the "Rat-House," justice one and all,
Shuffling the cards, campaigning through the day,
Kissing little babies, pulling ace to play.

International meetings in the dead of night,
Gather at the Summit, reducing pre-game fright,
Raking in the winnings, counting up the deadly toll,
Presenting ultimatums, riding on a roll.

Winning and losing mean something
In a black and white world,
But in grey mean nothing —
A game only for high rollers.

Intimating contact, what stands to be lost,
Captivate emotion, toying at all cost,
Sneaking subtle glances, conscious of the play,
Cautiously romancing, no one wants to pay.

Playing silent movie, newcomer to the screen,
Gesturing as to script, staging final scene,
Snake eyes on dice roll, big tears hinting the end,
Scoring on rebound, the game is on again.

Warren H. Wojnowski

MY LAST DAY

Yesterday is my last day
When the sun shines bright and true
For soon it rains in Nature's dismay
And mankind will lose His brilliant hue

Birds fly south never to return
To the land from which they hatched
While those of the wasteland fail to learn
The message the doves have dispatched

Salmon swim downstream towards the ocean
Leaving the waters from which they were spawned
As tragedy commences with one swift motion
And leaves a lingering stench which forever haunts

The brave wolf retreats in earnest
To the northmost sanctuary of his den
Turning away from a land where he once flourished
But where now the ox engineers his end

And, O, praise he, the stubborn ox
For he has crossed the forbidden boundaries with a devout flair
Those which even the most cunning fox
Would in his most brilliant moments have never dared

And yesterday was my last day
When the sun shined bright and true
But now it rains in Nature's dismay
And mankind has lost His brilliant hue

Warren H. Wojnowski

VACATION TIME

Parents send their children to
School to learn and get an education,
When school is finished they
Will have a summer vacation.

Children can stay home or go on a trip,
They just go to a park to lay on the grass;
Their happiness for sure
All day will last.

Vacation time is a happy time,
Children will do as they wish —
Even go to some bayou
To catch some crabs or fish.

Parents love to have them home
And have some good rest,
When their children go to Sunday mass
They like that best.

Having a good life they
Will need God and to Him pray,
Without His help they
Wouldn't know what to say.

Violet Ficovich Morovich

VIOLET FICOVICH MOROVICH.

A PROXY MATE

It's worth the wait, my time of arrival
I hope's not too late to aid your survival.
It's hard, I know, to want and wonder
A Proxy Mate will do while we're asunder.
There's no life in half a pair
Close your eyes and wish, I'll soon be there.
Amuse yourself in temporary delight
Then surrender to me and make it right.
My leisure play's a spicy game
But with one face, only one name.
The desire is real, sensations pure
A Proxy Mate, my viceful cure.
Soon, I pray, our souls will bind
Into one body and mind.
To be forever a love completed
No more *A Proxy Mate* is needed.
Until that day your own I see
I too wait on, endlessly.
But worth the time to savour true
Once united eternally, me and you.

Shelly Renee Wheaton

TO MY SON

Today, time is a chamber within reach
taming my repose.
And beyond the fluttering linen drapes
a lean vessel gently glides.
My heart, my eyes, held by a child,
my arms a still repository
a vertebral embrace.
Time sits in its idyllic diving-bubble
like a white clapper, as a prelude
to this dolphin, this amber jasmine,
this sprite of venerable ancestry.
The minutes are buried, flake by flake,
the ever-wistful hours soaked in lichen,
imbued in alchemy.
A breathing — not my own, and yet
still mine,
now drifting in the arrival of your halo.

Lourdes Gil

SOMETIMES

Who am I and what can I do
except enter into the movement
of branches and light,
be this ray of sunlight in which
my cigarette smolders away, this soft
and gentle passion in the air?
A cloud passes, a moment grows pale. I
die to myself.
There is everywhere a thin veil of sunlight
that could be split with the touch
of a fingernail, but clothes everything
in an eternal smile.

Eric Eckerberg

TRANSFERS

When I am on an Upper
How I lose the feeling
There will ever be a Downer.
As my heart expands in joyousness
There is nothing in my thoughts
That can transfer my attention
To the possibility I am
Headed for a Downer . . .
On this seesaw in my mind
I go from being in control
To the transfer of being
Overpowered by your need.
As your fragile arms enclose me
And produce a hopeless Downer
I know with time it will transfer
Into an Upper as I remember
Our greatest joys of yesterday!

Jerri Brillhart

A BREAK FOR BEER AND ONIONS

This is
like typing on one butterfly wing
the air yellow
like light through a white beer bottle
the space inside and the bubbles
poured across the fragile wings it flies —
Then soars higher and dries until it
smells like the inside green
of a beer bottle again.

This paper is thin
dangerously thin like a crystal piece
in the shape of an onion
the skin penetrated by the same
horrible yellow air until
the glass peels instantly and with
infinite grace into shapes
that take flight every day and
never give anything gentle in return.

Eric Eckerberg

ENDURING LOVE

Holding you, saying ''I love you,''
Is a total acceptance of all you are and
A realization of all your endearing frailties.
Knowing how wondrous you really are
Even when you forget and your voice
Sounds angry and impetuous
Or your eyes glisten with criticism,
Those are the moments I must remember
That underneath you are so magnificent.
Recognizing all your values are honest and
Sincere, even when you can't remember
What I asked you to do on Monday.
Recalling all the years of gentle ways
You were when abandoned to your amorous
Antics that now lie dormant on a secret shelf.
While love has mellowed and been tamed to
A tiny flicker, I sit in reverie still loving you.

Jerri Brillhart

WORDS

Perhaps words while being our mental tools
Can sometimes be used for destruction
Without thought and without care.
Words can be lethal weapons that escape
Our lips before we can retrieve them . . .
Such words burn in their power to
Sear our memories for a lifetime.
They can be so potent that their
Vicious effect can be seen in
Distorted lives that are filled
With discord, pain and misery.
Words that carry the power of love
Into manifestation for all to view
Are the precious tools we all can use
To bring beauty, joy and happiness
To everyone we shower them upon.

Jerri Brillhart

REFLECTIONS OF A WOMAN'S GRIEF

A woman's grief is as the sea in all its many moods.
Her deepest thoughts, most intimate feelings portrayed upon her face,
As changing moods of sea-green depths are seen upon the waves.

She thinks of one both loved then lost and melancholy sweeps o'er her.
Within her quiet eyes a mist of tears soon gathers,
As might the mists above the depths before the ocean storm.
In reverie, feelings of deep turbulence grow.
Tears spill down, pain and sorrow release in a torrent of emotion,
So too the heavens must release their burden upon the ocean,
Churning waves to towering heights,
    as feelings crash down upon memory's shore.

Storm spent, heart's pain and sorrow fade and are set aside,
Like parting clouds above the calming sea.
Light, like reflections of a new dawn upon the waters,
    dances within her eyes.
Her storm has cleansed her soul of grief,
    the void of loss is filled with love,
Even as now peaceful waves fill with life once more.

She feels each life touching hers and with each drop
    added to the sea of love within,
Ripples form to touch the hearts of others,
As waves must reach to touch the farthest shores.
With the gift of love she is bound to all and all to her.
Her love, her special spark will continue, as does the sea — forever.

Ann Zandie

THE PLAYER

Throw back the curtain, the stage is set
    for yet another masquerade.
The true self hides in backstage shadows
    content to play this quiet charade.
The critic's slur, the bright light's glare
    do naught to harm the bright façade.
The leers, the taunts, the audience stare
    can't bend nor pierce the true self's shade.
Alas, as cosmic rays pierce all, some
    arrows seem to tunnel through.
Discovered, naked to their sting, the
    true self writhes in pain anew.
It vows to build a stronger wall twixt it
    and pain and all the world.
Build and paint and cover again, thicker becomes
    the set and scene.
The play goes on and on again, an encore of
    what went before.
The wall's increased, the paint's renewed,
    until there's naught but scenery left.

Jean K. Norris

IN THE MOONLIGHT

The World was standing still;
The sky was filled with the glitter from millions of stars,
The moon was illuminated with light,
As if it were a candle burning with desire,
The ocean was calm and shimmering.

The only sound was the ocean caressing the shore,
The mist from the ocean spray sent chills throughout my soul,
And yet the ocean breeze was warm and soothing against the bare flesh,
The sand was as soft as a cloud, as my body nestled into place.

The World existed with only two spirits about to embody as one,
At last you can express your affection flesh to flesh,
Take hold, and never let go of this precious moment,
For as the dawn arises, you will see the light,
And know it was all only a dream.

No chance of ever returning; to this moment, this sensation,
    this pleasure or Lost Love.
Your Life will slip away slowly . . .
    With no ray of hope,
        of fulfilling,
            your Fantasy . . .

R. Kim Ingold

IF YOU WERE HERE, MY LOVE

For love of your country, you it did cost,
You went overseas, but now, you are lost.
My red eyes in tears, my sides are sore
If you were here, My Love, I'd love you more.

When I heard you were missing, at first
I knew my whole heart would really burst.
It hurts so, deep down to the inner core
If you were here, My Love, I'd love you more.

No matter what, I'll never forget you,
Each day I pray you're still alive too.
Love is for always. Loved you before
If you were here, My Love, I'd love you more.

People liked you because you did care,
Being without you it's hard to bear.
You wanted to help, it's you I adore
If you were here, My Love, I'd love you more.

Sometimes thoughts are going 'round and 'round;
Maybe you're in prison, or, in the ground.
Love for you, dear, comes from every pore
If you were here, My Love, I'd love you more.

Alice Charpentier

SONATA SEVEN

Sonorous notes
drip god-like through the air
    and hover
like wingless chariots above the ear.

Melodies
pour like honey from a pot
    and cling
to the brain and mind and thought.

Chords and discords
crash like storms without rain
    amid crescendo
decrescendo, clamor, clangor, strain.

A fugue
throbs in heartbeat time
    overlying
underlying, out of rhyme —
       out of rhythm.

Gail V. Baker

TWENTY-EIGHT DAYS

February's edge swallows everything.
The earth grows cold,
Clumps up against
A red and tinseled heart.
Even the flowers are fools,
Blooming in a lying sunshine,
Believing in the warmth they feel.
Soon the snows will come,
The blossom's tender hold
Upon this life, this thin green shoot
Of softly pulsing mystery,
Will snap and fall away,
To never understand
Why joy and sweetness,
Warmth and heart,
Must always end
With petalled faces
Crushed against the ice
In silent, shocked betrayal.

C. S. Parks

A NEW — A — KNOTT

First a man hurts his son.
The son hurts his sister;
He is given freedom to be
emotional.

The son becomes a man.
The man hurts himself.
And if hurt by a woman
hope is fleeting.

Eric D. Zuniga

DROPPED MY HEART

Dropped my heart
    on a string
      in the closet.
Locked it up tight
    so that nobody'd
      toss it.

Dangled the hanger,
    suspended
      in space,
just prayed that in darkness
    it'd germinate
      grace.

Laura L. Larkins

TONIGHT ALONE

Tonight I'm alone,
But you're here in my mind
And you're spending my time . . .
I'm with you.
I can touch you.

And to touch you again . . .
It's a test to my friends.
It unleashes the winds.
It's a thing to behold.
Awe . . . a thing to be told . . .
To Mariah, my love.
We're alone in my mind.

And we'll rush to the sea . . .
Where we'll laugh and we'll run,
We'll hold hands in the sun.
Yeah, we'll laugh then we'll cry
'Cause we'll wish we could fly,
But we'll fall in the sand.
We're alone yes, Suzanne.

Douglas S. Russell

SON

Your firstborn son for which you'd give
The very soul you need to live,
To share his joys, his health, his best,
To guide him through the bitter tests.

The sleepless nights, the dimpled knee,
The knots and falls he'll have by three,
The tree he'll climb, the race he'll run,
The many times you'll share his fun.

With body straight and shoulders wide,
You'll look at him and feel such pride,
You'll know he's yours, come good or bad,
To think that God gave you this lad.

Bonnie J. Scoble

SPELUNKING CROSSTOWN

Dutch-oven brick-city walls, trap
The heated summer's day,
Sirens and hydrants sizzling
A merry tune;
The clinging bustle and the sweat
The din's grinding gallows
The danger in the air
Brings to mind the shaping
Of urban predators and prey
Of children old before their time
But just a common city's summer's day.

Roy D. Benson

ROY DOUGLAS BENSON. Born: Bronx, New York, 5-27-49; Education: Rochester Institute of Technology, A.A.S., 6-69; Rensselaer Polytechnic Institute, B.S., 6-71; Cornell University, M. Engineering (Engineering-Physics), 1-73; Occupations: Chef, Locksmith, Factory laborer, Skydiver, Scientist, Engineer, Writer, Administrator, Artist; Memberships: Locksmithing Institute of America, U.S. Parachute Association, American Consultants League, Planetary Society, Cousteau Society, Wilderness Society, Police Athletic League, The Smithsonian Associates, The Nature Conservancy, National Arbor Day Foundation; Other Writing: "Neglected Factors," "The Macadamia-Nut Rhapsody," "Experimental Social Physics," "Abstraction As Facts," short stories, 11-25-86; "Is God Logical?" short story, 11-7-86; Comments: *I have been known to write on just about any subject you can think of: fact, fantasy, science, religion, law, art, philosophy, ESP, music, zoology, etc.*

WOODLAND

Darkness wears a silver cloak
A breeze for company
Nature breathes her gentle essence
The babbling brook a melody

Some secluded space, a forest fair
Where seasons cast the spell
Time weaves it magic here
Mysterious and everlasting . . .

Janine Lieber

WE ORIGINALLY SAID WE'D BE FRIENDS

We originally said we'd be friends
a friend for whom there's love
and a will to share what comes from above
nothing to win, nothing to lose
no need to improve, impress or prove
appreciating each other in a bond of trust
dearly affectionate and forsaking lust.

Complications arising all around
our agreements falling to the ground
and blaming the inability to refrain
then hitting the end just when we begin
thus taking heavenly mysteries all away
and leaving no innocent way to stay.

Yes, we originally said we'd be friends
and I don't see why we can't try again
no fault should be so fatal
as to make an end come consequential.
An affinity has grown in length and strength
the true offense to succumb to circumstance.

Cris Hernandez

THE ICE CREAM MAN

The   Bell ringing
Ice Cream Man
                    Rings
His
        Clang-clang-clang
Bell.
All the children
                Scamper
And
            Scramble
Across the close-cropped lawns.
            Raggedlyraging
They push and
        Shove,   cram,
And   squash
To get to that
Cold Slush,
            Ice Mush.

Linda Seiter McKay

STORM CLOUDS AND RAINBOWS

When storm clouds of sorrow sweep over your soul,
When teardrops, like raindrops, take over control,
When sadness invades you and fills you with woe,
Look up! for God paints your cloud with a rainbow!

When cyclones of sickness cross over your way,
When pain and discomfort take over your day,
When winds of impairment demolish your glow,
Be calm! for God paints your cloud with a rainbow!

When dark clouds of trouble blot light from your sky,
When tragedy threatens, and tears dim your eye,
When disappointments come and deal you a blow,
Be still! for God paints your cloud with a rainbow!

A lovely rainbow comes right after the rain,
A lovely rainbow soothes away all the pain,
The shining rainbow will banish all your woe,
After the dark clouds will come the bright rainbow!

Gladys Brewer

LITTLE TRAILING CLOUDS OF GLORY

Paula and Amy, two beautiful little girls,
You slid down a sunbeam from celestial domain.
Each earthly banner to you forever unfurls,
For you inhabited the heavenly terrain.
Truly you lighted the path with every step you trod.
For you are little trailing clouds of glory sent from God!

Little trailing clouds of glory, that's what you are.
Surely you have beheld the very throne of grace.
Without a doubt, you know each little star,
Perhaps, you have even seen the Master face to face.
At day's end when your little heads begin to nod,
Recall that you are little trailing clouds of glory sent from God.

Lay hold on life, dear diamonds rare,
Seize each opportunity to live it to the brim,
For out there in the future is reward so fair,
Out there is chance to live for Christ and always honor Him.
The choices that you make will never be forced with an iron rod,
For always remember, little trailing clouds of glory,
        you were sent from God!

Gladys Brewer

GLADYS SELVIDGE BREWER. Born: 1-3-13; Married: C. E. Brewer, 1936; Education: Northwestern State University, B. A.; Occupations: Teacher, Homemaker; Memberships: Louisiana Retired Teachers' Association; Grant Parish Retired Teachers' Association; Delta Kappa Gamma, Alpha Tau Chapter; Other Writings: *Cant Hooks and Dogwood Blossoms,* 1987; Comments: *My book,* Cant Hooks and Dogwood Blossoms, *is a history of Pollock, Louisiana. My poetry draws on my family and my spirituality.*

MARCHING SOLDIERS

As the sun shines down on the fields below, the wind blows ever so lightly, the tall grass sways and marches in the fields like a sea of soldiers ready for combat. But soon the snow will come and all of the marching soldiers will be beaten down by it, and this will be their last stand and here they will die. In the spring new soldiers will take their place only to die as the former soldiers had died when the snow falls once again. Then the process repeats itself over and over again for eternity. If there is such a thing as eternity, when the soldiers are lost in endless void, forever. If there is such a thing as forever. But what happens after forever. If forever has an after. What happens to the soldiers when the storm approaches? When the light wind increases in speed and the thunder clouds roll across the sky to cover the sun from the earth's view. And all of the marching soldiers are blown over so that the field resembles a defeated battleground, with millions of dead soldiers lying all over, never to rise again on sunny days. Then the dark skies crack open and pour their rain onto the soldiers to drown them, just to make sure. While flashes of light illuminate the sky sending bolts of lightning down to earth to strike trees, houses and whatever else might be in their path. After the storm is over, the sunshine is far away but the storm clouds linger on, and all of the marching soldiers, now they are gone.

Gerald M. Carter II

ULCER IS

an unshed tear
    a stifled word
a muffled drum
    that goes unheard.
        fear,
author of each compromise,
        assumes
the ultimate disguise;
by offering something
    less than whole
finds favor in
    a lesser role.
from ancient tyranny's
    dictates
'til loathing's poison
    ulcerates.

Untended-garden
    turns to seed to die;
Unquestioned — fact
    content to buy the lie.

Mamie G. Gibson

How fragile is my hold on silence
when I stand alone on a hill
a Saturday morning just watching the sun
tint the swirl of fog on Las Trampas Ridge
far from the freeway's roar
and near enough to swaying
grass and purple lupine
a mourning dove coos
from blue-shadowed slope
I inch my way and lean
on gnarled oak
smell its age
watch bees surge
from a hollow limb
And know that I am real.

Esther Anderson

PADDY DEARY

Oh little wonder clothed in fur
Rust and white with pinkish nose.
Eyes so big and mouth that smiles
Soft meows and little purrs.

Oh, what wonder, such delight
To have a creature here in sight.
Your little head rubs my face
Then your nose pats my neck.
You rush off to play your games.

Oh little wonder, paddy dear
What contentment holding you near.
The days were lonely lingering long
But now have changed and are short.

Just a kitten with a smile
Just a kitten running wild
But what a little wonder in my life.

Mary A. Egan

SICK UNCLE:

Shrinking dollar, drinking rum,
Smoking cigar, cousins of Uncle Sam.
Drugs and crime escalation,
Free inflation, terror toleration.
Character dips, spending picks,
Unemployment bids, debt licks.
Nation down, voice sharp,
Importing dear and up.
Closing mills, spreading green bills.
Bankruptcy abound, health on ground.
Ditch on dock, no export a shock,
Stocks and speculation rock.
Uncle hard sick. How to treat.
Turned pages, churned mental cages.
Put under microscope
To find edge of rope.
Every pill turned Uncle red.
Our votes became fade.
Uncle Same on final bed.

Than Anchlia

THAN AHCHLIA. Born: Bikaner, India, 10-18-18; Married: Jethi Anchlia; Education: Bachelor of Commerce, Diploma in Cost Accounting; Occupation: Service.

SING IN THE WIND!

Patriotic Song for Children

Sing in the wind,
Red, White and Blue.
Sing in the wind
All the day through.
Sing over hill and vale;
Sing in the rain and hail.
We love you,
Red, White and Blue!

Sing in the wind
Under the sky;
Sing in the wind
Where'er you fly.
Sing as you are unfurled;
Sing all over the world.
We love you,
Red, White and Blue!

Sing in the wind . . .
Sing in the wind!

Antonio Iantosca

DEAR NEWLY WEDDED:

As you go through life together,
You won't mind the whims of the weather
If you keep romance in your lives.

There's no trouble you can't dismiss
With a loving hug and a kiss,
If you keep romance in your lives.

There's no hope that you can't trust.
No prayer, when pray it is you must.
No deal from life you'll find unjust,
If you keep romance in your lives!

Antonio Iantosca

GLORIFY GOD!

Open, O eyes, and behold
God's handiwork unfold!
Glorify God, O Heart, as I delight
Through the wonder of my sight!

Open, O hand, to a need.
Stir the soil over a seed.
Glorify God, O heart, as I plant
By the strength of my hand!

Open, O self, as a flower.
This is your glorious hour!
Glorify God, O heart, as I try
This bit of earth to beautify!

O eyes, O hands, O blood,
You are the handiwork of God!
Glorify God, O heart, in joy, in strife,
For sight, for strength, for Life!

Antonio Iantosca

THE HAPPINESS BUG!

The wonders of just one smile is great.
Whoever sees that one smile
will give another smile back.
This will carry on
to many others.
It is a friendly bug.
The name is the *Happiness Bug.*
Everyone who catches it
will spread it to whoever they meet.
This bug is quite contagious,
but it is nothing to fear.
Once someone starts the first smile,
that smile will last and
affect the lives of many.
A smile fills someone's life with happiness.
The smile has the power to
cure sadness and lift that burden
by replacing it with joy.
Catch the *Happiness Bug*
and *smile!*

Janice M. Chang

THE URGENCY OF DAISIES

Screaming out your whiteness for attention from the sun,
Pleading with your posture to grab its ultraviolet ray,
Divinely disposed unto your purpose,
Constant fervor on display.

To what do you dedicate your passion?
How is it that your burning's so intense?
To what great task have you made promise?
What makes your little mission so immense?

You say your days must all be spent in glory,
Because they are so few then lost to cold.
So you spend each moment in pursuit of beauty,
I admit I've never seen you less than gold.

If I could but capture your dedication,
And plant it with the seeds of all mankind,
Then all could strive with your unbending resolution,
And in the striving save the battered mind.

M. Catherine Bunton

CAMEO CHASSIS

At first composure is the test,
a beating heart will race, not let you rest.
The ether starts to toss your head about,
and suddenly, though subtly, you're out.

So why the consternation at the thought,
of prodding parts that perhaps were never wrought?
Could be you're just a hollow heartless mass,
a finely blown cameo of glass.

"Impossible" you say, consider this.
Who knows beyond the corpus what's amiss?
Scalpels poised to pierce through dermal doors,
pass through unknown dimensions, virgin shores.

Rest assured is the recess that is void,
for the knife inside the aneroid,
is powerless where nothingness is whole,
yet where in this vast blankness is the soul?

If in nothingness the soul seems to abide,
cannot the body thrive with nought inside?
To recover unetched from a Passover in Brass,
like a finely blown cameo of glass.

M. Catherine Bunton

M. CATHERINE BUNTON. Born: St. Louis, Missouri; Education: University of Missouri, B.A., Cum Laude, English; Washington University, graduate work; Occupation: Congressional Staff Associate to William L. Cray, M.C.; Comments: *I hope that my poetry will someday rouse the populace from their air-conditioned coma, and break a new sweat of consciousness throughout the whole body politic.*

AESTHETICS PORTFOLIO

July 12, 1981, Westacres, Michigan

Horses galloping, cows mooing
Chickens clucking. Old MacDonald
Had a farm.

Fowl language — sin and filth
Degradation
"All Hell broken loose."

Power, power, who's got the power?
People in family dynamics — people in church —
But God has the real power.

"Blessed are the meek, for they shall
inherit the earth."

"Blessed are they who hunger and thirst after righteousness
for they shall be filled."

"Blessed are they who mourn, for they shall be comforted."

Oh God and Jesus — let Ron and Judy have a
Good time together. Amen.

Dennis Earl Garrels

TO DELPHINIUM

You are a skyscraper tall towering over all
The flowers that blow within our garden wall.
You are "the belle of the ball" when on us you call
In June. You nap July through while sun rain and dew
Fall on you. Refreshed your Heavenly Blue
Peers at the garden anew. Then while winds strew
Leaves, gold, rust, ecru everywhere, with ingenuity
You sometimes revive your blue array.
You are as blue as a jay, yet I have heard say
"You have a bee." Tell me, where. In your bonnet? Each day?
And the ribbons on it, tell me, are they
Blue or gray? Tell me, I pray without delay.
For, if the Pacific were to mingle with you
It would be *terrific** from a gardener's point of view!

Mollie E. Miller

HELL'S HOUNDS

It was Judgment Day quite clearly, and 'twas my turn next most nearly,
To stand before the bar and face the Judge.
My body commenced quaking as I saw His head was shaking — slowly
    left to right and nothing more.
        Shaking left to right but nothing more.
Freezing fright encased my spirit and like intense heat did sear it.
I fell upon my face before the bar.
With my wordless posture's pleading I presented thus my needing
His approval of my life long past before.
        Approval of the soul upon the floor.
'Twas in vain I sought and pleaded for my soundless voice, unheeded,
Was powerless to move this stern-faced Judge.
To the left I then was shunted where I soon became the hunted
By my sinful, wicked life in days of yore.
        Hunted by my sins long gone before.
Alas! how soon began their yapping and their barking, snipping, snapping;
Close upon my heels — they vex me sore!
With each bark I'm made to shudder for to me they seem to utter,
"He's ours! His chance is gone forevermore."
        All's lost, 'tis right, for here is Hell's wide door.

Sandra Schmidt

SPECIAL GIFTS — FRIENDS

Friends are the best gifts
anyone can ever have.
They can't be exchanged or returned.
In them, you'll find
comfort, joy, happiness, understanding, care,
and most of all —
Love.
A wealth in the love of friends
outnumbers and outlasts
the wealth in all material values combined.
Friends are indeed the most
precious and special gifts.
Once you have them,
you'll have them for life.

Janice M. Chang

JANICE MAY CHANGE. Born: Loma Linda, California, 5-24-70; Education: Loma Linda Academy, 6-14-87; California State University San Bernardino; Occupation: Student; Memberships: 5-24-70; Education: Loma Linda Academy, 6-14-87; California State University San Bernardino; Occupation: Student; Memberships: Loma Linda Chapter National Honor Society; Poetry: *My Treasury of Thoughts in Freeverse Composition, collection,* 5-87; Themes: *Love, Friendship, and the beauty of nature, which God has given to us, are aspects in everyday life.* Comments: *My poems portray these aspects which everyone can relate to. It is my desire that my expression of thoughts and feelings will affect the lives of people by bringing out happiness and by helping them to realize what they have is special.*

THINKING OF YOU

I sit her thinking of you
And it makes me feel somewhat blue —
For it was only once
That thoughts were only of you . . .

The reminder of you . . .
Brings out regrets;
And bitterness glows —
Where once warm red flowed . . .

So as I sit here
In the dark and gloom . . .
A lonely tomorrow surely
As it makes me think of you . . .

T. Umekawa

TWO TELL-TALE TEARDROPS

A moment ago she was crying,
And how do we know it was so?
On each cheek a teardrop is lying,
Though now is her face all aglow.

She's hurt, her desire is denied her,
And tears how quickly they run;
A toy or her mother beside her,
Her face is like after rain sun.

A joy takes the place of her sadness,
Forgotten her moments of pain;
How shiny her eyes are with gladness,
She's off now, new pleasures to gain.

Yet, still do we know she's been crying,
And how do we know we are right;
On each rosy cheek there is lying,
A teardrop so glist'ning and bright.

Beverly A. McElwain

LOST MEMORIES

Precious memories of long ago
Are now lost in time,
What a tragedy they're never put
In story or in rhyme.

To take each special moment
And mark it down with care,
Then add a touch of color
Just to brighten what was there.

To recollect all the things,
The happiness that should last,
And pass it on to others
For them to share our past.

Make the story of today
A precious part of tomorrow
And remember it with love.
For Lost Memories are a sorrow.

Jeanette Towns

MY TWIN COMPANION

Dedicated to Sheila Taylor

When I stop and think about our friendship
And what it means to me,
I think God has created
Another person just like me.
A person I can share a laugh with,
Sing and cry and understand.
Who creates a world of loving;
And is there to lend a helping hand.
In our lives there are many changes
That have happened now and then,
But when God took away my sister
He has returned her in a friend.
I never want to take our friendship for granted
Or hurt it needlessly;
Just enjoy a twin companion
That I have known in thee.

Jeanette Towns

ODE TO REASON

I think it is autumn that contents me most.
Crude, obscene winter holds no charms,
Shrieking banshee gales
That send the devil to cover!
Striking always at loveliness.
His one intent — to seduce spring.
And she, the tricky one
Summoning flowers from winter's bed
Before their time, to perish.
A weeping laughing hoyden
Dismayed, but not surrendering
Her virginity to winter's blandishments.
Summer, nor virgin she.
A full-bosomed nymphomaniac
Hot with passion of remembering.
Subduing winter, promised fulfillment,
Breathless loveliness that fades too soon.
Ah yes, it is autumn, exquisitely serene,
Quiet relief, sweet completion, dignity
That contents me most.

Ellen Grey Parks

MOTHER

Flowers may bloom forever —
sun, moon, and stars shine, too,
tho' nothing could compare with a
mother's love
for folks like me and you.

All during our life's existence
on this planet we call earth,
it is her prayers — her heart's desire
to give us sunshine, happiness and mirth.

During these troubled times unable to
purchase a bouquet,
even if we gave her a lovely wild flower,
she would with her heart, bless us —
each passing hour.

Someone may be a wanderer — and suddenly
a soft voice you may hear,
it may be the voice of your dear mother
who shall love you forever, dear.

Now, let you turn your steps,
hasten each step on its way,
until you reach your humble doorstep —
to love and cherish mother — each blessed day.

Francis X. Menz

A FATHER'S PRAYER

I was wondering what you think
ought to be done,
when you have a totally
ungrateful son?

This, I asked God
as I knelt down to pray,
at the end of a very
exhausting day.

He said, "Just love him
the way that I do,
for I strongly suspect
he learned that from you."

Carol Hudspeth

A GIFT FOR THE GIVER

You abound in thoughtfulness,
Always thinking of another,
Giving with a joyfulness,
That not a one could smother.

You have a treasure in your heart,
I know you love to share,
And many see from the start,
How much you really care.

You may become discouraged at times,
But just be patient with us,
For we are just humankind,
And are not known to trust.

This is my gift for you,
It may not cost a dime,
Just to say, ''I thank you,''
For sharing in my life — some time.

Kimberlee Ferris

YOU'RE VERY PRECIOUS TO ME

You're a very much shared part of my life.
You're like a rose full of loveliness.
You're like a priceless jewel with
Polish upon your beautiful face,
A pillar of support
A world of comfort when I'm feeling bad.
You're the one who makes my life so
Much easier to bear, because I know how much you care.
You taught me the reasons why
There's you and me together very close and lovingly.
Your sweet kisses and gentle loving touch,
These are just some of the reasons why
I love you so very much.
I'd like to be with you now and
Forever my lifetime through.
Reach out, take my hand, ease my soul.
Let us travel down life's pathway
Together and never let go.

Montgomery Rahrmann

A BRIEF ODE TO THE COMMA

A look at the comma gives us time for a pause;
    see how well it works on a non-restrictive clause.

Put a comma at the beginning and one at the end
    a most useful mark, this comma our friend.

It's used in a series of a number of things;
    ''he bought her diamonds in necklaces, in pins, and in rings.''

To set off a quote two commas are needed;
    without them, important words wouldn't be heeded.

The mark of the comma is used most of all;
    it's used in winter, spring, summer and fall.

It's used without thinking when writing our birth date;
    this wee little speck, it's really first-rate.

This mark, oh, so tiny, this mark, oh, so small,
    when used by a good writer, stands ineffably tall.

Shirley A. Bartelt

SILENT SPRING

I've bathed in the silent spring,
That fed ponds of no living thing,
That led to rivers of the dead,
Emptying into the sea's mercury bed.

I've swam the swirling sulphur fog,
That crouched low, like some mad dog,
While tentacles of warm choking death,
Come to steal your last breath.

I've walked playgrounds of toxic waste,
And cabbage patch graves, W. R. graced.
Choking on their see-through denials,
In their efforts to avoid just trials.

I've read of our nuclear mistakes,
Doesn't take much, and the world bakes.
They say it's safer than your own bed,
But only if you're already dead.

I've drowned in indifference without a prayer,
Government and corporate, an equal share.
They'll take everything, and return a spill,
Take heed, what nature doesn't kill, science will.
                    Silent spring.

Robert W. Sharpe

IT SNOWED

''It snowed!'' ''It snowed!'' Oh! what happy words;
    at this sound, the little girl in her stirred.

Peeking outside the world was now quiet and white;
    her past worries and cares were put quickly to flight.

This delicate change is from God's wondrous hand;
    to her it's like God's love is hugging the land.

Who could be sad on such a glorious day?
    She knew many others didn't feel the same way.

She felt sorry for them and hoped they'd turnabout;
    she dismissed them quickly with the tiniest pout.

This day was too special to fret and to worry;
    if she was to have fun in the snow, she must hurry.

And a great day it was, ''Oh, thank you dear Lord,''
    and now to the fireplace to burn wood by the cord.

Shirley A. Bartelt

SEEING DIFFERENT LIGHTS

You lit a candle in the living
Room and you
Lit a candle in your bedroom
And one night, years later,
I sat here, lit one
Candle before a giant
Mirror, and felt myself adrift,
As if in another room,
And then thought again,
The night, the day, the shadow
And shine of the
Distant city lights rising
Through the same window —
During the day a prism
Shimmering auras on the
Ivory carving of a fisherman
Holding a fish.
Minutes before sunset
I saw something move
Very fast across the sky.

Tom Dates

US

The leaches of life
are on you tonight
the night you were born
'til your role here is through

We are the actors
sometimes in the wings
seeing through the dark
to center stage the main part

With each his own
we often don't realize we
are being observed
until too late

You wonder if you
played your part right
whether they saw the luster
of your kindness and love that night

But one chance is all you get
so on your death may
many joyous memories
you not forget

Miriam Troxler

REMEMBER ME

Now that the end is here and tears
    are all that I have left,
If you should ever wonder if my love
    was really true,
Close your eyes and remember the
    feelings of love,
The touch of my hand in yours
    telling you I cared,
The warmth of my kiss on your lips,
    letting you know I was always there,
The pain in your heart and in my eyes
    each time we said good-bye,
If you should ever wonder,
    just close your eyes and remember
    the feelings of love.

Mary Wessel

A lovely warm sleep
In my lacy nighty
Somersaulting through
        the lazy sky
Swimming through open
        water unafraid
Floating unaided
Keeping out of the shade
I sun-dry
Tickled by the breeze
And browning
No moon in my dreams
No man in my comfy
        single bed

Snug and safe
        I am lulled
Back to life

Jane Fell

THE FERRIS WHEEL

Once upon a Ferris wheel,
Long time ago,
Saw a proper gentleman,
Hair white as snow.

Smiled at Johnny, bowed to me,
I remember that,
Flower in his buttonhole,
Feather in his hat.

Up, around and up we flew,
High above the crowd,
Music bursting in our ears
Made us laugh out loud.

Johnny took my hand in his,
Squeezed and held it tight,
Took my hand, took my heart
Up along the night.

Singing, swinging, on we flew
Gently to and fro,
Once upon a Ferris wheel,
Long time ago.

Beverly Beeton

I LIKE YOU

I don't like you for the way you look —
        Yet I do.

I don't like you for the way you speak
        Or the things you say —
        But I do.

I don't like you because you like me
        And you are my friend
        And I am flattered and grateful,
        But I am —
                And I do.

I don't like you for the reasons others do,
        Or say they do —

And I don't like you 'cause I love you . . .
        But I do.

Beverly Beeton

TO YOUNG LONNIE

(1956 - 1987)

Yesterday, tomorrow's dream was stilled
Nevermore another dawn to see,
So young to die with hopes ere unfulfilled
The silent dream lies weeping 'neath the lea.
An early frost has nipped the waiting bud
The beauty of the bloom forever lost,
A flood of tears cannot revive the arid
Waste — renew the petals, tempest-tossed.
Today the sun shines brightly on the mead
As gentle breezes soothe my aching soul,
And suddenly I smile — my pain is freed
I see a flower blooming on the knoll.
    An inner calmness now, a smile and love,
    If this be his, it will be enough.

Barbara Nell Lamb

COMPUNCTION

In my cupboard a pitcher stands
        to humble me,
        even make me sad;

For in its memories, simply said,
        unkindness tries
        to raise its head.

Its beauty often makes me think
        that wanting it
        brought injury.

But now I cannot give it back
        or tell her that
        I grieve for her;

Nor would she care for trifling things
        or feel at ease
        to see me thus.

So I must look and understand
        she loves me still
        despite my self.

Regina Golden

FUTILITY

You little black spider
with orange legs,
trying in vain, to crawl
through the window pane.
Your arachnidian sleekness
will get you nowhere
because you cannot grasp
nature's controversies:
The glass is liquid, yes.
But at the temperature of your existence
it must be solid.
The laws of physics are correct.
It is only our minds
that trick us.

Dr. GGisela Nass

254

TENAYA CANON, FROM GLACIER POINT.

THE SAD YOUNG GIRL

The young girl sat, her hair was gold;
  her face was youthful, but her heart was old.

The joy of life from her was taken,
  her father was gone; she was forsaken.

A young man but older than she
  once said, ''Father why forsakest Thou Me?''

When these words she did recall,
  her spirit came back, with warmth like a shawl.

Her father wasn't really away;
  she'd see him again, some glorious day.

As her happiness grew, she had to share;
  she gave to others who were in despair.

Her heart, that before felt so cold and so old,
  was bursting with love that just had to be told.

She told of her sorrow changed now to joy;
  in the telling, His love she began to employ.

She told of her loss that was changed by a gift;
  the gift that was given gave her heart such a lift.

The joy she felt is ours to know, too;
  just spread out your love, and God will help you.

Shirley A. Bartelt

GOOD GUYS ARE DESTINED TO MOVE ON

No matter when or why they came
They are all involved in the same exasperating game

You meet them by chance as the world goes by
You hope to be friends until all die

Good times you share and bad times forget
A true friendship that you will never regret

Laughing together and just having fun
They lighten your world like the rays of the sun

But deep down inside you wait for their reason
And so gloomy it will turn your brightest season

Always helping, or just knowing that they are there
I'll tell you right now, this game isn't fair

Together you can talk, for hours on end
And broken hearts they help you at once to mend

Dreams you share and experiences tell
Sometimes you think it was just as well

For soon comes the day of their reason why
And friends must part and say good-bye

Linda Marie Tracey

NUCLEAR MURDER

Guided missiles aimed at Dad
Dying children clinging to Mom
Crying faces looking sad
In the aftermath of a nuclear bomb

Nuclear war
Murder
What is it for
Murder
Nuclear war
Murder

Mushroom clouds illuminating the sky
Crumbling buildings all around
Screaming people as they die
Families hiding underground

Nuclear war
Murder
What is it for
Murder
Nuclear war
Murder

Lauri Jean Gerecke

THE CABIN ON THE HILL

Up a narrow, lofty hillside runs a winding little way,
  That I once journeyed now and then back in my childhood day.
A dwelling old and sturdy stood atop this little height,
  And from its creaky, wooden porch, the lake was such a sight!
Birds of many species dwelt among its nesting ground;
  I remember Mama made a point of hearing their sweet sound.
The summers there were special and their nights were full of hope,
  That we would always gaze at stars Dhrough daddy's telescope.
But I was young and, oh, so sure that God would give us years
  Of times like these, so full of joy, and keep away all tears.
But surely as the sun did rise one cold and wintery dawn;
  I awoke to feel an empty heart, for Mother now was gone.
Now change had stepped into my life and made her point so clear,
  That life would never be the same, yet memories are so dear.
Tho' change has made me saddened, taken with her what she will;
  She could never take my foretime of the cabin on the hill.

Amy Dunsha

AMY S. DUNSHA. Born: Chattanooga, Tennessee, 12-10-51; Married: Brian Lee Dunsha, 2-14-76; Education; Carson-Newman College, Jefferson City, Indiana; University of Tennessee, Martin, Tennessee; Occupations: PBX operator, Receptionist; Comments: *My poetry is emotional and spiritual and thus centers around what I feel are the two most important aspects of life. I like to keep each poem simple and true to my feelings, hoping that those who read my work will experience good memories. Then, whether they laugh or cry, it is good because I have achieved my goal.*

THE CHURCH

A nest where, as a child, we gain the strength to overcome all pain;
  And through the years we come to see that what we are —
    we choose to be.
A loft where we can store our dreams, upheld by wisdom's solid beams;
  Dreams that will never stale nor die,
    for we have heard the Savior's cry.
A lodging for our weary essence, strengthened by His Holy presence;
  Seeing us through times of grief, and testing our announced belief.
A church to share with young and old,
    where we can learn what prophets told;
  While young should lend attentive ear to those
    whose earthly time is near.
A structure, built by man's own hand, but standing fast on Holy Land;
  'Cause this is where a man may go, to stir the presence of his soul.
God bless her, love her, help her know that she's a place
    where souls may grow
  To wisdom's height and farther still,
    and teach us of our Father's will.

Amy Dunsha

MY GRANDMOTHER AND ME

"Your grandmother is very sick," my dad tells me,
"In the hospital where the doctors can watch her carefully."
"Can I go see her?" I ask my folks.
"No, you must be twelve, and you're not even close."

I got down on my knees and began to pray
For my grandma to get better some day.
God, please don't take my grandma away from me.
I need her as much as she needs me.

On my birthday she always remembers the day
And has something special for me hidden away.
She's old and wrinkled and in some places she's flabby.
When she doesn't feel good, you call tell — she's crabby.

She's pretty special, my grandma she is.
In fact, I like her just the way she is.
She always has a special smile
And a hug that lasts a mile.

When I do something wrong, she just grins
Shakes her head, and tickles my chin.
She reads me stories, she tells me tales
About lions and tigers and snakes and snails.

So Lord, now do you understand? Do you see?
I need my grandmother, and she needs me.

Kathleen Tomlin

VIETNAM

Vietnam, don't you care what you are doing?
Vietnam, the innocent lives you are ruining.

Vietnam, your people are running away,
Yes Vietnam, to save their lives some way.

Vietnam, your country is poor,
This, Vietnam, is what happens when there is war.

Your people are dying, your children are crying
    for the peace that never comes,
When you fight with bombs and guns.

Yes Vietnam, your people are running away,
Yes Vietnam, no one will be left some day.

All of your people are tired of death,
Tell us Vietnam, when it's all over how many people
    and soldiers will you have left?

Cry, Vietnam, for the people who have gone,
Then pray, Vietnam, that your people won't forget,
Then hope, Vietnam, that they will return to the homes
    they have left.

Susan M. Do

THE SEDUCTION OF TIME

Eternal is the pressure of knowledge,
Fastening itself to an idea.
Clinging there, waiting for man to discover what he has
    known all along.
Everlasting is the force that bathes the brain of man,
Nourishing a notion, bringing to light a spark of genius,
The gift that emerges in momentary glory from the dust of
    dormancy.
Neverending is the ebb of time,
Playing on the consciousness of man.
Creating immortality through man, with language,
Erupting from his throat of flesh,
Bringing light to human thought.
Up from the fundament of the soul;
Time losing her virginity to man, that upstart,
Who must conquer all;
Then in his greatest, and last triumph,
Man finally proceeds to do to himself in reality
What he has so far only proclaimed with words,
The aftermath of which is
Infinity.

William J. Russell

I'm just a little poodle, so what is wrong with that?
I didn't do a thing that's wrong — just ate Dad's stupid hat!
And just because I got a taste for leather shoes one day,
Is there really any cause for Mom to act this way?

I didn't chase the neighbor's cat just to get a thrill.
He was eating up my food — besides, that cat's a pill.
And, I let that old police dog stroll right on past the house.
I didn't say a single word. I was quiet as a mouse.

I didn't mean to mutilate Doug's little G.I. Joe,
I thought that I could find a knob to make the dumb thing go.
And Keith's guitar with all those strings made such a pretty sound.
I just thought I'd like to hear it when nobody was around.

I didn't know the burger on the table wasn't mine.
Steph didn't tell me it was hers — and, it sure tasted fine.
These humans, they're a funny lot. They never make much sense.
I don't see any reason not to crawl beneath the fence.

It's not as if I bit someone, or growled, or barked, or scratched.
And, if they really wanted to, that sofa could be patched.
I didn't do a single thing, I'm trying really hard.
So why am I now tied up in this lonely old backyard?

Josie D

DEATH OF A YOUNG PERSONHOOD
JUST 5 & 1/2

My spring lilies faded at dew's morningtide
Fall began to clip goldenrod too early, eagerly
and winter lingers at my door, still,
unwelcome imbiber of concealment

One dawn I was posies and tulips
Easter daffodils trumpeting love notes
then I learned daddy was having an affair
something punched me
                    at the heart of my knows
                            nose of my heart
hauling my springtime away like scrap metal,
to build great, sick pinnacles

There are tinged photos of that tragically ephemeral time
an ironic montage of happy people dancing near the precipice
                    ropeless, hopeless
all I see are the cold survivalist days following
and how I leapt off the same cliff as my mother
her pinky in mine

Carol A. Exton

TEMPLE BETH-EL

Could you translate a poem for me
Among the trees in desert sand sifted by sea?
Stars beyond a life of gifts, stars unfolded sheen,
Coiled around the spine of man, ones on which we lean.
Threaded in and out of view, sight beyond our eyes,
Concentrated birds-eye heaven, deeper than the skies.
Limited we are by day, Prince and Princesses of flesh,
Mortals striving to achieve, wisdom put to test.
Point and counterpoint is made, a repertoire of sounds,
Stringed instruments all laid at their stairs and grounds.
Landscape painted far within temple walls appear.
While gentle rocking tune, the Lamb of God is near.

Frances Naquin

WHISPERS IN THE RAIN

In each and every lone drop of rain,
There lies an answer to our pain.
Each minute driplet has a name and purpose.
The rain's whispered music gingerly wafts to the ears of our being.
Oh God, you must listen;
For only she is the music meant, this message to her heart.
How sad if these capsules carrying peace, love, and joy
    must fall in vain.
There is hope you see!
For once the droplets fall from the sky their wisdom pierces the earth.
From here each living thing drinks with thirst;
Hence, the wisdom, the key, is drawn within.
This knowledge is merely knocking at your door begging
    to be acknowledged.
So next time you distinctly hear golden leaves rustling in the wind,
Or a drip-drop, drip-drop outside your window on a calm grey day,
Listen, for you will hear a whisper so gentle at your inner door.
Open it, don't be scared.
What will you see?
A reflection of you, and in her hand a precious, golden key.

Poppy Gard

SONYA'S LAMENT

Sketches from ''Uncle Vanya'' by Anton Chekhov

I am concerned with earth, with growing things;
Spring sowing, harvest, animal husbandry.
You love trees; save life, curse men's sufferings;
We should be kindred spirits, you and I.
And yet you do not see me. My rough hands,
Plain looks, gauche ways, unable to ensnare.
I have no wiles, no languid silken strands
To bind you to me. Nor can I declare
My inmost thoughts, being afraid to know
The answer. Hope is all I can allow.
Orlando, in that forest long ago
Fastened his lovesick poems upon a bough;
But would you read, or would you even see,
Were I to hang my feelings on a tree?

Pamela Mant

WORDSMITH

I exist nowly,
but many fires have woven me
and bring me to the work I do,
in rhythm and concert with my spirit.

The essence of the moon rushes me
making sounds of the winds within the craft of me.
My fabric trembling,
I take to paper . . .

I seek out the brighter stones
that line the boundaries of heaven
to yield me my place
interfacing with earth and sky.

A Wordsmith,
I am on loan to the colors of my understandings
and wear my legacy in tune with my self.
To be and to work.
But, mostly,
to dance lovingly
and
to love dancingly.

Claire Burns Mille

DILEMMA

You rob me of my sleep with infant wails
Tearing the night away; and I must rise
And rock you back and forth till peace prevails,
Then face the coming day with red-rimmed eyes.
I am the centre of your little world,
Not you of mine — I have a life to lead;
The joys you give to me are thousand-fold
But they are not enough: I have this need
To use my talents, and in using, serve.
It is an offering that must be made.
Whatever God has given, strict preserve,
I hold in trust; a due that must be paid.
And yet I waver: who can think of Art
When small, fat fingers twine around my heart?

Pamela Mant

PAMELA MANT. Born: London, England; Occupation: Professional actress; Other Writings: ''The Black Brigand,'' co-author, BBC TV Drama Serial; ''East Lynne,'' Co-adaptor, Stage play; ''Day Out,'' writer and presenter, BBC Radio Series; Short stories for BBC radio; Comments: *At present I'm working on a collection of poems about theatrical life.*

SEASONS CYCLES

Life unfolds, time begins.
Curious innocence, newly born.
Nature's spectre gently descends.
Spring, whispering softly.

Life, busy and complete.
Season of laughter, joy and tears.
Ecstatic being, days replete.
Summer, bursting at the seams.

Life, golden and sweet.
Unending content, false illusion.
Bright promises none can keep.
Fall, arrayed in glory.

Life surrendered, astonished dismay.
Cycle fulfilled, gentle sorrow.
The Reaper came calling today.
Winter, cloaked and sleeping.

Billie A. Skelton

MIRRORED LIFE

Like the masses' eyes watching on the crowded streets;
heat, sweat dripping from brows, the confusion itching
their anger; noisy whistles, horns blaring, blowing,
whipping cars, crashing bodies into bodies, papers sprawling;
I am there.

Like the cobbled streets through the old world ville;
Or a serene summer field with child; Mother softly swings
the smiling youth from an oak bough; The robins sing but
unheard songs and yet without the pretty natural mixture,
silence would be too quiet; Though two enjoy this hill,
no doubt there are three.

Like a troubled tear from pale blue eyes, flowing, stopping,
continuing past a sad smile; A leaving train, blurred glass
by wet darkness; Grasping hope as if a hand; Sunken ship,
treasure lost by splintering wood; A vessel alone, floating
toward a country non-existent;
A mirror;
Familiar reflections;
Similar shapes;
I see myself.

Mark W. Sasse

APRIL VERSE

The flowers bloom, the robins sing.
The landscape moans in delight
to nature's playful caresses.
The sky is blue filled with billowy clouds
of a fluffy texture, and
the branches sway to the gentle touch of a breeze.

A bird flies overhead to the cadence of a musical
rainbow chiming away in celestial splendor.
The countryside is blooming with those little ones,
so long held dormant by the winter chill.

Spring is our season of delight where the snowy
storms of winter dissolve into rivulets of tinkling streams.

A man can feel the call of his inner being
leading him through what was once cold
and open him up to expression of sensual
feeling,
yielding to new vistas and enticing dreams.

Austin Gil

WALL

In the beginning egos lay low.
To please the other was the fare of the day.
We called it *Love*, although in retrospect
Serving really seems the better word.

But subtly, almost silently came the change.
What made egos rear their ugly heads?
When did *serving* turn instead to *taking*,
    or worse, *expecting?*

How did thin-edged *indifference* wedge between us
    and our thanksgivings
To cement this monstrous wall?

Bette Armstrong

LADY LIBERTY

Lady Liberty was shining very well,
Until the coup when Camelot fell,
John Kennedy inspired the world to dream,
His death was like a crack in the earth's seam.

Where once he planted compassion, honesty, and ideals from seed,
Now Ronald's team has replaced that with corruption, lying, and greed,
We will never know what would have been,
For the corrupt ones' fear of his leadership did him in —
    a mortal sin.

When Robert picked up the torch to lead,
The masses again looked upon goodness and ideals to feed,
As the campaign wore on — his stature grew,
The corrupt knew he was unbeatable — so they had to kill him too.

Now there are hundreds who could lead us right,
Instilling virtues of honesty, compassion, and sacrifice in our sight,
But it takes chances, money, and power to rise from the night,
Even if successful, you have to battle corrupt forces with might.

Lady Liberty — are you still here — do you still shine,
Protecting our freedoms, everyone's — including yours and mine,
The French sent a sympathy card after Robert died,
Saying ''Farewell America,'' leaders — please prove the card lied.

Daryl T. Olson

MESSAGE FROM MOLOCH

Entombed in subterrestrial space, they wait.
One hundred years now gone; it's soon to be.
In darkness sparked by phosphored light,
they wait for word, ''The party's on!''
Reverberating hammers ring. It's time
to break the stygian silence and begin.
Passion-possessed and inchoate,
desiring demons clasp the ground.
The earthy mistress, faulted, shifts, then breaks
her stillness with crescendoed breath that sways
the towered city far above,
now shakes to dust a shoddy mall.
The budget condos tumble into shards
of glistening glass and concrete-crumbled bones.
Moloch's minions lie in dreams;
entombed, no moans disturb their sleep.

Mary Freckleton

11:47 P.M.

The day fades out as it faded in,
With preponderances in silence ebbing hypnotically.
An indistinguishable duration.
Lights off! Chasing illusive images.
A strobbing reality.
Sight piercing the vacuum void of black,
Transfixed and struggling to see the lights behind closed lids.
Thoughts discursively ruminated —
It was — it wasn't — it was —
Induction: deduction — on and on . . .
Stop! Consciousness.
Being is paused forcibly!
Slowly
  Slowly fading
    Repose
      Sleep.

Nancy L. Hashemian

WHAT WE MAKE OF IT

Life sometimes hurts and makes one depressed
In time, the pain will subside and you'll continue
on your quest
Life is sometimes short, strange and unsure
And when you're alone, it can really be a bore.

Life is like a puzzle of a ship full of people,
in stormy weather
To survive, we must learn to join together,
We must learn to look beyond the color of the skin
And treat everyone as our neighbor and our friend.

There's hope, no matter what the case
We just have to take this world on face to face,
Life is a challenge that we all must meet
We must continue the struggle and never give in to defeat.

We must give of ourselves, learn to challenge life's pains
And we will learn to overcome its tremendous strains,
We're always complaining that life is the pits
When life is merely, what we make of it.

Ronald J. Smith

RONALD JEROME SMITH. Pen Name: R.J.; Born: Washington, D.C., 5-26-61; Education: Graduate of McKinley High School; Occupations: National Guardsman, Secretary, Security Guard; Themes: *My poems cover all aspects of life such as love, hate, depression, encouragement, religion, special occasions, etc.*

OFF-SEASON RATES

Children playing in hooded snowsuits
On the beach.
The mounds of sailboat hulls line the shore
Their exposed white bellies like huge beached fish.
The emptiness of the sea, a mirror of the sky
Summer's brilliant travel poster image
Shot in black and white.
Cottages huddle with their backs to the wind
Like a group of cold commuters waiting for a bus
Out of town.
The hotdog stand now a tomb
With its giant eye shut up tight.
A spoiled-child wind tugs at my clothes,
Runs around my legs, then leaps ahead
To jump out from around the next bend,
And run off along an alleyway
Sounding its teapot whistle.

Lisa R. Connolly

GREAT SPIRIT

Oh great Spirit;
Give me the strength and courage of a warrior.
Give me the wisdom of the council chiefs.
Give me the knowledge of the medicine man.
Give me the compassion of the squaw to her first born.
Let me be as gentle as a deer,
And as free as the Eagle and the Hawk.
Give me the fierceness of the Black Bear,
As she protects her cubs.

Let me walk in the prairies and the forest,
And know that they are yours and not mine.
Fill my lodge with many ponies, my baskets with corn.
Let me share with my brothers these gifts.
Oh great Spirit of the nations and tribes;
Let me share your waters and your earth.
Let me share your fish and your game.
Let me understand my enemies.
And oh great Spirit, let me count you as my brother.

Ronald R. Schauer

SOMEWHERE TO THE SOUTH OF US

All your leaders should be put to shame.
This thing you call a Revolution, is just a game.
You have a lot to lose and very little to gain.
Yes, you could say your country's in a lot of pain.

All the mothers worry about their missing sons.
You take away their school books and give them guns.
There's a dead young man lying on the corner.
There stands a frail old woman who is now a mourner.

The soldiers steal the food from the poor.
The people consider themselves lucky that they didn't do more.
There stands a young woman in mud that's caked.
How long will it be until she is raped?

There's a soldier that's flipped his lid.
He's getting his kicks from beating a kid.
I think whoever stands for freedom should control the land,
And I think that we should give them all the help we can.

Bradley S. Martens

THE FAT AND THE LEAN

Don't smash the cockroach crawling across my floor.
I'll bet ten dollars he heads for the door.
Like a bird in flight, you can't ask for more.
I just wish I wasn't so damn poor.

I don't have any faith in mankind.
I just hope someone there throws me a line.
All of us are living on borrowed time.
I can't just lay down and shut down my mind.

Most people seem to talk too much.
Even very small children talk Dutch.
Everyone has their own crutch.
Why do very few have the magic touch?

Now I know things I've never seen.
All my senses are very keen.
You can't eat fat when the meat is lean.
I'll bet you don't know what in the hell I mean.

Bradley S. Martens

WHAT'S HIS NAME AND ME

I walked along the beach looking for a place. I deliberately
picked the loneliest part of the beach because that is how
I felt alone. I sat down and stared at the sky and didn't even notice
the man approaching me. He began telling me that he thought the sky
was put on this earth as an escape world for dreamers and that
the sun was brought out to warm our hearts. This man, he understands;
he knew what I was feeling. I asked him his name, but, he kissed my
hand and said that his name wasn't important. The only thing that
mattered was that he was here. Then he grabbed me and held me
in his arms. It was so good to feel his presence. We talked and
laughed until the day ended. And I knew by the way he was holding me
tightly that I would never see him again. We stood up, he gazed into
my eyes, embraced me, then walked away without even looking back.
    The tears came down my face. They were not tears of sadness but
tears of joy, because in the world I may look alone but in my mind I
will no longer be. For I will always remember what's his name and me.

Judith L. Newbauer

SEEING IT THROUGH

We were sitting near the lake having a picnic one day
when 6 men with 6 guns pointed our way,
said gather your stuff and come with us, free you will no longer be,
and the one they called the master said — you now belong to me

So with no roof over our heads, but a master instead, we followed
this stranger home, and I whispered a silent prayer that our stay
wouldn't be too long

I washed your clothes, your hair, and your skin, took the blame for
the trouble you got in, through good times and bad times,
I held your hand, picked your cotton and plowed your land

I dressed you and blessed you, and fought your fights,
held candles for you when there were no lights

With herbs from the ground, I brought your fever down,
and nourished you back to health, while a few doors down,
I could hear the sounds of my brothers being put to death

But if this is my lot, I seek no plot to unlawfully get me out,
I accept my life however it comes, I'll take it round by round,
for greater is he who is within me, than he who can shoot me down

Fairretta Smith

SEASON UNCHANGED

As the periphery colors begin to turn gray,
in your mind from seeing them day after day,
and you subconsciously notice that all you can hear,
is the draft of the wind as it passes your ear,
then something is telling you, "Winter is near . . ."

And soon you will notice a goose pimple chill,
creating a warning but also a thrill,
as you think about Christmas, New Years and snow,
and bundled-up children with cheeks all aglow,
and the holiday parties to which you will go . . .

You start thinking that summer may have led you astray;
"You don't really need that warm weather to play,"
and you're really quite happy to see Winter again,
though you appreciate Summer for all it has been,
as you're reminded that happiness comes from within . . .

John Wren

THE ANCIENT TRAVELER

There is light and dark on the path of life,
there is love, there is joy, there is pain, there is strife,
and I ask for none of these to be removed from my life,
for if this is my mountain, I alone must climb it,
I am the Ancient Traveler

At my request, I asked to be blessed as I took on this humanness,
and like any other birth, I came to this earth disguised
     as a newborn child,
but in the pack on my back, I carry the facts of all my other lives,
I am the Ancient Traveler

Yes, everything that happens in my life is worth experiencing,
everyone I meet worth knowing, be they beggar, thief, or preacher,
everyone I meet is my teacher, for through this distorted game
     called *life*,
I am the Ancient Traveler

Never mind the color of my skin, that's just something that
     I'm in for now,
for I am my sister, I am my brother, I am every race,
I am every color, or I will be, for that is my destiny,
I am the Ancient Traveler

Fairretta Smith

FAIRRETTA SMITH. *I live in San Francisco, California. I am a writer, poet, songwriter, and composer who enjoys the journey of self discovery. I am creative, motivated, dedicated, and positive. My hobbies are dancing, singing, reading, and of course writing. My interests are understanding, knowledge, and wisdom.*

SISYPHUS REBORN

*Written upon reading ''Plausible Prejudices''
by Joseph Epstein*

Culture is here: culture is there:
Culture now is everywhere.
It sells! It sells! Come get it here.
Pile it higher! Pile it deeper my dear!
Look out! look out! It's going to fall.
Someone has called it a rubbish ball.
Pick it up! Put it back! Rebuild it tall.
We must keep culture on the through track.
We must keep people thinking it's back!

The Zeitgeist Express now roars along
With second and third rate culture in tow:
To fill up the windows
To fill up the shelves
To cover the walls
Of all who we know.
It's going for that mountain: the highest of all.
Look out! It can't make it, it's going to fall!
Save it! Please help it get over the top!
Poor culture is better than none at all.

Elesheva Campbell

TO MY CHILDREN

God give me the strength to go on. Help me to be able
to help my children with a happy song.
Give me your wisdom from day to day, in case one would
happen to stray.
Grant me their wishes in some way and give me the words
when sorrows strike them from day to day.
Hold my hand, lest I fall. Help me to get up when
they call.
Hide my sorrows and my griefs,
But most of all, give them the knowledge of your word
and my patient ways and good beliefs.

Helen Hinzman

JENNIFER

*I work with retarded and handicapped children;
This was written about a totally retarded child.*

That cute little smile as she runs to me each morning,
The way she says ''Helen'' or grabs and hugs you
without a warning,
A cute little shuffle of her feet, as she wants me to
see her clothes each day, the way she says ''See!''
A paper towel in her hand, she makes me understand
that she wants me to wipe her sleeve, she has gotten
wet by washing her hands.
The twinkle in her big brown eyes when she says
Oh, gee or *Dad.*
Long black hair that is always so perfect, if it gets out
of place she's ready to get me the brush.
The proudness of her ways when she wants people to
notice me, makes me feel like she is more perfect, and
like an angel. Don't you see, her name is ''Jennifer,''
but to me God made her just a little more special than
others someway. And I'll miss her, but in my heart there
will always be one girl who shines out more than others
— and I love that child whose name is ''Jennifer.''

Helen Hinzman

MANHATTAN

Manhattan: Stone-girt, seabourne,
The world has sent you her spawn
To create a new dawn.

     Beacon of the free,
Entrance to the golden Land of Liberty
Has there ever been a dream city more lovely than thee?

Chester M. Matzner

LET US WALK

Let us walk while I hold your hand
for tomorrow I shall leave this land.
Forget our sorrows and search our dreams
while we stare at sparrows by the stream.
Although we cannot deny tomorrow's tears;
today we can remember the fruitful years,
rejoice within memories of a love so true,
and from tomorrow through eternity remember I love you.

Kerry Michael Pilkey

THE CADENCE CALL

As the cadence is called the soldier moves,
Just like the waves when the wind blows through the air.

Once a boy but now a man, he's trying hard to do the best he can.
A soldier's life is something he will never forget; and when he's
out in the world he'll realize that what he learned will help him
get through the tough times.

The training is hard; the sergeants are rough.
But the rewards add up to be more than enough.

So as the cadence is called and the soldier moves;
The wind dies down and the waves float calmly through the sea.

Heather Crenshaw

SOARING SEAGULLS

As I sit and watch the water
As it ripples to the ocean's shore,
I see the reflection of the sunset
As it squints through the cotton-white clouds.

The seagulls soar through the pale blue sky.
Oh, the stories they could tell of rainbows
        gone by;
Of summer's gone and winter's past;
Of loves that have failed and of those that will last.

Holding its head high and proud,
It swoops to the sea to capture the feast it might have found.
For somewhere beneath the soothing waves lies unsuspecting,
        waiting prey!

Heather Crenshaw

Remember the winter not long ago
We were so young yet it made us old
The cold, the cold, the godawful cold
In the midst of four feet of snow
We found bliss in staying alive
Together snuggled 'neath piles of quilts
The child within my womb begging to survive
We let go of our shame, let go of our guilt
We found her a name — Christmas came
You gave me a kiss. Then came the pain
Through January and more eternal snows
Holey shoes that froze your toes
Towards the bleak month's end the labor began
All the infinite night long into the morn'
I screamed and flung myself at death's door
You stood in the threshold not letting me pass
And with strength drawn from your hands
Our child, our baby girl was born
The sun no longer hid, but came forth valiant and wild
And shone intensely upon the face of our fair child

Cynthia Clark Withers

WHAT WAS MEANT?

Suddenly you're here and I'm wanting you here with me but you're
        wanting to be with her.
And it hurts — your rejection of me.
Oh, I feel so lonely and blue.
Suddenly I'm alone, out on my own, and I just can't take it anymore.

Suddenly you're gone forever and I'm needing you more each day.
Why can't you see — what the loss of your love is doing to me?
Oh, why can't you love me again — like you did back then?
We had so much happiness being together all the time.
Now everyone I meet resembles you. I don't know what to do!

What was the fight even about? What happened? Who won?
All I know is that the consequences can't be undone.
I miss you!

Heather Crenshaw

HEATHER LEE CRENSHAW. Born: Greeley, Colorado, 1-10-70; Education: Senior at Clarksville High School; Occupation: Nursery Maintenance, McKenzie Methodist Church; Membership: National Honor Society; Comments: *My poems come from life experiences of myself and those around me and from dreams of what could be. They come from the heart.*

I CARE!

What is it that draws me back to him?
    Into that endless center,
Where time stands still,
    And no one else can enter.

What is it that makes me search for him
    in every face I see?
Wherever I go, I feel he's there,
    Why can't I tell him, how much I care?

I never told him how I felt.
    His smile makes my heart melt.
I think of every passing day,
    I do care, no matter what I say.

I didn't realize, I was afraid of being hurt,
    But the hurt I feel without him;
Is more than I can bear,
    I wish I had told him how much I care.

Summer is the worst time of year,
    I sit in the park and wish he were here.
I wish I could stop this feeling of pain,
    But if I had it to do over, I'd do it again.

I know that I've got to stop running away,
    So I think I'm going to tell him today.
The worst he'll tell me when I get there,
    Is simply, "I'm sorry, but I don't care."

Donna J. Steward

KENTUCKY BLUE AND YOU

Come — let us dance —
And run and sing
In the fields of rippling
Kentucky blue

Come — I will go with you —
Wear your blue jeans
And unshod feet
We will trample the cool Kentucky blue

Come — fire is lit in the heavens above
And will light ablaze your cornsilk hair
Twirl me 'round and spin me high
Amethyst and orange fill the sky

Come — laughter and music
Echo from the dark emerald hills
The mist will fall; the fog be low
Come, let me love you in the deep Kentucky blue.

Cynthia Clark Withers

CYNTHIA CLARK WITHERS. Born: Asheville, North Carolina, 10-26-63; Married: Tim Withers, of Monticello, Kentucky; Education: English & Theatre at Berea College, Berea, Kentucky; Occupations: Mommy, Actress (for love of it), Director (for $), Receptionist, Telecommunicator; You name it, I've done it — Dug ditches, cleaned houses, stacked mail, stuffed envelopes; Membership: Board of the Valley Community Theatre, Black Mountain, Kentucky; Comments: *I write about the happenings of life on "Poverty Street." It takes a mountain of courage to be able to look my failures (and relatives whom I love) in the eye and keep doing what my heart tells me to do. My writings embody the adventures my soul has taken me on as well as the traditional Appalachian values, thoughts & scenes embedded in my mind. To Mr. Wolfe I say one thing: "Sometimes you gotta go home again."*

UNTITLED

The plateau is flat, barren.
Stretching across the wastelands —
the mist rises and billows toward me.
Engulfed and briefly blinded by the
dead, stifling cotton of the mist's bumper,
I feel its icy tendrils caress and ooze into my soul
— where they linger — and harden.
My heart slowly beats against the bars
as the solidified tendrils rake
back and forth
— gently probing —
guided by the muffled pulse.
In another moment they will pierce my heart,
and my soul's tenuous existence will be
extinguished
— slowly —
as it drains, seeping into
the oblivion of the mist
and is blotted up
forever.

C. M. Doherty

QUESTIONS?

Why doesn't he see me anymore
    Is it because he thinks I'm a bore?
Can he trust me after what I've done?
    Does he still respect me after the fun?

Doesn't he know, it wasn't easy for me?
    Do you think I should just let it be?
Do you know what the ground rules are?
    Shouldn't I have gone that far?

Why did I go to the park that late?
    Why the hell did I make that date?
Didn't he care for me at all?
    Why didn't he at least call?

How could he think it was just a game?
    How can I give him all of the blame?
Could the truth be, I wanted him too?
    Why don't I know what to do?

Will I ever get to see him again?
    Can we go back to when we began?
If things were different, would I do it over?
    No! I wouldn't settle for being his lover.

Donna J. Steward

THE DEPARTURE

I hold my breath
while . . .
Our hearts count in rhythm,
                as one
A tear upon my lashes lay,
                heavy,
With unrequited sorrow
and as . . .
You and I touch, Skin upon Skin,
the hour passes nine; it is cold
My breath ceases
                Our hearts stop
A tear falls
        We die
and the world is stilled.

Virginia K. Calhoun

LOVE'S JOURNEY

Yes, he cut me clear down to the marrow of my soul,
In a place where I thought only God could dwell.

The anticipation of him knowing the entirety of my being
        exhilirated me.
And also frightened me. No one had ever read within my eyes my deepest
        thoughts or desires.

As he continued to search my heart what would he find? Would he reveal
my past? A compilation of what has made me what I am today?
Would these findings revolt him or would he find me
        all the more endearing?

Oh, the beginnings of love can be such a tightrope. My knees tremble
on the tenuous cord, not quite sure if I will make it to the end of
        my quest for love and intimacy.

Do not look down my heart, just look straight ahead to the Giver of
Love. That is the only way one can begin the most fulfilling journey
        of a lifetime.

Susan D. White

MY HEART'S BATTLE

My heart contemplates past feelings versus the lessons learned,
In desperation trying to discern the perilous opposition.

The past batters my mind like a tyrant demanding
    my undivided attention.

The battle continues its frantic feat,
Untold hatred gaining on the forgiveness of my heart toward one
    dearly loved.

The heated battle rages on only to allow the stench in my soul to rise
    to the surface.

Slowly the hatred is burned away by the continuous supplications of
    my heart.

Though heart drained by the raging battle,
                    Forgiveness won its triumphant victory.

Susan D. White

My friend is at work.
My only friend right now is myself and the telephone.
Let me dial:
One . . . two . . . three, here I come.
What a wonder modern time is.
You don't even have to be bothered
by doing it for real.
It's safe, they say.
Sure, baby, it's safe,
but unreal!
A new dimension is here to stay.
We don't need any longer to touch each other.
That's why we invented the telephone.
Communication.
Connection.
Where is love gone?
In the telephone.

Vittorio Maria Arimondi

FATE

My eyes slide from side to side
Like windshield wipers in the rain
My brain is like a vacuum
My heart is like a sponge

Soaking up the pain I feel till my emotions all run dry
I wonder why I love, I breathe, I wonder who I am

My thoughts are connected like freight cars on a railroad train
One long chain of memories that show where I've been

As to where I'm going, there's no way of knowing
If I'm headed in the right direction
Introspection
Seems to fill my days

But, it's too late for me to stop
For if I flop
I'll know I've done my very best
the rest
is up to fate.

Nicholas Sarro

THE DANCE OF THE SNOWFLAKES

'Tis late afternoon of a winter day,
The skies are promising snow, so they say . . .
        They come, one by one,
        Like blossoms they drop
A mantle of ermine from field to treetop;
Softly and slowly with fairylike grace
Glide daintily earthward tiny snowflakes;
        Faster and faster
        In gay ecstasy,
They dance to the north wind's wild fantasy;
The militant maestro's tempo is set
To the mad speed of a dream minuet;
        The revelry lasts
        'Til the dawn of day
When all the dancers drift slowly away;
The snowflakes have finished, their dance
        is o'er,
They've left white bouquets on the ballroom
        floor.

Dorothy M. Cahoon

MILADY'S BEAUTY NEEDS

Vanity Mirror: Humility brings the faults to
                view and reflects the heart
                condition true;

Finest Rouge: Modesty's blush is a tint to
                show the brightness of true
                virtue's glow;

Lipstick: Cheerfulness is the perfect
            shade of color that will never
            fade;

Beauty Cream: Good-humor is the perfect base
                To spread youth's charm upon
                the face;

Wrinkle Cream: Contentment is the magic way to
                smooth the aging lines away;

Eye Drops: Compassionate tears lend
            sparkle and shine to give the
            eyes a look divine.

Dorothy M. Cahoon

AD INFINITUM

A glimpse of yesterday
Is but a dream of tomorrow.
Happy times long gone
Sometimes remembered in a song,
Or the rustle of leaves,
Or in the breeze gently blowing.
Today becomes yesterday and
Tomorrow becomes today.
In the swirl of the world
Life travels on and on,
Until caught in the time called tomorrow.
The mind and body gone,
The soul travels on,
                to worlds unknown.

Patsy Greenway

THANK YOU!

Thank you for being there when the going got tough;
for smoothing out the times that seemed to be rough.

Thank you for being there to return my smile;
for making those challenging times so very worthwhile.

Thank you for being there to share my dreams;
for making me believe them, as crazy as they seemed.

Thank you for being there to share your advice;
for answering my questions without thinking twice.

Thank you for being there to show me the way;
for leading me past the pain to a brighter day.

Thank you for being there to laugh and have fun;
for talking of love and friendship; for treating me as one.

Thank you for "being there," whatever you do;
for being my friend . . . I thank you!

Tamara Stepan

HEAVENLY WONDER

As I lie in the grass and stare at the sky,
I look to the heavens, wondering when I'll die.

Don't be scared, I say, for it won't be all bad,
Wipe away those tears, and don't look so sad.

So I listened to myself, and lifting my head,
I began to wonder why it's dying I dread.

It will be peaceful and quiet "they" say,
but it's hard to think of it as being that way.

I know when I get "there," I'll be able to see,
that it isn't as bad as I thought it would be.

I'll be able to rest, and to think of my past,
watching the people below trying to make life last.

And as I'm peering down from that heavenly sky,
I will see the little girls with tears in their eyes.

The fear I once had I will recognize,
and I'll reach down and wipe the tears from their eyes.

Tamara Stepan

COME DOWN OFF THAT CLOUD

Hey, you wih your nose up in the air
Remember, you weren't always there
Since you acquired fame and money
You think you're sweeter than honey
For crying out loud
Come down off that cloud. Come down off that cloud

I cannot ignore what I see
And I plainly see you're conceited as can be
This is one fantasy you should definitely omit
Please, I wish you would snap out of it
For crying out loud
Come down off that cloud. Come down off that cloud

Get off your high horse and stop being rude
You must dispel this uppity attitude
Seriously, you're just fooling yourself
Because Honey, you are no better than anybody else
For crying out loud
Come down off that cloud. Come down off that cloud

Albert Humphries

EVERY DAY

Every day the sun rises and shines on most of the world, radiating
the cold spots, illuminating the darkness and evaporating the
waters, which produces clouds, which produces rainfalls, which
nourishes mother earth and her inhabitants.

Every day millions of Americans wake up, sit up, get up and
do push-ups, wash up, dress up, eat and drink up and
then dash out of their homes in an attempt to catch up and
keep up with a fast-pace, mixed-up and messed-up society.

Every day is somebody's birthday
Every day hundreds of thousands of babies are born
Every day hundreds of thousands of human lives are terminated
These terminations are caused by various reasons. Such as:
Drug abuse, starvation, droughts, diseases, wars, old age,
capital punishments, accidents, homicides, suicides and genocides.

Every day has its own unique course of action, its own positive
and negative aspects, its own headline, its own challenges and
its own destiny.

Despite whatever
Every day is a miracle.

Albert Humphries

THAT GOOD OLE SWEET LOVE

We were sitting in the backyard swing
Suddenly she started to sing
I placed on her face a soft and tender kiss
She sang about love and it went like this:

"What can more or less
produce tears of happiness
and at the same time be
capable of turning the situation around
I mean from one extreme to the other
Creating hostility toward one another
What is this force? The answer of course
is good ole sweet love
That good ole sweet love.

What can compel one to compete?
What can make life virtually complete?
What can stimulate the heart in countless ways?
Many different sensations for many different days?
What can make one mad, glad or sad?
What is it, that everybody wishes they had?
What is this force? The answer of course
is good ole sweet love. That good ole sweet love."

Albert Humphries

ALBERT LESTER HUMPHRIES. Born: Oglethorpe, Georgia, 12-28-47, reared in Columbus, Georgia; Divorced; Education: Queens College, New York City, 1968-70; Occupations: Freelance poet, Songwriter, Lyricist; Membership: Poets and Writers, Inc., New York City; Awards: Merit Award, Talent Association, Boston, 1983; Certificate of Achievement, New York Amateur/Professional Song Jubilee, 1984; The Harmonious Award, New York Amateur/Professional Song Jubilee, 1985; Certificate of Election, *Who's Who in the East,* 1986; Certificate of Inclusion, *International Who's Who In Music,* 1987; Certificate of Recognition, *Who's Who In Emerging Leaders of America;* Poetry: 'I'm Hungry For Your Love,' *Lyricists & Composers, Vol. IV,* 1984; 'Just Keep On Living,' *American Poetry Anthology,* 1986; 'Life Goes On,' *Best New Poets of 1986,* American Poetry Association, 1987; 'Nobody's Perfect,' 1987; 'Home,' *Cambridge Collection,* 1987; Themes: *Regardless of their social or physical status, I struggle to relate and communicate with all the people. In my writings I attempt to record and depict clearly my sincere and innermost thoughts. I feel that I have a lot to offer by harmoniously sharing my personal experiences as well as my personal opinion on the philosophical aspects of life and love.*

I LOVE BIRDS

I love birds.
When they come,
They always bring with them clinking songs.
When they stand beside me,
They are brave as soldiers,
Meek as lambs,
And lovely as flowers.
A photographer can't capture their delicate souls.
A painter can't depict their energetic strength.
Only the eyes of our minds can appreciate their perpetual beauty.

Li-Chung Wang

GIFT OF LOVE

So many dreams were shattered, 'twas more than I could bear,
    Struggling to carry on, there seemed no one to share.
Left alone to travel roads I could no longer care;
    Somewhere between the tragedies I lost my will to pray
God knew the need and sent a gift of love to me this day.

My empty arms cried out each day for someone dear to hold,
    My heavy heart was lonely when nights were dark and cold.
You promise now to stand by me until we both grow old;
    You brought to me a rainbow to brighten skies of gray
A very special gift of love God sent to me this day.

Thunderbolts and lightning made my body shake with fear,
    Many times the sadness brought an unexpected tear.
You promise now for years to come to always hold me near;
    You show me morning sunshine, make my heart feel young and gay
A very special gift of love God sent to me this day.

You've eased my pain and sorrow, I no longer dread the night,
    Looking forward to each morrow, you'll make everything all right.
We'll share and nurture new-found love, hold precious throughout life;
    I shall return this treasure in my most loving way
And thank God for this gift of love He sent to me this day.

Carol J. Riley

A SECOND CHANCE

God made of me a mother, the gift of love was great.
    I did the very best I could, oft times I made mistakes.
Many things we didn't do, I always thought we would;
    And now that she is all grown up, I feared we never could.
God knew I had to make amends, I loved my baby so,
    He said to me, "A second chance I've given you, you know.
Take time to answer questions, hundreds, even more;
    Teach her to plant flowers, you don't have to sweep the floor.
Sing her songs, play some games, help her ride a bike;
    Count her toes, tweak her nose, do silly things she likes.
Bake cookies in the kitchen, never mind the mess.
    All those things you didn't do before, but then I guess
You thought you were too busy, work had to be done,
    Never getting finished, no time left for fun.
Cooking, cleaning, shopping, laundry twice a week;
    Hardly time to listen whenever baby speaks."
I'm older, so much wiser now, I know how short the time
    To love, share, enjoy and teach this lovely baby mine,
God calls this baby grandchild, just as she's meant to be.
    She's quite like mom and daddy, and some like gramps and me.

Carol J. Riley

EASTER DAY

*"I am the resurrection and the life;
he that believeth in me, though he were dead,
yet shall he live." John 11:25*

When the redbud blooms, and the dogwood blossoms
out in white,
And the mockingbirds sing praises till the coming
of the night,
Then we know without a calendar, by their happy tune,
That Easter day, when Christ arose, will be coming
very soon,
And as spring's new life conquers over winter's
icy death,
We praise God for an eternity by every thankful
breath.

Curtis Nunn

267

TO TEACH US LOVE

To Troy our tiny miracle, God sent us from above
To be your family here on earth and teach us all to love.
    From infanthood you grew till you had just become of age
And fate determined time was right for you to go away.
    You left behind a seedling to grow to be a man
Entrusted us to cultivate since you no longer can.
    Your dearest only sister loves him as her own
Understanding devastation of being left alone.
    Your father teaches discipline, with firm and loving hand
I will teach him gentleness as only mothers can.
    Your elder brother wishes to provide for him a home
And raise him as he would a son, he has none of his own.
    We cannot fill the space for him, no matter how we try
His budding mind can't comprehend just what it means to die.
    He's angry 'cause you left him as a toy upon a shelf
He wanted to go with you, he told me so himself.
    God taught us all how very precious is a love to share
And we'll love one another, till God bids us join you there.

Carol J. Riley

WHY DO I LOVE HER?

Sonnett . . . To Eilene

Someone asked me today, "Why do you love her so?"
For the first time I thought, and wondered at the why.
Why do I stop breathing, whenever I see her go?
And when my breath returns, why comes it as a sigh?

I love the rhythm of her body as she walks,
The poise with which she meets whatever comes her way,
The music of her voice, whenever I hear her talk,
The honesty of purpose, she shows every day.

Ah yes, I love her laugh, it comes first to her eyes,
I love her gentleness, her love of flowers and life,
And her laughter, teases me, haunts me and taunts me,
  I love her understanding nature, that soothes my strife.

Like a benediction, this thought I clearly see,
I love her, yes I love her, for she first loved me!

Joseph H. Avellone

IN MY NEXT LIFE

Climbing through meadows of wild flowers,
Smells anew,
Reaching for the highest peak, when I saw you,
Bent on an ancient walking stick.
I passed you, knowing we'd meet again,
Continuing my journey of the internal continuity
Of becoming . . .
Higher and higher, on familiar paths,
Never touched,
Until the peak was under my skin.
Now, my hand outstretched, to help you up,
And hold you in the gentle breeze.
Viewing all God's acres, we knew,
Self realization had become
A part.
It was comfortable,
It was O.K. . . .
In my next life.

Dale Cowan

ON THE FLOOR

I stood on my head.
My cigarettes slid to the floor
Scattered and directionless
Like careless puffs of days.
But . . . but . . . no butts,
I dragged my fingers
Through the carpet fibers —
The weeds bending, breaking
Spilling cured grade A.
Sticking at random from my fist,
I dropped them in an ash can . . .
    Numbered days like a 20 per pack
    With so many draws to cheat you.

I find you on the floor
Sprawled and aimed at me —
An intense seductive beam.
You're bending, responding
Under my careful fingers
    And I know
    I need you.

R. Fain

YO' MAN

    Gonna take on out my great big ax.
Gonna chop me down some trees,
Take some shoestring an' lasso the world —
Gonna ride it where I please.

    Gonna suck some wind into my lungs
An' blow out a hurricane.
Gonna skin my knee on mountaintops,
Might bump my head on a plane.

Baby it's you I love, yeh it's you,
Tellin' it straight as I can,
Tell it to the sisters with they hats on too,
You my woman — I yo' man.

    Wanna snatch me up some clouds in my hand.
Gonna stick some in my ears.
Gonna watch some folks run around awhile —
Try to look back on some years.

    Gonna take you out come Saturday night,
Takin' you home when we're done.
Gonna love you baby with all my might,
I rise with the moon and the sun.

R. Fain

SHE IS SO DEPENDABLE

She is so dependable and trustworthy
That whenever I have questions,
I always come to her.
She never complains
And never avoids the trouble.
Her words like music from heaven
Suddenly disperse all the mysterious fog out of my mind —
Clear pictures take its place one after another.
She is like a magnet,
And I am like a nail:
When I get lost,
I know where I have to go.

Li-Chung Wang

A LIFE

A great gift that God gave me
Was a life different than thee.

The prisons are full of people like me,
That come from homes where good is hard to see.

Full of violence, the children were abused.
I was the lost sheep that God did choose.

He loved me so, he showed me the way,
Through all my difficult days.

God taught me to see, so that I can rise,
He'll be there, when I start my enterprise.

Someday I will die and the pain that I have felt,
Will all be gone because God will make it melt.

I'd like to be known for the good I've done,
The people I loved, and surely have won.

Thank you dear God, for putting me here,
Especially with the ones who were very dear.

Florence Tarolli

MY GRANDDAUGHTER

My granddaughter is so beautiful to me,
She brightens up my life like the sun on the sea.

Grandchildren, to grandmothers, are born without thorns.
They're there to love and keep our hearts warm.

Some people think that grandchildren make you feel old,
My Pamela, she makes me feel like I was gold.

I'm not saying she does everything right,
She's the one who brightens up my life.

I thank the Lord for letting me see,
The first part of my generation three.

Florence Tarolli

COVERED WITH
A BLANKET OF SNOW

We came from beyond a mountain, all covered with a
blanket of snow.
The clouds were like pillows, looking so high and soft
as they moved very slow.
The world looked different from beyond the mountain,
was it because we were there so long, or was it the blanket of snow
that made us blind, you know God only knows.
We looked to the land, we looked to the sky, we looked at each
other and almost cried.
We came from beyond a mountain, all covered with a
blanket of snow.
What made us different? What made us leave? For the destiny that lies
ahead of us is long behind us for we came from beyond a mountain,
and time has moved away, so we'll go back and stay covered with a
blanket of snow and still love the nights away.
I guess that's how we'll stay.

Wanda Leona Bell

LITTLE BY LITTLE AND WAS BY WAS

Little by little and was by was
He dreamt his dids and did his days
As dying had designed.

Sooner by sorry and later by sad
He sat the dance and chose to watch
As living took its leave.

More by minus and maybe by not
He wisht his will and went its gone
As sleeping settled in.

James Conti

TWO SHIPS

I was once like a lost ship upon stormy seas.
I became weary from battling a continual storm.
My sails were worn, tattered and torn.

It was like the dark before the dawn.
Like the tides of the ocean,
Constantly, I was in motion.

Our courses crossed and you extended hope.
You reached out with a lifeline and rescued me,
So strong, so gentle and your faith never wavering.

Thanks to you, I've found calm waters.
I'm in control from stem to stern
Because, of the ''Gail'' force who
Blew new life into my sails.

There are many new voyages left for my taking.
With faith as my compass and courage as my map
I will continue to sail; exploring and discovering.

The storm has passed me by and my course is set anew.
It will be clear smooth sailing from now on.

Never to be lost and now mended not worn,
No longer tattered and torn . . .

Marla Bearden

FOR ALL TIME

Perhaps, together in a past life, we have been.
One in which we had no chance to win.
Destiny has played a very important part
By once again granting us a new start.

In our hands A Gift Of A Greater Love has been placed.
Soulmates . . .
It's now left to us to determine the true fate.
A new beginning of which so many long and so few know.
A chance to discover the essence of an eternal pair in
Continual flow.

If the timing is wrong shed not a tear and let go of fear.
For joy and sorrow must be allowed to go hand in hand as one.
Always remember to hold onto faith even if we must separate.

No matter what, believe in your heart:
Together in eternal time we shall always reunite.

Our hearts beating as one
Never losing sight of the other one
Two souls not like one, but one —

Soulmates — Together — In all time . . .

Marla Bearden

Gray's Peak.

SIMPLY ME

For three decades, plus six, I've been around.
Like a fine wine, I become better with time
And at times can be quite profound.

I've sailed the various seas of life
And with great pleasure I've discovered
A very unique, timeless treasure.

Simply Me! A true free spirit,
Mixed with a wave of domestication,
Splashed with a touch of sophistication
And colored with many subtle distinctions.

A "homebody" I'm content to be, because
Of the writer who dwells within me.
Yet at times, I love to take new voyages,
Exploring new places and discovering new faces.

Only if I choose to be alone will I ever be alone.
Never to know loneliness which is one of the
Reasons for my emerging into my own seasons.

Thanks to the single life I've become
An independent lady of the eighties
And finally I've found —

Simply Me . .

Marla Bearden

GO FORWARD

Go forward and take off her veil,
I want to see her pretty face.
Clouds! Make way!
Let sunshine color the world
And light our minds.
Maybe there is violent clashing under the ground,
Maybe there is tremendous heat to release.
No matter how catastrophic the change will be,
Everything will fall on its solid basis.

Li-Chung Wang

LI-CHUNG WANG. Born: Taiwan, Republic of China, 10-27-50; Education: National Taiwan University, M.S., Mathematics, 1977; Comments: *All three of my poems are selected from my booklet* The Chinese Philosophy, Art, Life and Mathematics, *to appear in September, 1987. 'I Love Birds' illustrates that the pleasure of art comes from our direct and studious participation in it. In 'Go Forward,' the author indicates that an artist should be mission-oriented, especially if he discovers the need for change while the work of art develops. He should not hesitate to do his job even if it is frightening, frustrating, or extensively involved because any part of his work will be justly paid off some day.*

MY ONLY LOVE

Please! Tell my heart your feelings for me
There's already so much I don't understand.
Am I asking more than you feel for me
Did I miss the touch when you squeezed my hand?

This is not the first time my heart's been a fool
No longer does my heart have self-pride.
My heart is not ashamed of loving you
For too long my heart has tried to hide.

Did I misread the sparkle in your eye
When face to face our eyes would meet?
Did I misunderstand, no words good-bye
That someday you will still come back to me?

Through the tears, has my heart failed to see
The real reason you left?
Tell my heart this couldn't be
has my heart gambled and lost the bet?

Please! Don't put my heart on hold
Has this love in my heart been in vain?
Please! Tell this heart that's aching so
What is in store, even if the truth is pain.

Pat Whitaker Nichols

FLIGHT

What might have been Nature's loveliest sonata
Is a plaintive inaudible chirp,
A heartfelt plea from an appetite
Which yearns not for food.
What might have been graceful, incomparable flight
To previously unattained heights
Is reduced to frenzied futile wingbeats
Within cruel confines.
The finest specimen of its avian race
Is merely a household adornment, disregarded,
Insignificant.

Marina Rubio

FACES, NOT HEARTS

I see faces
    not hearts
You are images, reflections
    not realities.

You don't realize —
    you are a mirror.
You reveal the secret:
    Mankind is one composite person.

I am not Mankind.
    I think. I reason. I react.
I am different,
    I do these things without worrying about judgments.

You are Mankind.
You are faces, not hearts.

Your only distinction is
    your eyes
    your hair
    your clothes

You are faces, not hearts.

Christine Rossberg

PROVERBS OF A
CLOSET PROPHET

Graffiti

I cried the day I found out the wise man was
just a bastard magician.

The circles remain open, forever broken.

Honesty is too much for the human race.
It invokes too much fear.

Lamb's blood, drink deep.

The contented man says life is a mystery.
The poor man says life is a joke.

It is your Savior, it is your Nemesis.
It is the Truth.

Am I the freak in a circus of clowns?
Or the clown in a circus of freaks?

Life is the shadow of Reality.
Death is the release of Reality.

Litanies in the night,
fool's breath.
No guard against the Dark.
Offerings in the light,
fool's game.
No surety for the 'morrow.

Dave Wheaton

Drawn to her —
as my eye to forsythia
          springing yellowburst
(her favorite color) —
I am.

Eric Barker

DREAMSONG, HEARTSONG

We are two birds, soaring high and looking down
at the rest of the world.
Happy and content with the knowledge of the freedom
our flight brings.
The wind and air rushing past our faces and the sun
burning our backs, ecstatic that we are what we are.
And not wondering or longing for anything more.
We are two wild horses, strong and beautiful.
We race across the prairie,
our lungs burning with the exertion and choking on the dust.
Our hearts pounding and our legs pushing until it
sounds like thunder echoing through our brains.
But this is what we are.
And we are now truly free.
Without love, freedom only traps you into being alone.
And love gives you the freedom to be what you
want to be, and the power to be what you can be.
And we will always be young and fresh,
and we will live forever.

Dave Wheaton

A QUESTION AFTER
MOMENTS OF LAUGHTER

Where does laughter go
  As it echoes in the air,
  When we gather with our loved ones
  And free ourselves from care,
  As we while away some happy hour
  And our warmth of spirit share?
Tell me, friend, if you can:
  Just where *does* laughter go
  When it echoes in the air . . .?

Richard Alan Rieger

AN OPEN BOOK

Each man is God's creation
          Destined to be
          His own unfolding.
Like the petals of a flower
          The years drop one by one —
          Expanding, enhancing, destroying.
The choice lies within the soul.

Either beauty grows or rot corrodes
          Until man faces the end result —
          The evidence of his life
          An open book before his God.

Catherine Ray

HUNG

"It" —
  Knots the emotions,
  Smothers tolerance —
  Chokes out intimacy,
  Only —
  To abandon its victim to die,
  Inwardly alone —
  From the squeezing noose of,
  Rancid — ridicule.
                    "Rejection"

Venus Peek

WHO CALLS?

Is it the wind that calls to me
          And makes the forest seem to be
                    A magic land of mystery?

Pale moonbeams dance in wraithlike clouds,
          The tall pines sway in leafy shrouds,
                    Deep black shadow the valley crowds.

A startled deer breaks through the brush,
          "Who, who," an owl hoots from a bush,
                    Faint, far-off sounds the silence touch.

Listen! Murmuring waterfalls
          Echo through the murky forest halls.
                    I wonder, "Is it God Who calls?"

Catherine Ray

SILENCE

Let the silence speak to you —
    The soft murmur of the breeze.
    Distant t-whir-r-t-whir-r of a bird.
    Rustle of falling leaves.
Nature caresses you and speaks
    Of our Creator's love.

God, I pray you —
    Cleanse my soul of selfishness
    That would deny the need of others.
    That would consider my own imperatives
        Above the directives
        Of Your Son,
            Whose love did not ask,
            But gave to every task
            The unconditional measure . . .

Catherine Ray

OF REDEMPTION

From the beginning,
I have known you.
For the sake of a woman,
You gave up your life.
And the years have gone by since you last said:
I have pleasure in them.
Still your heart is hardened;
And, you shall have none of My reproof.
For man is the key to his destiny;
And, his worst enemy.
From the beginning,
You were rebellious.
And your Fathers, have taught you nothing.
They were even worse than *You.*
Give Ear, that you may learn,
And your Fathers need not bear their shame;
That it may go well, for *You.*
               Amen

Robert K. Walcott

OF ENDURANCE

And many nations, have come and gone.
And surely All have ruled.
And the wisdom of the few,
Is surely trampled, by the Fool.
And who can say look, see, this is new.
For your Fathers before them,
Also thought it was new.
And their Fathers before them,
Thought that things to come for *You,* were new.
"Therefore I say to you,
Do not worry" of things that are new.
For there is one who endures;
Before the dawn, and after the rain.
And it shall never be said of him,
Look, see, this is new.
             Amen

Robert K. Walcott

OF VANITY

I looked into my Vanity.
And I said;
"I shall be rich."
For what is Freedom,
If not Wealth?
And a fool and his money,
Shall soon be parted.
For what is Wealth,
Without Wisdom?
But, Man is vain;
And, secure in his finances.
And when his calamity comes,
And his wealth is gone.
He, who is without Understanding,
Stands naked and bare.
And the Truth,
Is overwhelming to him.
So he perishes,
Confused and lost;
And, is no longer remembered.
             Amen

Robert K. Walcott

CAN YOU?

Can you?
    Knit me close with a lovely loose stitch?
    Keep me in sight without watching each mole?
    Hear not words but the meaning I speak?
    See my differences, yet of me approve?

Can you?
    Hear my heart cry even tho' I should laugh?
    Answer questions I dare never ask?
    Share with me, silent conversation?
    And find the real me behind every mask?

Can you?
    Love me the best when I am my worst?
    Believe I succeed tho' failure you see?
    Believe in my dreams while I pretend?
    Join in my songs tho' I sing them off key?

Can you?
    How grateful I'll be
    For a friend like thee;
    And a friend like thee
    I desire to be.

Caroline Janz

REMEMBRANCES

The jumprope thwacks the sidewalk
And rhythms of childhood, darting and dancing,
Lift me up and take me
To the world of once-was that I thought was gone forever.
The songs float in through the window
With the warm glow
Of a sunlit trip on a forever day.
Not Mary and Ellen, or Suzy and Jane,
Now it's Kelly and Brigitte, Sofana and Tanya,
Their names sing out to me of places
My heart has known forever.
Flesh may be anchored inside the little box I live in
But my soul is riding high
Soaring and dipping as the spirit moves me
Along with my girls;
    And I sing!

Sandra Fox

. . . and now with cares arrested, much like small children safely tucked in for the night, I am able to sit quietly and think of nothing but what is here before me. The trees and the grass, the stars and the sky, and of memories of those who have brought smiles to my face. Be they real or imaginary, the pleasant are all I need now and all I shall entertain here in my moment of solitude and serenity. With God's hand on my shoulder we both can breathe easy and smile and rest until morning, when the cares like small children will awaken, and demand my attention once more, and I, like the most loving of mothers will attend to them to the best of my ability, all the while remembering this very moment of quiet restfulness, and knowing full and well that there will again be a time when they sleep, and my thoughts are my own . . .

Barbara R. Duva

HE ANSWERED MY PRAYERS

For the most wonderful husband in the world, Bob AcMoody, Sr.

With his head upon my pillow, as he lies here next to me,
Brings a warm flood of love and devotion that only God can see,
The prayers I said so long ago were answered one hundred fold,
I prayed for God to send me someone to be at my side, till we grew old.
The younger years were exciting, filled with love, passion, hard work and faith,
And four beautiful children, all because of this wonderful mate.
So many years have now slipped by, and our golden years are here, but deep in my heart, I feel such calm, I have no doubts, I have no fears.
As before my prayers were answered, I'm sure He hears me still.
I'll pray we'll be together in the world that has no end, for the man who lies beside me is the best that's ever been.
He's truly God's intention of what a husband and father should be.
And to think God's love was so great He gave this man to me.

Connie AcMoody

A FLOWER FOR A FRIEND

He sat by himself in an old rocking chair,
Near the mist-covered swamp where he lived.
On into the night, he sat and listened,
Awaiting his only friend.

His friend was there when the breezes brought,
The skeleton trees to life.
It cooled the marshes and stirred the mist,
As it started its chilly rounds.

He would talk to the wind, hour after hour,
Though it could not answer back.
He'd laugh and rock in his old squeaky chair,
He'd confide in his only friend.

But then the day came when the chair didn't rock.
The old man couldn't talk or laugh.
And upon his chair lay a single flower,
That was placed there by the wind.

Linda Fowler

FOR THE LOVE OF JAMIE

The face of an angel is the first thing I see.
Her tarnished little halo is overshadowed
By the sparkle of her smiles.
My firstborn child, my beautiful Jamie.
Maddening and alarming, friendly and charming,
One look in those eyes softens the hardest of hearts.
Bundle of energy, sweet ball of fire,
She can make me so angry but never ashamed.
Nothing she will ever do, can make me love her less.
When she's tickled her laughter rings like a bell.
She's not only ticklish,
But smart as a whip as well.
Of course these are my opinions,
You can probably tell.
Just look into your baby's innocent eyes,
And you'll feel these feelings as well.
She does have her faults, can't be good all the time.
But when I think of the love,
One little hug can bring,
For the love of Jamie I would do anything.

Linda Fowler

LINDA LOUISE FOWLER. Born: Fairfield, California; Married: Roger Fowler, 6-29-80; Occupation: Professional Dog Groomer for 8 years; Membership: Sacramento Aquarium Society; Award: $25 gift certificate for 'A Flower For A Friend,' 1976, when I was a Junior in high school; Poetry: 'The Buck'; Other Writings: *Count With The Animals*, counting rhyming book; ''Only The Innocent,'' short story; ''Bathtub Toys,'' article; ''The Dog That Barked Up A Storm,'' children's story; Comments: *I hope people enjoy reading my work as much as I enjoyed writing it. I dedicate all my writings to my family.*

EMOTION

I see my dreams crawl behind the reality of everyday living,
and every evening, I watch my rainbow fade from the sky —
Is it really wrong to be enslaved to feeling?
That's a question you put in my mind.

You think I'm foolish to open up myself
to the possibility of hurt by loving you,
But isn't it also wrong to close my heart and mind to you
In anticipation of the pain you may put me through?

If you stood silent, forced to watch your whole world crumble
I could never tell you that it's wrong to cry;
If you carried a heavy load and stumbled
and I met you on the street
I could never find it in my heart to walk on by —
Don't condemn me for these things I feel inside
If they frighten you, turn and run into the night

Because I am enslaved to emotion
too strong to be overshadowed

by any definition of wrong or right . . .

Katherine Spence

ONE SMALL CHANCE

What is this tiny miracle about to unfold?
It lies dormant, eyes closed — a body scarcely formed,
but with a mind vibrant and alive.
It hungers, taking nourishment from your body —
life from your life,
and one day will seek knowledge from your wisdom,
power from your strength,
and conscience from your convictions.

What is this apprehension, this uncertainty you feel?
Is it the threat of nuclear war, the rising cost of living,
the bleakness of the future?
Could it be the lack of honesty, corruption,
the rising rate of crime —
or perhaps the total loss of faith in mankind
that stops you dead in your tracks and makes you shudder
at the thought
of one so small, so innocent . . . one so trusting.

And what name will you call it by?
Conceivably, it could be "Faith" or "Hope"
because you have given this undeserving world something special —
ten tiny fingers to become two strong hands.
Like the hands of our fathers before us,
they will shape the future when you and I are gone.

You have given the world "one small chance"

one last hope for change . . .

Katherine Spence

REFLECTIONS

Feeling older today than yesterday
and looking back on days gone by,
It's easy to dream of a happier time
when love was "today"
and tomorrow never came.

But the sun steals softly through the window
to awaken me once more, and I rise to the same routine
like I've done so many times before;
But my mind slips back to days now past
when the summers seemed forever
and the hands of time didn't move so fast,
and I believed in my heart that my fate was my own —

Now, the cherub face and the tiny mind
have both developed and grown with time,
And the innocent trust that I placed in love
and the faith that I held in the spoken word
are gone —

I woke up this morning all alone

and I'm wondering why

I had to wake up at all . .

Katherine Spence

TWENTIETH CENTURY HABITAT

I wade on concrete streams
through wooded cities
where timbers scrape the sky.

Through synthetic leather
heat rises between my toes.
Sweat and dust is the mud that oozes
where no garden grows.

Denizens of my habitat
are chrome and diesel
chameleons in the smog.

Pungent fumes of flowers
are petroleum residues of silk.

Night masquerades in neon shades
and sunsets hide their glow.
Electric constellations
are the only stars I know.

Stephanie Conder

FRIENDS

You are my friend
Walk with me
Take my hand
Shelter me
When the sun hides its face in the clouds
And the rain spits its water at my feet
Hold me close

Hear my laughter
Feel my pain
Share my bread
Help me understand and forgive
Lashing, unleashed tongues

Feel my loneliness
When many seasons take their share of my life
Remind me of the joys of yesterday and the sorrows
Which helped me grow and live

You are my friend
And I am yours
This is God's gift which we share

Mabel Cummings Douglass

WATER-LADY

She rises in the sea, she sets in the sea
and she makes love under cliffs that overshadow the moon.
When the tide reaches certain heights, she loses all her balance
within — a natural turbulence through mind and spirit.

As the gentlest of waves wake and touch her supreme body curves,
she drifts unto ecstasy, nearing heaven — then the lady trickles
back down
Through all mysterious pain and ecstatic highs and lows, she always
clutches on to love: whether it is human, oceanic creatures or the
sea itself with its waves of basic fluidity and stimulation . . .

Bryant Fox Ostrander

FACES IN THE SUNSHINE

Faces reflect in ocean water
some are squinted and wrinkled
others are either hard or soft
still the sun shines

The eyes of many, can never hide
their deceiving eyes and those who have been lost
ignore ones of beauty and the thoughtful one
still the sun shines

The insides of many control their faces
by peering into others; leaning over beds
to capture a reflection of their own face
thus, keeping tears to flow along sunlit trees
still the sun shines

On dark nights and nights filled; faces of many
come to gaze in wonder like lost sheep; this is
a face of illusion, for they have never awakened to
entirely feel and live out the truth of the sun
on the next day, the shining of the sun shone

Faces came, faces left and all were waking with
smiles of sparkle; now, when a facial reflection was seen
there were no more tears within mirrors, ocean water and
most importantly throughout themselves: just happiness
still the faces within the sun, shine.

Bryant Fox Ostrander

STATISTICAL ETIQUETTE

No formal economic introductions are necessary
when a man's possessions and home are a bundle he must carry.

One homeless and one suburbanite were visually to meet
as he appeared in window view while walking down my postcard street.

The contrast between those who have
   and those who have not, hit me hard
with each category being represented in my front yard.

Statistics would then usher us to differing income strata
to wait while people are converted to numerical data.

From poorest to above average, our annual earnings range
Putting distance between us —
   making pleasantries hard to exchange.

To understand what separates those four categories apart
excuse yourself from the company of the bar graph and pie chart.

Poverty, affluence, pain, comfort: are four faces of social fact
when properly acquainted to numbers by the host leave impact.

Joan Flom

THE PREPOSITIONAL CRAZE

Some parts of the English language,
are impossible to teach.
Like the use of prepositions,
in formulating proper speech.

Now a correctly speaking person,
would surely rise above,
the use of certain phrases like:
"What are you thinking . . . *of* . . .?"

But some would look at a question like:
"Where did you get that . . . *at* . . .?"
And scratch their heads as they said to me,
"Dare ain't noth'un wrong wid dat!"

Still, others will look at this poem,
and claim that they always knew,
that there was impropriety in saying:
"Where are you going . . . *to* . . .?"

Of course, some will never understand.
They're illiterate, not really dumb.
They'll just wonder, as they read this poem:
"Where'd he get this idea . . . *from* . . .?"

John Wren

MOTHER'S DAY REFLECTIONS

I so often hear my friends complain,
that their mothers are a pain.
I think of reasons for me to complain,
when I realize with my mother I have so much to gain.
When I am hurt, she feels my pain.
She speaks with wisdom and tact
and I often wish I had that knack.
She breathes life into a room with her presence,
and brightens it with her laughter.
She has given me so many special memories,
that I will remember forever after.
When I offer her the sky,
she tells me that she is happy with the land.
When I tell her I would give her the world,
all she asks for is my hand.
When I place my hand in hers,
I feel warm and secure.
After all these years, of one thing I am sure,
I will love her still,
when the memory of my life is obscure.

Margaret E. Stevens

THE LIFE OF INDIFFERENCE

It grieves me to look and see
The indifference that sinners have for Thee.

In their ignorance, fear and pride,
They don't know why you suffered and died.

My only prayer for them is this,
That they no longer live in risk:

And find out one glorious day,
That You're truly the Life, the Truth and the Way.

Josceleyn Arielda González

MOTHER'S DAY IS EVERY DAY

It seems that the flow of life, is a rapidly moving stream,
and when we get caught up in it, we hardly have time to dream,
or even the time to rest, or time to relax and play,
or hardly enough time to take the time,
to be thoughtful enough to say:
"I love you . . . but . . . I do . . ."

I'm always thinking of you, but that, you surely must know.
For you are truly a part of me, the part that makes me glow;
the part that's full of happiness, and joy that others can see.
And maybe those feelings come from the phrase,
That you're always repeating to me:
"I love you . . . my son . . . I do."

So let me take this opportunity, to take the time to say,
that I love you, my dear sweet mother, and not just on Mother's Day.
I love you in everything that you do, on every day of the year;
and maybe by sending this message to you,
it will always be perfectly clear,
That I love you . . . my mother, I do.

John Wren

JOHN ANSLEY WREN. Born: Gastonia, North Carolina, 12-18-48; Married: Brenda Kalevas Wren, 4-16-81; Education: University of South Carolina, B.S., 1973; Occupation: Real estate developer; Awards: Member of Quill & Scroll, a national honorary society for talented journalists (high school 1967, 1968); Poetry: 'The Tranquil Sea,' 1985; 'Of Marriage and Love,' 'So Near, Yet So Far Away,' 'Pearl of Great Price,' 'Building Character,' 1986; Comments: *At the age of 35, I wrote my first poem, 'Staying Busy With Nothing To Do,' and discovered a wonderful way of expressing myself about things that come to my attention in going through the daily routine of life.*

DREAM TO REALITY

I dream the sea,
Flows past my feet —
Fish swimming among the coral reef,
Like dried leaves in the trees.
The sand shifts fast,
No meaning of time.
The dolphin swims,
The tiger runs.
The volcano erupts,
While the water freezes.

I awake to find,
The ground is frozen.
The water flows,
As the wind blows.
The horse runs,
The dog walks.
The sun comes,
The clouds roll in.
Flowers bloom,
And the bird sings.

Pat Moneybrake

MOUNTAIN WALK

Come, take my hand and walk with me
    thru the mountain greenery.
See the flowers so bright and gay
    nod their heads — as if to say,
"Enjoy our world; it's friendly here;
    there is not a thing to fear."
Look! See the chipmunk scamper by
    and disappear with the blink of an eye.
Sssh, listen to birds high in the trees
    sing to the sigh of a wandering breeze
    that touches your cheek with a gentle caress,
    so soft and so tender — it seems to bless —
    the mountainside from whence it came and
    dance away like a leaping flame.

Take a moment to stop and a second to care,
    and Thank God He gave you the right to share
    His work in the trees, so stately and tall,
    and creatures soft and friendly and small —
    that call this home, this mountain greenery,
    All part of God's triumphant scenery.

Nancy L. Johnson

HUMANIA

"League of Nations,"
"United Nations."
Why start with "nations?"
They did not serve us well,
they forced us through the painful unifications;
From the family, to the tribe, to the state.

Let's start afresh again!
Forge our people into a whole;
Create from each individual
a "United Humanity,"
or still better; "Humania."

What would be needed?
Some projects which could be efficiently attained
only with the cooperation of the whole of mankind,
or —
the arrival of the spaceship
of a *real* extraterrestrial.

George Mueller

MELODIES OF HOPE

The silence had fallen with the dark shadow over the city.
It made our hearts heavy and our minds still,
It tortured our bodies and desecrated our souls.
The one mistake that could not be undone.
We were afraid to hope, afraid to rise above the Shadow.
I was alone, walking through the rubble of the streets,
My hot angry tears splashing in the unmoving dust of a fallen empire
I could not understand why; none of us could.
The deathly silence holding no answers.
I listened, and then, above the quiet, I heard
The sound tugged at the unknown depths of my heart.
A lark's sweet melody, mending the hurt behind my eyes.
Lifting me, ever so slightly, above the darkness
Something I thought long lost, returned.
Music so sweet that it filled the air with its joy.
I shouted a challenge despite the desolation
Behold the freebird aloft on wings of light and love
The song of life smashing the nightmare of Shadow
Giving us hope, making our spirits rise high above the clouds.

CarolAnn Schmidt

MERCEDES-BENZ:
CYCLE AND CARRIAGE, MALAYSIA, 1981

Overlooking the N.U.P.W. students' hostel

Your neon-glowing insignia
Attracts those termites in their nuptials,
The once only, 'go get 'em baby' opportunists,
trailing substantial paths to devour and subdue,
leaving unrenewed husks with bloated
queen ants and a motley collection
of servile, sterile vermin
brooding in silent secret.

Christopher G. Jesudason

PARADOX

I am he: Who created his friends; loves them more than anything he
        can ever own
    Who writes for the benefit of others
    Who sings to chastise his soul
    Who lives life for what it can bring

    Yet

I am he: Who destroys his friends; crushes them without thought
        or feeling
    Who writes to control his sanity
    Who sings for material gains
    Who dies at his own hand

I am the endless Paradox:

Good yet evil,
Intelligent yet doltish,
Loving yet hateful,
Pure yet defiled,
Sane yet insane,
Thoughtful yet thoughtless;

The Creator and the Destroyer.

And it is ripping the very fiber of my existence.

Brian D. Worrall

RED LIGHT DISTRICT

*This poem centers around Kuala Lumpur,
W. Malaysia in the early '80s.*

The chic modern tarts tastefully
blending with the new shopping
arcades come and go like the
reproductive zeal of the earth
stoppered up, like the sight
and stench of rotting fruit and
garbage beside the stalls in
the market place; all these
signifying a hidden bottleneck
somewhere, so
with all the stuffy no-go areas,
rotting with excess, layer upon layer,
pile upon pile,
a virtual glut of what could
be but was not.

Christopher G. Jesudason

MY OLD FRIEND

Sunshine, my old friend — I feel your warmth engulf me.
    And I am replenished by your strength. I beg of you, old friend,
    please stay with me awhile, so I might breathe you in long
    enough to nourish my soul.

Sunshine, my old friend — Why are you so elusive?
    Is it that I demand too much from you? Or does a deeper being
    limit our time? Could it be that you would choose to stay if
    you could?

Sunshine, my old friend — Do I rely too heavily upon you?
    And, in turn, relinquish my own warmth and strength? Have I
    forgotten that I too possess these things? Perhaps, this is
    your way of gently reminding me of this.

Sunshine, my old friend — You are right; I must loosen my grasp.
    Now is the time to reach deep within and radiate my own warmth
    and strength. And, after awhile, perhaps I too may be able to
    give another what you have so freely given to me.

Sunshine, my old friend — I bid you a sad good-bye.
    I know you must go; And I must stay. But, you and I shall
    never be separated. For we have been bonded by an intangible
    gift: one of needing and being needed. A gift called Friend.

Tina Jochum

JUST THINK

Don't think about yesterday,
put the past all behind.
Just think about tomorrow,
what's in store you will find.

Don't think about sadness,
dry the tears from your eyes.
Smile, that's the way to gladness,
there's no reason you should cry.

The sands of time can run out,
so treasure every precious drop.
Don't pine or ever be in doubt,
treasure every minute of the ticking on the clock.

There's a rainbow waiting for you,
right after the falling rain.
Don't fret now whatever you may do,
smile and think about life's gains.

Remember those who love you,
they will be with you till the end.
Knowing this you'll smile right through,
thinking someone cares, a friend.

Bert M. Swanson

CHANGED FOREVER

You have ended our relationship. The electricity we once felt
Has been drained away. Without you I feel as useless as a rose's
Bud, forgotten and never to be used. I am that emptiness.
Your smile no longer brightens my day as it used to. I gave
To you my very essence. You took it and let it dissipate from
Your soul like a penny flung into the darkest corner of a fountain.
This act I can forgive with the civil disposition you have taught
Me to partake. This selfish act that you inflict upon my heart
Will leave it scarred. I hope and pray that I remember my well
Learned civilties, that I may never falter into this sort of
Act upon another.

Jeffrey A. Robinson

CABIN OF MEMORIES

The roof of the cabin is fast falling to earth
The stones of the chimney tumbling out on the hearth
Some hewn oak slabs that a door once had been
Are swinging and creaking as the breezes come in

The table and stools that I knew of yore
Have fallen to ruin, a heap on the floor
The windows all broken, their shutters nailed back
To the walls of this memorable log cabin shack

An air of regret, and of sadness still cling
Like the dusty cobwebs that from rafters swing
As I gaze from the window to a grass-covered mound
With its white, marble cross now felled to the ground

As I look from the window, with its rotting sill
I hear a soft rustle on the trail from the mill
The slow, dragging footsteps cause me to turn
And a man on the trail I quickly discern

The man's wrinkled face is a well written page
His work-scarred fingers all shrunken with age
The blue eyes are dim, the hair silver gray
Like the cabin, his days are fast fading away.

Fred V. Womack

DEAREST PLACE ON EARTH

There is a place that once I knew: the dearest place on earth
When as a boy I used to join the family 'round the hearth
Each evening after supper, on snowy winter days
We'd sit 'round the cheery fire and watch the leaping blaze

I'd dream of summer days gone by: of trails I used to roam
Or think of all the days to come, when I would leave this home
And then, I'd let my glances stray to loved ones 'round the hearth
As with a prayer, I'd thank my God for heaven, stars and earth

Then when at last the laughter, and the talk would nod my head
I'd climb the short, steep stair to the attic and my bed
And soon the talk below would cease, and in dreams I'd drift away
To roam once more as in days of yore, until the break of day

But the long years have a habit of rolling swiftly by
And each of us must strive our best, to fill them ere we die
With work, with peace and kindness, and love over all
That we may help a friend, or neighbor, lest they fall

That wars of strife, greed and lust; for all are born of hate
May all be shackled with God's great love before it is too late
And then, once more, peace will fall 'round that cheery hearth
With family, friends, and neighbor: the dearest place on earth.

Fred V. Womack

WOMAN OF BROWN

Of brown was she made, hair and eyes
thoughtful, considerate, and unforgivably kind,
a woman of worth, no poem could tell.

Her face, a beacon in the dark of night,
her smile, so pure, and most sincere,
a voice, whose sound grasps hold the heart.

All traits, in a woman so rare and wise,
just the picture of this; a portrait I find,
to never forget, oh nay, I know too well:

Radiance beyond belief, which blinds not my sight
a kinship is made; to us; all ye hear
a bond not to be broken, a life is to start.

Together, this woman of brown and I
walk to the ends, in search of a shore,
where we can be, away and alone.

And with love, spread our being,
in name, under the sun, shall it be,
our love, to forever prosper and grow.

Hand in hand we walk, and I sigh,
this woman of brown I adore
and sit, side by side, on the sea stone.

A sight for me, this woman worth seeing,
and I say, dear brown, listen to me,
for I love you now, and will tomorrow more!

Shane M. Kolbie

TO MY MOTHER

There could be no other, you are the best
I wouldn't trade you for all the rest!
In my troubles, you were there
And you've always cared.
You've done so much
That I couldn't praise you enough.
The love that you show makes me know
That you are near and always have a listening ear.
So I am of good cheer
For love will always be there!

Paul Marion Cox

REQUEST TO POE

Poe speak of death and despair.
Cry out through the void of death and enlighten my weary mind.
Talk of betrayal and ludicrous love.
Scream of madness and sorrow.
But most of all weep for me, and my closeness to your soul.
Poe you felt my grief and wrote of my despair.
A fool's love is a fool's payment for love of soft flesh so fair.

Allen Gatlin

MY WHEELCHAIR HAS WINGS

I can go anywhere I want with
   this chair
And I don't have to depend upon people
   taking me there.
For the first time in my life
   I can move by myself
And I have control over where and
   when I go.
Now I have independence and freedom
   you see
And it's right inside of me.
My wheelchair has wings to
   take me to new places
See old friends and greet new faces.
Yes, I can do many things on my own
   Because I have "wings"
My wheelchair has wings
But deep inside of me, I have the "wings."

Rick McQuaide

RELATIONSHIPS

Why don't men and women really relate
   and why not trust each other?
Is it because we don't understand
   the feelings of one another?
Or is it we just don't know the meaning
   of love from the other's point of view?
There must be something that we
   both can do.
Yes . . . feel love and accept
   each other just the way we are
and then our relationship will grow
   both for you and for me —

Donna Iavarone

ON SECURITY

Rainy days are good days.
They enhance our sense of security.
Peering out at the rain and ravage,
   we sit inside (warm, dry, and comfortable)
Telling ourselves how safe and secure we are.

Frederica Gibson

THE INNOCENTS

What are the mountains waiting for?
Why do the trees exist?
Why does the sky shout for breath?
Why don't they just desist?

Because they are wiser,
Because they care,
Because they do not despair,
Because they believe that man can turn greed
   into something more noble and fair.

Frederica Gibson

SHOPPING LIST

A slice of night sky
A bird awakening
A slant of sun
A breath of breeze
A mist upon the pond.

A spring meadow for roaming
A musty attic for remembering
A quiet corner for contemplating
A book for reading
A pen for writing.

A smile, a tear, a brief embrace
A touch of his fingertips
A body slumbering beside me
A baby at my breast
A quiet word in the dark
A last goodbye.

How little it takes to please me.

Frederica Gibson

QUESTION

   Why did I not tell you
While you had ears to hear,
   Just how much enjoyment
I knew when you were near?

   Why did I not show you
While you had eyes to see,
   Just how much I cared
When you were near to me?

   Why did I not give you
While you could know I gave,
   Just the love you needed
To keep you from your grave?

   Why did I not hold you
But let you wander on,
   To find yourself your death
And haunt me now you're gone?

Walt Summers

DON'T BE SO DUMB

Don't be so dumb, smoking
isn't that much fun;
Don't be so dumb, please
take care of your precious lungs,
protect your teeth and your gums.
Don't be so dumb, smoking
isn't that much fun;
 Some of it will make your brain numb,
break you down where you
can't jump, skip or run.
So don't be so dumb, tell the truth,
smoking isn't that much fun;
And it sure don't make your nerves calm.
So don't be so dumb, smoking
isn't that much fun;
'Cause the harder you breathe,
the harder your heart ticks
like a bomb.

Gregory Moore

TRUE LOVE

I've never known a love so dear.
So gentle like the breeze. I wish that I could
harness it so that it'll never go away.

What manner is this "love" — I seek?
A fortress though to speak.
Yet when you've entered it —
It takes *you* to a world unknown!

Because if you should fall in love —
It conquers these three things,
the fears and doubts and hates that you have
hidden through the years.

I wish someday the world could sing
in perfect harmony —
And know God really cares and loves
us all uniquely in his own way.

Enrique Avila

WHERE IS LIFE?

Unending dreams embrace each need
Of each longing soul in a desperate search
Each aching heart with a misplaced seed
Is painfully crying for its place on earth.

Willing minds are closed in pain
By misfortune's fate of the past and now
Unheeded pleadings again and again
Bounce back with a force, of "no, not now!"

Trampled and crushed beneath the tide
Are hope and faith in a better way
Yet, so thin the line to the other side
With fulfilled needs and a brighter day.

I ask the question, "Where is Life?"
Wrapped in all I can gain for me
Forgetting my brother's struggling plight
And turning my head when a need I see?

Life, is in knowing my own true self
And obeying my Creator's command
To love others as I could myself
And by serving each day, my fellow man!

Willa Elliott

I WONDER

   I wonder
How many tears must I cry
How many years till I die
How many ears heard my cry
How many hands passed me by
   I wonder

Gracie Greer

Life's road must be traveled from the cradle to the grave
All who start must go the distance and be brave
First it's easy road not bumpy, scenery something to behold
Then gets rougher, still is scenic, but at times so damp and cold
All those signs seemed unimportant in those early youthful days
Those warnings properly heeded would have helped me
    through this maze
Oh! A lighted sign at that crossroad, I must see what those words say —
Arrow points, ''Straight and Narrow'' sign says, ''Child I am the Way''
Those who've followed say He is perfect, has never lost a one
Should I? Yes I'll trust Him as these last few miles I run

    Milan McMains

If a man would write one little line
  Each leisure hour just to pass the time
He might say things that make a little sense
  And unlike talking folks would take no offense

Each line he wrote could be heard loud and clear
  Because folks reading have a much keener ear
I'm going to attempt it from this hour on
  Talking I've tried and I can't sing a song

There are so many things I'd love to say
  To my fellow man as I pass this way
The subject I best know on which I love to expound
  Isn't always popular and by some thought profound

So granted it is only spiritually discerned
  No excuse to go to the grave unconcerned
God plainly says man lives beyond the grave
  And only He can condemn or save

Wouldn't it be wise to look at it pro and con
  Tragic if the wrong data you've had all along
God makes it so easy expects one thing of man
  Accept His Son Jesus anyone can

    Milan McMains

Do you know the love of Jesus
  And how He died for you and me
Do you know Him as your Savior
  Or are you rejecting his plea?

All the world is at a crossroad
  Heaven or hell is out before
Hasten to take Him as your Saviour
  Before He closes the Door

Men act as if they don't need Him
  As if they could demand of God
Entry into His Holy Heaven
  As on the sacrificial Blood they trod

Don't walk the broadway with the masses
  That goes straight on down to hell
When you can walk the King's Highway to Heaven
  And with His help can walk it well

Oh! Be smarter than the average
  Accept God's plan and be made whole
Have peace and joy as your portion
  And heaven a harbor for your soul

    Milan McMains

THE FABRIC OF FAITH

My faith is weak when the storms of life beat upon me,
Sometimes it wanes and flickers and almost goes out
Much like a candle caught in a draft —
But though the flame dims, it never completely dies

In Him, I can do all the Lord requires of me . . .

The traumas and tragedies in living often make me waiver
Yet there was one who endured all things well
He suffered silently greater sorrows than I have ever known
Amazingly, it was how well He walked His path to perfection

Through Him, I can overcome temptations which beset me . . .

This heart of mine seems to stretch beyond my comprehension,
It breaks with sorrow, heals with time, expands in righteousness
Only to begin the process over again with new struggles
But when my strength is gone, He is still there to pull *me* through

Like Him, I can be clean and pure from spiritual pollution . . .

Yes, my faith is weak, but with each flicker
  the light grows brighter still
Amid the trials and heartaches little by little, it's added upon
Whatever personal Gethsemane or Calvary I must descend to
I shall not only pass it by, I will endure it well

With Him, my joy is full for He restoreth my soul . . .

    Donna Richardson

A TRIBUTE TO MY MOTHER

I build no monument of stone — this tribute meant for you
My tribute lies in all I am, in the things I say and do

For the woman that I am today is the reflection of another,
My childhood memories take me back to glimpse the face
    of my dear mother.

I sing no song of hit parade that all the world has known
My tribute is a lullaby I've sung to children of my own

It was from you I learned to love; watching you embrace each other —
The hands that taught me tenderness I learned from my sweet mother.

I send no costly gift of jewels, no crown for you to wear
Though queenly attribute you've taught; bright gems that now I share

And when the final trump is blown my tribute is none other
Than to meet her in celestial realm, and see again my angel mother.

    Donna Richardson

ANCIENT RITUAL

Swaying bodies move silently to inner rhythms of old
  An ancient story of love asking to be told
Necks straining in thoughtful dreamy contemplation
  Of a ritual performed ever since creation.
Without touching, they yet draw closer in a slow dance
  Electricity charging the space between them like a lance
Sounds of affection communicate passion in the air
  Signaling that the time is near for the final dare
Moving outspread arms, the male lifts his weight
  The female crouching, calmly awaiting her fate
A nonchalant good-bye ends the consummation, over too soon
  Like an interruption of a fine, lovely tune
Yet when one considers the agony of human love's traumas
  Who's to say pigeon partners don't have a better drama.

    Joanna Urquhart

THE SIGHTS

I watched the sunset
On Manila Bay,
The most beautiful
So they say.
I walked on Waikiki
Paradise to some,
Landed in Tokyo
Of the rising sun.
The sights I saw
Travelers may charm,
But serenity is found
On my Carolina farm.

Ruth L. Warrick

The butterfly is on the wall
Encapsulate, in plastic
It used to dance upon the breeze
But when I dance, it's spastic
And when I go, nothing is left
as large as that wall-hanging
But I'll be on some other breeze
    You'll hear a shutter, banging!

Peggy Dell

GOD IS PRESENT IN NATURE

Should you ever doubt that God exists,
Perceive His wonders in our midst.
Listen. The canary sings a song;
Her melodies to God belong.

Cast your eyes upon the setting sun,
To her lovely crimson rays succumb.
The dawn and the sunset shout with pleasure;
Search for God in nature's precious treasures.

Walk quietly along the shore.
Take time to think. Reflect. Explore.
Feel the cool waves splash against your feet.
In nature God's presence is concrete.

Throughout the jungle roam wild beasts.
Gardens hold lilies for our eyes to feast.
The mountaintops glisten with snow,
While sheep and cattle graze below.

God's love for us is plain to see
In every leaf on every tree.
Should you ever doubt that God exists,
Perceive His wonders in our midst.

Linda L. Finamore

In the backyard all
Dandelions turn white on the
Same day. Timetable.

Dana Gilbert

NO EXIT

Standing in the pouring rain,
drops trickling down my face.
Daydreaming comes so easy,
what's real and what's not.
My face is damp, my make-up smeared.
It's so cold and too moist.
My God,
it's not raining at all.
It's tears.

Terri L. Glazer

WIND SHADOW

I am born
Of wind and shadow
My blood flows
With wild mountain streams

I cannot lie
Beside man
Quiet . . .
Still . . .

No man shall own me
Nor bind me to him
I must reach for the stars
Let the clouds bed me down

My heart beats
With the pounding hoof
Of the wild mustang
On windswept plains

Free . . .
Bold . . .
Unbroken . . .

Kathleen S. Peterson

MY TURN

I remember

Watching children
Playing in the sun
Laughter spilling over
Dancing in the wind

I stood at the edge
Never joining in
A shadow in the trees
Waiting my turn

Childhood ends
Without a tear
Never missing
What wasn't there

Standing at the edge
Never joining in
Waiting my turn
To leave shadows behind

To enter life
To shout my name

Kathleen S. Peterson

I BELIEVE

I believe in the Father, Son and Holy Ghost
Knowing they all will give me the most
To help me cross bridges narrow or bent
No matter how hard things for me went
I believe I have a purpose to fulfill
And all that I do is by God's only will
He helps me or scolds me whenever I sin
He gives strength when I lose, pride when I win
I believe in the kingdom up in the sky
Where a Christian will go when he must die
To stand near God in this castle so pure
All pain he will help me to find the cure
I believe he is my one true friend and way
And that by my side he will always stay
To path my steps in this world of woe
No matter what I do or where I must go.

Wendy Burch

THE BROKEN-HEARTED DOLL

In the darkness lies the broken-hearted doll
In a box in a closet near to the wall
A torn dress and one button eye
It's kind of sad left alone to cry
No light shines through to help her see
She wonders where everyone could be
Endless days and sleepness nights
She prays for someone to turn on the lights
She hears a sound coming toward the door
Could it be the one she's been waiting for
The door is opened for a moment or so
The doll cries out Please, please don't go
The door slams shut, her heart is torn
Finally convinced she's washed up and worn
Then suddenly she hears a child's cries
She listened closely where she lies
The door opens as she's picked from the box
She wishes so badly that she could only talk
And tell the child not to forget her anymore
Inside the box behind the closet door.

Wendy Burch

I dreamt of moonlit nights
    and sun-filled days
Of walking hand in hand
    through time
Seeing ancient sites of
    sacred ceremonial grounds
Feeling our souls united
    in some ritual

Of star-filled skies
Of thrones
Of a masked priestess singing
    her praises under watchful eyes

I dreamt of walking
    hand in hand through time
Of our souls united in
    some ritual

Robert N. Vallie

BLESSINGS

Blessings are great, large or small,
We are thankful to God for them all.
There are times when we feel so low,
And we just can't see how we will ever go.
But with God's help we'll find our way
And go on living life from day to day
And his blessings we will share.

Blessings are there if only we'll see
That God has love for you and for me.
But he doesn't forget us if we'll go to him in prayer
And try to do what he taught us there
And his blessings we will share.

Blessings are for everyone to share
God gives them all because he cares
And if you don't believe God cares
Just wait until you have a burden to bear
Then go to God in prayer
And his blessings we will share.

Shirley A. Cox

HELP US LORD

Walk with us, Lord, through valleys so deep
Over mountains so high and steep.
Oh, guide us, Lord, and we'll always praise your name high
To the gates of heaven open wide.
Help us, Lord, to love our neighbors true.
Yes, yes, Lord, we're loving you.
Help us, Lord, to righteously stand
Yes, yes, Lord, we're loving you.

The blood you shed on Calvary tree
Is very precious to me.
Holy is your dear name
It must never be used in vain.
Oh, guide us, Lord, and we will always praise your name high
To the gates of heaven open wide.
Help us, Lord, to always be humble
Yes, yes, Lord, we're loving you
Help us, Lord, not to stumble.
Yes, yes, Lord, we're loving you.

Shirley A. Cox

FOREVER BE TRUE

Oh, life seems so hard to bear
And we have feelings at times no one cares
But when we tell our troubles to Jesus
His love he will share.
Oh! Jesus we're needing you, and will forever be true.

When burdens get so great
And we feel that it is too late
Go to Jesus, and he'll meet us at the gate.
Oh! Jesus we're needing you, and will forever be true.

Oh, when this life is over and with Jesus we will be
We will remember all the times he has said, "Come, follow me."
And at last we can say, "Dear Jesus, we have found much happiness
    being with thee.
Oh! Jesus we needed you and will forever be true.
Oh! Jesus we needed you and will forever be true."

Shirley A. Cox

RETIREMENT

I did not watch my youth slip away,
Engrossed was I in life's struggle, day by day.
The years marched by, in their orderly line;
Balmy spring, summer warm, autumn's cool and winter's cold;
So the cycle sped.
And one day I looked up from my life's routine with profound
    sadness-resigned;
Lo, I was old and perhaps soon I would be dead.
And still so much to do.
"Not yet," I said, aloud, defiantly, standing straight.
There are my young dreams, still to come true, the secret
    wishes, the wistful hopes to be —
All put aside till now;
And I am free to dare, to try, to achieve, if not complete
    success, at least in part;
(Ah the knowledge of compromise that comes with age —
    so sublime)
My head held high, I laugh because I know,
In spite of the inevitable,
I shall yet be young for a very long time.

Rachel Ellis

THE HEART

My tender and weak
my bold and so strong
my heart will not break
if you do me no wrong

My loving and so giving
my warm and endless heart
it will always be forgiving
if from me you do not part

My loyal and true
my music of song
my heart belongs to you
and to you my heart will always
                    belong

Carol A. Dixon

HURT

Do I have to fall, beg and plead;
Please, one more chance is all I need.

For me to prove my love to you
will always be forever true.

I know the past has been wasted years,
and for you your bless-ed tears.

Now I realize what you've been through
and once for good, I promise . . .
                    I'll always be true.

Carol A. Dixon

DRY CREEK

The summer caught
  The creek beside my house
    To stop its run.

But fall rains start
  And soon a trickle forms,
    The waters come.

Then winter nears
  To staunch the flow again
    With icy grasp.

And spring, at last,
  Releases gurgling flow,
    All dryness past.

As seasons pass,
  The dry creek of my life
    Knows seasons, too.

Oh, Lord, please bless!
  Keep well-springs of thy love
    In all I do.

Deloris Woerner

GRAMMA

You sit
and sew
while angels
gather
and fold
the material
around your
eyes,
and dust
your hair
with silver
dew.

The angels
are ageless
as you will be
when they
slip inside
to take
you home
at last.

Marcelle Soviero

CONTEMPLATION

If I should die and leave this earth
If I had no more tomorrow
Have I fulfilled destinies of my birth
Am I leaving more than sorrow
Did I offer aid to those in need
Have I lent a helping hand
Would I leave any unfinished deed
Have I helped the fallen to stand
Do I leave friends along the way
Not enemies mile after mile
Will they remember me from yesterday
A memory that brings a smile
Did I keep an always open door
Have I reached some hidden goal
'Tis not glory I'm striving for
But eternal peace for my inner soul

Sherial Wiser

SOLITUDE

Sitting upon
a craggy crest
high aloft
a private nest.

Looking out
across the sea
of endless fog
alone . . . just me.

Feels so food
to be alone
the time to think
all your own.

To have your thoughts
expand across
the ocean waves
then bounce and toss.

Sure to come
on back to you
all so fresh
with Life anew.

Glenn T. Fugitt

JUST A SHORT NOTE

Just thinking of you,
at times like this.
God, why aren't you here?
Ah, the one I miss!

The beautiful eyes,
the beauty of you;
all my Love forever Girl,
loves you what I do.

I'm smiling now,
expressing what's inside;
all my Love for you,
the Love, I just can't hide.

But soon, I'll be with you again,
and never shall I leave;
The Love and Trust once more, my Love,
your Love, that I believe.

So, until then Sweetheart,
when once again you're mine;
just know I'm thinking of you,
and hoping that you're fine.

Glenn T. Fugitt

FAITH

Come, my children, and do not be sad,
  This pain that I bear is revealing,
For when it is gone I'll surely be glad,
  And praise Him above for my healing.

Go, my loved ones, and grief not for me,
  And burn not your candles in mourning.
By fact we all know, through faith we can see,
  An end must precede each beginning.

Hugh Miles Ray

THE HULL

As the waves come crashing in,
and the fog lays light above;
the hull, glides safe within,
the next waves rolling shove.

Awesome, in their tremendous power,
crashing, crushing, thundering in their force;
mighty waves, with an impenetrable shower,
indomitable, from their source.

Mothers of a million graves,
molders of a thousand sands;
these, the relentless waves,
infinite, in their span.

Yet the steel hull glides,
steadfast and cold, distantly drawn;
and with each nomadic stride,
glides through . . . and Beyond.

Glenn T. Fugitt

DIDLIN' FOR DOODLIN'

It came my way
This didlin' day
The red orange and green for a picture

Two blinks of an eye
And I've painted the sky
With a few globs of blue in the mixture

Then a few strokes with white
For a few birds in flight
And I've drawn a volcano and named her

A foreground of trees
Just the tops if you please
As lava erupts from Mount Leter

I'll give it away
To the good girl today
— Just what I need to get her —
— Doodlin' my way

Patrick McGee

THE EDGE

A man Slowly walked
To the Edge and stared
Below, he saw the Ocean,
Bashing rocks Furiously.

"no," he thought,
"Not this way."

As he turned, he was
Startled by a gull.
He could Not be Heard.
He fell Forever.

Michael J. Grande

Karr's Pinnacles.

GROANING

When will unknown truth to me be sweet
Or love always abound?
Will the selfish leech inside my brain
In heart be ever found?
The convenience of providence
Just musing, maybe jest
I guess I couldn't resist myself
From having done my best
Darkened glass of time
And curse of old
Living corpse seeks the throne
Gazing into a mirror of filth
I never throw the first stone
Maker and made
Eternity and time
Omniscient and the known
Good and sin
Without and within
War and tension cause the groan

Jeff Stoudt

PARABLE OF PURPLE VELVET OVER GLORY

The glory of the day moved by,
As I gazed into the open sky.
Then as day reached out to touch the night,
I beheld purple velvet claim its right
To remove day's glory without a trace —
To place a velvet blanket over all, in grace.

Bart Casty

RAINY DAYS

Some people won't accept the rain
they only welcome sun
but with the proper attitude
a shower can be fun!
I like to watch the droplets fall
like marching, rhythmic feet
that form in puddles
making estuaries to the streets.
I like the pitter-patter sound
of raindrops as they bounce
upon my pane as though they're
keeping time in cadence counts.
No matter what the weather
each day's a day to behold.
But there's something in a rainy day
that is a joy untold.

Lois Reedy

A BROKEN HEART

Alone and hurting
because you lied
Crying softly
days of searching
I slowly feel the pain inside

Stephannie Opstad

TOGETHER

We spend moments together
You and me.
Alone, perfectly.
Happy and content.
Until the main event.
And then,
I cry.
I wait,
Until,
The next time, when
I'll see you again.
Happy I want to be.
Happy when you are with me.
Because when I'm with you,
Things are true.
They are real.
You know, you feel.
What can I say.
Will you talk to me?
Someday maybe.
Something is alive again, within me.
Like a warm and rushing sea.
The closeness,
I know you feel.
It's sweet, it's real.
It's us, you and me.

Helen Marie Vence

DEATH

Death comes along, so hard, so strong.
It picks on the weak, the old, the young.
It's not choosy, it claims all ages,
Families, friends and neighbors.

You're born in this life to play a part,
It's a written script right from the start.
Which road you take is your own choice,
Like a drifting spirit, or some inner voice.

You will do bad and you might do good.
It's a street we all must follow.
So many bends along the road, so many stories
That will be told.

But life is short as we all know.
And when it's your time, you must go.
There is a power stronger than ours,
Where we are weak, *this* power towers.

It is God, and it is his life,
That we act out and take in stride . . .

Helen Marie Vence

PREJUDICE

An ideal enmeshed in the web of
the mind,
Trapped, held at bay, by the widow
of prejudice,
Unable to free itself, the ideal
withers.
Clinging to the hope that a new
generation
Will discover it, before the spider
devours its remains.

Christina Ann Salisbury

I wrap your memory tightly around me
To keep out the loneliness that threatens
To creep in.

I tuck your image next to my ego
To encourage it not to shrink away.

How much longer do I rely on
Our past?

When I am old and death is the
Most the future holds,

Will I still be able to convince
Myself that you remember me and
Yearn for a relationship that
Almost was?

Christina Ann Salisbury

TIME

Time cannot be held still,
It quickly moves along.
It rushes swiftly by us,
And we wonder where it's gone.

Time is of the essence,
It's a highly treasured thing.
Our life is closely run by it,
To us it's everything.

Time tells us when to wake up,
And when to go to sleep.
Our daily chores are governed,
By this treasure that we keep.

By clock and watch and radio,
We trace the time of day.
Those possessive items tell us,
When to leave and when to stay.

Where would we be without it,
This small thing on our mind.
This wondrous small possession,
The one we know as time.

Elsie S. Eyamie

BELOW

I went for a dive the other day,
Down, down, down.
The water was cool against my skin,
Down, down, down.

I reached the bottom and looked around,
There's another whole world down there.
Where time stands still and cares are lost,
The water is peaceful and clear.

I swim with the fish and float with the tide,
What a grand way to spend the day.
Down where it's quiet and peaceful and slow,
Where cares seem to float away.

It would be great to stay down there,
With the fish, the snails and the sand.
But life must go on and I must leave
And go back to the world of man.

Elsie S. Eyamie

HERO OF RUNNING BIRD RANCH

The strings remain broken on the old guitar
And the metal frets are beginning to rust.
Cowboys don't sing on the prairie this year
And the old chuck wagon is covered with dust.

The colt-45 is still nailed to the wall
Three notches are turned where they show;
Steel-eyes stare from the picture above
With a calloused finger, proven once too slow.

Legend has it that love was the monster
And it could be, with all the lips that he kissed;
But, the girls in the bar did remove a star,
For each night in the week that he missed.

God covered the sky and darkened the night
And the "Lost Virgin" bar lit up its sign;
In memory of the hero of Running Bird Ranch
And the cowboy-poet, who wrote his last line.

The ladies of the night wore his mark on their garter
And "red-eye" flowed like a well.
Heaven traded a branded, "four star," Saint
For the best damn cowboy in hell.

I. J. Evans

GOD IS A POET

Oh, absurd little boy,
　　your eyes search the photograph for a meaning,
　　for the　　　other colors,
　　　　intangible . . . invisible . . .
　　they search and probe.
Smiling snowflakes conceal the crooked grass,
　　provoke the biting curiosity
　　in your intolerant head.
God, the poet, scratches out impossible verses
　　of puzzlement and mystery . . .
Wrestle with ignorance and blindness, oh little
boy . . . your weakness is your own!

Jon Saldivar

DANCING IN THE MEADOW

While I watched the little ballerina dance,
my thoughts drifted to a meadow
where once you skipped among azure forget-me-nots,
frolicked beside a small stream,
danced along the edge,
paused to sip the cool water,
dipped your toes into the ripples,
and knelt to gather golden daffodils.
The bees buzzed,
butterflies fluttered their wings.
You gathered wild violets
then left the meadow dancing,
carrying your bouquet of daffodils
and wild flowers.

Virginia Goland

TRAVEL ONE ROAD

Travel one road he said
for it will not lead you wrong.
Out into the night I ventured
not knowing what fate awaited me.

Mountains I climbed, rivers I swam
and deep valleys I rested to find solace.
My clothes worn from wear and spirit to seek the end.

The road split in two,
which way should I go?
Travel one road he said
for it will not lead you wrong.
Out into the night I ventured
not knowing what fate awaited me.

Split in two,
though I took one
to find the light of hope burning brightly.

Sharon Martinez-Headrick

INDIGO NIGHT

Faraway whispers of velvet-toned darkness
Echo through my ears;
My eyes are touched by the white-gold shimmer
Of fleeting stars.
My body is sensitized with a delicious craze of
Midnight mesmerization.
I see much more than I've ever seen before.
The indigo night has painted the sky in my eyes
A deep sapphire blue:
Of wishes and schemes and gossamer wings;
And she's brought me a three-quarter moon
To dance under, too.
Indigo night.
I love to dance on an indigo night.

Valerie M. Conti

WHEREVER YOU LIVE

Wherever you live,
　　In a room, an apartment or house,
　　All alone, with your family or spouse,
　　On a farm, in a city or town,
　　East or west, high up or low down,
Your problems are just the same — or are they?

　　There's the sun and the wind and the rain,
　　There's the cold and the heat and the strain;
　　There's the flowers and moonlight and bugs
　　And disasters like earthquakes or floods —
Your problems are still the same — or are they?

　　There'll be love, or just kindness and hope,
　　There'll be greed, even hunger and dope,
　　There'll be jealousy, hate and revenge,
　　(Nothing's changed since the days at Stonehenge)
So wherever you live
Your problems are really the same — aren't they?

Arlouine G. Wu

DISABLED

I may not have two legs like you,
Or I may just have one arm.
I may not think or talk like you,
But I really mean no harm.

Some say that I'm disabled,
Well maybe that is so.
But tell me, what is disabled,
I'd really like to know.

Does it mean that I'm unwanted,
Just because I'm not the same?
Does it mean that 'cause I'm different,
I deserve to be called names?

I may use crutches or a chair,
Or a hook where there should be a hand.
But I'm still human just like you,
I hope you understand.

I have feelings and I need love,
And a friend from time to time.
So if I'm disabled, I feel sorry for you,
'Cause it's only in *your* mind.

Elsie S. Eyamie

GOD'S PLAN

We conceive a person in our minds,
and build them up so tall.
We put them in a frame of glass,
a gleaming idol for all.

But, then they show their frailties,
their many faults come through.
The idol begins to tarnish,
the glass no longer new.

No more perfection, as we recall
from days when life was gay,
But able to hurt and steal and lie,
so human in every way.

These times when pain is hard to bear,
we must recall God's plans.
We can change ourselves, not others,
they are in His hands.

Ilene Cardinalli

WINDOWS

Morning mist hovers
Over the blue pools
Of your consciousness

The blowing wind
Stabs knives
In flourishes of pain

Beneath your ice
Down at your soul's core
The pressure is building a fire

You can't hide it anymore

I can see through
Those crystal tears
Your eyes are windows

Kevin Wilson

REBUTTALS

You said you were not good enough.
I said it wasn't true.
You said you were not rich enough.
I said that you would do.
You said you were not smart enough.
I said it was a lie.
But I didn't know just what to say
when you said goodbye.

But now I have an answer,
and it's true and not from spite.
After thinking of all the things you said,
I was wrong and you were right.

Cheryl Havens Kelch

TO BE A MAN

What does it take to be a man?
An open heart, a gentle hand.
A person there to understand.
I pray that someone out there can.

You know throughout this world today,
People run, people hide, from life.
A man is one who battles strife,
Yet never asks for praise or pay.

The thing that's most important is:
To be a man you have to feel
And show your heart what's truly real
By giving all that you can give.

To be a man is to believe
And take a chance on something new.
Yet still maintain your feelings through
The troubled times when you can't see.

You can be weak, you can be strong.
When strength within yourself is shown,
You never have to be alone
The gentle strength is never wrong.

Andy Prall

CHERISHED GEMS

Gold or silver
Stands no chance over gems;
You find them once . . .
Hold on tight,
For all of the money
In the world cannot buy one.

The roughness becomes smooth;
It slips as you grow.
Hold on . . . for love holds,
Your riches are losses,
But your gems are treasures.
Acres and acres of joy
Flow from gems.

You may only find a gem once;
Love it with all your heart.
Say, "I love you Mom, Dad, Sister, Brother."

Brian Briggs

THE SMITHY

*In memory of LeRoy C. Smith,
my husband, who died on 2-7-85*

Down in his shop beside the plum tree
Roy the smithy worked with glee.
Winter, summer, autumn and spring
You could hear his hammer and anvil cling.

He heated the iron and shaped it well
To whatever shape patrons would tell.
He repaired antiques and furniture, too,
Made the old and broken look like new.

Reproductions he cleverly made.
To do it well was quite a trade.
Collectors and dealers were all amazed
At such beautiful work on which they gazed.

His prices were most reasonably fair
For big profits he didn't care.
Work indeed was his great pleasure
Which he enjoyed beyond measure.

When work was finished they'd sit and chat,
About current events and this and that.
His time was his own; he was retired,
Never any danger of his being fired.

But now his tools are all at rest,
For God alone who knoweth best,
Has called to him, "Your work is done,
Come Home to Me, your Crown is won."

Catharine T. Smith

a darkened figure
standing surrounded by
    evening light
lost I tried to make a twig shelter
    far below
    the river black
all paths had gone nowhere.
Asleep,
slowly awakening to stars,
sun, sea and sand
flowers — trees — fresh air
and life.

Alan Williams

LESSON

Lest you live
The lesson of life
Learning and loving
Are legacies lost.

Nora Isabel Brandt

IMAGES

The eyes create powerful images for the mind.
It captures beauty and nature at their finest.
Profound images entice the senses and cause a chain reaction.
Simple gestures dig deep inside the human soul, with a powerful force.
An unknown force that captures the emotions.
A subtle gesture allures the senses,
A passion burns within the soul . . .
And the forces become one.

Amy I. Prebesh

THE TINIEST ROSE

Dedicated to Alberta Liz Sims

The rose I received was not the largest or the most grand . . .
In fact it was the smallest . . . and the shortest . . .
   of the ones in her hand;
But the love shown in giving it was far greater, you see,
For it showed a great love and trust in me.

The smaller the rose, the more care it needs.
For one must care for . . . and provide its needs . . .
   and care for it each and every day.
Watch it mature . . . as it grows up . . . out . . . and away.
Watch carefully as it is moistened and refreshed
   by the early morning dew.

Watch as the sun rises and dries it out, through and through,
Knowing that the love of this rose is here to stay . . .
   to comfort a glad heart throughout life's day,
    whether it's here, or far . . . far . . . away.
I can reach out and touch it, in my imagination,
   each and every day . . .
Knowing in my heart . . . my mind . . . and soul . . .
   that love is never far away.

Robbie King Harvey

ROBBIE C. JOHNSON. Pen Names: Robbie King Harvey, Robbie Colbert; Born: Gordonsville, Tennessee, 3-14-31; Separated; Education: Completed high school, college-level student; Occupations: Health field, General office, Writer; Memberships: Spring Street Missionary Baptist Church, Spring Street Baptist Church Choir; Comments: *Thanking God, who is the head of my life, for granting me the ability to express myself in words that other folk seem to enjoy reading and praying I will find the words to say something meaningful, beyond the trivial.*

HURTING IS LEARNING

Looking back at life I see,
How troubled times have set me free.
Through times of sorrow and times of pain,
I have learned to get back up again.
By forgiving myself and forgetting the past,
I have learned to be happy and to make it last.
Hurting is learning to be strong,
And once you have felt it, it is hard to go wrong.
Life may get rough, it may seem unfair,
But it wouldn't be life, if hard times weren't there.

Diana Martinez

THE JUNGLE

In the early light of this changing day
The bodies of young men in their gravesites lay
With all the gallantry that valor achieves
So many men die among the leaves
Grown plush by the rays of a tropical sun
In defense of their country, on the men run
Toward a goal obscured by a nameless face
That haunts at home a political race . . .

A young Kennedy dies and America weeps
Though the government with a clean broom sweeps
Away the foundation that valiant men laid
Of earth and sky and lives they gave
Toward a goal obscured by anonymity
And the dark nameless face of society.

And in the dusk of this changing day
How many more men in their graves will lay?
Their principles not by death were dimmed
But by a country that didn't look within . . .

And around them the jungle steams and waits
For the dawn of a new day, already too late.

Rene Denise Parker

LIMITED

Staring out over majestic waves,
At the calm of the ocean.
The same ocean that wouldn't hesitate to kill me tomorrow,
The bearer of good tiding, the reminder of sorrow.
Gazing deeply into the eyes of a beauty,
Contemplating losing all resistance.
The same eyes that hold promise, also hold a broken heart
In passion so narrow, in fury set apart.
Intensely trying to see through the eyes of God,
Studying people as diverse as pebbles on the beach.
The same people, so capable of doing harm,
I hold in contempt, he holds in his palm.

Dennis Michael Govoni

PLANS

What kind of plans do you make
When you're going to be alone?
My mind is like a merry-go-round,
With no plan of its own.
It just keeps going 'round and 'round
Not knowing where to stop.
After working together for fifty-two years
What can you do as one?
When you need someone on the other end
Of a bench or a box to lift,
Who do you get to help with the load,
When it's much too heavy for one?
Who do you look at across the table,
How do you cook for just one?
Who sits beside you as you come and go,
And carries your groceries in?
When you get tired of gardening chores,
Who picks up the hoe?
When something around the place needs fixing,
Who sees that the job gets done?
Who warms your feet on a cold winter night,
Who holds you in his arms?
How do you stop these questions from forming,
In a mind that goes 'round and 'round?

Florence Buckman

INNOCENT LOVE

What color we are
We do not mind
Our friends are different
Since the beginning of time
We are children of innocence
Who find joy in sharing
The smiles and the laughter
The love and the caring

So please, in our vulnerability
Take not the advantage to choose
Our friends; we have the ability,
But the advantage
Of the lesson we show you . . .
The outside is delicate
Holding our hearts

Angela Simon

DON'T LOVE

Don't open your heart
Or you might love.
Don't love
Or you might get hurt.
Don't get hurt
Or you might feel pain.
Don't feel pain
Or you might cry.
Don't cry
Or you might not stop.
Don't stop
Or you might break down.
Don't break down
Or you might be defeated!

Pahoua H. Chang

REMINISCENT DREAM

As I played the keys in time
He came into mind
My hands smoothed over the
  ebony and ivory
Like they had over his body

The music filled my senses
As I reminisced through
  mind-bound fences
Of the last time we were together
In the cold moonlit weather

They played faster and ever
  so powerful
Wanting him there by my side ever
  so gentle
The music, though, I realized
Brought only tears to my eyes . . .

I could only bring his memories
That my mind had seized
And not what I dream for —
To be by his side forevermore

Angela Simon

JUST ONE MORE TIME

I lived and died in Ireland
My cot near Shannon's flow,
Another dispensation, pray,
It's in the blood you know.

Set me down before a peat fire
Snug thatching overhead
Colcannon in the trencher
To enjoy with soda bread

And fish — fresh off the Curragh
A lively string of bream,
Herself in from the dairy
With slews of clotted cream

For the pudding warm and waiting
On the hob — oh root sublime!
Let me live and die in Ireland
One more time — just one more time.

Evelyn Pitel

UNDER THE STARS

Under the stars
we're living on the earth.
Under the stars
God gave us our worth.
Under the stars we fell in love.
Under the stars —
under the stars above.

Under the sky
people live and die.
Under the sky
people wonder why.
Under the sky
I learned to laugh and cry.
Under the sky
my spirit learned to fly.

Margaret M. Savitski

DREAM

Sometimes, at night
I visit you
And travel to you
Through valleys of clouds
Bright skies, distant melodies
And fields of flowers.

When I reach you
I take your face into my palms
And look into your shining eyes.
You kiss me gently
And the symphony begins again
As you lead me
To the mystic known — far away —
That is ours.

And when the shell bursts open
I have more than life
I have purity and innocence
Joy — creation of love.
And it is all right.

God understands.

Nora Isabel Brandt

YES

"Yes" and "Ja"
"Oui" and "Si"
Whatever the language
This word is for me!

"Yes" says: I do
"Ja" means: I will
With "Oui" I can flirt
And "Si" pays the bill!

"Yes" bears no limit
For letting me fly —
Whatever I give it
Is sure worth the try!

"Yes" is for winners
And people who dare
Sometimes maybe sinners
But always aware

That "Yes" and "Si"
And "Ja" and "Oui"
Are ours to keep
For life and to be.

Nora Isabel Brandt

LOVE ME

Love me
for what I am to you today . . .
And
I will give you more reasons,
for all
your tomorrows.

S. C. Brown

STARS CRY

I don't want to fight anymore
I don't want to cry
I don't want to dream about death or war
I just want to try to be free
To experience life and the way it may be
To find myself once again, but until then,
I will never be myself.
I'll only be a picture placed upon a shelf
Just the last thing to be seen by eyes
Just something that will only be noticed in disguise
Just something, not someone
What is left to be done?
Keep being ignored or yelled at all the time?
Or, go out and find a life that is fine?
. . . for me.
The only thing I ever lived for were my dreams;
Now it seems I don't even have them.

Theresa Campbell

GOOD NEWS

*A poem in the nuclear jargon,
written in response to Queen Elizabeth's call for
good news on the occasion of Christmas, 1985.*

Liz complained one Christmas eve:
''With bad news the world is replete.''
''Welcome,'' I wonder in my sleeve;
to MAD,* Starwars, goodbye, complete.
To those who pine for what is nice,
the bard in me can break the ice —

Good news: He's** here, once more He's here,
for Whom bells toll and the drums beat;
The wait is o'er in our hemisphere,
He herds His flock, the Beast His fleet.

Good news: He beckons a seeking soul,
''Behold the splendour veiled in Man!
Verily 'tis the cherish'd goal
we are all bound for and reach we can.''

Adieu, flesh foul! Adieu, wine vile!
No longer shall the twain defile
the spirit indwelling the clay;
'tis all and o'er; they've had their day.

* MAD: Mutually-Assured Destruction.
** Refers to the divine as manifest through the person
    identified as Baba Jai-Gurudev of Mathura, India.

Shambhoo Dutta Gupta

CAMP KENWOOD

Squirrels chattered, and chipmunks chased,
In the peaceful serenity of the place.
Soughing pines whispered in the evening breeze,
As needles fell silently from the trees.

Flowers bloomed, wild, in the shaded nook,
As well as in sunshine, near the brook.
Gold, brown, red and orange mirrored in the lake,
Smooth as glass, in the pictures we take.

While the Birch, Oak and Elm tree in Autumn dresses,
Pines are still green, near Sumac's red tresses.

June F. (Sutton) Grotte

FREE AS A BIRD

Wings spanned wide . . . they glide so gracefully,
And scan from aloft . . . the shimmering sea . . .
Swooping downward to meet the buoy's gently swaying dome,
Or feast as they will . . . partaking from the briny foam.
Now and then, to pursue an approaching fishing trow
In hope of catching morsels cast from the bow,
By seaworthy men returning to port,
Exhausted . . . weather-beaten . . . from their seafaring sport.
How I envy them all . . . my fine feathered friends,
For the heights they can reach, and the hours each spends
From dawn until sunset, by the lone oceanside,
Just riding the waves . . . their calls greeting each tide,
And as they waft gently between sky and sea,
I wish . . . how I wish I could join them and be
A part of their world . . . though it may sound absurd,
I'd like to be free . . . once . . . as free as a bird.

Irene Passarella

SOUL MATES

I reach out to the blazing sun, and touch each golden ray,
Bathe naked in the rainbow's vivid . . . dazzling display,
And drift upon the riptide, to strange lands far away
Where gentle winds caress me, and make me want to stay . . .
For you are there, Love.

I soar amongst the brilliant stars, and hear the cosmos speak;
Climb the highest mountains . . . conquering every peak;
Venture through vast deserts, not sure of what I seek . . .
And bide deep in the jungles, a feline . . . strong . . . so sleek,
And you are there, Love.

Perhaps these fleeting images, in the valleys of my mind . . .
Vague memories of places . . . and lives . . . I've left behind . . .
A longing for the ages past . . . that to the present bind,
Are the stepping-stones . . . of destiny . . .
    to the peace my soul must find.
Still you are there, Love.

I've known the earth primeval . . . weathered every clime;
Probed the depths of reason . . . for . . . immortal love sublime.
You were always there, my darling, though it seemed . . . in pantomime.
We've met before . . . we'll meet again . . . in the corridors of time,
'Cause you are there, Love!

Irene Passarella

IRENE PASSARELLA. Born: East Side of New York (Hell's Kitchen); Married: James Paul Passarella; Education: Dickenson High School, Jersey City, New Jersey; Raritan High School, Hazlet, New Jersey; Brookdale Learning Center, Eatontown, New Jersey; Occupation: Saleslady, presently retired; Awards: Golden Poet Trophy, 1986, 1987; Merit certificates include 'Master's Dilemma,' 3-31-86; 'Welcome Home,' 7-4-86; 'The Lily,' 1-16-87; 'Poet's Prayer,' 1-20-87; 'Saga of Flaggy Haggletooth,' Poetry: *Poetically Speaking*, collection of 15 poems, 3-86 to 6-87; 'Welcome Home,' *Modern Poems of Today;* 'The Master's Dilemma,' 1987; Comments: *I write and compose from the heart about everyday people, emotions, fantasies and the beautiful, but complicated world in which we live. I adore Nature, and often inject my thoughts (about the scenery, moods and serenity she offers) into my work. Reincarnation is also a strong point in some of my work.*

MARIANA

You now have climbed life's mountain
  And can see the other side
Just remember going down
  Is a fast and shorter ride
The birthday may be fifty
  That's no reason to fear
Just consider it a day
  Forget about the year
Live life to the fullest
  Have yourself some fun
Because before you know it
  It will be number fifty-one
Never let it slow you down
  Just keep in pace with Ray
Be it in the kitchen
  Or be it in the hay
Always keep them guessing
  In everything you do
We both are really wishing
  A Happy Day to you.

Earl F. Hamblin

WHAT'S YOUR HURRY?

Each day I look & wonder
  Why the people hurry fast
They don't seem to care about the future
  And even less about the past

If you my friend will take the time
  To stop and look around
You will be less in a hurry
  To be tomorrowbound

See the majestic High Sierras
  With their beauty unsurpassed
Once your eyes have seen their grandeur
  The vision will forever last

Have you seen God's mighty ocean
  Rolling in to kiss the land
Seen the little children running
  Playing in the sand

To see the sun slowly sinking
  As it puts the world to rest
Saying I will see you at the dawning
  Then you know you have been blest

So stop & look around you
  There's beauty everywhere
If you don't know where you're going
  What's the hurry to get there.

Earl F. Hamblin

JANUS

Lost in storms —
  Roses bloom;
Lost in mundane, worldly cares
  A sun also rises.
Lost in "conquest and glory"
  Stars beam brightly;
Lost in confusion
  Shines Wisdom, shines Truth.

Robert E. Jones

EVELYN

My wife baked a birthday cake
  She baked it just for you
She said that I could also help
  And told me what to do
She had me put some candles on
  A tradition that's not new
I asked how many would we need
  She said great quite a few
It was then I called the city
  They really had a fit
Said I couldn't light that many
  Without a Fire Permit
I finally solved the problem
  In a way I think is best
Just put one in the middle
  The hell with all the rest

Earl F. Hamblin

PEOPLE COME AND PEOPLE GO

People come and people go, as
dust in the wind.

The things they once said and
did are now only memories.

They were once close, as close
as could be. They were the
ones who shared our laughter
and grief.

But time and place have a
funny way of acting, they are
two factors that can cease
people to be.

Yes people come, and people
go, as dust in the wind.

Vanessa Mason

THE CREDIT GIRL'S CREED

No use debating
I'm "Miss Credit Rating"
I'm quick to pick up a tip
If you decide to skip
I'm always very nice
When telling you "No dice"
I have methods to make you call
When payments begin to fall
I patiently listen to all the baloney
When the records prove you are a phony
Confidence in yourself I'll help you gain
When you are under sincere strain
From this motto I'll never bend
"One always pays for what they spend"

Gloria V. Argon

GROWING PAINS

I used to be able to think
Brain cells had some links

Now I find I'm lost in space
Hoping to find my own grace

To love myself and seek forgiveness
For the lies that cause my world's distresses

Spirit and mind united in one place
Rooted, sealed and lovingly encased

Securely wrapped in folds of laughter
Leaving behind my soul's disaster.

Camille Brock Baumgartner

CAMILLE BROCK BAUMGARTNER. Born: Griffin, Georgia, 6-29-42; Single; Education: University of Miami, 1987; Chemical addiction professional; Occupations: Artist, Writer, C.A.C.; Memberships: Florida Writers Association, Florida Alcohol and Drug Abuse Association; Other Writings: "Sack Full of Lizards," 1980; "Cauliflower Connection," 1987; "Depression Born Males & Alcoholism," 1987; "My Best Friend Has Come Home!" *F.A.C.T. Quarterly Magazine,* 1985; all short stories; Comments: *My themes reflect the searching for wholeness within myself and life's changing forces.*

PLEASE UNDERSTAND ME

Please understand me
As you flip through these pages of my life.
What I feel,
What I live,
Is in all of them.
This is my book of life.
All of it in a list.
Why do people tear through them with a knife.
A knife cutting my wrist.
My heart pouring out
With each drop of blood
That is as thick as the thickest mud.
Please hear my tears of sorrow
Dripping slowly off my face like rain.
It won't be gone by tomorrow
Because of the pain.
Please listen to me
When I say nothing.
Please understand me.

Ramona T. Goodman

AT THE MOVIES

We sit in endless rows at the movies,
Staring through the darkness at the window out.
Then: voices making no sense in the pervading reality
Drag us back to the dingy darkness of the theater,
A woman quietly, pleading. A boy whimpering.
Angry, yet understanding the need for a mother to escape, too,
We scan rows for the source of intrusion.
Up front a shadow rises.
Holding out a hand for the figure beside it,
Its fingers suddenly connect to a hand much larger.
We watched horrified as a massive man rises,
Towers over the shadow and slowly begins to release
The wail that began as a whimper.
Projected onto the screen, his madness draws us into a world
So appalling we desperately try to repenetrate the
        fictitious world of film.

But the deep groans of a child-man cannot be ignored.
We listen to the echoes culminate in a resounding NOOOOO,
And watch as he feebly resists the frail but resolute shadow
        which leads him up the aisle.
His screams penetrate the silence long after
The swinging doors have ceased clacking.

Susan M. Hunt

CANNON

Silent are the trenches now where
    Once clashed giants, sword to sword, head to head,
Where columns of valorous comrades
    Left rows of wounded, crosses of dead.

Faces worn from weather and war
    Told the whole story, grim and grey,
Of huddles of men afraid of dark
    And their gritty defiance, undaunted, by day.

Heroes forged of mud and fire
    Felt the wind bite through what the rain had soaked cold.
But forsaking the human for something more,
    They stood like cannon, twice as hard, thrice as bold.

And o'er this very heap of ground
    Shouted scared volunteers through smoke and smell.
But each chose to sneer instead of run
    And plucked his soul from the jaws of Hell.

                Here I stand,
                Where greater men
                Once fell.

Shelton Harrison, Jr.

THE RAINBOW

I wish that all of life had the color of a rainbow,
But if this were so, I would not grow.
A caterpillar that hopes to be a butterfly,
Must spin a cocoon for a while to die.

The sunshine must give way to the rain,
Water it must bring to our terrestial terrain.
The tree in the winter must sleep,
So in the spring it will grow with a leap.

A seed that hopes someday to grow
The farmer, in the ground, must sow.
The bird, who wishes, the heavens to fly,
Must leave its sheltered nest so high.

As we travel our journey below,
Colorful rainbows will come and go;
When the waves of life become rough, let us never complain,
These are times when we must learn to grow;
Hasn't nature made that so plain?

Carl Allen Hilbrand

SOUL LONG

What is this creature so tall and gray,
    that feeds upon bales of fresh cut hay.

He runs, and jumps like a child at play.
    If I should approach him he scurries away.

I bring him gifts, a carrot, an apple, or two.
    He looks at me with eyes of blue.

He understand I mean him no harm.
    He rubs his head upon my arm.

One warm day late in the month of May
    I saddled him and rode away.

He took me to a long neglected grave,
    of a fallen cavalryman,
        killed in battle by an Indian brave.

I read the inscription upon the broken stone.
    I turned to see I was now alone.

If ever my soul does stray where cool breezes
    make tree limbs wave,
My faithful horse returns me to my grave

John R. Lenza

YESTERDAY, TODAY AND TOMORROW

We will take one day at a time
With no fears of the unknown.
Now is all we have to love and cherish.
The memories of yesterday will exist
Only in our minds forever.
Everything else will change,
Taking another form, size, and shape.
Tomorrow we will confront with dignity,
If we happen to wake up on the same
Planet, space, and plane.

Feliz Mosch

YOU TOLD ME

You told me
You wouldn't come back.
I thought it was a lie.
I never thought it was possible
For my father to die.
You're never coming back
That much is clear.
But, I often wish that you were here.
Because, I'm hurting more
Tear after tear.
My life has fallen apart.
I should have listened
But, I just couldn't hear.

Ramona T. Goodman

RAMONA TERESA GOODMAN. Born: Inglewood, California, 6-27-72; Occupation: High school student; Poetry: *Love & Life, Life & Love, Book I,* 1985-86; *Love & Life, Life and Love, Book II,* 1986-87; *Love & Life, Life & Love, Books III & IV,* 1987; Comments: *The common themes of my poems are obvious in the title of my books which I hope to someday get published. It's a sort of diary of my everyday life, the mature experiences I've had at my so-called young age.*

BOOK OF THE SEEDS

Thou comes to the seeds in their
    hour of pain.

Thou is coming to the seeds in their
    hour of sorrow.

Thou has more powers than the z-persons
    can think of.

Thou has come with power
    over all things.

Thou has saved the seeds once
    before from this z-person.

Thou doesn't confuse the seeds
    with vain ideas.

Thou has helped the seeds through
    the storm.

Felix Louis Wicks

ALONE

Today the sun is shining bright
The day drifts off into the night
I feel so alone, this seems so wrong
The days pass slow the nights are long
You and I were meant to be
Together for eternity.
My life goes on day after day
Not much changes, time passes away
Sometimes I feel like I just exist
I go through the motions, so much I resist
The sun comes up, the sun goes down
The nights are long, I must frown.
Here I sit feeling blue
There is nothing I can do
Life goes on day after day
I must live my own way . . . alone

Coralee A. Mollner

A wish,
a cup of wine,
I'm a child again.
Innocent,
pure,
such a wish,
such a fine cup
of wine.

I was told of old age —
but laughed in disbelief.
Until this morning image in
the mirror laughed back at me.

To appease the god of war
they sacrificed their
beloved sons.
To appease the god of war
they paid a royal tax.
To appease their conscience
they beat the family dog.

John Hagan

TANGERINE

They have flowers in Vietnam
those whose buds
open to a bloody wound
to pain that runs in rice paddies
and booby traps
to hunger-stricken faces
that share no love
with blasted skulls

the blossoms flutter and scatter
gather, flutter and scatter
like moths driven from light
a dark mosaic of quivering colors
that seeks an altar,
an arrival somewhere —

but for their growth
these flowers need no gardener
only the lesser man
whose finger on the trigger
draws the fatal bloom.

Gemma Racoma Clausen

HONESTY OSTRICH

I'm a bird, but I can't fly
Gosh kids don't ask me why
I got a long neck and great big feet
I thought I was always pretty neat

Till one day some kids made fun of me
I buried my head in the sand, you see
So I wouldn't hear their awful jeers
And they couldn't see my eyes with tears

Then Humility Pew came to call
And said what I looked like didn't matter at all
So I stood up as tall as tall could be
For all the world to admire and see

An ''Honesty Ostrich'' with a big heart inside
Who no longer had to run and hide

Margaret Womack

A need, the desire, an obsession —
    The game begins!
Hope, dreams, the excitement —
    Will it be —
    Agony or Ecstasy?

Is it lust — love
    NO! The Lottery!

Dolores Cudish

DOLORES JEANNETTE CUDISH. Pen Names: 'D,' Jeanne Cudish; Born: Acushnet, Massachusetts, 11-16-46; Married: Bruce C. Cudish, 9-28-70; Education: University of Maryland, European Division, A.A. (5-85), B.S. (6-86); Occupations: Wife and mother of five children, Substitute secretary for Denver School Department; Membership: Denver Art Museum; Comments: *My themes vary, however, most of my works are done as a form of therapy.*

THOUGHTS

They're nearly grown, they are going away,
Mother's heart goes with each one,
She longs for the day of their safe return
To her bosom, her daughters and sons.

How big must the hearts of parents be!
Each child takes a part of each one
With himself as he leaves the safety of home,
No matter how far he may roam.

When they return, there are open arms waiting,
Hungry eyes feast on the sight, of the one
Who's been gone and for whom she's been longing
Every day and long, lonely night!

Her prayers for your safety will always go on,
Her love for you never will cease,
You're part of her always, as alone she weeps silently
Then slumbers in deep, restful peace.

June F. (Sutton) Grotte

LOST LOVE

Oh, friend, do you remember those courting days?
Walking quietly in the woods,
Hand in hand, on pine-needle carpets,
The scent of pine all 'round, and
Sitting on the riverbank, listening,
Gurgling water, as it flowed around the rocks,
Its voice changing as it meandered on.
Breezes teased at the pines, whispering secrets,
As we spoke of "that little girl, sweet as pie,"
And the boy "cute as a squirrel," we'd someday have!
Oh, lost love, our dreams were tender and full,
Fueled by our emotions.
I remembered your crinkly-eyed smile, all encompassing,
As you held me, and remembrance still thrills!
In mind's eye, I see you, tall, dark curly-haired, handsome.
You went away for awhile, and I, forlorn, felt sure you had
Left for good! No word; what could I think?
Then you came in uniform! You had joined the army!
You brought a ring! But I was *so* young, and it was too late!
Where are you now? Do you still remember?

June F. (Sutton) Grotte

THE TRADE

Great globules of half-chewed,
sickeningly sweet pink bubble gum
permeate the air as the team gathers in huddle.

They try, try in vain
to contain
their excitement. "Ready, set, go!" is their call.

Fat fleshy fingers fight frantically
with cellophane wrappers.
The naked piles exposed, as the team goes to work.

Some are clearly admired, others chastised.
One, in particular, captivates and repulses.
"Say," one shouts, "who is this Babe anyway?"

"Think he played with the Yankees once,"
explains the team captain.
All in unison agree —

"Trade him!"

Anthony M. Millspaugh

DODGE CITY

The painted pony prances through the dusty road of town.
He halts, rider disengages,
swaggers to a hitching post.
Spurs jingle-jangle like loose change in a pocket,
as he ascends and travels through the swinging doors.

Seated in nearly empty room,
a dyed-hair woman approaches.
She is at his left.
A bottle of whiskey at his right.
Both at his command.

A swift swig.
He is parched.
He drains one draft and then another,
wiping ferociously at excess rivulets on
his dark, stubbled face.

A commotion outside.
He is oblivious as faint footsteps touch wooden planking.
The hinges haltingly cry out warning.
Shotgun blast.
Thirst quenched.

Anthony M. Millspaugh

EIGHTY-PROOF CATHEDRAL

Before the man-made altar of alcohol
many a man has cast his soul
to history's increasing toll
of social suicides.
Worshiping a whiskey sour
as if it had some special power
to cure the world's evil.

Man grabs the bottle as if it were the throttle
that controlled his life,
the answer to his daily strife.
When in reality it's nothing more than
a liquid knife, that cuts men to pieces
bit by bit.

Francis Dooley

RED LIGHT, GREEN LIGHT, ONE, TWO, THREE.

Deep within the womb of the city
a starving man who found a
hundred-dollar bill, died of
starvation because no one would
give him change for it.

He was found lying lifeless
in the gutter clutching a cheap
bottle of wine he earned
from occasionally washing the car windows
that stop for a red traffic signal.
We say it shines red so we avoid
death or accident.
But could there be another reason?

Francis Dooley

LONGING

Sunlight on the window sill,
The dust is plainly seen.
Outside the view is sharp and clear,
Even the dust looks clean.

But now I cannot pass the doors
Out into the street.
The beauty that the day begets
I've lost in vain retreat.

Children played another day
And never gave a thought
To sunlight on the sidewalks,
A sight their elders sought.

Gaye A. J. Feuer

MY CURLY HEAD

My little curly head, laying in your bed,
Only God knows what you mean to me,
Your dad's no longer here,
So to me you're twice as dear,
For a part of him in you I seem to see.
You took a step today, and I know in every way
You'll be the man he wanted you to be,
So sleep on as you lay there,
And I pray that one day, dear,
All of your dreams will come true.

Terry Hyland

WITH YOU

With you by my side, there's nothing I can't do.
In a time of darkness in my life,
You helped to see me through.
I found a friend, I found a love,
I found someone who's true,
I smile today, instead of cry,
It's all because of you.

Terry Hyland

ODE TO JOEY

Joey was only twenty-one,
He'll never be twenty-two.
A freak accident took his life,
and made his family so blue.
Working for the county on ''85,''
if they hadn't sent him down
he'd still be alive.
An apprentice and young
with orders to obey,
doing what had to be done,
he gave his life away.
But Joey, one thing I want you to know,
and it's all because of you,
new laws have been made on safety,
so other boys will reach twenty-two.

Terry Hyland

Let us talk again
Of peace on earth my friend
There will still be many wars
Attempts to even scores
When there's love we always win

Walter Timothy Hanna

For months on end
I worked across the globe
But always my thoughts were of you.
Sometimes it's hard to concentrate
Too many variables, too many distractions.
Then was the time to focus on the obvious
To be direct, with clarity and compassion
I returned; happy but with no direction.
Perhaps soon I'll understand
Until then I'll just keep believing
Of a better place, a finer life
And maybe, if I work hard and try my best
I'll have someone like you
To love until the end.

Walter Timothy Hanna

Maybe it is right
That you stay the night
We can talk about the news
You can tell me all your blues
I really want to hear
That you really care
Because you're a friend I trust
My spirit says I must
So let us build our lives
On rock instead of sand
Where our castles always stand
Through the thick and through the thin
We must trust in Him

Walter Timothy Hanna

TOO STRONG TO DESTROY

I am a man, I have a dream, but I
do not believe in dreams.
I see no dreams in man, I see no
warmth of dreams come true.
I hear the laughter of the cheated
souls and see the bitterness in their
haunted eyes of mirth.
I hear in their serious and wise voices
the true ring of madness and delirium.
''We must be men of strength and build
destruction to destroy ourselves.''
''How else can we prove we are too strong
to destroy?''

William Hamizides

A NEW BEGINNING

The nights now too few
Are times to set aside your problems
And to enjoy the sky and
The moon and all the starry host.

And when the sun rises
You should start anew
The day from beginning to end.
Enjoy life and give a toast.

Sad to say, I do not boast
Many a day I've wasted away.
Till now the days are too few
And Death in somber attitude.

Oh, a new day!
I vow! I promise this day I'll not coast
Nor sit idly by with regret;
I'll live my days, though few,
To the most exciting-est.

Ben Farris

BUSH CRAFT

Time will tell, I was child without wisdom
All my life, traveller without pretension.
Skirting the depths of empty spaces
Where red-hot pokers prod the blue,
And Protea burst calyces like stars.
Aloes alone have heralded my way
Through shadows of Mapani woods
Where elephants once thundered.

When cheeks are cracked in friendless lines,
Profile softened with unforgiving folds,
Eyes burning fervent as recurrent dawn,
Reflecting my image; monolith among clouds.
Where air slumbers under Mimosa umbrella,
My mind crouches, stolid as a Baobab trunk,
Between sandy rosettes; spoor of bashful buck;
My muffled footfall tramps forever.

Where light shines hard, metallic white,
Between blue shafts and rays of grass;
My irises, buried in myriad wrinkles
Mirror trails that criss-cross the veldt.
My youth tangles in my beard's bristle;
Rock-rabbits brushing the Savannah stubble.
May my brash life bubble irrepressively
Like monkeys scrambling or granite kopjies.

Mike Scheidemann

AUTUMN

The sun is so warm,
The sky so blue;
The colors so bright —
Can it really be true
That it is fall and
So much is dying?
It's Nature's show —
As though she is trying,
With one burst of color,
To bring us some cheer
Before the drab and chill
Of the end of the year.

Jill Vernon

THE LAST LAUGH

The last time I looked
Calvary Hill was crowded
with millions of maybe-next-time matryrs
along with Brooklyn Bridge barterers
and other such paragons of truth.

Below, the population of the
Sunflower Rest Home,
sit by themselves, all alone.
Forty strangers with only one thing in common,
society's demand for a quick demise.
Why do we despise
these early pioneers of our earthly existence?
Are their faces mirrors
we'd rather ignore?

We rationalize to ourselves,
the eternal snore
is all that's in store for them.

We have more in store, we surely must . . .

Of course, a few more children
to laugh at us.

Francis Dooley

PASSIONS

Hold me tight!
Keep me just for the night.
Fire me with your kisses.
Lie to me and tell me that you love me,
miss me, want me.
Show me your strength, my lion, my horse.
Ride me, ride me.
Make me scream the madness of this incompatible
steel world. Ride me under the hot sun.
Feel the warm soft sand under your calloused feet.
Ride me, ride me. Show me the fury and passions of
the ocean waves smashing into the rocks.
Ride me, ride me.
Take me where the sky is blue.
The ocean calm and cool.

Feliz Mosch

FELIZ MOSCH. Born: Lima, Peru; Education: Baruch College, New York; William Paterson College, New Jersey, Business Administration; Occupation: Teacher; Statement: *With my illusions no preaching and so-called "Words of Wisdom" I heard. Hopping and clapping, singing and dreaming, my carefree spirit flew over the meadows. Feeling and seeing the beauty, Thee created just for me to see! The river ran slow with crystal-clear waters. From stone to stone, I walked like an acrobat, up and down the stream. There I nourish my dreams. I would rise above the adversity of my conception, my birth and disenchantment of parental love. The highest star I would reach and make it my wish. I will see everything there is to see, I will learn everything there is to learn . . .*

ODE TO ANASTASIA — A LOST FRIEND

Her eyes were of green, her heart pure gold,
Her hair was of wheat and her spirit unchangeably bold.
Born the fourth part of a six-piece set,
Her untimely demise leaves the others with regret.
The fairest part now is missing, leaving
The other five with sweet, bitter grieving.
To have known and loved her was my treat,
But now ever gone leaves my heart set back a beat.
Is Life this unfair, cruel at its best?
Yet, to have shared some of her years gives me rest.
Anastasia was a daughter, a sister to five,
But above all, a best friend to me and those still alive.

Debbie T. Pearce

SYMBOL OF OUR ERA

The cross on the grave of a soldier who died in Vietnam
Marks the symbol of this generation,
For the world to look upon.
As a monument to freedom it stands tall above the grave,
To show this world of mass confusion
That precious life he gave.
No better way of saying: America stand tall;
Mark this time in era, freedom and peace for all.

The cross on the grave of a soldier
Speaks a language all its own,
Another true American will not be coming home.
For the freedom of our children,
For the need to live in peace,
Our soldiers keep on fighting to mend unsettled deeds.
And the symbol of our era, above him tall and kind,
Reminds us that our soldiers at last found peace of mind.

Lisa H. Meyer

SUMMER WINE

The fruit market
has the smell of dust and evening sunshine.
An apple rolls unnoticed beneath a table
full of strawberries nestling in grapeleaf-lined containers.
Neighboring melon vendors compete loudly
in hawking the lowest price.

We stroll amid the cacophony —
deaf to all but our own music.
Content in the knowledge of our secret love
we buy mulberries, cherries, and dusky grapes.
Our glances meet, then part.
In his eyes I see the caress of a kiss.

Beyond the market
the evening gathers into purpling dusk —
and we continue our peaceful promenade.
Our bodies may walk a yard apart,
but our souls stroll before us intertwined.

A distant nightingale serenades us —
a liquid note
in the effervescence of our love song.

Gail V. Baker

SHOW ME THY GLORY

When saddened by my remorse
Which pains my heart to no avail
When doubts have conquered
my faith and trust
and leave my weary soul in longing —
Show me thy glory.

When I long to know thee
But my heart is heavy;
When my prayer —
but a grumble
My mind crammed —
with thoughts of the day
Show me thy glory.

When I long to love
and be loved,
a shoulder to lean on —
But I'm alone
Lie clinging to my pillow —
tears softly caressing my cheeks
Show me thy glory.

Paulette Larmond

ORPHICS

You show your holy figure
in the garden, in the winter
crowned with grape clusters
among the barren branches.

Immortal son of unspeakable union
you shoot your arrows from afar
and dance in the swift waters
where there is no memory
of a time before or after.

I come to you moving
through the twilight
to hear all that you reveal
destiny and fate
the beginning and the end to come
a single note struck
on your lyre.

Pamela Hamilton Dunbar

FEELINGS

Have you ever felt so angry,
That you thought you'd nearly pop,
Then a voice inside said softly,
Count to ten before you stop?

It's a trick my mother taught me,
Helps my anger go away.
And you know it's really brought me
Better feelings for that day.

I've learned how to watch my temper,
I know how to think things through.
Now I see that it's much simpler,
If you try it you'll know, too.

Charlotte M. Hill

MORNING

Morning awakens around the lake,
Coming to life in the first light of dawn.
Steamy mist rises off the hazy surface,
Disappearing into the sky.

Startled by my presence,
A duck ruffles its feathers and
Waddles toward the water's edge.
In the reeds, a heron searches for its breakfast.

Small insects hover over the dewy grass.
Are they hungry, too, I wonder,
Or the birds, now in chorus
In the trees all around me.

I marvel at the peaceful activity,
The busy-ness of life.
Splashing, pecking, buzzing, chirping,
Everything dependent on the other.

A new day is here
Again.
And again.

Joyce Hartman

POSSESSION

Don't wait for warm winds of change
    to sweep the clouds away.
Never wait desiring the rainbow's end
    to cast its gold your way.
Don't expect something for nothing.
    The story is infallibly clear.
You don't get freedom for free.
    You don't get wise by dreaming,
    no matter what your dream may be.
All you own is your own heart.
    What you love is your only glory.
You are the oracle of your story.
    The unredeemed critic of your deeds.
In your head lies the answer,
    let it guide you along.
Let your heart be your anchor,
    and the driving beat of your own song.

Jeff L. Anderson

SONNET NO. 11

Once no more, but once more I plead
my cause, though moribund and fallow.
Fallen short of the divine fruit, a seed
simply sown, thrown from hand to shallow
grave to sprout tenderly, the pinnacle
of life, of the heart, of this emotion —
Yet wilted, love, for no precious miracle,
no hallow vitality such as your devotion
would rain upon love's lusty womb.
There is no elixir nor holy revival
come to kneel in the dust by my tomb
praying for relief, the kiss of survival
soft on its lips, save your touch,
which trickly essence I need so much.

Sandra Collins

EVENING

*To the memory of Dr. Jorge
Tirado-Romany, 1939 - 1985*

This is the hour when memory wakes
  Sweet dreams that could not last;
This is the hour when fancy takes
  A survey of the past.
It brings before the pensive mind
  Dear thoughts of earlier years;
And friends that have been long consigned
  To silence and to tears.

The few we liked, the ones we loved,
  Come slowly stealing on;
And many a form so long removed,
  And many a pleasure gone.

Friendships that now in death are hushed,
  Affection's broken chain;
And hopes that fate too quickly crushed,
  In memory live again.

I watch the fading gleams of day,
  I muse on bright scenes flown;
Tint after tint, they fade away,
  Night comes and all are gone.

L. A. Colón-Arce

HIS HIDDEN FACE

Where are you hiding your face?
Are you here with me?
Or, are you in another place?

Where are you roaming about?
Did you go into a heart
and then turn and go out?

No, I can't see your face,
but, I know you're here.
You opened my heart when
you lent me your ear.

The search is over.
You were always around
patiently waiting;
hoping to be found.

I realize now
never did we part.
You were always here,
right in my heart.

Karen Rocha

WALKING IN SILENCE

Walking in silence, I hear a lot.
I hear what I am not listening to.
I hear you speaking, yet you are not there.
  I still keep walking.
Will I ever catch up to the silence I hear?
Will I ever shake my fear?
Walking in silence, I do hear a lot.

Candice L. Lincoln

INTERLUDE

In the dawn
    I awoke to the smell
(Out of watermelon dreams,)
    of rain-cleared air
(curling beneath the sheets,)
    and smiled in the happy
      inspiration of sweet breath.

(I tried to slumber;)
    Past and present pin-wheeled
      in vague and hazy shapes
(thoughts of you intruded,)
      kaleidoscoping in my head
        until the morning birdsong
(pervasive and insistent.)
      lulled me back to sleep.

Gail V. Baker

HERE'S FOR NOW

Here's for the first time, here's for now,
really want to love you, don't know how.
    The day you left, I crawled into a bottle and I've been
there since. Never could handle singular suspense.
    Ten years later and I want to climb out, but it never will
happen, because when I crawled in, I plugged up the spout.
    Here's for the first time, here's for now, really wanted
to love you, but I'll never know how!

Chris Drury

THE OBTUSE

Fire-engine baby boats linger
Beneath the turbulent surfaces
Of serenities incarnate
To the single face of faces frozen
And caught, in the labyrinth of timeless crystalline forevers,
Wondering and wandering about the ice-castles of mind
    from matters
As red dripping bloodied moving targets
Rise into rainbow flowers and domestic unbearables,
Cool in the limelight,
Dark in the tragedy,
The wakened pull of life beckons thine every step
Onward.

Roy D. Benson

OUR SONG

Our time in life began
    When first our glance was met,
And has traveled through those yesterdays
    With happiness and regrets.
And tomorrow is that always,
    Just around the bend,
Where we shall love
    And we shall laugh,
        And some day we shall end.
For life goes on before and aft
    Our love's song is done,
But this world will be more blessed than not,
When our life song is sung.

Bonnie J. Scoble

HURT

The heart within me beats like a raging tom-tom
Trying to drown out the bitter memories of a false love.
Throbbing with my every pulse,
Beating, pushing resentment through my soul, like a raging river,
Awakening the raw primitive emotions.
Hopelessly balanced on that thin line between love and hate,
Aching to destroy — kill all memories,
Yet, searching, reaching for that last straw of survival.
Tormented, but afraid to forget —
Lest you have no reason for life.
So beat on, great and powerful heart,
Sound your drum so loud and clear that others may hear and learn,
The sardonic chant by which all fools must live.

Bonnie J. Scoble

LAURA

My minds drifts into a peaceful euphoria
When I think of my heart's desire,
The dreams I dream of Laura
Set my soul on fire.
The flicker becomes a giant flame
Melting my spirit like candle wax
And why should I be ashamed
For loving the girl who attacked
My heart with love's steely blade?
The girl who sliced it, making an incision,
Toyed with it, played, and then bade
Me to make a difficult decision;
Should I let her know on earth, she's the fairest upon it,
My love is hers to take, but will she want it?

Jacob Bembry

SHARE WITH ME A DREAM

Share with me a dream called the brotherhood of man
And stand united behind every peaceful purpose
As we try to scratch the surface
And break through the window pane
Called prejudice and then let our rain
Wet the flowers of the youth
Who are too young to know the truth,
That we are brothers in the eyes of God
And we must cease to trod
Through the fields that have been sowed
With the ever-ripe seeds of hate,
For years we've tried to escape
From the sheaves of the terrible wheat
Grown in this field,
We must cease to yield,
We must destroy the crop
And we must stop
The diabolical creatures who sow this seed
Because hate and war are things we don't need.

Jacob Bembry

Purgatory Falls, Head-Waters of the Roanoke.

THE PEASANT AND THE PEDESTAL

How does our friendship always work?
You run to me each time you get hurt,
Then I hold you to make you better,
But when I say "I need you," you say "Never,"
But I'll never turn my back on you
Tho' my heart may cry for lack of you
And I pray that one day, you will see
That, like my love was meant for you, yours was meant for me,
But, for now, I'll have to bear with my grief
While you grab snatches of my love, like a thief,
I'll keep putting you on a pedestal like a queen
And I'll keep being the peasant who can only dream.

Jacob Bembry

SILENCE

In the darkness one may find peace.
The street lamp speaks in a monotone,
quiet and more discrete than even a whisper.

In the silence of the night,
the whippoorwill spoke,
bringing hope in his whippoorwill song.

In the silence of the night,
I heard the river rush,
splash on the rocks did she, rolling back so silently.

In the silence of the night,
I strolled with you for a while — my love,
our minds enchanted by the sounds around us.

In the silence of the night,
we danced with our hearts,
recalling the gentle wind crying in the trees.

Darkness, my closest foe,
I long to listen in your silence.
Your shadows leer and I lie among them.
You help me find reason once past is turmoil of day.

Rachel Santine

ART IS

that neverending search whose struggle speaks
    from need's invinsible, intrinsic sway.
strikes core, strikes kernel,
    marrow, nucleus;
like wind, like water,
    fire, frost and air;
unceasing pulses, passion's rendering;
is spirit, sense — is ego, intellect
    defining more than camouflaged effect
    of form, or figment — costume or cosmetic.
    perceiving more than foil or fact,
    or sponge, or game, or noise, or act.

art is the stuff and fabric of soul's
unceasing struggle — striving to be whole.

Mamie G. Gibson

URBAN MALADY

Breeders of baubles, baffles 'n' bruises;
    of jive-dives 'n' mumbo-jumbo.
Bulldozers of yesterday's promises,
    with its ambitious-ambiguities
        of giving . . . getting . . . taking,
            Mostly taking.

That prey upon its dreamers without work;
and work upon its preyers without dreams.

Bulldozers of yesterday's promises,
    with its ambitious-ambiguities,
        of giving . . . getting . . . taking,
            Mostly taking.

Mamie G. Gibson

IF ONLY THERE COULD BE
(ONE MOMENT)

If only there could be one moment of stillness,
    The universe would show us realities;
thought, inconceivable.
    If only there could be one moment of silence,
    We could gain awareness of the here and now, long
forgotten.
    If only there could be one moment of blindness,
    We would all be individuals in search of any other,
a brother.
    If only there could be just one moment of togetherness,
    The universe would not have to show us these
realities, Heavens rejoice.
    If only that togetherness would be,
    We would surely endure the everlasting benefits of
harmony, that's unity.

Harry A. Russell

I cannot go on
Like this
I am lost in the galaxy of planets
A star that wanders endlessly
With no goal to be achieved
No destination in life
Just another faceless oddity.

Perhaps, soon, tranquility will come
In the plans that have been laid upon the void
For now my form is useless, a conversation
Of the epitaph of truth
The dusty saucers that lay naked
Where rivers have flown from each cup gently and unnoticed
In this whirlpool, one should search
Not for voices nor for life
Just for the emptiness of palms
Incidental to the depth of cracks
An end to hydrogen form

And maybe hidden amongst dust and tea leaves
One's imagination can perform a trick
A disillusion of image
To find a million faces scar the emotions of light

Carole Simmons

NEGLECTED WORDS

Did I tell you today that I love you?
Or did I take it for granted you knew?
I left the house so quickly
Our spoken words were few.

Did I tell you today that I need you?
Or did I conceal it deep inside?
Did I mention that I was the luckiest
or ignore it because of my pride?

Did I hug you or ask to be hugged?
Or did I think, maybe later —
Somehow, I let the minor things
always seem much greater.

Time is not meant to be taken for granted
for life can quickly pass us by.
Each day I'll tell you I love you,
how much you're needed and why.

Karen Rocha

Today, this moment,
this precious second of
time has been made by
God, for us to share, and
forever hold as a memory,
a good memory. This moment
is the beginning of a beautiful
segment of our life designed to
enrich our minds — to cherish,
to hold, to love. We love today,
  this moment.

Steven F. Shea

NEW YEARS' EVE

My heart is a searcher, lost and lonely,
It is unable to let you go.
I think of you now and think of you only
And wish that you could know.

Today I almost got into my car
To drive down South to find you.
But instead I wished upon a star
And asked that the Moon may remind you;

Might she tell you that you are so wrong
If you've thought you have been forgotten.
You have been beside me, within me, all along
Through every snare that I've been caught in.

Maybe it's just that I'm not quite as clear
As you are about our need and desire.
But I do know that I wish you were here
To ignite the flame, fan the fire.

I know that I still want to bear your child
But who can tell what's meant to be?
My soul is a hunter in an endless wild,
Seeking the love that will set it free.

Jeanne Heroux

ODE TO MY FATHER

Dads clothe, feed and educate
their children.

I haven't a closet full of clothes,
I wear the shirt from off your back.

Though there were times without food
on the table, I never went hungry.

You are my father, a man of quality.
You are the garden of health from which I eat,
the stream of knowledge from which I drink.
When I fail you show me new goals for
which to reach.

You are my father, a parent other
children can only dream of. You are the
one person I shall always love.

M. Shelton Blackwell

DEATH KEPT ME COMPANY

Death kept me company last night;
We talked 'til nearly three.
I came to know him rather well,
But he knew more of me.

Like a suitor paying court,
He wanted us to wed;
When I agreed, my fickle friend
Then changed his mind and fled.

There's much that I have learned of him,
This fellow we call Death:
His tight embrace won't suffocate;
He has no foul breath;

He doesn't dress in gray or black;
He makes no rattling din;
He doesn't smell of must or mold;
He doesn't leer or grin.

In fact, he is a kindly man,
An understanding beau,
Who knew when I said yes to him,
I really did mean no.

Sally Stembridge

The stillness of night enthralling
Sleep in darkness lost
Quiet
Careful not to breath
Eyes remain watchful
Take care not to close
Find no fear in shadows,
Unfortunate unrest
For comfort is the evil
Time, the clock with silent hands,
Brings the lightless dawn of death
Slumber too sweet and life the same
Both are snatched —
Abruptly

Andria Cantrell

The essence of time unfolds before me
My breath is stilled
Unlocked
My soul flounders — unsure
Lives —
All reconciled
Merge into one

The essence of immortality becomes clear
I am the earth
I fall
With breathless rain
I live in the sky
And in the hearts of mortal man

If eternity escapes me
Undulating from nothingness
One last search
The final vastness
Beyond humanity
Uncontained in spiritual realm
The last god, a final fear

Andria Cantrell

Adrift, lost
Laughter lingers on the fringes
Of nothingness
No world
No thought
Love, the only energy
Flows through breathless eternity
Long dead world
Takes no more
Clasped in perfect unity
The last spirits of humanity
Melt into dark spaces in time
Watch and wonder why it ever had to be
A useless farewell
To an uncaring stranger
Touch the world, then go.

Andria Cantrell

NO FLOWERS

Don't want no flowers
When I go
Don't want their
Pretty faces
Staring at my unseeing eyes
Don't want their aromatic smells
Creeping towards my unsmelling nose
Don't want them
Wanting me holding them
In my unfeeling hands
I want mine
Before I'm six feet
Down below
Don't want no flowers
When I go.

Olivette Morton

AN INVITATION TO STOP HURTING
AND TO START LIVING

Through all of your own doing of destruction,
you are hurting yourself the most.
You keep on persisting
in causing pain and
inflicting stabs at the delicate heart.
This hurts all who love you
and those whom you love.
Before you are totally blinded by
your destructive force,
open your eyes to the love
which lies before you —
ready to accept you
just as you are.
In fact, that love
is already yours,
even if you don't realize it.
So, stop hurting yourself
and begin to discover
the path to eternal life in heaven
with the One you can always count on.

Janice M. Chang

SUNRISE

DARK!
.
Then, hark!
A gentle glow
Growing, oh,
So very slow.
Streaks of pink
Push back the dark.
Hazy stars must disembark.
Living clouds reflect each hue;
Warming colors flood the view.
Silhouettes stand up to pose;
As their back unfolds the rose.
Then golden rays which take to flight
Like swords, reach out to lance the night.
See the red and orange of the frenzied flame
Eat the canvas through, then the smoking frame!
A yellow ball of glowing heat hangs low and hot and clean;
A blazing, blinding flash of light splits through the scenic scene!
So the eyes which watched with wonder must now turn to look away
For the *King of Life* has ushered in a new and radiant day!

Billy R. Zimmerman

TO HAVE AND HAVE NOT

If a ''have not'' had a knot of wood and that is all he had
Then he still would be a ''have not'' though there's something
   he would have.
But if a ''have not'' had a knot not made of wood but gold
Then he would not be a ''have not'' having something there to hold.
Where a knot of gold and a knot of wood would seem the same to some,
A ''have not'' would not have wood knots if a ''have'' he would become!

Billy R. Zimmerman

I CHOOSE TO USE MY BRAIN

The farmer plows and sows and sprays upon the fertile plain;
The net result — a livelihood through selling golden grain.
I need not know the skill to grow; I choose to use my brain.

The engineer a-swaying in his chuffing smoky train
Must suffer heat and noise and yet his family knows the gain.
I need not ride there at his side; I choose to use my brain.

The pilot, down the runway, guides with skill his roaring plane.
Like bird he flies among the clouds above the green terrain.
No time have I to learn to fly; I choose to use my brain.

The doctor uses pill and balm to conquer senseless pain.
The nurse gives comfort to the sick and guides the lost insane.
Now you can see, that's not for me. Just let me make it plain;
If given choice of work to do, I choose to use my brain.

The warden of a prison with his gun and lock and chain
Is lord and total master of his prisoners' domain.
Such grisly work I choose to shirk. Perhaps I should explain . . .

Through thought and time with words in rhyme I hope to entertain.
A poet am I and it's no lie (though it can be a strain!).
You can believe the words I weave; I choose to use my brain!

Billy R. Zimmerman

MY STRANGER

Today at last, it's come to pass, and I am made to see,
The little boy, that I loved so, is but a memory.
The one who stands before me now, I cannot understand,
The little boy that I loved so, is soon to be a man.

With glinted eyes and jutted chin; defiance plain to see,
It's a *Stranger* standing there glaring back at me,
He says that I don't know him, and now I quite agree,
I only knew the little boy; the boy he used to be.

As a Mother, he won't need me, I must let go of his hand,
Alone he must complete this journey, from his boyhood to a man.
Please God, help me to change with him, *Please God,* help me get to
   know and to understand this *Stranger,*
For you know, I love him so.

Sue Ragsdale

IN THAT TREE

You can say what you are thinking.
Words.
As I was under that tree.
Cold.
But, I would have slept there.
Waiting.
You were across.
Looking.
Quietly, I looked inside your mind.
You wondered how I was feeling and what I
was thinking.
Why did you dare not enter inside of me,
to find that I was thinking of no one else but you?

Susan Nalicat

I'LL NEVER SAY GOOD-BYE

The pain I feel is hard to bear,
It shows how much I'll always care.
A life-long friend has gone away,
I wish to God that he could stay.

He brought me joy for many years,
Now that he's gone, he brings me tears.
I feel my life is not worth living,
And the love I have is not worth giving.

I can't believe this day has come,
There was so much joy, and so much fun.
For thirteen years he was my friend,
My love for him will never end.

I'll remember him until I die,
But I know I'll never say good-bye.

Maryann Syrydynski

THE FINAL DAY

The sky was dark, and full of dust,
I was told to hide, I knew I must.
The sun was nowhere to be found,
and my feet were shaking on the ground.

The crowded land was full of screams,
and a lot of pain, or at least it seems.

The streets were gone and the trees were dead,
and a large grey mushroom was overhead.

There was nothing left but a lot of fear,
and the sound of death was growing near.

My years of life were passing by,
and I knew it was almost time to die.

The day had come for the world to end,
I looked so hard to find a friend.

But as I searched the air grew thin,
and I knew there was no way that I could win.

I lost my breath, and there I died,
with only one thing by my side.
The happy thought of being free
from this rotten world that hated me.

Maryann Syrydynski

THE POET

Page after page of scribbled
gestures gnaw at the
paper, screaming for an
exact meaning.

Effortless imaginings
blurt forth in an
unrhythmic pattern.

Fatigue sets in;
the element of thought ceases.
The poet ends his serenade.

Patricia A. Herrmann

THE DAY

Waiting for the day to come, yes,
it is to appear. When how and where
not known. But sure to show.
Harvest gathered from the field
is only shield, as much can be built.
Even the apparatus we belong
to hear, work, see and sing
not to hold among, when the bell bang.
Why not put a mark
to enjoy the park, before it is dark.
O dear, don't fear, when you hear
summons have come.
Be brave to share, boldly face tears.
Run the race, leave no trace.
Cross the goal, winning pole.
Don't miss life's role
before the call comes.

Than Anchlia

KING

His name was king
So he was king
King having no queen
King having no land
King having no house
King having no army
King having no money
Still he was king
When born mummy loved
'My little king'
Daddy said really a king.
He was king of his Cross
He was king of his boss
He was king of his friends
He was king of his ends
He was king in rebellions
He was king of millions.
Thank you king.

Than Anchlia

PROXIMUM DOMORUM

The Closest of Houses

I wonder sometimes:
How can two people so in love,
So wanting, so deserving, so close,
Be facing the possibility of seeing each other
Not but merely once a week?

'Tis not a promising situation to either
When it is but once a week they meet at
Any respectable length of time.
It is much worse when the two dwell in the
Same house and are committed to no other.

One may feel quite piteously for them —
As is expected.
But no two except they have that feeling
And know it for what it is, indeed.
It is painful, and makes them feel helpless.

Bernard Sulliban III

WELL GOD

I've taken my problems and chores
into my own hands again.
As you can see
I'm falling behind and growing weary
from the struggle.
I lie down before I sleep
and try to pray.
My mind wanders to things
I have failed to accomplish today
and the ever growing list
of things to do tomorrow.
I am too tired to even pray.
And I forget all I need to do
is ask for strength and help
and it shall be given to me.
I am fading off to sleep now
and I just can't seem to pray.
I guess I'll just add that
onto my list of things for tomorrow
that I've failed to do today.

Ann Benedick

ALONE

Alone — when the stars shine brightly
Upon the deep dark night sky,
The sweet smelling fragrance
Of delicate, ivory blossoms.

Alone — the dawning sun
Rises proudly against a fair sky,
A gentle breeze
Ripples the dark green grass.

A vast, open prairie field
Nothing breaks the shivering silence,
Scattered trees and violet fields
Alone — in a lonely place.

Alone — somewhere
Where the moon shines brightly,
Silence — all alone.

Ayesha Ahmad

GOD'S CHILD

To My Twin

Looking at you I often see me,
and when I watch you blink I think
    of sweet and kind and love and time
    unborn when we were one,
and when I watch you smile, your cheeks are
    soft and smooth and lightly pink
and your skin is pure and white and I think
of milk and children and bright sunshine
and the innocence of nature,
and you are truly beautiful.

Meryl Wolfson

A DREAM

Memories from the past, or the future yet to be,
Something once lived before, or something yet to see?
Pleasant occurrences, perhaps a love and life,
Or is your future — a detour, overcome with strife?

A fleeting glimpse of happiness or pain beyond compare,
Can you answer its revelation, or is it here or there?
A touch of softness — a caress to treasure so,
Or another journey yet to make, dreaming as you go.

Glancing into a crystal ball, scenes — you lived before,
Or is it but the key, that will open up the door?
Many years behind you, how many you do scream,
As you close your eyes at night, relive another dream . . .

Pleasure yet to come or joy from out the past,
Something to be yet explored or events that surely last?
Believe the feelings and the sights — papers piled in reams,
Future foretold or life once-lived, there within a dream . . .

Kenneth M. Snook

AMERICA

America, America, land of the free.
    America, America, blessed of God art thee.
Justice and liberty are for what you stand.
    Your patrons so reverent and loyal all over the land.
O Stars and Stripes, for freedom many have died.
    Our gratitude to them so that we may abide.
Our devotion and allegiance to you we give,
    for there is no other nation we desire to live.
Our hearts and our prayers go out to you.
    Wave, Old Glory, wave that Red, White and Blue.
Our forefathers dreams in you do they lie.
    Their foundation gave birth that fourth of July.
God bless their souls, now they're at rest.
    Their dreams now in our hands; we must do our best.
O direct and guide us Lord God above,
    for in You do we trust to protect the land we love.
America, America, we are proud of you.
    Forever let wave that Red, White and Blue.

Randy W. Teeters

I ONCE MET A MAN

    I once met a man who was quite unique,
he was not haughty but calm and meek.
    His love was one of many things he taught,
of how it was a gift and could not be bought.
    Many wondrous things did he perform,
from sickness to health did people transform.
    By a multitude he was falsely accused,
arrested he was then, beaten and abused.
    To his death a cross he did carry,
before a multitude and his mother Mary.
    Three days following his death he arose,
radiant glory shining from his head to his toes.
    He was alive to many a shock,
for of this prediction they did mock.
    Death was defeated and life is at hand,
for the way has been cleared to the promised land.
    His destiny had consisted of suffering and shame,
and after this a kingdom reign.
    His kingdom is different than what the world might conceive,
in order to get there you must believe.

Randy W. Teeters

DOWN BY THE SEA

    Why do I like to go down by the sea?
To watch the waves roll so wild and free.
    The ocean scent lingering in the air,
as the sea breeze blows through my hair.
    I notice a surfer out riding a wave,
to her subjection he has become a slave.
    The sun setting so beautifully in the sky,
as the sea gulls overhead soar by.
    Darkness beginning to settle around,
fires kindling and music the sound.
    The aroma of barbecues begins to arise,
the smoke ascending toward the skies.
    The people all with a smile on their face,
enjoying the surroundings of this fascinating place.
    Sometimes there's no place I'd rather be,
than spending a day down by the sea.

Randy W. Teeters

THE SHADOWS OF TIME

With each new dawn, alarms ring, children cry, horns blare,
        and doors slam.
Only the world's governments, procrastinators, and speculators
        give a damn.
The Shadows of Time are unrelenting, uncompromising,
        and very illusive,
Compelled by unknown forces to change policies, make money,
        then be reclusive.

Night falls with its bevy of fashionable dressed-up yuppies,
        phonies, and liars.
Unquestionably they come to the forefront with promises,
        schemes, desires.
The Shadows of Time, history knows, linger briefly for childhood
        and lovers,
Dispensing relief to welfare recipients, patients,
        and expectant mothers.

We forget time creeps effortlessly, day and night, through every
        mode of life,
Haunting, stalking, conquering, no matter exercise, affluence,
        or strife.
The Shadows of Time steal youth, health, ideals, and ambitions,
Removing these priceless assets in spite of race, creed, or traditions.

Despite its swiftness, Time promises to excite, challenge,
        tempt, enrage.
It also pledges to soothe, defeat, humble, and engage.
The Shadows of Time are sympathetic to prayers, death,
        marriage, healing,
Ironically asking in return for peace, commitment, an end to stealing.

Dean Moran

CALIFORNIA HILL NO. 2

Magic mounds of flesh you are a woman
        of the earth.
Your hills of cream are dotted with
beauty marks of black Angus cows
that peer through your folds of flesh
rolling and curving like the crevice
between breasts,
and far away some stallions stand on
the slope of a pregnant womb.

And my woolen jacket reminds me of your
dusty paths of soft suede, where I can
still see tan horses running and their
long wispy manes blowing.
And I see them in the valley deep within
your flesh
        and I see you caress them.

Meryl Wolfson

MERYL JEAN WOLFSON. Born: Boston,
Massachusetts, 5-6-48; Education: University of
Massachusetts, B.A., English; B.A., Psychology,
1970; Harvard University, Accounting and real
estate; Occupation: Controller for H.J. Davis
Development Corporation (real estate); Member-
ship: Registered real estate salesperson; Themes:
*Beauty and consciousness of the present. The in-
ward journey finds a beauty and a peace that no
physical sense, whether it be sound or touch,
etc., can experience. The wonderful joy of the
true love to be found within/inside one's own
self.*

CONFLICTS OF CREATION

Understand the mystery
Reasons for
Dark and Light, seasons change
Mystic seas
Movements of a star.

See the intellect
Little restraint
Sharpness of minds, truths bear
Questions hover
Still . . . bits not explained.

Fear causes anger
Self-contained
Love your enemy, as self
Love bolts
You . . . must continue on.

Centuries way ahead
Charted plans
Time drags, always in order
Learned or mystic
Where . . . will it end?

Elvin L. Jones

ME AND THE MORNING SUN

I'm just sitting here with me
No expectations. No fast movement.
Me and the morning sun.

We're awakening
To the sounds and the feelings of the day.
To allow the world to slow down
With me on it.

To sit in a space big enough for me.
Spacious. Room to breathe
Room to move.

But not moving. No need to run.
Comfortable staying here with me
With the world and the newness of the day.

Just stay. Sit. Be. Safe but not too safe.
Sitting with no attachment
Nothing to take with. Nobody holding on.

Just me. My space. My time.
Not knowing what the world holds for me
Not caring. Just sitting.
Me and the morning sun.

Arla Underberg

EMPTY SKI RUN

The falling snow muffles her cries
Soaking up sobs like a pale sponge
Intent on its duty.
The misty blue lake so close now
From this height.
How can this awe-inspiring place
Permit such sad goings on?
Perhaps the High Sierra knows
Something of endless loneliness
Isolated as it usually is
Under this vast gray sky.
Seasons go by and few come to comfort
Like being a rest home resident
With mostly Christmas visitors.
We are aligned today mountain
Like lovers. Breathing heavily,
And sighing deeply.
I can feel a soft shudder
Go through us
Silently.

Alannah Van Boven

Leave the fly alone —
        overwrought by misery
        succumbed by the grief
        of a new day's dawning.

A day of emptiness —
        of trials and temptations
        of love and war
        of hatred, deceit, lies

To go from place to place
        to achieve nil.
        Such is the fate of the fly
        with nothing to look forward to
        and even less
        to look back upon.

Chioma N. Onyekwere

MEMORIES AND REASONS

Dazzle me tonight
with the sound of your voice
the light in your eyes
the beauty of your face

The coldness of forever
separates us now
the memory is a dream
that I let slip away

I have another mistress
one I can never touch
she only comes to visit
when I'm exposed to the world

Choices were made
many years ago
sacrificed love
looking for diamonds in the ashes

They built a city in the desert
looking for paradise
thousands flocked to the temple
willing to pay any price

Chris Young

TODAY'S FOOLS

We live, we die
We laugh, we cry
We dream, we wonder,
In a world of fools and dreamers,
We live in fear of what will be.
We do not fear what is in the world today,
This is a world of fools.
We live, we die and all that we can do
Is to try to live the best that we can.

George Pol

LET ME BE FREE

Let me be free to breathe
the air of peace and serenity.

Don't bother me with your materialistic values
to which you cling so religiously.

I am not a piece of clay,
to be molded, shaped, and formed.
Like you, human am I
with all the flaws and imperfections.

Don't tell me how to dress, or think.
Or otherwise impose
your values on me.

I accept you as you are.
Though I may not agree.
Why must you be critical of me?

For who's to say what's right or wrong?
Do we mortals have the right?

The things we hold so dear on earth,
what good are they when we die?

Betty Watson McGrath

To sorrow a man is born,
to cause it and to know it.
Can this one born
escape his calling
to know sorrow, and to cause sorrow,
may he from this escape?
May there not be a path of bliss
that this one born can choose?

Such a path is not known to me,
and is it not well to let a mystery be?
But there is hope in what is known.
And if one man has trodden this path,
a path most wearisome and abounding in troubles,
if ten thousand men have climbed these mountains,
then so can this one born.
Then so can this one born,
whose heart is new, whose fears are few,
who of them all is strongest.

Julia Mbogho

THE BREAKUP

I have to wake each morning and begin another day,
And hope the sun outside my door will somehow find the way
To make my life much brighter ever since you went away,
Your leaving took away the joy of knowing you were there,
The laughter when you told your jokes, the way I laughed and cared,
Your leaving took away the sun, now rain is in its place,
And everywhere I turn and look I always see your face,
Your leaving took away my heart and now it cannot love,
A loneliness lies deep inside a heart without a love,
Your leaving took away my soul and now I cannot live,
Because, my love, you took it all, all that I could give.

Mary Wessel

LITTLE BOY

Wandering aimlessly down city streets
He's bent of head staring at his feet
Lonely soles worn thin, he's plodding on
Waging wars within, they've come and gone
Warm Mother Earth has slowly grown cold
Through time, through the ages, under treading souls

The sun is rising, hope dawns again
But beyond the horizon lies another sin
In the dark of the city a cruel wind blows
Seeking hearts of the lonely to turn to stone
Only time remains to grow him old
Will he find a song that will take him home?

Staring thoughts on crumbled page
The black and white eludes the age
Of foreign birth an idea grows
The desperate motto blind men know
A captured fate, a game of odds
One silent nation under God

Dream, little boy, *dream*
Close your eyes, let the world turn.

Paul Rosenberg

THE SYMPHONY

Waves rippling like a bellowing accordian
       across twisted pieces
             of driftwood . . .
As the sun gives way to night's
             own lights,
       she sits,
       knees to chest
       with her toes teasing
             the mud
       as she listens
       to the sounds of the night . . .

                  a connoisseur of its
                  symphony

Naidine D'Angelo

ARE YOU HOME, LORD?

I stopped by Your house today, a radiant forest of yellow and red,
   to see if You were home, and there was no answer.
I walked among the leaves and branches, while the sun shone
   on webs of spiders asleep.
I called You in prayer, asking, *Are You home, Lord?*
   But there was no answer.
I stopped by Your house today, an ocean of blue and green,
   to see if You were home, and there was no answer.
I walked along the golden sand and shells
   as the water baptized the shore with its salty touch.
I looked for Your footsteps near mine in the sand,
   and in prayer I asked, *Are You home, Lord?*
   But there was no answer.
I closed my eyes and stretched out my heart
   and You embraced it with your loving hands.
I am content . . .
You were home after all.

Naidine D'Angelo

LITTLE SISTER

My little sister, is not so little anymore,
Time has passed, memories that seem to linger.

Remember the way you pestered to go to the ice cream store,
We hardly agreed on anything, not even a favorite singer.
The feelings of being the older brother, to protect, to share,
Playing as kids, always getting the upper hand.
Even when fighting like cats and dogs, deep down to care,
Getting yelled at by dad, in the corner I stand.

The years have passed, you're a little sister no longer,
A woman to the world, a little girl at heart you be.
Just remember I'm the big brother, and I'm stronger,
So watch your step, you're still a little sister to me.

Salvatore LaFata IV

THE HOUSE OF SILENCIO

Caressed by a perpetual breeze,
Bordered by lonesome trees,
Overlooking neglected lawns,
And a weathered angel statue
Surmounted by a crow,
Lies the once proud House of Silencio.

The Master still lives there,
Without worry, without care;
A mere shadow of his former self.
Day and night he shuffles
Through labyrinthine halls
And in the kitchen
Pantomimes mealtime rituals.
The fragile staircase supports
His weightlessness, winter and summer;
And his dog trots to a different drummer.

If you pass the house by some whim —
Just give a wave. He will wave back —
But you won't see him.

Roger Reynolds

FREEDOM IS

Freedom is a word that few people know.

What does freedom mean to me?
Freedom is life,
Freedom is joy,
Freedom is the right to choose what
We want in this world.
The right to live,
The right to die,
The right to love,
And the right to hate.
The right to live in peace and love.

This is what freedom means to me.

George Pol

PASTEL EXPLOSION

Soft muted colors invade the sky,
Clouds blend across the purple hue,
Hazy shades of pink spread
Into the pale blue of dawn.
Suddenly, a burst of fiery yellow
Explodes across the heavens.
Reluctantly, the grandeur of pastels
Gives way to morning's light:
The victory cry of sunrise
Announces its capture of the sky.

Bobbi Mahala Drawdy

ASHES

Ashes to ashes
Dust to dust
The pain never ends
For some of us
Deliver me from evil
Take me from this place
What's so human
About the human race
Burn in hell
Heaven on earth
From the cradle to the grave
It ends at birth
Thy kingdom come
Thy will come undone
As life unfolds
We must learn to run
Ashes to ashes
Dust to dust
Ashes, ashes
Fall down, we must

Darcy Machado

THE HANGING TREE

The hanging tree
It's our history
In the middle of a field
In the middle of a dream

The dream was had
But the man is gone
A hidden rope
At the end of a gun

The gun takes another
See them fall
Their voices bounce
Off blood-stained walls

The walls can't hide
All the history
The black soul remains
On the hanging tree

Darcy Machado

THE DANGEROUS EDGE

The people sing, the people dance
They take what's theirs
They take a chance
They grab all they can, both day and night
They grab for this
Their God-given rights

Excuses hold a dangerous edge
Buying more time
To cling to the ledge
Hold on tight, dig in deep
Forget your fingers
They're gonna bleed

Come on and sing, come on and dance
Show 'em you're proud
Show 'em your prance
Hold your head high, don't look away
Tell 'em everything
That you came to say

Darcy Machado

WE THE PEOPLE

''We the People'' means to me —
Ourselves and our posterity;
Our Constitution made it clear,
That we should hold our country dear.

The future's in our children's hands
But first there's us to keep the lands,
And make them safe against a day,
When freedom could be torn away.

Some people think it's not their place
To meet our problems face to face;
They leave it for another day,
Then cry because they had no say.

So let's speak out for liberty —
Ensure its continuity;
It isn't just for our own sake,
But those who follow in our wake.

Our nation's strength is in us all,
But only if we heed the call,
To shape the country's evolution,
In keeping with our Constitution.

Brenda L. Bailey

CONSUMING LOVE

Quietly sitting,
Gazing into the flame of a candle,
I see the flicker in your eye,
The way you looked at me,
I envision a million scenes we shared,
Times of enchantment or hurt and pain,
A blazing fire burns within to remind
    me of my love for you,
A fire that will not be quenched,
An all-consuming fire that burns
    to my very soul,
And in the end will consume my
    soul for eternity.

Randi Kay Eden

DANCE OF CHRISTMAS

Christmas.
Chilling winds blow down the
    corridors of my heart,
Darkened halls,
Void of laughter and light,
No tree, no tinsel,
No presents or candles to
    warm my mind,
Sadness.
Emptiness.
Companions of me here.
Separated from love I once knew,
Loneliness and pain,
Dance my dance of
Christmas.

Randi Kay Eden

YOU AND I

Come, let us roam through a country meadow.
Let me look into your azure eyes while a breeze rustles the
leaves around us.
Let me take your hand and we'll stroll among the green
clover and Queen Anne's lace.
Let me see your hair blown by the wind as you bend to pluck a
blossom on your way
only to watch its delicate petals drop to the ground.
Little bird, sing for me, let your wings flutter as you lift
and fly away
only to sip the sweet nectar of our precious hours shared.
We'll gather tulips or sip wine and sway to music arm in arm,
or marvel at dew gleaming like diamonds on a spider's web.
Darling, you and I yearn to be near to one another,
and maybe some day we will find the way.

Virginia Goland

A NEW COMMENCEMENT

One plane comes, another one goes,
I listen to the coolness of the morning and in silence,
The Northwest Airlines, The United Airlines
Humming their songs of flight above the Philippine skies.

Last year, March 21st, my Lady Moon went aloft to the West
After the shadows had dimmed her radiance in the East.
The rising of a curtain, le premier pas
For a new beginning in the Land of the Angels.

This year, again, March 23rd '87, another satellite was flown
To train at Tennessee Valley, that he may learn
A better management of technology resources,
An envoy of peace for our third world countries.

A friendly program of the US AID,
A fresh start for progress we so badly need,
Giving us new dimensions for development
With America as our partner and guiding hand.

Thank you, America, for the friendship
That has linked our nations together,
The chain is made stronger from year to year,
The noble things you share hold you more dear.

May we continue to help one another
With the same spirit of friendly cheer,
When we have made our lives better
The job will become easier, our ties closer.

Gloria D. Reynaldo

Thomas is a fine little man,
He always helps me when he can;
He vacuums the shop, even tries to mop,
And goes until I tell him s is a fine little man,
He always helps me when he can;
He vacuums the shop, even tries to mop,
And goes until I tell him to stop.
Then there's little Baby Sam who is home with Mother,
Not old enough yet to help big brother
But one of these days he will be three,
Then he can come and help you and me.

Pa Pa Anderson

IT'LL BE OKAY

She looked up at me, with her baby blue eyes,
tears were running down her cheeks.
"Daddy," she said with a whimper and sigh,
"I fell and I skinned my knee."

"Don't cry, my girl, it'll be okay,
Daddy will fix it right up."
I washed it, I kissed it, then put on a band-aid,
she said, "Thank you, Daddy," and gave me a hug.

She smiled at me, and went back outside,
forgetting about the owie she had.
I watched her play through the window with pride,
she saw me and said, "I sure do love you, Dad."

I started to think of her growing up soon,
then the tears ran down my face.
She said, "Don't cry, Daddy, I'll fix it right up for you,
everything will be okay."

She kissed me, and gave me another hug,
then she started to play with her curls.
Then, just like she said, she fixed it right up,
when she said, "You're the best daddy in the world."

Glen G. Ohnstad

THE GREAT LIFE

*To Dolora Zajic on her triumphant debut as Azucema in
1986 Summer Season's "Il Ttovatore" on San Francisco
Opera stage.*

As we begin to travel world's wide roads
Uncertain, puzzled, but with gleaming hope for future bright
If fortunate and born with seeds of wisdom
We follow the guidance of *Great Life.*
  Her beauty is enchanting, captivating
  Her gifts are lavish, promises — unlimited in scope
  But rules are strict, direct, demanding, simple:
  "First — learn and work, then — dream and hope."
She leads us from the lowlands to higher mountains
To view the tops' magnificence, amazing, thrilling
She makes us walk through dismal gloom in "valley of the tears."
  No matter where we are — *Great Life* is always there
  Days can be dark and stormy or horizon clear and sky bright blue
  If we to *Her* are honest, fair, sincere
She helps our dreams sometimes come true.

C. S.

VICTORIAN ROSE

Victorian Rose delicately scents my room,
The flicker of candles dance upon my wall,
Bewitching and enchanting, I am taken back
    in time,
Taken to a time of grandeur and romance,
We're sharing this magic,
Just the two of us,
An eternal love story,
But then you vanish from me,
And I realize I have lost your love,
The very essence of my soul,
A love that I fear you will kill in time,
And I shall forever be in torment for
    losing it,
Somehow I am in another place and time,
My senses once intrigued, but now I
    feel desperately alone,
Because this fascination means nothing
    without you,
So to reality I must return.

Randi Kay Eden

Smiles are given due to delight,
Creating tears that shine so bright.
Smiles are given after a fight,
Creating tears that last all night.
Smiles are given out of fear,
Creating tears that do not appear.
Smiles are given when we *love,*
Creating tears as soft as a dove.

Sharon J. Davis

THOUGHTS ON A SPRING DAY

I like clouds
They're so nice —
In summertime, I like ice —
I like stars overhead —
In wintertime, I love my bed.

My friends I cannot do without —
Even those who sometimes pout —
This world we're in is a wondrous place —
Thank you, God, for making me
a part of the human race.

Margaret Montague Balcom

REBELLION AGAINST AGING

Sometimes with shock and disbelief
I see my friends — they're growing old —
Surely this can't be said of me.
My thoughts are bold, my heart still sings
While facing life with glee —

The mirror, though, points out to me
A person who is not a child —
A lady who has lived awhile.

So overlook my hair so white —
Love me for myself alone —
Be my friend and light my life!

Margaret Montague Balcom

TO BILL

I like the feel of you —
The smell — so much a man —
Your tenderness, I can't believe —
The soft touch of your hand —

You made my Yuletide joy,
You started my year off right —
You gave me memories that will last
All through my nights

I thank you —
But most of all, I've really
learned that I can love again.

Margaret Montague Balcom

THOUGHTS

profound thoughts on
animal crackers
simulations remind me
the humankind
lasciviousness of meat
eat heartily
no guilt
can gorge on this socialization
and still be free

Stephanee Pagano

BED TIME - HAIKU

Woman listens to
    ticking clock. Way 'cross town
bridegroom beds fresh new wife.

FISH FATE - HAIKU

Flying fish, sea gull
    merge o'er ocean's briny fr Way 'cross town
bridegroom beds fresh new wife.

FISH FATE - HAIKU

Flying fish, seagull
    merge o'er ocean's briny froth,
    fish meets Waterloo

Carolyn I. Hayes

THE GRIFFIN'S RAGE

With the sound of my own prophecy
Handwritten on the wall,
I became too comfortable,
So they came and took it all.

With wretched mornings mostly spent,
Ragged habit on my sleeve,
I would have gladly traded half my soul
For something left I could believe.
Or something smooth and warm to touch.
Or for just five brutal seconds
Without the taste of blood inside my mouth.

And when there was nothing left of fear,
And nothing left of time,
I then became the master,
And I came to realize,
    Within the final discipline,
    Within the order of all things,
    My spirit's endless destiny
    Was the reason for the journey,
    And blind existence of this fool.

Robert J. Pluss

ROBERT JOHN PLUSS. Born: Monroe, Wisconsin, 10-14-48; Education: Pratt Institute, B.F.A., 1971; Occupation: Artist; Other Writings: *Death Rays From Pluto,* book of poems, 1985; *Stories Laced With Hell and Tales of Leather Girls,* book of poems, 1986; *On The Outskirts of Town,* collection of music, 1984-1986; *The Griffin's Rage,* book of poems (in progress); Comments: *We are all blind, fragile creatures, easily tempted, who weaken and fall from grace with ourselves.*

IT'S A PARODY

They may say I'm crazy
But they don't really know
Life has no guarantee
And this life is my own.

Well, now you may not agree
That what I do is right
And you can say it's a parody
But the truth to that I'll fight.

So, if you want to disagree
I guess you have the right
But don't expect a symphony
Of dancers in the light.

Jenny Moline

THE GREAT LIFE

To Dr. B. L.

This world — Vast, strange, complex and enigmatic, resisting,
pushed by force, we enter with the anguished cry and meet
               its glorious and splendid *Hostess*
            Mysterious and beautiful *Great Life.*
Adventure of the journey is beginning: to learn, to grow,
to achieve or fail, fall low or reach high;
and *She* is Always there — guiding, teaching
            Enchanted, beautiful *Great Life.*
Like ancient *Goddess* — *She* is generous in kindness,
in anger — stern, unyielding, often cruel and severe;
Her gifts are oceans of emotions, *Her* punishment —
            The cups of tears.
How recklessly we often treat *The Time Eternal,* wasting
it foolishly, ignoring cautions and alarming signs, we follow
false promises, illusions, cheat on the rule and hide from
burning fury of *Great Life.*
The clock of *Time Eternal* keeps forever running; for humans
it begins to slow down, as in low tide; alarming obstacles appear
to block our ways and roads. And suddenly we feel abandoned
  by *Great Life.*
Where is *She?* Help is needed now more than ever, we suffer torture
of the sadness, anguish, pain and shocks

  But *She* is busy greeting new arrivals and trusts they will do
  better, trying harder, deserving and receiving higher marks.

      C. S.

THE GREAT LIFE 2

To Dr. M. L.

Alluring, forceful, fascinating *Life* leads us through
  the curves and bends
Majestic, powerful, but fragile in mystery *She* starts and ends.
She measures happiness with prudence, instructs to treasure
  what one gets
In troubled days of pains and losses directs to wisdom from regrets.
She sprinkles punishment with kindness.
One morning bright when sky was blue
She guided me to doors of healing and introduced to all of you:
Young handsome doctors, charming ladies — Pat, Gerry, Nancy,
Maggie, Sue, Hope, Bernie, Kerry, Bill and Eric
  and music-loving doctor — *You.*
In clear voice *She* was saying: "Remember, you are given best."
To precious *Life* I gave my promise not to forget that I am blessed.

If over struggle for the *Living* destructive forces
  win the deadly strife,
If Pearl of Planets — *Earth* — should perish,
Could *Life* be saved? Can *She* survive?
Creator *Great* in spare light years by sifting ashes
  and the sand may find the priceless remnants worth redeeming.
Will *He* restore for Universe to cherish *The Love,*
  The Music and Great Life?

      C. S.

THE POEM

African Poem on My Inner-Oracle

Thank God in heaven, that the mirror has no memories.

Today, the world knows the poetry of Shakespeare, the music of Wagner,
the art of Rembrandt, but alas, nobody knows about "my inner-oracle,"
known as "my instinct" in Africa,
and known as "my natural faculty" in Europe.

This poem advises — do more than look —
  see, observe, and understand,
Looking is like facing the mirror, in a darkened room
  or gazing at the sun ray.

Do more than touch — feel, observe, and understand,
Touching is like cupping the wind, initially there, then lost,
  lost forever & ever.

Do more than hear — listen, observe, and understand,
Listening is like waiting for an implausible, wandering vibration
  in the waited fog.

Do more than smell — taste, observe, and understand,
Sniffing dams the nostrils with heavy, damp dust flouted
  by the rushing steam.

Do more than think — exist as a people . . .
Do more than exist — live as a people . . .
I am only a soul in shining darkness, and I sincerely hope
  that this African poem on "my inner-oracle"
  will find a place in your heart.

      Dr. Akim Onojobi

YOU ARE . . .

The apple of my eye,
The onion in my stew,
The gentle rain on my garden
And the sunshine that makes it bloom.
You are the storm in my calm
And the calm in my storm.
You are the smile that flashes from your face to mine
  and lights up my life,
The silent, terrible tear that wells in your eye
  and wrenches my heart.
You are the unspoken thoughts which fly between us
And the secrets shared.
You are my swift, sweet hope for tomorrow,
The wisest investment I ever made.
You are the answer to my question, "Why am I?"
You are my baby girl, my child-woman, my brave beauty,
  my daughter,
      who grew up to be my friend.

      Beverly Beeton

UNSTRUCK SOUL

Time — thick as space
Slowly drifts by my face
Hours, minutes, years, days
Time, it comes in many ways

Lovers laugh and lovers die
Life, gone in a breath of a sigh
Time unwarped, time unfailed
Letter arriving before it is mailed

Time holds all the hurt and pain
Time holds sunshine and the rain
Time is growing, time is gone
Time is lingering on and on

Mountains, granite, stone and lime
Remain forever unstruck by time
Life so sweet, the best times past
You grasp holding on, so they may last
An empty shell within there lies
An unstruck soul that never dies

M. L. Hayes

I WAS LOOKING FOR YOU

I was looking for
Sunny dazes and happy ways
Long walks in the park and
Someone to talk with
Being alone no more
And much, much more.

I was looking for
A smiling face and no more tears
A hand to hold and no more fears
Warm sunny places and
Someone to be true to.

I was looking for
A bright blue sky
The end of a rainbow
Pretty ribbons and bows
And much, much more
I was looking for you.

Jenny Moline

ROCK PAINTING

This animal is a love carved from the sky
wanting to stay beside a man. The sun
waking up on the mountain made it run
beyond the fields where it would one day die.

It found a knowing hand to give it one
sure moment of existence, when its cry
echoed at night and sought human reply
while its creation on this stone was done.

So it adorned the thoughts and loneliness
with life upon the bare walls of the cave
and learnt the kindness which its master gave
as some eternal gift it could possess.

Within the simple outline of its art
it held a heavenly beauty in the heart.

P. Mihalik

SHADOW-SITTER

Oh, shadow-sitter,
    look you how
        in bright of
            gleaming day?

And do you seek
    in shadows dark
        to lose your
            haunted way?

And did you cry
    and shadows choose
        to keep the
            fears at bay?

And do you miss
    your counterpart
        or know her
            living ways?

Oh, shadow-sitter,
    dare you know
        the bright of
            gleaming day?

Alice L. Lewis

FREEDOM?

Is it random chance,
Or perhaps fate?
Forcing us to dance,
Forcing us to wait
On the stage of either one.
Who has won?
Who is lost?
What is the cost?
By Chance we are helpless,
By Fate we are selfless,
Some say, "It's plain to see
That we have free will."
Nevertheless, is that still . . .
Or is *anything* for free?

Gwynneth Gibson

PATHWAY OF TEARS

My thoughts are so chaotic
as I try to think things through.
But, life goes on around me,
so, I'll try to start anew.
But jumbled thoughts and feelings
are buried deep within.
They're trying hard to conquer me
with thoughts of what might have been.
My life seems locked in footsteps
on a pathway into tears,
and I have to end these feelings
of self-pity, doubt and fear.
Please God . . . I need your help now.
More than ever, so it seems.
To walk with me and guide me,
and return to me my dreams.

Carolyn J. Carruth

OCEANS 'n' MAN

Rivers to oceans
    commingle 'n' proceed
Man against man
    avarice 'n' greed

Oceans of water
    ebb 'n' tide
Man in his sorrow
    looks 'n' hides

Roar of the ocean
    waves lappin' beach
Man in his hunger
    searchin' for peace

Grains of sand
    to 'n' fro
Man wonders, stalls
    where to go

Majestic the oceans
    angry or calm
Man can surmount
    open fist — lay out palm

Glenda S. Thomason

YOU KNOW AND I KNOW

Dear God, you know all I've been through,
    You know and I know, so
    That's all that matters.
I'm growing older now —
    But the child I was still lives within.
I rejoice in the good she experienced,
I grieve for that which she suffered.
    But you know all about that —
    You know and I know, so
    That's all that matters.

Carolyn I. Hayes

OLDEN DAYS, GOLDEN TIMES

One large kitchen, shiny and bright,
Starched yellow curtains reflecting
        sunlight,
A glowing black stove used for heat,
Scent of apples baked — my, what a treat!

A windowsill and glass so clear,
Star-shaped snowflakes soon will
        appear,
A wild fixation to capture the snow —
And keep it, and hold it
'Til springtime's warm glow.

Some hot soup and tea all honey
        and milk,
A beautiful mother with skin smooth
        as silk,
A father who's happy — a baby that's
        crying,
Reliving those days — without even
        trying.

Marge Doran

I KNOW WHY DAISIES DANCE

Acres and acres of daisies, a sight to behold!
Like billowy clouds ere fallen to the ground
They whirl and swirl across the meadow, bound
To catch faint breezes as they doth unfold
To greet the sun, and bare their hearts of gold.
Heaven above, applauds the show profound;
Are these the Lambs of God the choirs expound?
Fallen angels parted from the fold.
And so they pirouette upon the verdant
Lea like ballerinas, a requiem
Ballet performed in silent beauty, ardent
Faces gazing ever skyward, valiant
In their quest to find Elysium;
And I am doomed — their parting to lament.

Barbara Nell Lamb

SONNET TO MY LOVE

My love, when winter's grey its gloom doth bring
As youth and all life's beauty fades away,
Will you often see me in my spring
With blushing rosy cheeks of yesterday?
When I feel the chill of fallen snow,
My love, as summer's tears have turned to frost,
Will you see the warmth inside me glow
Unchanged from the first taste of bliss not lost?
Please, I ask, don't gaze upon the lines
The fleeting years have sculpted bit by bit,
Turn not away to weep nor yearn for times
Long passed, the best of me is waiting yet.
   If love be cold, December's bloom will wither
   In its prime, and we will weep together.

Barbara Nell Lamb

TO SONG-QI

. . . and as i walked in the perfumed garden
of Buddha's Temple,
five-hundred pairs of eyes of the bodhisattvas followed me.
And i thought of your eyes —
smiling, sad, longing — speaking to me of love.

. . . and as the pink petals of the plum blossoms
performed their final dance
in gentle rhythm, they touched my face softly.
And i thought of your hands —
light, tender, loving — caressing me like a breeze.

. . . and as the white cranes spread their graceful wings
in the silver sky of the autumn moon,
their longing became part of me forever.
And I thought of your soul —
clear, honest, true — promising me love in all eternity.

Dr. GGisela Nass

A PLASTER WREN

A plaster wren fell from my shelf the other day
And broke — or shattered — I should say,
Like a water droplet's splash. I couldn't see
How fired-clay could smash so totally.

I stood there angry at myself for my emerging tears
At losing something both so trivial and small —
Its own fragility had long foretold its end,
An ancient gift from a vanished girlhood friend —
But this frail and foolish thing outlasted all
My cars and houses, marriages, careers.

I looked up at the empty shelf
Where my last scrap of permanence was kept
And, deciding to indulge myself,
I scooped the pieces up and wept.

Patricia Spicer

PARADISE LIFE

This life we live belongs to us, a life we cannot live again
or try to change the things we've done.
This life is ours and owes no pain.
If no one paves our path to run, we're free to take another one.
When we were young, we followed and listened, a choice we did not have.
But now we've grown and see ourselves a way that no one knows.
You have to choose a path that's yours, for it may never pass again.
And who's to say what we do is wrong and who's to say what's right?
We pay our dues as they come, and raise our heads to the sun.
Loneliness is a due we pay, it yields no time to heal.
If you choose to take your path, don't keep a love in vain.

We are our own prosecutors, and choose to suffer in vain.
God has more mercy on our souls than those who beg of our love.
This world is such a paradise, but hell is in our hearts.
If you love, desires and hopes are freed to our own will.
Then you can live a life that's yours, no echoing misery.
All it is is one true step, and the chains will set you free.
I only wish I could show you my soul, and reveal what secrets exit.
A world within a world of myself, and set your spirits free.
I'll show you all the love I hide and seek what's yet to find.

Joanne Valentino

GROWING OLD

*Dedicated to grandparents everywhere,
especially mine, Mr. and Mrs. Gerald Knierim
of Decatur, Illinois*

Growing old is just moving from the fast lane to the slow lane
From football to golf
From comic books to classics
From buying a sweater to knitting one yourself
From receiving gifts to giving them
From being ''on the go'' to settling down in one place
From going to work to getting Social Security checks
From driving a sporty car to walks in the park
From jumping out of bed to slowly rolling out with a
  touch of arthritis
From learning to being learned
From being taught to *Love* to *Loving*.

Brian Vandemark

WHEN DID THIS HAPPEN

When did this happen when this child
    cried out
To be heard not by her mortals —
To be heard but by her Master,
When did this happen — when anguish,
    remorse, became her total
    life disaster.

When did this happen when he whose
    carcass lay limp
With pain of past — became nothing
    but a knoll,
And she a figure of one tormented
    soul.

When did this happen when life, love,
    strong to impart —
Was severed, crushed, challenged —
    from the start,
Yet she alone carries the surge
    of pain in her heart.
Then lives only to remember —
    ''When did this happen?''

Marge Doran

NOT OLD

His hair has thinned,
His gait unsteady,
Her long brown tresses
Ashen 'fore she's ready.

They walk together hand 'n hand,
Each one rougher than sand
    and wrinkled faces.

Time has passed quickly
Yet it's slow they walk,
Wedding ring worn with age —
Yet they balk.

His hair has thinned,
Her tresses ashen,
Though deep in the eyes,
    the hearts — Ageless Passion.

Marge Doran

FINDING THE WAY OUT

Locked in a place
    a room
    a darkness.
Looking for a light
    something to guide me
        through this darkness.
I walk
    I travel little distance
        in much time.
Searching for a way out,
    out of the dark.
Groping for anything that will
        guide me.
I open my eyes
    finding the darkness gone.
Sleep was my darkness,
    my maze.
I am no longer afraid
    of the dark.

Barbara Allen

I COULD NOT SING
THAT SONG FOR YEARS

I could not sing that song for years
    because I did not know
the touch of unpretentious love
    upon my barren soul.

I never heard the melody
    that stirs when lovers meet
and never thought that there could be
    such songs that me would greet.

It's like the rare high mountain chimes
    whose solemn chords release
a gentle singing solitude
    for those who seek its peace.

A peace that stirs my brooding heart
    to seek a cleaner air
where two can dance the mountain dance
    and breathe a mutual care.

I never heard till she came near
    and looked into my eyes
and strummed on my neglected heart
    a tune of mountain skies.

Benjamin M. Eskew

IF LOVE

Love was roses
light kiss of desire
Sweet as honey
as ever I felt.
Passion like fire.

Soft baby blues
seduce
and melt the distance
between the clouds
that hide my tears.

Your strong arms
caress me with ecstasy.
One true flame
in the darkest night.

Peggy Hogan

TRAPPED IN HELL

Every time I see that room
I remember
The blood, the anger
Pain
It stabs me like a silver knife
Dark and cold.

Trapped inside the locked door
The dead soul screams,
Bangs against the walls
In the dead of night.
I can't make you live.

Peggy Hogan

HER TEDDY BEAR

She holds her Teddy bear
and holds her tongue
and holds her anger to her breast.
It is her love
it is her strength
it is her only hope for rest.
    She denies
    She nurtures
    She holds it dear.
    It's always present
    Always distant
        Yet —
    It's always near.
She hugs it close
and strokes its fur
and holds the rage at bay.
She strives for order
and strives for peace
amidst the burning pain.

Melba Ferguson

THE BEAST

Fearful eyes, forever watching.
The beast within, forever lurking.
Troubled heart and troubled mind
Working puzzles to make them bind
The troubled beast who never sleeps,
The fearful beast who always keeps
The searing pain just out of reach.
The pain of hate that seals the breach.
The lurking pain
That is
The Beast.

Melba Ferguson

RUSTED STEEL HEART

I wish I could turn off
my innermost feelings
with just a flip of a switch.
Turn it off,
Turn me off!

A machine will rust
if left out in the rain.
Sometimes I wish
I was a machine, for if I was,
Surely by now,
all of my fallen tears
would've rusted the compartment
which holds my heart,
permanently shut . . .
never to be opened again!

Juanita Mayer

Birmingham Falls, Ausable Chasm.

SOMEBODY CARES

For Mother

*Somebody cares
and we all know it,
with every breath,
you let it show.
You,
as always,
make me proud to say,
I am somebody
and
I love you*

J. T. Hawkins

PORK CHOP HILL

I love the look of Pork Chop Hill
The way I look upon it, it give me
the chills. The way I climb, the way
it thrills. You better be on the lookout
for Buffalo Bill.
The better he look, the better he feel
The better he cook, the better it fill
Thy shall not kill, without your skill
Just keep on the lookout for Pork
Chop Hill.

Leon Bernard

SUN

The sun is hot pink hanging
In the twilight sky

From the window eye
Can see through the mist

And cloudcover to the core
Of the sun in all its pinkness

Round and daringly pink
Hanging slightly off-center in the twilight sky.

Tom Pynn

MORNING PRAYER

Silently I pray before I rise
Lifting my heart to the skies.
Thank you, Lord, for all you've done,
This land, my life, Your Holy Son.
I pray today a Christian I'll be
A perfect witness for others to see.

EVENING PRAYER

As I now prepare to sleep
I pray Thee Lord my soul You keep.
Please guide my dreams to Eden's gate
To lose all evil, greed, and hate.
Watch my rest until morning's first light
While I gather strength against Satan's might.

Bruce Miles

AS THE PRESSES ROLL

While smiling underneath your sleep,
not counting sheep,
the politicians,
with their missions,
remain alert all night and day.
Soon they will say
their clever lies
which now belie
the purpose of all laws
that are worthwhile.
Calm and cool, they simply smile —
and for God's sake
I hope we wake!

Victoria Leigh Harlow-Emmons

JULY 4, 1976 —
UNITED STATES

It was a year of famine,
    but we didn't worry about that here.
We were more concerned about
    the high price of fertilizer.

1976. It was a year when we didn't know
    where our children were.
It was a year when everybody drank
    too much —at least on television.

Freedom meant shedding our clothes,
    and another year of rape of the land.

And the air.

And the water.

And it was a year of speed,
    and it was a year of greed.

Just a year to shed a tear
    over another great lost human dream.

Two hundred years, and a celebration.

Of what?

Victoria Leigh Harlow-Emmons

THE BLUE ROSE

A Blue Rose,
But only a bud,
Captivated His heart,
Among those . . . red as blood.

Although the rose,
Illuminated a strange colored hue,
It found favor with something holy,
In a world that wasn't blue.

A Blue Rose,
Grew from a vine,
And He picked it . . .
For something divine.

Lee Schweger

SEA GULLS

Sea gulls
Graceful angels
Catching light in their wings
Playing the beggars on the beach
Till dusk

Lee Schweger

A DREAM OF LOVE

I had a dream of love last night
So warm, so sweet and oh so right
We laughed, we talked and even planned
We were close walking hand in hand
We spoke of love so complete
Then all is still as our eyes meet
No more words were spoken then
It was all there from deep within
Awaken though I knew I would
I'd stay asleep though if I could

Dorothy Nickens

A BREATH OF SPRING

A breath of spring — you fill the air;
The flowers bloom — perfume is there;
The robins sing — a cheerful song;
A path winds down — you come along.

A breath of spring — the world is right;
The moon is full — a beautiful night;
The breeze it brings — a fresh new scent;
On happiness — the day is bent.

A breath of spring — the world is new;
The sun gently shines — the whole world grew;
Many a thing — may come from the past;
But only memories — of spring will last.

Mark Ashley

MY DEAR MOTHER

My dear mother, you have gone away.
Oh! how I miss you every day.

Someday we will be together
in that wonderful place called heaven.

But until then, I will pray to God in heaven.

On earth, you had problems, which is very sad.
They weren't called for and I was not glad.

You are now an angel,
and you have no problems.

You are happy now,
and until that day, I will see you.

Don't forget the fun we had,
and we can have lots more in heaven.

Until then I will see you,
in that wonderful place called heaven.

Billie Ruth Berkemeier

WALKING REFLECTION

a splitting mirror on two feet, your sarcasm cuts
with laser-sharp beams.

withering words of cold dancing light
   — chopping me
      — bating me
         — losing me . . .

I watch people bounce off your shiny exterior
before ever given a chance.

the "cool" one, hidden behind his silver shades;
your act has outdone itself, thank you very much.
clap clap says the audience.

I watch you slowly melt into the image you portray.

you've locked your Soul inside a sea of mirrors —
. . . before It joins those reflecting surfaces, you,
only you, have the power to open the door.

break free . . . !

and dare to be real.

Karen Trantow

THE CAESAR AUGUSTUS HOTEL

The Caesar Augustus Hotel was a movie star
from the forties,
I could hear the click of the projector.

From her balcony one could still gaze
down the craggy cliffs
to the ever-gentle breakers of the Mediterranean.

And from that balcony, off to the side,
one could catch a glimpse of the terrace,
where one might think to dance on a starlit evening.

But above, the once-manicured lawns had
given way to weeds,
crouching at the feet of the proud Roman statues.

And it was as though the must of the curtains and peeling wallpaper
was from those exquisite costumes of the past,
stale from the theatrical closet.

And now the tired winds of time had washed and muted
the once-magnificent palace,
waiting to fall from the Isle of Capri to the sea.

Allison Sutherland

FANTASY

I equate you with the Unicorn.
An animal of great stature and pride,
A creature of fantasy.
One with great heights of majestic prowess
At times, almost touchable, but elusive.
He gives you an assurance of nearness
And then darts off to worlds unknown.
The memory that lingers leaves a yearning desire
To be near, to touch, to love . . .
But the illusions fade
And leave you in wonder and awe
Of what might have been.

Judy James

WHERE CAN I FIND AN EMPTY NEST?

As my children grew from babyhood
And held claim to Mom, as they surely should
I hardly complained, for the fun was there
As we grew into a family, with joy to share.

I listened then to mothers that would say
How soon, too soon, they would go away
Leaving the nest you've built for them
And living their lives on a prayer or a whim.

Need not have worried my heart and mind
Mothers now tell me it's the signs of time
That feet still carry mud in from outside
And the table is set for four or five.

Today, it's as if it is engraved in stone
That this nest is forever and eternally, their own
So I'm pondering as the days and years go by
And wondering if I could learn to fly.

But, where on earth is there an empty nest
That I might flee to, for peace and rest

For I'm reduced from Mom to one who is begging
'Cause I'm now a tired, old-aged fledgling!

Willa Elliott

HER NAME WAS "LADY"

Her color was brown and black of sort
Her ears fell south and her nose turned north
Her mouth held more than too many teeth
For her mixture of Boston and Peek.

She learned to carry a tune and sing
And audibly say, "I love you"
On pitch, she moaned the sound of sirens
And frantically sought what she could do.

She stole from the neighbor's garbage and shoes
And often, on the porch, would lay
Cover-alls and clothes that were new
All covered with dirt and red Georgia clay.

Life has a way of altering time
But her response and love lingered on
Assuring us, everything with her was fine
But, sadly, we knew, not for very long.

Her spirit was much larger than her tiny size
And she was all things a dog should be
So in our hearts, she wins First Prize
Her name was "Lady," and a lady was she!

Willa Elliott

BORDERTOWN

Crossover
Unmistakable boundary limits
Remarkable changes, notably lacking unthought-of luxuries
Winding hills appear at peace in the distance. Approaching,
High society roughens to poverty
Asphalt to gravel, become dirt trenches engulfed
   in a mist of dust.
A Metamorphosis. Symbolic and Congruent
Monetary worth of sectional inhabitants
Downtown
Verandas, symmetrical gardens bursting with color,
Electric Values and operatable automobiles
Pavement
Midway on an upward slope
Shanties only half-spotted with light decorate rocky roads.
Wandering dogs and tires scattered everywhere
The maze begins farther into the lonely hills
Boxes of wood and tin become "home sweet home"
Darkness overpowers as heavy fog begins to settle in
   for the night.
Afar, a fire glows. Radiating warmth and direction
Direction to where?
The pavement? The bright side of town.

   Robyn K. Lee

ONE THOUSAND MEMORIES ABOVE THE BELT

Hey Old Man
I can see the story of your life, written all over your face.
Each crease, every fold, tells of many burdens. Laughlines
deeply embedded, are keepsakes of childhood pranks, the
cradle of a long-lived wit and sense of humor. Eyes reflect
great wisdom and truth. Sorrow, virtue, and brilliance;
complimentary reminders, success in life is not always easy.

Hey Old Man
Years of toil are read like Braille in the grip of your handshake.
Calloused, dry and cracking skin decorates fingers knotted and
bent at the joints. The gold band worn smooth through years of
tender fondling, awakens memories of home and the heart. A
deeply engraved lifeline intersects good fortune in your palm.

Hey Old Man
Your silhouette echoes laughter of many Saturday afternoons,
escaping from endless household chores, to the local café.
Your bulging belly pushes your belt toward your feet. Each
inch reminiscent of one thousand memories shared with boisterous
comrades. I can envision an indentation, to the right, just
below your shoulder blade. Years of friendly back thwacks,
each a greeting or a laugh.

Hey Old Man
It's been many seasons. But . . . each too short . . .
with so much time.

   Robyn K. Lee

DIPPED IN SOUL

Come to me,
   let me whisper it upon
      your face.

Hushed, the voice is wet
   when whispered.
   Then . . . it's the soul trying
      to escape.

Moist tears —
   the soul's totality glazing your lips —

Must touch your moist fingertips
   dipped every so cautiously
      in soul.

Come — let's find the grass.
   It will be wet now.
   The sun has not yet
      dried it.

It will be moist against us.
   And we'll be wet all over.
   — For a time —
      dipped in soul.

   Vanda Wark

GARDEN OF BEAUTY

In the garden of beauty someday I shall be
With the sweet fragrant flowers all around me
And the Angels all sing in glorious harmony
There's nothing but beauty in this garden to see

In the garden of beauty I'll dine with the King
There with the Saints, the victory I'll sing
As over the hills, holy echoes will ring
There'll be no sorrow in this garden of spring

In the garden of beauty I'll rest beyond the sky
With life-giving waters flowing nearby
From the tree of life, I'll feast and never die
There'll be no tombstones in this garden on high

In a garden of beauty I'm going to stay
There among the flowers dressed in white array
And the troubles of life will be passed away
By faith I will make it to this garden of day

   Gracie Greer

THE FLOWER PRAYER

Harmless as a flower, Lord help me to be
Though the storms of life blow around me
Harmless as a flower and smiled on from above
Please dress me, Lord, in the beauty of Your love

Harmless as a flower and free as a bird
Singing new songs the world never heard
Living a life that is kind, pure and true
I humbly request to be, Lord, like You

Harmless as a flower in the field growing wild
Noticed by many and loved by a child
Make me a blessing to everyone I meet
Hear me, dear Lord, I'm asking at Your feet

   Gracie Greer

THE UNTITLED

White playcards of a black day seek their origin
in the energies of space where rhythmic tunes of
melody exist in the vital disappearances of the
sun-rays. Where are the clout clumsy scenes of a
nefarious earth, speak o sky as a witness! In
silences that open the petals of lotus in the flicker
of a morning glory I have read meanings too deep
for meditation.

There have been many Easters in my life but Jesus
never came. The thudding leaves from the up and the
down have made me a bridegroom on many a solitary
evening. I create a saloon for my conscience and
display my bride in exhibitions without mirrors.
Show me my bones naked, o powers that be, and make
my life a cup of glory. Let narratives be small
and straight for crimson-nights to come and sing
poems of love. Let us all suffer and burn infidelity
like the all-conquering 'never-say-no' Job.

Charu Sheel Singh

THE STORM

Silver droplets of rain falling like a curtain slowly descending,
And behind it, the bees dance to a slow rhythm.
Silhouettes against a transparent backdrop,
Form bodies, with arms, many arms,
  moving slowly, gently to and fro,
    up and down.
      Executing a classical oriental dance,
        in bright oriental colours.

The wind quickens
. . . the tempo increases.
  . . . the music becomes louder,
And the dance changes through a ballet to a
      frenzied african dance
  . . . faster and faster
      until they fall
        exhausted to the ground.

Lorna McPherson

HEAVEN

Heaven is a pretty little cottage with a porch,
. . . two old folk in a rocking chair,
    rocking slowly with minds and hearts attuned,
    looking out into the sunset.

Heaven is a quiet walk along country lanes at the close of day
. . . tranquil animals, nibbling peacefully, dotting the landscape
. . . the soothing sound of a stream rushing over rocks
. . . birds going home for the night
. . . a pair of lovers walking hand-in-hand,
    stopping to kiss in the fading light.

Heaven is also loving and being loved by
    The Beautiful Ebony Prince,
    The Black Stallion
    Black Velvet
    Mandingo
    Winnie's Little Boy.

Lorna McPherson

DOWN BY THE RIVER

Down by the river listening to the waters
Telling me how to get the world back in order . . .

For the river knows why things come and go.
It can tell about the hell men have faced
And will face as time goes on . . .

Listen carefully to the waters of knowledge
For its *wisdom* didn't come from college. The
River is time, time is the river, each is one
Until there is none . . .

Down by the river listening to the waves, wondering,
Have I been saved? For the waters speak of me, of
Them, of all that is . . .

Trying to help me understand life and things that
Are wrong and right . . . river of *wisdom* you have
Taught me very much now I must awaken the rest of us . . .

You have cleansed my soul and uplifted my spirit
So that when I speak my words will be *deep* and
Reach all those who seek peace . . .

(For the river is time and time is the river)
      Those who understand will
      Succeed in all their
                  p
                l
                 a
                  n
                s . . .

Malik Canty

MY FRIENDS

The flowers are my friends
Now, you wonder why such a confession?
You see — I go in each day to work
In this work there is such a satisfaction
I work at O'Fallon Florist in Missouri
The flowers are my friends!
I design and deliver the flowers
In fresh and silk
Take a florist class
Am learning so much these days
Everything works out in so many ways
The flowers are my friends!
Before these arrangements go out
In my florist van
And I drive about
I make sure nothing's out of place
Like — balloons aren't missing out of arrangements
Plants and arrangements have enough water
These plants are shined and fresh or silk is added
The flowers are my friends!

Jennifer Kay Vroman Ruble

THE STREET WHICH I TOOK

To you I could be twenty or a hundred and two
Within all the paths that I have travelled through
Those filled with sorrow or those with joy
Making people happy or to really annoy
I can cause such a whirlwind or be silent or still
Go by the rules or by my own free will
I chose my way and the street which I took
As I go back and reminisce and take one more look.

All the ways that I acted, the things which I did
The tears that I cried, the feelings I hid
The moments I cherished, the loves which I had
Happiness, fears, and the times that were sad
But through all the paths that I calmly did walk
In all the discussions I needed to talk
I still am a human, and I can still surely feel
My tears and emotions, are still quite real
So please don't forget no matter the age
Its one more story, in life's turning page.

Wendy Burch

PERSISTENCE

As two bluebottle flies dance
the seemingly eternal hope for freedom
against a windowpane,
the temptation in an otherwise quiet bedroom
is to grant that buzzing wish
with an inch of fresh air and possibility.
But the next constant complaint would be against the screen,
and then the front door.

C. E. Courtney, Jr.

HE'S A CHANGED MAN, MAMA

Before I knew of tonka trucks or overgrown fields,
daddy had a scrap with a rusty axehead hidden in the weeds that
beat up on the bushog blade in seconds
and left him slumped and bloody,
nearly killed and surely saved by chance.
Now I know why mama hates the smell of fresh-cut grass,
diesel,
and the sound of metal against metal even more
than when he raves of anything except
how families can't recover when they wish that one of them was dead
or gone.

C. E. Courtney, Jr.

PERFORMANCE ANXIETY

Bet you can't stand on a bedpost and juggle two ghosts,
several whores,
and a lover's attention without falling.
Don't even try to avoid the performance
when they've crowded the bed
to laugh,
or applaud,
but never before have they all remained silent
and bowed to a locked bedroom door.

C. E. Courtney, Jr.

for Melissa

I long for you on a summer's day
When leaves are green
        and the air is warm

I long for you on a summer's day
When the world is full of women
I long for you

In the quiet of the night
My imagination soars beyond time
        to a place in my long-forgotten youth

If I say "I love you"
        Would it change the way
                you look at me
        Would your eyes meet mine
                with openness and trust
        Would you speak to me with the
                same intensity and caring

If I say "I love you" . . .

Robert N. Valli

DIAMONDS

The sea is like a mirrored glass, the sun is out by chance;
And when the breezes start to blow, the diamonds start to dance.

Atop the waves they sparkle bright — living jewels, all.
They tell us of another light, a memory they recall.

They speak of other diamonds rare, those gems beneath the ground.
The brilliance of the message there — is radiance profound.

For diamonds are the hardest stones, will cut through anything.
But starting out some years ago, they were the softest, then.

Coal and carbon, black as night, and soft — so weak as clay,
Hid in earth's recesses tight, away from light of day.

And with surroundings pushing hard, the black does turn to clear,
And prisms form, reflecting light, like tiny little mirrors.

From weak to strong, from dark to light,
    the growth is like man's worth:
The strength and hardness and the might —
    from pressures of the earth.

Hillary Hauser

VISION

The crystal palace of brilliant twilight
Sparkles paisley through vague eternity,
Ever encompassing distorted vision.
Illusions of sapphire rains and emerald fields —
Resounding elegance in gold-plated fantasy.
Canopies of opaled dusk
And dawns of fired ruby splendor
Emerge in diamond skies and topaz forests.

These images flash within the kaleidoscope walls of mind's eye,
While patterns from an eroded soul
Cascade furtively toward escape,
Yearning, yet perpetually imprisoned in feigned contentment
And satiated confirmations.

Daria Jaye Sambuco

LOST

When you left me I thought my life was through
I never thought I would get over you
I am found now that I've got someone else
Because I used to be lost without you
But now I'm found
You used to be the only woman in my life
And I was the only man in your life
But then you found somebody new
And I had to get over you
Now there's another woman in my life
And I'm glad to be getting over you
Because I was lost without you
But now I'm found with somebody else
You and me we used to be
All that I wanted to see
But now I know you've gotten over me
Now there's another woman in my life
And I'm glad to be getting over you
Because I was lost without you
But now I'm found with somebody else

Guy Wells

GUY DARREL WELLS. Born: Hamilton, Ohio, 8-29-72; Education: Wilson Junior High School; Occupation: Student; Comments: *I like to write screenplays and books. I usually use names of my close friends for the names of the characters. I get most of my ideas for poems and screenplays at 10-12 o'clock at night.*

PACING GIRL . . .

A poem to be played on a drum

Vibrating vertebrae . . . rippling stones
synchronized bones
neck laced to hip . . . side to side rock . . .
foot thrust and slink
pause
hip socket thrown . . . basin of bone
pause
rock . . . thrust . . . slink
head to side cup
hip angle up
pause
viniculum rock
hip out and swing . . .
swing-slink
pivot
profile
swing-slink
pivot
rest.

Kay Stewart

THE DON'T LITTLE KID

When I was a little child
Mama used to say,
Don't you get into trouble
When you go out to play.

Don't climb the fence
And don't climb that tree,
You know it will be trouble
For you and for me.

Just be a good child
And don't you stray
Don't open the gate
And sneak away.

Don't do this
And don't do that
And don't you chase
The neighbor's cat.

So I sat on the step
And that's where I stayed
That's all I could do
When I went out to play.

What can a guy do
With a mother like that,
Can't even play
With the neighbor's cat.

Helen T. Barker

GOD AND MAN
Not Lonely Anymore

Sitting in her rocking chair
  Combing her snow-white hair,
Looking around her tiny room
  That is so pitifully bare.

Her pride and dignity were all gone
  But she didn't even care,
Along the way she laid them down
  She wasn't even aware.

Her room it was so silent
  And pitifully bare too,
Nobody ever came by
  To see what they could do.

She picked up her Holy Bible
  And started to read,
Her heart it rejoiced
  As her soul she did feed.

She said why have I been lonely
  Now and long before,
That must be my Savior
  Knocking on my door.

As she sits there, in her rocking chair
  She is not lonely anymore,
Because she read her Holy Book
  And she opened up her door.

Praise God

Helen T. Barker

THAT OTHER LAMB

Little lamb on the green soft grass,
You did not know
That far, far away
And long, long ago
There lived another lamb,
  A little lamb like you.

Little lamb, you did not know
That that other lamb
Walked on stub and stone
And walked alone . . .

  And then one day was led away,
  Away to the slaughter —
  Away to die.

Little lamb,
You did not know,
But oh, little lamb,
It is so!

Francis Marquis DuBose

THE BEAUTIFUL SEA

I walk along the shores of the beautiful sea,
  Your warm presence is next to me.
Your smile is sweet, kind and sincere,
  It feels good to have you near.
The waves rising from the beautiful sea
  Let me know this is where I want to be.
Digging my feet into the cool sand,
  With you beside me, holding my hand.
Our thoughts flow as if they were one,
  Lifting a burden that weighed a ton
On my mind so heavily,
  As we walked on the beautiful sea.
Your presence filled me with pride,
  Standing there by your side.
Being happy is all I knew,
  Staring at the beautiful sea with you!

Belinda

ESTHER BELINDA OUTTEN. Pen Name: Belinda; Born: Pensacola, Florida, 8-23-52; Married: Lloyd Leon Outten, Jr., 8-23-80; Education: Pensacola Junior College, 1970-71; L.A. Trade Technical College, 1978-82; Occupation: Accounting supervisor; Awards: Six Award of Merit Certificates; Poetry: 'Positive Enchantment,' *Our World's Most Beloved Poems*, 1984; 'Rapture,' 1985; 'Black Diamonds,' 1986; Comments: *Through the hectic pace that life takes us, it gives my heart great pleasure to be able to put into words of poetry the serenity of life's quiet and peaceful moments that I receive.*

THE ROSE

I dreamt of you again last night,
You were holding me close in your sleep.
It felt so good, it felt so right.
I woke up feeling so happy,
Then so sad,
When I realized that it was only a dream.
I wish I could have that
dream every night.
So I could always feel like part of you.
My life is so empty without you,
I miss you so much.

You said our love was like a red, red Rose,
That slept in cold, but bloomed in spring.
You said our love would never die.
But you said it did for you,
And we went our separate ways.

God, I miss you so very much,
And I think that spring will never come,
I can only hope that you're right,
like you so often are.
And there is life after death.
Then maybe the Rose will
bloom again.

Judy Carignan

AMERICA MY OWN

When world confusion lies heavy on my shoulders
To go to a place of green grass and high boulders
As I sit at the top and glance toward the sun
My eyes open wide and I let my mind run
From trees to clouds I look and I see
The glorious beauty of this land of the free
As an eagle soars so high up above
I thank God for you, America, land that I love
I'm sorry to have been remiss with my appreciation
Of the people who gave their lives to make this great nation
My personal anxieties seem so petty and small
As I sit here and clearly contemplate about it all
I was born in a land with freedom to choose
A heritage taken for granted would be so easy to lose
My thoughts have lightened and as the sun sinks down
With a quickened step I descend to lower ground
My priorities are straight now and I vow to the sky
If you need me, America, I would gladly fight and die
To insure that old glory's stars and stripes wave forever
One nation, undivided, staying strong together

Sherial Wiser

REALITY

In which world is it that you are
You with your eye on the beckoning star
Your feet shackled firmly to the unyielding ground
Your arms reaching upward to territories unbound.
Lonesome longing within summons great urgency
By resisting the lure you display your dependency
On symbols of a life you did not create
Society's spider has spun your fate.
It extols of the freedom of property
And you weave the walls of prosperity
Ever higher they loom till you cannot see
Your beckoning star. Oh! Tragedy!

Norma Nixon

RECOGNITION

"Beyond the legend of the red, blue and gold lights flickering,
In the hazy distant shore, & beyond the ebb and flow of your need.
Reaching out for more, till the horizons of whiteness fill your vision.
And then the blur of peace, that lightly flashes knowing signs,
Before the meeting of our minds & much before that, the poverty:
Stricken crowds hungry with the impassioned roars,
Cast their bits gnawing eagerly at their morsels of pain.

Before the thunder clap of the first rain,
And the violence of the night in her silent pain.
I knew thee with the clarity of the eager brightness,
Of the vivid lightning & the flash of recognition:
It still burns strange . . . Remember i clutched the threads impulsively,
And rode the merry ride, i drank in the voices,

When heat came you prayed hard for snow,
And then came the chill,
Which you should never have wished for.''

Zareen Husain

A SHIELD OF COMMON SENSE

Man — let it not be the color of my skin,
The origin of my country, or my destination, be a breach.
Do not allow society to be the opportunist to be the arbiter,
Or the bitterness of your experiences, cast a shadow.
Hold a shield of common sense;
Something that is so scarce.
Absorb the sunshine into your heart,
And let the sunrays be your guide.
Do not let the harshness of the rain,
Or the snow, that freezes rivers, be your path,
Toward the freedom of color blindness be hindered.
For you must know, that it only exists,
In the realm of a misleading maze,
And will direct you straight toward a pitfall of ignorance.

Jessica Suh

WHEN I CROSSED THE OCEAN
I: TAHITI

When I crossed the ocean, I was alone
Somebody said to me, ''Bon jour!''
Others waved to me, ''Good morning!''
I gave them my best smile

When I played in the reef, I was alone
A tiny girl spoke to me, ''Kon-nichi-wa!''
Her father was from my country, ''Wow!''
We sang songs all starry night

When I met sunny Joyce, I was alone
Talked by the pictures on the sand
Walked by the palm trees, ''Watch out!''
Hibiscus to her, seashells to me

When I left the islands, words were gone
Kissing, hugging, tears in my heart

Yes, I was once in Tahiti

Fujie Fujikawa

THE SACRED STAGE

The sacred stage is a place of grief.
A faceless siege of time and vision
where shadows wedge in silence.

The sacred stage is a frameless void
of illusion, a charade in darkness
where dreams don't keep, and a ragged
sweetness overworks the flesh.

This sanctity where deception is conceived

       like a

passionless act without witness.
Where light is deceived into eternal death.

Louise Hagins

BRAVE SOLDIERS

The morning threw its warmth upon the beach,
Soldiers woke shivering in the shadow.
Souls hidden from glory alas beseech,
The darkness offered nothing to follow.
Spirits mingle together in the dunes,
Treading soft, waking no pain, healing love,
Warming Eden as the sun stalks the moon,
Solemn, soft, the gentle eyes of a dove.
The sun starts to settle, giving to night;
Yet there is no chill; laughter in the hearts,
Brave soldiers in arms welcoming twilight,
Darkness shrouds the beach; shredded fear
      departs.
As waves crumble their castles in the sand,
They carry their gifts in each other's hand.

Lisa Fisher-Hiller

TREACHERY

One's fatal spot is patted
By a foe, thought a friend
Thus the blade, plunged to its hilt
Is unresisted to the end.

Death comes so swiftly . . .
The lips, the eyes
Hold, still, that smile —
And reflect a faint surprise . . .

Lorraine Rice

WORDS

Don't take from man his words,
his own wealth even in silence,
words of love and those of hope.

Watch the human-like sleep of words,
watch the human-like rest of words.

Marcel Gafton

Silence brings fear
imagination wild
the noises you hear
could be real.

Daylight arrives
you can open your eyes
you think you were stupid,
yet maybe you're wise.

You think of escaping,
of places to hide,
just in case
your logic lied.

Your heart is beating quickly
so loud, you can't hear
your senses deceive you,

    As always with fear.

Debbie L. Weekley

BUILDINGS

Huge machines gouging
piles of lumber standing
ten thousand nails
cement and steel
skilled workmen.
Changing the face
of yet another space
that was once nature's reign
to man's domain.

John D. Merck

THERE'S MUSIC IN MY DREAMS

Did you hear the music up above?
It made me so sure of our love.
Though it stopped when I awoke it seems.
I know there's music in my dreams.
The music was so clear and loud.
It seemed to come down from the clouds.
To see you I crossed a crystal stream.
I know there's music in my dreams.
It was such a glorious time of the year.
We were both so full of love and cheer.
And if he hadn't come along,
It would be for you I'd dream my song.
He will not love you and be true.
I'm just not understanding you.
Though with you went my sweet love theme,
I still have music in my dreams . . .

Stanley Liston Rung

I BELIEVE IN YOU

For Cindy

I look at you and see the things
  you won't allow yourself to see
I see you being all of the things
  you don't trust yourself to be
I see you reaching all of your goals
  and making them come true
And using all of your talents
  helping them shine through
I see the dreams inside your heart
  the things you want to do
I know sometimes you feel you can't
  but I believe in you!

Twila Carter

TWILA CARTER. Born: Gallatin, Tennessee, 11-26-52; Education: Brigham Young University; Pierce College, Los Angeles, Psychology; Occupations: Public relations executive for the movie, television and music industry for 10 years; Nurse; Memberships: American Federation of Television & Radio Artists, Professional Business Women's Association, Media Publicist of America Association; Comments: *Since childhood I have wanted to write: to be able to express thoughts and ideas, fears and strengths; to have the ability to solve problems, on paper, that in reality I cannot solve; to comprehend things that are beyond my reach; to touch a side of life that is foreign to me. Writing is forever. It allows you to share a part of yourself with the world, and not just for the moment, for even one hundred years later someone, somewhere will read your words and know you lived. I do all types and styles of writing, but I especially enjoy writing poems and stories for children and teens. Their minds are so eager and their smiles so quick and sincere. It's very rewarding to know your work is enjoyed by children.*

SNOWFLAKE

A snowflake . . .
  crystallized
  mesmerized
shaped into stability
  liquidized
  energized
melted into debility

Sybil Holloway

I do believe that you are in love with me
But I need for you to tell me that it's true.

As you should already know, I truly love you so
Way more than you will ever, ever know.

Please tell me that you love me; Oh tell me every day
Wrap your arms around me and make me want to stay.

I dream about the things we used to do
The love we used to share and how we shared it too.

But now the truth has overcome us
Our love just has to end
We may never be together again.

Oh what am I going to do
Will I ever have you again
Or has my life just come to an end.

No matter what happens, I want you to know
I will always, always love you so.

Michelle Swavely

THE ATHLETE'S BEST FRIEND

Herded into a cathedral of professional leisure
We sit gazing upon the altar of sweat
Coaxed by boredom and the magnets of reality
The crowd pays the price for admission
And dons the cloak of spectatorship

Trick or treat
A furry mascot stuffed with plastic paid enthusiasm
Edge of seat
The proximity of popular fame fulfills our fantasies
Passions beat
Bare limbs pulsate to augment the sensory scintillation
Sportsexbloodandbeer is cool
Creed of the fan — TV fool
The tipoff and the ripoff
The playoff and the payoff
The kickoff and I'm sick of our distorted priorities

Jeff Stoudt

EXPRESS THOUGHTS

mechanical earthworm burrowing . . . subterranean pathways
concrete urban catacombs . . . a hallway of graffiti ghosts
haunting candelabra street lights . . . essence of horror as normative
discontinued alternation . . . light and dark
electrical spark, faces naked and stark
souls compressed in alienation
awaiting momentary destination
same old beginning in a technological unity of discord
long and lifeless labyrinth
flow of electrons on rails of steel
nothing to give and less to feel
metallic screeching precludes all
but the tacit communication of evasionary gestures
collision of human error and mechanical precision
fear is possibility in labor
reality is its birth
life at conception
death kills the deception
eternity hosts the parasite passengers
so goes it. O the rapture of a subway sonnet

Jeff Stoudt

PARABLE OF
AN OCEAN OF REFLECTION

The sea of life raged round about in commotion;
A form like a rock was born out of the motion.
The conditions were set by the Arcane Might;
There was no retreat — the rock form would fight.
Insistent wave after wave exploded against rock,
As if hoping to rend dedication by shock.
Then, as spray and spume rocketed down from on high,
The whole ocean seemed to retreat and to sigh;
For the rock once again, arrogant and proud,
Had slipped free of Neptune's tenacious green shroud.
Ah, if only with the vision of God I'd been born,
I could see that the rock was a little more worn.

Bart Casty

PARABLE OF
THE HOSTILE SWAMP

The sun's rays thread down through the trees,
Through gamboling green leaves, to tease;
To soothe denizen, predator, and huge alligator,
But none of the beasts are at ease.
For while the swamp glitters and glistens
And all nature listens,
Neither denizen nor predator agrees.

Bart Casty

THE WASHINGTON BOULEVARD TRAGEDY

He must have got in with the wrong crowd.
I watched as they pulled him from a pool
        of blood in the front seat.
He was unconscious.
The blood that seeped from his stab wounds
        was brown,
            like barrio rain.

A few blocks away . . .
An old woman and her grandchild were struck
        in route to the hospital.
They were death-still.
Reduced to clumps of white cloth on black
        pavement,
            like stray bullets jaywalking.

                    Through the barrio
                        In winter
                            At dusk.

Angela Allen

CLOUDS

As I gaze up at you so fluffy and white.
Sailing around in the sky what a beautiful sight.
You change shapes many times as you pass me by.
While you skip and dance about in the sky.
Like giant ice-caps floating in a sea of blue.
Just where are you going? I wish I knew.
Maybe to a fantasy land far far away.
Or just over the horizon and you'll return someday.
Sail away if you must but do come visit again.
And please give me a clue to where you have been.

Beverly Ernst

DREAM POEM

I'm stuffed into the pajamas I wore
as a child —
they hold my belly tight as I
bend to sit and
lie to sleep.
My hands can't grasp all the blankets
at once so they lift them
one by one until I'm
hidden,
quiet.
To lie here forever, curled embracing
ankles tucked under one another,
wrists tangled beneath my chin
as a child —
warm
dark
safe.
The black-haired violent
hand rips the layers
in one motion
and there I lie
head turned up, eyes startled wide
curled, holding my belly.

Trish Walsh

IMMORTAL MAN

My eye can't pierce the future,
and but little of the past.
I merely write the things I feel,
and hope that they will last,
or pray that they may bridge the gap
my life can never span.
By breathing my living spirit in words,
become immortal man.

Lauren R. Baum

THE BLUE ROSE

Blue rose petals fall silently
Fluttering to the ground
Waiting for the hand to pick them up
Waiting for the love

The blue rose standing silently still
Soaking up the sun
Wondering for your love

Violent rains make it weep
Winter snows
Shake its sleep

But it always stands
Waiting for the human hand

Once you touch it
It trembles and shakes
The frost is melted
The pain it takes
But then its lips are parted
And its hands uncurled
The sun is awakened
And the blue rose blooms

Melissa Martinez

NIGHT LIFE

Fear, despair, walk through the night
the lonely streets that echo
the shuffling and the easy glide
of older steps and younger ones
walking together and so apart.

Tuxedos, business suits,
good after-shave and plastic cards,
the faces haggard, empty the eyes,
propelling robots going through
gourmet food and senseless guiles.

The young flesh at their side
they try to make their own,
remorse and hatred bound together,
anguished smiles turn slowly
into macabre wholes, ever so wide.

The feet keep walking
shuffle, clip-clop, shuffle, clip-clop,
back and forth through the endless night,
older steps and younger ones,
walking together and so apart.

Ilse Wefers

THE DILETTANTE

There is no more the old anger,
no more the old fear,
left is the mute staring into outer space.
The knights are sleeping,
turned to poems, to songs of yore,
they left with dreams of better, of holy, of love.

A dilettante's pastime:
"The Survival of the Fittest,"
an apocalyptic film, in color,
the hero riding on four horses,
fulfilling his own vision,
of the ending of it all.

Let us, my friend, share sweet flowers,
watch joyfully the birds in flight,
let us find the shaded rainbow,
hold hands, sing softly about love,
drink endless cups of kindness,
smile gently, and finally

— blast off.

Ilse Wefers

MISTY CLOVER

Cherokee Indian bride
Flawless features of pride
Blue mist of magic arrows
Romantic world in the shadows
Dreamer with tiger eyes
Swirl of dreams in the sky
Grandmother bright eyed
Sky color hide
Around the campfire story telling
Following the romantic wings of morning
Enchanting Indian dance
Flame of romance
Wrapped in an Indian blanket
Unhappiness she will forget

Shereé Riggs

THE PERFECT LOVE

When our eyes first met, there
was an instant spark.
    She thought, This is it, and there
goes my heart.
    He said, Thank you God, my
life is happy again.
    We were meant to meet for
our lives to share.
    So we ran away together
just anywhere.
    Our short life was walking
on moonlit beaches, loving, and
caring.
    We had a storybook love.
    Now I'm gone, I am watching
my love from above.
    Thank you God.

Joetta E. Courtney

FAITH

We make our own sorrow here
on God's land
Because we are so weak we don't
seem to understand
Jesus died on the cross so we
could be saved
He asks us to remember Him
as He rose from the grave
He tells us to bring all
our heartaches to Him
Then He will walk with us and
contentment bring
If our faith is complete our
sorrow will be gone
Thank God for Jesus He is
so strong.

Bertha E. Hagen

GUINEVERE'S PRAYER

Take me away
away from cold biting eyes
eating the hearts
of those who hold warm dreams
in slender upturned palms.
The widest stroke of wisdom
did not intend this.
Leave your shadow
in the doorway
and plunge your voice
in stalled air:
Love is known
only to pilgrims
passing like smiles
through this surge of faces.

Jim Carr

FINGER PAINTING

You were purple, boy
purple as August sunrise discovery
gathered up flowers and twigs from the landlord's garden
Father placed in Mother's crystal
        on the window sill

A still life. you lay there quiet, boy
lessened of life and unconcerned
while the world scurried with hastened instincts
shook and demanded life
        from your limbs

A miracle. seemingly outraged but trembling
as they sucked and pulled fluid from your throat
lungs aching
        of new breath

A beginning. harsh as it is Divine
life's canvas pulls back the colors we endure
to reveal our sunsets with dimension
        and design

A masterpiece.

Angela Allen

TO THE CAGED LEOPARD

His slanted topaz eyes stare through the bars
Ears cupped to catch faint sounds unheard by day.
He dreams of freedom, lost 'neath jungle stars;
Soft footpads stalking the unwary prey.
Through wind-swept grasses tall and meadow green
He prowls in hungry purpose to his goal;
His ghost-like presence neither felt nor seen
By thirsting quarry at the water hole.
Dark silence bodes no portent of the kill —
The target clear — the net is swift and true!
Now, hunter and the hunted, caged and still,
Await their doom in man's barbaric zoo —
  He lives imprisoned in his concrete cell
  While man in self-made prisons lives his hell.

Marjorie V. Slater

SO SOFT A RAIN

Gently it fell upon the roof
 A rain so soft it did so soothe.
  A troubled mind, thoughts of unrest,
   Melted away by rain's request.
The old room of a young man's life
 Bringing peace of mind, in place of strife.
  Thoughts of old so clearly seen.
   Bolder notions of life's dream.
Drifting back to an uncluttered time
 When feelings for life were easy to find.
  So it goes — memory brings
   Happiness to present — by thought and thing.
So gentle, dripping water off the roof
 Rocking in chair, mind aloof.
  Thoughts fall back into place.
   To recall so many in such quick pace.
Gently it fell upon the roof
 A rain so soft it did so soothe.
  In waking at dawn, felt so rested.
   An easier mind with memories protected.

Michael V. McCann

ESCAPE

Alone again.
Lying on my dusty bed of memories,
Plagued by the neverending cry of despair,
I dream.

Of yesterday.
Of precious moments while loved ones lived,
But I, enraptured by self, slowly died,
To life.

Alone again.
Adrift in a world void of heart and compassion,
I flail my arms and beat my breast for want,
Of what?

Possessions perhaps.
Empty, lifeless forms of greed surround, engulf,
Pulling me deep within mire which binds me to earth,
Intense cold.

Alone again.
No companion to see the pain, hear the cries,
Just me, my possessions, and the essence of my being.
Precious bottle.

Ilene Cardinalli

THANKSGIVING PRAYER

Dear God I thank You for all that I am,
My goodness, my frailties, my unsteady hand.

I sometimes forget to thank You for life,
So caught in the whirlpool of pressure and strife.

But, then I remember Jesus walked this same path,
Encountered the hardships, the heartaches and wrath.

And through all that he suffered, his sadness and pain,
He thanked You for all, still praising Your name.

From this I must learn to be thankful each day
For all I encounter through life's unsure way.

I know You stay near me, Your touch I can feel,
As You guide and protect me, no love is more real.

Ilene Cardinalli

THE WIND

Hurrah! Spring has arrived.
We've weathered another winter.
Now summer is nigh. That wind!
Where does it go, when it lies.
From whence does it come,
When it blows hither and yon?
The breeze is so fresh and calm.
In a moment it gets strong.
Sometimes it's hot, sometimes it's cold.
Trees bend their heads, lose some leaves and twigs.
Then it seems the wind gets mad. Better take cover.
Quick! But where? That wind is everywhere.
It picks up houses like kites, sets them down again.
Most often not as a house but a mess.
People are not immune to its fury.
They are buried somewhere or oft
Carried elsewhere and dropped.
God must have a great automat behind the wind somewhere,
But never loses His control.

Pearl G. Ray

VARYKINO REKINDLED

Miss you?
Yes, even before
winter has died in the fires of tulips.
Lost in the wilderness of a heart
whose geography remains unmapped
I come to you a poet
naked and alone
speaking of faraway places
locked in willowy dreams.
Can love be known
in an occupied land
where time is the fuse
driving the circle of life?
Yet in the space of this moment
I feel I know you
as well as any night
that ever enveloped me
and seeing your face
would launch a thousand attempts
to split the heavens with fire.

Jim Carr

THE BUTTON

Who are you, friend or foe?
Weren't you ever told? Don't you know
That once you're pressed we'll all go.
Big or small all countries will know.
Button, you won't be such an issue anymore.
I wonder what you think will be the score,
Who will count the screams galore?
From all sides it will be an agonizing defeat,
As this dear earth it will shake
Right out from under our feet,
With no country left complete.
Never mind anymore friend or foe
We will all be as one, lost, searching,
Looking for a new place to go.
Then all powers will be no more,
I call that a pretty even score.
So what in hell is it all for?

Liz Forrest

HOMESICK

Silently slipping from day to day,
Feeling like nothing is coming my way.
Past memories of fun dance in my head,
From the early morning, until time for bed.
When sleep can release all your faces to me,
Dear friends so missed, you come back to me.
Then morning breaks, just like my heart
Because, my dear friends, we have to part.

Liz Forrest

MAUI

Wish I were a-goin'
On golden sands to run
Where tradewinds are a-blowin'
On my island in the sun

Where tall and slender palm trees
Bend low to greet the sand
And blossom-perfumed breezes
Gently blow — caress the land

Where vibrant bougainvillea
Stretch upward to the sky
And scarlet-bloomed poinsettias
With gold hibiscus vie

Where softly strummed guitars
Play a sweet Hawaiian tune
Under blue La-ha-in-a skies
 Or a Ka-pa-lu-a moon

Yes, beautiful Na-pi-li
Is calling me by name
By sands of Ka-an-a-pa-li
I long to roam again

Yes, I wish I were a-goin'
On Maui's shores to run
Where tradewinds come a-blowin'
On my island in the sun

M. M. Fidell

CANNING

Pleasant smells in the kitchen —
It's canning time, did I mention?

Mother made rainbows
With rows of jars
Marked beets, green beans, tomatoes.

I watched the pressure gauge,
Just helping was my wage.

Harvest time came but once a year,
But those memories are always near.

Nancy M. LaChance

INSECURE

A puzzle — unlocked pieces
Shuffle around
Not alike — not the same
Two faces (Conflicting character)
Somehow in disarray —
Controversial.
Now this, then that . . .
And they blend in.
You have a choice
Make your own puzzle.

Lydia Esther Lugo

SHE GIVES TO ME

She lives . . .
    few moments in a world
now, so new to her.
    In a world
now, so different to me.

Her eyes meet mine
and her fingers clutch my hand.
    She knows I gave birth to her
and I know she gives life to me.

She lives . . .
    precious dreams in a world
now, so unknown to her.
    In a world
now, so important to me.

Cassandra Brannan

TOO LATE

He stood atop a high cliff
Looking down at the rocks there.
His face was darkened by despair.
His life he knew must change, but
He only knew one way out.

Death stood below waiting.
Despair beside cheered on.
He closed his eyes tightly
And jumped into his arms.

Slowly he fell down.
He then too late thought
About his life's end.

His future called.
He cried, ''I changed . . .''

As his body struck the ground.

Jane Marchant

Remember penny candy
You bought en route to school?
That big glass case of goodies
That made your senses drool?
The butterballs and licorice sticks
The bubble gum and such
Those good old days and simple ways
When one cent bought so much?
You could hardly wait 'til recess
That penny joy to munch
More delicious than the sandwich
Your mom had packed for lunch.
It's fun to trip down Memory Lane
Sweet visions are so many
But best of all is to recall
The magic of a penny!

Beth Harris

WALLS

Built by time, built by men,
Purposed to let no one in.
Surrounding cities, surrounding me.
Barriers only few can see
Feelings, frustrations, fear and doubt
Brick upon brick, shutting out.
Spirits barred from singing,
Hearts denied their seeking.
Dividing husband and wife.
Room, left only from strife,
Built by time, built by men,
Purposed to let no one in . . . walls.

This that surrounds the hearts of man,
Surely, can be gone again.
Swallow all of the selfish pride!
Tear walls down from either side.
If love truly conquers all,
Love will cause the walls to fall.
Destroyed by time, forgotten by men,
Not from without, but from the soul within . . . walls.

Julia M. Peacock

THE GREAT COMPOSER

There is One who writes the symphonies of life.
He composes all joy and allows in some strife.
His melodies are sweet, His cadences clear.
With Him in control, what could we fear?
He writes every note, every passage with care,
And at each performance, He's sure to be there.

The beauty of His harmonies shine through, sing out.
Discord is brought by only our doubt.

Why don't we follow when He wants to lead?
An unled symphony is like a broken creed.
If we don't follow every note, each rest,
How can we expect it to sound its best?
There has been a symphony composed just for you,
Keep your eye on the conductor; He'll see you through!

Julia M. Peacock

ABILITY TO BE FREE

The ability to be free gives only the
courage to be you,
    the confidence to share the talents, that
you so uniquely do,
    with all the faith to guide you, through
the passages each day,
    and the security of knowing that you
did it your own way,
    the pride to say, "I did it," and the will
to carry on,
    the strength to hold your head up high,
when your hope is almost gone,
    the special way you show it, and take it
all in stride,
    as you fight to make that Dream come true,
that others criticize,
    there's a unique and special feeling, when
you make your Dream a reality,
    for that is the first, you actually realize,
you have the *ability to be free* . . .

Margaret E. Kerrigan

MARY'S PRAYER

"Morning talk with Jesus."
I got up early today.
To talk with you, Jesus, before I go on my way.
Sometimes things just don't go right.
But throughout the day or night.
I can just call you, and you are right there beside me.
You have always been there to guide.
If we only realize that you see all things.
Jesus, I know that you are my best friend.
You take care of me, no matter what the day may bring.
When I come to you in prayer.
All my cares and woes are easier to bear.
Because you give me strength to go forth with each new day.
Jesus helps me along life's way.
Thank you, Jesus, for caring, I love you.

Mary E. Phillips

ANGELS IN THE CLOUD

Today, as I looked out the window,
Away up in the clouds so blue,
Among the blue and white background,
A mist the morning dew.
The clouds had formed away up in the blue yonder,
As I was sitting with my beloved husband in the hospital today.
The clouds looked like a city in the distance so far away.
Right in the middle appear two clouds, that looked like angels.
What beauty to behold, such peace, and joy came over us?
As I try to share this with my loved one.
Jesus I know that you are leading us here below,
Where we are to travel on this hard road only you know.
I have no voice to sing, I only have my hand and pen.
I have always been timid and shy.
But today as I looked into the sky,
I just want to shout from this mountain top,
The things I had seen from on high.
Praises to my Savior, the King, he is coming by and by
I saw the angels in the sky.

Mary E. Phillips

A SONG OF MY HALF LIBERTY

Hundred years ago I was not being
    In the universe that birds always sing.
    What I was if
    The legends called me that was
    A Spiritual Dragon.
    How I was if
    The flowers whispered on me:
    "That your entire body we had never seen."
    And clouds flirted with me:
    "Would you not forget us, our dear venturer?"

I went down the Inferno to visit the freedom-seekers,
    After I left a note on Paradise:
    "Don't wait for me going back!
    I want to be merely a man!"

To exist as one human, I had the faith:
    That no jail, no church, no fort was strong
    Enough to keep the hearts and longs,
    But loves and rhythmic songs
    Were the castle did bind me in.

Nhon Tong Ong

FICKLE APRIL

April dawns so bright and rosy,
The grass is shimmery with dew,
Creatures awaken from hibernating,
And the sky is azure blue.

Away off in the distance
Is heard a resounding roar.
Seems but a minute instant
The sky is blue no more.

The sun by clouds is darkened,
Showers flood the earth,
Heavens split wide open,
The crack quivers as with mirth.

As we blink and look again
We see a patch of blue.
The clouds are parting one by one,
The sun is peeking through.

"Oh, April, with your cock-eyed days,
You know what's right and wrong,
You fool us with your fickle ways
And soothe us with a song."

Evelyn L. Lyons

OCTOBER MORN

With slim and magic fingers
The dawn cannot undo
The work of frosty fingers
Before she came in view.

With paints in snowy crystals
He changed all greens to reds.
The blossoms of each flower
In weariness droop their heads.

The dawn awakens humans
To look upon the earth
All glorified by nature,
A most radiant, splendid birth.

Evelyn L. Lyons

SPRITE

Wild wind,
Free wind,
Salt-bitter sea wind —
Fill the sails
Of my small boat,
And sweep me
Through the foam!

Sharp wind,
Fresh wind,
Misty rampant dew wind —
Blow my hair
And whip my shirt,
And make me
Always roam!

Jennifer McGraw

DREAMS COME TRUE IN NATURE

A rippling stream gurgles by.
Its waters are crystal clear.
It speaks to me in silv'ry tones
So pleasant for ear to hear.
The pastel wings of butterflies
Are dotted here and there.
The thrilling notes of the mockingbird
In cadence fill the air.
The billowy branches of the elm
Shade the ground around.
Pines that reach the highest realm
In stature straight and sound
Bear nestled homes of feathered friends
Within their lofty arms,
And hidden by the furry foliage
Tends to protect them from all harms.

As I sit here beside the stream
I see these glorious things.
I gaze in awe at God's creation
Making true my dreams.

Evelyn L. Lyons

EVELYN JOHNSON LYONS. Born: Kalamazoo, Michigan, 10-28-21; Married on 1-23-43 to Lawrence E. Johnson (deceased, 1976); Married on 12-17-83 to James E. Lyons; Education: Parsons Business College, 6-40; Lifetime Career Schools, Los Angeles, 6-76; The Institute of Children's Literature, Redding Ridge, Connecticut, 1985; Occupation: Executive secretary (retired), St. Regis Paper Co., Kalamazoo; Other Writings: "The Great Pretender," essay, *News-Sun Daily*, 11-12-85; "It All Happened in the Courtyard," short story, *News-Sun Daily*, 4-28-86; Comments: *I usually write about nature and birds or other animals. I make greeting cards out of flowers and sell them under the logo, "Nature's Own by Evie J."*

JOFFERY

Waves of emotion painted movements

Floating effortlessly, cutting air
And reforming in human line.

Swirls of motion glistened accents
Living flurriedly, as sculpture
Exploring brilliance in mankind.

Kevin John Cummins

TODAY

The days of my life have gone by,
Now, I look back and I cry.
So many things I could have done,
But all I did was look for fun.

The mistakes that we all make,
All the loved ones we forsake,
The things we didn't do,
That we never had a clue to.

The dreams of youth fade away,
Do we face the reality every day?
Living from this day to that,
Never knowing where love's at.

Moving here and there,
Hoping for someone to care.
Forwards, backwards, every day,
Yesterday's gone, now it's today . . .

Karla Jamison

BOTH BLUE AND GOLD

I sit alone it's almost dawn
Staring out my window toward the east
And I can't help but think there's hundreds
Out there watching to say the least

And I wonder how many minds
The thought of God has entered in
And how upon a prior time
He watched the dawn of dawns begin

With arms outstretched
The elements obeyed
A greater light a lesser light
On words alone were made

And as the void in darkness
Burst forth from the mold
The heavens did applaud
With streaks of light both blue and gold

Lonnie Collins

HER SYMPHONY

The dawn brings golden streaks
Like arrows pierce they ladened peaks
Down around shimmering glistening
Trickling notes for all that's listening

Keys begin to bounce in time
Knowing what's on nature's mind
I watch spellbound intriguingly
As nature plays her symphony

Lonnie Collins

WOOD DUCKS

I watch them catapult to the air
Their colors rare beyond compare
Their eeks siren in the morn
Wings outstretched, feathers torn

They lift up high
With all the grace
Fortitude
And endless haste

And soon are specks
On distant scene
Leaving nought behind
But waves

Lonnie Collins

LIFE AND DEATH

Art is smart
Science is true
I love to cotton to the red, white and blue
If a country is in peril
We dash to its aid
And don't forget the summer
With all the Kool-Aid
Jackson Pollack turns me on
There's no losing patience where I belong
Stare out bright stars of the firmament
Make our dreams a little more permanent:
Shout it out peace and good will
'Cause where we're going
There's not much of a thrill.

Mardene Butler

CLOSER LOOK

The upturned corners of a smile
A perfect place to hang rosy cheeks
In times of sadness the corners turn
As if to hold up a tiny, quivering chin

To look into those unpretentious eyes
And see the full promise of a lifetime
Tears only seem to magnify their color
And wash away each sorrow

A child . . .
The miraculous perfection
Complete, achieved, realized
The ultimate innocence, unknowingness
A gift freely given for benefit and pleasure

Look close and often
Don't miss the little things
Brevity of time steals from us
Special moments
That were meant to fill a memory

Connie L. Clarneau

GROWING

We were so young
But it was all we knew of love
Senior prom
Graduation
Trembling hands and gold bands
We had such dreams . . .

We were so young
So sure of our lives entwined
We would grow together
College — first year, second year
The joy of motherhood
Dreams changed
Diapers changed
We changed . . .

We were so young
We grew
As did the distance between us
The parallel of our lives was gone
One way streets going different ways
We grew . . . apart

Connie L. Clarneau

JUST WRITING

Sometimes I feel like writing
Even if there's nothing to say,
Sometimes I feel like writing
To take the blues away.
Sometimes I feel like laughing
Though no joke's been made.
Sometimes I feel like crying.
Sometimes I feel like jade.

Sometimes my guts are burning
With feelings I can't describe,
Sometimes my life is yearning —
Sometimes I just can't hide.

Sometimes I want to break down
With all the world's famine —
Yet then I want to make love
I can't remember when
I didn't get up one morning
To feel the love of God
Sometimes I want to make love —
Sometimes I feel so odd.

K. J. Deakin

MARCHING WINDS

Swaying branches
against a backdrop of grey
Damning squawks
and ruffled feathers
Trembling leaves
whipping back in defense
Nature merciless
in distribution of weather
A screen door slams
newspapers flutter
A yelping dog
wallows in self-pity
The sky darkens
and small children shudder
As the winds of March
descend on the city

Sue Rich

SMALL TOWN BLUES

In the dead heat of summer
    in a dull farming town
A woman lay naked on her bed,
    but no one was around.
Youth had nearly fled,
    leaving formless fears,
As she tried to face alone
    the coming of the years.
Was all her life just drudgery
    or remembered pain . . .
Nothing she'd accomplished had
    brought her praise or fame.
Were all her dreams and longings
    doomed to die in vain?
She closed her weary eyes
    wishing for more courage
So she could arise and face her
    middle age.

Beverly Clark

THE GIRL WHO DIED

She was only a "kid"
    of twenty
For whom life offered
    plenty,
But her parents denied
    the needs
        her therapist
            described . . .

The only good that
    would arise
From a young girl's
    tragic suicide
Is that on the day she died
    at least someone
        — her therapist —
            cried . . .

Beverly Clark

PLEASE, JUST LET ME LIVE

I could have been your *mother*
    I could have been your *dad*
I could have been your *sweetheart*
    Or the best *friend* you ever had

But you threw me out like garbage

I could have been a *genius*
    And cured your greatest ills
Or the greatest ever *President*
    And lived on Capitol Hill

But you threw me out like garbage

There are ever so many couples
    Who would love a girl or boy
But you threw me out in the garbage heap
    Just like a broken toy

What gives *you* the right to say
    Whether I should live or die
You may have to answer to the *God* above
    At the *judgment* by-and-by

Fred G. Howard

BRONZE MEMORIALS

In my travels I came to a little Manx village called Castletown,
On the lovely Isle of Man, in the turbulent Irish sea.
There before ancient castle Rushen in the village round,
Was a bronze plaque to honor men who died to keep their country free.
Young men who never had a chance to taste of life,
Whose life was traded for a place upon a bronze plate,
Who would never know of happiness or love,
    but only strife.
Simply a forgotten name in brass as payment by the state.
In villages, towns, and cities — round the world,
Are memorials to men who died in vain,
The ancient wars, civil wars, world wars,
    an endless swirl.
Men who traded their lives for a bronze refrain.
If all young men could rule their own destiny,
Guide their own lives, making decisions
    and meaningful history,
With a peaceful world,
With all men living in harmony,
There would be no need of trading lives for bronze memories.

Hank Dax

I'M ASKING YOU TO STAY

My heart is in your hand — And it will go away with you.
If you were to leave me now — I wouldn't know what I would do,
But as we go on walking — Past the flowers, and the birds,
Those things I notice just with you — ´
    I'm still searching for the words

Words that say 'I'm sorry' — In an entirely different way,
And in every word I think of — I'm asking you to stay.
I see you as a rainbow — The raining and the sun,
Where we used to cast a shadow — Two people casting one.

Only Poets can envision — The kind of *love* we've had . . .
So very ours and powerful — The rainbow . . . will be sad.
The daisies now are dying — The birds are going away . . .
Quickly, for a moment — I'm asking you to stay.

You say it's not your fault — And that neither is it mine,
But that the Pond has dirty water — And no one reads the signs.
As I'm standing here before you — So much running through my head;
I'm learning love, and losing it — Like a story I once read.

I'm refusing to surrender — 'Cause you'll take my heart away . . .
And I'm in need of both of you — I'm asking you to stay.

Joe Varela

MY MAMA'S THIMBLE

My mama's thimble I know it doesn't look like much
    to anyone but me.
For you would have to know my mama before the beauty
    you could see.
As I look at it I see not a single dent.
Nor do I see the way that it is badly bent.
I see only the many straight and perfect stitches.
Each sewn with love one of life's greatest riches.
Even though God called my mama back to heaven many
    years ago.
The sadness of losing her remains with me I still
    miss her so.
But as long as I have my mama's thimble old and worn
    as it might be.
I will always have a part of her to go through life
    with me.

Beverly Ernst

OCTOBER

Fall is here,
The ground is brown and bare.
The harvest's done, the crops are in,
The cribs and bins are full.
The trees are in their glory,
Their leaves are everywhere,
They're green and yellow, brown and red,
Glorious colors floating through the air.
The earth will soon be barren,
The death of fall is here.
It isn't only growing things
That meet this creeping fate,
It's also closing in
Upon my chosen mate.
For fifty years and more
We've walked along together.
Now the dim, dark shape of death
Is knocking on our door.
I sit and hold his hand in mine
"Please God, don't let him leave me."
But if it is "thy will" to take him,
Then show me Lord, how to accept it.
Show me how to live alone, when there's no one there to turn to.
And when my time on earth is gone, let me come up there to join you.

Florence Buckman

SEASONS

The seasons come and the seasons go,
Like footprints in the drifting snow.
Then spring comes in on tippy-toe!
Dancing past winter with all of its woes.
The plants and trees begin to grow.

Summer's here before you know it.
Different shades of green run riot,
The garden's in and there's grass to mow.
It's time to swim in the local pool.
Or put a line in the water as you sit on a stool.

Just as suddenly, the fall winds blow.
The leaves float down in huge, brown masses.
Jack Frost comes along and the garden wilts.
You can the vegetables and air the quilts,
As you get ready for the cold, icy, grip of winter.

Snow flies around like wind-blown feathers.
You find the scoop and begin to shovel.
Ice forms on the window panes,
When the sun shines through, it looks like crystal.
This is the season that lasts forever!

Florence Buckman

A BOUQUET OF LOVE

A small bouquet of dandelions that's what most would see.
I saw a bouquet of love my child had picked for me.
Held tightly in a little fist so not a single flower was lost.
Another bouquet wouldn't or couldn't be as beautiful no
    matter what it cost.
There's something special about flowers when they are
    picked by a child.
They might be the ones you planted or those that just grow wild.
My bouquet made of dandelions is as beautiful and special as it can be.
Because it came from my child who picked it just for me.

Beverly Ernst

THE LITTLE WONDER

It starts out as a little seed
So hard and smooth and round.
It looks so humble sitting there
And doesn't make a sound.

It doesn't know the beauty that
Is hidden deep within.
It sits there waiting for the time
Its destiny begins.

And now it starts to feel so hot.
It's ready to explode.
It moves so fast and makes such noise,
Its story now is told.

We look at it in wonderment
A sight no man will scorn.
It's fluffy white and hot and fresh
It's what we call *popcorn!*

Joan Voltz

MY LITTLE ONE

As I sit in slumber silence
I hear footsteps of my little one.
I know deep down in my mind
That my day is filled and silence is done.

Yet within the silence, as he runs
Towards me with his little feet
I know deep down in my heart
If he were silent, my day wouldn't be complete.

As he runs towards me
His feet are quiet on the rug.
But with open arms he rushes
To give his mommy a hug.

His kisses are as sweet and wet
As the morning dew.
Oh, my loving child, how I love you.
Even though I know my silence is through.

Even though silence is golden,
Noise, also, can be great.
So my precious little one, I love you
No matter how much noise you make!

Keith S. Huston

EVERLASTING LOVE

On a park bench, sits an elderly couple.
Not saying a word.
He gently puts a sweater around her shoulders.
As she slowly raises her head.
Their eyes meet, and you can see,
all the years of love they have shared.
He stands and offers her his hand.
As they start to walk away,
he gently slips his arm around her waist.
There are no words needed.
Theirs is an everlasting love.

Sandra Lockwood

FRIENDSHIP

What is friendship?
Oh, what could it be?
Is it what someone else
Sees special in me?

Could it be a bond between two people?
Like a sister and brother.
Or a bond that is so different
That there is no other?

Could it be a bond
Built on love and sharing?
Certainly it's not a bond of hate
Where there is no caring!

Could it be a bond between people
That is so hard to explain?
Could it be a bond between people
Willing to share each other's pain?

Whatever friendship may be
With its ups, downs, and clouds of doubt,
It is certainly something that the world
Can't live without!

Keith S. Huston

RETURN BY TRAIN

On a cool night
When the wind is right
And autumn's in the air
The lonesome cry of a distant train
Always calls me back again
To my old room — the first I ever had
Alone — as a boy — in my early teens,
And once again I am looking
From the window by my bed
Into the starkness of a moonlit night
Where a silver-studded roof below
Casts its dark and ghostly shadow
Almost to the little white fence
That protected a garden — and a path
That led to the smell of trumpet-lilies
Blooming wax-white by an open gate.

And I am home again —
    young again —

How many miles —
How many years —
Are of no concern to me
As long as I can return
So freely
Once again
By train.

M. E. Morrow

HOLDING ON

Some say that love is a shame
Some say that it's just a game
Some say it's a flame that will burn out
Before end of time
While never looking at the love of mine
My love for you is nothing but true
So i'll keep holding on to you

Robin Knight

A DAUGHTER'S PRAYER

This maternal being
with spirit so patient,
and self unsparing,

with caring so soft,
love so deep,
and much wisdom aloft,

such is a mender of tares and tears,
wasting no moment,
till all is done, she perseveres.

No hinder to young one's goals,
she is encourager, supporter,
God's director of tender souls,

an honor to her gender,
divine, yet reachably human,
and to God, in sweet surrender.

''I love you,'' I must tell her.
Thank you, Lord, for your grace.
Thank you for this, my mother.

Kathryn Lytle

A REMEMBERANCE

Her talents were many
The world didn't know
Her ''zest'' she did spread
Where'er she did go.

She's gone from us now —
But in Heaven above —
We'll all meet again
Who share her great love.

Those left behind
Who held her so dear,
Will remember her always
As if she were here.

We know in our hearts
What she'd want us to do —
''Go share all that love,
That I've shared with you!''

Her talents were many —
She wrote and she drew.
The love that she gave,
May it help us all through.

Terry Deane

FAITH

Faith is all too clear to see
Through you, and love, it comes to me
From times behind, and times to come
Learning how to be the one

Follow hearts and hummingbirds
Feel the rhythm of the words
Catch the breeze and falling stars
Faith will show us who we are

Travel roads and meadow lanes
On golden ponds, through silver rains
Heart to heart and truth be known
Faith is ours, and ours alone.

Debbie Wilson

A BROTHER

A brother is a person you've known since birth.
Someone you've shared parents,
Siblings, and more with.
We've shared joy and sorrow,
Through good times and bad,
And the loss of our father, mother and brothers.
There comes a time when your lives drift apart,
You grow older, and your choices in life are so different.
But there's still that tie, that binds you to him,
No matter what we disagree about.
He's the one you want by your side,
When you say "goodbye" to a husband.
We've argued a lot, about so many things,
And still seem to be doing the same.
This trait of ours will probably live on,
As long as there's life in both of us.
I still need you to share my thoughts;
Whether you approve them or not.
I know that I'm stubborn, and self-centered too,
But I still need and love you — brother!

Florence Buckman

DREAM FAIRY

The long day has ended, and the night has fallen.
Come and rest, for this night is mine.
Allow yourself to fall asleep so that you and I may
frolic in your dreams.
Tonight we shall play hide and seek with the moon, or
play catch with the stars,
Or, if you prefer, I will simply hold you close and
whisper the words of love I know you'd like to hear.
Come, hurry, close your eyes, close your eyes and sleep.
Sleep ever so long, and just as deep;
Please, dear one, dream . . . dream . . . dream.
For I, you see, am the fairy of dreams and this night
I shall haunt your slumber,
I am she who will caress you, love you, and hold you
near, and I am the same who wishes to comfort you when
you're in need.
Sleep, my friend, relax your mind, and I shall ease into
your thoughts, for I am she, the fairy of dreams.

Yutinna Price-Paige

SALUTE TO OUR FLAG

Our flag is flying high o'er land we love,
And waving in the breeze so high above,
With colors bright of
        red and white and blue . . .
Proclaiming *liberty* our land is due!

Our flag in battle many, many times,
So many years before our own lifetimes;
It proved our country
        freedom will defend . . .
Also, to others, freedom will extend.

Our flag imports its *peace* to whole wide world,
While fluttering on high with stripes unfurled.
We stand by our flag, whate'er times will be,
To keep this land unscathed,
                completely
                        free!

Helen Ehlers

TAPESTRY

46th Anniversary

Passion wove stitches of purple to thrill the heart.
Bands of cool green were added for serenity.
Separation and sorrow formed rows of gray
with a design of loyal blue, to mend the soul.
Splashes of orange blended with threads of
pale yellow to lift the spirit.
Now purple has toned down to a lavender hue,
Outrageous orange has become an apricot glow,
And wide strands of silver and gold thread
remain to be woven,
With nary a knot in view.

Olga E. Devereaux

THE PLATE

Found as often happens within the obscure confines
Of an antique shop's nook and crannies
A treasure. Round with slightly scalloped edges
Quite old. Hidden there, just for me
Brought to California from a farm in Lititz, Pennsylvania
The mark castle-like, excitingly old — Bonn, Germany —
    late 1800.

The face muted browns and greens
A peaceful woodland scene
With a proud and handsome stag
Nobleman of this woodland throne.
Overlooks a river, placid and serene
Like the river of Wagnerian opera fame — Der Rhine Gould!

Lending symbolic quality
Centered on this ceramic artifact
A setting sun; the final curtain
Depicting the last act
Of a once proud and prosperous Germany.
Symbolism and prophesy preserved in the potter's clay —
    The Plate.

Peggy Hoover

NOISE

Teacher's gone.
There is noise.
There is the sound of gossip
A blab, blab, blab.

The noise grows
A babel, clamorous
Hub-bub racket, a chit-chat
Chatty-chattery uproar.

The noise is reaching a deafening level
There is dissonance from this endless prattle
Indeed I can hardly think
The noise has finally reached a cacophonic pandemonium!

What's this stilly silence?
I must have a peep
I might have known
Teacher's back.

Peggy Hoover

The lightning cut through the sky
Opening its depths
Mingling with the clouds
Showing their whole selves
For an instant

But like the infinity of the lighting
I will always see the lines of the sky
My thoughts and electricity
Travelling together
Forever

Liesl Fowler

DREAMS

The future lies beyond the stars,
In the eyes of those who dream.
But futures as we know them,
Are seldom what they seem.

For these dreams of future promise,
Yield more heartache than success.
And many a man has fallen,
Chasing dreams that turn up less.

But where would mankind be,
Were it not for dreams of few,
That changed the lives of many,
And made this life for you.

Pete Meier

AFTER THE END

What seed has begun?
A fiction meant to be done,
In an edifice of darkness,
Of an all.

The cloistered thing,
Dwelt in the night,
But a shadow,
To gather all that live in fright.

Seeking the leaves,
In a symbolism of death,
A strange static,
Holds the air.

To which I owe,
I find this;
A shadow in the forest,
Of a long time, gone by.

Groans in the coffins,
And a beginning,
To a multitude of sins,
Vanquished by the other.

Suspended in the moist air,
From where it came,
Caught up together,
Being the drawl of the devil.

Russell Dagneau

So many times I have tried
To change my habits and my ways
So many times I have reached to God
So many times I have strayed.
Now I want to come home
And start my life again
But I am afraid
I don't know where to begin.
I know I need help
But no one seems to care
I am not needed
Anywhere.
I feel so helpless
I have nowhere to go
I'm just in the way
I have no room to grow.
So please forgive me
For the many times I have disappointed you so
Honestly, I love you,
Just give me time to let it show.

Debbi Severson

STORM

It is life
The metronome of burden
Pulsating to keep this pliable body awake
The angry cloud hovers
The downpour of conscience
Thrashing me into a daily fight

But . . .
But the wetness it leaves
Ah, the fresh moistness of my soul
Makes this misery sweet
My
Beloved misery
Spilling over their heads, stinging their eyes
They can't get away
It will seep between their toes
Until they, too
Feel the disgusting, soggy
Fabric

Sharlene Mark

HE CARES

Jesus cares so much for me.
It's really hard to imagine
That someone could care
As much as He does.

There are people here on earth
That care enough to listen
To other people and me
And give advice to us.

That's what we need sometimes,
Or maybe just a shoulder
To lean on or hand out
Comments on things we do.

But people here on earth
Can't care as much as Jesus does.
He takes you as you are
And loves you just the same.

Melinda Sorg

THE CONFUSION OF LITERAL THINKING

an afterthought: someone once said
that it would be easier for a camel
to pass through the eye of a needle
than for a rich man to enter the
kingdom of Heaven.
however, if you stand about twenty
feet away from a camel and look
at it though the eye of a needle:
  well, it fits perfectly.

Chris Gauthier

THE MISSION

Part of history
Was made that night,
As we watched the shuttle
Roar out of sight.

Excitement flew
Throughout the crowds.
Everyone watched,
We were all so proud.

Up in the shuttle
Were seven brave knights,
Who waved ''good-bye''
For their final flight.

And of the seven,
There were no remains.
But their hopes and dreams
Will stay the same.

Tracy Giraud

LOVE

Love is like a river,
Pure and yet disguised.
The day you think it's most alive
Is usually when it dies.

It's mystical and magical,
But somehow seeming real.
Describes a certain quality,
In how you really feel.

Love brings back the memories
Of how it's wished to be.
The dreams and disappointments,
Yet you still somehow feel free.

It takes in much excitement
And gives back tears and pain,
It's like a bright and sunny day
That suddenly turns to rain.

Love's the inspiration
That excites you when you're down,
It's something that should always be
Forever and always around.

Tracy Giraud

SCAR

Criticism intended maliciously
Terse words in anger spoken
Ridicule from an immature person
We remember, we remember

Not thinking, an unkind act is performed
We forgive, but often can't forget
Thus the scars time won't heal
We remember, we remember

And, in remembering
This, one of life's most bitter lessons
We act, intimidated, hurt, revengeful
Or determined to be careful not to inflict on another

A scar.

Peggy Hoover

THOUGHT FORM

At the foot of the pyramid she contemplates
her creation,
she remembers that her greatest anguish is to know
the future.

 Her parents have already left by plane,
 it's too late to change the course of her vision.
 Far away now, over the ocean, they fall in spirals of fire
 without time to think.

Her dream continues: at the bottom of the ocean
her parents are speaking with unknown people in the plane.
And by telepathy they send her their exact position
so that she will rescue them.

 "Get us out of here, reward us for our patience,
 remember that we are your parents and we put so much time
 raising you, get us out!"

She is now conscious of that blue ocean that imitates
another blue, a depth without sharks.
And in order to please her parents
she puts their names on the pyramid.

Lucia Fox

SANTA COMES JUST ONCE A YEAR

Santa comes just once a year,
And as I look upon his face
It is the Lord I see.
For only he can bring the joy
On this most Holy Day.
Cheerful, joyous, was the day
That Christ the Lord was born.
So, Santa, with his merry shout,
Sings out, Merry Christmas,
Merry Christmas,
Merry Christmas to all.

Mary G. Valdina

PUT YOUR HAND OUT IN FRIENDSHIP

Put your hand out in friendship
Put your hand out in friendship
Put your hand out in friendship
Whether white, yellow, red, black or brown.
Our country's for us all
With its hope of freedom's call,
Put your hand out in friendship
As we screen each one who calls
As some will surely fall.
Put your hand out in friendship
Put your hand out in friendship for them all.

Mary G. Valdina

OH! SON OF MINE

Oh! Son of mine, I love thee true,
Your love for me sublime,
What can one say when hearts entwine
With love so pure and true,
With tears of joy and happiness,
I thank the Lord, he gave me you.

Oh! Son of mine who's blessed by God
Whose cares are known to God alone,
What love is poured upon my brow
From God's most Holy Light,
No one can know the joy you give
 to mama's happy heart,
I thank the Lord most Holy, for giving you to us.

Oh! Son of mine, what can I say
 that's not already said,
Love's like a flower opened
 to show its lovely heart,
Dear son of mine may God bless and guide you
To be forever mine.
I thank the Lord most Holy for giving you to us.

Mary G. Valdina

SOLILOQUY

Loss of dream happiness very well very well I cry
You cry We all cry life gone I miss You miss
We all miss gravity attraction force Newton dark
dark all very dark black holes and nothing there . . .

Well, what are you doing?
I'm waiting for Godot.
Waiting for whom?
I'm waiting for Godot!

Hanging on a public telephone
I look like a . . .
I sound like a . . .

Well, are you still waiting for . . .
Yes, I'm waiting for Godot.
It's late. Let's go.
Do you think I can hang myself with this telephone wire?
Come on. Let's go.
O.K. . . . Let's go.
(I do not move.)

Sophia Nam

CHRISTMAS

Christmas isn't just the gifts
Or the pretty lights.
It's the gift that came from up above
Upon that glorious night.

It isn't just the candlelight
Or the star that shown above.
It's the present which Christ Jesus brought,
It's called the gift of love.

This gift is meant for all mankind
To share and give away.
It's something we could always use,
Each and every day!

Tracy Giraud

TRACY LYNN GIRAUD. Born: Trenton, Michigan, 11-19-71; Education: Junior in Carlson High School; Poetry: 'Barbara Mandrell Country,' *Fan Club Newsletter,* 11-84; 'Genesis,' *Michigan Synews Paper for the Reformed Churches of America,* 11-86; 'Love,' Carlson High School paper, May-June 1987; Comments: *Most of the poems I write are based usually on things that happen around me, and the way I feel. Writing poetry to me is interesting because it gives me a chance to explore my feelings and ideas.*

LENNON'S DREAM

Just seems like yesterday
Oh, how quickly time does flow
How people get together
Now their separate ways they go

Life is much too short now
Every second quickly passes by
Never think about tomorrow
Never sit and wonder why
Only live life to its fullest
Never let a bad day go by

For you are the universe
Only one little dot in space
Remember you are important
Every person of every race
Victory is everone's
Everybody in their own place
Remember, *love each other and preserve
    the human race*

Steven P. Surette

THE EYE

The eye carves out
a section of fading sunset
for the last glimpse of dimming rays
lingering warmly
in the glow of a memory.

Bonita Dostal Neff

THE ROPE

I fought hard.
Can you see what I did?
I climbed the very top,
But the top is not what I need.
There must be something for sure.
What is it?
I'm at the end of my rope!

James H. Nelson

SONNET

I cannot say how long
Half in love with death
I'd been before your siren song
Lured me — intoned on sweet breath.
At first, I did not call it "kiss of life,"
That reached my soul with respiration.
It brought me back to face the strife,
To live again in desperation.
But when you sang, I echoed with love,
Though all the while I must have known
Seduction in your heart should prove
Not life, but merely time my way you've blown.
Still, to sing the song, I learn to live
Though love's facade is all you give.

Joyce M. Sturgis

The wind blows across the sky;
    Over the land and sea,
The tree plants roots deep in the earth;
    As it stands tall in the breeze.

Both are strong in different ways;
    The tree's rigidness is hard to match.
But in the wind it must give;
    Or it will be cracked.

This means not the wind the victor;
    For the tree is in its path.
It must flow around to journey bound;
    Or be stopped as the tree snaps back.

By yielding to each other's might;
    No harm has come to either.
Peace and respect has been gained;
    As they both embrace the other.

Michael J. Roesti

E = MC ₂

Listen to the earth turn on
    its glass axis,
And the air break into little
    glass bits,
While the wind snarls staccato
    among the brittle trees.
The grey vacuum explodes
Around all the little stick
    figures,
The copper grass moves forward
    allegro —
Covering the bleeding marionettes.
Listen to the thick red dust
    sifting
Over their tangled strings.

Eunice T. Talbott

LAGNIAPPE

Deceptive summer now returns
And lulls my thought with dulcet
    song.
I lift my eyes to autumn skies
    and see —
A tattered monarch fluttering by;
Behold the glint of sun on
    snow goose wing
Wind borne aloft on cloud seafoam.
One feather from the great white bird
Falls softly down and comes to rest
Upon a treasure I have found,
A clump of violets fragrant, white;
Mistaking autumn for an early spring
Blooms out of season, pale unseen
Gratuities from Indian Summer.

Eunice T. Talbott

EUNICE TILLMAN TALBOTT. Born: Springfield, Missouri; Widow; Education: University of Florida, University of South Florida, B.S., Education, Post-graduate work, 3 years; Occupation: Teacher; Memberships: Included in *Who's Who in the World, 1984/85* and *Who's Who of American Women, 1987/88;* Poetry: 'Wild Geese,' 'The Wanton,' *Goliards,* 1965; 'Sandpiper,' 1973; several haiku poems in *Bardic Echoes;* Comments: *I've written poetry since I was a teenager. I love nature, and I have a philosophical interest in what goes on about me. I think that if there were more poets and poetry was read more often, perhaps the world would be happier.*

MY MAN

There stood a wine bottle
Transparent and greenish sight
That bears mystery and beauty.
When darkness sheltered me
From searching light, it whispered, softly to me.
Seductive scent flattered my heart . . .
Coolness of body spread through my fingers
And burned them like fire.
Should I . . .

Again and again, and again
I kissed
Until I could not remember who I was.

Sophia Nam

FREUD AND I

Night in the city
Reveals another face
Standing on my street
I'm like a stranger with a stranger beside me.

Creeping like nocturnal animals
We draw attention toward neon signs on the street,
Freed from the hypocritical smiles and pretentious beauty
Of day.

Deep inside the night,
Endless doubt and despair reside.
But we are drunk with pouring darkness,
Dream of happy illusion called future.

And while night cripples my consciousness
It belongs to me.

Sophia Nam

THE EXTERMINATOR

We decided to go camping
  One bright and sunny day,
With another couple
  Mariana and Ray.
We were out in the sage brush,
  Quite a ways from town;
When along towards evening
  We decided to settle down.
We got camp all set up;
  Figured we would stay the night.
But found the bugs and mosquitoes
  Really were a fright.
When one mosquito decided
  On my tummy he would sit . . .
That's when Mariana nearly had a fit.
  "Hold still Earl," she said, "so he doesn't fly,
Because that little mosquito is really gonna die."
  She drew back with her right,
And shouted out with glee.
  She killed that damn mosquito . . .
Came close to killing me.
  I got up from the ground;
Dusted off my pants and said,
  "Please, next time use the spray, dear,
It will kill them just as dead."

Earl F. Hamblin

BABY CAFÉ

Congratulations Ms. Jones, it's a boy.

And we have a special this week on
even temperment, courage and thriftiness.

The courage you say? Good choice.
How would you like some wisdom to go along with that?
They make a good combination.

Fine. And might I suggest a passionate burgundy?
1961 was a very good year.

All right. And for desert we have
good grades, clear skin, and natural rhythm.

Natural rhythm? Fine.

Returns? We have a strict policy on that.
But — maybe I can make an exception in your case.
You do look more like the tropical fish type.

Laura Smith

THE POET'S DEFINITION

Define poetry I was asked.
Very well.
It's an emotional outlet
Souls will tell.
Define emotion I asked myself.
Okay all right.
What makes you cry what makes you laugh what
Feelings sight.
For question three what do feelings mean,
Steps above thought,
Where the thoughts and their expression meet
What beasts have sought.
A poem is putting to paper
A mind's tale,
What an emotional heart hails,
To do what other writing fails.

Keith D. Alexander

Madison Avenue sinks its fangs into my jugular —
Draining my life —
Seducing me with false promises of immortality.
Twelve hours a day I serve my Neon god,
Electronic Master, and disappear nightly into the streets,
Veiled in darkness, amid the masses, all strangers.

Swallowed and regurgitated by the subway,
I emerge and look over my shoulder before
Hurrying home through the silent
Empty park that borders my apartment.

The rainy streets mirror and elongate headlights.
A misty drizzle tickles my nose.
I hunch deeper into my coat,
Fling my scarf around my neck.
(Whistling through the graveyard.)

Dana Gilbert

HE TOUCHED MY HEART

In my darkest hours, Lord
When filled with great despair
You reach out and touch my heart
And show me that You care.

You're "always" there to lift me up
When I am feeling low
You reach out and touch my heart
Because You love me so.

In my darkest hours, Lord
When filled with great distress
You reach out and touch my heart
And put my mind to rest.

Now I reach out to You, dear Lord
I pray that You will know
That You are "always" in my heart
Please stay there; never go.

Carolyn T. Mokan

HOW COULD I ASK FOR MORE?

Our Lord has "willed" to me His home
If I follow in His trace
And should I miss a step-or-two
He sets me back in place.

He gave to me the peace of mind
I was always searching for
The comfort of His love and grace
How could I ask for more?

He said to me, "My child,"
Just follow in my track
And every step take forward
Without ever turning back.

He gave to me His all — His life
And blessings by the score
He fulfilled His promise, to our Father
How could I ask for more?

Our Lord has "willed" to me His home
He's all I'm waiting for
Following tracks He left behind
How could I ask for more?

Carolyn T. Mokan

EOS

Dawn got up early to paint the mood
    of a summer morning.
She washed her palette and brushes
    in the North Sea,
And the pigments ran together
    in a glorious madras pattern.
Then she dipped her fingers
    in the colors
And traced them on the grey
    sky-canvas.

Eunice T. Talbott

I love you,
I love me.
But where are you now?
I can't see,
I can't see.

You said you would
always be there for me.
But where are you now?
I can't see,
I can't see.

I need your love,
I need your touch,
I need you . . .
But where are you now?
I can't see,
I can't see.

Linda Kizziar

My little girl,
see how you've grown.
It makes me remember
when you were just born.
I held you in my arms,
kept you safe and warm.
Now it's too soon,
you're starting to bloom.

My little girl,
now a young lady.
Soon to be a beautiful prize
for someone else's eyes.

As you grow remember this . . .
No other's love will be
    quite like this!
For I am your mother.

And this is sealed
    with a kiss.

Linda Kizziar

A FORGOTTEN PROMISE

You promised me
You would always be
That someone I could talk to.
Someone I could cry to,
Someone I could always come to.

You promised me
We would think together,
Be together.
Love together.
But you never promised
You would stay . . .
Not forever,
    Anyway.

Jennifer Thompson

Small are we . . . So unimportant.
    Specks in this universe,
        particles of dust
streaming in the sun's rays.

Still we toy with the
    human emotions.

Don't you see, it's all or nothing,
it's all or nothing . . .

Stop
the
games!

Let every living thing enjoy life.
This includes you and me,
the planet as we know it,
our children's destiny.
Please hear my plea:

Leave
life
alone.

                please let it be.

Linda Kizziar

MOLDMEN GROW . .

In the cold
Thrown from a neglected mother
Of old pickle and pimento loaf;
Perpetually delivering
Her fuzzy brown sons
In the dark.

With each explosive scission
They bound and they light,
Aspiring to a higher shelf,
By a carton of spoiled milk.

Sitting, dipping their fingers
In a frenzy,
Tasting the stagnant plunderings
Of an utterly vacuumed beast.
Unshaken by the motors' intermittent hum,
While ravenously smattering curds
In their salivating mouths;
Incessantly
In the frost-free tenement
by Westinghouse.

Michael Leggs

Love . . .
    A four-letter word,
    Trust and mistrusted.
    The smile of happiness,
    Torture of pain.
    Tainted or cherished,
    Only time will tell,
    How the word must be spelled.
Love . . .

Jennifer Thompson

WHERE THE LIVING WATERS FLOW

As the clock ticks out the minutes
  on our journey through the years,
Let us pause to check Life's blessings
  with its sorrows, pains and tears.
Do you know that smile 'twas given
  as the days pass swiftly by
Helped to make those trials lighter,
  like the sunbeams in the sky.
We may never know who's watching
  as we face Life's bitter sorrows
But somehow we'll face them calmly —
  all Life's battles, all tomorrows.
For the Love we show in passing
  through Life's battles day by day
Will provide all peace and calmness
  as we journey on Life's way.
Then I know the Hand that guides us
  as throughout that trip we go
Surely leads us toward that city
  where the Living Waters flow.

  R. Hazel Storm

WHIMPER AND A BANG

A Japanese winter. Pray that it's summer!
Blood in the snow? Turned to ashes.
The snow is gone. Only to return.
Black! Fatal! Hidden whimpers. Alone in shelters.
Acrid smoke. The taste of one's own flesh.
For two suns rose tonight. One rivalled the other.
Unheard! Approaching! Cataclysm! Shock!
Spreading flame. From where it came? I don't know!
Came a depilatory summer. Scars! Unseen sores.
Unseen by eyes. For lack of them.
Judgment falls. There is no rest for the wicked!
But those alive, share the blame.
We are faultless! So we said. So we thought.
Were we? Shame! A crucible, a testing ground
for humanity. Solomon was right! All is vanity!
All is fair! But not in love! And not in war!
What else is there? Humanity has played the game.
Has settled the score. Is this all there is?
There used to be more! And more overflowing.
Pressed down. Shaken together. Shaken were we!

  Jack Samorodin

CAROLINA CRIES

She shrivels in her wells of sand
And hears her hearty farmers cry,
And sigh; muttering, trying to understand
Why all the water in the sea
Cannot save tobacco, corn and barley.
Could she weep, she would, to hear their plaintive plea.

The anxious waiting's not a fitting rest
For struggling lives and crops that fail.
In the east, she hears, it's worse to the west.
And all the water in the sea
Would be to no avail,
As Carolina cries, echoing loss for you, for me.

  Janet Ann Wallace

DROUGHT DAYS

The worried farmers sit with heads down drawn together
All talk, all thought, all worries center on the weather.
No cloud, no rain, no chance with sunset ever red
From drought stricken days all life's humor's bled.
Fear is that which grows in sun's destroying fire.
More and more begin to wonder at God's so fearsome ire.
With each dread drought day, no saving shower;
Dried, dead and gone is the summer flower.

It's crisis in the making as crops won't, the heartaches grow.
Fists raised to God, provoked as streams no longer flow.
Trees are green and growing in memory's gift of shade.
The whys? The when? Of such, great calamities are made.
In the sun-slowed quiet, the mockingbird dares not sing,
The only sound the Sunday church bells' solemn grieving ring.
With each dread drought day, no saving shower;
Dried, dead and gone is the summer flower.

  Janet Ann Wallace

SUMMER WITHOUT ROSES

In the gilted glitter of a drought's long day
Life's fragile hold departs a dying rose.
Farm families suffer so from an absent needed dew.
With no loving drop of rain divine, the sun-parched spirit goes.

The bare-baked earth, as dry as bone
Is sterile; dead with sun's destroying gold.
Loved friends and neighbors bought-out so low,
If desert nomads, tents would fold.

Behind bleached barns reside a few successful briars,
It's dry enough to stunt a morning glory's creep.
A soothing tender rain, truly would be heaven
Sent and put an end to fruitless barren sleep.

There's beauty not without summer's rose,
No glory in a brown-brittle fall.
Oh, that the blessed boon of rain would soon
Quench the long born thirst of all.

A gentle rain, slowly to renew the land
An end would put to precious earth's great pain.
As nights stay clear, drought stricken dreams revile the stars,
Bowed heads are raised in vain, to have to hope to try again.

  Janet Ann Wallace

FELLOWSHIP WITH JESUS

I talked to Jesus this morning, I asked what must I do?
He answered, 'Abide in me, my word is true.'
Study to shew thyself approved unto God
A workman that needeth not to be ashamed. II Timothy 2:15
Lessons learned day by day until at last I
Stand before Him confirmed.

I meet with Him again tonight, thanking Him for
Helping me to shine today to show someone the way.
If I stumble and my light grows dim, then someone
Watching me, their faith in a conquering God weakens.
I'm at fault.
When waves of troubles swamp the boat,
Then know that Satan is at work.
There's an all seeing eye watching you.
Just hold on tight and call His name.
He speaks, 'Peace, be still.' The wind
And waves obey and all is calm once more.

  Pearl G. Ray

FEED THE FISH

Every day at exactly five o'clock
My fish swim in circles waiting
To see me pick up the bright yellow box
Filled with ground yellow corn,
Ground wheat, wheat middlings,
Meat and bone meal, fish meal, alfalfa meal,
Irradiated yeast, salt.
A healthy feast with crude protein,
Fat and fiber.
"Goldfish will eat anything,"
The man at the register told me
When I bought the fish.
And every day at five o'clock,
Whether I am home or not,
I think about my fish swimming
And waiting for their day's meal.
The starving little beasts
Eyeing the underwater plant at 5:05,
Leaping up when they see me
Sprinkle the brown flakes into the tank,
And I watch them fight over
Who will get the most.
The big fish always wins.

Nancy A. Brosky

ARGONAUTS

The age expands
    and minds explore
        in heads too tight.

This human frame
    of watered dust
        we shake. And seek

to wander between
    the galaxies
        of a billion years.

To push beyond
    in pitchy blue
        and silent cold.

To leave behind
    an earthbound view
        for lift-off flight.

The end is dark.
    God is hard.
        Twentieth century, someone says.

We dream and look for Supernovae.

Addie L. Bracy

A copper penny caught in a rushing
    stream.
A small puppy killed by a train.
An old man making sure his mother's
    clean.
A broken radio picking up static.
A dead man envied by the living.
All these things consist of life
Like a thunderstorm in the desert,
An earthquake underwater.
Without one there is no other.
And the two are constantly at war.

Rawn Simonds

REMEMBRANCE

Remember when it was just you and I?
So afraid of falling in love,
But needing each other.

From best friend to lovers,
Not all in one day.
We learned and we loved,
In our own special way.

Can't you remember
The past and the present?
It used to be us —
We were one, not two,
Sharing and loving all that we knew.

Two years have passed
Our memories will last.
But what about you and me?

Is remembering enough,
For you and for us?
Or will we be together?
Remember the past, future, and each other.

Jennifer Thompson

THE FIRST BOY

At twelve
the first boy I ever loved
would not love me back
but ran and hid
in an old garage
at the sight of me.

It took winter —
its white protection —
to lure him out.

We'd drag my father's toboggan
up the hill behind my house
to ride the icy wind down
our eyes blazing
our combined breath frozen in front of us.

He'd hold me between innocent knees.
I'd lean back against him, small.
Something inside me waiting, waiting
while we rode down that hill
into the dusk
over and over again.

Ann Carhart

PIGEON

Dirty pigeon, hungry,
Muddy bread crumbs
Too good for you.
And you too weak,
And too little,
Afraid to search them
Around feet and wheels.
Your fate you have accepted,
Just like motherless children,
Like peasants who are tired
Of walking, but got to go on!

Nike Kotsalos

IN THE PARK

With the breeze along
You did laugh and play,
Other children among
In the park today!

You ran here and there,
And much fun you had,
With your kites up in the air,
And the strings burning your hands!

Happy moments, yours,
Sweet memories of mine,
Tomorrow when of course,
All that will be behind.

Will you grow strong:
As the stout trees?
Patient as the tender grass?
For you'll be no carefree.

Will life be kind enough
To spare you happy times
More, rather than rough!
How I wish all will be fine!

Nike Kotsalos

MY JOURNEY

One sunny day I chanced to look,
Upon a sparkling, shimmering brook.
On this tiny brook I see,
A ruffled oak leaf that is me.
This leaf, comes from a calm lake.
Over rapids, did it break?
No, it is still strong.
Not always right, not always wrong.
Bobbling, toddling, and ambling along.
The leaf still on its way,
Now resting in a placid pool, which is today.
Where this oak leaf travels is my wonder.
How it arrives is my ponder.
Moving on its everlasting journey
On and on . . .

Andrew Thomas Richmond

VISIONS OF YOU

Visions of ocean waves . . .
    running through my mind.
Softness of sand;
    beneath my feet.
Thoughts are wandering . . .
    like magic.
    Visions of you, come and go.
The beauty as if a sunset scenery.
Neverending pleasures,
    are the serenity of you.
Like a rainbow's bright colors . . .
    across the sky.
The everlasting memory . . .
    will never fade.

Carol A. Marino

I AM THE ONLY ONE THAT CAN SEE

Why am I the only one that can see?
I can see the lies in everyone's eyes.
Why can't they see the pain in mine
That I have seen time after time.
No one likes the way I want to act and feel
So that I have to conceal.
When things are good or bad, happy or sad,
I have to act and look the same.
I'm sorry to say it's all become one big game.
And I realize there's probably no other way.
But, no one can see, but me.
I have loved,
But have never been loved;
I have given,
But have never been given;
I have been hurt,
But have never hurt.
Confusion is what it is.
My life is what it is called.
But, why am I the only one that can see?
Why only me?

Ramona T. Goodman

THY PRECIOUS PEACE OH LORD

I met God in my quiet moment, and His presence was like a warm
Sunshine embracing me . . . I prayed over my steaming cup of tea,
And pretended Jesus was there drinking and sharing my tea with
Me. Oh how I wish He truly was sitting there beside me . . . I
Could then tell Him all the troubles and burdens I am going
Through, and ask for His wisdom to cope with every passing day
Full of trouble and despair . . . Somehow, just pretending He was
Really there with me, I found the peace and assurance I was
Looking for! His warmth enveloped me and I was not alone any
More . . . Thanks and Praises I give Thee for always helping me.

April Avery

IT'S SPRING AGAIN

Today I woke up a little too early. When I opened my window I
Discovered that spring had tiptoed during the night and settled
Down for a spell! The whole place smelled so fresh and sweet I
Knew then that winter had gone into the usual slumber . . . Spring
Is here, I must make the best of its stay. The birds were
Singing loud and clear. Their chatter warmed my heart with its
Lively morning serenade! The neighbors' fence was a joy to
Behold as their pink camellias were covering the whole side and
Cascading into my yard! What a wondrous sight to my avid eyes!
At that moment I was happy I woke up a little too early. I could
Hardly draw my curtains and go back to sleep! The glimpse of
Spring was too precious to waste . . . I know the flowers will soon
Be sprouting and the whole world will be dazzling all of us,
Sparkling once more. The precious guest is back for the yearly
Visit. It's spring again!

April Avery

RESPECTFUL IBEX

The German forest is home to me
Sometimes I get my horns stuck in a tree
I play by myself, I like me best
I think the other kids are an awful mess

I climb the hill from bottom to top
Come to think of it I am alone a lot
Humility Pew said respect is what I should try
Respect for others and you'll see why

There's no one set of rules as kids go hand in hand
Respect for others' way of life is the rule of the land.

Margaret Womack

MY THANKSGIVINGS

When I thought I could tolerate no more . . .
More was given me.
When I thought I had nothing in this world that was mine . . .
A child gave me a smile.
When I cried for the losses I've suffered,
. . . I heard a baby coo.
When I thought that my mind was no longer within me,
I found a friend . . . in need of comfort.
When I thought my heart was truly shattered,
. . . I found someone lonelier than I.
When I wished I were no longer living,
I saw a young couple . . . loving.
And, when I opened my eyes,
To a breathtaking light . . .
A breathtaking sight . . .
It was God . . .
In all He hath created.

S. C. Brown

THINGS TO DO . . . THINGS TO BE

Pick up the pieces and try to put them back together. If they
won't fit, make some new ones. If *they* won't fit, borrow some of
mine . . . I've got plenty. Put your life in order. But if you
can't put it in order, at least put it in black and white . . . or
color. You've got to see it, before you can do anything with
it. Act your age. But remember, no matter how long you have
lived . . . you are still a child in God's eyes.

Care about something besides yourself . . . you are not alone.
One person can breed enough sadness for ten . . . so give the rest
of us a break.
You are better than you think you are, whether you like it or
not . . . but, you are no better than me or my neighbor.
We came into this world with the same breath of life,
. . . and it will leave each of us alike.
Kill no living creature, lest the Lord say it be so.
For He is here with you . . . irregardless.
And He love us all.
In your life, seek the meaning of love
. . . And all other questions will be answered.

S. C. Brown

VIETNAM: NIGHTMARES

I left the war in Vietnam
Returned home and tried to hide out

But the war never left me
So I had to hide within

For years the battles raged
Within my heart and in my mind

Searching for that inner peace
I know I'll never find

Countless nights I'd lie awake
And see faces from the past

Remembering their voices
And the cries that were their last

I shed my blood in Vietnam
Not that anyone really cares

But the blood I see upon my hands
Isn't mine dear God it's theirs

David J. Maloney

VIETNAM: NO SURVIVORS

I was stripped of all my sanity
The day the war began for me

Left naked
With only shame as my blanket

A blanket that would not cover
My face
So that the world might share
In my disgrace

Perpetual tears flow from these eyes
For only I can hear
The dead men's cries

Look at me, deep in my eyes
Into my soul and realize

There are no survivors
From a useless war

Only memories of men
That were once before

David J. Maloney

WET DREAM

I'm swimming in melancholy,
stroking up despair.
paddling my way to apathy,
gasping "I don't care."

The water doesn't burn my eyes
it's all made up of tears.
one last cry tries for a save,
too late, for no one hears.

I didn't think it'd be this way.
that death would be so wet.
there's a certain kind of peace I feel,
as I close my eyes and forget.

Bernadette Luckett

ROLL CALL

Roll call at the wall
Read by Dad and Mom

From commencement to war
On a foreign shore
In a land called Vietnam

A teenage son
Whose life is done
And now is laid to rest

No rewards
For this boy
Who tried to do his best

An American flag
Folded thirteen times
Handed to the next of kin

Twenty-one shots
Fill the air
As the sound of taps begin

Did he have to die
To make us cry
To see that we were wrong

To send our boys
To a place
That we did not belong

David J. Maloney

DAVID JAMES MALONEY. Born: Detroit, Michigan, 5-18-44; Married: Barbara, 1-5-66; Occupation: Pipefitter, Welder; Memberships: Vietnam Veterans of America, Oakland County, Chapter 133; Fraternal Order of Eagles, No. 2887; Poetry: 'Remembering,' 'Prisoner of War,' 'My Friend,' 'Thanks Uncle Sam'; Other Writings: *Corpsman Up*, novel; Comments: *My poems are messages from the hearts and minds of all the young men who served in Vietnam. They serve as a reminder that it should never happen again.*

AT THE BAZAAR

"Life is a cabaret . . ." to me,
Seems not quite apropos.
Bizarre bazaar would seem to be
A better way to go.
The trifling and the truly fine
Are all within my reach.
I pick and choose, and find, in time,
I've purchased some of each.

Mary Freckleton

THE KITE

The ocean screams a cry of anger
And tears at the cliffs with a violent rage.
The cliffs — tall, silent, proud, stand still.
On the cliff a boy runs —
His companion trailing behind him on
a cord made of heartstrings.

The kite itself is security, love, happiness,
and motherhood.

There is a rush of cool, sea air.
The kite is torn from the boy's hands.
It trails off indifferently out of the
boy's reach.

His life is forever changed.
No more tomorrow.
Yesterday is only a nightmare to keep
him awake.
Each tear falls like an atom bomb
to the hot sand below.
Sea gulls mock him, and the sea
laughs.

Rawn Simonds

TIME

Was it only last week
gray pin oaks
hatted
in green lace?

Overripened, yellow,
brown, ballerinas,
disowned by branch

They fall
in grace
on rainsilk

Winter hovers close
chill freshened
patient,
snow-covered
they wait.

Was it last week
gray pin oaks
hatted
in green lace?

Mary Ann Schacht

POET'S REBELLION

You always try to change me,
Bending me into society
With the Jesus-cry of mortal man.
You burn my paper, break my pen,
But my soul will always be free
Never changing to what
You want me to be.

Bill Rae

PHOTOGRAPH

A picture,
of you when youngest was your claim to fame.
But, now as I watch the refilming of the life you
lived so well,
I think deeply
and sleepily I look at your face,
the old problems and pains never erased.
I do picture you.
Vivid recollections brought by a camera new on Kodak
island.
In just one photograph,
a visual bath in which to immerse myself,
I encountered a flash.
Despite your sometime negative attitude,
your picture is food for my eyes.

Dennis Holter

OUR LIVES

Our past is so far away, just memories are all we have to hold,
  Just remember the good thoughts and try your best to forget the bad
Altho' today, right this minute, is all we can really have and know,
  Tomorrow is just another day in time
                            and no one knows how things can go.

All we can really do, it seems, is just the very best we can,
  Live our lives for this day, morning, noon and night,
Forget the unpleasant times of the past and just laugh at the good,
  Plans for the future are alright but still remember today as we should.

Our lives we live each day, sometimes, seem long or maybe too short
  But life goes on and on, day and night, as God's design for man,
It seems so unfair, sometimes, depending on the time we have to spend,
  But we can have a good feeling, for sure,
                            if we've done the best we can.

Life is a special gift and luckily, some of us receive the chance
  To live our lives in laughter and not just exist in a life that's dim,
No matter how our lives have been,
                            we wish a better way of life for our kids,
  This situation has been this way for many centuries now, I guess,
And will always continue the same for as long as there is man.

Lee Dennis

SOUL DREAM

My days are like walking in slow motion,
in a dream, I cannot wake from.
And I wonder what will happen when I wake.
The days drag on and on but the dream continues.
There is no spirit at all, just an everlasting slow
motion with no end.
I'm afraid if there were an end, it would be the end
of my life.
Yet every day I get closer to the end.
When I wake up from my dream, that will be the end of
everything.

The time is very near, I can feel it in my soul.
Aware of the loneliness and emptiness that come
with the end of time.
A light that you can see, but it is so far away,
like a shadow beginning at the first sign of
daybreak.
I knowing, at the end of the day, that shadow will
melt away into the darkness, into my heart, into
my soul,
never to appear again.

Beverly M. Whitmore

NO ESCAPE

There's no escape from reality, none that last at least,
        for I've looked far and wide in many things,
                and still I've found no peace.
Oh, peace, where art thou, peace? Why must you evade me so?
        Why is it that you run and hide
                each time I'm struck with pain's blow?
What can take away life's hurts? How can I hide for good?
        I've tried and lost and tried again,
                but nothing works as it should.
Through reading and writing and drugs and drink,
        I've searched both far and wide;
Through friends and lovers, but when they go,
        hurt is right there at my side . . .
Through food and tv, and play,
        and music, and sleep, and such,
I cry out for peace and serenity,
        but it slips right through my touch.
Alas, I guess I'll feel the pain,
        and grow up some . . . I'll have to I guess,
pick myself up, get strength from the Lord,
        and deal with reality's mess.

Carole Tucker Smith

CONFUSION

When I look in your eyes
    and try to understand what I see
                what you see,
        I don't understand —

When I try to interpret your actions
    your every word, comment and emotion
                what you feel,
        I don't understand —

When I think back in time
    to everything we have said and done
                what we have shared,
        I don't understand —

When I wonder how
    to act and what to say
                what you want,
        I don't understand —

When I wonder what went wrong
    to make things change so quickly
                what happened,
        I don't understand —

Lu Ann Glaser

SCENE AT FORTUNES ROCKS

On lofty rocks, the ocean's gallery,
Perch cormorants, wings spread umbrella-like
To dry; the matinee they've come to see.
The eiders on the pool-stage start the show,
Play follow-leader and perform grand dives.
On seaweed beds seals sleep through their tableau.
And while the jealous sea gulls screech in rage,
A lone blue heron does a *rond de jamb*
Across the pebbled apron of the stage.

Sally Stembridge

THE CAVE OF THE WINDS.

SMILE

You smiled at me today,
    in a way
        that I had never noticed.
A peaceful, almost grateful smile.
It set my mind at ease,
    and sent my heart racing.
You sent me a smile,
    a smile full of:
            desire,
                love,
                    and sensitivity.
You smiled at me today,
    in a way
        that I had never noticed.
Your lips never parted,
    and never rose
        from side to side.
You smiled at me today,
    with nothing more
        than your eyes . . .

Alysia Ann Poland

SWEET ARE HIS WAYS

Sweet are his ways in everything he does
Sweeter are his ways towards me
Wonderful and true he always has been
So how do I tell him I don't love him?
I see him not as a lover, but as a loving brother
His kisses are sweet, but don't create the passion I seek
His touches are gentle, but don't make me shake at the knees
When I look in his eyes, I'm not hypnotized
Just sad at the love I see shining out at me
So how do I tell him, I don't love him?
How do I say, you're gentle and sweet
But there's something more that I seek?
A passionate man whom with just a look
Will make my heart skip a beat
Sweet are his ways and always will be
Maybe I should accept his love so sweet
For how do I know the love I seek
Is the kind of love I need?

Andrea Raymore

LOOK INSIDE

I was always searching for that one thing
that would make me happy . . .

    Sometimes it would be a warm balmy day
        where I'd hear giggles of children happy at play,
    or laying by a window at my favorite place
        delighting as the wind breathed cool on my face,
    and so often I'd feel nostalgia at just being somewhere
        where my senses went wild from a certain atmosphere!

My faithful companions . . . I searched them out as if my very
life depended upon them . . .

    Now, years later I have come to see
    that those companions have depended on me

    for I am the one who is able to feel,
    it is me within me who makes all those things real.

        Yes, I am the source of my own happiness.

Karen J. Wolfson

IF YOU BELIEVE IN LOVE

I believe in the goodness of life
    in the riches that money cannot buy
    in a magic stronger than any wizard's spell
I believe the best is yet to come
For I believe in love.

Through the darkest of nights, a light shines
Through the heartbreak of loneliness, hope still exists
Through turmoil and confusion, peace will follow
Through sadness and despair, joy will overflow
For the best is sure to come
For I believe in love.

The goodness in life will go on forever
    the riches will never run dry
    the magic will always be seen
For the best is yet to come
For I believe in love.
And a life filled with love is the richest one can be . . .
    if you believe in love.

Mary Ellen R. Calitri

VOYAGER

Orville and Wilbur started it all, down at Kitty Hawk.
Still the adventure of flight continues while we sit and gawk,
As Rutan and Yeager circle the globe in their flimsy plane —
To do it all on one tank of gas was the plan and the aim.
While one sat up, one had to lay down, their cabin was so small.
With the constant noise and smell of gas it's a wonder
    they lasted at all.
For nine whole days the country watched as Voyager headed west —
Then just kept going 'til she touched down and her crew
    could finally rest.
With six years of work behind them, they did what they had to do —
To prove with new designs and materials the dream of flight's
    still coming true.

Jill Vernon

LIVING

I saw Life first
At dawn. A goblet to my lips he placed
To quench my thirst;
And when with wakened strength my blood-stream raced,
I learned his name.
He took my hand and led me towards the sun;
There in its flame
I warmed to him; our dancing had begun.

All afternoon
We danced to music sounding in my breast;
I felt too soon
My feet would weary grow, my heart need rest.
With sudden fright
At eventide I clung as lights grew dim;
But in the night
A stranger beckoned and I followed him.

Raphaella Kingsbury

THE SPANISH DINING TABLE

One day I crept beneath the table
the Spanish dining table
I felt the iron
and fingered the wood design
and marveled at how smooth it was
how dark it was
the cave was mine

In its midst, I made a me,
a gypsy me,
who laughed and banged
a tambourine,
a crazy colored gypsy lady
who read the future in a palm
Cast my mandala
on the ground
and vanish gypsy,
soundlessly
I will stay here
for I
am me
And I am tall
beneath the table
the Spanish dining table

Mary Ann Schacht

DECISIONS

The windowpane is streaked
with dust
I'm blooded out
wrapped in a bed sheet
I.V. sugar in my arm
Are those footsteps
in the new-mopped hall?
The Puerto Rican fellow
with his push brush mustache
hums cantatas as he sweeps.
My broadcast heart
is amplified on intercom.
Listen!
I don't want to be mummified
in plastic!
Is it immoral to want
so much
for you to listen?

Mary Ann Schacht

TENDER MOMENTS

Two lovers sharing
each other's existence.

Warm,

Flowing,

Entwined.

Exhilirating affinity to
a breath of fresh air on
a crisp spring day.

Ahh, the ecstasy of each
moment.

Moments that last
forever.

Arika Dark/Ann Lasley

ABSENCE

The empty drawer, the vacant wardrobe space
(Its hangers silent now) stare out to mock me.

A strand of hair clings to the bathroom soap;
Her warm, damp towel spread neatly out to dry
As if she had forgotten she would not be here
Tomorrow.

And in the kitchen, a crumpled shopping-list;
The cupboard full of little herbs and spices
That I shall never use, living, as I do,
Alone.

Her perfume on the pillow, pungent still.

Well, that's that.
So now I need not tidy up my clothes
Or clear away the dishes, or be home on time,
Or listen to inconsequential chatter.

And I must try
To go about the business of the day
Putting her from my mind.

Pamela Mant

AUTUMN

Golden, glimmering radiance
Like the warm morning sun.

Curative and tranquil; a
spectacular, prismatic array
that reach, search and cling
to life.

Sadden, yet joyous of the
infallible rite of spring.

Wintry breezes that gently
toss and caress the shriveled
agitated leaves;

Whisper the cessation of the
dawn from whence they came.

Once silenced, form a bed
on which I lie . . .

Waiting.

Arika Dark/Ann Lasley

WINTER EVENING

Snow scatters vision
    and smudges the landscape
Snuffing out its horizon.

Birds have disappeared to wherever
    birds go when it snows.
And the children, caps bobbing
    over sleds, laughter muffled
Trudge the hill in seeming silence.

Quiet creeps into folds of peace
    enlarging the white.
And the presence of your love in
    this corner of creation
Pulls a deeper "yes, Lord" from the
    inmost of my inner self.

Bette Armstrong

LOVE

Love, like a fragile flower,
must be nurtured, nourished,
treated tenderly,
or like a faded flower
'twill wither and wilt;
then like the setting sun
'twill slip silently away
and die, as does the day.
Love rekindled is refined, sublime,
truly becomes a treasure of splendor
more precious than crown jewels,
everlasting as the stars in the heavens,
and like the holy scriptures,
will be cherished through eternities.

Blanche Carson Reid

BLANCHE CARSON REID. Born: Payson, Utah, 8-26-07; Married: W. Eugene Reid, 6-30-27; Education: Studied voice at New York University and was admitted to the University Choir in 1931; Occupations: Receptionist; General office duties; Assistant to dentist, dental surgeon, medical doctor; Bookkeeper; Memberships: Literary Club, 25 years; Gave book reviews at women's clubs; Comments: *I have written poetry infrequently for some 30 years. This is my first submission. I have had articles read over the radio and printed in newspapers. I have read my poetry privately, and in public a few times. People respond very favorably to my poems and tell me I should do something with them. Most of them recognize God and His power in our lives and in nature.*

MARRIAGE ON THE WATERS

Branching away like wings of wind
streaming, whirling in waves
billowing wet
toward
a better place to be —
We are rocks . . . less than rocks.
We are two separate
grains of sand
buried in an ocean
under one single name,
hoping for miracles
that turn sand to air.

Deborah Newton Cooksey

VERSE: A CELEBRATION

I am the past, the present, the past present future.
I am poetry, history alive, dreams and reality.
I am the walls, the sides, the top, the bottom:
Smooth and soothing, passionate — emblazing.
I am war, I am peace,
I am love, hate, forgiveness, emotion:
Kindness, hardness, a spirit, a notion.
I am the month, week, hour, day —
Trivial, essential:
Primary blue, red, yellow, gray.
I am a universe, galaxy, system, sand,
Air, fire, water, earth,
The heavens, the pit,
Existence, Fantasy

— For —

I am the word,
I am the page;
I am the Verse.

Robert E. Jones

FEAST OF WAR

Today a black cloud covers the sky
    And hides all light from freedom's eye.

Sit at my table and feast with me
    Let's decide the future of what will be.

We hold in our hands the fate of creation
    We can give life, or choose devastation.

We can feed lightly on life in the air
    Or we can feed heartily if we don't care.

And eat the bodies of soldiers gone down
    Drink the blood of the broken crown.

But it's up to us to decide life's fate
    So mind you think twice before filling your plate.

Mary E. Hoerner

THE INHERITANCE CREED

Caught in a tumult of religions, how rare to achieve
    a confidence of being.
Torn between inheritance and legacy, deeds become
    a lone reconciler;
Trying to equate the creed of sin with
    the consequences of immorality,
Not realizing that the one has nothing
    to do with the other.
Sin being the business of the church; immorality being
    the business of the inner self.

They are planes apart.

Ultimate religion is an idea within an Idea,
Not an Idea within an idea.
Denial of greater experience than life is foolish,
But any search for it according to an impersonal premise
    is equally foolish.

A life is a legacy and its examples are
    the next generation's inheritance.

Kenneth E. Burchett

THE WAIL OF THE WHALE

*For my aunt, Vicki McAteer, who shares the
dream that the world may save the whales.*

Hear the wail of the whale, and you will agree
There's no better place to be, but in the kingdom under the sea
Where in the deepest blue tranquility, the true gods of life live free
And in mystic grace they call unto me, no matter how far from them
    I may be.

My soul yearns to sing with the whale
    my arms be fins, my legs be tail

Loyal my heart, wise my mind
    in the kingdom of whales I will find

The secret to life is not in the stars
    heaven's on earth and it is ours

Ours to view and ours to be
    when this life passes, a whale might I be

To live with the gods of kind heart and soul
    my brothers and sisters will make me whole
And I hear them calling in graceful song
    we brothers on land should do them no wrong

For hell, too, can be on earth
    when no whales are left
        to live or give birth.

Mary E. Hoerner

RACHEL

I close my eyes   again & again   I see
                    Rachel
Walking slowly   up   from the ocean depths
            Silently seeking revenge for her fate
I know not her reason   as she walks
                Stalks

The city's eyes   watch   in amazement
            This almost porcelain-figured body
Walks nude   radiating   a kind of innocence
        That   no man   can   ignore.
            (But how he should try!)

Tossing back   her long   black   hair
        She's caught!   in a young man's   stare.
She reaches out her arms   welcoming him   to all her charms,

            HARSH EMBRACE
No porcelain face   illusions gone away   years of salt water decay

            HARSH EMBRACE
The victim's face   lies dead on the street   at Rachel's feet.
        And as this Hag returns to the sea
I close my eyes   again & again   I see   *Rachel.*

Mary E. Hoerner

THE SEARCH

Based on 1st Corinthians 13:11-12

I looked for myself in the mirror of this world
but myself I could not see,
until I looked beyond the cradle to the Father,
through a glass darkly it is clear to see.

Tami Foxworthy

A PLACE TO BE

I am not looking for a man.
Not looking to exchange one problem
for another.
Just looking for peace of mind
and a place to *be*.

To be quiet
To be at peace
To sleep late
if I want to
To write all day
if I need to.

A place to feel whole,
not in fragments and pieces
like yesterday.

A place to be alone
with nobody watching
me putting on
and pulling off
all the intimate things
that I am.

Deborah Newton Cooksey

THE THINGS OF LIFE

The things that were so important yesterday,
Now don't matter much.
What matters most in life is love,
And a caring, friendly touch.

For time will teach us very well,
That earthly gold and mirth;
Are things that we can't take along
When it's time to leave this earth.

And the only things that we can carry with
To that next perplexing goal;
Is what we've learned and felt
And what we've kept and loved inside our soul.

Yes it's been said in all the centuries past,
For only love will now and ever last.
Don't save up all those earthly things;
For only love exceeds the worth of gold rings.

Ronald R. Schauer

RECOVERY

It was overcast
on a summer's day.
The nut tree sang outside our window,
dropping pods upon dead leaves
for rhythm.

Inside, the children flitted back
and forth like warm sand between
our toes,
whispering loudly
as children do
when they are sensitive to the need
of adults in deep thought.

We are quiet now.
The night had been long with talking —
the working out of gnarls.
We finished the doughnuts in the pink box
and somehow I forgot the many-footed worm
in the garden who was eaten
by a bird yesterday —
I had been hoping for a butterfly.

Deborah Newton Cooksey

DEBORAH NEWTON COOKSEY. Born: Houston, Texas, 6-24-52; Married: Ricci Elden Cooksey, 8-25-73, three children: Sybil, Nicole, Austin; Education: Pomona College, B.A., English literature, 1974; Claremont Graduate School, M.A., Education; 1976; Claremont Graduate School, M.A., English/American literature, 1987; Occupation: High school English teacher; Memberships: Tae Kwon Do Club of Pomona; Association of Pomona Teachers; California Teachers Association; Poets in the Schools; Scrutiny, Inc.; Awards: Second place for 'To the Lonely Artist,' 1985; First place for ''Love Without A Smile,'' ''How to Ruin a Perfectly Good Day in One Sitting,'' 1985; First place for 'Black Eyed Blues,' '' 'No' Was Never So Hard,'' 1986; First Place for ''The Riot — A True Incident,'' 'At Dawn,' 1987; Poetry: 'To The Lonely Artist,' *Mt. Sac Writers' Magazine,* 1985; 'Black Eyed Blues,' *Chaffey College Writers' Magazine,* 1986; Other Writings: ''Love Without A Smile,'' short story, *Mt. Sac Writers' Magazine,* 1985; '' 'No' Was Never So Hard,'' short story, *Chaffey College Writers' Magazine,* 1986; ''The Riot — A True Incident,'' Journal, *Mt. Sac Writers' Magazine,* 1987; Comments: *I am interested in writing fiction that tells the truth. In poetry my predominant themes are love and survival. I believe that the human soul requires real romance for sustenance — not the fluff and bubbles type that offers no tangible rewards. For me, writing poetry exorcises the day-to-day pain of reality and fires the imagination with hope for all possibilities.*

THE SOUL'S CANDLE

The candlelight softly flickers,
Inside it is a rainbow
That reflects in the eye and beyond,
Deep into the heart's fiery glow.

Simple, pure beauty.
The warmth quietly grows.
Tranquility and peace
The human heart seldom shows.

The candle lights the way
To the soul's eternal fire.
Smoldering in silence,
Burning with unfulfilled desire.

The candlelight dances and shimmers,
A flame flickering in the breeze.
Like the ignited soul
It is fighting for its release.

Pamela J. Timmons

MODERN DEATH

As I walked down the street,
I met a well-dressed man.
He asked me if I needed a ride,
I said, ''No.''
Then Death hopped in his DeLorean,
And drove away.

Bill Rae

BY THE SEA

I walk along the shore
senses all aware
fingers of golden sun
playing in my hair

by the sea.

Waves swirling around my feet
sea gulls gliding by
shells, rainbows of the sand
beauty personified

by the sea.

My peace is by the sea
joy is at its crest
here is where I shall come
to find eternal rest

by the sea.

Denise J. Ford

JUST MORE

Open up the door to my life
Just to see the way that you are.

By standing in the steps in between of me.
To maketh of my life as to be of you.

Just more
More enough to make it to us.

Let me take you will to my side
Just to see the other side as it has always been.

Moving into the threshhold
Moving in through the door

So that we both see
The way it can be.

As it always has been
Just enough to make it to us.

By standing in the steps in between of me.
Standing one in front of each other
As the door has been opened

Then side by side

Douglas Robertson

DEAR FRIEND OF MINE

I think that I shall never find
Another friend so true and kind
Who'll always be there day or night
Be with me through the morning light
If my need so be.

Our worlds are growing fast apart
But you know you're always in my heart
And will be there till the very end
Because you are my dearest friend
And always will be.

In time of trouble I will come to you
And in hours of need you'll find me true
When our days grow very "old and golden"
You will find our hearts still always holding
On to precious memories.

Now on this special day of mine
I want you standing close beside
To be with me as I start a new life
And to share my happiness as I become a new bride
Dear friend of mine.

Lori Hall

THE ROSE

I am a rose. My lovely petals always glow.
My fragrance engulfs the air, as you breath me deep
within your soul.

But don't try to hold me. I've warned you of the pain.
My thorns will prick you and draw your blood, like rain.

So please, just admire me from afar.
Close your eyes and inhale my fragrance.
But don't, please, don't try to hold me.

Candice L. Lincoln

MY FATHER'S BIRTHDAY

Today is my father's birthday
Or would be if he were alive.
And it's hard to imagine, but true nonetheless,
That today he'd be seventy-five.

I think of him often and the things that we did
Together, a long time ago.
When I was a child, he would take me to
Boatyards and airports. He taught me to row

At a lake, where each summer we'd swim
With my cousins, who had a small cabin nearby.
And those long summer nights would be spent
Catching fireflies in jars, if they dared to dart by.

Later on, in my teens, our summers were spent
At the beach, and the boardwalk at night
Was alive with excitement, music and people,
A colorful, carnival sight!

Today is his birthday, that man I remember.
I so wish that he were alive
To share in the memories and bask in the spotlight.
I wish he were seventy-five.

Joyce Hartman

UNSPOKEN FEELINGS

How shall I speak to you, my love?
My lips are mute.
I am tongue-tied.
What shall I say to you,
whom I admire and respect?
When your eyes gaze into mine
I want to hold you, protect you,
console you.
The sun sets as we
walk toward each other.
We stand near one another
afraid to touch,
but the dark acts as a shield.
We merge and embrace.
Oh! My love it is you
who gives me strength
to fight and defeat the tongues of malice
that surround us.
Like the snowflakes fall silently on an apple blossom
but do not destroy it,
so our love will kindle like flame
and never die.

Virginia Goland

LIFE

I think about life and to my mind it brings a fear,
contemplate the future and to my eye it brings a tear
I wonder about crime as it oozes through a city, all
the homeless children, and it makes me cry with pity
I ponder about the helpless fawn which no one ever
knows when lying beneath a bush it is unmercifully bulldozed
I reflect on the birds flying in the dirty atmosphere,
choking on the pollution and it destroys my cheer
I think about the acidic water and those poor little
fish, isn't there something I can do? Don't I wish.
My mind drifts to the sky, further than the eye can
see, isn't there a better place? *Lord, there must be!*

William F. Eardley, IV

ONE WOULD NEVER KNOW

My dream came true
and so I stand.

Maybe it is time

Time for me to make something of myself
Time for me to land.

I flew high in the clouds
looking down

Seeing the places I could go
if dreams were only reality

one would never know.

Judith L. Newbauer

SARAH

Sarah lived alone,
in the house she had known as a child.
The house was small.
The town was small.
Very few neighbors came to call.
Many thought she was strange,
living alone as she did.
They would see her at times at the store —
nothing more.
But Sarah wasn't alone.
So many memories she had known,
were in each room and on every wall.
The house was small.
The town was small.
To many, she didn't matter at all.

Mrs. James Wilmeth

THE SWEET SCENT OF LIVING

Buds, not yet in the bloom of their life,
Choose to cut their stems, giving up the strife.
Everyone knows this garden is not weed free,
But you mustn't choose death as a way to flee.
Listen you, and listen well,
I have a scent for you to smell.
There is the rose, the scent is sweet,
Choose to stay, and a prize you'll meet.
Yes, this is the sweet scent of living,
A prize beyond all.
Stay awhile, you'll get up from your fall.

Scott Phelps

SEASONS

I see the clouds turning from blue to grey.
Spoiling an otherwise perfect day.
The birds have sung but now they rest.
Their joy is their voices,
their home is their nest.
The leaves have all but changed their hue.
Trees standing naked in the autumn air.
Farewell, farewell red robin of spring,
and spend these wintry months in peace.

Frederic Exume

LUPINE COMMAND

On a steep slant of slope,
    next to a sudden vertex of shaling ridge,
heaves a density of blue purple,
rolling over bobbing white tips.

Waves pass and return in dashing beat.
Arterially red stems thrust downward,
rocking the earth.
Clusters of foliage reflect stars.

Turbulent scope of bloom blurs
by green deep grasses bounding in place
to sky whirled high with cloudy froth
pouring over earth.

Souls that drift to see are lost,
awash in a gulf of gully gales and
tranced by the quiet roar,
wondrously drained and defaced in
a culmination of imaginings.

Lindsay Wilhelm

THE BALLERINA

Silently she floats on stage,
her body lithe and full of grace;
Her head held high in gentle tilt;
Her graceful hands held nimbly so
that people watching felt that they,
like her, were all a part of the
graceful flow.

She leaped and twirled across the stage
in pirouettes and gliding strides,
and in at least a moment spent, the
audience felt full of pride,
that they were part of this great scene
and floated high along with her, in
leaps and whirls like some great tide.

Her heart of course was in her dance;
it reached beyond the dimension of stage;
and when the performance came to end,
she gracefully curtsied to the floor,
leaving all who viewed her there,
to praise and clap and call for more.

Doreen E. Baird

FOR A FRIEND

I have been dreaming
    of a man
whose face I couldn't
    quite see.
I knew you were he,
    when you
kissed me, held me,
loved me.
Why did you just run
through me like a train
on its way somewhere else?
Like a wave
headed for shore?

Debbie Billick

HER FRIEND

She heard a cry,
She ran in fright.
She stopped to look,
It wasn't a pretty sight.

The murderer was gone,
He did not care.
She knelt by her friend,
And started a little prayer.

There was no blood,
It was all internal.
Her best friend was gone,
And there would be no funeral.

They buried her in back.
She would always remember,
As she cried by her side,
How her cat was so tender.

Patti L. Hopp

MY FRIEND AND I

My friend is different than I.
We're like black and white,
She's as bright as the sun,
I'm as dark as the night.

We fight and quarrel,
Just like friends do.
But we'll be friends forever,
We'll show you.

We love each other like sisters,
And act like them too.
But when it comes to blood,
Friends will just have to do.

As the years go by,
We graduate.
Going with our careers, we
Separate.

We are miles and miles apart.
But we both write, and
Hope to see each other
On class reunion night.

As I pass away,
I'll remember,
My life with her, a friend, was
Much better.

Patti L. Hopp

VELVET GLOVE

He says I am his velvet glove —
    Warm . . .
        Soft . . .
A smooth, tight fit.

Now is *now* for love —
    Breathless . . .
        Urgent . . .
This is *it*.

June Rose Smith

VERSES FOR JOEY

Little Boy Blue, little boy true,
  Lost his way — what to do?
Helter skelter, hither and yon,
  Hast thou seen him, fleeting and gone?

Ask the ladybug, ask the yew, ask
  The bluebird, ask the gnu.
Say they no — what to do?
  Perhaps the lakeside, where first we knew.

The caves of wind, where once we played,
  The old man's house . . . nay, of there he's afraid.
Alas and alack — what to do?
  Pray not I've for always lost little boy blue.

There's but one spot where I must look,
  The house of truth, down by the brook.
The house of peace, the house of love,
  The house that God is fondest of.

I peek wtihin with cautious care, and lo
  And behold, what I see there.
Asleep among doves a bunny and a yew
  Asleep like an angel . . . little boy blue.

L. A. Colón-Arce

JANE, JANE

*To the memory of Dame Edith
Sitwell, 1887 - 1964*

Jane, Jane, tall as a crane,
  Where've you gone?
Come play again.

Tweedle fee, tweedle fye,
  Flowing gowns, serene of eye.

Turbans of old, rings of gold . . .
  Hands of marble, tears in your soul.

Cockscombed-ragged hair awry,
  Creaking light, pining sigh.

We miss you, Jane, we miss you dear.
  We miss your words, we miss your cheer.

Were you with us once again,
  What gem would you offer . . . what droll refrain?

Jane, Jane, tall as a crane,
  Where've you gone? . . . come . . . play again.

L. A. Colón-Arce

A MOMENT IN THE WINTER

    I gaze up at the sun, shining in the northern skies
burning so intensely, it nearly blinds my eyes
    Bringing a feeling of warmth to the frozen land,
perhaps a gift from God, ever there with an outstretched hand
    Soon to melt the snow from the mountainsides and fill
the rivers which flow deep and wide
    Causing the birds to sing with cheer and signal the world
spring is near
    Lending serenity and peace to the surroundings, as
the tranquility and quiet gently wrap around me.

William F. Eardley IV

WITHIN A THOUSAND YEARS

Spires of dust twist feral, shards of stone slice air;
Icy, biting winds scrape the rockscape bare

Darting, dashing, dipping sands, borne by freezing gale,
Trip the light fantastic, rip the dirty pale

Broken, battered, shattered rock, rigid in the night
Frozen, inky, empty time, latent, without light

At last upon a bouldered point, a spark, yet meager bleak;
A sunray wan and white-ish, spurts down a rugged peak

Unmindful of the world below, the sun rears rosy red
Pours across the scrawny sky, torching all ahead

The sun so hot it scars, brimstone at its worst,
Burning fire so stark, the earth by flame be-cursed;

The wind expires, no more its eerie moan
Awesome, murky stillness, fire and light and stone

The sun moves on, boring toward the west
Shadows and the breezes form, within the sand, unrest;
                and then,

Spires of dust twist feral, shards of stone slice air;
Icy, biting winds scrape the rockscape bare.

Lloyd Olson

THE MEANING OF GOOD MORNING

Good morning means so many things,
More things than I can name.
We say it for the joy it brings,
And gives out just the same.

It means I'm glad to see you,
Isn't it a lovely day?
It also means how do you do,
It's one more day to play.

Good morning simply means we care,
About the folks we meet.
It means I'm glad that you are there,
To know and just to greet.

Charlotte M. Hill

CHARLOTTE M. HILL. Born: St. Louis, Missouri, 1925; Married: Fred D. Hill; Education: Harris Teachers College, B.A., 1963; Webster University, M.A., 1975; St. Louis University, M.A. plus 30; Occupations: Classroom Teacher, Reading Specialist; Memberships: International Reading Association, Annual Fundraiser Committee for United Negro College; Comments: *The poems submitted here are from a collection of poems that I have written entitled 'Poetry For Wee Folks.' I write poetry mainly for my primary students as a tool for teaching values, building self-esteem and improving their reading skills. Someday I hope to have my book published.*

BOY OR MAN

When a little boy is hurt
And he doesn't understand
Why is he told to straighten up
And act like a man?

When he is hurting inside
It's better to let it out
Release your emotions
Go ahead and shout

It is not a sign of weakness
To let yourself cry
Don't act tough or indifferent
If you know it's a lie

To show you have feelings
Makes you no less of a man
It proves you are capable
Of trying to understand

Don't block out your emotions
Accept them and grow
Learn from your feelings
And a better person will show.

Roger D. Lee

WHO IS THIS MAN?

Who *is* this man?
Is he *me?*
Am I *I?*
I cannot grasp this locked-in
          feeling.
Will I ever be free?
Will I soar to ecstasy?
Or walk mean streets
locked inside myself?
Will I burst forth and be the
    man I am?
Or forever pass by
Never knowing who is me?

Chester M. Matzner

HALLS BY THE WAYSIDE

Numerous things happen occasionally,
Halls go through, they never stop.
One particular hall displays greed,
Self-destruction, hate, war, and such
like. Halls like this show and present
things that are not beautiful.
It is sad to think of such qualities
  as these to incriminate your soul.

Halls that display beautiful things
Like love, temperance, kindness,
  hospitality, meekness, and good will.
Sing them out and let others know that
  they can change a person's life.
The wayside shows other halls
That are famous and other halls that
  are musical.

Halls can bring happiness and grief
and others can bring happiness
  and joy.
Which hall are you going through today?

Margaret Blythe

WHEN DEATH COMES NIGH

One seeks the joys . . .
The pleasure dome . . .
The zest and swells of life . . .
The sparkling dew, the crackling twigs . . .
That soothe this world of strife.

  But when death comes
    (as come it must)

Let fear not us envelop . . .
But take this too
    As our just due
A part of life's reward.

Yes, reward it is — strange
    though that seems
For all that has been prologue.
    And we pass — in night or dawn . . .
To the path where all must tread . . .

Then do not look upon this friend
    with fear, remorse or dread.
    For it is, too — as much as
        dew or blue skies overhead.

Chester M. Matzner

SUDDEN SIGHT

A crashing sound
(thin glass crushing in
carpeting swept to
hard floor)
A huge deer
waries me brownly
clumsies out to the
woods behind me
Am I so terrifying
ask myself
the answer surer of
hoof is
moreso:
of course.

Phyllis Jean Green

IT'S NOT ENOUGH

You buy me candy and roses
    almost every day.
And it's nice,
But it's not enough.

You buy me jewelry of gold and silver
    even diamonds.
And they're beautiful,
But it's not enough.

You take me to fancy parties
    and the finest restaurants.
And it's exciting,
But it's not enough.

If you would just say
    ''I love you''
that
would be enough.

Kristin Shreves

A CHILD'S DREAM OF A STAR

I see my child asleep on his bed
and wonder what is dancing in his head.

He moves every once in a while
and on his face is a smile.

The stars are twinkling high,
and I see a lone star shining in the sky.

My child moves again, and every now
    and then
I see a smile on his face.

What are you dreaming of?
Is it the star above?

Tell me, my child, I long to know
    What unearthly dream makes you
        smile so.

Something about the star makes you
    sleep so peacefully
What could it be?

Up above in the heaven so bright
    shining like a beacon in the night.

Margaret Blythe

MARGARET EARLENE BLYTHE. Born: Floyd Medical Center, 1-16-56; Married: Emerson Blythe, 6-2-49; Education: Floyd Junior College, Rome, Georgia, 1979; Occupation: Assistant librarian, CETA Program; Membership: Homemaker's Club; Other Writings: ''Echo From The Past,'' short story, *Antaeus, The Ecco Press,* 1987; Themes: *I want to tell about life, its good times and the bad, the themes are blended into a pattern of love, joy, peace, and understanding. So are the ideas of the opposite.*

FARAWAY LANDS

Pink and yellow cats, with
bumblebee wings, live in
strawberry huts underneath
peacock skies.

Metallic fish, modeling fluorescent
eyes, guard the everflowing streams
leading to gingerbread houses
and lemon-drop trees.

On sand of cinnamon and rivers
of marshmallow cream, he sails
ships of gumdrops to reach
the lands of fire and mist.

Paula Faust

SONNET NO. 37

How often does love miss in its deadly aim
and strike a woman improperly, unjust and unfair
with a desire to mate and an attempt to tame
an unredeeming, unlikely fellow. One without care
or fancy for love, though she would brandish torch
and rally round love's simple cause, burning bay laurel
and rosemary, intoning cantos, waiting on the porch,
waiting, the well-versed sorceress pinching sorrel
and pot, spewing sonnets and incantations, voodoo
and votive, though in vain, for he sports no love dart.
These dreams my potent cauldron brewed in febrile love . . .
Ha! Were I to wear the very ashes of men, then too,
I could not win your damned reticent heart,
though would I, like a phoenix, from your ashes rise above.

Sandra Collins

GYPSY LOVE SONG

On one moon-drenched evening
I did not have to try
To fall in love with you.

Stars swept in sand-storm whirlpool madness
Across the sky;   Flurries in the head —
What do planets and galaxies sound like?
They must have a music all their own.

Whisper and glisten   Let us hold tight and listen
To converse without speaking
  To comprehend without thinking
    To know without asking
That we are together now, in spirit
  The heavens are ours for the moment
    And for the forever.

    Our lives in correlated variation
Free-form fantasy   Wordless imagery
There is always someone who will find you beautiful.

        Believe and listen;

  To my breathless sigh
    And wordless speech
      And silent serenade.

Jeanne Heroux

THE PAINTING

How sad is she. The silent painting. To cast a longing
  gaze upon your tender face.
To see the questions in your eyes and not be able to
  speak or touch.
In her silence, she will long for a soft touch from your
  fingertips.
She will pray for a gentle kiss from your warm lips.
For one moment she wishes she could step out of her
  painting,
Take you in her arms and repay you for all your warm
  and tender gazes.
For you will keep the painting young at heart,
Long after her paint has cracked and peeled.

Candice L. Lincoln

STILL YOUNG

I am still not ready to say goodbye to you
Although my words have stated it,
My heart cannot seem to agree.
For so long it was you and me
And now it's me, just me.
When will I ever see you again?

You called me your little girl
Although I was years older than you.
You made me feel young again.
I idolized you, as you represented strength;
I admired you, as you emanated beauty;
Yet, I released you, as we both anticipated freedom;
For it is what is necessary
    That you may grow into your stature.
You will need that
    So you may become who you must.
I shall get ready to say farewell to who you are,
In faith that one day, I am allowed to say hello
To who you have become.

Jeanne Heroux

JEANNE MARIE HEROUX. Born: Springfield, Massachusetts, 5-28-54; Single; Occupation: Commercial shellfishing; Memberships: National Writers Club, American Federation of Astrologers; Poetry: 'Beach Point,' fall 1985, and 'Hawks Nest Pond,' spring 1984, *The Cape Codder*; Comments: *I like to write about personal experiences, usually of a romantic nature. I feel good when I can communicate the essence of a particular relationship to my readers. I live permanently on Cape Cod.*

COLDBURN

My body leans against the stove.
My eyes are averted as they stare out of the window.
I hear your words but my mind is blank,
My tongue is still, my voice is silent.
My attitude is one of cold indifference to you
As a person at this moment.

I am an icicle.
I am frozen, solid, unmoving.

I am burning up with anger.
My frustration is a smoldering red hot ember.
I am a volcano ready to explode.
I cannot cope with the cold burn that I am experiencing.

''Just let me think! Just leave me alone!''

You leave . . .
And I continue to lean against the stove,
Wishing that you would return.

Michael W. Lee

SUNSHINE IN YOUR EYES

I see a sparkle, a glitter
and a glare.
I see hope; where once there
was despair.

For over the horizon, awaits
tranquility in the skies!
A new day is dawning, with
sunshine in your eyes.

Tomorrow will hence with it —
beautiful colors than before.
Tomorrow's a new — when again,
your spirits shall soar.

Awaken, oh you lonely soul —
let brightness so arise.
May reflections of a better day,
fill sunshine in your eyes!

As you look upon the many of clouds,
be reminded of the silver lining.
Not always will it be this grey,
for soon the sun will be shining.

Christopher J. Sando

CHRISTOPHER JOSEPH SANDO. Born: Corning, New York, 4-24-63; Single; Education: Painted Post West High School, Corning, non-regents diploma, 6-24-83; Occupations: Radio announcer at WCBA, Corning, and WEHH, Horseheads, New York; Poetry: 'From Where the Flower Grows,' 'A Nightingale's Lullaby,' 'Shining Star,' 'Sweetheart, Where Are Thou?', 'Along the Way'; Comments: *Most of what I write is, in general, centered around romance and love. It's a passion for me to convey that through my works: A love for humanity, a young lady, or with the word itself. But even more so, however, is that each piece is a reflection of my enjoyment of life.*

SYMPHONY OF A RAINY NIGHT

It is raining, I sit
before the fire,
warming myself.
Shadows dance
on the wall behind me;
moving in rhythm
to the music of the wind
singing through the trees.

Elaine B. Melloy

AN EAGLE'S VIEW

Eagle soaring
But I am imploring,
How does he fly so high?
I too want to soar the heaven's sky.

His vantage point is so profound,
And I am stuck here on the ground.

Oh, foolish one, rise above your circumstance,
A new mind's view is sure to enhance.

Rise up and fly and be not weary,
Only the Lord can give you wings to carry
You high above your muddled mind.

Oh, soaring eagle, I too can sail like the wind.

Susan D. White

TOMMY

Silence and darkness . . .

My eyes burn into the flame
And I am removed,
Again to be the little boy
I have locked up,
Again to be the friends
Once we were.

A million beams of dawn
Come crawling through the tangled branches
Each one brings an offering
Of laughing children
Lumbering through this wood,
The beams melt into a blinding sun.

A million miles between us
We've become society's
Alabaster pawns,
Raped by Time of friendship's love,
The morning invades my loneliness
My eyes slowly close.

Silence and darkness.

G. Paul Ray

CROSSROADS

Our thoughts we hide on the way
Only our actions do betray.
The feelings down deep
These we seek to keep.
We wonder why is life this way?
Mistakes are made each day.
Some to the world unknown
These to our self we must atone.
Our hearts lead us oft astray
Loved ones help us find our way.
Each must do all he can.
We will not pass this way again.
For some the crossroads are near
Others are a long time here.

Patsy Greenway

I AM GUINEVERE NO LONGER

The tambourine clattered
Clutter and confusion,
Sinning wildly crazily
Dancing like wicked fairies
Ringing bells
Golden goblets sloshing wine
We all cheered our victory
At the Guild Hall
Then I saw — I opened my eyes and saw —
Your black eyes shining
Teasing me with love — you had called me fair
I reached out to touch your hair —
I had to leave I had to run
Though my heart pleaded to stay
We had touched the audience's heart
But cannot touch each other's
For I am bound by oath and vow
To another
Camelot is over —
And I am Guinevere no longer

Cynthia Clark Withers

THE LONG RETURNING

Through a doorway, look around.
Find a particular web of destiny,
emit the first thread. Rewrite
the pattern many times, perfect
the intricate designs. Move on.

And through another doorway:
seven times . . . seven times with
so many pathways stretching in
all directions, so many other
lights along the roads which
all lead back. Dim and bright

and shades between. All ever
changing . . . some faltering,
others radiating as beacons
in the night. Struggling to
express, dimly recalling a long
ago time of lost perfection.
Ever trying to find it again.

Elaine Phillips

WE HAVE LOST

We have lost even the moonlight.
No one felt my feelings
underneath the sapphire sky,
no one knew my heart
while silver stars glittered by.

We have lost but a calm wind.
A silence flashed through
the sky, as I looked into
your unsound cobalt eyes.

We have lost even the rain.
Our fantasies are drenched
in reality, then buried
in the muddy almond earth.

Paula Faust

BUDDIES AND BEAUS, HUSBANDS AND WIVES

Our buddies are great — usually nice guys,
Who will be there in bad times to give us advice.
It's always nice to know there'll be somebody there;
Someone to talk to in time of need and despair.

Our beaus are our partners — for life, if you will.
We can't put into words exactly how we feel.
We befriend them, we like them, we praise what they do;
But most important of all, we love them too.

Husbands don't do much — at least inside the house,
Except dirty up dishes and keep company their spouse.
Their jobs around the house include the garage and outside;
And, while they're there anyway, by their rules all abide.

A wife is the same as a beau — but more committed.
To marriage vows and each other, our feelings we've admitted.
A wife's main job is rearing children and doing housework.
She usually has a job too, and on Sundays gets us to church.

Buddies are people we can have parties and fun with;
Beaus are people we have picnics and lie in the sun with.
A wife is someone who a husband looks to for love and support;
And a husband brings home the bacon, and holds down the fort.

Bernard Sulliban III

THE SEVEN DRUMMERS

There were only seven children playing in the street
The day the seven drummers stopped rapping out their beat.
And every seventh day of every seventh week
The seven elders of the town would pray and sing and shriek.
They'd pray for seven seasons but were given only four.
They'd sing their seven songs of peace but found themselves at war.
They'd shriek in shame for their seven sins but committed seven more.
And every day at seven when the sun began to rise
They'd find themselves awake again, wishing to be wise.
But there was one who came to them with five plus seven men
Who spoke of *love* and tried to prove that *God* forgave all sin.
And though the seven elders of the town would pray for seven days,
They'd curse the man of love who came and they'd spit upon his face.
They hung him from a tree, between two thieves, upon a hill
And stood and watched the sky grow dark just as his heart was still.
There were only seven followers there to hear his final cry.
One betrayed him, one denied him and three thought he would not die.
There were only seven children playing in the street
The day the seven drummers stopped rapping out their beat.

Michael W. Lee

TO TOM

I read this book of verse you left to me,
Revealing comments written in your hand;
I find in it a treasured legacy,
For who you were, I better understand.
You loved to fish at dawn in icy streams,
Your Irish heritage was a proud boast,
You would have been content to live in dreams,
And children were the people you loved most;
You often wept at Poesy's eloquence,
You learned the solace music can provide,
You tried to mask in wit your sentiments,
And every day your fears were multiplied.
 I hear the smug, sardonic laugh of Fate,
 Who schemed to let me glimpse your soul too late.

Sally Stembridge

WHERE SPRING IS BORNE

To stand where winter, stark and white, lies still,
To hear no song above the night, no thrill
Of magic, where the heart in lonesome plea
Trespasses, where the earth sleeps peacefully.

Restless this mind, impatient of earth's womb,
Mistaking now this ground for weeping tomb,
What promise here of joy escapes these eyes
Where spring is borne, and winter secret lies.

What mystic touch to waken now and change
To glorify in color, and arrange
A summer's scene in given time and space
Unequalled beauty, in this winter place.

Margaret Hancock

UNBLEMISHED CREATION

When I gaze at a child's astounding perfection,
I'm in awe of the *Lord's* unblemished creation.
A child's face can mirror distinct "orneriness,"
Or as easily reflect endearing goodness.
Their smiles are capable of moving mountains;
And its radiance rivals the noon-day sun.
An awarded kiss, however "*damp*", it may be
Renders the most poor, independently wealthy.
The *unknown* bewitches a child's curiosity,
It's vital in pursuing their identity.
They're busy as beavers, never idle minds,
Are constantly in — an inquisitive bind.
Children earn "*every*" inch of dirtiness —
Folks wonder if they've heard of cleanliness.
An adorable face peering up at you,
Alters any incident that may ensue.
Warm generous words can alleviate ailments —
But, a child's embraces excel all treatment.
Children are *God's* gift to be *loved* and *nurtured;*
And no greater *treasure* could He have ensured.

Nancy Olinger

MY TRUE LOVE

To my truest love — you know who you are:
I have long admired you, from afar.
I have so much to say to you.
For you, I know not what to do.
Wealthy I am not, and as for enough money — not nearly,
But I'd gladly give it to you, for I love you so dearly.

My feelings for you are impossible to state,
And I could not possibly write them all.
I'd like to go out with you, alone on a date,
That is, of course, before the next Fall Ball.

I miss you so much; it's gonna be rough.
But while you're gone, I'll just have to be tough.
I, like you, want a nice romance.
Haven't had one, but now's my chance.
If you ever wanna talk, or you just need a friendly face,
You can talk to me at any time — come over to my place.

I know that a lot of things are hard for you now;
I don't want you to feel that you're hurried.
I think that maybe 'fore long — I just don't know how —
You and I, we may someday be married.

Bernard Sulliban III

THE DARK SIDE

Beyond the realms of hell,
deeper than the bottomless pit,
is a dimension of the unknown.
Here lies an entity waiting
to consume your soul.

Onyx cauldrons boil with
 sinners' blood.
Pits of snakes writhe around
beating hearts.

Spirits flash like lightning.

Roses scorch through eternity, while
oxblood tears stream from hollow eyes.

Saffron mucous oozes
down sultry cave walls,
bats munch on fragments of flesh.

There is no escape.

Paula Faust

ALBINO

His orange-white head, curly capped,
 Bends to the task.
Hand, wrapped tightly in blackened gauze,
 Practiced and certain,
Moves from can to shoe, shoe to can,
 Again and again,
Till all the leather is made dull
 Enough to shine.

Done, the polished shoes seem renewed,
 But he is not,
His blue-eyed, broad-nostrilled face
Expressionless.
Is he made dull by drudgery,
 Boredom bred,
Or because, not black nor white,
 He is alone?

John M. Cornman

THE VIOLINIST

I was pleased to find you here
rubbing and bending ineffable tones
from strings relentlessly stretched
to the bare boundaries of a note.

The triumvirate scale of eye
to hand to bow
and a fretless composure
held horizontally under the chin.
Attentive to the fine, visceral
adjustment of spinous pegs
chromatically inclined to caress
or digress.
I am a captive audience,
hearing a voice
I've never known,
remaining the dancer
long after the piece
is finished.

Diane King

BUTTERFLY

This blue globe —
an icy sphere with skin
of rippling cellophane —
is stretched and punctured
by the beating
black and orange
Monarch razor wings.

Flowers of the field
bend gently
to a soft and painless death
beneath the cool
cupped hand
of October's dry breath.

In this blue globe —
my soft bed with blankets
of wet yellow wool —
I lie and trace your images
in the pool
of the darkening sky.

Susan Setteducato

CATHOLIC

In the Cathedral of my aging vision
it is raining
and sweetly bleeding
blue faces
of saints and sad women
on the stone shadowy floors,
diffusing
and quietly coupling
under a woolen cloak of Myrrh.

The gaping and toothless mouth of God
always is hiding
behind the silk purple draperies
and flamed spikes,
folded inside a ring
of black and singing maidens.

A thick brown angel floats forever
above the dark womb —
glove of the Sacristy.
Low and droning
is the tortured cantillation
of so many imprisoned sins . . .

Susan Setteducato

LOVE IN THE WORLD

Love can't become ol*d*.
Odd how we have al*l*
Varied in ou*r*
Evident need t*o*
Ensure to their lover ho*w*
Necessary love is to lif*e*.

Too few really believe fait*h*
Helps heal a broken hear*t*
Easily; no word need be spoke*n*.

When leaders use love as its radi*i*
Out comes peace; for no pric*e*.
Rated high should be L.U.*V*. —
Love United Virtues — it is *quo animo*
Declaring the humans' Golden Rule principl*e*.

D. Colleen Shuey

WINTER TREE

As eloquent in repose
Now,
The frozen maple,
As when blushed
By the rushing juices
Of the rogue, warm days.

There, a fine
Black charcoal line
Is splitting
 The white flanks of the hills,
Making filigree
On somber
Steel-sheeted sky.

The skeleton revealed —
All flesh
Torn off in mouthfuls.
A circling,
Screaming,
Solitary bird
With wings of ice,
Razor cold . . .

The deer have returned to the winter tree.
Silhouettes
And white flags
Decompose
In the crimson belly
Of night.

Susan Setteducato

A GIFT BESTOWED

Is it not a myth,
That for better or worse,
A gift bestowed,
Reaps a blessing or curse?

For if we cling tightly,
To all earthly things,
Daring not part,
Naught but emptiness brings;

The intangible thought,
Captured in word or rhyme,
Somehow endures,
Throughout ages and time;

So I choose to live,
And with humbleness leave,
Where my feet have trod,
But a small part of me.

Dorothy K. Wheeler

Sometimes I'm following God's light,
and as I travel, I learn to depend and trust in Him.
Then as I travel the light at times seems to
dim or sometimes even disappears. I m I learn to depend and trust in Him.
Then as I travel the light at times seems to
dim or sometimes even disappears. I must remember
in these times God has not abandoned me, but is letting
me have faith by following my own light. At these
times I must create my own light and let Him shine
in and through me.

These are the times I can help others and show
them the way.

Sometimes it's scary and I feel alone, but I
must always remember I'm doing God's work and He
knows me better than I know myself. He would not
let me be harmed or place me in danger. I must
remember this and know this and go on with faith
and love and confidence and do His work.

I must always believe we are a team and go
everywhere together.

Ann Benedick

ILLUSION

I had a son.
A beautiful, happy, crying, wetting, suckling, tiny
Baby boy.
And he ate. And he grew. And he learned.
And he played. And he dated. And he laughed.
And he drank. And he drove. And he died.
And . . .
He's gone.

And I try to remember . . .
Did I have a son?

Michael W. Lee

CALIFORNIA HILL NO. 1

Sitting on top of a hill where foxtails
have turned white from the dry heat,
and I feel like a little girl,
    my cheeks are red and soft,
and I am aware of being loved as one gentle
flower caresses my face,
    and I'm high up in the mountains
    away from the comings and goings from
somewhere to nowhere and back again.

All that is life is below me and as I sit and
watch the day die, my view looks like the
inside of a transistor radio and I hear the
music of an electrified city — too much static
to stay high.
But me, up here where it's cool and calm,
I feel the contradiction of life as prominent as
my own heartbeat.
I paint a picture in my mind of all the colors
around me, and it looks like a picture of me,
just another flower in an atmosphere where
I can stay for a while and be happy.

Meryl Wolfson

TEHACHAPI PRISON

He remembered his friends —
And often wondered, if they remembered him?
He thought about the scent of the sea . . .
How the taste of it upon his tongue —
Reminded him of me . . .
In brief moments of time passing —
He remembered books and poetry he'd read,
Of thoughts spoken aloud to him
By people whose faces were now fading
From his memory . . .
He remembered the first love and how he'd lost it.
He remembered all the broken dreams of yesterday
Every one . . .
He wanted so much to cry but could not . . .
There were a thousand uncried tears locked inside.
Where's the boy who sang to the stars?
The boy with a rainbow in his heart —
Where has he gone?
Tehachapi . . .

Sharon Kennedy-Shapiro

FIRST LOVE

When you were just a boy, and I was just a girl,
    We met for the sake of another.
But when we met, we were made for lovin' each other.

At first our troubles were so few.
    As time went on, they seem to have grew.

Our words and bodies just went through the motions.
    But deep down in each other's eyes we saw the emotion.

The times that you thought were so good,
    Were really the times that were of a sexual mood.

I once thought it was love for me, for you,
    for one another. *I once thought it was love.*
That's why it hurt us both to leave one another.

Now you're a man and I, a woman.
    Our feelings will never be the same.
Because, *inside* we both have changed.

I once thought it was love for me, for you,
    for one another. *I once thought it was love.*
That's why it hurt us both to leave one another.

Jamie Marie Lee
(written in high school)

AS A SHIP SAILETH

As a ship saileth from sea to sea,
    Help me, Dear Lord, to put my trust in Thee.
And as the ship is tossed to and fro,
    By the current of the sea,
Let the winds of Your Holy Spirit
    Completely control me.

For without Your precious Spirit,
    Where on earth, would I be?
So help me put my trust in You,
    Then, I'll have victory in Thee.

Judith E. Reed

DREAMS AND GOALS

Dreams are usually only make-believe
The kind you usually wake up from,
Dreams can keep you going though
When all else seems to fail,
They are inside your mind and your heart,
Some dreams you can share with others,
With some others, they're just kept inside.

Some dreams can certainly be realistic
It's possible that those, sometimes, can come true
But some dreams are just dreams, dreams of a fool,
To know the difference, it takes someone wise
Because when dreams are just dreams
The ones you really know can't come true,
They are the ones that hurt you
That wreck your mind and make you blue.

Set your dreams and goals just shortly out of reach,
Realistic plans that you might dream and reach for in time,
And then you can have your faith and hopes,
Your family and friends and new friends, yet to meet,
Dreams and goals, when combined, sheer happiness you'll soon reap.

Lee Dennis

THE STRANGERS

The strangers came one stormy night.
The strangers came with open hearts.
They brought joy to the town . . . to us all.
The strangers changed the hearts of the children
to joy and laughter.
Where there were sadness and despair,
they made it good again.
The strangers are God and his son Jesus.

George Pol

GEORGE CAMPALANS POL. Born: Caracas, Venezuela, 12-19-59; Naturalized: 4-26-73; Education: Owasso High School, 1981; Poetry: 'Today's Fool,' 'Freedom Is,' 'The Strangers'; Comments: *I write what I feel about the daily conflicts that exist in our lives. I write about things most people in America take for granted, such as freedom.*

DELAYED PHOENIX

A strong wind swept across sweltering plains
Swirling dust in mesmerizing clouds,
Flinging worn, tattered rags aimlessly about
To abandon them in hollowed shrouds,

Imperious, relentless, indignant waves
Beat incessantly against the shore,
And with each impassioned salt-licked kiss
Eroding the wall of the heart, even more.

Bobbi Mahala Drawdy

HEALING WIND

The soft breeze swept through the leaves
Leaving them scattered like torn pages . . .
Then, almost as if in regret
The air became still and warm
Only to rise again in a gust
Clearing the sidewalk of all debris
Leaving behind a fresh scent . . .

. . . airing out the closet of my life.

Bobbi Mahala Drawdy

TOMORROW

As I gaze upon my loved ones from the heavens up above,
they're grieving needlessly, missing all my love.
Wishing I could tell them how happy I would be,
if they but knew the beauty of this place that's made for me.
To know someday they'll join me, whenever the time appears,
fills me with great happiness and many joyful tears.
Never mourn for those who have gone away, you will surely meet again.
Be patient, loving, giving to each other until then.

Jeri A. Wilson

THE PLAY

At last, a part for me, little or not.
Hours of practice and many lines to jot.
Nervousness precedes each performance date.
Everyone trying desperately not to be late.
Coughs and measles equally shared.
Among the cast no one is spared.
Sharing smiles and all the tears,
they reach the end amidst the last cheers.
The play is over, the audience gone —
The sound of applause still lingers on.
It is a time of joy but sadness, too,
so long together exchanging colds, gossip, the flu.
Quietly, the cast in opposite ways go, hoping to
meet again for *just one more show.*

Jeri A. Wilson

YOUNG MR. FORESTER

A long-time American friend; he is loved by many people.
He can burn your lips, lift your spirits
and lower your morals.
He is unique, humble and well-mannered. He is loved
mostly by adults.
He is one of the few people who is not loved by children.
He is extremely nice in summer; on holiday and vacation.
He loves to party as a symbol of good living,
as he got older he got better.
He is always well-dressed in his bottle tan suit,
black shoes, white underwear.
He looks great and smells nice.
He is the showman of the big parties; with his whiskey
flavor cologne splash.
The lovable American friend.

Eulalie Herring

RAMAPO RIVER.

LOONEY BEN GARDEN
OF MOUNT BEACH HAVEN

This may be parliamentary broadcast to the unknown

Hi! Bill Bailey. What are you doing on this side of the mountain?
There is a thunderstorm of love on the west side plateau,
can sweep you off your feet;
walk careful, sunshine is romance.
Have you ever heard of the beach haven where the sun only shines
when romance is in the air?
That kind of love can woo your body;
enter Mr. Looney Ben Garden, scratching for help.
Some people go to the mountain beach haven to negotiate power
and come out whoo-whee!
Still fixing their faces straight to catch the
daylight-savings time.
Unless your performance is good, don't make the presentation
or certainly you won't be back to comply with the vote of
confidence. Catch your breath, there's more to come.
Don't go to Mr. Looney Ben Garden without a companion
or a convenient cook, or you will be denied carrots!
The decline of Indian corn is the insect of love;
The only cure is the bird. The absolute tomorrow.

Eulalie Herring

FOLLOW THE STATEMENT

We seldom give ourselves privilege to believe or understand
how much compassion we all need to whisper the word *love*.
Everyone should accept the honor to love and be loved —
it is a courageous feeling!
Not everyone knows how to introduce the soft-spoken word
that keeps the world in tack and on track.
The decency of it is the difference. The difference is feeling.
You can apologize for not being nice; but it takes so little
to be nice, so why not?
Let us love with the love that was meant to be.
We were born equipped to love and should be applauded
when we have done a good job of it.
Many people were placed in a straitjacket for many things,
but never for the love that is so beautiful it glows
like the flowers in springtime.

Eulalie Herring

EULALIE MARNA HERRING. Born: Barbados, West Indies, 9-8-39;
Education: Community College, 1978-80, speedtyping, english letter writ-
ing; Occupation: Nurse's Assistant; Comments: *I am new in the writing
profession. I love writing poetry and short stories. Poetry is an art on its
own, the true talent of the mind.*

SO YOU THINK YOU ARE SUPERIOR

So, you think you are superior
You think you can belittle me
You undermine my every word
And you think that you know me.

Well, let me say just once more
Before you give me that all-knowing look
That what I have left is still worth more
Than the world from me you took.

Jenny Moline

FOOTSTEPS

The anguished moment when the child would die
was caught and held dear as transparent noon.
The steps that lingered in the mountain soon
would be the last within that burning sky.

Trailing fresh beaches, where the night had strewn
edges of cloudy froth, some voice could cry
chilling the fish that caught the cormorants' eye
curbed in the water of the tidal moon.

Roaring, adrift from a departed sun
the ocean weed clung to the surfaced brine
presenting earth with what was made undone.

But sometimes understood, man's thoughts would shine
into the unknown, where he went and won
admission, not to die of fear and time.

P. Mihalik

THE DOVE

White-cast, air-soft, it landed near its mate
on the veranda where the man of stone
half-sculptured stood, unmoved, cold as cut bone,
it seemed helf-merged within an unsought fate.

And in the house the owner dwelt alone,
distressed, that dry grass rustle still this late
in dying fields: that wind thrust through the gate
as it turned, disturbed, upon its heavy groan.

His conscience so awake, yet, could not sleep
hurled from the rising earth and ruined by storm.
There was no peace for him in some judged form
and certain value which rock statues keep.

A life in him was cruel, he could not give
the beating rate, that make creations live.

P. Mihalik

HOW DO YOU SAY "I LOVE YOU"

How do you say, "I love you"?
Flowers? Candy? Money? Jeweley?
No, that's not how you say "I love you."
You say "I love you!"

Sandy Dieu

FALLING DREAMS

December 21, 1986

In the twilight, in the evening,
In the black and darkened night
That hovers over me;
Through the silence of sleep
This is such a secret place to be
That even the fallen stone should dream.

Voices come far away in the night,
Rage within the enemy
Stirs the mystic night profound,
Dull and dead the dreams rebound,
While the stagnant sky is still
The open road runs deep to falling dreams.

Laura J. Lawrence

undefeated

old beat up cars
filled the yard
the drive stained with oil
and grease barely showed a spot of concrete
trash had replaced the grass
and there she sat middle-aged
on the hood of a tireless
jacked-up car
more than an ornament
drinking coffee
from an oversized cup
the sun formed a crown
undefeated her head up
royalty is more than
circumstance

B.E. Crawford

MY LIFE

I have found peace among the rocky places
I've found calm in the middle of the storm
I have seen love in all the hard hearted
I've seen beauty in the midst of the thorns
I have lived a hard life
I've seen many sad things
But since I have been reborn
My spirit only sings
Of the peace, calm, love, beauty
And the joy that Jesus Christ brings

Rick Redmill

FRIENDS

What is love?
I sometimes ask myself
And I see you . . .
A vision of smiles, of warmth and bliss,
Like golden sun through autumn leaves
In a blaze of light
Shining down
Upon me.

When I'm sad
I look to you, my friend,
And you're there . . .
When I'm happy I share my joys, my friend,
And away we fly high above cares
To the land of dreams
High in the sky
Where we're free.

When alone
I think of you, my friend,
And you're there . . .
Side by side we share a bond, my friend,
There's no pretense, just selfless love,
Like a mountain stream
Rushing forth
To the sea.

*Karen Sri Kartomi
and Michael Peter Kennedy*

POWER

In the glory of the sun
A meadow of daisies bloom,
Their beauty is astonishing
Shedding scars and wounds.

Soon the skies turn against them
Each daisy is cast in gloom,
They know not what to do
And wither and wilt in doom.

But one flower holds fast its beauty
Enduring the turmoil of the skies,
His strengths and warmth bring joy
And it alone survives.

Karen Sri Kartomi

HANDS

for t. w.

i love your hands — their gentle touch
tender, yet they thrill so much;
fingers that express devotion
yet evoke so much emotion.

hands that to my great delight
send my feelings up in flight,
then in moments that surprise
tempt and tingle . . . tantalize.

small wonder that my thoughts return
to memories that within me burn;
i hope for other moments when
you'll touch me, darling, once again.

Cy Jenkins

THE WORLD UPSIDE DOWN

Today I saw . . .

The world upside down,
Through trees with leaves that looked like
Fall butterflies.
The clouds were billowy and white,
And moved fast.
Airplanes did cartwheels —
A palm tree in the background was
Waving its branches,
As . . .
One child hung beside me and laughed,
The other child below me laughed,
I laughed too!
I like the world upside down.
It was fun seeing the world from the
Jungle gym,
I did not want to get back on
My feet again!

Dale Cowan

OH, BEAUTIFUL WEB

Oh spider,

You weave a web so fine,
The morning's sunlight caught on
Every detail.
Take me into your patchwork of
Fine beauty
And
Design,
And let me so
Resign.

Dale Cowan

PREPROGRAMMED

Don't wanna read,
Just wanna write.
You programmed me
To do just right.

Don't wanna go
Just wanna stay,
It's all preprogrammed
Any damn way.

I confess to Merrill Lynch
I held out with Johnny Bench,
My bankroll is in a pinch —
The rest of life is a cosmic cinch.

Don't wanna hear,
Just wanna tell.
Got an apple
Programmin' hell.
Programmin' you,
Programmin' space . . .
Can't compute your touch,
Can't compute your face.

R. Fain

CENTER

First you must find your center;
It is the key you know,
It is strong, it is yours, depend on it
For what you need to know.

It is the base for higher life;
All your soul has been,
Wisdom of many centuries, lives and reasons within.

It is darkness if you can't feel it
And light that knows no bounds,
It is silence, listen to it,
All music in one sound.

You'll find there all your secrets,
Though you still may know them not.
There lies the future knowledge
With the past that you forgot.

I thank the highest powers
For the mind in me that flowers,
In the light of some, it towers,
And in the light of some, it bows.

Valli Pizza

UNITED IN WEDLOCK

We stand in matrimony with trust in our hearts
Loving each other forever, never wanting to part
Being cheerful and understanding for our special reason
And sharing the respect for this joyous occasion

In wedlock our rings have no ending with the value we express
We share a love together with a gentle tenderness
With remembrance of the good and the bad times
Knowing that I will be yours and that you will be mine

We will grow strong with God as our faithful foundation
We shall overcome fear and evil as our spiritual inspiration
A love for God in our marriage and with a knowing smile
We will be happy together forever as we walk down the aisle.

Ozell and Kim Paulk

SHYNESS

My heart is pounding. I stand unable to speak.
My thoughts rushing, yet my mind feels so weak.
Anxiety twisting its knife in my intestine.
All I want is a favorable impression.
Why do I feel this way? Wishing to disappear
And be away from this horrible fear.
In a crowded room, nowhere do I feel so alone.
For what sins must God, in this way, make me atone?
Someone addresses me and I clutch in desperation,
At old phrases, my palms wet with perspiration.
Soon they leave and, with tears of rage,
I exit the party, my social life still an empty page.
I arrive at the safe and secure womb
That is my bedroom.
I see my books and familiar walls,
Where one never falls.
And the words flow with expertise and precision,
Never with dullness or indecision.
I lie on my bed in the position of my birth
And dream that the meek inherit the earth.

Gwynneth Gibson

LIFE

The sublime strength that is God's power
Can be discovered in the majestic peaks,
Or something as delicate as a flower,
Or, perhaps, in the softness of a baby's cheeks.
Then there are the everyday miracles of life,
From working for your daily bread
To kissing your wife.
When the Jews from the Pharoahs fled,
Miracles occurred that cannot compare
To the birth of a child;
Whether in a hospital amidst the urban snare,
Or hidden deep within the wild.
Yes, in the wind, God's flag is unfurled,
Blowing in the vibrant breezes of the living world.

Gwynneth Gibson

If I were my feet would I want to walk where I have
taken them? Would my eyes choose to see what I have
commanded? Would my voice sing the same song? If I were
my hands, would they still write what I have instructed
them to write? I pray that I am giving them things they
would want to do.

Nancy Jo Clifford

Do not be afraid . . . to try again.
   Within us is *always* a strength to grasp.

A realm to hope lies dormant.
The pond's ruffled surface masks the depth below.

Reach into your soul that core of life.
It pulses within and beats to its song.
   It shines! A day of its own, a time, a season.

Seek out its peace. Hold it quietly within your heart.
   Appreciate its tears. Bask in its love.

   Feel it, growing in spite of it all — to be alive!
Don't die. It's much too beautiful! To be wilted is only
   to feel the glory of the rain
      softly falling . . .

Oh, but the sadness! It too must have a place within you.
But, doesn't the flower die, only to cast its seeds upon the soil?

Take heart — for the spring of your being shall bloom anew
   With the glory of those blossoms.

   Love again! Yourself . . .

For only then can you truly once more, give to another.

Nancy E. Sherman

THE CARVER

Fresh pungent odor of pine
Lately vibrant with leaves and bark
Now from death — a new calling.

A life born of man's quick mind
Made with hands that seek expression
New concepts, fresh perspectives.

Crude beginnings now take shape
For souls of each become as one
Together now — birthing's done.

Lois Banks

THE WALL

I built this wall because of you
A shiny fortress; brave and strong
From which I look upon a world
That cannot hurt me now.

It keeps me safe. I need its shield.
For you once reached into my heart
And stole from me my very soul
Then walked away unmoved.

You speak, I smile. I'm free of you
You can no longer bring me tears.
Do not reach out and touch my wall
I fear that it may shatter.

Lois Banks

EXTRAORDINARY

The winter is so cold and gray,
The wind blows — and then the next day.

The snow falls so cool and white,
This makes the winter much colder at night.

The rain comes on a cool day
To wash some of the snow away.

The leaves spring up to do a dance,
With the wind, how they make romance.

The sun shines on a clear day,
The wind blows the clouds away.

The birds are up at five to sing,
Now you know that it is Spring!

Gary D. Smith

COMMITMENT

Please God, oh Lord I pray,
That you will help me through each day.

Keep me safe all day long,
Never let me do things wrong.

Watch me and guide me in the night,
Wake me in the morning light.

Guide me safely through the years,
And if I fall hold back my tears —

For I have sinned and that is why,
I know that I must still try.

So I'll stand and walk tall,
Now I know I'll never fall,

For thou art with me and I'll withstand,
All complaints and all demands.

Gary D. Smith

SENTIMENTAL SEDUCTION

Passion man sends trembling sparks
through the body.
The limbs gain strength then weaken.
Lust entraps the soul and mind.

Passion man speaks bold silence;
then shouts pleas of perversion.
Shamed are the experienced enticing the naive.

Passion man consumed by the act
relives his love-making past.
The intensity delights the shy one.
Passion lady murmurs goodbye.

Pamela Rose Downer

ELUSIVE BLISS

At the night's hour of intimacy,
two bodies unite.
An entanglement of heartlessness
and non-existing love,
A likeness of devices which perform
with the perfection of Beethoven,
but play no Fifth Symphony.

Pamela Rose Downer

NATURE'S FORTITUDE

Just a placid desert beneath the sky —
Hardened soil; unfertile.
Clouds appeared,
It began to rain.

The tears of God replenished the earth.
Clouds vanished; the sun understood.
A stem emerged —

A rose was born.

Pamela Rose Downer

IMPERFECTIONS

Survival should not be
taken for granted. We should
remember how delicate and
beautiful a human life can
be. As we constantly seek
a higher level of perfection,
something should rise above
the differences among men.
And that should be a bond
between the less evolved members
of our society and those reaching
down to pull them out of
their world of darkness. Very
sadly, and much too often,
human potential is wasted
because we are blind to
imperfections . . .

Jerry Moskos

BEST FRIENDS

Teresa's nails split open
the pomegranate's curve,
she offers me half,
her cheeks match red flesh
of the fruit.
seeds and laughter spill
from our lips,
we sit at lake's edge
wriggling our toes in cool mud.
she screeches at some
strange larval creature
her toes have uncovered.
we try to run
Teresa gets stuck,
when i pull her
the clay pulls back.
we cling to each other
and sway like cattails,
laughing   at the   sucking sounds
the wet clay makes.

M. D. Williams

A LONG WAY HOME

Cast adrift in a sea of stars,
far from the home I love.
Going from star to star looking
for friendly face.
I have seen suns and stars of
different colors and shapes.
I've been to see a black star
and have come back again.
From here to there it is
a long way home.

I've watched the birth of stars
and the death of others.
But I miss my family and the friends
that I left behind.
It's hard to think of anything
else, except of going home.
But I have to push on, until
I have finished my job.
From here to there it is
a long way home.

Rosanne Hoagland

ROYALTREE

Your majesty, how grand you are in your crown of green
  What wonders have, you could but speak and tell me all you've seen
Within your shade how many'd rest, as they toiled along the way
  Upon your sturdy branches, how many children played?

How many storms you've weathered. How many summers shone
  Birds have nest within your breast and off away have flown
And what say all those carvings upon your toughened face
  How many lovers wandered to your beckoning embrace?

One by one your leaves do fall, and naked there you stand
  Shamelessly awaiting the winter close at hand
And my — but we can wonder of all the wonders there
  How you can be alive, great tree, when all of you is bare!

No I would not bend upon one knee and kneel before a king
The crown he wears, I could not care in such a tritely thing
His grace is but so ordinare, impressed — I would not be
But curtsey me most humbly
  I am bowed before a tree.

Nancy E. Sherman

NANCY ELAINE SHERMAN. Born: Detroit, Michigan, 5-14-57 (I have an identical twin sister, Frances); Single, have traveled extensively throughout the world; Occupation: Antique collector (I grow roses and orchids as a hobby); Comments: *I feel that in everyday life there are encounters of poetic reflection. There is always a great abundance of expression within those who feel deeply. Little whispers of appreciation for the wonders of nature, the great joy in living, sorrow and compassion, a seeking of comfort with ones who have also suffered. My writing is simply those capturings of the sights and emotions that abound in being alive. And that most all of us, in some way, share a poet's heart.*

POETRY, WHAT I LIKE ABOUT IT

One thing I like about poetry is:
Some rhyme, some don't.
Here are other reasons:
Some people give dimes, some won't.
Some people write about sadness and fear;
sometimes the sadness is too much
that you may have tears.
Some people care enough to write about the sick and homeless.
Some people don't even care.
But when you think of it
I hope you will share.
All of this came from my heart,
so please understand
this is all true,
it is not for a marching band.
Some people might say,
Are you crazy?
Have you gone mad?
Are you a stray girl?
Don't feel sad.
But you know what?
I'd rather listen to my heart than listen to them.

Jocelyn Quijano

DREAMS OF AMBITION

The world is full of people with ambition,
People dreaming of seeking their goals.
Some young men dream of becoming a pilot,
Of flying a plane, soaring through the sky
Like a bird, trying to reach the nearest star,
Or dashing right and left, up and down,
Like lightning in a storm.

Some of these men might hope to join the Air Force,
So while in the air, risking their life,
They protect our country's freedom.
Other men might seek to risk their life
As a stunt pilot, doing breath-taking tricks
Flying with ease, and thrilling the audience below.

The world is full of people with ambition,
Some seek their goal, some reach it,
Yet some dreams vanish, fading away into the clouds
Never seen or heard of again.

Ginger Chapman

I HEARD THE WOODS TODAY

I heard the woods today.
  She talked to me softly
    In words only I could hear.
      Gentle rustles, which said,
        "Love me, for this may be your last chance.
        "Look at me! Remember me!"

I heard the woods today.
  Tall, majestic monarchs
    Speaking tenderly of long ago days
      When pleasures were more simply taken.
        The scent of warm wood and sun-glazed leaves,
        Leafy arms reaching toward the sky.

I heard the woods today,
  She brought me a peace I can get nowhere else,
    Whispering softly to my soul,
      Calling me to her warm bosom.
        I went there sick and was healed.
        I went there in sadness, and found joy.

Jonni Bantz

AUTUMN

There's a certain feeling in the air,
  A tang, a special scent that whispers, "Fall."
    A crisper caress to the wind
      As it fingers its way from tree to tree.

There's a new delight to the eye,
  A vision, nature's colors on display,
    A bounty, rich and rewarding,
      A symphony for the soul and mind.

There's a waiting quiet to the world,
  A sense of peace, a final content,
    A knowledge of the eternal cycle,
      And of the renewal soon to come.

Jonni Bantz

THINK CAREFULLY

If you think things are worse
   than the things you think of;
Then the things you think worse of,
   can get as you think them.

So, the worse that you think of things,
   the things you think of will
   become as you think of them.

Then you must not think the worst
   of the things that you think of;
And the things that you think of
   will be allright.

I think?

Rosanne Hoagland

ROSANNE JEANETTE HOAGLAND. Born: Milford, Connecticut, 7-21-56; Education: Graduate, Sacred Heart University, Fairfield, Connecticut, A.A., Creative Writing; Comments: *I'm just starting in the poetry writing field. This is the first time I have had any of my work printed. I don't have a set plan for writing my poetry. I write by whatever inspires me at the moment.*

I see you walk by
I see the gleam in your eye
When you smile for me
I hear words unspoken
Your heart is one with mine
Your mind is your own
We are separate, but one
We are free
Yet never alone
There may be miles between
Of oceans and land
Yet all is forgotten
As you take my hand

Cynthia Landers

When you say ''I love you''
My heart beats
Faster
My insides
Tingle
When you hold me close
My breathing becomes
Shallow
And my knees
Weaken
But when you kiss me
My body melts
And I am yours
So
When you say ''I love you''
Hold me tight
Kiss me and
Let me give myself to you

Cynthia Landers

AS WE LAY

As we lay
   Dawn is gently kissing the earth
   The world is as new
      as a babe at birth

As we lay
   The early warmth of the waking morn
   Paling to the splendor of
      the love we've born

As we lay
   There is no gift greater than
      the ground we lay upon
   And no sight more beautiful
      than that of the dawn

As we lay
   For now and forever
      each day we shall share
   The touch of the sun
      and a love so rare

Cynthia Landers

LAMENT

I hate to shut the draperies on
   The fading light of day;
To feel that loss of sunshine as
   The daylight steals away
And slips across the mountains,
   Dipping slowly 'neath the sea . . .
The night's a velvet beauty, yet
   Old Sol means all to me!

Richard Alan Rieger

FROM THERE TO HERE

Onto the round stone I was thrown
from darkness into the light
By choice or divine mold
I do not know
But I crossed the open door

Onto the round stone I was thrown
by the fellow of fateful fate
A one in a billion chance
Or maybe more
On that evening of being born

Onto the round stone I was thrown
Promised not only to suffer
But to work for what is better
in biting cold
While avoiding the double-edged sword

Onto the round stone I was thrown
and the world was not meant to be fair
What is fair is that I got there
A chance for a life
I ask for nothing more

David W. Konow

THAT CERTAIN SMILE

It came through again yesterday
And as always, ever shines.
Your smile, one of the greatest
Treasures that a man can find.

For when you smile you become
Such a wondrous gal to see.
'Tis a very lovely, joyous glow
Present, 'specially then to me.

The warmth within your laughter,
A sparkle in your eyes.
Creating one as beautiful
As you, the Lord was wise.

If the day should come when I regret
All the bad times that I've known,
Thanks to your love, I can recall
Riches that are mine alone.

Richard Novak

TWILIGHT

In the west the fiery ball
Called the sun has set, and all
Nature sinks to quiet rest.
Time of day we love the best.
In the east the moon rides high,
Lighting up both earth and sky.
Whippoorwill calls from afar.
O'er the mountaintops a star
Twinkles with a friendly light,
Keeping tryst with me tonight.

Mary Hoffman

ACCIDENT PRONE

Accident prone?
That's one way to put it, I guess.
Bad luck, you ask? Well, what can I say?
There's only one answer . . . Yes!
Last night, for instance, a party was held
and I did *so* want things to go right.
I wanted to impress with my charm and my wit,
and, I tried very hard all night.
Is it too much to ask, just one good day?
Nothing bad from dawn to dusk?
Instead of the way mine usually go,
accidents, mishaps and such!
But, at last it was over. I turned to leave,
and much to my chagrin,
I'm standing too close to the side of the door,
OOPS! . . . poor nose . . . you're in the way again.
I wanted to make an impression, oh yes!
And as the saying goes —
the *Lasting Impression* that was made last night,
was made . . . by the door on my nose!

Carolyn J. Carruth

SINCE I'VE KNOWN YOU

Here's a poem for the pretty girl I hope to always see
When you wear jewelry or make-up,
   it just distracts from your own natural beauty
You have taken looking good to a new high, a new degree
You might not think so, but that's the way you appear to me

The time I spent getting to know you seemed short
In that time, I could see that you're the type
   to show a lot of support
But in that time, the time seemed very well spent
'Cause in my imagination, girl, you put one hell of a dent

These are some words for a girl who is awfully nice to know
Since I've known you
I just wrote this to say *Hi Denise, hello*
Since I've known you

I really hope you like these words I have written with my pen
'Cause in knowing you, girl, I know I'll never match
   the beauty of it ever again
You're on my mind quite a bit during the day, until the night
And you're in my dreams a lot, when there is no light

Try to always keep alive that pretty smile, one I couldn't ignore
Very few smiles like that I have ever seen before
You're a very fine example of the saying that the best gifts are small
To have known you for a little while, is sure better than never
   to have known you at all.

M. R. C.

STILL-QUIET TIME

I sit and listen to the morning as it passes by.
Only the gentle whisper of the wind reaches my ears.
The soft light of a day just born touches my eyes
   and I am awed at such morning beauty.
The grey clouds, they drift easily.
The soft song of a bird touches my heart, softens my soul.
Tranquil dawn, you have brought peace again.
Such wonder does touch my eye, softens my soul in the gentle
   morning hours.

Clifton Jackson

SPRINGTIME

When springtime comes around each year,
   And trees are full of buds,
With April showers in the air,
   And flowers all abloom,
Limbs suddenly no longer bare,
   Blue skies, green grass, we all assume.
Children playing everywhere,
   Hats no longer on their hair,
With puppies running along beside them,
   Nipping at little girls' hems.
Happy cries
   And laughing eyes,
Each busy with his game.
   Then mothers calling their child's name.
Come home, dear child,
   The weather's mild,
But now the day is done.
   Tomorrow is another day,
For you to have more fun.

Nancy J. Grenier

REFLECTIONS

Midnight calls to a destiny clear.
Father brings me home.
Sunlight pauses as an owl calls.
I see her face in my eyes.
Winter is as summer does, dear heart, and all our actions
like the ripples on a pond will affect us later in life.
Past actions like a ghost will haunt us.
Life you see is a circle.

Clifton Jackson

FAITH

I believe in miracles.
I believe in people who believe in themselves.
The people who hear, you can't but say, I can.
I believe in the people who have the faith to persevere.
The people who pursue their dreams.
I have faith in God, who will give us the strength and the
vision to reach for the stars and make our dreams come
true, as long as we believe in ourselves.

Clifton Jackson

Look for solid things, like window stains.
Granite towers in the sky's own blue.
The man said, ''Over all of this I flew.''
I sat holding on with all my nerve, feeling our earth's pulse.
Let me feel the heavings and help to caress away the throbbing.
''Whyfor, wherefor,'' the caretaker cries.
''Who poked out the hummingbird's eyes?''

Mary Jane Burgess

A moment of silent laughter,
As our eyes meet across a room,
Thoughts interwoven
Like threads on a loom.

Evenings of talking,
What was it we said?
Fuel for the fire;
The flames of love well fed.

A soft, gentle touch;
Whispers in the dark,
Many are the ways of loving you,
Many the ways of my heart.

Penelope M. Towle

I looked in your eyes
And knew we had met
In centuries gone by
In futures not yet.

Eternities passed
As I looked in your eyes
And the world fell away
Before lightning skies.

The know continues
For me and for you
Always fresh;
Constantly new.

For you are my lover,
My child, my friend;
You are a beginning
That has no end.

Penelope M. Towle

Where is the love
I promised myself
When I was just a child:

The magical prince
Who would come along
And carry me off in style?

Who wove his way
Into all the dreams
Which filled my head in the night,

It all seems
Oh, so hopeless now
With no one yet in sight.

Penelope M. Towle

THE WATCH

Hurtling, unyielding
empty of compassion
a river of hope
never conceiving

The faces fade
and streak away
left behind no one
is saved and yet

Continuous peace
in the wreckage of change
unlooked for
eyes, blind and knowing

The sorrow returns
again and again
no thought is offered
no bargain struck

Sightless, heartless
prejudice denied
resisted without odds
hold the weight of eternity

James R. Greenfield

TRINITY

The tie that binds
brings more than two
searching, seeing
disbelieving

Closer than touch
pain at the distance
hoping, loving
dreaming

A life of doubt
unrealized guilt
spectral deeds
promises unspoken

James R. Greenfield

DEATH DOESN'T WAIT

Written the day my father died.

Death rode a swifter horse than I
It flew along while I
With heavy heart and dragging feet
Went through the night wind fast
When I reached him at last
To do the things that only love can do
To make his passing easier
Death had swooped down and took him
And left an empty place.
Oh, had I traveled faster
Oh, had I reached him sooner
Oh, father dear, isn't it queer
That winter should come
And you are not here?

Violet Simon

RAZORBACK

Running the edge — RazorBack.
Running so fast, the blade goes on forever.
No balance, just those forces beyond control,
some pushing, some pulling.
RazorBack — so sharp.
Stop and you fall,
cutting your soul free.
But can you survive the pain?
Running the edge — RazorBack.
Surreal nights, endless days in the burning sun.
The twilight of reality.
Where the impossible tries your sanity.
No right, no wrong.
Just survival.
Dreams are a joke.
Nightmares the norm.
And it just goes on and on.
Running the edge,
running so fast — RazorBack.
So this is insanity.

Dave Wheaton

SEE OTTER?

Furry clown in sunlit sea,
  he floats upon his back
Drifting, as quite lazily
  he dines upon a snack —
Hapless fish or ab'lone,
  to catch them is his knack.
Quite a guy this otter, see?
Oops! See ya later, Jack!

Richard Alan Rieger

BEATRICE

Beside the sea whose ruthless energy
Endlessly spends itself in crushing might
Against the shore, to break in battered white,
Then foams again in tireless majesty:

Remember, dear, a dream of ecstasy
In which we knew short hours of sweet delight,
Caring naught but for the spell of night,
Ensnared, yet never wishing to be free.

Disconsolate, alone, in psychic pain,
I wander there tonight in memory,
Vainly seeking peace beside that shore
I used to roam with you, and would again;
Ne'er daring hope, though longing constantly,
Another time to know like times before.

J. Eugene Blair

WASHROOM ATTENDANT

For years he has been a washroom attendant,
Diligently refining and perfecting the art
Of how to hand towels to rich men with wet hands,
And opening stall doors as rich men depart.

He has labored and pondered and experimented,
Assiduous as an alchemist of old,
Mixing tap water in different proportions
Until it flows just right — not too hot or cold.

While poets waste ink on descriptions of lovers
And priests ponder whether men have cause for hope
And dumbfounded pedants make metaphysical blunders,
He queries, ''Could the soap dispensers be out of soap?''

His shoes shine bright as the washroom mirrors,
His jacket's as white as a clean, folded towel,
He wears on his pocket a label saying ''Luther,''
His face shows the profundity of an owl's.

And when his shift ends in the morning at two,
He leaves the washroom with the trace of a smirk,
He thinks, as the janitor commences the washing
Of toilets: Good God! Such menial work!

John Mumma

GOOD-BYE

It's hard for me to say goodbye. But through this poem
I'm going to try.
The wealth I found in each of you, helped me find a life
anew.
It doesn't seem that thanks enough. What we went
through was really rough.
We shared our thoughts and feelings so deep. We sought,
we searched, our memories to keep.
To me you mean an awful lot. A warm feeling of love is
what I got.
I will never forget what we have shared. I will never
forget how much you cared.
You're special to me, what can I say. I plan to return and
visit some day.
I write these words from deep within. To all of you,
you're my best friend.
I will feel a loss when I depart. But I shall hold you
always within my heart.
So, I shall go, but forget you not. I want you all to
remember I love you a lot.

Larry Boatman

TO SYLVIA

When I was young, the earth seemed old, for the leaves would brown,
wither, and as snow fall to the ground.
In a while Spring appeared and helped me grow unaware I was
growing old.
In pain we suffer defeat. Sorrow forces our attention within
and we look for our guide of tomorrow.
Hope eases our defeat.
My sun-gold darling with the sky-blue eyes,
you are loved, yet you've seen the evening.
We will ride out this storm,
ocean crests will hide our wake.

Mary Jane Burgess

SOMEONE WHO CARES

We sat at tables and spilled our guts. Most of the
people think we are nuts.
Our way of life they can't understand. To give up
our will, and put it all in God's hand.
We stand in a circle heads bowed, what type of life do
they offer, that draws such a crowd?
They will take you in, hungry or broke. They'll prop
you up, give love, strength, wisdom and hope.
They say they're not perfect and never will be. But they
are so alive, so honest, so free.
Far and wide you need only look, page after page of
stories, just like mine or yours, make up the big book.
If you're feeling low or just need a friend, walk through
their door, you'll be met with a grin.
It's just like a family, lots of love to share. Just
walk through that door, you'll find that they care.
A desire to stop drinking, that's all that they ask. It
matters not how big or small the task.
Where do you find this? Most truly where, they call it
AA, unselfish, free of charge, and they care.

Larry Boatman

HANDS OF CHINATOWN

Gnarled knots wringing the crying change purse
Twisted knuckles straining the way between calloused fingertips
and chapped palms
Bubbling veins streaming down the backs of survival-hardened
washboard hands
   (Woman in line for a pay toilet, Pier 39)

Thumb and fingers snapping at the chrome bar like Aesop's crow,
greedy for precious cheese
The beaklike appendage turning from pink to yellow
to pale olive
As Bus #30 climbs Grant Avenue from dockside to her
hungry home
   (Woman carrying seafood wrapped in newspaper, Bus #30)

Long spindles getting mixed up with his knitting needles
Bonded wrists and narrow palms folding inward like
lotus leaves
Stamens of sallow uncooked lomein noodles
in a flurry
Bearing a bloom of yellow yarn
   (Man knitting on bus, Columbus Avenue)

Allison Barlow

POETASTER

How tough it is seeking fresh thoughts to write,
Baring one's self to endless love and hate,
Tempering combinations wrong and right
Metered beats falling too soon or too late.

I'm no study of those masters and bards
Exalted in homes, libraries, and schools.
My poems are born in bedrooms and backyards
Where Truth, not meter, is the style that rules.

I can only write of life that I know,
Penning emotions we each feel and share,
Taking my cues from life's endless sideshow,
Venturing to write what most hearts don't dare.

Bruce Miles

TREASURES

In land of plenty
With abundance great,
I gathered treasures;
I barely could wait.

A house and two cars
And some acreage green;
A cottage and yacht;
A young man's great dream.

A satellite dish;
A large TV screen;
A computer set,
The best to be seen.

One day the truth came:
The treasures I owned,
Belonged to the bank
From where I did loan.

In land of plenty
With abundance great,
I owned no treasures
because I couldn't wait.

Caroline Janz

ELDERLY PLIGHT

Aged with days,
Aged with years,
Wisdom, strength,
Why these tears?

Hair now grey,
Pace grown slow,
Life full spent,
Heads bent low.

Sight is dim,
Hearing lost,
Who will pay
Health Care cost?

Prices rise,
Pension fixed,
Rent soars high,
Mind is vexed.

Love grown cold
For the old,
Mocked and scorned,
Long foretold.

Caroline Janz

I see your hair, shimmering
Among green grass
Like sparkling waves catching the breeze
Beyond the sun.
And in the motionless silence
I see the surface of time
I hear light
I hear you.

Sandra Fox

Hurtling down the mountain
Proclaiming freedom from winter's grasp
A stream issues its press release;
The coming of a new season.

Waking, the world revises
Its wintry colors from brown to green;
The earth's changing its story line
To a spring-softened theme.

In the warmth of spring's dawn
The wakening bears, the fledgling birds
Punctuate the air with sounds of life
Editing the birth of spring.

Sandra Fox

I walked surefooted on the hill
through clover, grass and daffodil,
and as I moved through where they grew
I heard a far-off gentle moo
and wondered how we ever came
to hate and fight and play this game.

To no one had I been so near
in heart and mind than you, my dear.

The love we shared had been so strong
we thought it never could go wrong,
but now it has and I can't seem
to find my hope.

I've lost my dream.

If hope is dead, I should be too.

Our love is gone, my life is through.

Barbara R. Duva

GROWING UP GOY

The neighbors fight a lot.
No one knows why;
Well, I don't.
They yell about everything.
I listen from my window
Until I'm late for Bible class.
My mother tells me I'll go to hell
For being nosey
But she can't show me
Where Christ said so;
And when I leave she sits down
By the window and sighs.
They're better than the radio soaps
Except on Saturdays
  (Their Sabbath)
When they call a truce.

Lynne A. Wilkins

TEARS IN THE SHOWER

No one notices if you cry in the shower
With a radio on
Your tears can mix with a D.J.'s drone
During the Morning Show.
While you shower
No one hears tears running down the drain
So you pour out fears and regrets
Into streams of hot water
And soap suds
Hopeful that it will get better
Before the hot water runs out.

Lynne A. Wilkins

STILLBORN

Innocence
white swirls of
tiny
falling flake

leaving
pale blue heavens
racing skyways
home to earth.

Amassed
by wind and storm
to bank and drift
along concrete streams

muddied
by
earth-smudged
scars of living.

In my hand
a single pattern
caught too soon.
DOA

Stephanie Conder

WINTER'S A-COMING

I heard the honk of the first old goose
I felt the changing breeze
I saw the cloud of the eager flock
As it soared over the apple trees

In my child's mind I flew along
Going places of my dream
We stopped a while in a shaded glen
To dip in a wooded stream

"Wait for me my feathered friends
Carry me through the breeze"
But they felt the call of the warm deep south
The land of magnolia trees

Mabel Cummings Douglass

THE SEVEN ATTRIBUTES OF RUM

Sometimes life could be so fun,
but my brown bottles weigh a ton!

There will never be a time,
when I don't say, "Got a dime?"

Some men can drink a wine so fine.
Double-time down the hatch go mine.

People know I don't play dumb.
They all know I'm just a bum.

Fifty carloads, not a case.
For more and more, I'll always chase.

Under a bridge in wintertime,
nevermore knowing warmth sublime.

Well, seems the bottle won hands down,
and soon I'll be resting underground.

Victoria Leigh Harlow-Emmons

CRADLED PEARL

On a rose petal pillow,
Rests a shimmering drop of rain,
Like a cradled pearl.

A reflection is mirrored,
In the prism of nature,
The tranquil tiny pond . . .

The dewy stem,
Is plucked by a hand,
And the pond . . .
                becomes a shower.

Lee Schweger

There is a young artist named Marni Renee
Whose viewpoint is farthest from social mainstay
Her keen eyed perception
Scans every direction
Then weeds out those hustlers with blarney decay.

Kevin John Cummins

FLOWERS FOR YOU

Daisies I would give to you, bright yellow, deep rich brown;
To see a smile upon your face, to chase away a frown;
Chrysanthemums are better yet, to brighten up your day;
I set them here for all to see this colorful array.
Poinsettia you may well enjoy, a deep rich red you see;
They whisper softly in my ear, the love you have for me;
Edelweiss I could always choose, a flower full of soul;
A guiding light when all is lost, to fill an empty hole.
Orchids, I am positive, through all they will endure,
To symbolize an endless love, so simple and so pure.
Tulips yet, may better suit, how I feel for you,
A sign of deep devoted love, not so often but so true.
However, roses most of all, I give with all my heart;
To give you flowers is not enough, but the only way to start.

Mark Ashley

NO MORE

Anger rises swiftly
  Vengeance takes its tour
Lightning flashes through the sky
  The breeze whispers — no more

Arrows come to apex
  Great white birds will soar
To all concerned the greatest lie
  The wind says — no more

A great white blaze of folly
  Brilliant to the core
A thousand voices seem to sigh
  The gale screams, the people cry —
            NO MORE, no more

Mark Ashley

NATURE'S LAW

It's nearing dusk, the sea has calmed in preparation for the storm
        to come.
The surfers have gone home, a good day's fun.
But now the ocean's mellow warning beckons us beware
For soon the sky will turn its coat to grey
And westward winds in full array will plunge the ocean depths;
A challenge, once again a test.

Protecting its domain the sea in anger must respond.
The battle may be long but in the end the waters will defend;
It's nature's law.
The sea will crush the storm against the shore.

A silence now.
"Go home, frail one" is echoed in the wind.
"Go home, I'm waiting to begin."

And yes, I guess it's time to go.
No need to watch the battle's end;
It's nature's law.
Invader crushed, defender shaken yet the balance stands.
A pity justice such as this is seldom witnessed man to man.

Betty W. Hervé

DUST

The old do not disturb their houses settling in as they sit,
We count the respirations, we feel the pulse,
They wait, afraid, and there are none who comfort.
Who has been old and then young and old again?
The old must be translated for they are complicated and seldom
        listened to.
Bewildered in their pain they lay and slowly drift away —
We look for them and wonder why they ceased to stay.
They once worked hard for the crust they shared.
Muscles knotted and cramped and now they stare
    as dusk meets the dark of the evening damp.
Beware of being so young that upon becoming old
You are taken by surprise.

Mary Jane Burgess

DEATH

There's a bright star over the meadow
There's a deepening wane of the moon
There's a wilderness cry in the far-away
Coldness comes too soon
Where are those who have loved me
Dressed me in raiment bright
Don't ever dare to know me
I'm an illusion; an illusive light
I am wafted away in the shadows
I am carried on wings so sprite
I'll wait 'til I hear your footsteps
When darkness sweeps out the light

Mabel Cummings Douglass

OCOTILLO

Pirouetting
    on
        its
Slender stems
    to
        the
Rhythm of the wind.

Fingers
    of
Electric red blossoms

Warmed
    by
        the
Sun and spawned
    by
        the
Rain.

A desert bouquet
    in
        a
Cactus cradle!

Maggie Ramsay

GUIDANCE

Help me, O God, I pray
Make this a sinless
Day
Help me do all things
Right
Guided by thy forceful
Might
Help me to curb my
Tongue
Before the final bell
Is rung
And when I face
The call of death
When I have drawn
My final breath
I'll partake of
Eternal rest
And hope, O God, I've
Passed your test

Lawrence E. Hays

A LESSON OF A FLOWER

A flower gently plucked
    is beautiful to see
But, alas, it will wither
    and be no use to me.
So there in my hand it
    lay all forlorn,
Yet little I knew of the
    savour that's born . . .
When it's broken and crushed;
    for a fragrance it brings
That permeates the room
    and every other thing.

And so is my life
    down on this earth
All broken and crushed
    and lacking in mirth.
But God up in heaven
    with His loving concern
Can make my life beautiful,
    this — I must learn;
So others might smell His
    sweet fragrance of love,
And glorify Christ
    our Savior above.

Marcia Berger

SAVIOR

Mentally unstable due to lack of rhythm
Blindsided by fatal diseases
Jesus suffers for the world
But who suffers for Jesus?
All my long distance traveling
Leads me to circle around and find
That it's important to be gentle
It's important to be kind.
So I shall take the nails out of His hands
I shall take the nails out of His feet
I shall lay Him down on the cold, wet ground
And leave Him there with no one around
But that's all right, yes that's all right
'Cause Jesus Christ can rest tonight
With nothing on His mind

Steven McGill

FOR KAREN

Busy nurses go running down the hallways
Minds busy, gotta think of something quick
Where do we turn, who do we trust
What do we do when the doctor is sick?
Children wail in agony at night in their beds
"Oh mommy mommy what is there to do?
All my life has turned to heartbreak
All my nightmares have come true."
Voices emanate from distant shadows
Say "Let the light come shine on you
All is love, love is all
Watch your sorrows fade from view."
I'll always remember Children's Hospital
I'll always remember Karen too

Steven McGill

A FEELING I GET WHEN FLOWERS ARE GROWING

A feeling I get when flowers are growing
A crash of waves upon the rocks
Is it enough to keep the river from flowing?
Teardrops falling on a musical box
Thoughts that come from another world
Faces lost in concentration
Awaiting the moment of unclenched fists
Awaiting the moment of utter elation
Letting go oneself despite all the tension
Getting closer and closer without even knowing
Creating illusion, another dimension
A feeling I get when flowers are growing
Quiet, reflective, releasing the power
Man unfolds as does the flower

Steven McGill

FECUND WITH LOVE

As sobs softly sever the silence of night —
    I, travail in tears — body riven by fright,
Aborting past wounds, so the mind will mend —
    Love yearns to impregnate my heart again.

Venus Peek

BRIDLE THE NEGATIVE

"It's Wisdom" before you speak —
    To pause for time to pray,
So caring, comforting words will flow —
    To brighten someone's day.

For critical, cutting words —
    Can sever a "Loving Heart,"
Then love flees, emptiness sets in —
    Life's meaning also departs.

Words can heal, or words can kill —
    It matters what you say,
"It's Wisdom" before you speak —
    To pause for time to pray.

Venus Peek

WENDY'S

To work at Wendy's
isn't much fun

Because you work one
hour on the run

Then you are sent home
because it's so slow

With a paycheck that
is worth very little to
blow.

Elaine D. Barber

IF I WERE AN EAGLE

If I were an eagle I'd soar above the mountains, fly through the
    valleys, glide across the sea.
I'd climb and fall and turn with the wind.
I'd circle creation again and again.
And then in the eve when nature is still
I'd rest in content on some faraway hill.

In spring I would sing of the life of the land;
Cows grazing in the pasture, children playing in the sand.
Summer would bring the warmth of affection
So dancing through sunlight I'd pause in reflection of love.
The colors of fall I'd love most of all,
And surely I'd fly from the east to the west a hundred times o'er
    if I could without rest.
Then winter would bring a glistering white,
And amazed at the sight I'd gather my feathers for warmth in the
    weather and fly without fear.
And then a new year and before very long I'd be singing a song for
    the spring.

Yes, if I were an eagle I'd fly and I'd laugh
    and I'd dance and I'd sing . . .
And I'd probably wonder while grooming my wings
Why man hasn't mastered such beautiful things.

Betty W. Hervé

BETTY WIGHT HERVÉ. Born: Boston, Massachusetts, 2-3-52; Married:
Philip A. Hervé; Education: University of Connecticut, B.S., Nursing, 1974;
Occupations: Registered Nurse, Mother of two little boys; Poetry: 'Nature's
Law,' 'If I Were an Eagle,' 1976; 'A Place in the Sun,' 1982; Comments: *I
see the beauty in nature and the pain in mankind. My writing reflects my
struggle with pain and my drive to become as happy, self-fulfilled, and con-
tent as I can in this life. I wish life were more fair and people were less
cruel to each other.*

EGO

What is this animal man seeks in vain the horrible
Culprit by which Satan shall be slain, a hideous
Creature that lies on every plain, seeking individuals
Who want to acquire fame. It is because of this
Creature that man decided to go on his own, turning
Away from Jesus, leaving his eternal home.
To roam in the desert of stress and pain, until if ever
He decides to go home again.

Man created pagan gods to dwell in their lust. So
Corrupt was this cycle that babes were taken from bust,
To satisfy the hunger of the mighty hunter's lust. Through
Him were signs developed, and to them the people gave
Their trust.

It would be so simple if in God we truly trust, to
Glorify and worship Him from the dawn unto dusk.

Australia W. Banks

THE GOOD OLE DAYS

What ever happened to Gertie Klepner?
    linoleum kitchen
    cozy fragrance of fresh rolls, real butter, gefilte fish?
Mrs. Klepner, Flour Queen of Maple Ave.
    in a Bamberger robe
    a *real* mother
Saturday, and "Let's Pretend"
Let's pretend we never heard of
    saddle shoes and bobby sox
Dad's school ring on a chain 'cause I didn't have a steady
Those days when a Sloppy Joe was a sweater
When a Peter Pan was a collar on a dickey
When a dickey was a false front we wore to
    the socials in the rumpus room
Girls on one side — boys on the other
Spin the Bottle 'til we played Post Office
Post Office was the bathroom
    dark and close
Braces on my teeth
    fear of chapped lips, strange tongues
    sweaty hands and trying not to giggle
It seems like only yesterday when Helen Trent wondered,
    "Can life begin at forty?"
And now I know . . .

Marcia Marx

QUEST

When summer's song retreats
    And vital streams begin to ebb;
When worried wings glide down the dome
    Their goal to find a kinder home;

When night advances on the day
    Making longer bolder strokes,
Encircling the vale and shrouding the hill
    In a glittering boreal chill;

And summer's smoke unwinds
    And hides in cooler skies
When August's embers throb into the night
    And fade to ashes feather white . . .
Then is the time to fly or stay:
    To follow summer down the sky
Or walk among the fallen leaves
    Where every heart the truth perceives.

And taste of all that autumn weaves.

John A. Geller

THE HATCHING

Little by little a fissure as fine as a young girl's hair
Cracks the smoothness of the shell
And in its infancy the small brown puff
Becomes vulnerable to the world.
It stands quivering on new legs
But grows stronger with each day
Until it tires of walking and dares to fly.

Jill M. Brininger

THE SPROUTING OF MARY C.

What a joy it is
that slams me to the wall
to come upon you, Mary, sunbathing,
still dripping from your shower.
(For a second you took me
back to the old skid road
that cracks the forest open —
I found red newts there,
lying in the sun.)
What a joy to see you
a snake in air afire
content to let the blood burn,
a fern, too,
coolly hugging the moist earth,
root and fiber storing sunpower,
p   o   etic
photosynthetic
green again.

Eric Barker

BEING HUMAN

Great on the outside
Churning on the inside.

What did I do wrong?
Did I do it right?
Did I hurt someone's feelings?
Why can't I do it right?
Why can't I keep my big mouth shut?
Why am I so stupid?
Am I going to get yelled at?
Am I pretty?
Am I ever going to be happy?
Am I a healthy person?
How can I get this done?

The hardest thing about being human
Is forgiving yourself
For being human in the first place.

Rosann Claeys

Keep the ship afloat.
Keep the fire burning.
Keep the fear remote.
Keep the passion yearning.

Don't pull down the shade.
Don't turn out the light.
Don't miss the parade.
Don't give up the fight.

Keep intact your drive.
Keep avoiding foes.
Keep yourself alive.
Keep passing open windows.

Ann de Schweinitz

ANIMALS

Animals are beautiful people too
They need love and attention just
as much as we do.

A pet can bring laughter and joy
when you're feeling down

Especially when they act like such
little clowns

You can't help but laugh when they
act so funny

Especially when your day at work went
just like a Monday

Pets are always fun to come home to
They love you no matter what you do

Treat your pet kindly with love and
respect

Because animals are beautiful people too.

Elaine D. Barber

WE WERE ONE

Tears in our parting, we go
our own ways.
  Alone once again, alone.
  We once were so happy to-
gether as one,
  But so far apart we have grown.
  Two different people, no
longer in love
  As we once were a long
time ago.
  Now we are leaving 'cause
we stopped believing
  Our love would ever grow.
  Empty hearts searching for
a new love to fill
  The void from our drifting
apart.
  Once we were one, but now
we're alone
  With two equally broken
hearts.

Debbie Michael

SUMMER SHOWERS

O!
How welcome
Is
Thy succor —
Showers
For
A thirsty earth!

Skirts of rain
Like
Sweeping mantle;

Refreshing summer days
Of
Dearth.

Loran Allen

IN DUE SEASON

A worm
     must
              turn
     and
crawl
              and
     squirm
and

              then
          in capsule
         seem
           to
          die
        before
          its
         flight
          as
      butterfly.

Loran Allen

GETTYSBURG, JULY, 1863

Blue and Gray — O, Blue and Gray —
Sweet love of life beat strong that day
When Johnny Reb and a Yankee boy
     Met
On Little Round Top.

Blue and Gray — O, Blue and Gray —
How red the blood that flowed that day
When Johnny Reb and a Yankee boy
     Fought
On Little Round Top.

Blue and Gray — O, Blue and Gray —
Sad, sad mournful day —
Dreadful — memory won't go away —
When Johnny Reb and a Yankee boy
     Fell
On Little Round Top.

Loran Allen

VAIN AUTHORITY

War and strife, to take a life
of a youth in Asia;
Still a sin for euthanasia.

Take a knife, to the battered wife
faux pas, blah blah;
But never euthanasia.

The cat has pain, kill without shame
such misplaced vainglory;
Is euthanasia as gory?

Are we insane, to punish the claim
of a loved one who did comply?
Euthanasia is not to simplify;
Euthanasia allows one to die.

Carolyn Pikula Gallagher

Cypress-Swamp.

QUID PRO QUO

Foremost and so forth
we rush on today;
Quid Pro Quo
with the words that we say.

Counterpoint while out of joint,
Simply being the case in point.

Forestall and Henceforth
we smile then betray;
Profess to bestow
while looking for prey.

Counterpoint while out of joint,
Simply being the case in point.

Forebode and so forth
we make it risqué;
Quid Pro Quo
with a doomsday touché.

Carolyn Pikula Gallagher

A POET

We all experience things
We all feel things
We all know things
But these things are hidden from us
Until some seeing person
Selects the right set of words
To tell us
What we have known
Ever so long
And had no knowledge of.
That person who
Does that service
Is a
Poet.

Rupert Hawkins

The leader is a dealer
'cause he strikes a deal
with the people whom he is to lead.
So that they support his need.
And he be called to lead.
And when he does lead.
He squares his deal.
To fulfill the dealer's greed.
And fills his creed.
In the positions of need.
When people cry their need.
He fails to heed.

Ramesh C. Shah

THE GREEN, GREEN GRASS

*Lalang is a very coarse grass
(suitable for cows)
that grows in Malaysia.*

Luxuriant lalang, fibrous grasses
like a coarse mat upon the ground,
Perhaps concealing the bones of
past treachery,
Time's many dispensations
clothed in green now,
very quiet and forgotten; bones
dissolving gently, peacefully
beneath still, muffling grass,
or maybe, the present scene
remains purely innocent
and at rest.

Christopher G. Jesudason

TIME TO BEGIN

Lying in bed at night
Falling into sight
Are all the girls lost and never won
Not a one.
Believing all the worst
Thinking virginity's a curse.
Is it true
That society controls you?

A lost and lonely soldier on a road
Carrying his dead friend's load.
Does he have time to think of death
As he catches his breath?

A deaf farmer stands in a field all dry
Dust flying in his eye.
Does he hear the ringing in his ears
Borne all these years?

You look away
When you should turn and stay.
For there is nowhere to run
When you're melting into the sun.

Paul Eldreth

COMES AND GOES

I have a slumbering intelligence
    in a dark and obscure place
deep within the recess of my mind
    Sometimes it bursts into
a million fireflies, and even I am
    dazzled by its shine

Sometimes it's mesmerized by a
    lazy transfixed mood
Content to lie idle, without care
    Till I am beset with problems
that have to be solved, And I scream out
    Wake up now, if you dare

Santina Hartung

ON CIGARETTES

Some think it's real cool,
smokin' and puffin' on cigarettes.
Breathin' in and out like fools,
the big "C" is all you'll get.

Burnin' the lungs away,
fillin' stale smoke in the air.
What a high price you will pay,
it's not stated in Medicare.

Lighting one right after another,
the dangers this will do.
It will make your heart flutter,
then hit, then your life is through.

All the doctors say,
Stop smokin' before it's too late.
Throw those cigarettes away,
watch food have such a better taste.

Some say "oh I can quit,"
but then they don't even try.
It's only a bad habit,
and no good for you, that's why.

Bert M. Swanson

BERT M. SWANSON. Born: Chicago, Illinois, 12-8-33; Married: Jean Madolyn Swanson; Education: Lane Tech, Elmhurst, 1951-1953; Occupation: Tax examiner; Memberships: B.M.I., AFSCME; Honorable mentions for: 'Fishing Story,' 1986; 'Love,' 1986; 'Smile,' 1987; Poetry: 'The Fishing Story,' 'Love,' *Quill Books,* 1986; 'Smile,' 1987; Other Writings: "Love Can Say Hello," "The Hills Of Carolina," songs, *Hitsource,* 1987; Comments: *I believe that by writing and composing I express my inner feelings. I acknowledge that all that is within me, and all that I give, is first given to me by a higher power — one whom I believe is helping me create and do. I believe with the Lord's help all is possible and can be done.*

MOTH WINGS

I am compelled to the center of my burning
To flee my own ashes
And rise to eagle edges,
Turning the corners of the sun.

It is the seventh day and I am risen
Beyond any beneath but the sky.
This,
This is my strong song.

Claire Burns Miller

GLANCES

A chance for romance,
A verse to converse,
When looking for romance,
This is definitely the place to glance.

Guys and gals are entering apart,
Waiting for a come-on to start,
Guys circling like sharks waiting to feed,
Gals showing interest and the intimacy need.

If someone throws you a glance and makes an advance,
Asking you to talk or to dance,
Try really giving them a chance,
You really never know in the game of romance.

I'll give you another chance,
But this is absolutely the last glance,
If your pretty eyes don't signal me soon,
I'll be history to you by the very next tune.

With a wink or a glance I'll take my chances,
On meeting fun, sexy people wanting dances,
So for romance or just fun,
Try a sultry glance — it makes my motor run.

Daryl T. Olson

HOPE

Where is the kindness?
Where is the grace?
Where is the light that she saw in his face?

The hopeful nights, explosive fights,
the fear, disgust, the deadened walls.

The cracks through which warm rays
danced through jagged edges,
melting worn, torn hearts.
Another try — why?
They began again as if their lives
depended on it.

Quiet, lilting laughter like gossamer threads
floated out like unattached hope between the two,
back and forth,
back and forth . . .

Where is the kindness?
Where is the grace?
Where is the light that he saw in her face?

Clo Wilson

FREEDOM

Bubbling streams, slaves to the rivers
Shining sun, slave to day
A moon so bright, slave to night
And I, slave to life
How I wish to have my freedom
To come and go as the breeze
Oh, how I distrust just lingering on like the seas
But, alas I shall linger
And alas, I shall never be free
Until my dying day, when this life my Lord extracts from me.

Quanda Dawnyell Johnson

UPON THE THOUGHT OF RACIAL PREJUDICE

The sorrow in my heart will it tear me apart,
Delivering my soul into vanity destroying my
Mortal heart?
It is the result of pigmentation an end result
Of the Lord's creation that I must suffer a
Pseudo cross.

Must I suffer the grief in tears for the past
Several hundred years?
I am guilty without a trial, no courtroom judgement,
To receive shall I.

It's hereditary they say, for along with the pigment
Comes much dirt.

Jesus the tears I cried, when will thou wipe from
My swollen eyes?
For the Lord shall judge my character and in Him
I shall abide.

Australia W. Banks

THE CREATURE I AM

I am a man who has the highest thoughts of himself.
To myself I am strong, graceful, full of nature, vigor,
Valor and might.
I don't care what other men think I am or who I should
Be, for I see all the glory and wonder that God bestowed
On me.
Though I am sometime boastful, but I am still no fool,
For God is my Savior, and I am His tool.
I am not even worthy to sit upon the mucous He would spew
Upon the ground,
For it is too divine, for such blood as mine.

Australia W. Banks

AUSTRALIA WILFORD BANKS. Pen Name: Oskar; Born: Forrest City, Arkansas, 3-11-60; Married: Ellen, 5-8-83; Education: University of Arkansas, Pine Bluff, B.S., 1983; Occupation: Soil conservationist; Themes: *Man's spiritual and carnal aspirations in relationship to God.*

SOMETHING BEAUTIFULLY UGLY

Here glint two warm wet sparks
within the poke-faced skull
worry line and lip curled careless
on ski run nose
triangle ears and chicken-breasted torso
ride on stumpy feet and bench-legged axles . . .
tail a maestro's baton on a long, thin arm
carrier of wit, caprice and ridicule
. . . dachshund!

Kay Stewart

THIS LONG NIGHT

The world will swallow me
Or shun me.
People will save me
Or destroy me.
Can family sanctify me,
Or will I wince
At the final twist of the knife?
Friends will walk away
Without another glance;
One may linger.
She smiles, now;
She knows.
You reach for my hand
In the darkness
As tears fall.

Walking alone through the valley
On this long night
I will fear no evil.

A. E. Winans

JOURNEY TO THE SEA

Waves
fill me up
pull me out
to the sea.

Ride
on the waves
through the spray
to the sea.

Back
to the sand
draw me in
and consume.

This moment of conception
The instant of pure joy
This feeling of oneness — of belonging!

The sea and I
alone and together
struggling to unite
each a part of the same spirit.

Two directions — one destination.

A. E. Winans

In my hands I hold yesterday,
In my hands I hold today,
In my hands I hold tomorrow,
But,
In my heart I hold forever.

Collene P. Maier

JOSHUA

My son got up early today,
He said, Come mommy and let us play.

I said, Not now — there's work to be done.
He said, Ah mommy we never get to have fun.

I hung my head, I wanted to cry,
Then I saw a tear in Joshua's eye.

I said, Son please it's got to be done
He said, Ah mommy we never get to have fun.

The guilt was there like always before,
This time I knew there was room for no more.

So much time had already passed with *wait*
and *maybe later, son,* that I knew this time
my work was really done.

I stopped my excuses that very day 'cause
someday I might need to play.

Someday Joshua will grow up and I'll say,
Remember how we had fun, and he'll say,
Not now, mommy, there's work to be done . . .
    Then I'll know and feel how I
rejected my son . . .

Pamela Nidiffer

GIVE ME YOUR HAND

"Reach out and take my hand,"
A stranger said one day.
"For if you let me lead you
I surely will show you the way.

"I will show you the wondrous creations —
Flowers and trees that grow on this land.
And all you do to see this
Is only to give me your hand.

"Blue skies, white clouds and sunrises;
Morning dew on rosebuds and green grass.
We'll take time to see these things,
And in memories they will last and last."

The dear, the antelope, the squirrels,
Children playing in the parks,
The song of a canary, the music of a lark.

So He reached out His hand and put it in mine,
And He told me who He was.
For the beauty you see was created by Me.
The hand I took was God's.

Judy Berteau

ONE SIZE FITS ALL

When I see a sign: "One Size Fits All"
I know it doesn't mean that at all.
It means too big for twiggies,
And too small for biggies.
I get away fast
Until I find at last
My right size, else I'll be as uncomfortable
As a snake still wearing last year's skin
Or Baby Brother wearing Big Brother's coat!

Bettye Ellis Owen

TO MY LITTLE BOY AND GIRL

I made a wish and it came true
On the day that I had both of you
My little son, how sweet you are
My precious daughter, my shining star

A boy full of mischief, climbing a tree
Throwing a ball, a cut on his knee
A girl with her doll, in her rocking chair
Playing mommy, a bow in her hair

I'll treasure these moments
With you while you're small
For you'll only stay little —
Just for awhile

So I know for sure
That wishes come true
For God loved me so
That He sent both of you

Judy Berteau

I'LL STAY HERE

How can I see where I am going
    when I don't know where I've been
Heavy shadows cross the mountains
    they want to keep me in

Where is the golden sunshine
    where has the sun gone to set
I need its rays to remind me
    of what I never can forget

Daffodils blow in the moonlight
    instead of yellow they're green
Washed by a bath of moonbeams
    or was it only a dream

Wicker buggies and bonnets
    Was it yesterday, when the sun
and the moon came together
    and the buggy turned into hay

How can I see where I am going
    memories blind my eyes
I'll just keep the door shut
    I need no new surprise

Santina Hartung

HOPE

Will February never end?
I think not.
It's Nature's plot
To offend me.

But May will emerge
Renewing Earth's face
With gentle green grace —
Life on the verge.

Mary Ann Jefferies

THE FISHERMAN

He wanted to be a fisherman
to go out on his boat with his poles, and then
find the peace from the sun and the water and sand
and never have to leave there again.

I went along a few times with this man I called Dad
to this different kind of world that he had.
I saw all the troubles and the worries fade
in this piece of God's heaven he'd made.

We'd call out to the other boats, big and small.
Or sometimes we'd sit, saying nothing at all.
And when we were out on the Sound all alone,
it seemed to me that he'd found his home.

When the angels came and took my dad away,
I could almost hear him gently say,
"What I loved most about the sea so blue,
was sharing a part of my life with you."

And now, that summer begins anew
I think of him, as I often do.
As I look way up on the clouds going by,
and picture him sailing off in the faraway sky.

Susan Barichko

HUMAN AM I

Lord, this existence is so shallow,
I wonder if it matters at all,
Are you really up there listening,
When one of us mortals call,
And are you up there watching,
When one of us, being human, falls.

I wonder, Lord, does it matter,
How we sometimes are hurt by thoughtless others,
And I have to stop and remember,
They're as human as me,
They're my brothers.

Being my brothers shall I forgive them?
As you bade in your word to do,
I turned the other cheek,
And they slapped it,
The same as they did to you.

So please help me sweet Lord to be humble,
In my search for a deeper meaning to life,
Please continue to watch over and protect me,
As you have all the days of my life.

Annette L. Derr

US

Though we've parted now and our romance has ended,
You'll be a part of me for all
Eternity . . . some essence of you blended
With my essence. Sometimes I shall recall
The happiness we once shared and again, untended,
Across the mirrors of my mind shall fall
Reflections of *us* that unendingly enthrall
And for just a moment in time shall be relived, extended
Until awareness encounters that wall
Closing off the past, demanding the present be attended.
My life moves on without you; my heart has a secret place,
Though small, in which some part of *us* endures
And never shall be ended.

Lorraine Rice

The fields were white with flowers like snow,
with Socrates and Plato discussing what they *not* know.
A sense of wonder, a sense of awe,
about law and beauty which encompass us all.

The foundations were laid by these men — the two,
our knowledge, our morality, or growth, a few.
These great minds, they fueled the fire,
for Aristotle, for Rome, for others to inspire.

The search for answers, the truth is the quest,
for laymen, for ministers, for atheists, the rest;
to learn, to discover, to overcome the odds . . .
may you find your journey is accompanied by God!

And herein lies man's destiny to date,
"To be or not to be," said Shakespeare of late.
The choice is critical, the outcome is known,
to live or to perish, the result is our own!

Stan Heffner

BLACK ROSE OF LOVE

*I dedicate this poem to a beautiful, kind person
who inspired me to write it — Mr. C. Mayers*

You are my black rose of love
  Sent to me by a messenger dove;
Your kiss is as soft as the black rose petals that shine
  On the black rose bush of love that is only mine;
Your smile reminds me of a beautiful sea
  Where the water changes its color only for me;
You are my black rose of love with charm and grace
  I can feel every part of you whenever we embrace;
You touch me inside with a feeling so rare
  I know only my black rose of love can be there;
The thought of you brings love to my soul
  With dreams and feelings that can never be told;
You are my black rose of love for now and ever
  For I know we will always be together!

Belinda

LOVE CHILD LOST

*I dedicate this poem to my niece Monique.
May it help put back a smile that was lost that day.*

Love child lost her mother one day,
The angels whispered in her ear and took her away.
They said to her, "Little darling, it's time to go,
There's another world for you, we are going to show."
Love child lost her heart and soul,
To heavenly angels taking a stroll.
They took her mother in the clouds so high,
Love child lost didn't have a chance to say good-bye!
Love child lost now hurts deeply within,
Depending on her relatives and a friend.
Love child lost her mother one day,
Now she knows not what to do or say.
She takes each day one challenge at a time,
Hoping one day her light will shine.
Love child lost her beginning of life
To go through the future with struggle and strife,
They left her with plenty of love behind
In her relatives and a friend,
Love child lost, can start all over again!

Belinda

LONELINESS

There's no feeling like the feeling of loneliness.
What was once a family,
are now strangers.
What was once thought to be love,
is now deceit.
You are alone.
No one to tell you bedtime stories,
or play with you in the park.
No one to tell you they love you,
or comfort your fear of the dark.
Now it's just you, kid,
to play in a grown-up world.
No more lullabyes.
No more children's laughter.
But was there ever love
for this child you once were?
Or just the feeling of
    Loneliness.

Berneta Reid

NORTHERN SPRING

The sun revels in awesome
power
as we recover from
winter's cold curse
and dead air,
when the summer nears its
approach and everything
except the solemnity of nature
becomes a memory of
no lasting merit,
since man is no longer
in bondage to the forlorn
but never forsaken image
of front and cold air
breathing in every sense
except the weary expectations
born of summers past.

William J. Lyttle III

NATURE'S MESSAGE

A leaf fell and gave a cry of pain.

The sky soothed it with a gentle rain.

The tree thanked the sky
    and sent its branches high
with a gift of grateful leaves
through which the dancing air weaves.

The sun smiled about its observation
and beamed its rays in admiration.

And a rainbow shared some of its colors
    with the sun's rays
just so we could have a Purple Haze.

So, all got along
    held by a Force so strong.

And Mother Nature approved,
she was deeply moved.

Diane Staiano

A POEM

I tried to write a poem
        but
        it died
so I buried it.

I tried to write another one
        but
the letters switched themselves around
to form words other than
those I had intended:
''Letter Liberation!
    Alphabets of the world *unite!*''

So, I tried to write a third poem
        but
those letters escaped
    and ran off the page.

So, I wrote this.

Diane Staiano

UNFAITHFUL?

Hint of a smile
    or was that a sneer?
Glisten of sweat
    or was that a tear?

Burn of a blush
    or was it the heat?
Sigh of regret
    or was it defeat?

Caress in your sleep;
    clasping for covers?
Caress in your sleep;
    dream of other lovers?

Susan Nasmyth-Miller

FAITH

Faith is a Promise from God
        that He will deliver you
        from the dark shadows
        of want and despair.
And you will stand
        in the honor of His presence
Refreshed and Renewed,
        And He will adorn you
        with the light
Of His Almighty love.

Bonnie Flint Podgorski

WHO IS A POET

I love . . . but I did not create love.
I sing my songs and sonnets,
But also does the dove.
The perfumed fragrance of the flowers
Speaks to me from some celestial power.
I hold my spirits to be free,
But yet I envy the rolling sea.
It is not I who write poetry.
Yea, my heart would pound, my pen but thrill
To praise the splendor of yonder hill.
A poet but shares in some small part
What life has writ upon his heart.
Nay, no man living or no man dead
Could create a verse like He has said.

Bonnie Flint Podgorski

I COULD DREAM

the night pulsed in and out
of my being — a shiver —
so faint! — ran down my spine

a hand so gently touched me then —
it banished my thoughts away
and replaced them with my hopes —
for a while I could dream

a hand so softly caressed me then —
I thought it was the wind
for it stirred the leaves that
    had fallen — long before

I thought I felt the sun kiss
my cheek — but it was you

and you came in and covered me —
you gave to me —
    you gave to me!
and for a while I could dream

Debbie Gaier

DREAMS ON THE HORIZON

I watch the sun go down,
It's burning the sky.
Fires abound over me.
I'd think of you now but I'm
Much too afraid.
How could I take you there
    with me?
And life is a sunset
That's burning in me.
Even my tears turn to sand.
I'd think of you now but I'm
Falling asleep.
I'll meet you in my dreams,
So near me . . .

Debbie Gaier

ARKANSAS RIVER POEM

Some waves you can't ride.
The stars dim, dew sparkles on the grass,
moss-covered earth lies cool and spongy.
The world oozes around you.
You can't just put your finger in existence;
it rolls over you, covers you like molasses.

Some waves pull you under.
Throw that empty wine bottle to the trees.
Nothing breaks. Darkness grabs it.
The world sucks itself in.
No, this isn't your night to die.
The black waters tease you on this side of despair.

M. Anson Harbour

THE QUEST

Small, fawn-hued bird with heaving breast, wildly beating
Heart and eyes filled with fright,
Why flail so desperately against the barrier,
Wings bloodied by your futile efforts at flight?

Again and yet again you forward lunge — high, low,
Then high again, but there seems no passage through.
Helplessly I watch the struggle, straining to understand
The desperation that impels you.

When finally, overcome and powerless,
Your fragile wings unequal to the fight,
Death claims you . . . tiny, gentle creature,
The place you sought — unreached — yet within sight!

"Don't die," I scream. "Don't die before I know!"
Breath chokes in my pain-seared breast.
"Were you on the 'inside' seeking out?
Or was getting from the 'outside' in, your quest?"

Desperately, I pursue! "I *must* know! Can't you see —
I'm you! You're me!"
Only death's silence greets my shrieked request . . .
Beyond caring now, at last you are at rest . . .

Lorraine Rice

LORRAINE RICE. Born: Los Angeles, California; Comments: *After graduation, I became the wartime bride of an Army Air Corps navigator and had two sons. Alone again in the early '60s, I set out to travel around the world. During the five years the trip took, I taught English in Tokyo, worked for a secretarial/translating service organization in Rome, gathered information for an English diplomatic corps publication while in London and spent time in Zurich and Paris. I will celebrate my 4th wedding anniversary this year with architect/photographer husband, Ernest H. Elwood. I recently retired as office administrator after 16 years with a Los Angeles trade association. Having taken an extensive trip through China last year, I am currently working on articles about the China adventure in collaboration with my husband, who did the photography.*

CAT SONG

So many voices called and called again
The Other kind . . .
And she would run in answer through the kitchen door.

Each eve at an appointed hour the din would start
And she would leave her ease upon the bed
And fly into the darkness

Last night
She ran out past the kitchen door
The air was dead . . . still . . .

She sat alone,
Tail curled 'round her feet,
Lapping moon.

Kay Stewart

ONCE A YOUTHFUL AGE

Melancholy, my warm coat,
at least to have you,
my forehead to rest in my hands,
as the first thought.

All horizons have died by turns.

The roads pass without travelers, without dogs.

No signpost anywhere,
but the blood gallops
like eager horses.

Marcel Gafton

A SAD GOODBYE

Some children were playing on the beach one day
There were four, or maybe just three
When off to the east, in the deep blue sky
A most curious sight they did see

A Pegasus flew over the mountain so high
And landed down by the sea
Just in time to meet a unicorn
Who had been grazing under a tree

They waited together by the oceanside
For their friend the mermaid to rise
Then all of the whales and dolphins came 'round
Shouting out their goodbyes

The Pegasus fluttered her lovely wings
The unicorn pranced in a wave
The mermaid wiped a tear from her eye
Trying to act very brave

"We hate to say goodbye," she said
"We really don't want to leave
But we do not have a choice, you see
For the children no longer believe."

Twila Carter

FOOTSTEPS IN THE SNOW

A stranger passed our house last night,
Yet all I'll ever know . . .
A stranger passed our house last night,
There were footsteps in the snow.

Oh, was he lonely? Was he cold?
Had he a place to go?
A stranger passed our house last night,
There were footsteps in the snow.

None but a poor and lonely soul
With heart so full of woe,
Could travel on a night like this . . .
There were footsteps in the snow.

A cold and wretched winter 'eve
When mighty winds do blow,
A stranger passed our house last night,
There were footsteps in the snow.

Sandra J. Snider

GOD'S MASTERPIECE

God painted all the trees last night
With brushes long and free.
He mixed His paint of misty white
And went from tree to tree.

He touched the mighty branches long
And cast on them a spell,
And when the dawn came slowly up,
The story forth did tell.

And then the masterpiece of God
Came forth for all to view.
It sparkled as a mighty sun
On grass so damp with dew.

The wonder of a mighty God —
This beauty I conceive,
And now it dwells forevermore;
God lives! And I believe.

Sandra J. Snider

LOST IN LOVE

When moon and stars are gone from view.
 So lost in love I seem to be,
As if a flow'r wants so to bloom,
 Or as a ship lost out at sea.

I stand midst storm with wind and gale
 Alone to fight for nothing gain,
The waves toss high their heads of white,
 I'm bound by doubt; my fears remain.

I turn to find a love as mine,
 When empty heart . . . I feel it pound,
No love as mine can be so strong,
 Endure, entwine, be e'er profound.

And so I stand, I stand so far . . .
 So far from land, so far from sea,
And ever in this love I turn,
 So lost in love I seem to be.

Sandra J. Snider

MOMENT

The feel of you to such a moment,
Has never brought me sorrow.
But away from you I feel alone,
Like today without tomorrow.
I need your love to help me through,
The dark of a lonely night.
'Cause when we touch I feel renewed,
As a songbird lifted to flight.
I will not say a word of what,
Might make you drift away.
But all my love I give to you,
In every special way!

William J. Martinson

FIND ME

I'm lost in the changes of life,
I can't find my way around misfortune.
I need so desperately to find a love
As warm as yours, to keep me from
Losing my way again. Telling you
This I feel needed, but what
I really need is you. So
Please help me find myself, and help
Me find the love I need. Let it be yours.

William J. Martinson

WILLIAM JOSEPH MARTINSON, JR. Pen Name: Billy; Born: Manhattan, New York, 10-5-57; Married: Erzebet Siladi, 4-23-76; Education: Valancia C.C., Orlando, Florida, A.A.; F.I.T., Florida, B.S.; Occupation: Owner of construction company; Memberships: Pershing Professionals Association; American Legion Post 194; Awards: Army European Community Service award for poems in Army community service newspaper; Poetry: 'Everlasting Understanding,' High School newspaper, 1971; 'Memories Not Forgotten,' Hometown newspaper, 1974; 'A Mother's Soldier,' Hometown newspaper, 1976; 'Find Me,' Army community newspaper, 1981; 'Endure,' Army community newspaper, 1982; Themes: *I try to share the feelings of being separated from loved ones. I know this feeling so well due to serving 10 years in the U.S. Army and 8 of these years in Europe. I want others who share this feeling to know everything will work out for the best.*

What do you want?
 words that came from your lips.
If you only knew the truth,
 you may not be here, tomorrow.

If I say what I feel,
 I may scare you away.
I don't know if you
 can handle my honesty.

On the other hand,
 if I don't say what I feel,
And you never knew,
 you may not be here, tomorrow.

Tom King

What can I say
 that I haven't.
When you feel a closeness,
 are there more than words,
Or can you look into my eyes
 and know the way I feel?

After tonight, I may never
 see you again,
But I have a memory,
 a thought of you,
You were
 part of my life.

Tom King

I face the world
 during the daylight hours,
But when the sun sets,
 I die in a world of loneliness.

No one likes
 to be lonely,
Everyone needs a closeness,
 or just someone who cares.

Life is a constant
 learning experience,
Always looking for that someone
 to make two people never lonely again.

Tom King

WAITING FOR THE POEM TO COME

"Don't leave!" I said to the expectation gathered in me,
that itself has been awaiting me.

It has been awaiting me, together with me, to come with myself,
hand in hand with me.

Equally we awaited the encounter with me,
and the life mirror image is troubled, stealing my ego.

Marcel Gafton

MARCEL GAFTON. Born: Romania, 1925; Education: N. Balcescu High School in Braila; Studied law at Bucharest University; Occupation: Poet; Membership: Romanian Writers' Union; Awards: Bucharest Writers' Union Award for Poetry, 1977; Collected Works, partial list: *Non Possumus,* Bucharest, 1972; *Wondering,* Bucharest, 1977; *So What!,* Bucharest, 1982; *Sixty Poems,* Bucharest, 1986; Comments: *Marcel Gafton began publishing poems while a young student in high school. He also made scores of translations into Romanian of various works from universal literature. Basically, however, he remained a poet.* Themes: *Marcel Gafton's poetry is described by the literary critics as a performance of words communicating an intellectual vision of distress and difficulties.*

PRETEND

The boy sat on the back porch step, dreaming of what he could play
A fireman, a pilot, a cowboy, a judge, who should he be today?
He couldn't play with matches so a fireman was no fun
He couldn't be a cowboy because he did not own a gun
To be an airline pilot you can't be afraid of heights
And if you want to be a judge you must know the Bill of Rights
He thought of being a hero, so fearless and so brave
But he didn't think that would work, for he had no one to save
The little girl next door called out, "My kitty's up a tree,
I tried to get him down and I fell and skinned my knee!"
The boy rushed over and climbed the tree and brought the kitty down
He put a bandage on her knee and wiped away her frown
And now he was a hero and he'd also made a friend
But the little girl wasn't real, of course
Because the whole thing was pretend

Twila Carter

PAINFUL MEMORIES

The loss of my brother has torn me up inside, feelings I have will
never subside.
The pain and suffering I see in my mom, make me want to cry and
never be around.
The quietness and pain I see in my dad, make me believe he'll
always be sad.
I know that it hasn't been easy for them, if only they'd realize
they'll see him again.
For when their time comes they'll go through those pearly gates, and
none other than he will be there to wait.

Brenda Carver

SECRETS

I like to smell bad
soap loosens the dirt I spent
days carefully collecting —
artfully assembling.
Oh, wait — now I've lost the connection
between aphasia and Searle's speech act theory.
Don't go yet. Don't go —
I don't understaaaaaand
the ever spraying luke-hot water
takes my collections and dissolves them
into greyish dirt suds at my feet.
The razor blades flash a crafty,
sinister smile; waiting until they
can yank the innocent hair from under my ivory arms and tear
the scratchy stubble from my casty legs.

Trish Walsh

LOVE IS LIKE A WARM SUN

A sunlike smile a happy face reflects love mirrorlike
Warm words handshakes embraces kisses turn echo like
Love is like mercury
In an open palm it stays in sympathetic bliss
Close your palm tightly it climbs out
Restricted love grows retarded like a tree on
Stony ground but still with a will of its own
Blissful love is a state of the inner man
Mercury broken in anguished clutch
Little bowls trickle through fingers
Thousand drops streaming irretrievably
Love is perennial like grass
Love can't be bought sold taught given away
Love like mercury is ever moving
Wise men's form gave method called alchemy
Alchemic knowledge stills it once stilled becomes silver
Silver melted mixed with herbal juice turns gold
Becomes comforting life giving sun
Moving without restlessness.

Elisabeth Locke Ellis

IT WAS ME

Who is the one who's always been with you?
And who always let you run free?
And who held your hand when you lost your first love?
My darling, my dear it was me.

Who always worshipped the ground that you walk on?
Who was with you when you got that scar on your knee?
Who waited at home till you got through running?
My darling, my dear it was me.

And who'll be beside you when you cross that river?
Who'll hold your hand till your spirit is free?
And who'll grieve your passing, till the angels weep with me?
I guess you know who, it's still me.

Now who's sitting alone in this cold, silent room?
Who waits by your side for your farewell to me?
And who'll kiss the last smile as it fades from your lips?
After seventy years it's still me.

Now we've come to that river where you must cross alone,
I can't walk beside you like I have for so long.
Then he reaches to kiss her, as he did yesterday,
and with a soft whispered sigh, his love slips away.

Lauren R. Baum

GET AWAY

A weekend of love and romance —
A remote hideaway just for two.
Time to get to know each other all over again.
I wish this for just me and you.

A time for laughter, a time for tears;
All emotions finally let go.
No interruptions from anyone or anywhere.
Let out all that we want to know.

Slow and beautiful seduction.
Maybe time to reach cloud nine.
A new beginning or an ending —
Hoping to one day make you mine.

Janice Skinner

Coming home
the door swings open
to the inner courtyard,
bouganvilla blooms
fuchsia silk drifts down
to kiss the paving stones.

Here my heart meets all,
fire floats upon the water
small points of light flicker
at the feet of Buddha's smile
as I join the reflection pool.

A steady breeze
stirs the trees to murmur envy,
sighing at the beauty,
and at the All.

Like the blooms in the breeze
I am uplifted
to float
at the feet of Buddha's smile.

J. S. Nichols

ASPIRATION

To live
To work
To love
To be, creating
Myself, this fragile creature
My world, this crystal sphere,
reflecting
light
perfect
harmony, illuminating
Balance, this solitary stillness
Beauty, this tender kiss,
truth
a miracle
freedom
grace, this aspiration.

John E. Davidson

THIS MIGHTY WAVE

I know of no one unaffected,
by this wave, this mighty wave.
Lover-child-poem-song-dance,
this light in flesh transforms.
Our memory awakened, by,
these visions of the future,
in a moment, an instant,
we are everywhere, alive.
Our eyes flash, in recognition,
seeming madness, save intent.
We dare to touch,
to re-connect,
our bursting hearts, divine.
We know we have this power, yet,
to know is not enough, for,
we must live,
truly live, beyond survival's confines,
beyond these prison walls,
of self-inflicted wound,
our Dream.
Immortal, yea,
of Gods.

John E. Davidson

THE LAUNCH AND THE SEVEN

All was ready, Time to blast
Then ignition call was given
Fiery hands pushed ever upward
As the Launch was borne toward heaven

Not a hint was ever given
That there would be something wrong
Gleaming white with fires surrounding
She seemed capable and strong

Up-lifted faces scanned the sky
Searching hard if in some way
They would see the thrilling moment
When the boosters break away

Tell me, Was it somewhere written
That today for you and me
Seven names would be engraved
Forever in our history

They loved life and country too
Giving freely of their worth
Their sacrifice to explore space
Has made them stars, For this our Earth

Santina Hartung

ACE

Oh how I wish to fly
The mighty wings of steel.
Warrior's passion, do or die
With a patriotic zeal.

If I must certainly fall
Tell me that I earned my wings.
I hear, now, the final call.
Angel playing harp and sings.

John C. Erianne

FIRST SIGNS OF WINTER

Scarves unfurl as forms are bent
Trying hard the sleet to miss
Tearing eyes began submitting
To the winds they can't resist

Lacey patterns form on windows
Where just earlier raindrops lay
Frosty etchings take their places
Swirling pictures on their way

Common ordinary paths
Turn to glass of silver hue
Leaving icy winding trails
Where the children have walked through

Santina Hartung

SANTINA M. HARTUNG. Born: Chicago, Illinois, 1-1-20; Married: Howard E. Hartung, 10-22-38, 3 children, 6 grandchildren; Education: high school, 2 years college; Occupations: Director City Art Center, 12 years; Director William Hodges Gallery, 4 years; Awards: Golden Poet Award, 1987, 'Artistry of Winter'; Poetry: 'Unfaithful,' 1970; 'Halley's Comet,' 1986; 'Why Me Oh Lord,' 1985; Other Writings: "My Bonus Baby," article, *Chicago Sunday Tribune*, 1960; Themes: *Nature, animals, historical events, family memories, early Chicago events.* Comments: *I never send greeting cards, only poems. Working on a book of early Chicago, have been for several years now. Only recently have I begun to share my poems with out-of-my-family contacts.*

The warmth of your body
Close to mine
As you caress my soul
By the soft glow
Of the firelight
I reach out to you
Tenderly
Anticipation
In my every breath
You hold me
Whispering words of love
Softly in my ear
To lead me
Yet again
Into ecstasy

Cheri L. Stocker

THE STREETS OF NASHVILLE

As I passed through the streets of Nashville one day,
    an old man I happened to meet.
His face was creased with the ravage of time, he had rags tied 'round
    his feet.
In his pocket I saw a familiar bulge, like a bottle of Dago Red.
''What a bum,'' I thought, as I started to pass, he won't work to
    keep himself fed.
I stepped aside to go on my way, when I heard him begin to speak,
and these are the words that I heard him say that day on a Nashville
    street.
''You know what I wanted to do with my life? Go ahead, bud,
    take a guess.
I've always wanted to sing for the world, reckon you've heard the rest.
But sir there must be a million or so broken down relics like me,
that got hooked on the booze and settled for less than they started
    out to be.
Some maybe got caught by their shirttail in a crack in the boardwalk
    of life.
By the war, an accident, maybe jail, or children and an unplanned wife.
Or maybe they was just never there at the right place or at the right
    time.
And it's possible that just for a phone call they missed out 'cause
    they hadn't a dime.
But don't get me wrong, it's not money I want, but a chance before I
    die,
and don't be put off by the tears of this fool, it's the drink that
    makes me cry.
No sir it's not a handout but a hand up I want, one time before death
    draws near.
Let me sing for the world, if it's in your power, one good song, if
    only God hears.''

Lauren R. Baum

A LONELY OLD PRISON

In this lonely old prison, I sit alone in my cell.
Just how long I'll be here, only time will tell.
For I was found guilty of killing my wife.
So the judge sentenced me to do time for life.

We both were so happy our lives full of joy.
With two lovely children, a girl and a boy.
Then she started drinking and staying out late.
With no time for the children or me. Just her date.

I said I'd forgive her. We'd start a new life.
For life's not worth living without her as my wife.
But she turned around, looked me straight in the eye.
And she said, I'm sorry my darlin', but this is goodbye.

She said, I no longer love you. I found a new love.
And swore to be with him by stars above.
So you raise the children and pretend that I'm there.
And please reassure them that I'll always care.

Then I became angry, and I took my knife.
Three times I stabbed her and took her life.
The judge found me guilty and sentenced me for life,
So in this lonely old prison I'll spend the rest of my life.

Rita Landgren

JEWEL OF THE NIGHT

Although the sky is blue, the way is gone;
The further from the night, the longer the road;
The more beautiful nature is, the more one gets lost;
The wind is blowing and the air is clean.

The sun steals a jewel only night can offer;
Many times this truth slips through my grasp;
Only through the pen will it be known;
At each precise instance it is right in view.

Only to be replaced by the next moment in time;
The more I search, the more it eludes my mind.

Misha

PRETTY LADY

    Take my hand, pretty lady — and I will lead you to the place
where the woodbine twines.
    A carpet of grass, a leafy tree, a tinkling brook — and a
bird for company.
    We will rest — and listen to the sounds of nature.
    Without a spoken word — we will let our souls mingle — one
unto the other.
    Time will become meaningless, because we will have forever,
together.
    The setting of the sun will be the silent lullaby that lulls
us to sleep.
    The cover of darkness will be our blanket for the night.
    Our protection will be our faith in the Lord — and our trust
in our fellow men. We will sleep, hand in hand — and dream until
dawn. I will awaken you with a gentle kiss. You will open your
beautiful eyes — and look at me — and smile contentedly. We will
frolic in the woods — and watch the chipmunks play. We will
listen to the songs of the cricket, the contented sounds of the
bullfrog — and watch the eagle soar, high overhead.
    We will be as two lovers, without a thought or a care —
except for each other.
    Will you take my hand, pretty lady, and go with me?

Roy D. Johnson

FINALLY

Thanks to Gertrude Stein

The red neon light is burning.
The red neon sign is burning.
The dark pink light is lit.
The dark pink sign is burning.
The dark pink sign is lit.
The dark dark pink light is a sign.
The dark dark pink light is lit tonight.
The deep pink light tonight is aglow.
The deep maroon of the light is aglow.
Tonight the deep maroon of the sign is aglow.

Alan W. Freeland

WHITE STAR

As I walked in the woods,
Cool pine rousing me,
I stared at the heavens
Searching for I-don't-know-what.
Blue-black sky and, most surprising,
White lights, barely seen.
They struggle to be noticed,
Surrounded by Darkness, ever hungry.
Waiting to consume them.
Yet, as small and insignificant as they were,
They still gleamed,
Staving off eternal night.
Shedding light in the dark,
And giving hope to the world.

Scot Robert Carr

SCOT ROBERT CARR. Born: Newton, Massachusetts, 11-30-66; Education: 3rd year student, Framingham State College, Framingham, Massachusetts; Graduate Holliston High School; Occupations: Freelance Writer, Part-time Sales Clerk; Poetry: 'Man in the Chair,' *Many Voices, Many Lands,* 6-87; 'For Me,' 6-87; Other Writings: Various articles, *Japanimation* magazine; Comments: *I really have no common themes in my work. The fancy of a particular item, person, or song will hit me, then I write. In fact, some of my best stuff was first written on notebook paper, old store receipts, matchbook covers, etc.*

LOVE IS

Love is a baseball game on a hot summer day.
And watching the children play.

Love is having your child miss a day of school.
While you try and keep your cool.

Love is telling your child to brush his teeth,
Before he gets a cavity.

Love is being yourself,
When you can't be anyone else.

Meridell W. Merritt

INNER SPHERE

Colors bounce
About my head
Mixing
Nondescript

Thoughts tumble
In and out
Concepts
Without words

Memories fade to black
Come to light
Time past
Becomes present

Words crush
My inner sphere
Of colors
Of thoughts

Pretty pictures
In a peaceful place
Where words
Only interfere

Debra McLaughlin

Come to me
In silence
For it is silence
That remains
When that
Last part of you
Is taken
From me
You will leave
And I will stay
Alone
With my memories
And your silence

Cheri L. Stocker

Within the realm
Of dreams
My lover lies
And dreaming
Takes me
And yet again
Until at last
The dream
Is real
And I
The illusion

Cheri L. Stocker

TRUE LOVE

No greater love on earth we find,
It is the true and perfect kind;
Christ came to earth to love us so,
To give His life, that life we'll know.

No truer love can we receive,
From friends or kin, we do believe;
The love of God exceeds it all,
He listens when He hears us call.

No deeper, sweeter, purer love,
Can we receive than from above;
We do believe and we do know,
The love our Father can bestow.

We love as we are loved by Him,
E'en though we're full of woe and sin;
As He forgave and gave His all,
We too forgive when others fall.

This perfect love of God will be,
Ours too in heaven eternally;
We eagerly await the day,
When True Love we will have for aye.

Ruth Roehrs

PAS DE DEUX FOR THREE

We danced from the beginning
To music heard by none.
What was once a graceful pas de deux
Is now just danced by one.

We danced so softly on the stage
While she waited in the wings
And lured you gently with a song
That only death can sing.

She moved so swiftly on the floor
And danced into your face.
A pas de deux, I know, for two,
Don't let her take my place.

I watched her perfect pirouette
I skip, I fall, I leap.
I watched her perfect arabesque
I try, I fall, I weep.

Don't take her for your partner
We do not need three
What was once a graceful pas de deux
Is now just danced by me.

Rebecca Hutton

A CIRCLE OF LIFE

We cannot shelter her from this world
    just help her to understand
        and to know
  love is more powerful
      than war, hate, greed.

It can overshadow dark images
    and breathe life into
      her hopes and dreams
        friendships and memories
    for her to cherish
          forever.

    And we,
      forever knowing
    our hopes and dreams
        friendship and love
    created someone
        as beautiful as our daughter.

Cassandra Brannan

WINDS

I stood alone atop the mountain of life,
The east and west winds colliding against me.
Both wanted to be my master.
Both fought for control.

The east wind blew strong and sure.
It promised sweet balm of peace and rest.
All seemed safe and secure,
But did I want it that way?

The west wind blew wild and fierce.
It spoke of things captivating and new,
But the way was full of dangers and uncertainties.
I feared to go that way.

They waged their war, savage and long,
But I, I let neither win.
I stood there, hand-in-hand with fear,
Until the mountain crumbled,
    and life itself ran out.

Jane Marchant

BENNIE

You were a part of my dream
I made you up that night
I wanted you a part of my scheme
I wanted to love you tonight

    But deep inside
    A child was I
    So afraid to let you know
    That I had loved you so

But you were a part of a dream, and I made you up tonight
So why does my heart hurt so and I hated to let you go
You made me laugh and now I cry
But you were a dream lost in the night
And when I awoke I had realized that I had tears in my eyes
How could this be, you were just a dream and I had loved you so.

Helen Topalovich

THE DIFFERENCE

An August storm is gathering now; there's a grayness in the air,
The clouds are shredded cotton batton and swirling angel hair,
A billowing mother cloud is filled to brimming over,
She releases one of her offspring — set free!
A glistening, gleaming raindrop becomes a reality.

Slate and charcoal and rose and lavender peach, and as the tiny
Newborn raindrop begins its descent, the trees and grass and
Flowers greedily reach; its life is joyous, bounding and buoyant,
Befriended by the wind, lower and lower, slower and slower until
With an almost unheard, gentle, indiscernable *plop* — into a lazy,
Grazing, glossy river the raindrop came to a brave stop.

But it wasn't the last stop and it wasn't the end; a strange and
Wonderful thing began — the tiny ripples grew in multiples and
Spread, gaining and growing and passing on to reach to each opposite
Shore, the tiny raindrop was a part of something, caused the start
Of something much bigger than before!

In a flash of lightning that sizzled in neon and thunder that
Roared and rolled, a torrent of tiny raindrops burst from the
Tearful, voluptuous mother clouds they could no longer hold —
Like that first courageous, pretentious raindrop,
I wish for when I could make the difference in my lifetime.

Rita Schmitt

BLURRED VISION

    Shallow empty eyes of gluttonous ambition
Reveal the murderous deed of chronicled tradition

    Rotten stench that tears the soul
Denounces the unceasingly wretched toll

    Plunge forth the dagger of personal gain
Foul imaginings of blood and pain

    Dark elements passionately possessed
Domineering and brutal ready to molest

    Haunting shadow envelops its prey
Final destruction is now on its way

    Prison of conscience induces betrayal
Put to an end this search for the grail

Jill Kaplan

THE SEA

I hear it calling me as I push open the veranda doors
I become engulfed by the awesome vastness of the sea
It crashes and thunders as it rolls upwards reaching towards the sky
The rippling motion moves it closer to me as I stand by the edge
Its continuity fills me with contentment when I walk along its shore
Its white foam covers my feet
I hear the sea gulls call as they search for fish
The children's laughter adds happiness to my scene
Its crystal clear blue water relaxes my body and lulls me to sleep,
For this sea may be a dream in my head, but its feeling is all too real.

Barrie Elizabeth Luftman

*JUNE NIGHT

I love the drowsy hush of evening
Just before the waiting night,
When the pale gold light
Of the reluctant sinking sun,
Knowing that his day is done
Lingers on to color twilight,
And perchance to challenge starlight
To a race for beauty run.

The sleepy chirruping of birds
And slow lifting of drooping leaves
To catch the first faint evening breeze
So gentle that one gropes for words
To speak of beauty, subtle as these
Half silences from the waking trees.

Marjorie V. Slater

FOREVER WEEP NIOBE

Weep for my love, Niobe,
O cold and empty stone;
My tears are locked within my heart
And all emotion flown.

Arise from out your sheltered pool
Beneath the willow tree,
Where lies my love, forever lost;
Awake, and weep for me!

Let fall your shining hair of gold
To trail in paths of dew,
Where memories are buried
Which life cannot renew.

The blackbird sings a requiem;
His music fills the air,
And in the evening shadows
My love, once more, is there.

So, forever weep, Niobe,
Beside the flowing water,
And in the waking breezes
Let me hear, again, the laughter.

Marjorie V. Slater

DAFFODIL HILL

Heaven and nature's beauty
In full bloom on the hill
I drive closer,
So that my eyes may get their fill

My soul becomes captive
Of the Spring's golden flower
As I watch hour after hour
In this flowery land
So beautiful, so grand

Rose Mary Gerlach

TRINITY

God the Father, God the Son,
  God the Spirit, three;
One in three, three in one,
  Divine Unity.

The Father, Creator and Ruler
  Of earth, of sky, of sea,
Of birds, of trees, of flowers;
  He created you and me.

The Son, our promised Savior,
  He died on Calvary
To redeem us back to God again
  After we from Him did flee.

The Holy Spirit comforts us
  Through word, and faith and love;
He lives in us and we stay close
  To our Lord in heaven above.

Ruler, Savior, Comforter
  Praise to Thee ever be;
One in three, three in one,
  Holy Trinity.

Ruth Roehrs

RUTH CLARA ROEHRS. Born: Defiance, Ohio, 5-1-15; Married: Edgar E. Roehrs, 11-13-38; Education: Defiance High School, 1933; Occupations: Homemaker, Former Sunday School Teacher; Children: 3 sons, Don Roehrs, Hicksville, Ohio; Norman Roehrs, Findlay, Ohio; and Kenneth Roehrs, Ft. Wayne, Indiana; 9 grandchildren & 1 great-grandchild; Memberships: Church Choir; Poetry: 'Victory,' 1986; 'Looking To Calvary,' 1987; 'Adoration,' 1985; 'Easter Song,' 1987; 'Right to Life,' 1986; all published by *The News Tribune*, Hicksville, Ohio; Comments: *My idea is to publish the gospel of God's son, Jesus Christ, through poetry. I find this to be a type of mission work, to show God's love for all His children through my poems.*

MORNING PRAYER

Father we thank thee for this day
Bless everything we do or say
May we give kind words and a friendly smile
And try to make this life worthwhile
That others may see that we walk with you
That we love them and you do too.

Sylvia Boxell

MOLECULAR EVENING

Evening's presence
Molecular
Fibers of hands
Invisible
Touching, reaching
Feeling the dark
Pencil sketches
Of clouds
Trailing, dancing
Calling the night

Evening's soft face
Your smiling eyes
Longing for answers
Asking, waiting
Searching the sky
Touching, reaching
Feeling the dark
Trailing, dancing
Calling the night
Asking, waiting
Searching the sky.

Corinne Cykiert

REFLECTIONS IN A STILL SKY

Dedicated to those who died with the Challenger.

The soul that swings in endless flight
Throughout the eon blue,
Will find its depth and width and height
And venture forth anew.
There is no end to life and love.
The clouds that rim the sky
Cannot hold back the quickening joy
Of dreams that never die.
The thread is woven deep and strong
Within the burgeoning breast.
The fingers brave have held the loom
And given it their best.
There is no hope that cannot reach
Beyond the ken of man,
And bridge the darkest gulf between
The widest breadth and span.
Though heart is stilled, and race is run,
The spirit is set free,
To lend enchantment, love and hope
Through all eternity.

Thora M. Astle

CREATIVE WORK

Creative work, done in the name of Art
Must first, in my mind,
Come from the heart
The inner soul alone can find
Sweet utterances to describe
All God's Greatness and Beauty
With pride
We hail the sun, moon and stars
That shine above
And all Nature's wealth, that He supplies
With His Love

Rose Mary Gerlach

UNFINISHED SERENADE

Harmonious composition, petal-soft, alluring,
Tiptoeing across the mind, mesmerizing my thoughts.

Slow, gentle melodies, soothing subtleties,
Tempting the listener,
Into submission.

Single rhythms into doubles,
High tunes into lows,
Chords and resonance.

Delightful turbulence of music,
Fusions of octaves,
Pairing of notes.

Symphonies of sound,
Scampering, dancing, joyful notes,
Raising the spirit of expectation.

Alas, comes the pause,
The moment of anticipation, doubt, disbelief . . .
Denial of the ending.

Harmonious composition, petal-soft, alluring,
Begin anew to tempt and mesmerize,
Or leave behind the unfinished serenade.

Bernadette Court

TRAFFIC SCHOOL

Oh accused one, come forward with your innocence.
Remove the offending garment from your pride,
That portrays you as the guilty one.

Lift the heavy weight you have brought
From off your shoulders, *and* your good name,
So that you can once again breathe freely.

Wash the shame from your face,
Cleanse your spirit *and* your ego,
And leave behind the lack of proof.

Who can appease this taunting feeling,
Assuage the anger brewing,
If not yourself?

Lay the burden at the feet of the accuser,
No one can force you to carry it
If you refuse to oblige him.

Guilt is self-inflicted, self-absorbing,
Fed from the inside and encouraged
By those wishing to place the load on you.

Yes, officer, I saw the stop sign.

Bernadette Court

RAINBOW

Look to the rainbow for there you will see
My everloving dad smiling at me.
He's up in the heavens serene and at peace.
He's up there with God where love does not cease.
So when I miss Dad with smiles or with tears,
I look up to heaven and a rainbow appears.
Dad always will watch me wherever I roam,
And show me a rainbow to follow him home.

Joan Voltz

RETROSPECTION

You think they are yours forever
Diapers and feedings plague your dreams
Little kisses reach to the very core of your heart . . .
Their giggle as they cuddle their first puppy,
The soft touch of their cheek as you share a hug.
How many times have I been too busy for bedtime prayers?
You want to give them the very best of everything . . .
                              better than you had.

You cry as you give them up to the first day of school,
And laugh when they laugh . . . their smile warms you.
Like leaping track hurdles, you meet each new fear:
First dance, first date,
First time you see them sharing a kiss.
''Mom, can I borrow the car?''
Don a cap and gown . . .

Did I ''raise up a child in the way he should go''?
Did I tell them enough that I loved them?
Was I there when they hurt?
Did I really hear? Did I care?
I just need a little more time.
Too late . . . they're gone.

Connie L. Clarneau

The paints have faded
Faint traces remain, alone in the canvas of life
Abandoned to die in silence.

The words are no longer clear
Pages have turned yellow with age
Crisp rhymes are now forgotten
In the weakness of today.

The music has ceased, at last
Melody but hovers in the morning air
The memory of harmony now finds refuge in darkness.

But this joy.
Ah, this home I have found in your smile
The fulfillment I have seen in the color of your eyes,
The warmth I have felt in the strength of your hands,
The peace I have heard at the sound of your voice . . .

These things, in man's fleeting earth, will prove lasting.
These things, I know, like God's love, will stay.

Mary Stephanie A. Amargo

BEACHCOMBERS

Combing the seashore, wave carved and terraced
we roam for miles and sift the white silt,
bend to collect pale quartz crystals, pumiced
pink and red garnet in patterns occult.
Heaping sea pansies, lavender and luminant
anemones, sand dollars, moon snails and limpets
starfish, seawhips, conchs with horned crescent
sealace and rockweed for astral coronets.
Beached by spring tides with bottles and barrels
tossed from anchorage, planks, shells, spars
drifting to shore despite many tangles . . .
finding existence on marginal floors.

Addie Lee

WALLS OF THE GRAND CANON.

MY SISTER

She was my oldest sister and she meant so much to me.
She did so many things etched in my memory.
One wintry day I walked to school, the snow up to my knees.
In front of me Alberta said, ''Walk in my footprints, please.''

And so I lifted my feet high, stepped in the prints she made,
With woolen stockings o'er my shoes, warm and dry I stayed.
Once I teased a fat chum. ''If you were in her shoes
How would you feel?'' Alberta asked, ''Watch the words you choose.''

She chased away my foolish fears, taught me empathy,
To sing and laugh, love and care, face life fearlessly.
Years later she was dying, and we knew she knew it.
We went to cheer and comfort her. Instead she helped us through it.

She still lives within my heart and I still hear her say,
''Step in my footprints carefully through the snow today.
I follow Christ as best I can. He taught these things to me.
Read His words so you can be the best that you can be.''

Ruby Tippit Peacher

RUBY TIPPIT PEACHER. Born: Indian Mound, Tennessee, 8-5-17; Married: Joseph William Peacher, 6-13-36 (died 1976); Education: Austin Peay University, Clarksville, Tennessee, B.S., 1958; Occupations: Retired teacher, Writer, Mother of five, Grandmother of eight; Memberships: Stewart County Historical Society, Tennessee Retired Teachers Association, Tennessee Library Association, United Methodist Women; Poetry: 'Family Tree,' *The Seay Side,* 1985; 'Spring Is a Child,' *The All State,* college paper, 1934; 'My Sister,' Mother's Cookbook,' 'Not in the Cookbook'; Other Writings: ''Indian Mound'', family histories, *Stewart County Heritage,* 1980; Themes: *Our past heritage, love of nature, inspiration to be all we can, belief in God.* Comments: *I write song-poems with melodies, but have not tried to have any published, and I write short stories based on childhood memories.*

THE UNICORN

A unicorn stands on his smooth oak dresser
Glazed china figurine like the whiteness of Paul
''Gift for me,'' he shyly said, ''from a magic land,''
when he nudged it neighing against his cheek
mythical visitor of childhood dreams.

With knights of old, medieval scenes
this son unveiled his cast of mind
I wander now in vacant rooms
my young man gone in an armored tide
his flag draped 'cross battle sworn.

They sent ribbons and a Medal of Honor
which lie quietly inside the drawer
beside his neatly pressed uniform
What land does the mort of his bugle keep?
Born to an early death; so fast the rose.

Sunset streams red on the unicorn's horn
distant taps break through my paling dream
the hollows in my ears burn
as I fold his lifeless coat on the chair
Agnus Dei, donna nobis pacem.

Addie Lee

LOST WITHOUT LOVE

Trapped in a world
    full of half-hearted faces
True intentions are not known
    as fake feelings surround all places.

You look in every set of eyes
    for a glimmer you once knew
Yet the elusive sparkle you seek
    stays away, waiting to come out of the blue.

No one risks the honesty
    hidden away in their heart
Not for one night of happiness
    or possibly a loving life to start.

Wondering around in this world
    drunk from loneliness; with a heartache chaser,
Stumbling over lights in a stupor of darkness
    you're lost without love: the magic of nature.

    Love is . . .
        finding the one you desire.

Ken Malin

DEATH

What happens
    and where do you go
Questions, of thought
    the gone only know.

It seems ironic
    the ones picked from day to day
Why should this one be taken
    and this other stay.

Some say it's fate
    or maybe it was their time
Cause or age doesn't matter
    striking without reason or rhyme.

    A part of life we all know
        Because it marks the end,
    Yet remember, you start a new life, with death
        even, in this life, at the loss of a friend.

    Love is . . .
        LIFE! before and after death.

Ken Malin

YOU NEVER REALLY LEFT

Did you think about me
the night you left?
Didn't you know
that every corner I'd turn
I'd catch you walking away.
At every unguarded moment
I'd hear your quiet laugh.
Will I ever be free?

Can I ever go on?
While all the memories
still hold me down.
Just when I think you've gone
you haven't really left.
You're still there
with your haunting smile.

You make me so angry at times.
In your world of peace.
While I fight and struggle
to become what you wanted.
But, will you ever know?

Alisa L. Fuller

AND SO IT GOES

We take for granted
    golden sand
that stretches over
    coastal land

Some spilling into caves

Before its shape
    reduced in size
was other matter
    I surmise

Ground by winds and waves

Sometimes I walk the
    swirling surf
small shells and pebbles
    grind and hurt

My tender toes

The constant motion
    of the sea
will grind them fine
    as sand for me

And so it goes

Santina Hartung

AND THEN I KNEW

I searched my heart everywhere,
My people, my people, land of my birth.
Hoping to find them, did I dare,
Searching forever the elusive worth.

Hidden within me always mine,
A presence of happenings that I must discover.
Holding me with an invincible vine,
As though I might reach out and touch her.

And then you reach across the years,
A father I had thought gone forever.
You touch my soul, you dry my tears,
And still that loneliness haunts me ever.

But now a child, so small I hold her,
Screams and wails, she knows not who,
In her eyes her anguish I suffer,
I reach out for it . . . and then I knew.

Ann Victor

THE LAND

Uncover,
know what I am.
I am here,
everywhere.
to be shared and felt,
seen by all.
if beauty is to be held,
so direct that I cannot be revealed
but known, if not searched,
for I am here.
find me,
and feel my embrace.

Wendy A. Bauer

NIGHTWORDS

Nights,
waiting for
sleep,
we speak.

Words.

Smooth,
silvered words
in tendrils of
smoke.

Whispers
and sleep:

gentle
friends
to
strangers.

Margaret L. Somers

WISHES AND PROMISES

I do not wish for you roses without thorns
Nor rainbows without gold
Nor rain without umbrellas.
I do wish for you to cast off the thorns —
See the beauty of God's perfect creation —
    the rose.
I do wish for you rainbows where you find
    God's strength and peace
At each glowing shining end.
I do wish for you rain with God's umbrella
    of love
To protect your every move.
Life is made up of thorns that hurt
Of dreams of wealth that soon disappear
Of rain that saddens the soul.
Hold fast to God's promises, for —
Only then will thorns turn to roses
Rainbows to lasting dreams come true
    And
Rain will become God's sunlight of hope.

Dorothy McGaughran

DOROTHY ANN McGAUGHRAN. Married: Joseph, 7-26-41 (now deceased); Education: University of Redlands, B.A., English; Occupation: Teacher, in Pennsylvania for 23 years; in Redlands, 30 years; currently teaching accelerated students in a private school; Memberships: Past member, N.E.A.; Lifetime member, C.T.A.; C.E.T.A.; Comments: *Last year, I taught poetry scanning and basic guidelines for poetry writing to accelerated seventh graders. The poem published here is my first ever!*

WHEN EVENING FALLS . . .

When evening falls, they used to sáy:
Night steps ashore.
But that was long, too long ago
Before your time.

Your brilliant nights of charted skies,
No matter how intelligibly clear,
Twice bend our separate souls
In darkness.

My night still steps ashore,
Its hem still trails through oceans;
It ripples in the puddles on your street
And leans with half a smile
Against your door.

Ursula Korneitchouk

AN OASIS

An oasis in the heart
    a walk in the sand
The sunset a part
    holding hand in hand.

An oasis with life
    fulfilling without demand
Between husband and wife
    they do what they can.

An oasis like the sea
    open and endless
A relationship to be
    never defenseless.

    An oasis that is true love
As white and pure as a beloved dove.

    Love is . . .
        quenching your thirsts from the oasis
        two have made; and now, and always
        will share.

Ken Malin

THE COLD WOODS

    The woods are cold. Winter falls away as I walk by the young
bright aspens. I walk through and remember how long I have to
live, how long I follow this path, how long the petals move
inside me. These woods are cold, and a young blue jay looks from
one of the aspens, and everything happens at once. Winter falls
away. Small gray stones, and I know the way of seeing the
leaves again. I know the way of seeing the fresh dark soil. I
know the way of listening to the voices in stones.

Alejandro Venegas

MAN AND BOY

There's a little boy in me who loves to go fishin'
Sit on a log, dangle bait, do some wishin'
Who gets his clothes muddy and walks in the water,
Winks his eye, says things he really shouldn't oughter.

There's a man in me who likes things just right,
Who likes his co-workers all to be bright.
When the going gets tough, he doesn't shirk,
But determines to find a way to make it work.

There's a struggle within me 'twixt the boy and the man.
The man needs to win it, at least if he can.
The boy seeks to act out whatever's his passion,
The man leads his life in a role model fashion.

Which one will win out? Nobody can say,
Now winning, now losing, each one has his day.
The twosome within me will not suffer a loss
If the boy is the lover, and the man is the boss.

Paul Duffey

I CALLED . . . TO YOU

I remember calling to you
As you stood at the ocean's edge.
I remember smiling at a child's play,
And looking . . .
To see if you were smiling, too.
But you weren't. Nor did you answer my call.
I remember wondering if the roar deafened you,
And at any moment you would look my way.
I etched our names in the sand, and smiled in our memory.
And then I looked at your profile. So silent.
Foamy traces sent ''I love you,'' in swirls,
Past me, and to your bare feet.
I thought surely then that you would turn,
And wonder why I was so far from your side.
But you never did.
And so I called to you again. Called from the depths of me.
Still you didn't respond.
And then it came to me . . .
It wasn't the ocean's roar, or the spirit of the moment . . .
It was you, and it was us — some things never change.
                    Like loneliness.

Wendi Guerette

LADY WITH A TORCH

As I came drifting into the bay
My eyes came to see
A lady standing in the water with a crown
That stood for all men to be free.

As I came closer
Her clothes looked all tattered and torn
But as I came to understand her
She was in good shape for the troubles she had borne.

She stood on a platform
With a torch in her hand
It was a symbol of freedom
Of each woman and man.

She was one hell of a lady
Standing as tall as she could be
Standing for her country
And people like you and me!

Keith S. Huston

GRAY MATTER

In the rain . . .
The trees and grass are lush and green —
The pavement glitters, sparkles, shines,
And the shadows gather under
With no regard for time.
But the bay has lost its colors
And is only gray with flecks of white
From where it nudges earth
To where it gently weds the sky.
And even though I strive to think:
''How green the grass, how glist'ning every tree,''
My mind is swayed by only what is gray
And all that I can really see or feel
Are those same currents — convolutions —
Screaming something wildly from the sea
That I recall as drawings of the brain
Still coiled to spring within the skull
And buried deep in *Gray's Anatomy.*

M. E. Morrow, M.D.

A CHILD

A tear streamed down with no reason
A frustration, it just broke free.
There's a well that knows no season,
It just knows it has to be.

To want so much in just one day,
To stifle your sense of right?
To just depend on what others say,
Just lose without a fight?

As quickly as this sadness came,
It just gets wiped away.
Life just passes steadily on,
And you grow a bit each day.

A child is small, so very small,
With a heart as big as he;
So handle that heart as you would your own,
The rest — the future will see.

Love him gently, but love him hard;
For that child is you . . .
And as much as you can love yourself,
Love that child times two —

Brianna Douglas

THE HOUSE

It is night, and I'm alone
My children to bed long gone.
Outside I hear the wind, the rain
beating softly against my window pane.

Suddenly, I feel a gentle longing
for company, for friends,
but yet the house
embraces my life.
Somehow, it takes me to places
where I've never been.

This dwelling nurtures my feelings
that lie deep inside, hidden
from all who cannot possibly know
what to me has true meaning.

If not for my house
my own private place,
I could never experience
this exquisite solace, this space.
For intimately, the house and I share
all earthly pleasures, and sorrows and pain.

Lourdes C. Gonzalez

QUALITY OF LIFE

I echo forth mute, trite words
muffled voices distract on the absurd
one tries to recall what was the myth
that created this miracle to assume forthwith
we live our lives a day or two
at a time when the world is not reborn
unable to replenish what was new
tribal man lives with his daily scorn
managing to destroy the leftovers
for future generations to enjoy moreover
what have we done to the quality of life
freedom beckons us to have strife
so that we martyrs can save
what is left of the world's built grave
giving the last rites solemnly so
to the world that will never know
that we are dead on this dirt
we didn't even leave time to hurt.

Christine Alison Bennett

CHRISTINE ALISON BENNETT. Pen Name: Cab; Born: Ventura, California; Single; Education: Attending Santa Barbara City College to obtain A.A.; Occupation: Executor, Bus driver; Poetry: 'Tom, My Earthly Father,' *The American Muse*, 1984; 'The Mirage,' 'Corner Shadows,' *Ashes to Ashes*, 1984; 'Awakened,' *Poetry of Love*, 1982; 'Devil's Hell,' *Glowing Embers*, 1984; Comments: *I was born in Ventura. I now reside in Goleta, California. I wrote my first poem at age 12, often writing late into the night. My poetry has appeared in several anthologies. I'm also working on my first romance novel, entitled* The Quest.

WINTRY TEARS

There are so many words that I need to say,
so many thoughts to be expressed,
as wintry tears fondle the earth
climaxing the blossoms of tomorrow's petals,
cascading into collective patterns,
forging into oblivion.

One word, each a drop,
a thought,
fragmented, forlorn,
unadorned, imprisoned,
must be released,
in or out of season,
for no reason
than,
just
I love you.

Edward Kagel

SNOW

snow's soft pearly
        white essence
                smiles
            upon all
    in blinding
                rage
blocking life
                        movement
            till
        death
            joins
                    the partnership
        and both
        become
        one.

E. Ann Rauer

E. ANN RAUER. Born: Oxnard, California, 8-21-59; Education: North Idaho College, Coeur d' Alene, Idaho, 1981-83; currently enrolled at San Bernardino Valley College, majoring in Graphic Arts and English; Occupations: Part-time Photocomposition and Assistant Night Production Supervisor at *The Sun* Newspaper in San Bernardino, California; Awards: Golden Poet, 1985 and 1986, Honorable Mention 1985; Poetry: 'Friend,' 7-85; 'Growing,' 9-85.

HAIKU TAKEN FROM HAWAIIAN VACATION

Vacationtime near
Sailing along in the sky
All is white below

Beautiful white clouds
Cushion our jet in the sky
Hawaii appears

Sunbathe in the rain
Hawaiians hang loose
Ala Moana

Flight over Maui
Leaving Honolulu sights
Haleakama

Whales jumping up high
Enjoying the Pacific
Seaflite excursion

Sunset disappears
Over the blue Pacific
Will we meet again?

Jo Bivin

HEFFALEFFASTING

It's a heff.
It's a leff.
It's a heffaleffasting.

What the heck do I care
if anything goes wrong?
What the heck do I care
if a frog should turn into a drosophila
instead of a prince?
What the heck do I care
if the weight of a hanky
causes the Dreadnought to sink?
What the heck do I care
if George Washington's wife, Martha,
had a mole on the end of her nose?
And what the heck do I care
if Dan Rather should be replaced by Don Rickles?

Because it's a heff.
A leff.
A heffaleffasting.

Bobbi Sinha

WALLS

You can still see the newspaper clippings, plaques
and trophies that won your father fame
hanging on the dark walls of your house.
Your mother sits quietly by the kitchen window
drinking coffee and staring blankly into her toast
while your sister, still naive,
talks to her about the costume she needs
for the school play, and your brother
has yet to come home from the night before,
and you, dear friend.
You can still remember racing insanity,
yet you never said a word. You vowed
to remain solid and faithful, your mother's rock,
you longed to scream through the house
and hide from its presence.
Now when you think, you wonder
what to do when you are free.

Nancy A. Brosky

GOD CRIES

Furious! Verging on tornadic; whipping violently
through leafless branches!
Screaming! The pitch deafening; not quite vainly seeking entrance
into still, silent abodes . . .
The wind!
A great flurry, sending leaves and debris crashing into every
obstacle that dares get in its way . . .
An old woman and a skinny, frightened child, plunge through the
flurry — staggering; trying desperately to reach their destination.
Their cheeks, exposed to the squall, are raw and tender.
Pines and Maples bow low in feigned humbleness as the Devil's icy
breath races through their limbs.
Suddenly, an angry, black cloud descends, muffling
treacherous howls!
A moment passes; deep silence prevails . . .
And then,
God's tears rain down on a torn and beaten earth.

Cindy L. Hartman

MY NATIVE WISH

I wish my feet could dance in the sands of Africa
Dance, to the beat of my ancestors' *drum*
If I knew the way my people danced
Then, my heart and soul will have succumbed

I wish my soul were in Africa,
Mind and spirit free
And everything there was green again
My people speaking in our native tongue —
Beneath a tatu* tree

I wish my tribal grandmother could show me
The sita** worn on her wedding day
And we could share all the joys and laughters
That were celebrated in their tribal and cultural way

I know now, I may never get there
But, my heart still wishes it so —
When my soul leaves this foreign soil,
I yearn for my future Kumi*** to know
I wanted my feet to dance in the sands of Africa . . .
To the beat of my ancestors' drum.

*   *Tatu* (ta-too) *Swahili for coffee bean tree*
** *Sita* (see-tah) *Swahili for clothing*
*** *Kumi* (koo-me) *Swahili for children*

Roz Henry

ROSALIND RENEÉ HENRY. Born: Fort Worth, Texas, 12-16-52; Education: One year of college; Occupation: Receptionist at the Dallas Museum of Art; Poetry: 'Same Difference,' 6-87; 'Plight of the Black Woman,' 6-87; Comments: *The common themes in my poetry are Black heritage or ideas. My poems are all very personal to me and are written from my point of view, coming from a Black family heritage and ancestry.*

He marched with all his buddies through Viet Nam's muddy soil.
He shared the heavy burdens and he shared the endless toil.
He seemed to walk on angels' wings. So strong, so sure, so bold.
Protected by his destiny. The bells had not yet tolled.

While others all around him fell to plague and serpent's bite.
And many wounds were suffered in the battles — day and night.
Not for him this torment, his tale as yet untold.
He walks in silent dignity. The bells still have not tolled.

He walked right through the gates of Hell, a twinkle in his eye.
Nothing seemed to touch him, it all just passed him by.
No illness did befall him, not even just a cold.
But fate awaits this young man. Have the bells for him now tolled?

He didn't fall to war wounds — he never bore a scar.
But, he came home to die upon the freeway — in a car.
At seventeen a young man, at eighteen growing old.
By nineteen he was dead and gone. For him, the bell had tolled.

Josie D

ONE IN 25,555 +\- SOME

Today is a special day.
It will only pass, but once, by my way.
It will provide once in a lifetime opportunities.

Today is not yesterday or tomorrow.
Today is neither that of Christmas,
Or May, or Washington's Birthday.

Today is today.
Today is this moment.
Today is a diminishing 24 hours long.
Today is here, tomorrow unsure.

Today is the first day of the rest of my life.
Today is only what I make of it, be it bland or grand.

Today will I take to my knees, take a seat, take a stand?
Of today, what would I say, if bade,
Today was good; today was a blow-off?
What will I do with this day?

Today is "the day that the Lord hath made,
I will rejoice and be glad in it."*

*Psalms 118:24

Kathryn Lytle

MY WEDDING SONG FOR YOU

At last, no longer two,
You are as one
Eagerly walking the narrow path,

Crossing mountaintops,
Hewing through deep valleys,
And looking unto the Son,
Remaining blind to diverging shadows of darkness,
In pursuit of growth-giving visions,
Taking with you creativity and flexibility.
Your blessings, I pray, be as numerous as the
 dimples upon the orange peel.

Kathryn Lytle

THE REWARDS AT THE END OF THE ROAD

When life becomes a battlefield
With its obstacles too great to overcome —
When you have no strength
To inhale the country air
Or the scent of the spring flowers —
When a stroll in the park
Doesn't allow the old limbs
To sway in the breeze anymore —
And when the sweet melody
Of nature's orchestra
Becomes but a faint murmur to thine ear,
Look to the heavens above
And say a silent prayer.
Pray that you've earned a place in His kingdom,
And upon your arrival
You will find your robe
And starry crown waiting there.

Angela Yvonne Baker

EGO-MAGNIFICENT

So many people tell me that they want to be all that they can be,
But how do they avoid the traps of not seeing what they should see?
Where ego clouds up all the senses; lost Alices in Wonderland,
With distorted and maimed perspectives — putting up their
 very own fences.

Looking into a mirror of distortion
 Where all psychic energy flows through the glass.
Needing no one; abandoned with only the touch of fear.
Nothing returns back to the soul —
 Loss of honesty and clarity soon takes its thunderous toll.

I think I've found the answer to be all that we can be,
By acknowledging that we're all in this together,
 sharing each gift we hold,
We don't have to lose that precious self-identity.

Ego now becomes a magnificent word and bears no evil seal,
Meaning only the strength to know ourselves and use
 those talents wisely,
All of us as one, revelling in its fruitful feel.

Exchanging energies without fears, planting and harvesting each seed,
Balancing ourselves through others, taking only what we need.

Let's all be ego-maniacs and dance our dances of joy!
Knowing it's right to say what we believe, never drowning
 in self-importance,
Praying that we give ourselves gold stars for all that we achieve!

Adele Williams

A WRINKLE IN MY SOUL

Awoke with a wrinkle in my soul this morning.
Desperately struggling to free it,
but a voice deep inside said
Nothing will change —
The wrinkle will always remain.

Days go on and melt into weeks;
My fortieth birthday
and no goals to seek.

I touch moments like butterfly wings
brushing lightly on the tips of my fingers.
Reminders of the past: a haunting voice, a smell, a certain song.

Walking in this closet, I deeply fear,
because when I'm back there it's all so real.
Hold on to me — so I don't disappear.

Reaching out, you give me your touch.
Crossing this ocean of misery, your hand leads the way.

I'm ironing out the wrinkles now,
lightening the burdens I bear.
"You cannot remain in the past," you whisper,
"Only try to understand it so you may progress into the Future . . ."

Adele Williams

DAWN

In front of me
is a canal
The sun not yet risen
The grey-tipped white birds waking
gliding over my head
The grey-blue sky in the water under my feet, playing
like I am the Indian
The waves clap because they are the cowboys
It is a game
the cigarette smoke plays, too
Roping around me
all the different lines, all those drawings
one after another
As long as he keeps blowing it out
Him
that person over there
Reveling in defeat
as the sounds, the breeze, the smoke
make their kill
Devouring him
into the silence of their pictures

Sharlene Mark

MISSING

A child taken by chance
Worrying, your days are a mindless trance.

Today the children are playing,
Tomorrow there's a child who is missing.

Morning of sadness; you can pray
Strengthening the mind and soul everyday.

What can you do? Keep caring!
Don't give in; Don't give up.

Don't forget your life or other people keep giving.
Share your good memories; live for the missing.

Watching over each other's sisters and brothers.
Child helping child; Fathers helping mothers.

Maybe we can't find or save everyone,
But working together to help a few is . . .
    . . . better than helping none.

You can help all the people who are missing.
Alive or dead they will get your help from your praying.

Laura A. Knapp

SAND CASTLES

I saw a tiny grain of sand, upon a lonely beach.
I wondered how it got there, beyond the ocean's reach.
Was it once a giant stone, upon a mountain peak?
Standing like a royal throne, it's glory there to seek.

Then did a storm come rushing by,
And unleash all its might?
And stones crashed down with booming cry,
And scattered left and right.

Then gradually, the years went by
And stone was rubbed by stone,
And tiny little grains of sand
Were washed into the foam.

Then once again, a storm came forth
And swept the ocean clean,
The waves threw sand upon the shore
And made the beaches gleam.

Who knows how many centuries past
It took to bring it near?
I sit upon the sand, at last,
And know God put it here.

Mary L. Ross

FROM "YEARS" TO
"SECONDS" OF TIME

Lord, grant me *years* — enriched with Your love
Eager to serve You; as You watch from above.

Lord, grant me *months* — enriched with concern
For the helpless and needy; with hearts that yearn.

Lord, grant me *weeks* — enriched with Your grace
To set good examples; at just the right pace.

Lord, grant me *days* — enriched with Your spirit
That others may see; what there is to inherit.

Lord, grant me *hours* — enriched with Your word
And try to tell others; who may not have heard.

Lord, grant me *minutes* — enriched by a few
Never failing to thank You; for all that You do.

Lord, grant me *seconds*
Before I close my eyes
To know I'll "soon" be with You
In "Your Kingdom" in the sky.

Carolyn T. Mokan

DIXIE

I came up from the South,
The dusty-rained wind in my mouth,
From the tar-papered shacks and furrows of fields,
Through thorn-tangled thickets
And dank, smoky forests of crickets
Who, to my onslaught, serenity yields . . .
The dirty cotton strands, never picked by hard, black hands
Stick fast in my beggar-liced hair and shredded trappings;
And I tramp on, heaving in gulps of stale air, branches
Snapping. The sugar cane I broke, carved and chewed
In the clear swelter of the cruel morning
Has ceased its poor nourishing,
And my stomach and blood howl for substance,
Sustenance, as I pass a pod-withered garden
Where once, in an eternity far away, It Did
Flourish.

Roger Browning Moreland

CELEBRATIONS

For all that has been, is now, and shall be
For color and vibrance, dancing and sea
Mountains and rivers, forests and glens
Butterflies, unicorns, rainbows and fens
Hummingbirds, sailing ships, mountain rams, swans
Music and laughter, evenings and dawns
Bubbles, balloons and songs of delight
Sun in the mornings, stars in the night
Journeys and trips with things still to see
Adventures and tales, distances free
Waterfalls, rimrocks, canyons of might
Mem'ries just waiting for time-seekers' sight
Seasons of summer, of winter, of fall
Simple, full grandeur, beauteous all
Spring's dance of newness and white singing streams
Castles and candles, worlds of dreams
For all that has been, is now, and shall be
We give thanks to you, Lord, we give thanks to thee.

M. D. LeDoux

ONLY A ROSE

No other flower grows quite as elegantly as a rose,
  The rose, no matter the color, is the sweetest one that grows,
Orchids, poinsettias, daffodils, jasmine, forget-me-nots and violets,
  Some are African violets and no one can deny their beauty and grace;
So many colors and hybrids are now ours to silently grow,
  God's gift to us just simply to beautify our gardens so
But a rose is so fragile, dainty and delicate,
                        so gorgeous for us to view,
  Just to mention a few of the prize ones are Caribia,
                  Voodoo, Double Delight
Also Show-off, Blue Girl, John F. Kennedy, Mint Julep and Lemon Spice
  All just for our sense of pleasure and to only decorate our homes;
Flowers are, even sometimes, compared to our loved ones and friends,
  So very beautiful are the colors but beware of the thorns;
Seemingly so, no flower grows as graciously and gently as a rose,
  The rose will stand out over all the other beauties that grow,
The petals will wilt though, this we all can conceive,
  Unlike our friendships that are true and will never deceive;
The relationship will just grow sweeter and more precious, you'll see
  As the delicate petals of the most exquisite flower we know,
If this writing should seem, somehow, unrealistic to you,
  Just for one second, seek its beauty
                        and inhale the fragrance of a rose.

Lee Dennis

A LIFE BEYOND

for Kenneth D. Capodagli

So you flicked the channels of your energy.
Dramatic voice to achieve your liturgy.
How glorified you must have been, throned to your selected kingdom.
What you believed to perceive, eternal peace – pain deceased.

Was it memories attracting your return?
Peaceful flotation a knowingly yearn.
Patience unyielding to stive life's rewards,
You chose to abandon all life's discords.

Temple of kingdom's love soothes your afflictions,
Caressing your soul's altered awareness.
Upon awakening you walk but are not seen.
Reflections in the pond quickly forgotten.

Realization, Frustration, Confusion –
Alteration, Elation, Illusion.
Inner turmoil creates lessons,
A better soul yet to become.

A life beyond life beyond life,
To forever grow, To forever know,
Inner peace, the karmic lesson,
Time to endure reincarnation.

Suzanne Joy

FOR A FLEETING MOMENT

Oh, for a fleeting moment
back in time I did peer,
a glimpse at times gone by
and people I still hold dear.

When childish ways so precious were,
giving way to more grown-up days.
Days when responsibilities were light,
days when all seemed just right.

Oh, for that fleeting moment I held to
so very tight,
the dark days had faded,
leaving only the light.

Precious days, precious times,
times to treasure.
Memories to keep in
my heart always, forever.

Carol M. Iacona

OUR LOVE WON'T
EVER CHANGE

Now that I'm so far away
I love you more and more each day
I'm so afraid love will leave me
Just one day you might want to be free
I know I shouldn't feel this way
The love we share has got to stay
I know you love me
With me you'll always be
Tell me that we'll never part
And you will never break my heart
Our love will soar to the greatest heights
In love together each day and every night
It hurt so much to see you cry
Now I hate the day I said good-bye
The memories we shared will remain the same
The love we share will never change

S. M. Young

MOTHER'S DAY

Mother's Day is on its way,
Remember your Moms on this special day.
They care for you in every way.
Try to heed whatever they say.
They help you in what you do and say,
Please be kind to her in every way.
She's there for you whenever you need her.
Whether you're fine, or have a fever.
She always helps you when you're ill.
It is Mom's special skill.
She's always there to comfort you,
Whenever you have a nightmare.
You can see, she really does care.
So be good to her, while she is here,
So she will know, you also care.
Cherish each moment, each day, each year.
Be thankful for every hour she's there.
Tell her you love her when she's near,
It is what Moms like to hear.

Carol Bourdy

MISS YOU

*To Woody,
my forever friend*

When Eventide unveils a dying day
   and slumber fills the air –
Into twilight vanish the heavens
   of azure blue;
Stately trees lift up up their faithful arms
   in prayer –
And I – I miss you.

Night winds soar up to embrace
   a proud enchanted sky –
The last ember fades from sunset's glow;
Though the cares of day have gone –
I sigh – for I miss you so.

Ilse H. Ehret

THE REALM OF LIFE

For each day we live yesterday it will
always be tomorrow

For each day we live tomorrow it will
always be yesterday

For each day we live with our wrongs or rights
it will always be the past

For each day we live negatively it will
be impossible

We must live for today and forget the
past wrong, and look for the future

If you can do this in your lifetime
it will be the sphere or the Realm
of your Life

Linda S. Fulton

ALAS THE PUPPET

Move, move, move upon a string,
Soaring there, now leaping here.
Jump, dance, laugh and sing,
But alas, I see the puppeteer.

Cut the string and see you fall,
Onto laughter, hiss and sneer.
Not to answer curtain's call,
For alas, I see the puppeteer.

The theater's cold, dark and sad,
A chamber now for children's fear.
The echoes of the laughter had,
For alas, we saw the puppeteer.

But alas, the puppet, for we loved him dear.

Scott Bradley Gushwa

THE SKY ABOVE,
THE CLOVERLEAF BELOW

Datsun, Mazda, Subaru,
It furthers one to cross the great waters
in search of dependable transportation,
there is no blame,

The superior man ignores the rebates,

Hiroshima, Nagasaki, the great sun rises
over the still blue waters,

Honda, Yamaha, Kawasaki,

Thus is revealed the true meaning
of the missing hexagram,

Flame above,
Earth below,
Steadiness brings good fortune,
Three receptions beneath one sun,
Toyota, Nissan, Mitsubishi.

(Independent financing is available).

Ron Savage

TREASURES GROWN OLD

As a child I heard and believed
the legend so often told –
At the end of every rainbow
sits a pot of gold.

Now when storm clouds gather
I hang my head and cry –
For I have chased the rainbow
till life has passed me by.

So please hold back the lightning,
don't let the thunder roll –
Please hold back the death-watch
that threatens and seeks my soul.

Oh yes, I've chased my rainbow,
searched yonder far and wide;
but, I overlooked the sunshine –
ebbing with each tide.

I overlooked the meadows –
green and filled with flowers
much too busy – face turned upward –
waiting for the showers.

Jean Lockamy Kaplan

The practice of being gentle
Is as much physical as it is mental
Softly spoken words
Are much mightier than swords
Quiet, deliberate movements
Are graceful improvements
For a person, large or small
We would most likely all
Benefit from the practice
Of being gentle and the fact is,
We would love the life
We would find
When we practice being kind.

Jill G. McDowell

HORSE SENSE

I hear the whispering of an American pony
He prances unhaltingly inside his stall
Unable to break free of his prison . . .

Oh, maybe he's able – but he just doesn't know
Which way to go – what direction to take
So he stands and prances in place – waiting, just waiting . . .

Waiting for something that may never arrive
Not a grooming, or new saddle or anything like that
But he stands waiting, for something – a chance . . .

A chance to be something more than himself
Maybe a grand stallion on a beautiful carrousel
Maybe to be – maybe to grow wings . . .

To grow wings, to fly high, out above the mundane
Maybe then to escape, at least be free for awhile
Oh, to grow wings, he'd be a Pegasus in Paradise . . .

Alas, I hear the whisperinghen to escape, at least be free for awhile
Oh, to grow wings, he'd be a Pegasus in Paradise . . .

Alas, I hear the whispering of an American pony
Prancing unhaltingly inside his stall
Unable to break free, but able to dream.

Shelly Smith

ON GOD

God is my inspiration,
God is my only need.
From God all things come.

God is beauty and . . .
When you see beauty, you see God.

Life is beauty.
The laughs, the tears, the joy, and
Sorrow,
These things are but a part of God.

When you laugh, say "Thank God it is
great to be alive." And you will laugh
with God.
And when you cry, think of God,
for God cries with you.

But think not that you are God,
for now man is God.
He is but a part of God.

Think not that you need,
for God fills all needs.
Think but you want and . . .
if you need you will receive.

John J. Francis

LAST YEAR'S LEAF

I saw you old leaf, skipping by my window one more time
Before gliding in spring's breeze
On to earth's everlasting recipe.

Last year you were on our maple
First, in nature's wondrous form, a bud,
Then as if by magic, a beautiful bright green leaf
Always faithful, contributing to a cool shade
Or a shelter in a sudden shower.

You chose gold for color in the fall
And I watched you mellow to a soft brown
One dawn, with the slightest sigh,
You floated to the ground, your work done
Soon snow came softly covering the resting place you found.

Now another spring has arrived
Though it is sad to see old leaves blow away
Indeed, you have such a short time in life's minute,
I will not grieve, for you know you're one of nature's perfect schemes
From beginning to end you have given
And always you have been so beautiful
Thank you old leaf, goodbye, goodbye.

Melba Barber

The pavement,
hot and grit
beneath his feet
   Jesus walked,
long and thin
   and beside him
   his companion dog,
ragged fur and dirt,
   panted along in pace

"The roads
   are much straighter these days," said Jesus,
   observing the placement of his feet.

The dog laughed –
   "It seems that straight roads
   leave much less to see."
– as he chased his tail
'round Jesus' knees.

Mark Anthony Squires

STAGES OF MY LIFE

You've taught me things since my life began
First to crawl and then to stand.
Soon came school, such a big day
Off to learn, then home to play.
Before we knew it the years had passed.
High school graduation had come at last.
With Bob's proposal came one of the biggest choices of my life.
I made my decision and became his wife.
With the birth of Josh and then Hanna, our family grew to four.
Now we were blessed with two little ones for all of us to adore.
You've been there for me through all of the above
Sometimes with discipline, but always with Love.
So every time you read this I hope you will see
How so very important you both are to me.
I feel that I've been very lucky through the good times and bad
To have always had the both of you – My Mom and Dad!

Patty Maben

DEPRECIATION

Automobiles are fine things;
Alive almost, once a man knows them.
But the older ones aren't worth much
   (needing body work and such).
I own a car that's half my age;
And the upkeep's getting harder –
Now it needs a clutch and fresh rubber.
But these days, I don't care much. I mean,
Even the hottest rods get rusty with age,
The new highways too fast for them.
I am thirty-two, past the stage
Of being used, and not quite ready yet
To be collected or driven in parades.
I run good. And even though my price
Is no longer listed in the *Bluebook,*
There must be someone who needs parts
   (mine are still intact);
Or perhaps a handy second for the wife?

Gregory J. Smith

HAIL! HAIL! THE LORD ABOVE

Hail! Hail! The Lord above
Open your hearts, feel His love
For He is reaching out to you
Longing to show you His love is true

Forget your pride and take His hand
For He loves you, He'll understand
For His love is so strong and true
That He alone will help you through

He can make things right again
He's your father, He's your friend
He can make the darkness light
He can make the wrong all right

For His love is everlasting
He's your Father, He's the King
Praise Him when you speak
Praise Him when you sing

Danette G. Balsam

MY PRAYER

Reach out Lord – and take my hand
Help me with – my Christian stand
Let me feel – your loving grace
That saves me from – this evil place
I'm still watching – that eastern sky
Because when you come – I know I'll cry
But the tears will be – of great joy
As Satan will lose – his only toy
This world he has told – his great lies
Will soon see clearly – through his disguise
Thank you Lord – for your everlasting love
And the Holy Spirit – you sent from above
Praising you now – with all my might
May it be pleasing – to your sight
Returning your love – and keeping your will
For that soul-saving trip – up on Calvary Hill

James R. Norris

BACKWATER CHILD

Backwater child, slant spoon fed,
   late arrival at the fair.
Behold! With all banners flying red,
   his own demons hosted there.

Faith and Doubt and Absolute
   Allegory, Myth and Maybe;
Man or Ape or question moot;
   Son of David – Virgin Lady.

''Hush my child, do not ask.''
   Contradictions! Paradoxes!
When a smile is only mask,
   put the sky in little boxes.

Sweet relief unto the bone,
   O' feel his burden ease.
His, they are not his alone;
   hosts are they who ride the seas.

Gray bearded his revelations!
   Many others man the oars;
Seed of all the generations
   visit only open doors.

Gene W. Abbott

THE DAY THE RIVERS ROSE

Dayton was a pretty town
   With three rivers flowing by.
The hand of God had there touched down
   And brought beauty to the eye.

Its buildings were the finest
   The dreams of man could build.
Its citizens the kindest
   This cold world ever filled.

Then one rainy morning
   The rivers marched from their beds.
They crept over everything
   Even people's heads.

Where once there was beauty,
   Now lay just mud.
A town filled with life
   Was now filled with blood.

But Dayton didn't crumble
   Though her heart was filled with pain.
For an even greater Dayton,
   Was born in that spring rain.

Judy A. Deeter

A BEST FRIEND

I will always have a special friend.
   She will be sometimes yours but always
   mine until the end.
She has her good days and her bad days, too.
   But I can bet she is as good as you.
That is one thing I know for sure.
   Just like two plus two is four.
She is me, can you believe that?
   You better! Because my name is Pat.
My best friend is very special to me.
   I treat her with a lot of respect
   even on our bad days.
I am sure she is me. We match down to
   our last name.

Pat Motola

FINALLY SEEING

In vanity's mirror
   i disappear
  No more searching
   for reality isn't there
Seeing a face
      painted to please
     Completely believing in
     the desire to be
No longer a possession
   transition of age
Inside a developing soul
   and vanity is true
  A simple vase
     holds beauty for me
A love for him
shared between two hearts always
  A portrayal of beauty
   in essence
  Believing in all that i am
   and could ever be

Dianna Michelle

IMAGINATION

My daughter is a weasel,
At least she is today.
She sneaks around the house,
Stalking out her prey.

There was a time she felt
Like being a giant frog;
And pretended to eat horseflies,
While sitting on a log.

And her very special friend,
I never could hear or see;
A dolphin named Jennifer,
Who lived by the sea.

Oh, the imagination
Creates a fantastic world;
A hideaway from grown-ups,
For an inventive little girl.

Linda Susiene

JUST A TECHNICALITY

So what, green hair
Chains and leathers everywhere
Gender really has no bearing
On the hideous stuff we're wearing
Lots of guys
Paint their eyes
Thinking of a new hair-do
Well, come on ladies, get a crew

New wave, punk rock
Mega volts of future shock
Well, go ahead and stand and stare
You don't like it, we don't care
We are a disease of a new variety
And we've come to join your sick society
With flower children in three piece suits
And city boys in cowboy boots

Being strange is just a technicality
Of one's own individuality . . . of your own individuality
So what, green hair . . .

Jeri K. Rooks

A POET

When you are a poet,
your work is never done.
    Thoughts rush into your head by the dozens,
never one by one.
    Our thinking is different from all others,
with a deeper appreciation
    for all that binds us together,
to ourselves and all creation.
    We are in harmony with ourselves
and put our thoughts into view,
    so that others may understand
what we have to say to you.
    We try to convey our messages
in songs, riddles and rhymes,
    but we are often laughed at
and misunderstood at times.
    We're trying to be at peace with the world
and express it through our word,
    for though we are few in number,
we try our best to be heard.

H. Thomas Huben

THE STORM KING

Over the meadows the storm king rode,
Scattering snowflakes, the north wind he bore
Howled like a banshee fresh from the lease,
And crashed every town, shaking window and door.
Stalked every house and howled 'round the flue,
Waited for prey that was foolish to dare
Brave the cold wind and the ice and the snow.
He would swoop down upon them with terrible glare,
Then he would chuckle at shivering folk
Watching them huddle and draw close their cloaks,
His laughter still echoing far down the canyon
As if he thought it a wonderful joke.
On through the woodlands he rides with the gale,
Piling the snow in such fantastic way.
All was a pattern of deep ribbed whiteness,
Figments of artistry, beautiful and gay.

Bessie Mittick

HAWKESS

You,
thrown into relief by your own sweet surprise . . .
the dew of mating falling from your lips
                    to the floor of me
                        elevates.

I need your love
            to recall the truth in madness,
            the divinity of abandon.
But, mostly,
It is the art you make of me that I need.
    The I,
    so well founded in the soft moans
living beneath your skin,
that linger on your tongue,
and promise themselves behind your coalshine eyes.

Oh yes . . .

        Let us burn!

Claire Burns Miller

402

TIME IS OF THE ESSENCE

Did you know you only have 500 days
    To really be able to live
The time that is left over for you
    From what you already give.

The time it takes to eat and work
    And take care of other things
Such as chores, sleeping & traveling
    And whatever the day brings.

The next 36 years you will have
    The equivalent of 550 days
To spend in actual living
    In better happier ways.

So spend your days wisely
    For when they're gone each day
They will never come back again
    We can't afford to waste away.

Each one of us is called to weave
    A unique tapestry of time
And how he spends his days on earth
    Should be what is most sublime.

Jeannie Urban

HEAVY

The world of the heavy
Causes so much pain;
A world full of tension,
A world full of gain.

The world of the obese
Is made of constant refrain;
Continual denial,
Full of pressure and strain.

Rejection of others,
And even more of oneself;
Feeling terribly ugly,
And fearing for their health.

May those who are spared
This plight in their life;
Show kindness instead of repulse,
For others who face this strife.

Linda Susiene

FLAMES OF THE HEART

Flames fill my heart on this
    And every day
Because you showered me with
    Your love . . .
The touch of your lips made my heart sing
    When we kiss we kiss with
Passion as if it's for the very
    First time
Our love grows into a rose bursting forth
    With both of our loves coming
    Together as one
Yet giving each other time
    To branch out on our own
To be free and strong in our love

Queenie Archer

I'm a wife and I'm a mother –
    who has chosen to stay home,
So when people say, "Oh, you don't work?"
    I just smile and hide my groan.

Well, as I did my laundry –
    in between loads two and three,
I thought, maybe I should get a job,
    to help out my family.

As I bathed the dog, put towels away,
    and made up all three beds,
I thought, I shouldn't sit at home,
    but go back to work instead.

While I feed and clean eight gerbils –
    the two birds could use it, too,
I can feel the slightest headache –
    let's just hope it's not the flu!

After dusting and the sweeping,
    and when dinner's in the pot,
If I've got time, with coffee in hand –
    I'll sit down and give working some thought!

Deborah A. Judisch

THE PLIGHT OF THE FARMER

The rack body sagged
As the farmer's truck
Struggled beneath its weighted load

Already the turgid
Green beans
Had begun to release their ripeness
Wilting in the rays
Of daylight's early heat

Dawn painted its last
Blood-red streaks across the sky
As a farmer, passing by
Shouted, "Going to market?"
"I'm heading home.
Got nowhere near a fair price."

He paused a moment
At the edge of earth
Whose hollows held household garbage
Then with a single motion
His calloused hands
Dumped the load

Angelina Rossetti

GOODWILL

When you visit home folks,
And notice jobs undone,
Mention his accomplishments,
You'll find a friend is won.

If you talk of people,
Their good points strongly stress.
Sure, they have faults aplenty,
Yet, truly, have you less?

Life's a trial to most folks,
We all want grand world things.
Needs are few, don't moan and groan,
Of blessings all can sing.

With goodwill your pattern,
Jest-plain-folks become fun,
And when they speak of their loves,
Here's thanks – you will be one!

Grace Pierce

ONE LOVE IN MY LIFETIME

You have many friends throughout your life.
Some are good, some are not.
But you are one of the good ones because you
Really seem to care and make me feel like
I am someone and that your life is there.

There are many things that you do
Every day to help people out.
That makes me proud
To know someone special like you.

The one love in my life time is
Having a friend like you to guide me
Through the good and bad of everyday life
And that's what friendship is all about.

Phyllis Fogel

LET GO OF THE PAST

Let go of the past
    Let life go on.
Let your life be free
    Just like a swan.
Don't grab at it and hold it
    And keep it in the dark.
Let your life be joyous
    Let it be like a lark.
You have better things to do
    With your time
    Each and every day –
Than sitting around moping that way –

Open your eyes
    And hear what I say –
For there's more to life
    And it starts today.

Mark Stoddard

FADED MEMORIES

This picture that I came across today
        brought back a smile and a tender thought . . .
But photographs don't often show the pain
        of the hard times or the love that was lost.

My reflections are of feelings pure and kind.
'Twas a bond that was unselfish and refined.
And real love keeps on giving; I know it should.
But it seems we'd given and we'd taken all we could.

Isn't it funny how our lives just slip away,
        and the hands of time are something we can't fight.
Yet I can't help wondering if you still do care . . .
        while I'm aching for your warmth in the night.

We mapped our future to the end of our days;
        but the best laid plans will often go awry.
Now I'm thinking it's the price we've got to pay
        for the wisdom that will help us to survive.

Faded memories gone by . . . Tracks of tears cried long ago . . .
Looking back and wondering why
        all our dreams went up in smoke.

Darlene Bergeron Valentine

DEAR MOTHER

*Written April 24, 1987,
for Mother's Day*

Dear is the truest word, when describing you.
    It shows in all you say and do.

With your words of encouragement and praise.
    When lost, there to guide me in my ways.

Even a mother to those friends around us.
    Helping, caring and worrying regardless.

There's nothing in this world worth as much.
    Having you there with advice, or just a tender touch.

You're the type of mother that every girl and boy wishes for.
    You know when to hold me, or just let go to soar.

Whatever I lacked, you gave me all you had.
    You loved me all the more, when good or bad.

Dear Mother is so true, when I think of you.
    You are truly like no other, and
I Thank God for giving me – *You!*

Jamie Marie Lee

THIS LIFE

In a day: 24 hours seems to end
    before it begins

In a week: 7 days, what were
    you to seek?

This Life: of yours and mine,
    is it just a waste of time?

All you can do is wait, for this or
    that, or until it's too late

In a month: 4 weeks have passed,
    how long will this last?

In a year: 12 months, that's how fast
    this life can pass

This Life: of yours and mine,
    very few are even given the time

People are born, and people die,
    some without an explanation why

Jamie Marie Lee

In our back yard there used to be a grand, majestic old oak tree.
We tied a rope to its strongest limb and made a seat to swing us in.
When I would swing, toes touching sky, I was sure if I let go I'd fly
    like birds in the blue, never touching ground.
        Just soaring, flying and gliding around.

As all small children, I learned one day it just plain doesn't work
    that way. Oh, I let go – Oh boy, did I. But, as you can guess,
        I did not fly. I hit the ground with a thud – kerplop!
And came to a most unpleasant stop. I jumped up rubbing the seat
    of my pants – I'd landed smack dab on a hill of ants.

I made up my mind right then and there that I'd never again try
    to fly through the air. But, after awhile, so determined was I,
I thought I'd give it just one more try. So I figured and planned.
This time I know I'll be able to fly when I let go. Let go I did –
and where did I stop? Back on the ant hill with a thud – kerplop!

With childish determination I knew I'd just done something wrong –
    but this wouldn't do. I figured some more and tried it again –
        and again and again – but I just couldn't win.
At last, discouraged and tired and sore, I decided I just couldn't
    try any more. My mind said "Give up, you silly girl.
        You weren't meant to fly out of this world."

I wanted so badly to try it once more but I couldn't, the seat of my
pants was too sore. Many summers have come and gone since the day
I decided that I would just fly away. Sometimes I wonder, with a sly
    little grin, if I'd tried just once more – but then
        I shake myself soundly, I know I can't fly
        (But if I had tried – Could I? Could I?)

Josie D

MIRRORS OF THE SOUL

I am drawn
By the sparks in your eyes
Like a moth to a flame.

I am captured
By the color in your eyes
Like a light to a prism.

I am bonded
By the care in your eyes
Like a mother to her babe.

I am pulled
By the need in your eyes
Like a tide to a shore.

But most of all
I am attracted
By the love in your eyes
Like a woman to a man.

Susan A. Remeika

SITTING ON THE PALE MOON

Riding on a rainbow
Across the darkened skies
Sitting on the pale moon
I listen to all your lies.

I saw a falling star
Burning through the air
Sitting on the pale moon
I can see you standing there.

Clouds fill my head
And my tears fall like rain
Caught in total confusion
Stung by all the lies and pain.

I sit upon the pale moon
As the sun starts to rise
I'm looking for all the answers
And the words to say goodbye.

Evelyn DaCunha

THE CLOUDBURST

A flash of light
Comes into sight,
It brings a moment
Of day to night.

It is followed by
A fearsome cry
Of angels singing
In the sky.

The dancing of rain
On my windowpane,
Lasting awhile,
Begins to refrain.

Moving on
The cloudburst is gone,
Just passing through
En route of its marathon.

Michael Geyer

SONNET OF WAR

The grass is tilled
The seeds are spilled
They wait for the new season
When the harvest will grow without the sun
Each year a new crop comes in
Each year the field uses more men
The harvest is lined row by row
With no need for a scarecrow
The seeds won't yield a garden
However, it will yield many of our own kin
The crops were once young and strong
But they shan't see another dawn
For, the seeds are of flesh and bone
Which lie dormant, in the garden of stone

Look at the row of white crosses
And understand the burden of our losses

David Hartman

SHARING A MOTHER'S LOVE

Another year has come and gone
    as we travel on life's way.
So let's review the love we share
    for tomorrow is Mother's Day.
For in God's plan to guide us all
    and thus respect each other,
He gave to each a special love,
    to each a precious mother.
Her tender care all through the years
    with lessons that she taught
Gave strength enough to bravely face
    Life's battles to be fought.
May we repay that precious love
    that was so freely given
With hopes that we shall meet again
    with the angels up in Heaven?
Oh! Yes indeed we may repay
    that love to one another
By passing on that Mother's Love
    to one who has no mother.

R. Hazel Storm

OUR CHRISTMAS CELEBRATION

Through clouds of grey time slips away
    as wintertime draws near
It's time to renew our friendships
    sending forth sweet words of cheer.
The Christmas Lights shine far and wide
    across our Blessed Land
With holly wreaths and mistletoe
    and waving tinsel bands.
Our family gathers full of joy
    as happiness abounds
To celebrate the birth of Christ
    the whole wide world around.
Then as the old year slips away
    may all our heartaches cease
As we look forward to the new
    guided by Our Prince of Peace.

R. Hazel Storm

THE LION SINGS

Silence broken forever
by a single note,
borne aloft and gliding
like a bird new to flight.

Out of the void
and the pitch-black night,
the far-off song
builds and rejoices,
destroying Emptiness,
and creating far-flung Space.

Galaxies fill the Heavens,
the stars join the refrain,
first light touches virgin soil
and flashes gold on the Lion's mane.

Sun and Moon molded from dust
by a single baritone phrase,
and out of the soil,
trees and creatures are called out to play
by the Deep Magic
that set Time on its course toward Home.

Richard Newswanger

TYRONE TOBY

A Black Scotty

To Toby with wistful eye of brown;
Chases flies upstairs and down.
Fly small insect of destruction;
Major receiveless attention.
Intent eyes upon a creature;
Poor fly you have a dark future.
Only a few hours ago you were born.
Toby with life ahead;
Can only please each and every whim.
Like fly catching art they;
To frightening a forlorn cat.
Opening doors you certainly can;
Shutting them never. Licking pans;
A first class dishwasher you'd be.
More gentle; faithful and as kind
A better dog you couldn't find.
Tyrone Toby after a brushing;
    why, he's *blushing*.

Evelyn Hefflon Agro

LOOKING FOR JESUS

Composed by inspiration, 8-11-61
Dedicated to my aunt.

I looked for Jesus beyond the stars but I never found Him there.
I searched the woods among the trees – I know He's everywhere.

I walked along the highways and into the crowded street,
Why can't I find Him? Where can He be? Where do the saints all meet?

The day was spent and nightfall came and I was filled with sorrow;
''I'll not give up,'' I told myself, ''I'll go again tomorrow.''

Alone I sat in my secret place and devised a noble plan
But Someone touched my aching heart and Someone patted my hand.

''Here am I,'' I heard Him say, ''I've been here all the while;
But you were filled with carnal thoughts
    and selfish deeds of worldly style.

''I looked at you from every star; I bowed from every tree,
I walked with you upon the highway but you were too busy for Me.''

''I'm sorry, Lord, I was so vain, too blind and lost to see
That You have always been so near to love and comfort me.

''I didn't need to leave this place to wander off so far;
For when I breathe, I use Your breath,
    that's just how close I know You are.

''I need not search afar again, I'm glad You're here with me.
Where'er I go; whate'er I do, I cannot stray from Thee.''

Bertha O. Whitterson

BERTHA ORR WHITTERSON. *Rooted in the vicinity and the city of Lockland, Ohio, are Bertha Whitterson's birthplace, her family training and influence, her educational beginnings, and most of all, her spiritual birth and nourishment in the family of Mt. Zion Baptist Church. After leaving a long period of teaching in the high schools of Lockland and Lincoln Heights, she was called to a new experience in the teaching field in Los Angeles, California. From here, she became the assistant to the Girls' Vice Principal in one of the senior high schools. During the crucial racial upheavals and forceful demands for racial equality in education, Bertha was asked by the Human Relations Department of the Board of Education to write a course of studies concerning minorities. Aside from the teaching career, Bertha Whitterson was active in the work of missions of the American Baptist Churches. She has held offices on the local, district, and regional levels. She also served on all the boards of management that extended throughout California and into the states of Arizona, Nevada, and Hawaii. Also, she holds the record of having been the first, and so far the only, Black president of the Los Angeles City Mission Society, an organization consisting of 66 churches. Since retirement from public schools, Bertha served in Christian schools, as the principal of one.*

NATURE'S GLORY

Nature in all her glory, unveiled before my eyes.
Below me lies the greenest grass, above me the
bluest skies.
    In His will God created it flawless beyond
a doubt. As I gaze in awe at its beauty, it
makes my flaws stand out.
    Untouched by man's uncaring hand, unspoiled
by changes and time. Such a splendid sight
for my eyes to behold, not another of its kind.
    Just the sound of the crickets pierces
the air, their eternal chirping song. As I
gaze at the sky, I hear the wind sigh, and
know this is where I belong.
    No words, no matter how many, could sum
up this sight I behold. Follow me, be silent
and you will see all of nature's glory unfold.

Dawn Stanton

ast night I put my hands together and I hoped He'd hear my call
to put a wall around my brother deep within South Africa.
He dropped a match in a dead forest and a fire's about to start.
Let the flame blaze across the world and singe the fists of blackened hearts.

Please keep Him in mind — please keep Him in mind. The world is
baking now — soon it's going to burn. For none of us — none of us
get in except by the Grace of God.

A child reached from my TV set and then he clutched my eyes —
instead of baby fat he had tired bones in place of thighs.
Nothing filled his stomach but a dream to stay alive — so far
his screams for a hope seem to be whispers that die.

Howard Dantzler

CLIFFS ON THE YELLOWSTONE.

Index

A

Abbott, Gene W. . . . 44, 99, 401
Abbott, Gregory S. . . . 230
Abulencia, Charles, Jr. . . . 121
Ackley, Lorrie . . . 176, 239
AcMoody, Connie . . . 274
A'cs, Bernhard R. . . . 3, 4
Adams, Aylwin . . . 116, 127
Adams, Betty . . . 32
Adams, J. C. . . . 24
Agro, Evelyn Hefflon . . . 405
Aguero-Tjiong, Robin L. . . . 83
Ahmad, Ayesha . . . 304
Albrecht, Janice F. . . . 94
Albright, Lou . . . 226
Alcorn, Ruth Elder . . . 110
Alexander, Keith D. . . . 338
Alires, Mystery . . . 127
Allen, Angela . . . 324, 326
Allen, Barbara . . . 314
Allen, Calee . . . 43
Allen, Clinton . . . 21
Allen, Loran . . . 374
Alswager, Tom . . . 133
Alvarez, Monnet . . . 132
Alvis, Donna . . . 121
Amargo, Mary Stephanie A. . . . 389
Amick, Pat . . . 58
Anchlia, Than . . . 250, 304
Anderson, Esther . . . 250
Anderson, Jacqueline M. . . . 194
Anderson, Jeff L. . . . 298
Anderson, Marge . . . 18
Anderson, Pa Pa . . . 309
Angell, George Irl . . . 158, 163
Angell, Philip J. . . . 168
Anglin, Frank E. . . . 109
Anne, Renatta . . . 3, 4
Arabia, Anita . . . 35, 37, 39
Archer, Queenie . . . 403
Argon, Gloria V. . . . 292
Arimondi, Vittorio Maria . . . 265
Armstrong, Bette . . . 259, 347
Arnold, Joy A. . . . 216
Aron, Randy B. . . . 50
Arthur Lisa . . . 190, 209
Ashbough, Annette M. . . . 164
Ashley, Mark . . . 316, 371
Astle, Thora M. . . . 388
Atkins, Carleen Y. . . . 126, 130
Avellone, Joseph H. . . . 268
Avery, April . . . 342
Avila, Enrique . . . 280
Ayer, Anne . . . 26, 220
Ayres, Lilian L. . . . 24

B

Babinsky, Tom . . . 68, 69, 70
Bahl, Dianne . . . 18
Bailey, Bernadine . . . 238
Bailey, Brenda L. . . . 308
Bailey, Victor . . . 96
Bailey, Zorrine . . . 50
Baird, Doreen E. . . . 351
Baird, Jimmy Rimmer . . . 91
Baisley, Emma Enberg . . . 218
Baker, Angela Yvonne . . . 396

Baker, Gail V. . . . 248, 297, 299
Baker, Helen . . . 8, 10
Baker, Vera Lee . . . 32
Balcom, Margaret Montague . . . 310
Ballantyne, Carl D. . . . 187
Balsam, Danette G. . . . 95, 99, 401
Banks, Australia W. . . . 373, 377
Banks, Lois . . . 364
Bantz, Jonni . . . 365
Baral, Aven R. . . . 174
Barber, Elaine D. . . . 372, 374
Barber, Melba . . . 133, 400
Barbour, Miriam . . . 179
Barger, Joann . . . 94
Bargmann, Joan . . . 188
Barichko, Susan . . . 379
Barker, Eric . . . 272, 374
Barker, Helen T. . . . 321
Barlow, Allison . . . 369
Baron, Linda . . . 204
Barreto, Miguel . . . 144
Barrett, Linda . . . 140
Bartée, Mitzi J. . . . 38
Bartelt, Shirley A. . . . 253, 256
Bartholomaus, B. W. . . . 19
Bates, Lori L. . . . 107
Bauer, Wendy A. . . . 92, 392
Baum, Lauren R. . . . 325, 383, 385
Baumgartner, Camille Brock . . . 292
Beard, Deborah . . . 106, 119
Bearden, Marla . . . 269, 271
Bedwell, Don . . . 32
Beeton, Beverly . . . 254, 311
Belinda . . . 321, 379
Bell, Valerie Jean . . . 102, 137, 139
Bell, Wanda Leona . . . 269
Bembry, Jacob . . . 299, 301
Benedetto, Kathleen . . . 176
Benedick, Ann . . . 304, 358
Bennett, Arline . . . 176
Bennett, Christina Anne . . . 49
Bennett, Christine Alison . . . 394
Bennett, Monica L. . . . 194, 196
Benson, Annie M. . . . 242
Benson, Clara M. . . . 9, 12
Benson, Roy D. . . . 87, 248, 299
Bentler, Mary . . . 212
Berger, Marcia . . . 372
Berger, Rosalie . . . 59
Berkemeier, Billie Ruth . . . 316
Bernard, Leon . . . 316
Berry, Gail . . . 58, 110
Berteau, Judy . . . 378
Bertolino, Vincent . . . 158
Bethea, Carroll R. . . . 242, 244
Betker, Jane . . . 118, 129
Beyer, Ruth Ann . . . 102
Biasetti, John Albert . . . 16
Bice, Marcine . . . 159
Bignell, Rob . . . 233
Billick, Debbie . . . 351
Bing, Shirley W. . . . 203
Birch-Madgett, A. . . . 184, 199
Birkenfeld, Derek . . . 116
Bivin, Jo . . . 182, 394
Bjorkfelt, Christine M. . . . 220
Black, Gayla E. . . . 233
Blackwell, M. Shelton . . . 302
Blackwood, Frank M. . . . 89, 91
Blades, Dee Anne . . . 20
Blair, J. Eugene . . . 368
Blake, Vincent R. . . . 128
Blakeslee, David Joel . . . 59
Blaney, Shannon . . . 203
Blue, Douglas J. . . . 187
Blythe, Margaret . . . 353
Boatman, Larry . . . 369

Bock, Sharon . . . 53
Bode, Christine . . . 58, 59
Bollman, Tina . . . 38, 41
Bolouki, Matty . . . 128
Bond, Harold . . . 87
Boney, Anita Hill . . . 221
Boothe, Sandra R. . . . 192
Borchardt, Olga . . . 175, 198, 215
Borden, John F. . . . 95, 97
Bostic, Linda . . . 58
Boughan, Thomas R. . . . 200
Bourdy, Carol . . . 399
Bourque, Andra Marie . . . 26, 29
Boxell, Sylvia . . . 388
Boyd, Robert S. . . . 233
Bracy, Addie L. . . . 341
Bradley, Ruby McKay . . . 124, 130
Brainin, Frederick . . . 43
Braman, George N. . . . 16
Brandli, Henry W. . . . 193
Brandt, Nora Isabel . . . 288, 290
Brannan, Cassandra . . . 327, 387
Bray, Georgia . . . 207, 209
Breitzke, Margaret Bennett . . . 26, 27
Brennan, Gail . . . 112
Bretschneider, Paul J. . . . 174
Brewer, Gladys . . . 231, 249
Brian, Maria E. . . . 42
Bridges, Charlotte Snowden . . . 58
Briggs, Brian . . . 288
Brillhart, Jerri . . . 246
Brininger, Jill M. . . . 373
Brittingham, B. A. . . . 18, 23
Brosamle, James Garland . . . 53, 55
Brosky, Nancy A. . . . 341, 395
Brower, Douglas . . . 49
Brown, Marlene . . . 31
Brown, Paula Jayne . . . 153, 218
Brown, S. C. . . . 290, 342
Brum, Olivia . . . 232
Brumfield, Audrey . . . 196, 198
Bryant, Angel Y. . . . 222
Buchanan, Patsy B. . . . 213
Buckman, Florence . . . 290, 332, 334
Buckner, Linda F. . . . 216, 239
Bunton, M. Catherine . . . 222, 251
Burch, Wendy . . . 282, 320
Burchett, Kenneth E. . . . 348
Burgess, Mary Jane . . . 367, 369, 371
Burgin, Sylvia Bothe . . . 179
Burke, Barbara L. Dietz . . . 13, 14
Burke, James "Jock" . . . 5
Burke, John . . . 59, 61
Burr, Lola . . . 164
Burrell, L. . . . 116
Burton, Sara . . . 203
Buseman, Bill . . . 188
Butler, Mardene . . . 331
Byrum, Linda A. . . . 157

C

C. S. . . . 309, 311
Cacyuk, Alexis . . . 10
Cahoon, Dorothy M. . . . 265
Calhoun, Susan Eppers . . . 47
Calhoun, Virginia K. . . . 264
Calitri, Mary Ellen R. . . . 346
Calkins, Ruth . . . 50
Callahan, Frances G. . . . 50, 242
Cameleon . . . 217
Campbell, Elesheva . . . 262
Campbell, Leona . . . 17
Campbell, Lisa . . . 140
Campbell, Madelyn . . . 112
Campbell, Maureen Redden . . . 14

Campbell, Theresa . . . 291
Cantrell, Andria . . . 302
Canty, Malik . . . 319
Capozzi, William . . . 8
Capper, Judith M. . . . 176
Caputo, Joy . . . 236
Caraway, M. . . . 121
Carbone, Lorella . . . 236
Cardenas, Gerald L. . . . 33
Cardenas, Ruben . . . 38
Cardinalli, Ilene . . . 288, 326
Carestia, Hazel . . . 76
Carhart, Ann . . . 341
Carignan, Judy . . . 322
Carmody, James P. . . . 160
Caro, Marie-Jose . . . 202, 206, 227
Carr, Daniel Thomas . . . 138, 140, 151
Carr, Jim . . . 325, 327
Carr, Scot Robert . . . 386
Carruth, Carolyn J. . . . 312, 367
Carson, Cathy S. . . . 52
Carter, Gerald M., II . . . 249
Carter, Lena J. . . . 222
Carter, Twila . . . 323, 381, 383
Carter, Wanda . . . 58, 62
Carver, Brenda . . . 383
Casolari, Albert B., Jr. . . . 7
Cassill, Lewis . . . 35
Casty, Bart . . . 286, 324
Cates, Mary E. . . . 232
Cerrato, Vickie . . . 213
Cersosimo, James . . . 146, 147
Chang, Janice M. . . . 250, 252, 303
Chang, Pahoua H. . . . 290
Chapman, Bonnie . . . 129
Chapman, Cynthia . . . 141
Chapman, Ginger . . . 365
Charpentier, Alice . . . 220, 247
Chechile, Maria . . . 193, 197
Cheshire, Tere . . . 62
Chiesa, John R. . . . 146
Christianson, S. A. . . . 152
Claeys, Rosann . . . 374
Clark, Betty . . . 222
Clark, Beverly . . . 331
Clark, Laura J. . . . 184
Clarke, Furman . . . 86
Clarke, Robert Emmett . . . 189
Clarneau, Connie L. . . . 331, 389
Clausen, Gemma Racoma . . . 294
Clayton, James G. . . . 179
Clemons, Chuck . . . 61
Clifford, Nancy Jo . . . 363
Clinton, Dorothy Randle . . . 164
Clostio, Kim . . . 226
Clothier, Kathleen M. . . . 174
Clyman, Shep . . . 239, 241
Coates, Elizabeth Diane . . . 10
Cody, John A. . . . 10
Coffee, Carolyn J. . . . 214
Cohen, Mara W. . . . 208
Coleman, George T. . . . 226, 233
Coleman, Jeanine G. . . . 61, 62
Collett, Ruth . . . 115
Collier, Donna . . . 14, 17
Collins, Linda . . . 31
Collins, Lonnie . . . 329, 331
Collins, Sandra . . . 298, 354
Colon, P. G. . . . 34, 39
Colón-Arce, L. A. . . . 298, 352
Colson, Leslie . . . 52
Comberiate, Josephine Bertolini . . . 74, 123
Conable, Phyllis C. . . . 145
Conder, Stephanie . . . 275, 370
Connolly, Lisa R. . . . 260
Conque, Dana . . . 154
Conrad, Harold K. . . . 168

Conti, James . . . 269
Conti, Valerie M. . . . 287
Cook, Bradley . . . 145
Cooksey, Deborah Newton . . . 347, 349
Cooley, Stephanie Ann . . . 232
Cooper, Bobbie . . . 198, 204, 221
Cooter, Terri . . . 52
Cornman, John M. . . . 357
Courouble, Bea . . . 103
Court, Bernadette . . . 389
Courtney, C. E., Jr. . . . 320
Courtney, Joetta E. . . . 325
Cowan, Dale . . . 268, 362
Coward, Mary Ann . . . 62
Cowen, Maria . . . 34, 40
Cox, Nadine . . . 34
Cox, Paul Marion . . . 226, 279
Cox, Shirley A. . . . 283
Craig, Shawna . . . 112
Cravens, Holly . . . 100
Crawford, B.E. . . . 362
Crenshaw, Heather . . . 263
Crisamore, Debra . . . 156
Crosby, Fawn . . . 154, 156
Cruea, Cary S. . . . 186
Cudish, Dolores . . . 294
Cumbie, Phyllis M. . . . 106
Cummins, Kevin John . . . 329, 371
Cummins, Paul . . . 6
Cunningham, Mary Jane . . . 110
Curenton, Ginevar . . . 140
Curran, Timothy G. . . . 26, 31
Curtis, Jan . . . 188
Cykiert, Corinne . . . 234, 388

D

D'Angelo, Naidine . . . 307
DaCunha, Evelyn . . . 405
Dagneau, Russell . . . 335
Dahlhauser, Mary C. . . . 62, 63
Daley, Sharon M. . . . 156, 161, 163
Dame, Frederick, Jr. . . . 52
Dantzler, Howard . . . 406
Dates, Tom . . . 254
Davenport, Leila . . . 78
Davidson, John E. . . . 384
Davis, Allan, Jr. . . . 62
Davis, Sharon J. . . . 310
Dax, Hank . . . 332
de Bergerac, Anthony Livingston . . . 98, 101, 109
de Schweinitz, Ann . . . 374
Deakin, K. J. . . . 331
Deane, Terry . . . 333
DeCesare, Linda . . . 112, 123
Dee, T. . . . 194, 211
Deerfield, Laura A. . . . 129
Deeter, Judy A. . . . 50, 99, 401
DeGraca, Desiree . . . 214
Delisle, Jennifer . . . 32
Dell, Peggy . . . 282
DeLong, Leon F., Jr. . . . 63
DeMarinis, Monica M. . . . 9, 11
Dempsey, Tina . . . 126
Dennis, Lee . . . 344, 359, 398
Derr, Annette L. . . . 379
Derrico, Sharon . . . 152
Desmond, Heather . . . 112, 115, 123
Dess, Dori Rolando . . . 44
Dess, Jeff . . . 44, 46
Detwiler, Miwa . . . 64
Deuso, Anna Maria . . . 38
Dever, Charles H. . . . 52
Devereaux, Olga E. . . . 334
Dickey, Joyce E. . . . 9

Didjurgis, Hilde K. . . . 158
Dieu, Sandy . . . 362
Dillinger, William W. . . . 96, 144, 146
Dilmore, Diane . . . 18, 23
Dinger, Craig R. . . . 133
Dixon, Carol A. . . . 77, 234, 283
Dmytrasz, Denise . . . 5, 6
Do, Susan M. . . . 230, 257
Dobrovolny, Kathy Jacobs . . . 50, 54, 70
Dodd, Buddy . . . 26
Doherty, C. M. . . . 264
Donnelly, Royston W. . . . 137
Dooley, Francis . . . 295, 297
Doorley, Mary Grasinger . . . 74
Doran, Marge . . . 312, 314
Dougher, Colleen . . . 164
Douglas, Brianna . . . 394
Douglas, Carmelita . . . 152, 163
Douglass, Mabel Cummings . . . 275, 370, 372
Douglass, Steffanie S. . . . 218
Dowden, Kayla . . . 48, 94
Downer, Pamela Rose . . . 364
Downs, Diane Gause . . . 128
Drawdy, Bobbi Mahala . . . 308, 359
Drummond, W. H. . . . 174
Drury, Chris . . . 299
Dubas, Daryl . . . 33
Dubiel, Christopher . . . 190, 192
DuBose, Francis Marquis . . . 321
Dubya . . . 98, 130
Duckworth, Cheryl Yvonne . . . 220
Duffey, Paul . . . 393
Dugan, Mary . . . 7
Dulin, Tracy . . . 92
Dunbar, Pamela Hamilton . . . 298
Dunn, Michelle L. . . . 98
Dunsha, Amy . . . 256, 257
Duva, Barbara R. . . . 274, 370

E

Eardley, William F., IV . . . 350, 352
Earwood, Jeff . . . 128, 133
Eccleston, Shari . . . 216, 241
Eckerberg, Eric . . . 246
Eden, Randi Kay . . . 308, 310
Edenfield, Mary Ann . . . 142
Edgar, J. D. . . . 57
Edmonson, C. E. . . . 100, 153
Egan, Mary A. . . . 250
Ehlers, Helen . . . 334
Ehret, Ilse H. . . . 399
Ehrhardt, Bonnie . . . 96
Eichmeier, Neola M. . . . 80
Elaydi, Ghada . . . 96
Eldreth, Paul . . . 376
Eldridge, Lou . . . 175
Elliott, Willa . . . 280, 317
Ellis, Elisabeth Locke . . . 383
Ellis, Rachel . . . 241, 283
Elwartowski, Darlene . . . 216, 241
Eme, Udeagha . . . 129
Enright, Frank J. . . . 69
Erianne, John C. . . . 88, 384
Erickson, Gina . . . 52
Ernst, Beverly . . . 324, 332
Escobar, Aida . . . 224
Escobar, Mickey M. . . . 158
Eskew, Benjamin M. . . . 314
Esposito, Carol . . . 170, 183
Esposito, Gary . . . 216
Estrada, Lourdes M. . . . 141
Estrada, Phyliss . . . 157
Evans, I. J. . . . 287
Evans, Jon S. . . . 158, 160
Evans, Mark A. . . . 101

Everette, Ada Waters . . . 190
Everhart, Lora . . . 230
Exton, Carol A. . . . 258
Exume, Frederic . . . 351
Eyamie, Elsie S. . . . 286, 288

F

Fain, R. . . . 268, 362
Farquhar, Cynthia . . . 158, 160
Farris, Ben . . . 296
Faulk, Jason . . . 186
Faulk, Thomas A. . . . 201, 203
Faust, Jeanne . . . 188, 192, 209
Faust, Paula . . . 353, 355, 357
Fawers, Ida . . . 111
Federici, Annie G. . . . 141, 143
Fell, Jane . . . 218, 220, 254
Fellman, Stanley A. . . . 181, 194
Feltner, Lori J. . . . 34, 64, 65
Ferguson, Melba . . . 314
Fernandez, Lydia . . . 182, 197
Ferris, Kimberlee . . . 224, 253
Feuer, Gaye A. J. . . . 296
Fidell, M. M. . . . 327
Finamore, Linda L. . . . 282
Finn, Gabriel . . . 115
Firth, Terry J. . . . 201
Fischer, Carla . . . 110
Fisher, Julia . . . 190, 192
Fisher-Hiller, Lisa . . . 323
Fiyad, Naddeem . . . 168
Flom, Joan . . . 276
Fogarassy, Helen . . . 170
Fogel, Phyllis . . . 403
Folks, Jeanne C. . . . 102, 113
Folus, Alice . . . 149
Ford, Denise J. . . . 349
Forrest, Liz . . . 327
Foster, Dawn . . . 139
Foster, Lisa . . . 64
Foster, Nina J. M. . . . 235
Foster, Suzanne . . . 98
Fowler, Liesl . . . 335
Fowler, Linda . . . 274
Fowlkes, Juta H. . . . 142
Fox, Lucia . . . 336
Fox, Sandra . . . 273, 370
Foxworthy, Tami . . . 349
Francis, Bertram . . . 21
Francis, John J. . . . 400
Fratta, Rose . . . 92
Freckleton, Mary . . . 111, 260, 343
Freel, Ed . . . 145
Freeland, Alan W. . . . 385
Freshour, Regina . . . 176
Frigo, Grace . . . 148
Friis, Irene I. . . . 74
Frodhe, Anders . . . 28
Fudge, Rudy A. . . . 65
Fugitt, Glenn T. . . . 284
Fujikawa, Fujie . . . 322
Fuller, Alisa L. . . . 392
Fulton, Linda S. . . . 399
Furman, Ray . . . 213

G

Gafton, Marcel . . . 323, 381, 383
Gaier, Debbie . . . 380
Galbraith, William J. . . . 95, 97
Galipeau, Angela . . . 236
Gallagher, Carolyn Pikula . . . 374, 376
Garcia, Debby . . . 131
Gard, Poppy . . . 258

Gardner, Cynthia L. . . . 87
Garland, Omer Ray . . . 182, 197
Garnier, Lynn . . . 56
Garrels, Dennis Earl . . . 251
Garrett, Gerald . . . 196
Gascoigne, Harold D. . . . 160
Gatlin, Allen . . . 279
Gatti, Lauren . . . 11, 36, 40
Gauthier, Chris . . . 335
Gawin, Michael E. . . . 2
Gayzik, William J. . . . 192, 209
Gearhart, Donna E. . . . 205
Geller, John A. . . . 373
George, Katie . . . 188
Gerecke, Lauri Jean . . . 256
Gerlach, Rose Mary . . . 72, 78, 97, 388
Geyer, Michael . . . 405
Gharbawi, Ayad . . . 134, 136
Gibson, Frederica . . . 280
Gibson, Gwynneth . . . 312, 363
Gibson, Mamie G. . . . 250, 301
Gil, Austin . . . 259
Gil, Lourdes . . . 246
Gilbert, Dana . . . 282, 338
Gilbert, Susan . . . 219
Gilden, Kathy . . . 4
Gilead, Tom . . . 8
Gilliland, Jean A. . . . 123
Gillis, Bonnie K. . . . 164
Ginther, Ruth . . . 196
Giordano, Gloria . . . 182
Giraud, Tracy . . . 335, 337
Girgenti, Margarette J. . . . 9
Givham, Benny . . . 166
Givings, Sherry . . . 110
Glaser, Lu Ann . . . 344
Glazer, Terri L. . . . 282
Gochenaur, Leslie M. . . . 76
Goforth, Shirl-Leigh Porter Temple . . . 80
Goland, Virginia . . . 287, 309, 350
Gold, Richard Ellis . . . 160, 167, 169
Goldberg, Barbara . . . 207
Golden, Regina . . . 254
Gomez, Elizabeth . . . 154
Gonzales, Jesse-Diego . . . 40
Gonzalez, Josceleyn Arielda . . . 276
Gonzalez, Lourdes C. . . . 394
Goodman, Ramona T. . . . 292, 294, 342
Goodwin, Charles R. . . . 32
Gosnell, Pamela . . . 156, 167
Govoni, Dennis Michael . . . 289
Goyette, Reneé . . . 52
Graham, Gennie . . . 153
Grande, Michael J. . . . 284
Grasso, Frances . . . 55
Gray, Sarah N. . . . 192, 209
Greco, Jim . . . 204
Green, Phyllis Jean . . . 353
Greenfield, James R. . . . 368
Greenway, Patsy . . . 265, 355
Greenzweig, Chanie . . . 51
Greer, Gracie . . . 280, 318
Greer, Lona . . . 198, 217
Grenier, Nancy J. . . . 367
Grogan, Earlean S. . . . 84
Gropper, T. . . . 26, 27
Grotte, June F. (Sutton) . . . 291, 295
Guerette, Wendi . . . 393
Guerrero, Ada . . . 118
Gupta, Shambhoo Dutta . . . 291
Gushwa, Scott Bradley . . . 399

H

Hagan, John . . . 294
Hagen, Bertha E. . . . 325

Haggerty, Charles . . . 20
Hagins, Louise . . . 162, 323
Haid, Arcadia . . . 114
Haile, Tamara . . . 38
Haldy, Allene . . . 156, 167
Hale, David J. . . . 242
Hall, Anthony James . . . 81
Hall, Lori . . . 350
Hall, Mary Sue . . . 242
Hall, Shannon . . . 164
Hamblin, Earl F. . . . 292, 338
Hamby, Samantha . . . 34
Hamilton, Joyce Elaine . . . 213
Hamizides, William . . . 296
Hamsher, Paul . . . 226
Hancock, Chris . . . 133, 141, 169
Hancock, Margaret . . . 356
Handley, Jaemi . . . 7
Hanes, Marty . . . 6
Hanford, Joan . . . 142
Hanley, Inez S. . . . 43
Hanna, Walter Timothy . . . 296
Hansberry, Nancy Jean . . . 137
Harbour, M. Anson . . . 381
Hargrove, Rosemary F. . . . 16
Harkness, Roger S. . . . 35
Harlow-Emmons, Victoria Leigh . . . 316, 371
Harris, Beth . . . 327
Harris, Denton . . . 64
Harris, Kathy . . . 108, 112
Harrison, Shelton, Jr. . . . 293
Hartman, Cindy L. . . . 395
Hartman, David . . . 405
Hartman, Joyce . . . 298, 350
Hartung, Santina . . . 87, 376, 378, 384, 392
Harvey, Dorothy H. . . . 12
Harvey, Hazel . . . 19
Harvey, Robbie King . . . 289
Hashemian, Nancy L. . . . 260
Hass, Kim . . . 196
Hatcher, Mary Elizabeth . . . 221, 228
Hauser, Hillary . . . 320
Hawkins, Carole Rutledge . . . 174
Hawkins, J. T. . . . 206, 316
Hawkins, Rupert . . . 376
Hawley, A. S. . . . 5
Hayes, Carolyn I. . . . 312, 310
Hayes, Edwin K. . . . 131
Hayes, James R. . . . 46
Hayes, M. L. . . . 312
Hays, Lawrence E. . . . 372
Hayward, S. Glen . . . 236
Healy, Andrea . . . 191, 197
Heffner, Stan . . . 379
Heffner-Schweitzer, Megan . . . 14, 16
Hefty, Shirley Strain . . . 88
Helton, Tony . . . 10
Henry, Christine B. . . . 22, 25, 27
Henry, Roz . . . 395
Hernandez, Cris . . . 220, 249
Herndon, Davie M. . . . 100
Heroux, Jeanne . . . 302, 354
Herrera, Cynthia R. . . . 64
Herring, Eulalie . . . 359, 361
Hermann, Patricia A. . . . 304
Herve, Betty W. . . . 371, 373
Hestand, Debbie . . . 107
Hester, Gloria . . . 227
Hewson, Robert . . . 115
Heymann, Hartwig . . . 110
Hibbs, Vera . . . 21
Hicks, Elsie L. . . . 64
Hicks, Lorraine . . . 166
Hilbrand, Carl Allen . . . 293
Hill, Charlotte M. . . . 298, 352
Hill, Kathi . . . 94
Hilton, Larry W. . . . 71

Hines, Melva Lea . . . 226
Hinson, Louise . . . 237
Hinzman, Helen . . . 262
Hoagland, Rosanne . . . 364, 366
Hobart, Kathleen S. . . . 42, 44
Hodge, Edward W. . . . 18, 23
Hoekstra, Nancy . . . 143, 145
Hoerner, Mary E. . . . 348
Hoffman, Mary . . . 366
Hogan, Peggy . . . 314
Holland, Lauren . . . 112, 114
Hollis, Karen H. . . . 47
Holloway, Sybil . . . 323
Holter, Dennis . . . 344
Honan, Jack . . . 206
Honey . . . 170
Honza, Carol Grey . . . 35
Hoover, Peggy . . . 334, 336
Hopp, Patti L. . . . 351
Houdek, Laverna A. . . . 43
Houdek, Mary Kay . . . 52
Houlihan, Patricia A. . . . 224
Howard, Annie M. . . . 179
Howard, Fred G. . . . 331
Hryhoryk, Bonita J. . . . 74
Huben, H. Thomas . . . 402
Huber, Tina L. . . . 175, 177
Hudspeth, Carol . . . 252
Hull, Dorothy L. . . . 106, 108
Hulse, Gloria D. . . . 81
Hummel, Robert W., Jr. . . . 107
Humphrey, Dennis . . . 199
Humphries, Albert . . . 266, 267
Hunt, Susan M. . . . 293
Hurta, Diana L. . . . 160
Husain, Zareen . . . 322
Huston, Keith S. . . . 333, 393
Hutton, Rebecca . . . 88, 386
Hyland, Terry . . . 296
Hynak, Michael J. . . . 168

I

Iacona, Carol M. . . . 399
Iantosca, Antonio . . . 250
Iavarone, Donna . . . 280
Ingles, Jim . . . 123
Ingold, R. Kim . . . 247
Irving, Joanne . . . 72
Ishmael, Dr. Don M. . . . 44
Ivan, Thelma D. . . . 124, 129, 132

J

J., Francis John . . . 76
Jackson, Clifton . . . 367
Jackson, Jeanine M. . . . 20, 25
James, Judy . . . 317
James, Larry . . . 208, 212
James, Tammy . . . 138, 140
Jamison, Karla . . . 329
Janwich, Lori . . . 168, 214, 216
Janz, Caroline . . . 273, 370
Jarvi, Beryl . . . 177
Jefferies, Mary Ann . . . 84, 378
Jenkins, Cy . . . 362
Jenkins, Edna . . . 169
Jennings, Christopher . . . 142
Jennings, Kathryn Anne . . . 38, 41
Jesudason, Christopher G. . . . 278, 376
Jochum, Tina . . . 278
Johns, Arthur J. . . . 86
Johnson, Charles William, III . . . 125
Johnson, Constance L. . . . 124, 131
Johnson, DeElla . . . 13

Johnson, Doris Bowman . . . 136, 138, 151
Johnson, Evelyn M. . . . 171
Johnson, Kathryn . . . 94
Johnson, Michele . . . 115
Johnson, Nancy L. . . . 277
Johnson, Quanda Dawnyell . . . 377
Johnson, Roy D. . . . 385
Johnson, Sandra Lee . . . 238
Johnston, Naomi L. . . . 178
Jones, Elvin L. . . . 306
Jones, J. . . . 148, 157
Jones, Norma Dean . . . 241, 243
Jones, Robert E. . . . 292, 348
Jones, Ruby A. . . . 81
Jones, Stephen . . . 37
Jones, Theresa L. . . . 123
Jordan, Peggy . . . 43
Jordan, Sandra Larcher . . . 64
Jordan-Faulkner, Laurietta . . . 228
Josie D . . . 258, 395, 404
Joy, Suzanne . . . 76, 398
Jubelirer, Sherry Shea . . . 238
Judisch, Deborah A. . . . 403

K

K., Mary Elizabeth . . . 209
Kagel, Edward . . . 394
Kahler, Antoinette . . . 137
Kalmes, Jean Reed . . . 9
Kaltenbach, Babette Elaine . . . 172, 185
Kaplan, Jean Lockamy . . . 399
Kaplan, Jill . . . 387
Karol, Eileen . . . 114
Kartman, Leo . . . 200, 217
Kartomi, Karen Sri . . . 362
Kassinger, Holly . . . 134
Kau, Edward . . . 76, 78
Kaufmann, Gail . . . 82, 83
Keating, Mildred . . . 228
Keefe, Sandra Jean . . . 79
Keene, Jennifer . . . 218
Kelch, Cheryl Havens . . . 288
Kellogg, Veronica S. . . . 184
Kelly, Anne . . . 145
Kelsey, Kim (Moore) . . . 214
Kelso, E. L. . . . 8
Kempf, Kimberly . . . 119
Kendall, Pamela Sue . . . 200
Kennedy, Michael Peter . . . 362
Kennedy-Shapiro, Sharon . . . 358
Kerrigan, Margaret E. . . . 328
Khosrofian, Harry . . . 82
Kibler, Wally . . . 95, 97
Kiihn, K. Lynn . . . 104
Kilburg, Paula . . . 100
Killion, Armella C. . . . 32
King, Clemmie . . . 162
King, Diane . . . 357
King, Jamie L. . . . 98
King, Tom . . . 382
Kingsbury, Raphaella . . . 346
Kirkbride, Laury . . . 223
Kirkpatrick, Thomas N. . . . 22, 23
Kish, Mary Jane . . . 136, 183, 185
Kizziar, Linda . . . 339
Kleinwachter, Pam J. . . . 146
Kline, Ramona . . . 4
Knapp, Laura A. . . . 397
Knight, Robin . . . 333
Knutson, Kelly D. . . . 96
Koch, Jeff . . . 18
Koerner, Colleen . . . 152, 159
Kolbie, Shane M. . . . 279
Konow, David W. . . . 366
Koons, John F. . . . 28

Koontz, Norma . . . 66
Korneitchouk, Ursula . . . 392
Korth, Jacqueline . . . 16
Kotsalos, Nike . . . 341
Kubashack, Genevieve B. . . . 28
Kuhl, Karen . . . 66
Kuntz, Cathy . . . 10
Kunze, Jay Douglas . . . 66
Kurpjuweit, Wayne J. . . . 182, 184, 199
Kuykendall, Patricia Gayle . . . 48
Kvande, Marta . . . 48

L

LaChance, Nancy M. . . . 327
LaFata, Salvatore, IV . . . 233, 307
Lafkas, Melissa S. . . . 85, 86
Lagerlof, Mabel . . . 31
Lamb, Barbara Nell . . . 254, 313
Lamb, Catherine Stockton . . . 82
Lampe, Joseph M. . . . 41, 47
Landers, Cynthia . . . 366
Landgren, Rita . . . 385
Lane, Laura Brown . . . 147
Langer, Cassandra . . . 208
Langston, Raymond . . . 201
Larkins, Laura L. . . . 248
Larmond, Paulette . . . 298
Larocque, Donald, Jr. . . . 16
Laska, Lisa . . . 96
Lasley, Ann . . . 347
Laster, Clara . . . 101
Law, Dorothy E. . . . 17
Lawrence, Laura J. . . . 362
Lawrence, Suzanne M. . . . 104, 117
LeDoux, Delphine . . . 136, 138
LeDoux, M. D. . . . 126, 130, 398
Lee, Addie . . . 389, 391
Lee, Jamie Marie . . . 358, 404
Lee, Michael W. . . . 354, 356, 358
Lee, Robyn K. . . . 318
Lee, Roger D. . . . 353
Leeds, Morton . . . 107
Leggs, Michael . . . 339
Lehnig, Cynthia . . . 131
Lemasters, Marie J. . . . 224
Lender, Stuart K. . . . 28
Lenzä, John R. . . . 147, 293
Lestina, Janette . . . 176
Levack, Virginia . . . 229
Lewis, Alice L. . . . 312
Lewis, Karen Janice . . . 187
Libero, Karen Aileen . . . 78
Lichtenfels, T. Christy . . . 32
Lieber, Janine . . . 248
Liechti, Elizabeth . . . 202, 204, 206
Lincoln, Candice L. . . . 298, 350, 354
Lindholm, Nicole . . . 205
Linville, Patty J. . . . 205, 207
Litterer, Robert A. . . . 168, 188
Lockwood, Sandra . . . 333
Lonsford, Florence . . . 146
Lorraine, Nancy . . . 219
Lucas, Doreen . . . 104
Lucas, Susanne . . . 69, 73
Luckett, Bernadette . . . 343
Luftman, Barrie Elizabeth . . . 387
Lugo, Lydia Esther . . . 327
Lui, Lawrence . . . 198, 200, 217
Lumsden, Lois . . . 127, 132
Lunsford, Barbara . . . 37, 39, 40
Lunt, R. E. . . . 52
Lutz, Priscilla J. . . . 128
Lynn, Hazel T. . . . 119, 126
Lyons, Evelyn L. . . . 329
Lyons, Markham H. . . . 162, 171

Lyons, Ronnett (Crafton) . . . 17
Lytle, Kathryn . . . 333, 396
Lyttle, William J., III . . . 380

M

M. R. C. . . . 367
Maben, Patty . . . 22, 25, 400
Mabrey, Valerie Taylor . . . 114
Machado, Darcy . . . 308
Mackey, Sheyla . . . 8
Maddy, Edith W. . . . 118
Mahony, Ronald L. . . . 217, 230, 232
Maier, Collene P. . . . 378
Makar, Dorothy . . . 10
Malin, Ken . . . 391, 393
Maloney, David J. . . . 343
Maloney, Karen B. . . . 136
Mansel, Christopher Alan . . . 244
Mant, Pamela . . . 258, 259, 347
Marchant, Jane . . . 327, 387
Marchin, Lynn . . . 111
Marian, Donna . . . 117
Marino, Carol A. . . . 341
Mark, Sharlene . . . 335, 397
Marner, Dorothy . . . 203
Marquardt, Ethel . . . 154
Marshall, Ollie . . . 178
Martens, Bradley S. . . . 261
Martin, Debra A. . . . 56
Martin, Debra K. . . . 125
Martin, William F. . . . 137
Martindale, Nancy . . . 214
Martinez, Diana . . . 289
Martinez, Melissa . . . 325
Martinez-Headrick, Sharon . . . 287
Martinson, Martha Mae . . . 208, 212, 237
Martinson, William J. . . . 86, 382
Marx, Marcia . . . 373
Mason, Vanessa . . . 292
Massimini, Nicholas . . . 33
Matthews, Annette M. . . . 235
Matthews, Barbara . . . 200
Matzner, Chester M. . . . 262, 353
Mauro, Jean . . . 65, 66
Mayer, Juanita . . . 314
Mayo, Lauren M. . . . 161
Mbogho, Julia . . . 307
McAdams, P. . . . 170, 183
McAnally, Elizabeth Haynes . . . 74
McBride, Elizabeth V. . . . 61, 63, 66
McBride, Kara . . . 176
McCann, Michael V. . . . 326
McCants, Donald . . . 170
McCormack, Paula . . . 3, 6
McCormick, Tonia A. . . . 72
McCoy, Christina . . . 78, 93
McCoy, Paul Brian . . . 215
McCracken-Cooper, Mary Anne . . . 24, 27
McCrory, Paul D. . . . 142
McCulley, Carolyn . . . 31
McDowell, Jill G. . . . 56, 70, 399
McElwain, Beverly A. . . . 252
McGaughran, Dorothy . . . 392
McGee, Patrick . . . 284
McGill, Steven . . . 372
McGrath, Betty Watson . . . 306
McGraw, Jennifer . . . 329
McInnes, Luanne . . . 234
McIntyre, Juanita . . . 29
McIvor, Barbara . . . 56, 57
McKamey, Beverly Hirsch . . . 189, 193
McKay, Linda Seiter . . . 249
McKenzie, Kevin . . . 168
McKinney, Michael . . . 142
McKinnon, John, Jr. . . . 114, 118

McLaughlin, Debra . . . 386
McMains, Milan . . . 281
McMillin, Marilynn M. . . . 10
McPherson, Lorna . . . 319
McQuaide, Rick . . . 280
Meek, Richard W. . . . 89
Meers, Kyle . . . 54
Meier, Pete . . . 335
Mellgren, Leslie . . . 148
Melloy, Elaine B. . . . 355
Menz, Francis X. . . . 252
Mercer-Capps, Patricia . . . 98
Merck, John D. . . . 323
Merritt, Meridell W. . . . 386
Mesaros, Lisa . . . 151
Meyer, Lisa H. . . . 221, 297
Meyer, Susan Lee . . . 66, 67
Michael, Debbie . . . 374
Michelle, Dianna . . . 126, 401
Mihalik, P. . . . 312, 361
Miles, Bruce . . . 316, 369
Miles, Randall David . . . 146, 157
Millard, Laurie . . . 164
Miller, Alice . . . 5
Miller, Claire Burns . . . 258, 376, 402
Miller, Karen . . . 18, 23
Miller, Melinda L. . . . 205
Miller, Mollie E. . . . 251
Mills, David A. . . . 176
Mills, David Allen . . . 43
Millspaugh, Anthony M. . . . 295
Minacci, Lisa . . . 134
Minsky, Diana Stanton . . . 6
Misha . . . 385
Mitchell, Martin . . . 102
Mittick, Bessie . . . 402
Moen, Zamir . . . 8
Mohammad, Rasaan Abdula . . . 8
Mokan, Carolyn T. . . . 339, 397
Moline, Jenny . . . 310, 312, 361
Mollner, Coralee A. . . . 294
Momy, Gerald . . . 188
Moneybrake, Pat . . . 277
Monte, Joanne . . . 1, 2
Monteith, Michael . . . 238
Montelius, Susan A. . . . 36
Montgomery Linda . . . 236
Mood, Cyndi . . . 154
Mooney, Barbara . . . 68
Moore, Craig S. . . . 154
Moore, Flora Ellen . . . 189
Moore, Gregory . . . 280
Moore, Kathleen . . . 142
Moran, Dean . . . 305
Moreland, James E. . . . 46, 51
Moreland, Roger Browning . . . 21, 36, 398
Morgan, Russell . . . 74
Morovich, Violet Ficovich . . . 246
Morris, C. K., Jr. . . . 110
Morrison, George . . . 51, 157
Morrow, M. E. . . . 333, 393
Morrow, Stan . . . 93
Mortis, Frank Allen . . . 32
Morton, Olivette . . . 302
Mosch, Feliz . . . 244, 293, 297
Moses, Leroy L. . . . 200
Moskos, Jerry . . . 364
Motola, Pat . . . 401
Mowery, Gilbert . . . 166, 177
Mueller, George . . . 277
Mueller, Kurt . . . 36, 38, 41
Mueller, P. A. . . . 92
Mumma, John . . . 369
Munson, Bertha . . . 137
Murray, Tamara L. . . . 212, 237
Murray, Terri Lea . . . 48, 50

Myers, Darlene . . . 8
Myers, Kimberly . . . 19

N

Nalicat, Susan . . . 303
Nam, Sophia . . . 336, 338
Naquin, Frances . . . 258
Nash-Bienaimé, Beryl . . . 124
Nasmyth-Miller, Susan . . . 380
Nass, Dr. GGisela . . . 254, 313
Nathan, Geraldine . . . 5
Navarrette, Andrea . . . 33
Neal, Sandra . . . 19
Neff, Bonita Dostal . . . 337
Nelson, Deborah J. . . . 163
Nelson, James H. . . . 337
Nevarez, Lydia . . . 56
Newbauer, Judith L. . . . 261, 351
Newswanger, Richard . . . 405
Newton, Brian Floyd . . . 161
Nicholas . . . 206
Nichols, J. S. . . . 384
Nichols, Pat Whitaker . . . 271
Nichols, Ruth . . . 33
Nickens, Dorothy . . . 316
Nidiffer, Pamela . . . 82, 378
Nissinen, June Ann . . . 218
Nixon, Norma . . . 322
Noble, Robert . . . 228
Norella, Pete P. . . . 13
Norris, George B. . . . 94, 103
Norris, James R. . . . 143, 401
Norris, Jean K. . . . 247
Norris, Nena Lynne . . . 200
Novak, Richard . . . 366
Nunn, Curtis . . . 267
Nuttall, Lucy . . . 226, 227
Nyberg, Vivian Sprinkles . . . 223

O

O'Donnell, Beth . . . 134
O'Guinn, Denise . . . 5
O'Keefe, Shirley B. . . . 190
O'Key, Helen W. . . . 28
Obakoya, 'deolu . . . 181
Ocain, Frank . . . 171
Ochs, Alice Ruediger . . . 91
October, Dene . . . 122
Ohnstad, Glen G. . . . 309
Okecha, Steve A. . . . 74
Okorie, Rinkart Eze . . . 100
Olinger, Nancy . . . 356
Olson, Daryl T. . . . 260, 377
Olson, Lloyd . . . 352
Ong, Nhon Tong . . . 328
Onojobi, Dr. Akim . . . 311
Onyekwere, Chioma N. . . . 306
Opstad, Stephannie . . . 286
Orbeliani, Andre . . . 68, 182
Oregel, Ernesto . . . 172, 183
Ostrander, Bryant Fox . . . 275, 276
Oswalt, Tiffeny . . . 230
Owen, Bettye Ellis . . . 83, 84, 378
Owen, Robert . . . 14, 38

P

Padgett, Tom . . . 19
Pagano, Stephanee . . . 310
Parenti, John J. . . . 104, 106
Parker, James . . . 1
Parker, P. J. . . . 154

Parker, Rene Denise . . . 238, 242, 289
Parks, C. S. . . . 248
Parks, Ellen Grey . . . 252
Parrinello, Violet W. . . . 156
Parrish, Deirdre . . . 74
Parron, Hazel Mae . . . 185
Passarella, Irene . . . 291
Patton, Kenneth D. . . . 47
Patzman, Florence Dorothy . . . 35
Paulhamus, Mary . . . 162, 171, 173
Paulk, Ozell and Kim . . . 363
Payne, Zelia . . . 152, 159
Pazoureck-Lucy, Lilibel . . . 136, 151
Peacher, Ruby Tippit . . . 85, 391
Peacock, Julia M. . . . 328
Pearce, Debbie T. . . . 297
Pearson, Robert S. . . . 78, 93
Pederson, Debbie J. . . . 229
Peek, Venus . . . 272, 372
Pelcman, Jodie . . . 134
Penne, Russ . . . 186
Perry, Sherry . . . 118
Peter, Bonnie S. . . . 242
Peterson, Craig . . . 142
Peterson, Kathleen S. . . . 282
Petro, Valerie A. . . . 17
Pettit, Beverley . . . 98, 101, 109
Phelps, Scott . . . 351
Phillips, Elaine . . . 355
Phillips, Mary E. . . . 328
Piazza, Louis Arduin . . . 218
Pierce, Brian . . . 148
Pierce, Grace . . . 403
Pilkey, Kerry Michael . . . 262
Pillsbury, April . . . 121
Pimentel, Laurie A. . . . 94
Pisacane, Ernie . . . 202
Pitel, Evelyn . . . 54, 290
Pizza, Valli . . . 363
Plotnikova, Alla . . . 18
Pluma, Aquilla . . . 53
Plumley, Elizabeth . . . 12
Pluss, Robert J. . . . 310
Podgorski, Bonnie Flint . . . 84, 380
Pol, George . . . 306, 308, 359
Poland, Alysia Ann . . . 346
Pollock, Michael D. . . . 166
Pons, Angie . . . 110
Porter, Gianna . . . 194
Porter, Nancy . . . 46
Porter, Sandie . . . 196
Potjan, Renate . . . 94, 103
Pounder, Ann Marie . . . 125
Prall, Andy . . . 288
Prebesh, Amy I. . . . 289
Preston, Kenith . . . 113
Price, Gregory . . . 148
Price-Paige, Yutinna . . . 334
Privee, Noel . . . 162
Prose, Meg . . . 172, 185
Pynn, Tom . . . 316

Q

Quijano, Jocelyn . . . 365
Quinn, Mary . . . 37
Quinterno, Anne T. . . . 230

R

Rae, Bill . . . 343, 349
Ragsdale, Sue . . . 303
Rahrmann, Montgomery . . . 253
Raithby, Cheri . . . 70
Ramet, Susan . . . 89

Ramey, Diane . . . 87
Ramsay, Maggie . . . 372
Ramsey, Larry J. . . . 2
Ramsey, Vicky K. . . . 7
Rance, Paul . . . 74
Randall, Marcia A. . . . 117
Ranew, Joyce . . . 47
Rathje, Cindy . . . 28
Rauer, E. Ann . . . 124, 394
Ray, Catherine . . . 272, 273
Ray, G. Paul . . . 355
Ray, Hugh Miles . . . 284
Ray, Pearl G. . . . 326, 340
Raymore, Andrea . . . 346
Rea, Sherri L. . . . 56
Redmill, Rick . . . 362
Reece, Evelyn C. . . . 206, 229, 231
Reed, Judith E. . . . 358
Reedy, Lois . . . 286
Regan, Donna M. . . . 8
Regan, Patricia M. . . . 91
Regehr, Lydia . . . 236
Reichenbach, Gregory . . . 68
Reicino, Dalia . . . 186
Reid, Berneta . . . 380
Reid, Blanche Carson . . . 347
Reimus, Donna J. . . . 212
Reinhart, Eve . . . 189, 191
Remeika, Susan A. . . . 405
Reppert, Lisa R. . . . 35
Reynaldo, Gloria D. . . . 309
Reynolds, Roger . . . 308
Rice, Lorraine . . . 323, 379, 381
Rich, Sue . . . 331
Richards, James D. . . . 102, 113
Richardson, Donna . . . 281
Richardson, F. L. . . . 34
Richardson, Gerald . . . 186
Richmond, Andrew Thomas . . . 341
Richter, Jan . . . 178
Riedthaler, Bernice . . . 181
Rieger, Richard Alan . . . 272, 366, 368
Riggs, Sheree . . . 325
Riley, Carol J. . . . 267, 268
Rinehart, Connie . . . 127
Ringereide, M. . . . 214, 243
Riojas, Cruz . . . 53
Ritter, Valerie R. . . . 134
Robbins, J. Stone Gramm . . . 184, 186, 188
Roberts, Gene . . . 128
Roberts, Kris . . . 161
Roberts, Mrs. A. A. . . . 199
Robertson, Douglas . . . 350
Robinson, Jeffrey A. . . . 279
Robison, Bob D. . . . 55
Robison, Shane P. . . . 100
Roceric, Alexandra . . . 28
Rocha, Karen . . . 298, 302
Rodgers, Jeannette L. . . . 114
Rodning, Charles B. . . . 126, 128
Rodriguez, Amanda . . . 155, 159
Rodriguez, Robert E. . . . 228, 230
Roehrs, Ruth . . . 386, 388
Roesti, Michael J. . . . 337
Rogers, Catherine H. . . . 7
Rooks, Jeri K. . . . 93, 402
Rose, Eric . . . 198, 204, 223
Rose, Julie . . . 47
Rosenberg, Paul . . . 307
Rosenborg, Margaret . . . 244
Ross, Mary L. . . . 397
Rossberg, Christine . . . 271
Rossetti, Angelina . . . 403
Rotella, Emma . . . 20
Rowles, Rodney H. . . . 182, 197, 199
Rowley, Ruth C. . . . 234
Rowls, Alfred G. . . . 28

Rubarts, Virginia . . . 22, 24
Rubin, Cindee D. . . . 122
Rubio, Marina . . . 271
Ruble, Jennifer Kay Vroman . . . 319
Rudloff, Kim . . . 166
Rudrow, Rhonda Michelle . . . 236
Runch, A. . . . 236
Rung, Stanley Liston . . . 323
Runyon, Tracie L. . . . 218
Rupar, Diane . . . 178, 189, 191
Russell, Douglas S. . . . 248
Russell, Harry A. . . . 301
Russell, Jerry . . . 172, 187
Russell, William J. . . . 257
Russo, John F. . . . 196, 215
Rutte, Carol Ann . . . 6

S

Sadowski, Josephine . . . 7
Saldan, Richard . . . 81
Saldivar, Jon . . . 234, 236, 287
Salerno, Ellen L. . . . 16
Salisbury, Christina Ann . . . 286
Saliscente, Anita R. . . . 206, 231
Salvato, Frederick J. . . . 201
Sam, Augustus G. A. . . . 208
Sambuco, Daria Jaye . . . 320
Samorodin, Jack . . . 340
Sanciprian, Kathleen Rose . . . 148
Sandefur, Ron . . . 224
Sanders, Bonnie J. . . . 161
Sanders, Wanda T. . . . 147
Sando, Christopher J. . . . 355
Santanna, Paul M. . . . 4
Santine, Rachel . . . 301
Sapp, Daniel O. . . . 28
Sarro, Nicholas . . . 265
Sasse, Mark W. . . . 259
Saunders, Sally Love . . . 6
Savage, Ron . . . 399
Savitski, Margaret M. . . . 290
Sawyer, Eleanor L. . . . 191
Scanlan, Steven J. . . . 218
Scarpa, Carmine J. . . . 202
Schacht, Mary Ann . . . 343, 347
Schact, Mary Ann . . . 347
Schauer, Ronald R. . . . 261, 349
Scheidemann, Mike . . . 11, 13, 296
Schiebler, Rachel . . . 94
Schifferli, John "Bud" . . . 49
Schmidt, CarolAnn . . . 277
Schmidt, Sandra . . . 251
Schmitt, Rita . . . 387
Schock, Gerhard . . . 194, 211
Schoener, Dorothea . . . 24
Scholar, Deborah J. . . . 54
Schroffner, Ingrid . . . 181
Schulman, Arlene . . . 231
Schultz, Clyde L. . . . 144, 155
Schuth, Roni J. . . . 134
Schwab, Joy . . . 103
Schwartz, Sue Ann . . . 83
Schweger, Lee . . . 316, 371
Schweiger, Karen . . . 51
Scoble, Bonnie J. . . . 248, 299
Sconfienza, Dawn A. . . . 29
Scott, Hope . . . 54
Scott, Ronald . . . 79
Scurlock, Dolly . . . 77
Selby, Lois L. . . . 99
Serrano, Carlos . . . 205
Serrano, Marriane . . . 106
Setteducato, Susan . . . 357
Severson, Debbi . . . 335
Sewing, Michelle . . . 67

Shah, Ramesh C. . . . 376
Shambaugh, Joan . . . 219
Shaner, Jeanine . . . 11
Sharp, Amber . . . 202
Sharp, Charles S. . . . 68
Sharpe, Robert W. . . . 226, 253
Shea, Steven F. . . . 302
Sherman, Nancy E. . . . 363, 365
Shields, Kerry Ann . . . 138
Shirk, Katherine Priestley . . . 4
Shreves, Kristin . . . 353
Shuey, D. Colleen . . . 357
Shukis, Gary C. . . . 184
Sickels, David R. . . . 24, 27
Sigler, David A. . . . 21
Sills, Susan . . . 68
Silva, Isabelle . . . 224
Silvia, Linda . . . 65, 69, 72
Simmons, Carole . . . 301
Simmons, Mary E. . . . 68
Simon, Angela . . . 290
Simon, Violet . . . 368
Simonds, Rawn . . . 341, 343
Simpson, Inda B. . . . 107
Sincavage, Steve . . . 111
Singh, Charu Sheel . . . 319
Singletary, Patricia . . . 155
Singletary, Patricia A. . . . 155
Sinha, Bobbi . . . 395
Sittre, Dennis . . . 142
Sivels-Rodgers, Joy C. . . . 1, 36, 39
Sizemore, Korene Cleo . . . 118, 122
Skaggs, Gary . . . 10
Skelton, Billie A. . . . 259
Skinner, Janice . . . 384
Skinner, Jauneth . . . 55
Skvarka, Joe . . . 134
Slade, Robert K. . . . 67
Slater, Marjorie V. . . . 326, 388
Sloan, Shari . . . 167
Slowick, Monica . . . 158, 167
Smith, A. L. . . . 116
Smith, Carole Tucker . . . 344
Smith, Catharine T. . . . 288
Smith, Evan . . . 154
Smith, Fairretta . . . 261, 262
Smith, Gary . . . 122
Smith, Gary D. . . . 364
Smith, Gregory J. . . . 78, 97, 401
Smith, Gregory Neil . . . 238
Smith, Irene . . . 219
Smith, Jeff . . . 242
Smith, June Rose . . . 351
Smith, Laura . . . 338
Smith, Marla . . . 202
Smith, Michelle L. . . . 243, 245
Smith, Ronald J. . . . 260
Smith, Roslyn D. . . . 83
Smith, Shelly . . . 76, 400
Smith, Victoria . . . 48, 51
Smith-Banks, Linda . . . 49
Snider, Sandra J. . . . 382
Snook, Kenneth M. . . . 305
Snow, Timothy B. . . . 76
Solek-Fritsche, Patricia Anne . . . 44
Somers, Margaret L. . . . 392
Sorg, Melinda . . . 335
Sorgani, Deborah L. . . . 202
Sorrells, Leslie . . . 96
Soviero, Marcelle . . . 284
Spence, Katherine . . . 274, 275
Spicer, Patricia . . . 313
Spierdowis, Portia . . . 55
Spinney, Linda Lathrop . . . 108
Spriggs, David . . . 31
Squires, Mark Anthony . . . 400
Stacy, Henrietta M. . . . 213

Staiano, Diane . . . 380
Stanley, Dorothy M. . . . 181
Stanton, Dawn . . . 406
Staples, Ross . . . 223, 227
Stapleton, Valerie A. . . . 12
Steamer, Kathleen M. . . . 12
Stembridge, Sally . . . 302, 344, 356
Stepan, Tamara . . . 266
Sterner, Paula . . . 184, 190, 207
Stevens, Edgar H. . . . 214, 243
Stevens, Margaret E. . . . 276
Stevenson, Theresa . . . 36
Steward, Donna J. . . . 263, 264
Stewart, Betty . . . 107, 162, 173
Stewart, Kay . . . 321, 377, 381
Stewart-Tornai, Nancy . . . 178
Stites, Genée . . . 16
Stocker, Cheri L. . . . 384, 386
Stoddard, Mark . . . 403
Stone, Nancy Marie . . . 42
Stone, R. N. . . . 54
Storm, R. Hazel . . . 340, 405
Stormont, Edith F. . . . 109
Stoudemire, Danita . . . 110
Stoudt, Jeff . . . 286, 324
Strohmyer, Monica B. . . . 44, 154
Strong, Robert M. . . . 72, 77, 79, 80
Stroud, Katherine G. . . . 42
Struller, Patricia A. . . . 218
Strusz, Ed . . . 235
Sturgis, Joyce M. . . . 337
Styles, Mark . . . 239
Suh, Jessica . . . 322
Sulliban, Bernard, III . . . 304, 356
Sulzdorf, Alice Ekern . . . 222
Summers, Walt . . . 280
Surette, Steven P. . . . 337
Susiene, Linda . . . 126, 401, 403
Suter, Marie . . . 194
Sutherland, Allison . . . 317
Swalley, Thomas L. . . . 192, 211
Swanson, Bert M. . . . 278, 376
Swartz, Rita B. . . . 116
Swavely, Michelle . . . 324
Sykes, Debra . . . 152
Symon, Terry L. . . . 2
Syrydynski, Maryann . . . 304

T

Talbott, Eunice T. . . . 337, 339
Talton, Patricia S. . . . 148
Tarolli, Florence . . . 269
Tatum, Chester A., Jr. . . . 235
Taube, DeEtta . . . 18
Taylor, Joanne . . . 67
Tebo, Ernestine J. . . . 193
Teeters, Randy W. . . . 305
Tenorio, Jennifer . . . 103
Thacker, Mike . . . 22, 41
Thair, Ben . . . 178
Thomas, Carolyn Smith . . . 202
Thomas, Susan . . . 3
Thomason, Glenda S. . . . 312
Thompson, Jennifer . . . 339, 341
Thompson, Marjory Lee . . . 216, 245
Thompson, Mary E. . . . 175
Thompson, Raeford E., Sr. . . . 57, 58
Thompson, Robert J. . . . 124, 145
Timmons, Pamela J. . . . 349
Titus, Julianne . . . 122
Tollakson, John E. . . . 54
Tomlin, Kathleen . . . 257
Topalovich, Helen . . . 387
Towle, Penelope M. . . . 368
Towns, Jeanette . . . 252

Tracey, Linda Marie . . . 256
Trantow, Karen . . . 317
Treihart, Karen . . . 189
Trent, C. W. . . . 122
Tribulato, Diane . . . 26, 27
Troxler, Miriam . . . 222, 254
Tucker, Mary Margaret Louise Peery . . . 190
Tucker-Pickens, Mary Olive . . . 98, 100
Turner, Ginny . . . 96, 128, 133
Turner, Sia . . . 26, 29

U

Ulisse, Peter . . . 144
Umekawa, T. . . . 252
Underberg, Arla . . . 306
Urban, Jeannie . . . 143, 201, 403
Urquhart, Joanna . . . 281
Ursini, Rae . . . 232

V

Valdina, Mary G. . . . 70, 73, 336
Vale, W. . . . 16
Valentine, Augustine Ephrem . . . 223
Valentine, Darlene Bergeron . . . 215, 404
Valentino, Joanne . . . 313
Vallie, Robert N. . . . 282, 320
Van Boven, Alannah . . . 306
Vandegraft, Debra A. . . . 42
Vandemark, Brian . . . 313
VandenHeuvel, Robert E. . . . 234
Vanderbrugen, Robert . . . 148
VanSickle, Paula . . . 128
Varela, Joe . . . 332
Varela, Joe F. . . . 89
Vashey, Denie . . . 140
Vence, Helen Marie . . . 286
Venegas, Alejandro . . . 393
Verdino, Gregory T. . . . 235
Vernon, Jill . . . 296, 346
Vezzoli, G. C. . . . 147, 153
Victor, Ann . . . 392
Virata, Marc P. . . . 216
Volkman, Mary M. . . . 65
Voltz, Joan . . . 333, 389
von Bothe, Barbara . . . 179

W

Wade, Normay M. . . . 219
Walcott, Robert K. . . . 273
Walcott, Ruth . . . 85, 92
Waldrop, Ed . . . 237
Walek, Jennifer . . . 182
Walford, Joanna . . . 183
Walker, Jason D. . . . 166
Walker, Katherine S. . . . 228
Wallace, Janet Ann . . . 340
Walling, Paula . . . 108
Walsh, Trish . . . 325, 383
Walters, Troy L. . . . 172, 176, 187
Wang, Harry . . . 148, 235
Wang, Li-Chung . . . 267, 268, 271
Ward, Barbara . . . 168
Ward, C. . . . 229
Wark, Vanda . . . 318
Warren, Doris I. . . . 212
Warrick, Ruth L. . . . 282
Waterman, Sharon M. . . . 48, 53
Watkins, Anita . . . 20, 25
Watkins, David A. . . . 65
Watkins, T. Steven . . . 37, 102, 143
Watson, Billie J. . . . 153

Watson, Johnny P. . . . 49
Wayne, Timothy P. . . . 220
Webb, Michelle . . . 202
Weber, Deanna . . . 32
Weber, Kathy . . . 33
Weekley, Debbie L. . . . 323
Wefers, Ilse . . . 325
Weigert, Gladys . . . 117
Weiss, Abe . . . 67, 70
Welker, Mary D. . . . 190
Wells, Elizabeth . . . 54
Wells, Guy . . . 321
Weppener, Barbara S. . . . 164, 173
Wessel, Mary . . . 254, 307
West, Honey . . . 104
Westerhoff, Amy Kathleen . . . 244
Wetzel, Calvin G. . . . 108, 119
Wetzel, Mary Kathryn . . . 50
Wham, Mary . . . 55
Wheaton, Dave . . . 272, 368
Wheaton, Shelly Renee . . . 244, 246
Wheeler, Dorothy K. . . . 357
Wheeler, Nancy J. . . . 144
Whitacre, Susan . . . 14, 17
Whitaker, Alisa . . . 122
Whitaker, Dan . . . 113
White, Susan D. . . . 264, 265, 355
White, W. D. . . . 74
Whitenburg, Steve . . . 54
Whitfield, Valerie . . . 149
Whitmore, Beverly M. . . . 344
Whitson, Debra . . . 161
Whittaker, Lois . . . 237
Whitterson, Bertha O. . . . 406
Wick, Myrtle . . . 42
Wickett, Laurie . . . 76
Wicks, Felix Louis . . . 294
Wik, Timothy A. . . . 140
Wilhelm, Lindsay . . . 351
Wilkie, T. . . . 96
Wilkins, Lynne A. . . . 370
Willett, Anna Hart . . . 222
Williams, Adele . . . 396
Williams, Alan . . . 288
Williams, Dorothy E. . . . 173
Williams, Joseph R. . . . 130, 139, 141, 147
Williams, Lisa . . . 127
Williams, M. D. . . . 364
Williams, Ronald . . . 181
Willingham, Craig . . . 42, 99, 101
Willits, T. . . . 238
Wilmeth, Mrs. James . . . 351
Wilson, Bill . . . 224
Wilson, Clo . . . 377
Wilson, Debbie . . . 333
Wilson, Jeri A. . . . 359
Wilson, Kevin . . . 288
Wilson, Linda L. . . . 16
Wilson, Madeline H. . . . 22
Winans, A. E. . . . 378
Winslow, Susan . . . 206, 231, 233
Winters, Shirley . . . 172, 187
Wirth, Dorothea . . . 138, 149, 151
Wise, Donna . . . 14, 17
Wiser, Sherial . . . 284, 322
Withers, Cynthia Clark . . . 263, 264, 355
Woerner, Deloris . . . 284
Wojnowski, Warren H. . . . 245
Wolf, Tracy L. . . . 83, 84, 92
Wolfe, John Roberts . . . 220
Wolford, Carrie . . . 166
Wolfson, Karen J. . . . 346
Wolfson, Max M. . . . 239, 243
Wolfson, Meryl . . . 304, 306, 358
Woltman, Crystal . . . 149
Womack, Fred V. . . . 279
Womack, Margaret . . . 294, 342

Wood, Shannon G. . . . 228
Woodard, Frances E. . . . 149, 152, 159
Woodward, Mary . . . 200
Workman, Dee . . . 56
Worrall, Brian D. . . . 278
Wren, John . . . 261, 276, 277
Wren, Karen . . . 103
Wright, Angela S. . . . 104, 113
Wright, Donna . . . 106
Wright, Stephen J. O'Slavin . . . 104
Wu, Arlouine G. . . . 287

Y

Yarges, Lin . . . 70
Young, Chris . . . 306
Young, S. M. . . . 399
Young, Shirley A. . . . 104, 106, 119

Z

Zandie, Ann . . . 245, 247
Zapata, Antonia . . . 24, 26
Zarb, Sandra . . . 208
Zarensky, Hope F. T. . . . 28
Zimmerman, Anna Rita . . . 198, 215
Zimmerman, Billy R. . . . 303
Zobenica, Janet . . . 148
Zuck, Matt . . . 116
Zuniga, Eric D. . . . 248